HANDBOOK OF RESEARCH M
MIGRATION

Advisory Board

Professor Stephen Castles, Research Professor of Sociology, University of Sydney, Australia

Professor Robin Cohen, Emeritus Professor and Principal Investigator on the Oxford Diasporas Programme, University of Oxford, UK

Professor Josh DeWind, Director of the Migration Program, Social Science Research Council, USA

Professor Raúl Delgado Wise, Professor of Development Studies, Universidad Autónoma de Zacatecas, Mexico

Handbook of Research Methods in Migration

Edited by

Carlos Vargas-Silva

Senior Researcher, Centre on Migration, Policy and Society, University of Oxford, UK

Edward Elgar
Cheltenham, UK • Northampton, MA, USA

© Carlos Vargas-Silva 2012

All rights reserved. No part of this publication may be reproduced, stored in a retrieval system or transmitted in any form or by any means, electronic, mechanical or photocopying, recording, or otherwise without the prior permission of the publisher.

Published by
Edward Elgar Publishing Limited
The Lypiatts
15 Lansdown Road
Cheltenham
Glos GL50 2JA
UK

Edward Elgar Publishing, Inc.
William Pratt House
9 Dewey Court
Northampton
Massachusetts 01060
USA

Paperback edition 2013
Paperback edition reprinted 2016

This book has been printed on demand to keep the title in print.

A catalogue record for this book
is available from the British Library

Library of Congress Control Number: 2011939344

ISBN 978 1 84980 311 3 (cased)
      978 1 78100 542 2 (paperback)

Typeset by Servis Filmsetting Ltd, Stockport, Cheshire
Printed and bound in Great Britain by
Marston Book Services Limited, Didcot

Contents

List of contributors viii

Introduction 1
Carlos Vargas-Silva

PART I FUNDAMENTAL ISSUES OF SCIENTIFIC LOGIC, METHODOLOGY AND METHODS IN MIGRATION STUDIES

1. Understanding the relationship between methodology and methods 7
   Stephen Castles
2. Migration research between positivistic scientism and relativism: a critical realist way out 26
   Theodoros Iosifides
3. Migration, methods and innovation: a reconsideration of variation and conceptualization in research on foreign workers 50
   David Bartram
4. Transnational – transregional – translocal: transcultural 69
   Dirk Hoerder
5. Contemporary migration seen from the perspective of political economy: theoretical and methodological elements 92
   Raúl Delgado Wise and Humberto Márquez Covarrubias

PART II INTRODUCTION TO DIFFERENT TECHNIQUES AND APPROACHES

6. Interviewing techniques for migrant minority groups 117
   Luis Sánchez-Ayala
7. Collecting, analysing and presenting migration histories 137
   Jørgen Carling
8. Empirical methods in the economics of international immigration 163
   Fernando A. Lozano and Michael D. Steinberger

9. Using longitudinal data to study migration and remittances   186
   Edward Funkhouser
10. Measuring migration in multi-topic household surveys   207
    Calogero Carletto, Alan de Brauw and Raka Banerjee
11. Migration and its measurement: towards a more robust map
    of bilateral flows   229
    Ronald Skeldon
12. Experimental approaches in migration studies   249
    David McKenzie and Dean Yang

PART III   INTERDISCIPLINARY APPROACHES AND MIXED METHODS

13. Mapping movements: interdisciplinary approaches to
    migration research   273
    Pablo S. Bose
14. Even a transnational social field must have its boundaries:
    methodological options, potentials and dilemmas for
    researching transnationalism   295
    Paolo Boccagni
15. Mixing methods in research on diaspora policies   319
    Alan Gamlen

PART IV   EXPLORING SPECIFIC MIGRATION TOPICS

16. Diasporas on the web: new networks, new methodologies   345
    Jonathan Crush, Cassandra Eberhardt, Mary Caesar,
    Abel Chikanda, Wade Pendleton and Ashley Hill
17. Approaches to researching environmental change and
    migration: methodological considerations and field
    experiences from a global comparative survey project   366
    Koko Warner
18. Chasing ghosts: researching illegality in migrant labour
    markets
    Bridget Anderson, Ben Rogaly and Martin Ruhs   396
19. Using qualitative research methods in migration studies: a
    case study of asylum seekers fleeing gender-based persecution   411
    Connie Oxford
20. The importance of accounting for variability in remittance
    income   430
    Catalina Amuedo-Dorantes and Susan Pozo

PART V PRACTICAL ISSUES IN MIGRATION RESEARCH

21. Ethical challenges in research with vulnerable migrants 451
    Ilse van Liempt and Veronika Bilger
22. A guide to managing large-scale migration research projects 467
    Melissa Siegel

PART VI MOVING FROM RESEARCH TO PUBLISHED WORK

23. From dissertation to published research: so close, yet so far 483
    Anna O. Law
24. What the textbooks don't tell you: moving from a research puzzle to publishing findings 502
    Irene Bloemraad

PART VII EXPERIENCES FROM THE FIELD

25. Immigrants and 'American' franchises: experiences from the field 523
    Jennifer Parker Talwar
26. In the factories and on the streets: studying Asian and Latino garment workers in New York City 545
    Margaret M. Chin
27. Three mistakes and corrections: on reflective adaptation in qualitative data collection and analysis 560
    Johanna Shih

Index 573

Contributors

Catalina Amuedo-Dorantes, Professor of Economics, San Diego State University, USA.

Bridget Anderson, Senior Research Fellow at the Centre on Migration, Policy and Society, University of Oxford, UK.

Raka Banerjee, Extended Term Consultant at the Development Research Group, World Bank, USA.

David Bartram, Senior Lecturer of Sociology, University of Leicester, UK.

Veronika Bilger, Programme Manager, International Centre for Migration Policy Development, Austria.

Irene Bloemraad, Associate Professor of Sociology, University of California at Berkeley, USA.

Paolo Boccagni, Assistant Professor of Sociology, University of Trento, Italy.

Pablo S. Bose, Assistant Professor of Geography, University of Vermont, USA.

Mary Caesar, Researcher in the Southern African Migration Programme, Queen's University, Canada.

Calogero Carletto, Senior Economist at the Development Research Group, World Bank, USA.

Jørgen Carling, Research Professor, Peace Research Institute Oslo, Norway.

Stephen Castles, Research Professor of Sociology, University of Sydney, Australia.

Abel Chikanda, SSHRC Post-Doctoral Research Fellow, Queen's University, Canada.

Margaret M. Chin, Associate Professor of Sociology, Hunter College, City University of New York, USA.

Jonathan Crush, Professor of Global Development Studies, Queen's University, Canada and Honorary Professor, University of Cape Town, South Africa.

Alan de Brauw, Senior Research Fellow, International Food Policy Research Institute, USA.

Raúl Delgado Wise, Professor of Development Studies, Universidad Autónoma de Zacatecas, Mexico.

Cassandra Eberhardt, Researcher in the Southern African Migration Programme, Queen's University, Canada.

Edward Funkhouser, Associate Professor of Economics, California State University, USA.

Alan Gamlen, Lecturer of Human Geography, Victoria University of Wellington, New Zealand.

Ashley Hill, Researcher in the Southern African Migration Programme, Queen's University, Canada.

Dirk Hoerder, Emeritus Professor of History, Arizona State University, USA.

Theodoros Iosifides, Assistant Professor of Social Science Methods, Department of Geography, University of the Aegean, Greece.

Anna O. Law, Associate Professor of Political Science, DePaul University, USA.

Fernando A. Lozano, Associate Professor of Economics, Pomona College, USA.

Humberto Márquez Covarrubias, Professor of Development Studies, Universidad Autónoma de Zacatecas, Mexico.

David McKenzie, Lead Economist at the Development Research Group, World Bank, USA.

Connie Oxford, Assistant Professor, State University of New York, Plattsburgh, USA.

Jennifer Parker Talwar, Associate Professor of Sociology, Pennsylvania State University at Lehigh Valley, USA.

Wade Pendleton, Emeritus Professor of Anthropology, San Diego State University, USA and Research Associate, University of Cape Town, South Africa.

Susan Pozo, Professor of Economics, Western Michigan University, USA.

Ben Rogaly, Senior Lecturer in Human Geography, University of Sussex, UK.

Martin Ruhs, Senior Researcher at the Centre on Migration, Policy and Society, University of Oxford, UK.

Luis Sánchez-Ayala, Assistant Professor of Geography, Universidad de Los Andes, Colombia.

Johanna Shih, Associate Professor of Sociology, Hofstra University, USA.

Melissa Siegel, Assistant Professor of Governance, Maastricht University, Netherlands.

Ronald Skeldon, Professorial Fellow in Geography, University of Sussex, UK.

Michael D. Steinberger, Associate Professor of Economics, Pomona College, USA.

Ilse van Liempt, Assistant Professor in Qualitative Research Methods at Utrecht University, Department of Human Geography and Planning, Netherlands.

Carlos Vargas-Silva, Senior Researcher, Centre on Migration, Policy and Society, University of Oxford, UK.

Koko Warner, Head of the Environmental Migration, Social Vulnerability and Adaptation Section at the United Nations University Institute for Environmental and Human Security, Germany.

Dean Yang, Associate Professor of Public Policy and Economics, University of Michigan, USA.

Introduction
Carlos Vargas-Silva

Migration research has expanded significantly during the last three decades. Nowadays there are many graduate programmes around the world (both at the master's and doctoral level) in which students can specialize on migration-related topics as distinct as integration, discrimination, forced migration, labour migration and development. Many of these programmes are discipline specific (for example, Anthropology, Demography, Economics, Geography, History, Law, Political Science and Sociology), while others (probably the majority) follow a interdisciplinary perspective. At the same time many academic outlets, including several migration-specific journals, have come into existence in order to disseminate this increasing stock of research.

The key policy implications of migration research suggest that this interest in migration will keep expanding in the future. Immigrant receiving countries are constantly looking for better ways to attract the most talented individuals to fill labour shortages in the high skilled sector and low skilled workers that may allow for the provision of services at a lower cost. At the same time there is a growing preoccupation in these countries about the impact of population growth as a result of immigration and the possible impacts of immigration on the provision of public services, local culture and the labour market outcomes of their citizens. These countries are also concerned about the arrival of new asylum seekers from the increasing political instability of some countries in the developing world. Developing countries, on the other hand, want to exploit the opportunities that arise from their citizens moving abroad. For instance, channelling remittances for more productive uses is a policy priority in many countries of the developing world. These countries also worry about losing their best through the brain drain process. Finally, many developing countries want to look after their citizens abroad, and protect them against human rights abuses. For these, and many other reasons, we can expect migration to remain an important issue in policy discussions.

The permanent importance of migration for policy in the developed and developing world, in addition to the large stock of migrants around the world (over 200 million), suggest that learning more about migration research is a great investment for anyone interested in shaping the future of the world we live in. That is where this handbook becomes handy.

This handbook is an interdisciplinary collection, which can be used as a learning tool and reference for anyone interested in migration research methods, including students, academics, policymakers and other professionals. The chapters of the handbook maintain an introductory level of discussion in all topics and provide readers with the references necessary to go deeper into the topics.

The handbook is divided in seven parts. The first part has two purposes. First, it introduces and defines key concepts in migration research. For instance, the chapter by Castles (Chapter 1) makes a distinction between the concepts of methods and methodology, Bartram (Chapter 3) explores the concepts of variation and conceptualization, while Hoerder (Chapter 4) discusses the methodological consequences of using terms such as transnational, transregional, translocal and transcultural. The second purpose of this first part of the handbook is to introduce different perspectives on migration research. Iosifides (Chapter 2) offers an interesting introduction to the critical realism perspective, while Delgado Wise and Márquez Covarrubias (Chapter 5) provide the perspective of the political economy.

The second part is in essence the core component of the handbook with regards to introducing the reader to a range of techniques and approaches in migration research. The techniques introduced range from those that are qualitative in nature such as the interviewing techniques by Sánchez-Ayala (Chapter 6) and migration histories by Carling (Chapter 7), to the quantitative discussions of Lozano and Steinberger (Chapter 8), Funkhouser (Chapter 9), Carletto et al. (Chapter 10), Skeldon (Chapter 11) and McKenzie and Yang (Chapter 12). Lozano and Steinberger introduce readers to the methods used by economists to explore the nature and impacts of immigration, including immigrant assimilation, immigrant selection and impact on receiving labour markets. Funkhouser explores the potential for using panel data in migration research, a key discussion given the increasing availability of longitudinal data on migrants and their families. Carletto et al. discuss sampling techniques, and survey instruments to collect data on migration. This discussion is expanded to the macro level by Skeldon, whose chapter highlights the difficulties in interpreting the data on migration that is contained in international databases. Finally, McKenzie and Yang introduce natural experiments and policy experiments in migration research. The experimental 'route' proposed by these authors is a novel and resourceful way to conduct quantitative research in migration given that it avoids many of the existing econometric challenges.

The third part of the handbook moves into interdisciplinary territory. Bose (Chapter 13) explains the advantages of interdisciplinary approaches, including triangulating research strategies. Boccagni (Chapter 14) makes a strong case for mixed-methods approaches in the study of transnationalism, while also highlighting the need for further methodological elaboration. Finally, Gamlen (Chapter 15) delineates a mixed-methods framework for exploring the policies of migrants' sending states.

In the fourth part, researchers present ways of exploring different migration topics based on their research projects. One common idea across some of these chapters is to explore migration in relation to current events, themes and innovations. For instance, Crush et al. (Chapter 16) discuss the use of several internet networks such as Facebook to collect data on the diaspora from African countries. Meanwhile, Warner (Chapter 17) discusses the methodology of a project exploring the impact of environmental change on migration, another very current topic. This part of the handbook continues with a discussion of the challenges in researching undocumented migration (Chapter 18 by Anderson et al.) and asylum seekers (Chapter 19 by Oxford). Finally, Amuedo-Dorantes and Pozo present evidence on the variability of remittances and the importance to account for this fact in order to avoid biases in statistical results (Chapter 20).

Towards the end, the handbook turns into a guide, instead of just a discussion of research methods and projects. It starts this guidance by introducing some practical issues in migration research, including ethical challenges that researchers encounter while doing research with vulnerable migrants (Chapter 21 by van Liempt and Bilger). In this part there is also a discussion of the logistics of conducting a migration research project by Siegel (Chapter 22). In the sixth part there are two chapters (Chapter 23 by Law and Chapter 24 by Bloemraad) that discuss the process of research from the personal perspective of the researchers, putting emphasis on the process of converting research into published work. So, this guidance works very well as it provides information on how to conduct an academic investigation (including ethical and logistical issues), followed by a discussion of publishing those research findings.

Finally, the handbook concludes with a testimony from several researchers with regards to their research experiences and the methodological challenges that they encountered along the way (Chapter 25 by Parker Talwar, Chapter 26 by Chin and Chapter 27 by Shih). This final part of the handbook is intended to provide a more intimate view on the experience of being a migration researcher. Therefore, it adopts a more relaxing and storytelling point of view, while at the same time making explicit reference to all the methodological challenges that are present during migration research. As such, this handbook starts with a fairly dense discussion of research concepts and approaches, moves into specific techniques and practices and then shifts to actual research experiences. The goal of these transitions is to expose the reader to the diverse universe of migration research methods.

PART I

FUNDAMENTAL ISSUES OF SCIENTIFIC LOGIC, METHODOLOGY AND METHODS IN MIGRATION STUDIES

1 Understanding the relationship between methodology and methods
Stephen Castles[1]

Methodology and methods are often confused, or used as if they meant the same thing. Many articles in the social sciences have a section on 'methodology' that merely describes the methods used in a study, but does not actually discuss methodology. Methodology and methods are closely connected, but they are not the same thing.

Methodology is about the underlying logic of research. It is closely linked to the branch of philosophy known as epistemology – literally 'the theory of knowledge'. Epistemology asks such questions as: 'What is knowledge?' 'How is knowledge acquired?' 'How can we know something to be true?' A key dispute in epistemology is between 'positivists' who claim that there is an objective world outside ourselves as observers, and 'constructivists', who believe that meanings are constructed, interpreted and constantly reconstructed by people in their perceptions and social interactions. Methodology involves the systematic application of epistemology to research situations. It deals with the principles of the methods, concepts and procedural rules employed by a scientific discipline.

Methods, by contrast, are specific techniques used to collect and analyse information or data. Data collection methods include, for instance, literature reviews, censuses or other large datasets, surveys, qualitative interviews, household budget analysis, life histories and participant observation. Data analysis methods include, for instance, literature analysis, content (or textual) analysis, qualitative analysis, simple tabulations, cross-tabulations, regression analysis, social mapping, network analysis and socio-grams. It is important to specify the methods of data collection and analysis in any report or publication describing a research study.

Each discipline has its own methodology and methods. Here we are concerned with those of the social sciences and their specific application in migration research. Methodology is our chart to navigate the social world while methods are the tools of our trade. An important starting point to understand this is a discussion of the place of the social sciences in contemporary society.

8   Handbook of research methods in migration

1.1   THE TASKS OF SOCIAL SCIENCE

According to the famous book on *The Sociological Imagination* by C. Wright Mills, a feature of all classic work in social science is the distinction between 'the personal troubles of milieu' and 'the public issues of social structure'. 'Troubles' have to do with the character of the individual and his immediate relations with others, while 'issues' have to do with matters that transcend these local environments of the individual and the range of his inner life. Mills illustrates this point by looking at unemployment: if one man in a city of 100,000 is unemployed, that is his personal trouble, and the solutions lie in his own character, skills and opportunities. But if in a nation of 50 million employees, 15 million are unemployed, that is an issue that cannot be resolved by an individual, but requires action by the economic and political institutions of society (Mills, 1959 [2000], pp. 8–9).[2] In *The Sociological Imagination*, Mills argued for the need to link history and biography – that is, to 'understand the larger historical scene in terms of its meaning for the inner life and the external career of a variety of individuals' (Mills, 1959 [2000], p. 5).

This is a simple but profound statement of the tasks of social science: it needs to analyse the collective behaviour of human beings and how this is linked to social structures and institutions, the changing historical context of specific societies and the character types prevailing in each society. No social action can be understood without an understanding of the broader context in which it takes place. Isolated studies of single issues (or 'social facts') do not help people to grasp the complex processes that are at work, nor do they lead to adequate strategies for public policy. Social inquiry should be relevant to the pressing issues facing individuals and groups in society, and should be grounded in historical understanding. This is particularly important for migration research: it is indeed important to carry out micro-level studies of specific migratory experiences, but they should always be embedded in an understanding of the macro-level structural factors that shape human mobility in a specific historical situation.

1.2   HOW CAN WE UNDERSTAND SOCIAL ISSUES?

But how can social researchers implement such principles in practice? What social scientific methodology and what specific research methods can be used to develop our understanding of social behaviour and issues within their historical context? The debate on this topic continues to play an important part in the social sciences as a whole and within each individual discipline. For example, the American Sociological Association publishes an influential journal entitled *Sociological Methodology*. University libraries contain shelves of books on the methodology of economics, political science, geography, demography, anthropology and indeed all the social science disciplines. Professional conferences include workshops and training sessions on how best to plan and implement research.

Yet there are wide divergences between and within disciplines in methodological approaches, ranging from the emphasis on quantitative analysis of large datasets (that is, econometrics) and the relative absence of fieldwork in economics, to the reliance on in-depth case studies and ethnographic fieldwork in anthropology. Other disciplines are somewhere in between, but all grapple with problems of knowing and understanding. In recent years, the rise of 'mixed-methods' approaches within disciplines and the call for interdisciplinarity in addressing complex real-world issues (such as migration or development) have made things even more complicated. A key problem of interdisciplinarity is the very different definitions of knowledge and the assumptions on how to obtain it, which social scientists absorb during their specific training in the various disciplines.

In the USA, quantitative methods were dominant until quite recently in such disciplines as sociology and political science, and a great deal of social research has been concerned with refining statistical techniques to improve analysis of large datasets. For many years, critical thinkers (such as Mills) have argued that such approaches may advance the description of social phenomena, but do very little to increase understanding of the processes which bring them about or indeed to find solutions to the pressing dilemmas of society. In recent times, recognition of the need for qualitative research and case studies has grown, and professional bodies (such as the American Political Science Association) encourage training in such approaches. However, their advocates in the USA sometimes seem to be trying to justify why qualitative methods can be a useful 'second best', and some advocates of 'mixed methods' appear to have an almost patronising attitude to qualitative approaches, trying to introduce forms of analysis and automation (for example, in textual analysis) that turn quality into quantity (see, for instance, King et al., 1994).

This emphasis on the quantitative has been driven by two factors: the availability of high-quality statistics in large datasets such as censuses and labour-force surveys, and the declining costs and growing power of computer analysis packages. These factors do not necessarily prevail everywhere in the world. In many developing regions, censuses and other official data collections may be absent, irregular or unreliable. Similarly, high-quality computer equipment is often not widely available to researchers. Reliance on official data can be especially problematic in migration research. Even in the most developed regions, migration statistics are based on differing definitions and categories, and are collected in different ways from country to country, because they reflect national migration policies and ideologies. Even the Organization for Economic Cooperation and Development (OECD) has taken some 30 years to work towards comparability in the data published each year in its annual Migration Outlook reports (formerly known as the SOPEMI reports). Many users of this data would argue that comparability, although improved, is still far from perfect.

Migration researchers therefore need to be very cautious in aggregating national data into regression models. This applies all the more in migrants' origin regions, where statistical data may not be available or reliable, and where international comparisons therefore require great care. Researchers in such regions need to develop methods of data collection and analysis that reflect the realities of the society (or societies) concerned. However, such approaches should not be seen as a 'second best'. Rather researchers working in the Global South can draw on a range of traditions in the social sciences, which emphasize the importance of understanding social phenomena and the processes which bring them about, rather than merely describing and counting superficial indicators. A precondition for innovation in migration research methods is an examination of the epistemological basis of the varying approaches.

1.3 OBJECTIVITY VERSUS SOCIAL CONSTRUCTION

In the social sciences the dispute between positivists and constructivists has been particularly important (see Iosifides, Chapter 2, this volume for an expanded discussion). Positivists believe that there is a single objective truth or 'reality' that can be found in studying social institutions or practices. The influential early French sociologist Emile Durkheim spoke of 'social facts', which he characterized as 'ways of acting, thinking and feeling, external to the individual, and endowed with a power of coercion, by which they control him' (Durkheim and Catlin, 1895 [1938], p. 3). His 'first and most fundamental rule' of sociological method was to 'consider social facts as things' (Durkheim and Catlin, 1895 [1938], p. 14). The implication was that social practices and institutions take on an objective and hence measurable character, which is independent of human action and agency. Later US functionalist sociology followed this approach (see Parsons, 1951).

By contrast, early German sociologist Max Weber argued that the observer has to try to understand the 'meaning' of social action and

Understanding the relationship between methodology and methods

institutions for the people involved, leading to the idea of 'interpretative sociology'. He argued that 'an "objective" analysis of cultural events, which proceeds according to the thesis that the ideal of science is the reduction of empirical reality to "laws" is meaningless' (Weber et al., 1949, p. 80). An important reason for this was that social and cultural knowledge was always conditioned through 'evaluative ideas'. He therefore argued that value judgements – especially about the relevance of social matters – could not be banished from science. Rather, the principle of 'value freedom' meant that the researcher should strive to make a clear distinction between values and knowledge (Weber et al., 1949, pp. 49–112). Thus, Weber argues: 'both for sociology in the present sense, and for history, the object of cognition is the subjective-meaning complex of action' (Weber, 1947, p. 101) (quoted from Berger and Luckmann, 1966, p. 16).

In an important work on the 'sociology of knowledge', Berger and Luckmann argue that this apparent gulf between the two great theorists actually reflects 'the dual character of society' leading to the central question for sociological theory: 'how is it possible that subjective meanings *become* objective facticities?' (Berger and Luckmann, 1966, p. 17, emphasis in original). Berger and Luckmann make a strong argument for social constructivism – that is, the principle that knowledge about social relationships and practices is constantly being created, modified and recreated through processes of social interaction. People in society perceive social phenomena as a reality that is independent of their own volition, even though these social phenomena are constructed by human beings and can therefore be changed by them. Judgements on reality are socially relative: 'what is "real" to a Tibetan monk may not be "real" to an American businessman'. 'Reality' and 'knowledge' pertain to specific social contexts – and these contexts must always be analysed before a social scientist can understand the meaning of these concepts for the people concerned (Berger and Luckmann, 1966, pp. 2–3). This concern for context harks back to Marx's recognition that 'man's consciousness is determined by his social being' (Berger and Luckmann, 1966, p. 5).

1.4 THE CONSEQUENCES OF METHODOLOGY FOR CHOICE OF RESEARCH APPROACHES

For positivists, social science is a matter of improving research methods to the point at which they can accurately describe and measure social facts. For constructivists, social sciences have to interpret the social meanings that they find, and may actually influence these in the process. Positivists believe in objectivity, while constructivists believe that there is no single truth in social phenomena. Early positivists claimed to be bringing the certainty and objectivity of the natural sciences into social research. However, the questioning of the immutable laws of Newtonian physics by early twentieth-century quantum mechanics undermined this approach. Quantum mechanics works with probability rather than certainty and its 'uncertainty principle' (proposed by the physicist Heisenberg) states that by measuring something, the researcher actually changes it (Heisenberg et al., 1977). Nevertheless, many quantitative social researchers have come to believe that ever more sophisticated statistical packages and computer analysis can lead to objectivity.

Constructivists, by contrast, point to the complexity of social situations, and the impossibility of building models that can really include all possible factors. They argue that the dominant approach to social science (often imposed through the peer review process of influential US and international journals) is inherently reductionist: the researcher carries out a literature review and derives a research question from existing theoretical and descriptive material. The question has to be narrow or limited enough to be answered by linking a set of variables available in recognized datasets – fieldwork is rarely carried out by users of advanced statistical techniques. The researcher puts together a list of 'stylized facts' seen as the state of knowledge on the topic concerned. Then a hypothesis is tested by preparing a model of factors and interactions between them seen as relevant by the researcher. The data is fed through a regression analysis, and the researcher can then publish the results, which usually confirm his or her hypothesis. The reductionism is visible at various stages of the process: the existing understanding of the problem may be incomplete or flawed; the factors chosen for the model may not reflect the complexity of human decision-making so that important factors may have been left out; the people concerned are not asked about the meaning they attribute to practices or actions; the interactions of variables in the model may not reflect the importance of various factors in social processes, and there is a danger of detecting spurious correlations.

Emphasis on the social meanings constructed by people in diverse communities and societies, and on the relativity and context-dependence of these meanings implies quite different ways of doing research. The aim must be to understand the historical and current processes through which social meanings develop and change, and what they signify to people. The methods needed to understand processes and meanings include ethnographic study, qualitative interviews (using open-ended questions to allow people to explain their own meanings), case studies and participant observation.

Understanding the relationship between methodology and methods 13

But both positivistic and constructivist approaches can be one-sided. The social scientist needs to find out both what actually happens in society – that is, what are the forms of social behaviour, practices, customs and institutions – and why and how it happens. Thus there is a need both for big-number analysis using descriptive and analytical statistics and for micro-level studies using ethnographic and case-study methods. Mixed-method approaches seem the best way to develop greater understanding of social issues and of their relevance to individual and group life. Ideally, research teams should include people with knowledge of a range of approaches, and – hardest of all – with the ability to cooperate across methodological and disciplinary boundaries.

1.5 METHODOLOGY AND METHODS IN MIGRATION RESEARCH PRACTICE

Methodology asks such question as:

- How can we obtain knowledge about a social practice or a relationship, such as about its frequency, its significance, the process through which it emerges and its links with other aspects of a social situation?
- What leads us to believe that the methods of data collection and analysis we want to use will actually provide valid and reliable data?
- How can we understand the significance and meaning of a social practice or institution for those involved?

For example, if we use the method of a sample survey in an African city to answer a research question about people's intentions to migrate to another country, how do we know:

- That our sample is representative of the population we want to study?
- That our respondents have the same understanding of the questions as we do?
- That they are willing and able to tell us what they really think?
- That their stated intentions provide an accurate guide to their actual behaviour?

Many further issues could be added. These are methodological questions that cast doubt on uncritical use of quantitative methods. They require us to ask if the methods we use will really provide accurate answers to our research questions. The use of increasingly sophisticated data analysis software has led some people to think that if they feed quantitative data (numbers) into a regression analysis package, they will get scientifically valid results. However, if the quality of the data is poor (due to mistaken or narrow assumptions, lack of reliable statistics or inadequate survey techniques), then the results may be misleading. Of course this applies to use of qualitative methods too: if sampling techniques are biased or inadequate, or if the researcher's understanding of the factors involved in the process under investigation are wrong, then the findings are unlikely to be valid.

To address such problems, it is important that a migration study (just like any other social scientific study) should include reflection on methodology as well as a justification of the methods used. Ideally, a research paper or report should have a section on methodology and another one on methods. At the least, an author should always address both themes, even if in the same section. A migration research proposal should:

1. Outline the issue or problem to be studied, and explain why it is significant.
2. Discuss existing literature on the theme.
3. Outline migration theory and broader social scientific theory relevant to the theme.
4. Develop one or more hypotheses or research questions based on the previous steps. These should include both 'descriptive questions' (for example, 'what forms of migration are taking place and what are the motivations and decision-making processes of the people involved'?) and 'analytical questions' (for example, 'how do the studied migratory behaviours and practices relate to each other, to other migratory patterns and to more general processes of social interaction and change?).
5. Discuss the methodological challenges to be faced in answering these questions in the research situation concerned.
6. Describe and justify the methods to be used for data collection and analysis.
7. Outline the type of outputs that are expected from the study.
8. Provide a research plan that shows how the work is to be carried out with the resources and time that are available.

A migration research report should cover the same themes, with the addition of a presentation of the information collected, a descriptive account of the data collection and analysis processes and any problems that arose during these, and a discussion of the findings. All publications arising from a migration research project should provide summaries of the methodology and methods used, and provide the reader with links or contacts to obtain fuller information on these matters if required (for example, by reading the full report and accessing the archived research data).

A methodological discussion of how a social scientist can know something or answer the research questions will often highlight the limitations of any one method of data collection and analysis. The methodological conclusion will frequently be that there should be a 'triangulation of methods' – that is, a range of different methods should be used to collect and analyse data on any specific migratory process. If the answers are the same with a range of methods, this allows a much higher degree of confidence in their accuracy. If the answers are different, then it is likely that the methods are not actually answering the questions as the researcher had expected. In addition, use of multiple (or mixed) methods provides broader and more profound information on the topic.

Another important methodological point is that different types of method can answer different types of question, for example:

- A cross-sectional survey (a study covering a representative sample of the individuals, families, groups, regions and countries that make up a specific population at any one time) can answer such questions as current levels of income or mobility, but it cannot tell us anything about how a phenomenon has changed or developed.
- A longitudinal study can show how such indicators have changed over time, but cannot explain the motivations or the social meanings attached to behaviours, practices and institutions.[3]
- Use of qualitative methods (non-directive interviews, social biographies, asking about family mobility trajectories) can help us understand intentions and social meanings, but cannot give an accurate measurement of the frequency of certain attitudes or behaviours.
- Historical studies can help show the development and significance of social practices, but cannot show their current extent.

This list could be prolonged. The point is that it is usually necessary to use a range of methods. For instance, the Mexican Migration Project has used a mix of large surveys and qualitative studies to describe and explain patterns of migration from Mexico to the USA. Because the project has carried out several waves of research over a long period, it also has a longitudinal (or historical) dimension (Massey et al., 2002 [2003]).

A valuable collection of reports on migration research experiences argues that 'the validity of social science knowledge derives from making manifest, and exposing to critique, the process by which meaning is derived from research'. That means demonstrating the 'credibility of the procedures by which factual information and interpretations of its significance have been acquired and produced' (DeWind, 2007, p. 9). This book – available as a free download from the website of the US Social Science Research Council – is highly recommended to migration researchers for the many useful lessons on research practice that it provides (DeSipio et al., 2007). Most of the authors of that book have also contributed updated chapters to this handbook, including the process of moving from writing a dissertation (the focus of those chapters) to publishing in academic journals and finishing book manuscripts and experiences doing post-doctoral research.[4]

One of the most important lessons concerns the need for 'flexibility' on the part of the researcher: repeatedly, unexpected issues and obstacles encountered in the actual research process caused researchers to question and modify their original assumptions and their research strategy. Indeed, one might conclude that anyone who starts research convinced that she or he already knows the best way of getting the answers may have a tacit belief in already knowing the answers, and will therefore probably find what he or she expects – whether it is accurate or not. In other words, the results will reflect mistaken or inadequate assumptions which have influenced the problem definition and the choice of methods.

Flexibility implies 'adaptability': the willingness of the researcher to respond to the lessons of the field and to hear what respondents are saying by changing the research strategy. This may well involve concluding that the original research question was not the best one, or that the starting hypothesis was mistaken.

1.6 GLOBAL SOCIAL TRANSFORMATION AND HUMAN MOBILITY

A deficiency of much migration research lies in its rather atheoretical nature and particularly in its failure to connect adequately with social theory. Many studies on migration and its consequences are driven by predominantly descriptive objectives – often linked to the short-term policy interests of the agencies that commission research. The result can be narrow empiricism that does little to explain social action and how it changes. But if we understand methodology as the bridge between social theory and research methods, then it is crucial to start all migration research projects with objectives and questions that are grounded in broad theoretical frameworks.

I will conclude this chapter by sketching briefly my own perspective on social theory and migration research. This starts from the principle that migration researchers should always site their research in the context of broader processes of social transformation, which, for the contemporary epoch, means examining the way neo-liberal globalization and reactions against it have reshaped societies, communities and cultures (see Castles and Miller, 2009, especially chapter 3). According to this approach, migration studies should analyse movements of people in terms of their multi-layered links to other forms of global connectivity. Macro-trends in economic, political and military affairs are crucial in reshaping the global space in which human movements take place. The closely related shifts in social and cultural patterns are also important in influencing the forms and volume of mobility, and the social meanings they have for those involved.

That implies, first, seeing migration not as something exceptional or problematic, but as a central part of processes of social change everywhere. Migration should be analysed therefore not primarily as a result of social transformation, nor a cause of social transformation, but as an integral part of most processes of social transformation (Castles, 2009). This means questioning the widespread understanding of 'migration as a problem to be solved' that is expressed in many official statements on migration policy as well as in official rationales for migration research (IMI, 2006). The dominant role played in migration research by governments and intergovernmental bodies has led to a 'sedentary bias' – that is, the belief that development should take place in rural areas and that poor people should not move (Bakewell, 2008; Bakewell and de Haas, 2007). This sedentary bias may block understanding of the significance of migration as a way of accessing opportunities, improving human rights and security, and developing sustainable livelihoods (UNDP, 2009).

Second, it means reflecting on the nature of processes of contemporary social transformation, and including in our analytical models such key trends as neo-liberal globalization (and the resulting growth in inequality); the increasing economic, political and cultural integration of local communities and national societies into cross-border interactions; and the growth of transnationalism as a form of human agency.

Contemporary trends to cross-border economic and political integration lead to processes of social transformation in all types of society. The idea of 'transformation' implies a fundamental change in the way society is organized that goes beyond the continual processes of social change that are always at work.[5] This arises when there are major shifts in dominant power relationships. Massive shifts in economic, political and military affairs since the mid-1970s (and especially since the end of the Cold War in the 1990s) represent such a fundamental change. Globalization has uneven effects. Indeed it can be seen as a process of inclusion of particular regions and social groups in world capitalist market relations, and of exclusion of others (Castells, 1996).

Rural-urban migration in the Global South is driven both by the erosion of older forms of rural production and the growth of new urban opportunities. Often social transformation starts in agriculture. The 'green revolution' of the 1980s involved the introduction of new strains of rice and other crops, which promised higher yields, but in return required big investments in fertilizers, insecticides and mechanization. The result was higher productivity but also concentration of ownership in the hands of richer farmers. Many poorer farmers lost their livelihoods and had to leave the land. The process continues today with the introduction of genetically modified seed-stock. The pressure on farmers in poor regions is increased by farm subsidies in rich countries – especially US cotton subsidies and the European Union (EU) Common Agricultural Policy (Oxfam, 2002) – which depress world market prices.

At the same time urban employment opportunities have grown – albeit unevenly. In the early stages of urbanization, most urban growth is the result of rural-urban migration. As cities grow, and rural labour reserves are used up, natural increase in cities outstrips new rural inflows, although that natural increase can also be seen in part as a consequence of earlier inflows of young adults. Cities also grow through the outward expansion of their boundaries, as formerly rural areas are absorbed (Skeldon, 2009). Industrialization in emerging economic powers such as China, India and Brazil has been linked to a rapid growth in inequality between urban and rural incomes (Milanovic, 2007, pp. 35–9). The cities of the South, like Sao Paolo, Shanghai, Calcutta or Jakarta, are growing at a rate of about 70 million a year – and most of the new inhabitants can only find accommodation in informal housing or slum areas (Davis, 2006). Labour market entrants with the skills, education or good fortune to find jobs in formal sector activities may do well, but formal employment growth cannot keep pace with labour market growth, so that large numbers of workers end up in precarious informal sector jobs, or in cycles of sporadic work and unemployment. For these groups, standards of housing, health and education are low, while crime, violence and human rights violations are rife. Such conditions are powerful motivations to seek better livelihoods elsewhere, either in growth areas within the region or in the North.

Inequality has not been reduced by the global economic crisis that started in 2007 – indeed the overall effect may well prove to be even greater redistribution of wealth from poor and middle-income groups to the already wealthy. The social transformations inherent in globalization do not just affect economic well-being – they also lead to increased violence

Understanding the relationship between methodology and methods 19

and lack of human security in the Global South. The great majority of those affected by violence are displaced within their own countries, or seek refuge in other – usually equally poor – countries in the region. But some try to obtain asylum in the richer states of the North, where they hope to find more security and freedom – as well as better livelihoods.

Social transformation drives emigration from poorer countries, but it is also a process that affects richer countries, shaping the conditions for immigration and incorporation. The increased export of capital to low-wage economies since the 1970s had a reciprocal effect in the Global North: old 'rustbelt industries' declined, blue-collar workers lost their secure jobs, and often found their skills devalued. Factories were replaced by distribution depots, shopping malls and call centres, employing de-unionized and casualized labour. The neo-liberal turn in economic policy meant a decline in welfare states, trends towards privatization and individualization and the erosion of community solidarity. At the same time, declining fertility, population ageing and changes in work locations and requirements created a strong demand for immigrants of all skill levels. Immigration and settlement thus took place in a situation of rapid change, uncertainty and insecurity for host populations. Immigrants became the visible symbol of globalization – and were therefore often blamed for threatening and incomprehensible changes. This helps to explain the rise of extreme-right racist groups since the 1980s (Schierup et al., 2006).

1.7 CONSEQUENCES OF A SOCIAL TRANSFORMATION APPROACH FOR MIGRATION STUDIES

The processes of social transformation that arise from globalization are the crucial context for understanding twenty-first-century migration. The flows and networks that constitute globalization take on specific forms at different spatial levels: the regional, the national and the local. These should be understood as elements of complex and dynamic relationships, in which 'global forces' have varying impacts according to differing structural and cultural factors and responses at the other levels (see Held et al., 1999, pp. 14–16). Historical experiences, cultural values, religious beliefs, institutions and social structures all channel and shape the effects of external forces, leading to forms of change and resistance that bring about very different outcomes in specific communities or societies.

For most people, the pre-eminent level for experiencing migration and its effects is 'the local'. This applies especially where processes of social transformation create conditions which encourage people to leave their communities of origin to move elsewhere. Development processes may help people obtain the education, knowledge and financial resources needed to access opportunities for better livelihoods in other regions or countries. On the other hand, changes in agricultural practices or land tenure may drive farmers from the land, or development projects (such as dams, airports or factories) may physically displace people. Migration itself may become a force for further social transformation: the departure of young active people, gender imbalances, financial and social remittances can all transform conditions in the local community – in ways that may be either conducive to or detrimental to economic and social development. Similarly, the impact of immigration in migrant-destination areas is felt in the way it affects economic restructuring and social relations in local communities.

'National'-level impacts of global forces are also important. Nation-states remain the location for policies on cross-border movements, citizenship, public order, social welfare, health services and education. Nation-states retain considerable political significance and have important symbolic and cultural functions. But it is no longer possible to abstract from cross-border factors in decision-making and planning. One result of this is the growing importance of 'regional' cooperation through bodies like the EU, North American Free Trade Agreement (NAFTA) or the Economic Community of West African States (ECOWAS).

Researchers therefore need to be aware of the way migration processes – like all forms of social transformation – work across socio-spatial levels. Whether we start from the level of global phenomena – like the overall expansion of international migration – or local phenomena – like changes in a specific village brought about by migrant remittances – we need to take account of multi-level linkages, and to examine the complex processes that shape these. Understanding migration as an integral part of social transformation has important consequences for the theory, methodology and organizational forms of migration studies.

1.7.1 Theory

Migration theory is concerned with the social consequences of transnational or cross-border human movements. Migration studies should analyse movements of people in terms of their multi-layered links to other forms of global connectivity. Macro-trends in economic, political and military affairs are crucial in reshaping the global space in which people movements take place. The closely related shifts in social and cultural patterns are also important in influencing the forms and volume of mobility.

Understanding the relationship between methodology and methods 21

Theorists of neo-liberal globalization often argue that contemporary economic and political relationships imply shifts away from hierarchical power structures towards network patterns, in which centralized power is being replaced by transnational functional cooperation. Multinational corporations or international organizations are seen as representing rational divisions of responsibilities, rather than top-down power hierarchies. Yet the differentiation of migrants between privileged possessors of human capital credentials and disadvantaged groups with weak legal status who can be easily exploited casts doubt on this positive view. By linking hierarchies of migration and citizenship to the power dynamics embedded in economic and political institutions, migration researchers can contribute to the analysis of new forms of social relationships.

As already pointed out, a key dimension of migration theory lies in conceptualizing the way social transformation processes act at different spatial levels (local, regional, national and global) (cf. Pries, 2007). Analysing the mediation and transformation of global forces by local or national cultural and historical factors can help overcome the division between top-down and bottom-up approaches. This implies that attempts to create a 'general theory of migration' are unlikely to be helpful, because such a theory would be so abstract that it would give little guidance to understanding any real migratory processes (Portes, 1999). Rather migration theory needs to be historically and culturally sited, and to relate structure and action.

1.7.2 Methodology

Migration researchers need to take a 'holistic approach', linking research on specific migration experiences to broader studies of the transformation of whole societies and how this is connected to global trends. This in turn implies the need for interdisciplinarity: migration processes affect all dimensions of social existence and cannot be reduced simply to the subject areas of specific disciplines like anthropology, law, sociology or economics. Migration researchers should work in interdisciplinary teams in larger projects, and make use of the published research findings of other disciplines in smaller ones.

Clearly, most forms of migration research are likely to require 'mixed-methods approaches' (for an example see Gamlen, Chapter 15, this volume). Quantitative research is important for obtaining comparative data to describe macro-social changes linked to migration. At the same time, 'qualitative approaches' are needed to provide understanding both of individual and community-level social action, and of the history and cultures of sending, transit and receiving societies.

Castells, M. (1996), *The Rise of the Network Society*, Oxford: Blackwells.
Castles, S. (2007), 'Twenty-first century migration as a challenge to sociology', *Journal of Ethnic and Migration Studies*, **33** (3), 351–71.
Castles, S. (2009), *Development and Migration – Migration and Development: What Comes First? Migration and Development: Future Directions for Research and Policy*, New York: Social Science Research Council, available at http://programs.ssrc.org/intmigration/2Castles.pdf (accessed 11 May 2009).
Castles, S. and Miller, M.J. (2009), *The Age of Migration: International Population Movements in the Modern World*, 4th edn, Basingstoke and New York: Palgrave Macmillan and Guilford.
Davis, M. (2006), *Planet of Slums*, London and New York: Verso.
DeSipio, L., Garcia y Griego, M. and Kossoudji, S. (eds) (2007), *Researching Migration: Stories from the Field*, New York: Social Science Research Council.
DeWind, J. (2007), 'Preface', in L. DeSipio, M. Garcia y Griego and S. Kossoudji (eds), *Researching Migration: Stories from the Field*, New York: Social Science Research Council, pp. 9–12.
Durkheim, E. and Catlin, G.E.G. (1895 [1938]), *The Rules of Sociological Method*, 8th edn, New York: Free Press of Glencoe.
Heisenberg, W., Price, W.C. and Chissick, S.S. (1977), *The Uncertainty Principle and Foundations of Quantum Mechanics: A Fifty Years' Survey*, New York: Wiley.
Held, D., McGrew, A., Goldblatt, D. and Perraton, J. (1999), *Global Transformations: Politics, Economics and Culture*, Cambridge: Polity.
IMI (2006), *Towards a New Agenda for International Migration Research*, Oxford: International Migration Institute, available at http://www.imi.ox.ac.uk/pdfs/a4-imi-research-agenda.pdf (accessed 14 October 2011).
King, G., Keohane, R.O. and Verba, S. (1994), *Designing Social Inquiry: Scientific Inference in Qualitative Research*, Princeton, NJ: Princeton University Press.
Massey, D.S., Durand, J. and Malone, N.J. (2002 [2003]), *Beyond Smoke and Mirrors. Mexican Immigration in an Era of Economic Integration*, New York: Russell Sage Foundation.
Milanovic, B. (2007), 'Globalization and inequality', in D. Held and A. Kaya (eds), *Global Inequality: Patterns and Explanations*, Cambridge and Malden, MA: Polity, pp. 26–49.
Mills, C.W. (1959 [2000]), *The Sociological Imagination*, Oxford: Oxford University Press.
Munck, R. (2002), 'Globalization and democracy: a new "great transformation"?', *Annals of the American Academy of Political and Social Science*, **58**, 110–21.
Oxfam (2002), *Rigged Rules and Double Standards: Trade, Globalization, and the Fight against Poverty*, Oxford: Oxfam.
Parsons, T. (1951), *The Social System*, London: Routledge and Kegan Paul.
Polanyi, K. (2001), *The Great Transformation*, Boston, MA: Beacon Press.
Portes, A. (1999), 'The hidden abode: sociology as analysis of the unexpected – 1999 Presidential Address to the American Sociological Association', *American Sociological Review*, **65** (1), 1–18.
Pries, L. (2007), *Die Transnationalisierung der sozialen Welt*, (Frankfurt am Main: Suhrkamp.
Schierup, C.-U., Hansen, P. and Castles, S. (2006), *Migration, Citizenship and the European Welfare State: A European Dilemma*, Oxford: Oxford University Press.
Skeldon, R. (2009), *Migration, Urbanization and Development*, New York: Social Science Research Council, available at http://essays.ssrc.org/developmentpapers/wp-content/uploads/2009/08/23Skeldon.pdf (accessed 1 December 2009).
Stiglitz, J.E. (1998), 'Towards a new paradigm for development: strategies, policies and processes', *1998 Prebisch Lecture UNCTAD*, Geneva: World Bank.
Stiglitz, J.E. (2002), *Globalization and its Discontents*, London: Penguin.
UNDP (2009), *Human Development Report 2009: Overcoming Barriers: Human Mobility and Development*, New York: United Nations Development Programme, available at http://hdr.undp.org/en/reports/global/hdr2009/ (accessed 14 October 2011).

Weber, M. (1947), *The Theory of Social and Economic Organization*, Oxford and New York: Oxford University Press.
Weber, M., Shils, E. and Finch, H.A. (1949), *The Methodology of the Social Sciences*, New York: The Free Press.
Wimmer, A. and Glick Schiller, N. (2003), 'Methodological nationalism, the social sciences and the study of migration', *International Migration Review,* **37** (3), 576–610.

2 Migration research between positivistic scientism and relativism: a critical realist way out
Theodoros Iosifides[1]

In this chapter, I discuss some crucial ontological and epistemological dimensions of migration research methodology that have significant repercussions on the ways migration research is designed, practised and utilised. As meta-theoretical (ontological and epistemological) dimensions are inevitably implicated and closely related with any methodological strategy in social research, including migration research, the main aim of this chapter is to highlight the consequences of positivist and relativist epistemologies for contemporary migration research methodology. Discussion starts with some central premises of contemporary scientific positivism and relativism and continues with indicating their consequences for contemporary migration research methodology. The way out from the *Scylla* of scientism and the *Charybdis* of relativism is offered in Section 2.3 and entails the adoption of a critical realist meta-theoretical approach. This approach prioritises ontology over epistemology and can serve as a guide to substantive migration research, enhancing its explanatory power and potential. In Section 2.3, I briefly refer to some central features of the realist approach and discuss more extensively its advantages for migration research practice through concrete examples. Finally, the chapter is concluded with some brief remarks about the emancipatory and critical potential of a critical realist rationale in migration research.

2.1 WAVES OF IRREALISM, REDUCTIONISM AND ONTOLOGICAL FLATNESS: POSITIVISTIC SCIENTISM AND RELATIVISM

In this section and before discussing the consequences of positivism/scientism and various forms of contemporary relativism in migration research, I briefly refer to some of the most serious limitations of these rationales in general, notably irrealism, reductionism and ontological flatness. Waves of irrealism in the philosophy of traditional and contemporary social science are responsible for most of the problems, inadequacies, limitations and distortions that plague current social theorising and methodological choices.

2.1.1 Positivism and Scientism

Although there are certain differences among the traditions of 'logical positivism', 'positivism' and 'logical empiricism' (see Hibberd, 2005, section 4.2), here I discuss crucial dimensions of the positivist tradition, notably empiricism, methodological individualism and modes of inference such as inductivism and deductivism. Right from the start, I have to assert that positivism commits the 'epistemic fallacy' due to the fact it adopts an empiricist epistemology that corresponds to a 'flat ontology' of sense experiences and data (Collier, 1994; Cruickshank, 2003; Morgan, 2007). For positivism, 'knowledge ultimately derives from sense experience' (Morgan, 2007, p. 169).

The central premises of positivist thinking may be summarised as follows (see also Iosifides, 2011):

- First, positivism takes as reality (ontological position) what it renders possible to be known as reality (epistemological position) and because what is known derives exclusively from sense experience, reality is reduced to sense experience, that is, to the levels of the empirical and the actual. Thus, positivist epistemology is 'actualistic' despite that in practice 'empiricists selectively violate the criterion of that theory. In doing so, they refer to intransitive structures, practices or sustaining possibilities that fall outside actualism' (Morgan, 2007, p. 170). The differentiation between intransitivity and transitivity, that is, between real objects/entities and theories about objects/entities, is clarified in Section 2.3.
- Second and closely linked with the previous point, positivism adopts a successionist or a regularity view of causality. This means that positivism accepts as causal the 'constant conjunction' of empirical, observable events and facts (Archer, 1998) and locates causality in the association or correlation between different variables. This, of course, entails the qualitative invariance of social objects and entities across time and context, which is at least uncommon (see Sayer, 1992, p. 177). Moreover, it presupposes 'closure', that is, the stability of both 'the object possessing the causal power in question' (Sayer, 2000, pp. 14–15) and 'external conditions in which it is situated' (Sayer, 2000, p. 15). However, '[W]hile closures of concomitance are plentiful in both the natural and social realms, closures for causal sequence are found to be rare' (Faulkner, 2007, p. 67).

Hence, the positivist notion of causality and its application in social science and research has major negative consequences regarding explanatory power and potential due to the confusion of causal with associative-correlative relations.
- Third, positivism advocates a fact-value dichotomy, which derives from its premises according to which science is about 'objective' facts, that is, about observable empirical events, while values are mere judgements that cannot be verified with empirical methods.
- Fourth, positivist explanatory models are based on inductivism and deductivism. The former entails the formulation of universally valid conclusions from a definite number of observable events (Danermark et al., 2002) while the latter means 'To derive logically valid conclusions from given premises' (Danermark et al., 2002, p. 79, table 1). Both, and especially the deductive-nomological or the covering law model of explanation derived by deductivism, try to establish 'universal laws' based 'upon the Human principle of empirical invariance; viz., that laws are or depend upon empirical regularities of the form "whenever event x then event y"' (Pratten, 2007, p. 194).
- Finally, positivism is atomistic and individualistic. It adopts a social ontology of atomistic, discrete events that can be observed, measured and arranged in empirical-regularity schemes and methodological individualism according to which social explanation is based on the dispositions and the supposedly 'rational-utilitarian' actions of individuals (Archer, 1995, 2000; Iosifides, 2011). The adoption of this kind of ontology is inadequate to link structure and agency as social structures are conceptualised as epiphenomenal, as reducible to properties of individuals or as the aggregate outcomes of individual actions (Archer, 1995; Sawyer, 2005).

As is conspicuous from the above discussion, positivism and empiricism in social sciences are forms of 'reductionism'. Social reality is reduced to observable empirical events and social causality is reduced to regularity and constant conjunction of quantitative variables. Ontologically, positivism is characterised by 'flatness', as it exhausts reality to what is rendered knowable about it; that is, empirical, observable events. Also this 'ontological flatness' of positivism results from its inability to conceive social reality as 'stratified' and from the absolute prioritisation of the probably least important stratum regarding adequate social explanation, that of empirical, observable events. Thus, positivism is deeply 'irrealist' as it does not take into account deeper levels of reality, exhausts reality to surface appearances and makes knowledge dependable on abilities of observation (Patomäki and Wight, 2000). Methodologically, positivism advocates the use of quantitative methods in a highly uncritical and foundationalist manner. This is because positivism makes the false assumption that measuring empirical events and phenomena with precision results in an 'unmediated' and 'value-free' access to reality, ensures 'objectivity' and the advancement towards the 'Truth'. In this sense, positivism is a kind of 'scientism'; that is, a position that portrays itself as *the* scientific, value-neutral, objective position. Scientistic arguments are quite 'useful' both politically and ideologically, because they serve purposes of legitimation of certain policy decisions and actions. For while these decisions and actions are value- and interest-laden, they are portrayed as based on 'evidence' and 'data' which, because they derive from positivistic research are to be 'objective'. This scientistic, political/ideological use of contemporary positivism-neopositivism-oriented social research is one of the most important reasons for its proliferation and persistence (for another reason related to methodology see Yeung, 1997).

2.1.2 Relativism

While much of contemporary quantitative methods in social research are tacitly or implicitly characterised by positivist/scientistic rationales, qualitative methods have largely embraced another fashionable trend – that has been on the rise from the end of the 1960s onwards (Wood and Foster, 1997) – that of relativism or even extreme scepticism. Relativist thought characterises in different degrees much of contemporary qualitative research practice inspired by theoretical frameworks such as interpretivism and, primarily, strict social constructionism, post-structuralism and post-modernism. The whole turn to relativism and contemporary forms of idealism (cultural, linguistic, conceptual or others) has been the result of an exaggerated reaction to traditional positivist thinking (see Fleetwood, 2005). Of course, a reaction to something largely flawed as positivism does not guarantee the constructiveness and fruitfulness of the result. As in the case of relativism, the outcome could be equally flawed and fallacious, having severe negative consequences for social theorising and research practice.

Relativism takes many forms but in general is the doctrine according to which a phenomenon, notion or object acquires its identity and character through some other 'background factors' (Baghramian, 2004, p. 3); in other words, it is 'relative' to one or some of those factors. Baghramian (2004) refers to the various types of relativism by listing a series of phenomena, notions or objects and the background factors to which these phenomena, notions or objects are allegedly relative to. Thus, according to relativist thinking:

(1) Meaning is relative to (a) language.
(2) Reference is relative to (b) conceptual schemes.
(3) Truth is relative to (c) theory.
(4) Metaphysical commitment is relative to (d) scientific paradigm.
(5) Ontology is relative to (e) version, depiction, description.
(6) Reality is relative to (f) culture.
(7) Epistemic values are relative to (g) community.
(8) Moral values are relative to (h) individuals.
(9) Aesthetic values are relative to (i) historical periods. (Baghramian, 2004, p. 6)

Space constraints prevent me from analysing each type of relativism in depth. Instead, I focus on a series of problems of what is common in its various kinds along with some remarks regarding its consequences for social research methodology.

First, the strict social constructionist version of relativist thinking reduces the totality of social reality to language and discourse. It reorients (and limits) social inquiry from asking questions about real social, economic and cultural processes and forces and how they interact with individual and social agency to the 'discursive practices' by which social phenomena and processes are 'constructed' (Best, 2007). Thus, as Hammersley (2008, p. 173) points out, 'The focus becomes, not the phenomena themselves, and certainly not what might have caused them or what effects they produce, but rather the discursive processes by which they are constituted and identified by culture members.' This comes largely from viewing discourse and language as a closed, self-referential system of signs where words and terms acquire their meaning solely from within a conceptual scheme or a set of conventions that a linguistic or cultural community accepts (Cruickshank, 2003; Hibberd, 2005). The outcome of this line of thinking is 'conventionalism' (Hibberd, 2005) or a form of 'internal realism' (Cruickshank, 2003) that cannot be maintained in a consistent way as it is self-refuting and self-contradictory. Thus, as Hibberd (2005, p. 109) asserts:

> The notion that the meanings of terms and relations are given solely by a closed, autonomous system or framework cannot be maintained consistently. It requires making a distinction between the framework and an external domain of things, and this requires getting outside the framework and seeing it in relation to something else. But, given internal reference, such a distinction cannot be made. It is not possible to 'break out' of the system, whether that system be narrowly geometry or, more broadly, the discursive practices of communities . . .

Furthermore, relativism, characterised by epistemic and genetic fallacies, acts back on its advocates and seriously undermines their assertions too, along with any meaningful argument, academic or other (Hammersley, 2008; Sayer, 2000).

Second, discursive/linguistic relativism – common in the strict social constructionist and post-structuralist thinking – results in an implicit, flat and surface ontology where the deep levels of reality are rendered either unknowable or non-existent. This line of thinking 'suggests that things can be known at their surface level. This brackets off what lies behind the language games and effectively denies that this reality has any bearing on the description of social objects' (Joseph, 2002, p. 153). By asserting that reality is constructed by discursive practices and is relative to the linguistic conventions of social groups or to various language-games, strict constructionists and post-structuralists make claims that are essentially 'empirical', as they presuppose the reality of discursive practices themselves and knowledge about how exactly language operates (see Iosifides, 2011). However, empirical claims cannot be made by these kind of relativists given the axioms that they accept. Thus, despite the fact that strict constructionists, post-structuralists and post-modernists accuse literally everyone else as crude 'foundationalist' and 'essentialist', their rationales entail 'a combination of "identity thinking" or inverted foundationalism and wishful thinking – "the world is what our concepts say it is"' (Sayer, 2000, p. 34). Moreover, their thinking 'essentialises' discourse and language, as the basic principles of their workings and functions are assumed to be stable and universal.

Third, by reducing the social world to discourse, by relativising truth and denying the possibility of any kind of objective knowledge about the world, relativists undermine any notion of causal explanation and are unable to adjudicate between different theories and interpretations of reality. As Patomäki and Wight (2000, p. 217) rightly point out:

> If discourses construct the objects to which the discourses refer, then the discourse itself can never be wrong about the existence of its objects, in any meaningful or methodologically interesting way. Nor can an alternative discourse possible critique another discourse, since the objects of a given discourse exist if the discourse says they exist. External criticism of the existential claims of discourses seems impossible. Ontologically, if discourses do construct their own objects, then what constructed the discourses themselves?

The preceding remarks show that the consequences of relativism for effective critique of social injustice, exploitation and domination of any kind may be far more serious than imagined, mainly because such a critique presupposes true, that is, practically adequate (see Sayer, 2000), knowledge of the structural arrangements of the social world and their causal powers.

Fourth, it is impressive how much and how unproductively the relativist thinking of the type I discuss in this section is divorced from everyday practice and ordinary experience (see Sokal, 2008, especially chapter 6).

32   *Handbook of research methods in migration*

For its consequence is epistemic scepticism while 'it is impossible to engage in any form of action, to *live one's life* or even to do empirical research, if one treats epistemological skepticism as valid' (Hammersley, 2008, p. 96, emphasis added).

Finally, as positivism based its project on an imitation of the way that natural sciences supposedly gain objective knowledge, strict constructionist, post-structuralist and post-modernist relativism borrow their rationales from art and literature (Hammersley, 2008; Yoshida, 2007). Yoshida (2007, p. 293), criticising the 'interpretive-symbolic' approach of the prominent anthropologist Clifford Geertz, points to the negative side effects of this attitude for social scientific inquiry:

> Geertz suggests that a factual look or conceptual elegance is not so important to decide whether anthropological research is serious or convincing. What then is important? Geertz claims that grounds of acceptance 'are extremely person-specific' in anthropology, basing himself on Foucault. That is, what matters most is the name of the author who writes the research. Geertz argues that in this sense anthropology is on the side of *literature* [emphasis added] rather than on the side of science . . . Since the merit of a work turns on the name of the author, we are faced with authoritarianism.

However, this is not the only element that contemporary relativism of either the constructionist or post-structuralist version shares with positivism. It also shares together ontological flatness, reductionism, irrealism, prioritisation of language and acceptance of common definitions of what counts as knowledge, truth and objectivity (Hibberd, 2005; Moore, 2007; Patomäki and Wight, 2000). While, positivism and contemporary relativism are often viewed as antithetical (see Hibberd, 2005), in reality, they are not genuine alternatives to each other as their flaws and fallacies derive from the same or similar origins.

2.2   SCIENTISM AND RELATIVISM IN CONTEMPORARY MIGRATION STUDIES

2.2.1   Positivism/Scientism

Positivistic and scientific rationales significantly influence contemporary migration research, and especially, but not exclusively, the economics of migration. This influence is related to the implicit or explicit conceptual and theoretical assumptions of migration research practice, the ways that migration data are collected, interpreted and used and to the strong interdependencies between the 'scientific logic' and the dominant discourses of 'effectiveness' and 'problem management' (see IMI, 2006; Jones, 2003). Boswell (2008) describes the basic assumptions of contemporary positivist thinking – that largely characterised the neoclassical rationale of much of today's economic studies on migration – as follows:

> – Methodological individualism. This is the thesis that facts about society and social phenomena can be explained in terms of facts about individuals . . . Thus the onus of social explanation lies in individual preferences and behaviour, and structures that can be derived from their interaction, rather than institutions, intersubjective meanings or culture. This in turn implies that the preferred methodology focuses on the observation and analysis of the behaviour of individuals.
>
> – A utilitarian ontology of the self. This is the assumption that individuals seek to maximise their own utility. This is not so much a claim about the individual as being the appropriate unit of explanation, but rather about the psychological disposition of individuals to be interested in promoting their own well-being or happiness. It draws on the eighteenth- and nineteenth-century tradition of utilitarianism in political philosophy.
>
> – A uniform concept of rationality. The assumption here is that individuals wish to maximise utility through rational means. In other words, individuals will act in a way that maximises their personal utility, given available information and subject to external constraints. (Boswell, 2008, p. 552)

These assumptions have had important repercussions in the ways migratory phenomena are researched and theorised. They have resulted in the formulation of various conceptual schemes and models for explaining and 'predicting' migratory phenomena, 'flows' and movements such as, for example, 'economistic cost-benefit models', 'value-expectancy models', 'stress threshold models' and others (see Faist, 2000, pp. 35–46). What all these attempts to explain and 'predict' migratory processes share in common is their empiricist social ontology and a utility-maximisation notion of individual action. What they all lack is the ability to account for ontological depth and to move beyond appearances, empirically observable, discrete events and behaviours and a regularity conception of social causality. Of course, the flaws of empiricism and positivism do not result solely from theoretical and methodological faults and limitations (see Jones, 2003; Patomäki, 2003). The irony is that they are strongly value-laden despite positivist ambitions and declarations for value-neutrality and 'objectivity'. As Jones (2003, p. 236) rightly argues:

> The [positivist] orthodoxy is ideological: its errors 'are not just mistakes, but ones which function in the interest of a particular social system' (Collier 1994: 104). It consists of a set of false ideas about society, which necessarily arise within and serve to reproduce the structure of society. A full examination of the ideological status of the orthodoxy would reveal how the atomistic assumptions at its core arise spontaneously from the appearance and experience of capitalist society.

Jones's insights lead to a brief discussion of what role 'scientistic' knowledge about migratory phenomena plays in contemporary societies. On the one hand, the increasing 'technocratisation' and complexity of policies concerning, for example, 'the control, entry, stay and integration of immigrants and refugees' (Boswell, 2004, p. 6) leads to simplifications of policy issues and to usages of knowledge of migration for purposes of legitimation of certain political beliefs and actions (see Boswell, 2007). Migration research findings are often used for constructing various categorisations related to migratory phenomena, which serve certain political or socio-economic rationales and interests, 'the state's need to find new patterns of mobilisation to shore up legitimacy' (Boswell, 2004, p. 6) and for masking the deep systemic causes of social antagonism and its consequences. On the other hand, migration research studies inspired by implicit or explicit positivist and empiricist assumptions present distorted and biased versions of social reality as value-neutral, objective and scientific. They usually take certain background assumptions for granted, such as, for example, the co-identity of the 'national' and the 'social' (see Wimmer and Schiller, 2002) and the alleged 'causal' relationships between external, discrete, atomised events and behaviours, resulting in legitimisation of existing social arrangements of domination and unequal power relations at different levels and scales. Closely linked to the above arguments are the consequences, both epistemic and political, of the positivist assumptions of the so-called Human Capital Theory (HCT) which mainly informs 'economists, some economic geographers and sociologists of immigration, and many policy-makers around the world' (Samers, 2010, p. 125). HCT is a predominately quantitative, variable-oriented framework that seeks to address the determinants of labour market outcomes of immigrants. Nevertheless, because of its intrinsic positivist assumptions, HCT is characterised by a series of problems. For the purposes of the discussion developed in this chapter, I briefly refer to two of these problems. As Samers (2010, pp. 126–7) notes:

> First, many HCT studies rely on an oversimplification of migrant experiences and characteristics (such as 'holding English skills constant' or other questionable assumptions about the homogeneous character of immigrant groups). Second, and with respect to the assumptions of homogeneity, human capital theorists are guilty of 'naturalizing' social distinctions that occur in both labour markets and the wider society in which these labour markets operate.

The consequences of the overall positivist assumptions of the kinds of migration theorising and empirical research practice such as HCT lie in the reproduction of 'racial and cultural stereotypes' (Samers, 2010,

p. 128). Worse than that, these stereotypes are 'supported' by seemingly 'objective', that is, 'scientific' data and analyses.

An assumption that characterises much of contemporary migration research, despite the increasing focus on transnationalism, derives from what is called 'methodological nationalism', that is, 'the assumption that the nation/state/society is the natural social and political form of the modern world' (Wimmer and Schiller, 2002, p. 301). Thus,

> In quantitative studies, following the logic of methodological nationalism, immigrants have usually been compared with 'national means' of income, with children per family, with percentages of unemployment and welfare dependence, taking for granted that this would be the adequate unit of comparison ... They are rarely compared with sectors of a national population that they resemble in terms of income and education. (Wimmer and Schiller, 2002, p. 310)

Moreover, internal migration is distinguished from international (Wimmer and Schiller, 2002), and research questions about the impact of 'flows' and the effectiveness of control pertain more to the latter than to the former. Freedom of movement is considered a natural and undisputed human right within the national territory (and the European Union with some exceptions), but it is perceived as a 'threat' when the debate moves to the global level (Pécoud and de Guchteneire, 2009).

An example of the consequences of positivist/scientistic rationales in contemporary migration research concerns numerous economic studies, which estimate the degree of competition/substitution and complementarity between immigrants and natives in the labour market and the economy (see Lozano and Steinberger, Chapter 8, this volume for an overview). However, the quantitative sophistication of much of these studies and the precision of measurements of empirical regularities that they entail do not guarantee their 'scientific' status, that is, their value-neutrality and objectivity. This is due to the fact that certain assumptions, which are taken for granted in a highly uncritical manner, are underlying these studies. Thus, while competition in the labour market between job-seeking individuals is an inherent feature of capitalist social relations, a specific kind of competition (that between immigrants and 'natives') is rendered 'negative' and 'undesirable'. This kind of competition is portrayed as a serious 'problem' that needs 'management'[2] and 'mitigation'. Migratory movements are treated in a 'utilitarian' manner and dominant categories such as 'nationhood', 'national economy', 'foreigner', 'illegal immigrant' and others are stabilised and reproduced. This results simultaneously in accounts of social reality derived from surface appearances of things and of reproduction of deep structures of inequalities and divisions that in

36 *Handbook of research methods in migration*

the case of migration-related phenomena and processes are apprehended in distorted forms through 'ethnic' or 'national' thought categories (see Fenton, 2003).

2.2.2 Relativism

While positivistic/scientific rationales underpin much of contemporary quantitative, 'evidence-based' (Wells, 2004) studies on migration, various forms of relativism are common to qualitative migration research inspired by social constructionist, post-structuralist or post-modernist assumptions. Relativists place almost exclusive emphasis on immigrant subjectivities and identities or on various public discourses, about migration-related phenomena and processes, which, methodologically, usually engage in in-depth interviewing, discourse analysis and ethnography. There are certain differences in the employment of these methods and the rationale of accounting for migration-related phenomena among relativists, but there are also marked commonalities such as discursive reductionism, irrealism, distrust towards causal explanations and an emphasis on description.

Of course, there is nothing wrong in studying in depth and in a qualitative manner, immigrants' lived experiences, subjectivities, identities, meanings, interpretations and discourses and engaging in descriptions of various aspects of their biographical trajectories or of the ways they make sense of their lives and reconstruct them in their narratives. The problematic elements in the relativist rationale lie in the ways of conceptualising immigrants' identities, subjectivities and lived experiences, the ways of employment of various methods for their investigation and the ways of making sense of data collected through these methods. Thus, reducing reality to the discursive level or to semantics and interpretation relativises identity formation experience and subjectivity, and divorces them from any objective, relatively durable and non- or extra-discursive aspect of the social world. Nevertheless, this has further consequences; it leads to abandonment of any ambition to explain social reality in any meaningful way, to the rejection of the possibility of adjudicating between different interpretations and, eventually, to 'judgemental relativism' (Sayer, 2000) or even worse to radical scepticism (Hammersley, 2008). Extremely interesting questions about the adequacy (Manicas, 2009) of immigrants' interpretations of their situations and lives, the relations between immigrants' subjectivities and identities with their social locations (Henze, 2000) and of the embededness of immigrants' agential (individual or collective) action within certain, either constraining or enabling (Archer, 1995), cultural or structural contexts are left unanswered. Moreover, social research methods are confined to the extremely narrow task of investigating the 'discursive practices' of research participants and the ways participants co-construct (with social researchers) versions of social reality and meaning (see Hammersley, 2008). The possibility of employing qualitative methods as a 'window' to realities beyond the context of interaction between the research participants and researchers is rejected (Hammersley, 2008). This of course results in extreme scepticism, which – besides being self-refuting – has negative consequences for the endeavour of social inquiry as a whole (Hammersley, 2008). In relation to this, Hammersley (2008, p. 131), referring to post-modern ethnography, asserts that: 'It came to be emphasised, more than before, that ethnographers *construct* their accounts of the world, and that in doing so they draw on the same techniques as writers producing fictional literature. Moreover, what they write cannot but reflect who they are, in socio-cultural terms' (emphasis in original).

Now, to refer to some examples from 'ethnic' and migration research, Bader (2001), criticising Baumann's relativist and constructionist rationale in analysing 'ethnic' and immigrant cultural practices and identities in the highly diverse and multi-ethnic area of Southall, London, refers to the epistemic, political and moral consequences of discursive and processual reductionism of social constructionist thinking. In the author's own words:

> Constructivism as a *sociological or anthropological theory* tends to dissolve culture(s) (i) into narrative discourses, (ii) into processes, and (iii) into identities. This triple reduction . . . prevents rich descriptions and adequate explanations of processes of cultural change, of community formation and identity definition. Concepts and theories which clearly distinguish between perspectives of cultural change, perspectives of group- or community-formation and perspectives of (re)definitions of identities provide more successful strategies and methods for historical and comparative research. Constructivism also has some counterproductive consequences for *practical politics* . . .: 'strategic essentialism', for example, does not help to resolve practical dilemmas, it tends simply to reintroduce liberal myopia into the debate on affirmative action policies and on group representation. Moreover, as a *moral philosophy*, constructivism is explicitly opposed to any concept of cultural rights for specific groups. It ends up in a self-contradictory criticism of all normative notions of individual autonomy. (Bader, 2001, p. 252, emphasis in original)

Bader's remarks illustrate some of the most serious problems – discursive reductionism, irrealism, ontological flatness – of relativist constructionism and post-structuralism and their consequences for investigating specific topics related to migration (immigrants' identities, subjectivities, cultural practices and lived experiences). Relativist usages of notions of 'identity' and 'subjectivity' are rather narrow and incomplete as they fail to relate identities and subjectivities to extra-discursive social realities and to ascribe to them ontological depth. Walby (2009) criticises such relativist conceptualisations of 'ethnic identities' and highlights the potentialities for a constructive account of them within a complexity and realism-oriented theoretical framework. She points out that:

> The use of the concept of identity tends to lead to a cultural reductionism, to flatten the ontology . . . The deployment of the concept of identity may lack or leave unspecified any link to wider macro concerns and thus any macro theoretical framework within which identities are to be analysed . . . Ethnic regimes of inequality have ontological depth, just as class and gender regimes do. (Walby, 2009, p. 266)

Another research practice that gained prominence in contemporary migration studies is related to the employment of biographical/narrative methods in studying migrants' life histories (see Apitzsch and Siouti, 2007; Halfacree and Boyle, 1993). The value of researching subjectivity, intentionality, lived experience and meaning of migration-related phenomena and processes and understanding crucial aspects of migrants' lives through biographical methods lies in an effort to overcome the flaws and inadequacies of the variable-oriented, positivist-empiricist migration research. However, the reaction against empiricism in researching migration-related phenomena and processes, through the employment of qualitative, biographical methods, took, in many instances, a relativist or even an extreme scepticist twist. Thus, for example, social constructionists reject any reference of biographical narratives, material and data to social realities outside the life-history reconstruction by narrators and the biographical narrative itself (see Tsiolis, 2006, p. 141). The focus of investigation turns to the 'discursive practices' that narrators use in order give an 'account' of their life trajectories (Hammersley, 2008; Iosifides and Sporton, 2009). Thus,

> a narrative of an immigrant about her trajectory of spatial and social mobility in the host country, about passing different stages and phases resulted in modified social situation and relations, have value only as 'accounts' that is as interpretations or discourses. As those accounts or interpretations/discourses exhaust the domain of the social, they cannot inform us about any 'reality' behind the told story . . . (Iosifides and Sporton, 2009, p. 105)

This one-sidedness is also evident in the interpretive use of biographical research, material and data. In this case, agential intentionality, meaning-making and interpretations are given prominence and understanding social action is restricted to understanding ascribed subjective meanings to it. The role of materiality, social relationality, structural and cultural contexts, unacknowledged conditions and unintended consequences of action is underplayed or ignored. Both constructionist and interpretative applications of biographical methods in migration research prevent us, to a great extent, from viewing subjectivity and objectivity, agency and structure not in opposition but rather in dialectical unity and asking really interesting questions about how the interaction between the analytically distinct agential, structural and cultural causal powers produces certain outcomes and phenomena. Employing biographical and qualitative methods in general, in a non-relativist and extreme subjectivist manner, may allow us to pose these critical, explanatory questions and give adequate answers. 'Especially in the field of migration studies, biographical narratives may lead to deeper understanding of social processes and inform policy making, subject to their conceptualisation not just as "stories", but as reconstructions of the complex and dialectical interplay between agency action and meaning making with certain structural and systemic conditions, constraints and enablements' (Iosifides and Sporton, 2009, p. 106).

2.3 A CRITICAL REALIST WAY OUT

A promising solution to the conundrum of positivism/scientism and relativism in social sciences and in contemporary migration studies and a viable alternative to both are offered by the philosophical and meta-theoretical approach of critical realism. In this section, I briefly sketch the basic principles of this approach and their methodological consequences, placing special emphasis on migration research.

2.3.1 The Critical Realist Approach

Critical realism is a philosophical and meta-theoretical framework in the social sciences that prioritises ontology over epistemology and, in contrast to positivism, empiricism, interpretivism and various modes of contemporary idealism and scepticism – such as strict social constructionism, post-structuralism and post-modernism – avoids the long-standing epistemic and linguistic fallacies (Cruickshank, 2003; Hartwig, 2007). Thus, critical realism does not conflate reality and real objects with our knowledge of them and maintains that the former exist independently of our identification and our conceptions of them (Fleetwood, 2005). The former are the 'intransitive' objects of science while the latter are the 'transitive' ones (Danermark et al., 2002, pp. 22–3). This distinction between transitivity and intransitivity is crucial, and it is a presupposition for scientific practice itself (either natural or social), if it is to be successful in intervening in nature or in society, for it takes into consideration the dynamics of conceptual and theoretical change and of error both in everyday life and in scientific practice. Although reality is always concept mediated, approximately valid (although always fallible), knowledge of the intransitive realm is possible because of the constant interaction between concepts and an external reality that exists independently of them. Thus, while critical realism accepts the epistemological relativity (and fallibility) of all knowledge claims, it allows for validity judgements of different conceptual schemes, theories and interpretations. In other words, it integrates in one scheme 'ontological realism, epistemological relativism and judgmental rationality' (Archer et al., 1998, p. xi quoted in Danermark et al., 2002, p. 10).

Now, the kind of ontology that realism embraces is an ontology that avoids the epistemic and linguistic fallacies. Hence, and contrary to positivism and relativism, realism's ontology is a deep and stratified one. Critical realism distinguishes the reality domains of the 'empirical' and the 'actual' from that of the 'real'. The domain of the 'empirical' consists of experiences, concepts and signs, the domain of the 'actual' consists of experiences, concepts, signs and events while the domain of the real includes experiences, concepts, signs, events and generative causal mechanisms (Hartwig, 2007, pp. 400–1). Experiences are events that are known and/or conceptualised by social agents and researchers alike. Experiences are known through concepts and signs, that is, through various conceptual schemes while events consist of whatever happens in the world irrespective of its conceptualisation or knowledge. Lastly, generative causal mechanisms are interactions between different causal powers and structures of social objects that tend to produce events (see Danermark et al., 2002; Sayer, 2000). Generative causal mechanisms are largely unobservable at the level of the 'empirical' and tend to produce observable events, processes and phenomena. Now, this depth ontology has serious repercussions in conceptualising social causality. For critical realism, causality is a matter of real causal powers exerted by social objects due to their structure. '"Structure" suggests a set of internally related elements whose causal powers, when combined, are emergent from those of their constituents' (Sayer, 2000, p. 14). Causal powers of social objects may remain unexercised or modified due to the 'openness' of social reality and the contingency of interaction between them and other causal powers and mechanisms (Sayer, 1992). The relational conceptualisation of structures and their causal powers by critical realism entails the rejection of a successionist, regularity view of social causality embraced by empiricism and positivism along with its surface and flat ontological assumptions. It also entails the rejection of relativists' discursive and ontological flatness which results in the abandonment of the notion of causality in the social world altogether. Moreover, the realist-relational conceptualisation of causality focuses on the phenomenon of 'social emergence' (Sawyer, 2005). 'Social emergence' describes 'situations in which the conjunction of two or more features or aspects give rise to new phenomena, which have properties which are irreducible to those of their constituents, even though the latter are necessary for their existence' (Sayer, 2000, p. 12). Giving emphasis to the phenomena of social emergence, critical realism offers a viable solution to the long-standing problem of linking structure (and culture) with agency (Archer, 1995; see also Bakewell, 2010). Instead of conflating them or reduce each to the other, realism maintains that structure, culture and agency are analytically distinct, are characterised by different emergent properties and causal powers of their own and the task of the social sciences is to examine how their interplay results in social transformation or social reproduction (Archer, 1995; Carter and New, 2004).

The next sub-section contains a brief discussion of the repercussions of realist principles – ontological realism, reality stratification, social emergence, relational causality – in social science methodology, with special emphasis on migration research.

2.3.2 Realist Methods in Migration Research

Critical realism does not propose any novel and radically unique array of methods that correspond to its premises. It rather sharply reorients existing methodological paradigms and traditions (quantitative and qualitative) towards achieving consistency between ontological assumptions and presuppositions, social theorising and methodological strategies (House, 2010). This entails the disconnection of quantitative methods from positivism and of qualitative methods from interpretivism and relativism, as there is no inherent necessity in these connections (Iosifides, 2011). Both quantitative and qualitative methods, or better extensive and intensive research, can be utilised and fruitfully combined, under realist ontological and epistemological premises. Critical realism advocates methodological pluralism in empirical social research, the main task of which is to '[I]dentify generative mechanisms and describe how they are manifested in real events and processes' (Danermark et al., 2002, p. 165). Thus, the ultimate purpose of realist social research is explanatory, in other words, it is to address social causality but in a way fundamentally different from that of positivism.

Disconnecting quantitative methods from positivist assumptions means the abandonment of a notion of social causality based on correlations between variables. It also means that quantitative methods are used to identify important and persistent empirical regularities or demi-regularities (Danermark et al., 2002) and to account for the measurable aspects of social reality. Moreover, it means the employment of these methods in order to investigate 'formal relations of similarity' and 'taxonomic groups' (Danermark et al., 2002, p. 165) and to come up with 'descriptive', 'representative generalisations' (Danermark et al., 2002, p. 165). Realist researchers – instead of treating empirical demi-regularities as causal explanations of phenomena – treat them as pointers for further research about the deeper, generative mechanisms that produce them.

Now, disconnecting qualitative methods from interpretivism and relativism means the reassertion of the centrality of qualitative methods as means for facilitating causal explanation. Since what is fundamental for critical realist thinking is the elucidation of the character of social relations and their emergent results (Archer, 1995), along with the distinction between internal and necessary from external and contingent relations (Sayer, 1992) – essentially qualitative tasks – intensive methods are in a better position to contribute to the identification of generative causal mechanisms. This contribution can be realised because intensive methods are more appropriate for the investigation of 'substantial relations of connections' and of 'causal groups' (Danermark et al., 2002, p. 165). This does not mean that 'interpretative understanding' of social agents' meanings, intentions and reasons is of no use in realist methods of social research. Quite the opposite! It is an integral part of realist methodology as for realism human reasons are (partly) causes of action since they can produce changes in social reality (Sayer, 1992, 2000). Therefore, for critical realism interpretative understanding 'provides "a good initial heuristic for understanding what it is to think" in the mode of totality . . . However, only when conjoined with concepts of intransitivity, transfactuality,[3] dialectical process and agentive agency[4] – which presupposes that reasons (that acted upon) are causes – and struggle can it be regarded unreservedly as a friend of emancipatory science' (Hartwig, 2007, p. 234). Similarly, realist qualitative-intensive methods are more appropriate in investigating the social role of discourses and discursive formations but without the presuppositions and doctrines of constructionist, post-structuralist and post-modernist assumptions. Discourse is just one moment of the social (see Chouliaraki and Fairclough, 1999), does not exhaust it and is always related to other non- or extra-discursive realities, such as social relations, networks of social practices, individual identities, emergent social forms and objects and so on (Chouliaraki and Fairclough, 1999). Discourses do not only 'construct' reality and orient social action but they themselves are conditioned and influenced by emergent social properties and realities (Fairclough et al., 2004).

The combination of extensive and intensive methods, within the critical realist framework, aims, as already noted earlier, at identifying causal generative mechanisms, often unobservable in the empirical domain of reality. To achieve this, realist social researchers utilise modes of reasoning that go beyond induction and deduction. Rather than using induction and deduction as an end in themselves, realist researchers use them as means for 'abduction' and 'retroduction'. Abduction is theoretical redescription of events, phenomena and processes using certain conceptual schemes and frameworks whereas, retroduction aims at identifying the necessary conditions for the occurrence of certain events, processes or phenomena (Danermark et al., 2002). So, according to Danermark et al. (2002, p. 80), retroductive reasoning – the most central mode of realist reasoning – aims to answer '[W]hat knowledge must exist for something to be possible?' Effective retroduction '[P]rovides knowledge of transfactual conditions, structures and mechanisms that cannot be directly observed in the domain of the empirical' (Danermark et al., 2002, p. 80). Retroduction can be achieved in various ways; that is, by employing 'counterfactual thinking', by engaging in 'social experiments and thought experiments', 'studying pathological circumstances and extreme cases' or 'comparisons of different cases' (Danermark et al., 2002, pp. 101–5). Realist social research is theory driven and aims at theory development. It utilises existing theories – which are subjected to immanent critiques – it appreciates the role of general theories as tools for investigating social reality and for facilitating retroductive reasoning, and links theoretical and conceptual abstractions to concrete phenomena and processes in a dialectical manner (Danermark et al., 2002; Sayer, 1992; Yeung, 1997). The process of conceptual abstraction and its dialectical linkage with concrete phenomena are central for realist explanation. As Sayer (1992, p. 86) puts it 'knowledge must grasp the differentiation of the world; we need a way of individuating objects, and of characterizing their attributes and relationships. To be adequate for a specific purpose it must "abstract" from particular conditions, excluding those which have no significant effect in order to focus on those who have.'

Now, migration research has been dominated (and still largely is) by forms of theorising and research practice that are conflationist or reductionist. In other words, it has been dominated by research-guiding theoretical rationales that fail to effectively account for the complexity of linkages and interactions between structure, culture and agency regarding migration-related phenomena and processes. The commonest of these rationales reduces social structure to agency and agential action, preferences, meaning-making and choices (for example, the various neoclassical push-pull models along with interpretivist theoretical schemes), and human agency to powerful structural determinations (for example, Marxist and neo-Marxist models) (Ratcliffe, 2007) or conflates structure and agency at the level of 'social practices' (for example, structuration theory) (Cruickshank, 2003). Another fashionable trend is discursive reductionism, mainly of constructionist and post-structuralist – Foucauldian style – where 'The social world is seen as constructed by authorless discourses which themselves become agents; rather than tension between actors, agents and discourses, concretely negotiated in particular historical settings, there are merely discourses constructing objects and human subjects' (Carter, 2000, pp. 38–9). What all of the above share in common is their inability to account for the analytically distinct and emergent causal powers of structural, cultural and agential properties and how they interplay over time producing either social change or reproduction (Archer, 1995). Migration-related phenomena are 'paradigmatic' of this constant interplay between structural, cultural and agential emergent properties over time (see Carter, 2000) and at different levels and spatial scales. Discourses of 'nationhood' and 'national belonging', local, regional and global economic forces and structures, regimes of immigrant incorporation or exclusion, social stratification patterns, immigrant organisational forms and action are only some of the emergent elements that interact with each other and produce new environments that condition subsequent action and interaction.

Critical realism can act as a meta-theoretical underlabourer of empirical, migration research, supplying the general 'precepts of emergent properties existing in open systems'(Cruickshank, 2003, p. 143) that guide both theorising and research practice. Moreover, generic theoretical and conceptual schemes, either explicitly realist or highly compatible with realist meta-theoretical principles, can become powerful means for guiding applied migration research. Such frameworks have already been developed either in migration studies or in the social sciences in general. A first example of such a framework is the 'complexity theory', which explicitly adopts the premises of 'complex realism' (Walby, 2009). Based on a renewed systemic thinking and utilising notions such as 'path dependency', 'coevolution of complex adaptive systems in changing fitness landscapes' (Walby, 2009, pp. 99–100) and the dynamic relationship between social systems and their environments, complexity theory can guide empirical research on the multi-dimensional 'social interconnections' (Walby, 2009, p. 99) that underpin migratory phenomena and the dynamics of 'intersecting multiple systems of social inequality' (Walby, 2009, p. 99) (ethnic, gender, class and other) within which migration takes place, reinforces, reproduces or modifies them.

Another example of a generic framework that is quite compatible with realist premises, and can guide empirical migration research[5] in a fruitful way, is that of 'social transformation' (Castles, 2007). It is a framework that concerns explicitly migration and migratory phenomena and processes advocating interdisciplinarity, historical and holistic understanding of migration-related phenomena and processes, multi-level analysis, transnationalism, comparability, linking agency with the features of wider contexts and participatory research methods (see Castles, 2007, p. 367, Chapter 1, this volume). This framework, by focusing on the multi-layered character of social reality and migration processes, on the need to effectively relate structure and agency and to the employment of 'depth' participatory research methods, avoids much of the problems that characterised conflationist and reductionist theorising and research practice on migration.

It is true that migration research, inspired by explicitly realist principles, is not common in the contemporary era. Nevertheless, the 'explosion' in social scientific studies that adopt the theoretical and methodological premises of critical realism in other domains and fields creates favourable conditions for the proliferation of realist thinking and methodological practice in migration research. Indeed, there have already been some indications. First, I should mention the paradigmatic study of the transition to a restrictive immigration policy regime in the UK between 1945 and 1981 by Bob Carter (2000). The study is based on the realist 'morphogenetic approach' of Margaret Archer (1995). Methodologically, the study employs the 'historical narrative approach', and its development is based on evidence derived by primary documentary sources (Carter, 2000, p. 109–10). Another example of explicitly critical realist research on migration is the study of migratory movements of Finland Swedes between Sweden and Finland by Hedberg (2004). The author adopts an explicit critical realist approach in order to identify the ways that the complex interaction between structural (internal and necessary relations) and contingent factors produce certain outcomes, notably migratory movements, identity formation and social integration patterns. Methodologically, the study is based on a combination of qualitative (biographical) and quantitative (survey) approaches that were integrated in such a fashion that the identification of generative mechanisms could become possible. In the author's words: 'An individually based, statistical data set focused on the extension of the Finland-Swedish migration pattern, whereas an in-depth interview study was used to analyse the deeper causes of migration and integration'(Hedberg, 2004, p. 2). Finally, a mode of ethnographic research practice that is implicitly underpinned by realist principles, and is often combined with critical realist meta-theory (see Prowse, 2008) – the so-called 'Extensive Case Method (ECM)' – is employed as a guiding framework for contemporary ethnographic migration research. Thus, for example, either by researching the relationships between class and gender in transnational migration through accounting for the experiences of nurses migrating from India to the USA (George, 2000) or by investigating the social transformation and structural conditionings of immigrants' domestic work arrangements through the examination of the characteristics of two job-distribution cooperatives in San Francisco Bay Area (Salzinger, 1991), ECM ethnography transcends the local level, effectively links micro- with macro-levels, engages in causal explanations of migratory processes and phenomena and avoids the pitfalls of both relativism and positivism.

2.4 CONCLUSION

Social research practice guided by critical realist principles is inherently characterised by a crucial 'critical' element. This element lies in the fact that explaining social phenomena and processes (for example, restrictive migration policy regimes, inequalities and selectivity in the social distribution of opportunities for legal geographic mobility) presupposes and results in critiques of existing systemic features of domination, inequality and exploitation. 'Explanatory critiques' (Lacey, 2007) are thus integral in the realist project and necessary for a truly emancipatory social-scientific research practice. Neither positivism – with its a-historical, atomistic assumptions – or relativism – where the enduring relations of power inequality, domination and exploitation are viewed as mere 'discursive constructions' – can be really 'critical' (see Moore, 2007). In an era of enhanced efforts of mobility restrictions of immigrant labour and relatively unrestricted mobility of capital, goods, information and persons with 'enough' 'economic and human capital', realist explanatory critiques of social relations of injustice and of their effects and consequences are urgently needed and are worth engaging with.

NOTES

1. I am grateful to the editor of this book Carlos Vargas-Silva and to Oliver Bakewell for their constructive comments. I also thank Dr Ekaterini Nikolarea (School of Social Sciences, University of the Aegean, Lesvos, Greece) for language editing.
2. Regarding the conventional views that portray 'asylum' or 'illegal immigration' as a 'problem' and 'threat' and legitimate practices of strict border controls and 'migration management' see Squire (2009). It should be noted that legitimation of such practices and of associated unequal power relations across different spatial scales requires the production of 'evidence' which are portrayed as 'scientific', that is, as 'neutral' and beyond dispute. It is in this legitimation of contemporary neoliberal relations of domination at a global level that the 'truth' of positivist-style 'evidence' lies. Thus, as Düvell (2003,

p. 205) rightly puts it: '[E]thically, borders and the policies of exclusion on grounds of immigration are hardly justified when economically borders seem to be a prerequisite of capitalism'.
3. 'Transfactuality' or 'transfactual conditions' refer to the fundamental structural characteristics of social objects that are responsible for their causal powers and liabilities. As Danermark et al. (2002, p. 77) put it, transfactual conditions are 'the more or less universal preconditions for an object to be what it is'.
4. 'Agentive agency' refers to the unique and distinct causal powers of human agency. These powers are agential emergent properties and are irreducible both to biological features and to societal-discursive effects (see Archer, 2000).
5. 'Empirical' research should not be confused with 'empiricist' research. The former means merely any engagement and effort to understand and explain reality while the latter entails the confinement of these engagements and efforts solely to the level of observable events.

REFERENCES

Apitzsch, U. and Siouti, I. (2007), *Biographical Analysis as an Interdisciplinary Research Perspective in the Field of Migration Studies,* Frankfurt am Main: Research Integration, Johann Wolfgang Goethe Universität, University of York.
Archer, M. (1998), 'Introduction. Realism in the social sciences', in M. Archer, R. Bhaskar, A. Collier, T. Lawson and A. Norrie (eds), *Critical Realism, Essential Readings*, London: Routledge, pp. 189–205.
Archer, M., Bhaskar, R., Collier, A., Lawson, T. and Norrie, A. (eds) (1998), *Critical Realism, Essential Readings*, London: Routledge.
Archer, M.S. (1995), *Realist Social Theory: The Morphogenetic Approach*, Cambridge: Cambridge University Press.
Archer, M.S. (2000), *Being Human. The Problem of Agency,* Cambridge: Cambridge University Press.
Bader, V. (2001), 'Culture and identity. Contesting constructivism', *Ethnicities*, **1** (2), 251–85.
Baghramian, M. (2004), *Relativism*, Abingdon: Routledge.
Bakewell, O. (2010), 'Some reflections on structure and agency in migration studies', *Journal of Ethnic and Migration Studies, Special Issue on Theories of Migration and Social Change*, **36** (10), 1689–1708.
Best, J. (2007), 'But seriously folks: the limitations of strict constructionist interpretations of social problems', in J.A. Holstein and G. Miller (eds), *Reconsidering Social Constructionism. Debates in Social Problem Theory*, New Jersey: Aldine Transaction, pp. 129–47.
Boswell, C. (2004), 'Knowledge transfer and migration policy making', Special Lecture on Migration, International Institute for Labour Studies, Geneva.
Boswell, C. (2007), 'The European Commission's use of research in immigration policy: expert knowledge as a source of legitimation?', Paper prepared for the panel Driving and Legitimising Contentious EU Policy-Making: The Case of Immigration Policy, EUSA Conference, Montreal, 17–20 May.
Boswell, C. (2008), 'Combining economics and sociology in migration theory', *Journal of Ethnic and Migration Studies*, **34** (4), 549–66.
Castles, S. (2007), 'Twenty-first century migration as a challenge to sociology', *Journal of Ethnic and Migration Studies*, **33** (3), 351–71.
Carter, B. (2000), *Realism and Racism. Concepts of Race in Sociological Research*, London: Routledge.
Carter, B. and New, C. (2004), *Making Realism Work. Realist Social Theory and Empirical Research*, Abingdon: Routledge.
Chouliaraki, L. and Fairclough, N. (1999), *Discourse in Late Modernity. Rethinking Critical Discourse Analysis*, Edinburgh: Edinburgh University Press.

Collier, A. (1994), *Critical Realism. An Introduction to Roy Bhaskar's Philosophy*, London and New York: Verso.
Cruickshank, J. (2003), *Realism and Sociology. Anti-foundationalism, Ontology and Social Research*, Abingdon: Routledge.
Danermark, B., Ekström, M., Jakobsen, L. and Karlsson, J.C. (2002), *Explaining Society. Critical Realism in the Social Sciences*, Abingdon: Routledge.
Düvell, F. (2003), 'Some reasons and conditions for a world without immigrations restrictions', *ACME: An International E-Journal for Critical Geographies*, **2** (2), 201–209.
Fairclough, N., Jessop, B. and Sayer, A. (2004), 'Critical realism and semiosis', in J. Joseph and J.M. Roberts (eds), *Realism, Discourse and Deconstruction*, Abingdon: Routledge, pp. 23–42.
Faist, T. (2000), *The Volume and Dynamics of International Migration and Transnational Social Spaces*, Oxford: Clarendon Press.
Faulkner, P. (2007), 'Closure', in M. Hartwig (ed.), *Dictionary of Critical Realism*, Abingdon, Routledge, pp. 66–7.
Fenton, S. (2003), *Ethnicity*, Cambridge: Polity Press.
Fleetwood, S. (2005), 'Ontology in organization and management studies: a critical realist perspective', *Organization*, **12** (2), 197–222.
George, S. (2000), '"Dirty nurses" and "men who play". Gender and class in transnational migration', in M. Burawoy, J.A. Blum, G. Goerge et al. (eds), *Global Ethnography. Forces, Connections and Imaginations in a Postmodern World*, London: University of California Press, pp. 144–74.
Halfacree, K.H. and Boyle, P.J. (1993), 'The challenge facing migration research: the case for a biographical approach', *Progress in Human Geography*, **17** (3), 333–48.
Hammersley, M. (2008), *Questioning Qualitative Inquiry. Critical Essays*, London: Sage.
Hartwig, M. (ed.) (2007), *Dictionary of Critical Realism*, Abingdon: Routledge.
Hedberg, C. (2004), 'The Finland–Swedish wheel of migration. Identity, networks and migration 1976–2000', PhD Thesis, Uppsala University, Sweden.
Henze, B.R. (2000), 'Who says who says? The epistemological grounds for agency in liberatory political projects', in P.M.L. Moya and M.R. Hames-Garcia (eds), *Reclaiming Identity. Realist Theory and Predicament of Postmodernism*, Los Angeles, CA: University of California Press, pp. 229–50.
Hibberd, F.J. (2005), *Unfolding Social Constructionism*, New York: Springer.
House, S.R. (2010), 'Critical realism, mixed methodology, and institutional analysis', Working Paper No. SPP10-02, Lee Kuan Yew School of Public Policy, National University of Singapore.
International Migration Institute (IMI) (2006), *Towards a New Agenda for International Migration Research*, Oxford: James Martin 21st Century School, University of Oxford.
Iosifides, T. (2011), *Qualitative Methods in Migration Studies. A Critical Realist Perspective*, Farnham: Ashgate.
Iosifides, T. and Sporton, D. (2009), 'Editorial: Biographical methods in migration research', *Migration Letters*, **6** (2), 101–108.
Jones, B.G. (2003), 'Explaining global poverty. A Realist critique of the orthodox approach', in J. Cruickshank (ed.), *Critical Realism, The Difference it Makes*, Abingdon: Routledge, pp. 221–39.
Joseph, J. (2002), *Hegemony. A Realist Analysis*, London: Routledge.
Lacey, H. (2007), 'Explanatory critique (EC)', in M. Hartwig (ed.), *Dictionary of Critical Realism*, Abingdon: Routledge, pp.196–201.
Manicas, P.T. (2009), 'Realist metatheory and qualitative methods', *Sociological Analysis*, **3** (1), 1–15.
Moore, R. (2007), 'Going critical: the problem of problematizing knowledge in education studies', *Critical Studies in Education*, **48** (1), 25–41.
Morgan, J. (2007), 'Empiricism', in M. Hartwig (ed.), *Dictionary of Critical Realism*, Abingdon: Routledge, pp. 169–71.
Patomäki, H. (2003), 'A critical Realist approach to global political economy', in

J. Cruickshank (ed.), *Critical Realism, The Difference it Makes*, Abingdon: Routledge, pp. 197–220.

Patomäki, H. and Wight, C. (2000), 'After postpositivism? The promises of critical realism', *International Studies Quarterly*, **44**, 213–37.

Pécoud, A. and de Guchteneire, P. (2009), *Migration without Borders. Essays on the Free Movement of People*, New York: UNESCO Publishing and Berghahn Books.

Pratten, S.B. (2007), 'Explanation', in M. Hartwig (ed.), *Dictionary of Critical Realism*, Abingdon: Routledge, pp. 193–6.

Prowse, M. (2008), 'Locating and extending livelihoods research', BWPI Woking Paper 37, Brooks World Poverty Institute, University of Manchester.

Ratcliffe, P. (2007), 'Migration studies', in M. Hartwig (ed.), *Dictionary of Critical Realism*, Abingdon: Routledge, pp. 193–6.

Salzinger, L. (1991), 'A maid by any other name: the transformation of "dirty work" by Central American Immigrants', in M. Burawoy, A. Burton, A.A. Ferguson et al. (eds), *Ethnography Unbound. Power and Resistance in the Modern Metropolis*, Oxford: University of California Press, pp. 139–60.

Samers, M. (2010), *Migration*, Abingdon: Routledge.

Sawyer, K.R. (2005), *Social Emergence. Societies as Complex Systems*, Cambridge: Cambridge University Press.

Sayer, A. (1992), *Method in Social Science. A Realist Approach*, 2nd edn, London: Routledge.

Sayer, A. (2000), *Realism and Social Science*, London: Sage.

Sokal, A. (2008), *Beyond the Hoax. Science, Philosophy and Culture*, Oxford: Oxford University Press.

Squire, V. (2009), *The Exclusionary Politics of Asylum*, New York: Palgrave Macmillan.

Tsiolis, G. (2006), *Life Histories and Biographical Narratives. The Biographical Approach in Sociological Qualitative Research*, Athens: Kritiki (in Greek).

Walby, S. (2009), *Globalization and Inequalities. Complexity and Contested Modernity*, London: Sage.

Wells, P. (2004), 'New Labour and evidence based policy making', Paper presented to the PERC Research Seminar, University of Sheffield, Sheffield, 16 May.

Wimmer, A. and Schiller, N.G. (2002), 'Methodological nationalism and beyond: nation-state building, migration and the social sciences', *Global Networks*, **2** (4), 301–34.

Wood, E.M. and Foster, J.B. (eds) (1997), *In Defence of History. Marxism and the Postmodern Agenda*, New York: Monthly Review Press.

Yeung, H.W. (1997), 'Critical Realism and realist research in human geography: a method or a philosophy in search of a method?', *Progress in Human Geography*, **21** (1), 51–74.

Yoshida, K. (2007), 'Defending scientific study of the social. Against Clifford Geertz (and his critics)', *Philosophy of the Social Sciences*, **37** (3), 289–314.

3 Migration, methods and innovation: a reconsideration of variation and conceptualization in research on foreign workers
David Bartram

There is a methodological balancing act to be performed by researchers who hope to produce something genuinely innovative. On the one hand, one's work must not depart too wildly from the practice of established scholars in the field. On the other hand, there is little to be gained from merely repeating and recapitulating their creations; one can hardly accomplish something innovative if one doesn't try to break – or at least reshape – the mould that has crystallized around the dominant perspectives in a field. Go too far in one direction and one's work is likely to be irrelevant, even unnoticed; go too far in the other and one's role becomes that of an apostle or acolyte.

The institutional production and reproduction of academic researchers probably reinforce the second tendency. One who spends years reading and writing about a particular topic, especially in the context of a PhD programme, might come to take certain ideas for granted. Pressures for specialization and disciplinary identification might fortify this tendency even after one has acquired a stable job. A professional scholarly perspective undoubtedly brings advantages relative to the common sense understandings of informal observers, but there are potential costs as well.

In this context, a serious and sustained engagement with research methods can be a mechanism for innovation. This chapter argues that consideration of some core principles of social science research methods is likely to catalyse some productive thinking on a number of migration-related topics. The discussion here highlights two aspects of migration studies that in my view remain underdeveloped in methodological terms and which might therefore be fertile territory for new varieties.

One core research methods principle is the importance of studying variation, particularly variation in one's dependent variable. In the context of migration research, this principle carries an implication that might be unsettling to some migration scholars: to understand instances of migration, one must also devote significant effort to the analysis of instances where migration has not occurred. This implication is particularly intriguing and compelling insofar as it suggests that migration scholars might benefit from studying countries that have experienced only limited immigration.

Another issue concerns the way migration researchers deploy some core concepts. In particular for comparative work, it is sometimes possible to discern that concepts are used in ways that do not sufficiently take account of their inherent complexity and the different contexts in which they are applied. It does not help that the meaning of concepts is sometimes determined by the available data rather than vice versa. The argument presented here, advanced via a discussion of 'foreign workers', is relatively simple: the study of migration would likely benefit from further reflection on the meaning and use of key concepts. Such reflection is in fact an ongoing necessity, because the reality those concepts are meant to capture is constantly changing.

3.1 VARIATION

One fundamental goal of social science research is to create 'general' explanations.[1] Even if we only want to understand a particular instance – say, why people migrate from Estonia to Finland – the answer we give to that question has to be generalizable in principle. That is, the answer would have to apply to other cases that are similar in relevant respects, and it would have to distinguish this particular case from others where the outcome is different. For purposes of illustration, consider an example simplified for ease of presentation: perhaps preliminary research suggests that people migrate from Estonia to Finland mainly because of geographic proximity and linguistic affinities. For this answer to be valid, it would have to be true that, in general, people migrate from one country to another when there is geographic proximity and linguistic affinities between those two countries. If one were to find cases – indeed, even a single case – where those two factors did not lead to migration, this explanation for Estonia-to-Finland migration would be, at a minimum, underspecified, and perhaps simply wrong. Perhaps these factors are actually relevant only in a context of historical domination by a larger power; if so, then that context is a necessary part of one's explanation. Or perhaps those factors are simply irrelevant – the conjunction is not significant, instead merely a coincidence – and the real answer lies elsewhere.

The best way to be sure that one's explanation is robust against this type of risk is to consider instances where migration has not occurred, searching in particular for conjunctions of geographic proximity and linguistic affinities; if one is not successful in finding such conjunctions, one will have greater confidence in one's argument. Again, this general point holds even when one is really interested only in the one particular case. Doing research only on a single case would seem unwise if one's goals involve explanation. One reason is that comparison is a fundamental cognitive operation (Bechhofer and Patterson, 2000), and all explanations are at least implicitly comparative. But while comparison can mean analysis of similar cases, a more productive approach to comparisons includes the analysis of different cases (that is, contrast) as well.

Insofar as our goal is explanation, then, our research ought to take variation in the dependent variable as its main focus (King et al., 1994). This point is taken for granted in quantitative/survey research where the use of representative samples means that one studies an entire 'population' (however defined) as a matter of course. But in other types of research it is not taken for granted in the same way. In ethnographic studies, where explanation is not the usual goal of research, it is more reasonable to assume that one's cases will be instances of the phenomenon of interest; it can make sense that ethnographies of migration involve studying only cases where migration has actually occurred. If variation is not an explicit focus of the research, then one might wonder about whether that research is well suited to offer generalizable claims about migration – and indeed many ethnographies are not undertaken with the objective of offering generalizations.

But the issue is more urgent in relation to research in the 'comparative/ historical' mode. Research in this mode sometimes draws on the methodological work of Charles Ragin – in particular, his discussion (1987) of John Stuart Mill's distinction between the 'method of agreement' and the 'indirect method of difference' (where the former involves investigation of similar cases and the latter entails investigation of contrasting or negative cases). As Ragin notes, it was apparent already to Mill that the method of difference is preferable to the method of agreement (though the former also has its own flaws). Even so, comparative researchers are sometimes content to draw what they perceive as strong conclusions from analysis of similar cases.

This tendency can be found in some areas of migration studies, for example, in work that compares small numbers of cases, particularly when 'cases' means countries. Deep knowledge even of a single case, let alone several, is a demanding task. The tendency also expresses a kind of common sense: if one is a 'migration scholar', then naturally one investigates migration. In the absence of methodological reflection, it might seem appropriate to believe that cases where migration has not occurred are inherently uninteresting.[2]

Migration, methods and innovation 53

In concrete terms, the case that has particular relevance along these lines is Japan. Migration to Japan has received a great deal of attention in recent years, much of it entirely interesting and useful; Japan has become a significant destination for migrants of various types (Cornelius, 1994), including descendants of emigrants from Japan (*nikkeijin*) particularly from Latin America (for example, Sellek, 1997), highly skilled workers (Fuess, 2003) and migrant/foreign workers (for example, Komai, 1995; Mori, 1997).

But for certain purposes the wrong question has been asked about Japan. (Or, if that formulation is too strong: some researchers have overlooked a more interesting question.) Particularly in relation to labour migration, the question often posed is: what accounts for migration to Japan? This question makes sense to a degree: Japan had mostly refrained from adopting a 'guestworker' policy (or other forms of labour migration) during the period when a number of countries in Europe were importing workers in large numbers, but in the 1990s Japan witnessed inflows of foreign workers in non-trivial numbers.

Even so, the numbers involved point more to a difference between Japan and Europe (Germany, Switzerland and so on) than to a similarity. Depending on how one treats certain types (on which more below), Japan has roughly 800,000 foreign workers – approximately 1.3 per cent of its labour force (including undocumented workers and the 'side-door' categories of 'trainees' and descendants of Japanese emigrants (Iguchi, 2005)).[3] When one compares this figure to certain European countries where the number is closer to 10 per cent, what stands out is how small the Japanese numbers are. It is also worth recalling that the increase emerged much later than in other countries at similar stages of economic development.

The most interesting question about Japan, then, is: how/why has Japan (mostly) refrained from importing migrant workers? More precisely, how was Japan able to achieve rapid economic/industrial growth without using large amounts of foreign labour – something that was ostensibly an essential element in other countries (cf. Kindleberger, 1967)? Finland is also interesting in this respect, for having achieved significant economic success despite a very small proportion of foreign workers in its labour force (Bartram, 2007).

These questions imply that Japan and Finland are best thought of as 'negative cases' of labour migration. Ragin and Becker note the importance of asking, in the context of comparative research: 'what is this [the research subject] a case of?' (1992, p. 6). Most migration researchers studying Japan in recent years have assumed that Japan is a 'positive case' of migration[4] (and have paid little attention to Finland). That assumption is useful for certain purposes and has produced some valuable research. But in the context of comparative research about labour migration, particularly where it would be important to consider variation in outcomes, the opposite approach for Japan and Finland seems more compelling.

In more general terms, a negative case of labour migration is an instance (that is, a country) that has few migrant workers even though it appears in other relevant respects to be similar to countries that have significant numbers of migrant workers.[5] What matters is not simply that there are few migrant workers: no one is likely to be surprised if a country like Laos is not a significant destination for migrant workers, particularly as theoretical understandings of labour migration would not lead to that expectation. A 'negative case' is a country that appears to be anomalous with respect to existing theory. Anomalies in these terms are typically valuable objects of research – but they are likely to be discerned as such only when researchers are open to the study of instances that embody the 'absence' of their research interest.

In practice, negative cases are consequential only to the extent that overlooking them has contributed to the construction of arguments or theories that need revision once those cases are considered. An overview of explanations for labour migration in these terms suggests that research on Japan and Finland as negative cases is indeed a useful exercise. Existing theories lead to the prediction that these countries ought to have become a destination for migrant workers in similar measure to that of the main European guestworker countries.

The most obvious challenge to existing theories arises in relation to a standard neo-classical explanation for labour migration, which suggests that migration is driven mainly by differences in wage levels, that is, the fact that workers in poorer countries can earn more by gaining employment in a wealthier country. Differences in wage levels are no doubt relevant at some level. But the history of Japan and Finland shows that differences in wage levels are by no means a sufficient cause of migration flows. (A fair amount of labour migration takes place between countries at similar levels of economic development (cf. Ratha and Shaw, 2007), which means that differences in wage levels are not even a necessary cause of migration.) Restrictive policies in (potential) destination countries are an obvious reason, a point explored in more detail below.

The basic neo-classical economics argument is no longer taken seriously in most research on migration. But other/later perspectives encounter similar difficulties. Piore's dual labour market theory (1979) holds that migration is driven by the fact that native workers in wealthy countries reject jobs in the 'secondary labour market': such jobs bring low status and lack of job security, and in many countries natives can rely instead on welfare payments or other means of support. Migrant workers, on the other hand, are not concerned with local status hierarchies and do not have high expectations of job security (though both preferences can change as they become rooted in the destination country). But Japan's labour market is arguably no less dualistic than elsewhere (for example, Pempel, 1978). Piore's argument emphasizes the notion that labour market dualism is a universal feature of advanced capitalist societies – a consequence of the business cycle.[6] But the experience of Japan shows that dualism, like wage differences, does not lead inevitably to use of migrant workers. Dualism might well lead to employer 'demand' for migrant workers, but it is not inevitable that this demand will be satisfied (cf. Weiner, 1995). Again, restrictive policies need to be considered.

A similar observation can be made about a world-systems theory argument. In this perspective labour migration follows from the incorporation of previously peripheral areas into the capitalist world system (Sassen, 1988). Incorporation destabilizes local 'survival strategies', forcing people to seek out new sources of livelihood. Particular migration flows develop from connections of various types between sending and receiving countries – in particular, connections based in a history of colonization, trade and investment. Thus it is no mystery that there has been migration to the UK from former components of the British Empire, or to the USA from Vietnam and the Philippines.

Here as well one would have expected the development of significant migration flows to Japan from a variety of countries in east and south-east Asia, given Japan's status as a regional (not to mention global) economic superpower and the nature of its relations with particular countries. This perspective certainly helps us understand the migration flows that have in fact taken place to Japan from countries such as Korea. But given the relatively small numbers involved, one would have to wonder, from a world-systems perspective, why those migration flows have not been much more extensive. World-systems theory is useful in explaining why migration flows take place between particular pairs of countries and not between other pairs. But its failure to account for the overall immigration history of Japan suggests that it is less effective in the more general task of explaining variation in the occurrence of migration, that is, why some countries have experienced more immigration than others.

I have suggested that certain perspectives give insufficient attention to the role of restrictive policies in limiting the migration that other factors or processes (for example, wage differences or labour market dualism) would otherwise foster. In fact, migration scholars have paid greater attention to politics and policy in recent years (for example, Hollifield, 2000). But it is not clear that these contributions are markedly more successful in explaining variation in migration outcomes. The reason might have to do with implicit ideas about what the core relevant research question is. Migration research is permeated with a broad assumption: there has been a very significant increase in international migration in recent decades, leaving virtually no part of the world untouched. That assumption is, mostly, correct. But the qualification 'mostly' brings us around again to the way research questions sometimes overlook the utility of focusing on variation: the global increase in migration has been uneven, occurring more in some places than in others.

The utility of this focus is likely to be especially relevant to the study of migration policies. The insightful work of Gary Freeman (1995) sets itself the task of explaining the expansionism of migration policy among liberal democratic destination countries. Freeman argues that the interest groups favouring more open migration are better placed than those favouring greater restrictions to see their preferences translated into policies: pro-migration interests – particularly employers – are smaller in number and more easily organized, while the more diffuse preference of voters for less immigration does not find expression in an effective lobbying apparatus. The nature of policy-making in liberal democracies, then, feeds a structural bias towards more open migration policies.

This perspective emerges from consideration of what is held in common by significant destination countries, an approach consistent with Mill's method of agreement. We then see an example of how the picture changes when we turn our attention to variation. Freeman's argument – pointing to a policy-making dynamic characteristic of liberal democracies – identifies a factor that is also present in certain countries that have not experienced immigration to the same extent. When we take on the task of explaining why some countries have many immigrants while others have relatively few, we must look for a factor that distinguishes the one from the other. The Japanese case – insofar as it is no less a liberal democracy than the countries of western Europe and North America – emerges again as an anomaly (as does Finland). Even if one were to doubt that Japan is a liberal democracy without significant differences to the more classic cases, it is hardly self-evident that migration policy in Japan would be any less responsive to the perceived needs or demands of employers than in other advanced capitalist democracies.

Attention to policy is likely to be productive because there is greater potential for a successful effort to distinguish between positive and negative cases. Other approaches point to factors that appear to be (or are sometimes even argued to be) universal. They thus run up against a basic methodological axiom: one cannot explain a variable with a constant. If migration policies mediate the effect of the various factors that produce pressure or demand for migration – and it is therefore policy that determines whether pressure or demand actually results in migration – then a focus on variation in policy might be a promising way to explain variation in migration outcomes.

Investigation of negative cases, then, could lead to better arguments about the causes of migration. The observation that migration scholars have not devoted significant efforts to countries with few immigrants/foreign workers is valuable only if such efforts have potential for generating new insights. The discussion in the preceding paragraphs suggests that this potential arises from the notion that investigation of negative cases is likely to sharpen our questions about the role of migration policy in shaping different migration outcomes.

3.2 CONCEPTUALIZATION

The preceding section builds on the assertion that there are countries with many foreign workers and countries with few foreign workers. That idea requires clarity on what might be considered a prior issue: whom to count as a 'foreign worker', or even an 'immigrant'. Some of the same considerations identified above come into play for this issue as well. When researchers investigate a single case, there is no obstacle to developing the depth of familiarity with the case sufficient to establish unproblematically whom to count. But for comparative research across many countries, one might be tempted to use an approach that emphasizes ostensible consistency, at the cost of overlooking the specificity of particular cases. In practice, concepts such as 'foreign worker' or 'immigrant' become quite complex when comparing across a diverse range of cases. This complexity has significant implications for our appreciation of variation in migration outcomes.

A temptation to use standardized approaches to conceptualization arises in part because of the availability of data collected by international organizations such as SOPEMI (the Organization for Economic Cooperation and Development's (OECD) 'continuous reporting system on migration'). On one level, such resources are a boon to researchers precisely because they facilitate international comparison with standardized data – indeed this is one of the major purposes of their production.[7] One can take figures directly from tables in the SOPEMI appendices on a variety of concepts: stocks of foreign workers, stocks of immigrants and so on. The question, however, is whether doing this is too easy, at least for certain purposes.

In developing this argument in relation to 'foreign workers', it is useful to begin by making explicit the intuitive understanding the term is likely to evoke in general. As with many topics of social science research, we are often interested in foreign workers because they represent a 'problem' at some level (cf. Castles, 2010) – a problem that might arise from political considerations (voter discontent and resentment) or from concern over their own marginalization. (That is, I am not asserting that I consider the presence of foreign workers in wealthy countries to be a problem.) The essence of the problem of foreign workers is captured in the oft-quoted aphorism: 'We asked for workers, and people came' (Frisch, 1967, p. 100; cf. Zolberg, 1987, 'wanted but not welcome'). In other words, foreign workers are useful as workers but are considered unsuitable for full membership in the societies in which they are employed; if they were full members, they would not be useful for the specific types of employment that brought them to the destination country. The long-term marginalization of significant numbers of people – something that has arguably been an active policy goal (even if not explicitly framed in those terms) – is, inescapably, a problem in liberal democracies, one that attracts sustained attention from social scientists.

The paradigmatic case of foreign workers is Germany's use of 'guestworkers'. The word itself describes the expectation underlying the various agreements signed in the 1950s and 1960s between Germany and Italy, Greece, Turkey and so on: the presence of the workers would be temporary, a solution to temporary (cyclical) labour shortages, such that there was no need to contemplate the prospect that they would become permanent members of German society. The amount of research conducted on guestworkers in Germany is surely rooted in the failure of this expectation to be matched by reality: if 'guestworkers' had been integrated into German society as full members (that is, in a way that resolved their socioeconomic as well as political disadvantage), it seems likely that less research effort would have been devoted to them.

One wonders, then, whether it is sensible to count all non-citizens in the labour force as foreign workers (as SOPEMI does). Such rules capture a number of people whose situation is quite different from the paradigmatic case of German guestworkers. The categories thus created are excessively heterogeneous, in part because they include people who do not embody the 'problem' indicated by the foreign worker label. It seems implausible to work with a category that implicitly claims that (for example) Norwegians working in Sweden have a great deal in common with Turks working in Germany or Thais working in Israel.

Drawing on an intuitive sense of what it means to be a 'foreign worker', the argument here is that the operationalization of the concept should capture those who are significantly disadvantaged by their foreignness (relative to natives). Foreign workers are an addition to the labour force of the destination country – but more specifically they are an addition not of generic workers but of workers with an inferior labour market position, impaired by restricted economic, political or social rights/assets. Non-citizen status is a marker that indicates a potential for disadvantage of this sort, but certain types of non-citizen workers might not in fact be disadvantaged by lack of formal citizenship. Perhaps, then, it will make sense to exclude these types from the category of 'foreign worker', so that the latter captures the concept as we really intend it.

Some sub-types clearly fit the concept, without ambiguity of the type I am indicating. Workers on restricted visas limiting the period of their residence and/or preventing them from changing jobs are obviously disadvantaged, by design, in ways that express the intuitive meaning of 'foreign worker'. Some workers essentially enter a relation of indenture as a condition of gaining access to higher wages; the word indenture suggests an outdated arrangement, but it persists in a variety of settings, for example, foreign workers in Israel (Bartram, 2005) (the practice was declared illegal in 2006 but still exists in modified forms). In other cases, restrictions are looser, but workers are required to remain in particular economic sectors, or particular regions.

Another type for which there is little or no ambiguity is illegal/undocumented workers, whose vulnerability is often exploited by employers aware that such workers are unlikely to complain about ill-treatment. Undocumented workers typically do undesirable jobs for low wages and encounter limits to their ability to improve their situations markedly. Even so, the risks they run are real. There might be rare instances of undocumented workers whose formal status does not amount to actual disadvantage,[8] but it seems reasonable to assume that disadvantage does in fact follow from lack of documentation/status.

In many instances, then, there is no question about the fit of people's situations with the concept of 'foreign workers' as described above. But there are other types for which a degree of ambiguity arises in relation to our intuitive sense of that concept; if we follow commonly used markers such as citizenship status we would speak in a prima facie way of foreign workers, but on further reflection there are grounds for considering a different view.

The primary type for which that ambiguity arises is: workers who migrate under the auspices of a common labour market arrangement such as the European Union (EU) or the Nordic Common Labour Market. A French citizen employed in the UK simply does not face nearly the same degree of disadvantage, as a consequence of being 'foreign', as a Thai worker employed in Israel. Provisions for mobility within the EU mean that EU nationals do not usually face significant restrictions on employment (for example, limited to particular sectors or regions), nor are they barred from eligibility for welfare benefits. Perhaps just as importantly, in most cases they are unlikely to face disapproving public attitudes of the sort encountered by non-EU workers, particularly those from poorer countries. Being a foreigner might entail some degree of disadvantage – perhaps one lacks familiarity with local job search/hiring practices – but on balance the situation for such workers suggests a difference from rather than a similarity to the situation of the types discussed above. Thinking in terms of similarity and difference, a Norwegian working in Sweden surely has more in common with a New Yorker working in Connecticut than with a Jamaican working on a restricted visa in Canada. Part of the rationale behind common labour market arrangements is that the countries involved are willing to enter them because the similarity in levels of economic development means that they do not have to worry about being 'swamped' with 'cheap labour' from the others. The emergence of a common element of identity, as a condition for and/or consequence of the larger supranational project (of which labour mobility provisions are a part), is also relevant here. The concept 'foreign workers' suggests that the workers are different from natives in significant ways – but to a certain extent workers moving within Europe share a common European identity.

The preceding paragraph speaks of ambiguity rather than clarity on the point being made. It is not obvious that workers enjoying the mobility provisions of the EU are always lacking disadvantage in the way described. The situation of Polish workers in the UK following Polish accession to the EU in 2004 is sometimes difficult (for example, Weishaar, 2008): British newspaper articles recount experiences that read very much like those of prototypical foreign workers, including mistreatment, substandard housing conditions, discrimination and prejudice and so on. In the end, there is no substitute for contextual knowledge of the cases one is including in one's research. At the very least, however, the existence of a common labour market arrangement might suggest beginning with a rebuttable assumption that workers benefiting from that arrangement should be excluded from the category of foreign workers.

The logic of the argument regarding common labour markets can perhaps be extended to the migration of workers among countries at similar levels of economic development even where there is no common labour market arrangement. Workers from other wealthy countries in general might not fit with our intuitive sense of the concept of foreign workers – even where they are employed on a restricted visa of the type described above. As an American sociologist employed on such a visa by a British university in the early 2000s, I enjoyed a relatively lower degree of labour market and social disadvantage than many UK citizens, let alone foreign workers of the conventional type. Many employed foreigners in

Migration, methods and innovation 61

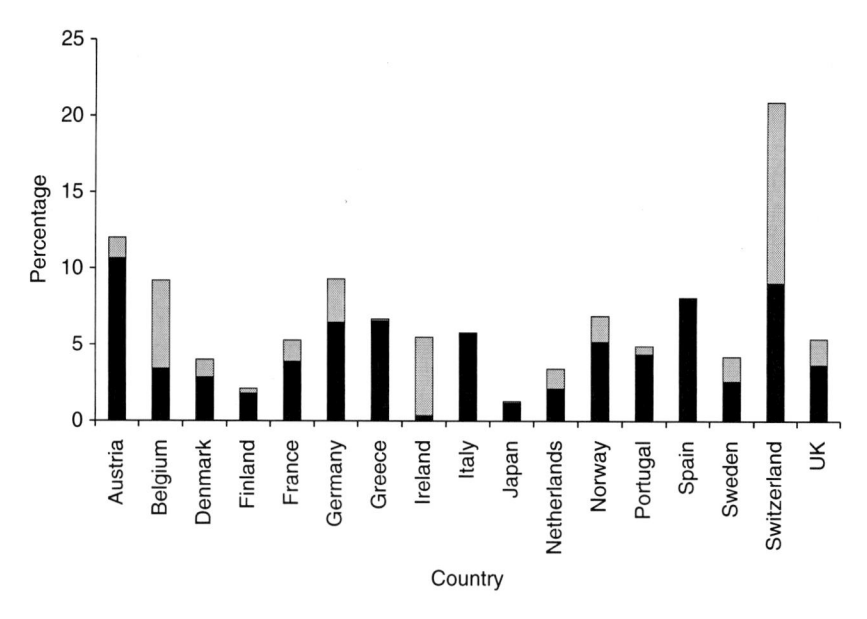

Note: Sources are OECD (2008) and Iguchi (2005) for Japan (data relate to 2003). SOPEMI offers data for Japan, but the figure (180,500) is implausibly low. Iguchi (2005) data include *Nikkeijin*, 'trainees' and 'overstayers' (undocumented workers).

Figure 3.1 Percentage of foreign workers in selected OECD countries, 2005

Japan are skilled workers/professionals from North America and Europe (Fuess, 2003); some are transferred among the various offices of large transnational corporations. Migration by high-skilled workers from wealthy countries has increased significantly in recent decades (Böhning, 1991) adding to the number of ostensible foreign workers. But the practice of including such workers into measures of a concept that originated in an entirely different sort of experience might well hide more than it reveals.

As with other issues relating to research methods, the significance (or otherwise) of this discussion turns on whether a different approach leads to a different picture or conclusion. A consideration of data on stocks of foreign workers in selected countries shows that there are indeed significant differences. Figure 3.1 presents data from SOPEMI; the top portion of each column identifies the size of the categories that, following the logic of the preceding discussion, would be excluded from the concept of 'foreign workers'. The bottom portion, then, indicates the percentage of foreign workers in the labour force that accord with the definition elaborated here.

A striking difference emerges for Switzerland: more than half of the almost 21 per cent of the labour force consisting of foreign workers are from other wealthy countries (most in western Europe), though the remaining 9 per cent is still a substantial figure. For Belgium, SOPEMI data suggest that foreign workers make up 9 per cent of the Belgian labour force, but the majority are from elsewhere in the EU (many are probably associated with the EU institutions in Brussels). If we adopt the view that they are not really foreign workers in a way that accords with an intuitive understanding of the term, we arrive at a 'real' figure of 3.4 per cent.

The difference is even more dramatic for Ireland, which has recently gained much attention as a new and rapidly growing destination (for example, Fanning, 2007) The vast majority of people identified as foreign workers in the SOPEMI data come from elsewhere in the EU (as well as the USA and Australia). There are other types of immigrants (for example, asylum seekers from Africa), and immigration from the 2004 accession states became significant after 2005. But using unadjusted data on 'stocks of foreign workers' in Ireland in general might produce a misleading impression – one in which it is perhaps surprising that almost half of the individuals counted in this category originate in the UK.

There are smaller differences for Finland and Japan: an adjustment for Finland that removes workers originating from elsewhere in the EU lowers the percentage to 1.8 per cent, reinforcing the assertion that Finland has not been a significant destination for labour migration in the way that characterizes other cases. Japan has no international free labour mobility arrangements and relatively few workers from other wealthy countries – but then the overall numbers are not large to begin with.

3.3 QUESTIONS AND ARGUMENTS

The discussion in the preceding sections suggests a research question that might effectively supplement the questions underpinning a fair amount of migration research in recent years. Some migration scholars hold that a main task is to address a question akin to the following: why has international migration increased so significantly in recent decades, becoming a truly global phenomenon? As indicated above, this is a useful question for certain purposes. Even so, additional insight might emerge from addressing a different question: alongside this significant increase in many destinations, why do certain countries that might be expected to attract large-scale immigration fail to do so? More generally, how do we explain variation in migration outcomes?

I have already indicated that a focus on variation in migration policies is likely a productive direction for addressing these questions. Other well-known arguments highlight factors that account for why 'migration pressures' arise – but to a certain extent government policies determine whether those pressures lead to actual migration.[9] Some governments adopt more restrictive policies than others. Restrictive policies are sometimes effective in preventing immigrants from entering (or in preventing people from gaining employment in violation of the terms of a tourist or student visa). There is variation on both counts (adoption of policy and effectiveness of adopted policies).

As described above, Freeman (1995) argues that liberal democracies have similar dynamics of policy-making processes, such that there is a structural bias towards more open immigration policies. This argument overstates the extent of uniformity among the wealthy liberal democracies one might expect to attract immigrants; it particularly overstates uniformity in policy-making on labour immigration. Basic market incentives lead employers everywhere to want access to cheaper labour – and labour is usually cheaper when there is a greater supply of it, especially when it comes with political and social impairments rooted in foreign status. Why, then, are some governments more able than others to resist pressure from employers to allow them access to cheap foreign labour?

Here it becomes highly relevant that there is variability in the degree to which the state (and individual policy-makers) is beholden to employer interests. Research on the autonomy of the state (for example, Evans, 1995) demonstrates that state officials are sometimes able to pursue policy agendas contrary to the preferences of powerful private interests (as against older Marxist ideas about the state being the agent of the bourgeoisie).

Research on the 'developmentalist state' in Japan (for example, Johnson, 1982) is particularly useful here. In Japan (at least, post-war Japan through perhaps the mid-1990s), significant areas of policy-making were controlled more by civil servants in key ministries than by politicians in the Japanese parliament (Diet). As such, policy-making was insulated – to a greater degree than in more 'clientelist' settings – from the pressures of private interests such as employer organizations. A key difference in policy outcomes emerged in particular from the fact that civil servants, not being subject to the short-term dynamics of electoral cycles, could take a long-term perspective on desirable outcomes and the appropriate means to achieve them. The ability of the state to adopt a long-term perspective was also supported by the long-term dominance of the Liberal Democratic Party; electoral cycles were less of an issue because of the generally lower level of political competition.

The general mode of economic policy-making in Japan supported the ability of the Japanese government to resist employers' pressures for permission to import migrant workers.[10] Japanese employers began lobbying for access to migrant labour in the early 1970s in response to labour shortages. But the government's response, in contrast to the accommodationist approach in many European countries (not to mention the USA), was instead to require and/or facilitate (via support for investment and research) the adoption of a less labour-intensive mode of production. A key example was rapid mechanization and use of prefabrication in the construction sector (which in other countries typically makes extensive use of foreign workers). The result was that construction workers in Japan are mainly (though by no means exclusively) Japanese – attracted to the sector by the fact that they could earn higher than average wages, in part because of their higher labour productivity. Needless to say, another supporting condition was the decision to restrict immigration, that is, the fact that wages for Japanese workers were not subject to effective competition from immigrants.[11]

The extent of rapid structural transformation of economic sectors in Japan was not necessarily consistent with maximization of profits for Japanese businesses, at least in the short term. Again, the reason employers in particular sectors typically want access to foreign labour is that they believe that by lowering their costs they can gain greater profits. Japanese employers have in general continued to be profitable – but perhaps not as profitable as they would have been with access to foreign labour. Nor have they been able to gain profits via the externalization of costs that typically go with use of immigrant labour in the 'guestworker' mode.

A similar set of conditions and outcomes is found in Finland, the European country with membership in the OECD having the lowest proportion of foreign labour (properly conceived), barring Ireland. In common with other wealthy industrialized countries, Finland has experienced labour shortages, particularly in the late 1980s and again in the late 1990s. As in Japan, however, the Finnish government simultaneously refrained from opening the doors to migrant labour from poorer countries and supported the transformation of the construction industry into a sector that could employ native workers in relatively high-wage, high-productivity jobs (Bartram, 2007). This interventionist approach was possible in part because of the greater role of civil servants in policy-making, also evident in the highly organized corporatist mode of economic governance (Schienstock and Hämäläinen, 2005; Vartiainen, 1997).

3.4 CONCLUSION

The central methodological argument of this chapter is that certain aspects of migration research would be advanced via more explicit attention to variation in migration outcomes. One is likely to discern variation of the sort just described only if one starts by explicitly incorporating variation into one's research questions. In the context of migration studies, this means that migration scholars would benefit from giving consideration to cases where migration is more an absence than a presence. This point has been addressed productively at the level of individuals: Hammar et al. (1997) emphasize the need to study 'immobility' along with migration. But it is less common to find this approach when one's unit of analysis is countries.

The issues of variation and conceptualization are heavily interrelated. As argued above, one can only define the nature of a case when there is clarity on the concept that feeds the definition of the case. In other words, thoughtful conceptualization sharpens the question: variation of what? The section on conceptualization argues for a more subtle approach to the concept of 'foreign worker' in particular.

There is substantial scope for conceptual development in other areas of migration studies, even with reference to the more basic concept of 'immigrant'. Most definitions are implicitly oriented to determining whether/how particular individuals 'enter' the status of immigrant so that it then makes sense to include them in one's measures. I am not aware of research that explicitly addresses whether/how particular individuals might 'exit' from the concept, apart from via emigration. Implicitly, some approaches to measurement carry the implication that one who moves permanently to another country remains an immigrant for the rest of one's life (by virtue of being 'foreign-born'). In other approaches, one ceases being an immigrant via naturalization. In both cases, we might wonder whether these measurement rules are used primarily because of the availability of data rooted in administrative rules, rather than emerging from a serious effort at conceptualization. As with the definition of 'foreign workers' above, that effort would depend on contextual knowledge of cases: in some places one might exit 'immigrant' status more quickly than others. A telling example is Israel, where immigrants can become 'veterans' (*vatikim*) quite quickly, in part because they are quickly 'replaced' by new cohorts. In observing how Israel is relatively extreme in this regard, we can become more attuned to the fact that other countries are likely to be dissimilar from one another as well as from Israel.

Another example for further development emerges from the observation that the analysis above assumes that the categorization of individuals as foreign workers requires use of a dichotomy: one is either a foreign worker or one is not. Ragin's discussion of 'fuzzy sets' (2000) offers another possibility: to the extent that arguments above concerning the complexity of the concept (particularly for cross-national comparative work) are convincing, we might be tempted by a fuzzy set approach in which particular types of individuals are deemed to have 'partial' membership in the category.

To add yet another (related) layer: the degree of membership in a category (concept) can change over time, for example, as with the progressive accession of countries to the EU. The fact that Polish and other eastern European workers now enjoy free mobility throughout part of the EU cannot sensibly be taken to mean that on one day it was right to count them as foreign workers and on the next (as mobility provisions came into force) it was right to count them as not foreign workers. A fuzzy set approach might help mitigate some of the anomalous implications that would seem to inhere in the use of dichotomies.

Over the course of several decades, migration researchers have produced large volumes of insightful work, frequently by giving careful consideration to methodological issues. Research on migration presents significant challenges, arising both from the international nature of the topic and the speed at which it changes. Continuous methodological reflection is thus an essential aspect of any researcher's work. This chapter demonstrates the added value of such reflection in one extended example and suggests some areas that might yield further development (where the need for further work is evident in the underdevelopment of the suggestions). An ongoing engagement with research methods is probably the best means of sustaining the potential for one's work to lead to innovation and insight.

NOTES

1. We might even say that the goal is to produce 'causal' explanations. Some social scientists reject the notion of causal explanations on epistemological grounds. But causality is an inextricable part of our language: we often start questions by asking 'why . . .?', and we then naturally begin to answer them with 'be*cause* . . .'. See also Elster (2007).
2. For an interesting exception, see Seol and Skrentny (2009).
3. This figure does not include the Korean permanent residents, most of whom are not themselves immigrants.
4. An exception is Reubens (1981).
5. For a more general discussion of negative case methodology, see Emigh (1997).
6. To the extent that Finland's labour market might be less dualistic than in most countries, one would then have to account for the fact that this apparently universal dynamic does not characterize Finland.
7. See Skeldon (Chapter 11, this volume) for further discussion of international migration databases.

8. I found myself in such a situation as a PhD student conducting research abroad: I violated the terms of my student visa by editing a manuscript for an academic whose native language was not English.
9. Whether/how that statement applies to undocumented migration deserves an extended discussion (not provided here). In brief: the failure to take effective action against undocumented migration is itself a policy matter – one can argue that the growth of the undocumented population in the USA, for example, results from a deliberate strategy to eschew effective enforcement (on which see, for example, Calavita, 1994).
10. For a more extended version of this argument, see Bartram (2004).
11. Japanese concerns about racial homogeneity are sometimes considered an important part of the explanation for Japan's more restrictionist approach (cf. Kibe and Thränhardt, 2008). But such concerns were no less a feature of the Israeli debate over foreign workers – and those concerns were quickly swept aside in the government's subservient response to employer demands.

REFERENCES

Bartram, D. (2004), 'Labor migration policy and the governance of the construction industry in Israel and Japan', *Politics & Society*, **32** (2), 131–70.
Bartram, D. (2005), *International Labor Migration: Foreign Workers and Public Policy*, New York: Palgrave Macmillan.
Bartram, D. (2007), 'Conspicuous by their absence: why are there so few foreign workers in Finland?', *Journal of Ethnic and Migration Studies*, **33** (5), 767–82.
Bechhofer, F. and Paterson, L. (2000), *Principles of Research Design in the Social Sciences*, London: Routledge.
Böhning, W.R. (1991), 'Integration and immigration pressures in Western Europe', *International Labour Review*, **130** (4), 445–9.
Calavita, K. (1994), 'US immigration and policy responses: the limits of legislation', in W. Cornelius, P. Martin and J. Hollifield (eds), *Controlling Immigration: A Global Perspective*, Cambridge: Cambridge University Press, pp. 55–82.
Castles, S. (2010), 'Understanding global migration: a social transformation perspective', *Journal of Ethnic and Migration Studies*, **36** (10), 1565–86.
Cornelius, W.A. (1994), 'Japan: the illusion of immigration control', in W. Cornelius, P. Martin and J. Hollifield (eds), *Controlling Immigration: A Global Perspective*, Cambridge: Cambridge University Press, pp. 375–410.
Elster, J. (2007), *Explaining Social Behavior: More Nuts and Bolts for the Social Sciences*, Cambridge: Cambridge University Press.
Emigh, R.J. (1997), 'The power of negative thinking: the use of negative case methodology in the development of sociological theory', *Theory and Society*, **26** (5), 649–84.
Evans, P.B. (1995), *Embedded Autonomy: States and Industrial Transformation*, Princeton, NJ: Princeton University Press.
Fanning, B. (ed.) (2007), *Immigration and Social Change in the Republic of Ireland*, Manchester: Manchester University Press.
Freeman, G.P. (1995), 'Modes of immigration politics in liberal democratic states', *International Migration Review*, **29** (4), 881–902.
Frisch, M. (1967), *Öffentlichkeit als Partner*, Frankfurt am Main: Suhrkamp.
Fuess, S.M. (2003), 'Immigration policy and highly skilled workers: the case of Japan', *Contemporary Economic Policy*, **21** (2), 243–57.
Hammar, T., Brochmann, G., Tamas, K. and Faist, T. (eds) (1997), *International Migration, Immobility, and Development: Multidisciplinary Perspectives*, New York: Berg.
Hollifield, J.F. (2000), 'The politics of international migration: how can we "bring the state back in"?', in C. Brettell and J.F. Hollifield (eds), *Migration Theory: Talking Across Disciplines*, New York: Routledge, pp. 137–85.

Iguchi, Y. (2005), *Possibilities and Limitations of Japanese Migration Policy in the Context of Economic Partnership in East Asia*, New York: UN Population Division.
Johnson, C.A. (1982), *MITI and the Japanese Miracle: The Growth of Industrial Policy, 1925–1975*, Stanford, CA: Stanford University Press.
Kibe, T. and Thränhardt, D. (2008), 'Japan: a non-immigration country discusses migration', in D. Thränhardt and M. Bommes (eds), *National Paradigms of Migration Research*, Göttingen: Universitätsverlag Osnabrück bei V&R unipress, pp. 233–58.
Kindleberger, C.P. (1967), *Europe's Postwar Growth: The Role of Labor Supply*, Cambridge, MA: Harvard University Press.
King, G., Keohane, R. and Verba, S. (1994), *Designing Social Inquiry: Scientific Inference in Qualitative Research*, Princeton, NJ: Princeton University Press.
Komai, H. (1995), *Migrant Workers in Japan*, London and New York: Kegan Paul
Mori, H. (1997), *Immigration Policy and Foreign Workers in Japan*, New York: St Martin's Press.
OECD (2008), *SOPEMI: Continuous Reporting System on Migration*, Paris: OECD.
Pempel, T.J. (1978), 'Japanese foreign economic policy: the domestic bases for international behavior', in P.J. Katzenstein (ed.), *Between Power and Plenty: Foreign Economic Policies of Advanced Industrial States*, Madison, WI: University of Wisconsin Press, pp. 139–90.
Piore, M.J. (1979), *Birds of Passage: Migrant Labor and Industrial Societies*, Cambridge: Cambridge University Press.
Ragin, C.C. (1987), *The Comparative Method: Moving Beyond Qualitative and Quantitative Strategies*, Berkeley, CA: University of California Press.
Ragin, C.C. (2000), *Fuzzy-set Social Science*, Chicago, IL: University of Chicago Press.
Ragin, C.C. and Becker, H.S. (eds) (1992), *What is a Case? Exploring the Foundations of Social Inquiry*, Cambridge: Cambridge University Press.
Ratha, D. and Shaw, W. (2007), 'South-South migration and remittances', World Bank Development Prospects Group, Working Paper No. 102.
Reubens, E.P. (1981), 'Low-level work in Japan without foreign workers', *International Migration Review*, **15** (4), 749–57.
Sassen, S. (1988), *The Mobility of Labor and Capital: A Study in International Investment and Labor Flow*, Cambridge: Cambridge University Press.
Schienstock, G. and Hämäläinen, T. (2005), *Transformation of the Finnish Innovation System: A Network Approach*, Helsinki: Sitra.
Sellek, Y. (1997), 'Nikkeijin: the phenomenon of return migration', in M. Weiner (ed.), *Japan's Minorities: The Illusion of Homogeneity*, New York: Routledge, pp. 178–210.
Seol, D.-H. and Skrentny, J.D. (2009), 'Why is there so little migrant settlement in East Asia?', *International Migration Review*, **43** (3), 578–620.
Vartiainen, J. (1997), 'Understanding state-led industrialization', in V. Bergstrom (ed.), *Government and Growth*, Oxford: Clarendon Press, pp. 203–39.
Weiner, M. (1995), *The Global Migration Crisis: Challenge to States and to Human Rights*, New York: HarperCollins College Publishers.
Weishaar, H.B. (2008), 'Consequences of international migration: a qualitative study on stress among Polish migrant workers in Scotland', *Public Health*, **122** (11), 1250–56.
Zolberg, A. (1987), 'Wanted but not welcome: alien labor in Western development', in W. Alonso (ed.), *Population in an Interacting World*, Cambridge, MA: Harvard University Press, pp. 36–73.

4 Transnational – transregional – translocal: transcultural
Dirk Hoerder

This chapter presents a historicized approach that integrates levels and concepts: Transcultural Societal Studies. Methodologically, this interdisciplinary approach is capable of combining the advantages of discipline-constrained approaches. Since the early 1990s, scholars have increasingly used 'transnational' as an anchor term for interpretations of migrants' continuing relations with their nation-states of origin. The concept is complex, contested, and ambiguous. It has both a long history – transnationalism before the nation-state in one awkward formulation – and is applied to diverse phenomena. As a practice it has been interpreted as liberating migrants from the constraints of nation-states and their bordered identities or as destructive to social cohesion and as opening countries to assumed threats of the most recent globalization. In contrast to 'inter'-national which posits two distinct polities in formalized contact by diplomacy, warfare, border-crossing trade, or other, 'trans' dissolves the separating qualities of borderlines to a degree. It combines lived spaces with the 'beyond,' conceptualizes the national as connected to the distant 'other.' 'People, ideas, and institutions do not have clear national identities. Rather, people may translate and assemble pieces from different cultures.' Instead of taking things and ideas to be distinctively national, elements may begin or end somewhere else (Bentley, 2005; Thelen, 1992, p. 436).

This chapter will first discuss historic practices and conceptualizations of 'transcultural,' and will then discuss usages of 'transnationalism' in the nineteenth and twentieth centuries and outline the debate since the concept's reintroduction in the 1990s. In a second section it will develop translocal and transregional approaches as the levels on which migrant connectivity is acted out and can be empirically traced. Third, the alternative concept 'transculturation' as developed from the 1930s to the early 1950s, will be introduced. Finally, a historicized approach that integrates levels and concepts, Transcultural Societal Studies, will be presented.[1]

4.1 TRANSNATIONAL: USAGES, CONCEPTUALIZATIONS, CRITIQUES

In its 1990s version 'transnationalism' takes nation-states as the frame for analysis. The term 'nation-state,' however, compounds two distinct and contradictory entities. States, as political theory since the Age of Enlightenment postulated, were to treat the diversity of their inhabitants as equal before the law. Nations, the corollary of subsequent Romanticism, added a cultural unity of a people. Resulting nationalism hierarchically ranked members of the cultural 'nation' above different groups designated as 'minorities' or segregated as immigrants. From this new regime, members of minorities emigrated because the nation-state prohibited equal access to societal resources. Nationalist-republican states demanded uniformity of culture before equality before the law might be granted. Internal inter- or transcultural relations were not part of nation-state political theory and historiography. This European construct – or, perhaps, ideology – became the paradigm of political organization in the North Atlantic (white) World. Transnational implies a 'translation' of national cultures which, however, are difficult to locate since most states are – at least to some degree – composed of many cultural groups. In the one century during which most nation-states have existed, institutional regimes have come to fuse some political and cultural aspects.

Historicizing the concept of state indicates that dynastic states combined peoples of many cultures and social positions into polities with all inhabitants unified as 'subjects' of the ruler. No further homogeneity was required. In medieval Iberian societies such many-cultured living was conceptualized as *convivencia*, in the Ottoman Empire cohabitation of different ethno-religious groups became the organizational basis, the nineteenth-century Habsburg Empire was a self-designated 'state of many peoples.' When the concepts of 'peoples' and 'nations' emerged during middle-class ascendancy, the Age of Revolution, and Napoleonic imperial expansion, they were still open. Cultures were distinct but not clearly bounded, territorial states contracted and expanded according to dynasties' marriage alliances, treaties, and warfare. Wilhelm and Alexander von Humboldt emphasized the value of comprehensive histories of 'nations', that is, all its strata, as opposed to dynasty-centered narratives. From their worldwide perspective, they commented on the interactions between cultures. Johann Gottfried von Herder studied the distinctiveness of local peoples and their connectedness in the many-cultured and -layered Baltic societies with noble cultures, urban cultures of in-migrant burghers, and rural 'vernacular' peoples. Mid-nineteenth-century observers commented on how improvements of transportation and communication were breaking down nationalities, connecting remote peoples, were even 'making the world one' (Hoerder and Blank, 1994). In the late nineteenth-century United States the new transcontinental railroads were called 'transnational' in the sense of across a nation's, a state's territory.

Early twentieth-century usages refer to the increasing density of economic relations between states or to the Catholic Church's near-global web of relations. From the 1950s, 'multi-national companies' acted beyond the borders of the state in which they were incorporated. The field of 'international law' was, to some degree, reconceptualized as 'transnational law' to include legal subjects acting beyond the confines of nation-states as P.C. Jessup first argued. In the 1970s, R.O. Keohane and J.S. Nye questioned the social and political sciences' nation-state centeredness by including non-state actors whose cross-border agency was trans- rather than international. While historians from the mid-nineteenth-century on constructed 'national' narratives, much of Europe consisted of empires of several peoples, whether the Hohenzollern, Habsburg, Ottoman, or Romanov ones, or states like Great Britain and Switzerland (Patel, 2008).

For migration research, US public intellectual Randolph Bourne introduced the concept in 1916, when the 'melting pot' imagery reigned: 'America is coming to be, not a nationality but a transnationality, a weaving back and forth, with the other lands, of many threads of all sizes and colors.' The image of weaving would be taken up by scholars of cultural interactions: braided or entwined, of many threads, tapestry-like. Such perspectives focus on human agency as well as the labor of both men and women and *homo migrans* and *femina migrans* (Harzig). The story of clothing and cloth-making countered the nation-state-industrialization narrative centered on the steam engine-blast furnace view of history, as male-centered and top-down as stateside approaches. By 1900 the early 1800s views of peoples' histories had been reduced to ideologies of superior race-based nations threatened by inferior immigrant masses. US author Madison Grant's *The Passing of the Great Race* (1916) is a prototype. Bourne had noted that societies need not 'panic' about migrant cultural expression; Horace Kallen conceptualized states like the United States as federations of nationalities with 'cultural pluralism' when state-imposed school curricula propagated and media advertised monocultural nationalism.

Nationalist historians saw borders as militarized dividing lines, states as self-contained, and national identities as essentialist – in the very decades when European states in the transatlantic migrations 'lost' some 50–55 million men and women. These selected the economic options of migrant-admitting societies over the bloodline constructs of their states of birth. Elsewhere in the world, in the Indian subcontinent-Southeast Asia-southern China migration macro-region similar numbers moved. Still, borders were not conceptualized as permeable and migration historians postulated a nation-to-ethnic enclave paradigm which has migrants move from a bordered state to a bordered ethnic community. Continuing the Chicago School of Sociology's emphasis on social and personal disorganization, O. Handlin labeled migrants 'uprooted,' others saw them as 'in limbo' or 'in between.'

In this frame, the (re)conceptualization of 'transnationalism' by US cultural anthropologists N. Glick Schiller, L. Basch, and C. Blanc-Szanton (1992) opened new perspectives. Their study of late twentieth-century Caribbean and Filipino/a migrants was adapted to Mexican and other Latin American migrants by sociologists, A. Portes most prominently, and by feminist scholars to women migrating as domestic and caregiver workers from Asian societies and Europe's post-communist countries. Much of this research assumed transnational mentalities to be specific to late twentieth-century changes in the world economy, especially a new global capitalism that forces people to migrate from capital-dependent countries globally to centers of capital to earn a living. The emphasis on the global is salient but world historians emphasize that globalization emerged since the sixteenth-century European expansion. The Portuguese outsourced the production of Catholic devotional objects to their colony Goa in India early.

In the initial formulation transnationalism referred to processes by which 'immigrants' or 'transmigrants' build 'social fields' or multi-layered relations linking their countries of origin with those of settlement, they establish networks in two or more nation-states and 'maintain activities, identities, and statuses in several' locations. Such exchanges are legal and structured. Scholars ensconced in 'bounded' concepts' like 'tribe' or 'nation,' the anthropologists acerbically noted, were simply blind to ongoing relations. The transmigrants live in complex systems, reformulate identities, and deal with global and national hegemonic contexts. In a disparate global word their countries of origin, meant to be protective of citizens and their rights, become 'labor-exporting states' and 'remittance societies.' Discussing the 'pitfalls and promise' of the emergent transnationalism studies, sociologists suggested to limit the concept 'to occupations and activities that require regular and sustained social contacts over time across national borders.' They considered such interactions 'truly original phenomena' – thus overlooking the historicity of transborder migrant spaces (Portes, 1999; Portes et al., 1999). After a decade of debate (Fitzgerald and Waldinger, 2004; Levitt et al., 2003) the German, Swedish-trained political scientist T. Faist (2000) provided a differentiated synthesis of transnational approaches. Proponents of the new approach agree with Bourne that the presence of multiple cultures within one country does not imply disintegrative tendencies.

The new approach countered state-generated data by information from migrants. Macro-level, stateside data reflect migrant and remittance flows between states. Both for scholarly analysis and state policy making, more specific data on migrant destinations both as regards regions and economic sectors are necessary. Sending as well as receiving societies do not merely exchange undefined populations but specific groups: miners or caregivers, factory workers or rural laborers. The specific goals that these pursue can be gauged only from migrant-created sources whether communications with the family of origin, life-writings, or interviews. Goals may include higher wages (related to living expenses), increased labor market options, less rigorous social hierarchies, or – in terms of family and intergenerational goals, lower infant mortality, better healthcare for pregnant women, more educational opportunities for children. Statewide trends, growing unemployment, for example, are translated into migration on the level of individual decision making within a regional frame of information about conditions at specific job-providing destination regions in another state. Aggregate data indicate population loss or gain, migrant-generated data indicate reasons for and trends in selection of destinations. To understand rather than merely describe (quantity of) migration the motivations need to be analysed. Such data would also be the basis for encouraging, reducing, or deflecting migration routes.

Critical assessments of the concept of transnationalism, which became a catchword and center of a scholarly citation cluster, emerged quickly. First, the term 'transmigrant' did not come to replace 'migrant' in general; it was defined to refer to migrants whose actual move covers an extended period of time and who live temporarily in a transit society like South and Central Americans transiting Mexico to the United States or Russian Jews transiting the Germanies and other European countries on their way to Atlantic ports. In historic Asian overseas migrations, where departure regions were often close to ports, the issue of transit was of less impact. Second, the scope of transnational spaces and designation of cultural groups were problematized. Designations like 'Chinese' or 'Salvadorians' or 'Poles' refer to national language or, since the end of the nineteenth century, to passport and citizenship. They emerge from the inability of receiving-society residents to distinguish multiple local cultures afar, from an increasing role of nation-states in establishing migration regimes, and from a need in everyday communication to simplify and generalize. Migrants, however, connect translocally to keep ties to kin and community. They could, in nineteenth-century receiving societies' political arenas, increase political clout through self-organization by nationality. Such national identification reflects a post-migration practice as has been shown for 'Italians' in North America. Similarly, migrants from Fujian at their destinations face a double identity/ identification, a self-definition by region of origin and a labeling as 'Chinese.' In the (white) North and South Atlantic Migration System around 1900 tele-communication through millions of letters annually and high levels of return migration – on average one third of the migrants – indicate the translocal and transregional connections (Foner, 1997; Kivisto, 2003).

Third, a multi-generational perspective indicates transcultural ties to be specific to the first generation. Over time they are transformed to constructed symbolic celebrations of roots. In the Southeast Asian migration region sequential migrations and returns of Fujian men in contexts of extended families did perpetuate transregional ties but balanced these by the emergence of permanent institutions in communities in the receiving society. The same pattern has been traced for Czech men and women in Vienna. Such circular migrations and structures have been compared to a hotel: the building is in place, the managers are settled, the occupants come and go. Thus ethno-cultural communities are often 'turntables' rather than 'enclaves.' The nineteenth-century juxtaposition of a 'sojourner'-image associated with a 'Chinese' and 'immigrant' image with Europeans was but an ideological indicator that 'Orientals' were not to become permanent immigrants. European and Asian migrants developed similar patters of 'trans'-linked exchanges, though some cultural frames, like Chinese demands on sons to return, explain specifics. It might be asked whether the concept of diaspora does not already theorize related spaces. In the original formulation, 'diaspora' includes a memory of a homeland (that need no longer exist), postulates relatedness of the dispersed diasporic communities among each other, and (perhaps) a desire to return to or recreate the homeland. Diaspora is an interrelated web, a transnational space defined by region of departure and arrival, perhaps multiple arrivals.

Once the double cliché of emigration, that is, permanent departure, from one nation and 'assimilation' in another, never supported by the data, is jettisoned, transsocietal ties reappear in view. Thus the 1990s concept of transnationalism emerged as a needed antidote to a nationalist ideological construct. Across the globe and the centuries migrants negotiated cultural adjustments, accommodated or inserted themselves, accepted some but not other aspects of the receiving society, rejected some but not all aspects of the culture of birth. They intended to adjust because their respective 'home' was unsupportable or, at least, extremely constraining. They adjusted in steps and to some segments of the receiving society – labor markets for adults, schools for children. They connected societies in multiple forms of 'trans.'

The terminological ambiguity of 'transnationalism' may to some degree be clarified by a differentiation between transstate and transnational. States, as institutions and processes of rule, with increasing intensity since the early twentieth century set frames for exit and entry. Nations, the respective dominant ethno-cultural group, sets territory-wide parameters for acculturation. State-generated refugees and labor migrants from Mexico, Caribbean societies, and Central and South American countries originate in specific social stata, rural or urban locations, disadvantaged or fully participating segments of their societies. 'Transstate' captures migrations of people of different cultures out of one (nation-) state. Poles from the pre-1914 German Reich, though citizens, were not nationals. When after the coup in Guatemala in 1954 – by an exiled army officer with involvement of the US state and the multi-national United Fruit Company – 'Indios' had to flee, they could hardly be called 'transnational' since they had been denied national-cultural belonging. Both the German Poles and the non-Guatemalan 'Indios' did create transstate spaces.

If the nineteenth-century self-defined nation-states of birth lost tens of millions of 'their' inhabitants, late twentieth-century states with high demand for workers and aging populations have to compete for in-migrants, as Canadian sociologist L.L. Wong (2002) argues. Such migrants, rather than cling to essentialist national identities, search out the best options available and acquire citizenship, that is, membership in the polity. Their very presence transforms the society's culture, migrants make national cultures fluid.

'Transnationalism' concepts subsume all or most of the world's societies under the nation-state category. Is this justified for formerly colonized, now independent states and the former colonizer states from where capitalist relations and dependency structures, informal empires, radiate out? The transcultural colonizer-colonized 'contact zones' involve strategies of power: imposition of cultural frames of reference, of establishing hegemony, of dominance (Pratt, 2007). Post-colonial migrations need to be analysed in terms of global hierarchies whether under concepts of dependency theory, world systems, or center-periphery concepts of which A. Appadurai (1996), C. Hall (1996), S. Hall (1995), and H. Bhabha (1990) are proponents. Macro-regions of migrations may be discerned under approaches such as global apartheid (Richmond, 1994), subalternized peoples (Guha and Spivak, 1988), former imperial zones turned zones of a common language (English, French, Spanish), informal economic empires, governance of multi-national capital over lesser developed countries. Such hierachizations have been successfully merged with

76   *Handbook of research methods in migration*

transnational approaches in research on present-day women's migrations from countries with low income levels and options, within the globalized yet state-specific service sector, to countries with better options.

4.2   MULTI-LAYERED SPACES: TRANSLOCAL AND TRANSREGIONAL

Migrants create integrated social spaces that follow logics other than those of nation-states. Empirical data on migrants' choice of destination in the past and the present indicate local and regional connectivity, analysis, and theoretization best begins on these levels. Migration decisions are made and migrations start from a family space of birth and family economies. For refugees and other displaced persons, the starting point may be a camp or other dis-location. In the case of stepwise movements intermediate spaces are involved. They target a destination about which a maximum of information and, equally important, where help from kin or acquaintances is available. In the process migrants in networks transfer their individual human capital but also need to rely on social capital, specific to social spaces, and thus not easily transferable. Migrants leave societies in which they have learned to be (deeply) distrustful of institutions and, often, upper strata. Rather than rely on 'official' sources, they search information from trusted earlier migrating relatives or neighbors. Such a communication relationship has been depicted as 'rosy' pictures conveyed in emigrant letters. However, in networks and with expectations of help overly positive reports act as a 'pull factor' for sequential migrations and the originator of the letter or, in the present, of a cell phone message would have to provide assistance. This auto-corrective helps assure reliability of information between the community of arrival and origin.

States were of limited importance in the nineteenth century when few immigration restrictions existed. Within networks, around 1900, 94 percent of all Europeans went to local spaces where kin or friends lived rather than to a vague 'America,' the United States as state, or an imagery of unlimited opportunities. They moved along known routes – as migrants do across the globe. 'Chinese' never originated from across the empire but from highly localized spaces in two coastal provinces, Guangdong/ Kwangtung and Fujian/ Fukien as well as from the island of Hainan. Around 2000, women from the Philippines depart from particular localities and retain ties to families there. The twentieth-century development of migration control systems has reduced accessibility. While Italians before 1914 could choose between specific destinations in Europe, North and South America, and other regions, Filipinas in the present, may legally enter only some states. Entry without documentation increases options of destination selection but decreases options at the selected destination.

The destinations, in addition to supportive communities, need to provide immediate access to income-generating jobs in specific labor markets. The latter aspect dominates in agent-mediated migrations – to a Malayan mine, for example. In view of their very limited means, laboring men and women move to specific labor market segments upon just-in-time information by acquaintances, nineteenth-century women in domestic labor to a Chicago neighborhood, for example, today's Filipina or Somali migrant women to a neighborhood of Rome or Beirut. Men would migrate to factory jobs in Budapest or Cleveland; or, in a craft circuit, like cigar-making, between Manila, Havana, Ybor City, or Hamburg. Distance was no deterrent; routes were well traveled. Around 1900 every eighth passenger on transatlantic steamers had been in North America before and could advise first-time movers. Once an economic and language base had been established, migrants might explore other options in the region, in the same labor market in another region, or target a better paying job in their range of skills. The intensity of communication before 1914 is revealed in statistics indicating a decline of immigrant arrivals within a year after an economic downswing in the United States. Translocal information led to hundreds of thousands of decisions to postpone departure. Statistics for Singapore, the transhipment point for Fujian workers to Southeast Asia, indicate similar patterns for middlemen-organized labor supply.

Beyond retaining emotional ties, migrants establish material connections. Remittances were and are destined for the exact locations from where migrants originate: family, local institutions, perhaps a community. They might help a family survive in a marginal economy (and thus reduce departures), permit visible consumption to improve community positioning, or help the community by paying for a school or providing relief in times of crisis. Patterns of remittance have been studied for Mexican migrants in the US 1920s and 1930s, migrant associations in Africa's metropoles, and Bangladeshi women's savings transfer from the Eastern Mediterranean region in the present. Translocal connections decline when migrants begin to develop aspirations for their own material and emotional well-being. The more family and acquaintances on the spot, the more advanced the process of acculturation, the more material resources are needed at the destination. They decline further when the immigrants' children no longer have personal knowledge of family and culture in the region of origin. Remittance-dependent states try to encourage continuity of exchanges and, in some cases, facilitate transfer of assets. The fact that whole state budgets – Italy in the past, the Philippines in the present – depend on such remittances is an often cited transstate effect which emerges as a corollary to migrants' intentions and translocal connections.

The regions in which community of birth or embeddedness are the frame for the socialization of migrants as infants, children, and adolescents. They speak their language with region-specific intonation or dialect. Proximity of ethno-cultural groups of different languages may permit bilingualism or even (rudimentary) multi-lingualism. Since variants of some languages are not mutually understandable – examples are the Chinese dialects and some German ones – same-dialect rather than transnational language communities emerge at destinations. In many regions, the South Asian subcontinent, for example, regional and ethno-cultural language variety would preclude any discussion of generic 'Indians,' but receiving societies and scholars have labeled men and women as such. Migrants are audibly recognizable by region – which may be a tool for discriminatory distancing or a marker of cultural proximity.

Economic regions – whether agriculture, mining, software production, or other – provide potential migrants with specific skills usable in specific segments of distant labor markets but not in others. Historically, mining was a macro-regional or global economic sector connected by migrants regardless of states and borders. In the multi-national Habsburg Empire regional patterns of training explain migrants' selection of particular intra-imperial but distant labor markets. In many-cultured northeastern India defined recruitment regions provided seasonal labor migrants to the tea plantation economy, others permanent workers for the West Bengal coal mines. With factory production and deskilling of tasks (Taylorization), expanding from England (with internal inter-regional migration) to the Atlantic World and Russia, Europe's economy – at the height of nationalism – was not characterized by nation-states but by a bifurcation into industrializing core and labor-exporting periphery. Migrations between the two were special to meso-regions by culture, language, and skills. The parallel transatlantic migrations from eastern and southern Europe after 1885 appear as one mass movement from highly aggregated data but, in fact, connected specific sending regions with specific destinations. Fujian migrants might select labor markets in Manila or in Malay mines – the availability of jobs was and is the prime determinant of regional connectivity.

Regional spaces are layered and change over time: urban or rural regions, regions of language and religion, regional economic sectors and labor markets. Where either only men or only women departed, another layer, the regional marriage market, became imbalanced. Depending on where at what time which jobs were available migratory connections and the extent of regions adjusted. 'Processual geographies' or adjustable spaces replace the named and fixed territories of physical geography or bordered states. The primacy of labor markets, that is, job options, is entwined with aspects of culture. Communities of earlier migrants serve as a station on a trajectory into the new culture and provide mediators. Regions of shared language – often former empires – facilitate access to institutions.

The delimitation of regions also depends on the stage of economic development. From the late nineteenth century, the deskilling of factory work increased rural migrants' range of target regions. While skilled and professional migrants, intent on finding a better market for their human capital, are restricted to the respective labor market segment, unskilled migrants may choose from a wider array of destinations but, being easily replaceable, have less clout to negotiate acceptable working conditions and thus realize migration goals. This is similar for the mass migrations to the industries of the Atlantic World, to the Plantation Belt, and to service jobs at the turn to the twenty-first century. The inter- and transcontinental layered and complex economic spatializations as well as the regional and local ones make nation-states but one more level. Again, such aggregate labor-attracting regions are culturally differentiated. West African women depart from specific, if changing, regions, move along specific migration corridors, to arrive in other defined, if flexible, spaces with service jobs (which often do require skills). In nineteenth-century Brazil, but not at other destinations in the Americas, 'unskilled' male and female slaves could reconstruct complex ethno-cultural and spiritual practices of their home regions.

The physical-geography view of global migrations – between continents – and the high visibility of transatlantic migrations perhaps explain scholarly disregard for the regionality of moves. Nineteenth-century intra-European and twentieth-century intra-Asian labor migrations were and are vastly larger than out-bound ones: around 1900 only 5 percent of all migrants of the Habsburg Empire moved to other European economies or North America, 95 percent moved internally, with Prague and Vienna the largest receivers. In the present, the vast majority of North or sub-Saharan African migrants move inter-regionally. In the Indian Ocean system, Gujarati-migrating merchants from northwestern India traded with and settled in Arabia and East Africa, those from the southeastern Malabar Coast connected to Siam and the Malay Peninsula. Since voyaging is costly in terms both of time and conveyance, migrant traders and artisans establish branch firms and communities at their destinations. Thus, voyaging turns into migration and the 'pioneers' bring in personnel from the region of origin, circular migrations develop, families are formed.

The translocal and transregional approaches, beyond reflecting migrant experiences, involve further methodological advantages. Statistics collected at international borders exclude intra- and inter-regional movements within states from consideration. These are in the vast majority of cases quantitatively larger than transborder ones. Local and regional data – the levels on which each and every person counts and is counted whether as taxpayer or cost factor – register men, women, and children. They correct national data and narratives that privilege men. On the local level, women's mobility and their economic contributions usually were not recorded on the assumption that their political, citizenship status is derived from men and that they are mere 'associational' migrants to be registered under the male household head's name. Gender bias in migration data occurs on the national level. As late as 1991 a United Nations Expert Group noted massive bias in nation-state data collected by male census-takers from male heads of households under a value regime that underrated women's roles and (unpaid) labor.

The ideological-interpretive frame of male-headed household units prevents analysis of family-based departure decisions as well as family labor or individual contributions of all family members in the society of origin and at the destination. Labor market insertion of in-migrating families as well as strategies of acculturation through schooling depend on family strategies: do men and women work outside of the home in paid labor? If cultural assumptions restrain women to work inside the home, do they substitute purchase of consumer goods, like clothing, by home production? Do they, perhaps, produce garments or paper flowers, assemble technical parts or toys as paid piecework in the home? Furthermore, since under ascribed or even societally cemented roles women care more for children than men, the inclusion of women into the analysis permits a better understanding of strategies for the second generation as regards education, socializing, and marriage options – decisive factors in acculturation. Though the shift to service economies in many developed societies has made women's migrations more visible, in the past much plantation labor and some factory labor involved families; employers in the nineteenth-century garment and electrical industries and in the twentieth-century clothing and electronics industries sought migrant female rather than male labor. Some importers of labor such as plantation owners encouraged family formation in order to gain their next cohort of workers through family reproduction. Inclusion of both genders is also a requirement to analyse post-migration family formation in terms of emotions and sexuality and, thus, societal insertion strategies including the decisions about numbers of children per couple which impact population growth and social security systems. Only gendered and inter-generational approaches – in statewide economic structure provided all data required for comprehensive research approaches.

4.3 SPACES AND INTERACTIONS: CONCEPTS OF TRANSCULTURATION, 1930s TO 1950s

Migrant-agency centered concepts in regional contexts and for many-cultured new societies emerged from the 1930s to the early 1950s on the margins of the Atlantic World's knowledge production: In 1935, Gilberto Freyre published his Portuguese-language study of African- and Portuguese-background cultures in Brazil. In 1940, Fernando Ortiz's Spanish-language path-breaking 'Del fenómeno de la transculturación y su importancia en Cuba' appeared. In 1948 and 1952 Helen MacGill Hughes and Everett C. Hughes's *Where Peoples Meet* became available. Though Freyre's and Ortiz's studies were translated in 1946 and 1947 respectively, they hardly influenced US research. The mind-numbing Cold War period not only exorcised economic approaches, including labor market analysis, from national scholarly agendas; the reductionist 'free world' against the 'communist bloc' paradigm also resulted in a self-centered narrow-mindedness. In the United States, Caroline Ware's fascinating gendered and inter-generational community study of Greenwich Village, New York City, with its immigrants from Italy, Ireland, and elsewhere was forgotten – 'the uprooted', arriving from post-war Europe's ruins, became the template of interpretation of all migrations.

Freyre studied Brazil's sugar plantation economy, which due to soil exhaustion underwent far-ranging regional relocation. Other region-specific sectors included ranching, marginal family agriculture distant from markets, and, of course, the urbanized regions. He argued that African-background men and women – which he differentiated into the constituent 'nations'/ peoples – and European-background Portuguese led entwined lives in power hierarchies and jointly developed the society's culture. The Portuguese had intended to replicate Portugal in Europe, a 'transoceanism' (Capistrano de Abreu), which was also reflected in (other cultures') naming practices: New Spain, New England, New France, or New Amsterdam, and others. The 'unlooked-for phase' of imperial expansion and institution-building involved adjustment to the tropics in general and Brazil's regions in particular. Freyre's emphasis on community formation and creation of a culture rather than on colonial institutions demanded a gendered approach to 'an entire economic, social, and political system.' In sexual hierarchies – including sexual violence – enslaved women, and we should add: free African-background families, of many African ethno-cultures, bore the children that formed each next generation. Freyre's view of Portuguese-Brazilian paternalism was overly positive and later research has emphasized urban life and underclass cultures.

Fernando Ortiz, in 1940, forcefully argued that terms and concepts like 'acculturation' or 'assimilation' assume an existing frame to which newcomers adjust. For Cuba he discerned a sequence of Ciboney and Taino migrations and the merging of cultures; the coming of 'the Spanish,' a problematic aggregate for Castilians, Andalusians, Portuguese, Galicians, Basques, and Catalonians; of other groups like Genoese, Florentines, Jews, Levantines, and Berbers; and sub-Saharan Africans, that is, Mandingas, Wolofs, Hausas, Dahomeyans, Yorubas; as well as Asians from Macao and Canton (Guangdong). Others, US planters, for example, came subsequently. Power relations – Africans came with bodies and souls but without institutions or implements – and size of each group involved rigorous hierarchization. But in a process of 'transculturation' all contributed to the emergence of Cuban society in the frame of a sugar plantation economy capitalized first from Europe then from the United States. Again, cultural-regional differentiation, the plantation regime as economic frame, and imperial political institutions are analysed comprehensively.

In Canada, bi-cultural and bi-lingual Montreal with immigrants from many other European cultures and the presence of African-background migrants provided an opportunity to test the Chicago School's theories on metropolitan regions and immigrant disorganization. E. Hughes and H. MacGill Hughes studied urban 'race' relations and the effects of industrial change in a French-Canadian community. Their approach was contextualized by the divinity schools' and social work departments' attention to poverty, social welfare, and ethics. It was also contextualized by Montreal's economy. State, province, and city would provide all institutions necessary to stable communities, while deteriorating or slum ones would be characterized by 'imposed' or 'elevating' institutions. Institutional completeness characterizes self-determined societies; institutional deficiencies open communities or regions to outside – stateside – imposition. They, too, concluded that migrants arrive in complex societies rather than in mono-cultural nations, that no society or state offered only one single model of adjustment to newly arriving migrants.

Such conceptualizations were not isolated. In Trinidad and Tobago, historian (and, later, statesman) Eric Williams explicated the relations between British capitalist development and slavery's abolition. Trinidadian C.L.R. James, journalist and activist, using the Haitian revolution as case, researched culture- and class-based resistance of the enslaved. Mexican anthropologist Manuel Gamio in the 1920s studied migration from Mexico to the United States and back with detailed attention to region and to translocal connections. Some of this research was completed at the London School of Economics. Many researchers were influenced by the German scholar-migrant of Jewish faith, Franz Boas, and by Bronislaw

Malinowki, scholar-migrant from Poland's highly developed ethnology, both at Columbia University, New York. Edward Sapir, of Lithuanian-Jewish background, and Ruth Benedict also taught there. Of their 1930s students Katherine Dunham researched African-background dance ritual in Martinique, Haiti, and Jamaica; Eleanora Deren African cultural adaptation in Haiti, and Zora Neale Hurston Caribbean migrants in Harlem, Bahamian songs, and African-American folklore from Florida to British Honduras. This vibrant research was hardly noticed by US and other migration historians. Was race an issue, Jewishness or Blackness? Or gender, the role of women in the research?

These scholars were primarily concerned with the question of how a particular society was created – the cultural 'trans' involved the translation of imports through migration and capitalism. All recognized cultural input of the laboring men and women who neither duplicated 'old world traits' nor assimilated unconditionally. The 'trans' was also transoceanic, implying movement and ties across vast but connecting distances. At the time, scholars in the US-British-French-German core of knowledge (or ideology) production who held the power to define in the Atlantic World and the power to hire younger scholars of their mindset into academia did not incorporate these transcultural theoretizations.

4.4 SYNTHESIS AND CONCLUSION

4.4.1 The Translocal, -Regional, and -National: A Transcultural Approach

From the range of concepts of transculturation, translocal, and transregional spaces, and recent discussions about transnationalism, a new synthesis may be developed. Since transnational is an ambiguous term and translocal as well as transregional capture the multiple internal and cross-border spaces created by migrants but not necessarily the twentieth-century stateside entry frame and aggregate impact of family-directed remittances on state budgets, the term 'transcultural' provides both comprehensiveness and the openness to empirically determine the spatial extent of migrants' (overlapping) arenas of agency.

Expanding on Luis E. Guarnizo and Michael P. Smith (1998) as well as Anthony Richmond (1994) the present is characterized by (1) a new level of globalization of capitalism and financial institutions which, in a frame of global apartheid, have destabilizing effects for less industrialized countries, (2) technological innovations that reduce cost and time of long-distance transportation and communication, (3) worldwide political transformations such as decolonization (with continuing links to the former colonizer countries) and the universalization of human rights (which challenges the inferiorization of minorities and migrants within states), and (4) a parallel rise of expectations – literally in view of wealthy segments of the world though media projections – among people in countries with lower standards of living, in fast developing societies with regionally uneven development like China, India, Brazil, Russia, and in regimes that institutionalize high levels of inequality like Mexico and India. In consequence, nation-state gatekeepers' postulated mono-cultural essentialized identity dissolves into relations and belongings, into embeddedness and plural context-depending identifications. The myriad of residents' and migrants' decisions and actions transform fixed into processual structures which retain continuity and thus agency occurs in structured processes. Migrations appear as counter-narratives to nation and ascribed national identity; mobile life trajectories and multi-locality counter bordered territoriality of unsatisfactory (home?) states and unsustainable lives in them (Osterhammel, 2001).

The traditional interpretation of migration as occurring between nation-states and its theoretical reach is highly problematic for migrant-sending and -receiving states that are not nation-states – Britain's or Indonesia's multi-nationality may serve as examples, for colonies-to-colonizer-states moves as well as for those from post-colonial to post-imperial states and societies. Migrants deal with political structures but move to societally framed communities. Rather than a state as a whole, particular regional frames like labor markets, schools, and neighborhoods are the spaces of migrant insertion and of interactions and these contribute to individual and societal transculturation. The intensity of the process depends to some degree on whether large numbers of migrants arrive in a short time (as in Brazil and Cuba) or in small groups over long periods of time (as in Europe's and North America's cores). Migrants transport and transpose practices and values of one social space to another and translate their ways to resident community members while, at the same time, trying to translate residents' ways of life into categories and interpretations familiar to themselves. This migrants achieve with the 'funds of knowledge' they bring from their socialization in the (regional) society of origin.

A study of migrant experiences provides the empirical data for such inter-regional continuities including what might be called 'continuities-in-breaks': cultural ruptures that demand high capabilities of coping and negotiating to develop adjustment strategies. Methodologically, mass data on migration 'flows' in the frame of economic upswings or downswings cannot provide information on how a multi-year recession or a perhaps single-year harvest failure stimulate the propensity to migrate. Local or regional as well as individual data are necessary to understand the range of options, of coping strategies. Under economic duress people may decide to stay and reduce their standard of living, even minimize food intake; in relief-providing societies they may apply to the relevant institutions of mutual aid, religious bodies, or municipality/state. They may send out one or more family members both to reduce food needed locally and to earn income afar. They may decide to depart as a family (or group). The range of options varies from locality to locality and region to region in terms of structures, mental frames, actual options for departure as well as information about and actual options in potential receiving societies in particular regional and sectoral settings. Rural out-migration in Peru, in one microregional study, could establish the class interests, ethno-cultural interactions, and short-term crises that drove decision making: large landowners could force an independent peasant class to leave only after a (natural) dislocation by a flood; when the in-migrating sharecropping tenants were no longer needed because of mechanization, their departure became a viable strategy only when highland Native peoples began to migrate as laborers. No general paradigm of out-migration from rural regions, correct on the aggregate level, has explanatory value for the specific case. Similarly, in-migration and 'creating of societies' in Canada, was (and is) region-specific. Research needs to establish the range of options for each sociologically defined group and move to generalizations from this empirical basis. The top level, states, provide only the exit and entry options, the frames for acculturation.

The Euro- or Atlanto-centric paradigm of bordered and homogeneous nation-states, on which the transnationalism concept is still based, has been questioned by intellectual migrants who moved between colonial/post-colonial polities and the post-imperial 'mother countries' since decolonization from the 1950s and 1960s. The reconceptualizations of states and their master narratives and the colonizers-colonized struggles involved militants and theorists with migratory experience of their own: Frantz Fanon in Martinique and Algeria, Jacques Derrida and Pierre Bourdieu in Algeria, Roland Barthes in Romania and Egypt. Others experienced two (or more) regimes in one society. In Italy and Russia respectively, Antonio Gramsci and Mikhail Bakhtin lived and suffered the regime change to fascism and Stalinism. In Britain, Stuart and Catherine Hall, the former of Jamaican origin, questioned imperial-national master narratives. Experiencing two or more societies permits recognition of the specificity and interest-driven limitations of master narratives. Each particular one is but a discourse in the context of one state and society. In migration common people act out counter-strategies to nation-state demands and frames in local and regional spaces, the intellectual migrants question national ideologies on the society-wide level of academic and political production.

In Latin America, where each and every society in the many variations by region and status emerged from multiple migrations and from Indio-Euro-African ethnogenesis in processes variously called *métissage*, *mestizaje*, and *créolisation*, interaction occurred in 'contact zones' rather than in whole states of which the nations were only being formed (Pratt, 1992 [2007]). Concepts like *négritude*, developed by intellectual migrants of French-Caribbean and French-African origin, were transcultural in the literal sense. The cultures of the mobile colonizers and the colonized, of oppressor and oppressed were (and are) inextricably entwined, the worlds the immigrant slaveholders made with the worlds the force-migrated slaves made as much as the worlds of capitalist industrialization and the worlds of 'free' male and female workers living in economic constraints to expand on Eugene Genovese. In such contexts of hierarchical mixture or imposition of brutal power, processes of *hibridación* or *tranculturación* occurred and varied by region, economic sector, and social class.

Spaces, imbued with specific meanings, become 'scapes' (Appadurai, 1996). They are fields of action and of production of meanings; physical-territorial geography changes to 'processual geography' (Roberts, 2006); and the creation and appropriation of structures creates 'processual structures' and 'structured processes' (Hoerder, 2005). The arenas of contest have been called 'third space,' neither the space of the powerful nor the space of the subalternized, but spaces in which the contestants have adapted their distinct ways as to be able to engage the opponents (Bhabha, 1990). Such transcultural third spaces may, of course, also emerge out of more peaceful tranculturalization.

Translocal, -regional, and -national spaces are flexible, fluid, and have fuzzy boundary definitions as well as permeable borders. While a migrant's place of origin may be relatively fixed, his or her outreach can adjust to options and constraints as long as adjustment is within the range of the person's human and social capital. Human capital refers to an individual's abilities, skills, and knowledge to enable him or her to lead a life in terms of – under the larger circumstances and constraints – satisfying material, emotional, intellectual, and spiritual needs. Social capital refers to the networks and other non-material resources people may mobilize, it requires communities and may provide access to societal resources, material goods, and funds. Human capital is transferred in the persons of each and every migrant; social capital, in contrast, is located in communities and thus is space-specific and not easily transferable. Pioneer migrants, the first ones to arrive in a new space – then still merely a place – have nothing but their own human capital. By forming a community through sequential migrations and entering into relations with others they increase their access to material, cultural, and institutional resources. Examples in the present are the global networks of Indian, Chinese, or Filipino sailors or of women from many origins in caregiving and domestic work. Some such resources may be transferred back to the community of origin by return migration, density of exchanges, money remittances, passing on of organizational or other capabilities. Such spaces are created by human actors and, since each and every participant pursues personal interests and goals – as long as these do not damage his or her network relationships – they are highly flexible ones.

Post-migration ethno-cultural associations, established by late twentieth-century West African migrants, provide an example for such spaces and the complexity of usages. Usually founded by middle-class professionals and businessmen, they formalize informal networks and bridge spatial distance. They provide protection against discrimination, give credit when banks refuse loans, and attempt to improve a group's social standing. From the cities, Lagos or Port Harcourt for example, the associations establish backward links to the region of origin and may superimpose a 'culture of modernity' on non-cash-based ways of life. Given the persistence of traditional gender roles, women's associations support maternity and child welfare clinics. Such spaces also extend back- and forward from and to New York, London, and Paris.

To research and understand such transcultural spaces in societal, economic, and political frames, an integrative and interdisciplinary approach is fitting which has recently been developed for migrations in the medieval period (Borgolte, 2009) and as Transcultural Societal Studies from Canadian research (Hoerder, 2005 [2010]). The transcultural perspective – the comprehensive term for transsocietal, transstate, transnational as well as translocal and transregional levels, requires a systems approach to connect migration decisions and patterns (1) in the society of departure on all levels from local to global; via (2) the actual move across distance given an era's means of transportation and communication; to (3) the society or societies of destination again in micro-, meso-, and macro-regional perspectives; and (4) linkages between the communities in which migrants spent or spend part of their lives. The transdisciplinary agenda, comprehensive as to class, race/ethnicity, gender, and generations, would combine the discursive sciences (that is, the humanities); the social sciences (that is, the study of state institutions, societal structures, statewide as well as family economics); the life and environmental sciences; and the normative sciences (that is, the study of law, religion, and ethics). Transcultural Societal Studies capture the diversity of human lives and the diversity in each and every human being's life in the frame of institutions and power hierarchies across spaces, local and regional, in different societies, in national or many-cultured polities. They may deal with macro-regions of the same (former colonizer) language which facilitates insertion or with small regions like the borderlands of the Mexican US-capital-dependent northern region and the Hispanic or hispanized US Southwest.

Methodologically, and to some degree theoretically, this interdisciplinary approach is capable of combining the advantages of discipline-constrained approaches: The study of law, prerequisite for immigration admission, but assuming – as in political science – equality before the law may be supplemented by sociological and gender studies' finding that gender-neutral laws may have gender-specific (and discriminatory) results in application. Thus a normative science and a social science combine their frames of thought and research procedures to achieve an integrated answer. The 'information' about a change in exit laws (in fascist Germany, for example) and entry laws (in societies of the Americas, for example) is colored by interests, hopes, fears, even actual threats to life – discourses emerge that neither Law nor Sociology capture – the Humanities provide methodologies. Economics of transportation may explain destinations: in the nineteenth century, rural migrants close to expanding urban centers often opted for a short-distance move to the next city; those from hinterlands, northern Sweden, for example, assumed to be less informed or even backward, had to get on a boat to travel to Stockholm and could, for little additional fare, stay on board and debark in New York. The cultural barrier to be overcome was not Sweden versus the United States, but rural life versus urban life. The issue of language would not occur since the destination would be a culturally and linguistically similar 'ethnic' community.

Life sciences have not usually been considered part of migration research. However, the change of food parameters leads to healthier or unhealthier lives after migration. The flight from famine in colonized Ireland is a case in point; movement from a peasant village to an urban slum or *favela* increased options while decreasing sanitary conditions and availability of fresh foods. The shift from 'folk remedies' to professional medical care, if accessible, may be an advantage but involves cost and loss of everyday health knowledge. In modern societies with complex health-care systems, utilization of such systems by migrant groups depends on culture and gender restrictions. Non-usage of preventive care may have cost-effects on the system as a whole later. The life sciences may also counter the utilitarian 'body parts' approach to migrants – hands or arms (*braceros*) or muscle in general (sexual organs in 'entertainment' migration of women used by men) are needed for labor markets, not human beings. The equally utilitarian 'reproduce and elevate the next generation of worker' approach encourages families to come and expects cost-cutting by a locally raised labor force. Rotatory labor migration schemes, like the West European or Singapore's guestworker one, assume that once muscle is no longer needed, the whole human beings depart. A Transcultural Societal Studies approach might not have predicted the stabilization of guestworker populations but would certainly have included the option into analysis and planning.

The inclusion of the environmental sciences seemed self-evident in societies of departure – under visible ecological conditions farm land cannot be expanded and migration is the only alternative. However, post-migration housing, for example, next to potentially toxic industrial sites requires as much attention. Under industrial farming ('factories in the fields') food production for export may increase but the local residents may need to depart because food production for local consumption declines; resulting soil erosion may accelerate massive out-migration. The comprehensive 'systems approach' would include all factors, structural and personal, Transcultural Societal Studies provide not only the broad array of tools and methods from all disciplines but also the encompassing questions to be asked and answered.

Socialization – a process which cannot be captured by a single discipline – provides people with their human capital, that is, their individual capabilities. These are transferred in the process of migration though at the destination they may not be usable given a different stage of economic development or internationalized access to only some segments of the labor market. The locality and region of birth and socializations also provides potential migrants in gendered and status- or class-specific social environments with social capital, that is, connections to others and to societal resources. These are dependent on space and cannot automatically be 'taken along' in migration. They need to be recreated, often by early arriving men or women ('pioneers,' 'founders,' first-comers) who provide a nucleus or anchor-point for subsequent migrants moving in networks of acquaintances and along shared routes. Jointly, they recreate the social capital in ways viable in the changed societal frame. The combination of human and social capital permits each and every individual to fashion a scape, a person- and group-specific social land-scape for him- or herself. Young migrants construct scapes distinct from adults, women's scapes are different from those of men, non-moving producers view and live markets differently than mobile traders.

Transcultural Societal Studies reach out globally to the diversity of origins of the some 180 different transcultural groups in capital-circulating metropoles like Montréal, London, Moscow, Hong Kong, Nairobi; or to fewer interacting ethno-cultural groups in the internationalized labor markets of small meat-packing country towns in Minnesota or fish-packing towns on Lake Victoria. Transcultural Societal Studies analyse relations, interactions, and networks; they approach peoples' lives and their roles in creating ever new societies or scapes. Diversity of cultures and interactive negotiation permit options, creative energies, and development – as H. Kallen and R. Bourne noted almost a century ago. Individuals combine multiple cultural capabilities and decide where to invest the results of their labor – at the destination, at a future destination, in the community of origin, or elsewhere.

NOTE

1. See Boccagni (Chapter 14, this volume) for further discussion of the methodological options in the research of transnationalism.

REFERENCES

Appadurai, A. (1996), *Modernity at Large. Cultural Dimension of Globalization*, Minneapolis, MN: University of Minnesota Press.
Bentley, J.H. (2005), 'Regional histories, global processes, cross-cultural interactions', in Bentley, R.B. and Yang, A.A. (eds), *Interactions: Transregional Perspectives on World History*, Honolulu: University of Hawaii Press, pp. 1–13.
Bhabha, H.K. (1990), 'DissemiNation: time, narrative, and the margins of the modern nation', in H.K. Bhabha (ed.), *Nation and Narration*, London: Routledge, pp. 291–322.
Borgolte, M. (2009), 'Migrationen als transkulturelle Verflechtungen im mittelalterlichen Europa. Ein neuer Pflug für alte Forschungsfelder', *Historische Zeitschrift*, **289**, 261–85.
Bourne, R.S. (1916), 'Trans-national America', *Atlantic Monthly*, **118**, 86–97.
Faist, T. (2000), *The Volume and Dynamics of International Migration and Transnational Social Spaces*, Oxford: Oxford University Press.
Fitzgerald, D. and Waldinger, R. (2004), 'Transnationalism in question', *American Journal of Sociology*, **109** (5), 1177–95.
Foner, N. (1997), 'What's so new about transnationalism? New York immigrants today and at the end of the century', *Diaspora*, **6** (3), 354–75.
Freyre, G. (1935), *Casa-Grande e Senzala: Introd. à Historia da Societa Patriarcal no Brasil; Farmação da Familia Brasileira solo o Regime de Economia Patriarcal*, Rio de Janeiro: Olympio, translated as *The Masters and the Slaves. A Study in the Development of Brazilian Civilization*, New York: Knopf, 1946.
Glick Schiller, N., Basch, L. and Blanc-Szanton, C. (eds) (1992), *Towards a Transnational Perspective on Migration: Race, Class, Ethnicity and Nationalism Reconsidered*, New York: New York Academy of Sciences, especially Glick Schiller, B. and Blanc-Szanton, C., 'Transnationalism: a new analytic framework for understanding migration', pp. 1–24.
Guarnizo, L.E. and Smith, M.P. (eds) (1998), *Transnationalism from Below*, New Brunswick, NJ: Rutgers.
Guha, R. and Spivak, G. (eds) (1988), *Selected Subaltern Studies*, New York: Oxford University Press.
Hall, C. (1996), 'Histories, empires and the post-colonial moment', in I. Chambers and L. Curti (eds), *The Post-colonial Question. Common Skies, Divided Horizons*, London: Routledge, pp. 65–77.

Hall, S. (1995), 'New cultures for old', in D. Massey and P. Jess (eds), *A Place in the World? Places, Culture and Globalizations*, Oxford: Oxford University Press, pp. 175–213.

Harzig, C. and Hoerder, D. with Gabaccia, D. (2009), *What is Migration History?*, Cambridge: Polity Press.

Hoerder, D. (1996), 'From migrants to ethnics: acculturation in a societal framework', in D. Hoerder and L.P. Moch (eds), *European Migrants: Global and Local Perspectives*, Boston, MA: Northeastern University Press, pp. 211–62.

Hoerder, D. (2005 [2010]), 'From interest-driven national discourse to transcultural societal studies', in D. Hoerder (ed.), *'To Know Our Many Selves Changing Across Time and Space': From the Study of Canada to Canadian Studies*, 1st edn, Edmonton: Athabaca, pp. 316–26.

Hoerder, D. and Blank, I. (1994), 'Ethnic and national consciousness from the Enlightenment to the 1880s', in D. Hoerder, I. Blank and H. Rössler (eds), *Roots of the Transplanted*, 2 vols, Boulder, CO: East European Monographs, 1, pp. 37–110.

Hughes, E.C. (1948), 'The study of ethnic relations', *Dalhousie Review*, **27**, 477–82.

Hughes, E.C. and MacGill Hughes, H. (1952), *Where Peoples Meet: Racial and Ethnic Frontiers*, Glencoe, IL: Free Press.

Kivisto, P. (2003), 'Social spaces, transnational immigrant communities, and the politics of incorporation', *Ethnicities*, **3** (1), 5–28.

Levitt, P., DeWind, J. and Vertovec, S. (eds) (2003), 'Transnational migration: international perspectives', thematic issue of *International Migration Review*, **37** (3).

Ortiz, F. (1940), 'Del fenómeno de la transculturación y su importancia en Cuba', *Revista Bimestre Cubana*, **27**, 273–8; reprinted in Ortiz, F., *Contrapunteo cubano del tabaco y el azúcar*, 1940, translated as *Cuban Counterpoint: Tobacco and Sugar*, New York: Knopf, 1947.

Osterhammel, J. (2001), 'Transnationale Gesellschaftsgeschichte: Erweiterung oder Alternative?', *Geschichte und Gesellschaft*, **27**, 464–79.

Patel, K.K. (2008), 'Überlegungen zu einer Transnationalen Geschichte', in J. Osterhammel (ed.), *Weltgeschichte*, Stuttgart: Steiner, pp. 67–90.

Portes, A. (1999), 'Conclusion: toward a new world: the origins and effects of transnational activities', *Ethnic and Racial Studies*, **22**, 463–77.

Portes, A., Guarnizo, L.E. and Landolt, P. (1999), 'The study of transnationalism: pitfalls and promise of an emergent research field', *Ethnic and Racial Studies*, **22**, 217–37.

Pratt, M.L. (1992 [2007]), *Imperial Eyes: Travel Writing and Transculturation*, New York: Routledge.

Richmond, A.H. (1994), *Global Apartheid. Refugees, Racism, and the New World Order*, Toronto: Oxford University Press.

Roberts, A.F. (2006), 'La "Géographie Processuelle": Un nouveau paradigme pour les aires culturelles', *Lendemains*, **31** (122/123), 41–61.

Saunier, P.-Y. (2009), 'Transnational', in A. Iriye and P.-Y. Saunier (eds), *The Palgrave Dictionary of Transnational History from the Mid-nineteenth Century to the Present Day*, New York: Palgrave Macmillan, pp. 1047–55.

Thelen, D. (1992), 'Of audiences, borderlands, and comparisons: toward the internationalization of American history', *Journal of American History*, **79**, 432–62.

Vertovec, S. (1999), 'Conceiving and researching transnationalism', *Ethnic and Racial Studies*, **22** (2), 447–62.

Wong, L.L. (2002), 'Home away from home? Transnationalism and the Canadian citizenship regime', in V. Roudometof and P. Kennedy (eds), *Communities Across Borders: New Immigrants and Transnational Cultures*, London: Routledge, pp. 169–81.

5 Contemporary migration seen from the perspective of political economy: theoretical and methodological elements
Raúl Delgado Wise and Humberto Márquez Covarrubias

Contemporary migration studies tend to consider this phenomenon as an independent variable excised from the context of global capitalism. Research approaches are mostly descriptive and schematic and often split by disciplines, all of which limits the understanding of migration and any opportunities we might have to influence it. Political economy provides an analytical alternative with which to engage this subject, addressing it from the historical, structural and strategic viewpoints. This approach constitutes a source of critical thinking through which the complex reality of contemporary capitalism and the role of international migration can be understood and transformed. This chapter proposes political economy as an alternative theoretical and methodological tool with which to uncover the nature and elements of contemporary migration.

5.1 THE FOUNDATIONS AND VALIDITY OF POLITICAL ECONOMY

Political economy studies the social relations present in production, distribution, exchange and consumption processes. They are meant to cover material living needs in accordance with the extant degree of productive development and in interaction with existing institutions and power relations. The relationship between the bourgeoisie, who own the means of production, and the proletariat, a workforce deprived of means of production or subsistence, is of peculiar importance, although landowners, the peasantry and other subaltern social classes also play a role. In the words of Engels: 'economics is not concerned with things but with relations between persons, and in the final analysis between classes; these relations however are always *bound to things* and *appear as things*' (1859 [1977], no. 16, emphasis in the original).

When Marx undertook a critique of classical political economy as embodied in the work of Adam Smith and David Ricardo, he revealed the double nature of work (concrete and abstract). This led to the understanding of surplus-value. Capital is seen as a social production relation belonging to the capitalist production mode, where the bourgeoisie appropriates surplus-value while the proletariat receives a salary equivalent to the reproductive cost of the labour force. Generally speaking, political economy studies the development of capitalism – conceived as a historical mode of production – and analyses its main contradictions, trends and transformations. Some of the most important subjects addressed by this discipline include accumulation and crisis; exploitation; the role of the State; class struggle; imperialism; the nature of social networks; and social transformation.

The method of abstraction is particular to political economy and entails separating and analysing simple, condensed elements in order to address a specific relationship in the object of study. For instance, in order to build up a conceptual apparatus to understand social reality, Marx envisaged the realm of production as the most general and, henceforth, as a law-like endeavour. This realm encompasses one of the highest levels of abstraction for disentangling the nature of capitalist societies. Distribution and exchange correspond to more particular realms of reality, accidental and conjunctural in their nature, mediated by class struggles. Consumption expresses the singularity, the most chaotic and unpredictable realm of reality. All these elements are underlying aspects of social reality representing different and interrelated levels of abstraction. This procedure is based on analytical concepts and categories that explain underlying social relations in order to reconstruct the 'rich totality of many determinations and relations' (Marx, 1973, p. 101). This is how social relations and processes are organized and fitted into a hierarchy. In addition, political economy simultaneously combines the historical and critical aspects: while the historical trajectory of capitalist society is examined, the validity of the concepts and relations currently taking place in it are also evaluated.

The method of political economy does not imply a unidirectional move from the abstract to the concrete, but rather a two-way, dialectical, enquiry. In this process, a permanent tension between the abstract and the concrete is forged, which entails the necessity to unravel the essence of the analysed phenomena and transcend its surface. This is not evident from a laid-back approach based in simple observation. From a political economy standpoint, it is thus inappropriate to establish an immediate relationship between the researcher and its object of study. In order to comprehend social reality it is necessary to disentangle its historical and social substrata which is not apparent from straightforward observation. At the heart of the political economy method is an interaction of the 'twin couples abstract/concrete and essence/appearance, and the latter can be rendered as content/form' (Tarbuck, 1991). Most theoretical and methodological approaches in migration studies depart from the surface of the phenomenon and have contributed to the extraordinary mythology prevailing in the field which distorts the root causes and implications of the migratory dynamic. The political economy approach, on the contrary, allows for an appropriate contextualization and interpretation of the phenomenon avoiding any descriptive and mechanical use of theory where the 'process of abstraction is not abstraction from reality, but rather a process whereby we can truly perceive the reality' (Tarbuck, 1991).

The benefits and validity of political economy can be listed as follows:

1. The social whole. Political economy, especially in its critical, Marxist-derived tendency, seeks to theoretically address the complexity and historical nature of the social whole. That is, it privileges the reconstruction of reality as a concrete totality.
2. Reconstruction is carried out using a trans-disciplinary critical apparatus that delves into the system's major relationships and regularities. This approach contrasts with the fragmented and disjointed analyses, excess of descriptive studies and distribution of knowledge across disciplines that characterize neoclassical economic theory, rational choice in political science and social action in sociology. It also differs from the reductionism espoused by quantitative epistemology, which condenses complex social phenomena into a few variables.[1] Additionally, political economy's encompassing approach, where the whole is more than the sum of its parts but where the parts are also important, refutes the oft-quoted criticism that this discipline is an economics-driven field.[2]
3. The historicity of social phenomena. Social conflict is omnipresent, to the point where history can be conceived as a display of social contradictions. In this sense, history is always a mode of production. Contrary to what conservative, ahistorical and decontextualized approaches suggest, political economy posits that institutionality and bourgeois social practices are historical and transitory phenomena, as are the private ownership of production means, capitalist democracy, salaried relations and the mercantilization of social life. History is seen as a dialectical relationship between social agents, structures and junctures with their own historical/structural limits. This view contrasts with the hegemonic view of the end of history and the final prevalence of a market economy and liberal democracy.
4. Dialectic analysis of society. Political economy is an analytical tool that seeks to transform the contemporary world. A dialectic approach enables us to analyse social contradictions on several levels: generally

speaking, we can look at the contradictions between the development of productive forces and social production relations while, on a more specific level, we look at the concrete developments of class struggle. This crucial aspect of the method employed by political economy requires situating 'the part' within 'the whole', identifying different levels of abstraction. This is known as the dialectics of the abstract and the concrete, where the concrete represents the synthesis of multiple causal determinations at the same time that it stands for the whole of diversity. 'Capital in general' is the highest level of abstraction for the analysis of capitalist reality, and it is this level that Marx addressed in his *Capital*.
5. Bringing theory and practice together. Theoretical reflection and research are not carried out in a purified environment excised from the dynamics of social reality. On the contrary, there is an attempt to unearth the key relationships at the heart of the social organization. Attempts at social transformation must bring together theoretical constructs and strategic social practices. In this particular, there is a point of contact between transforming theory and practice. In contrast, neoliberal hegemony, both political and ideological, upholds methodological individualism while obscuring potential social transformation. At the same time, given its historical and dialectic character and its emphasis on social praxis, political economy refutes determinism, an element often ascribed to it by its detractors. The possibility of social transformation requires a dialectical evaluation of the social agents participating in structural dynamics and practices.

Even so, political economy cannot be taken as an immutable and irrefutable paradigm. Its bases are historical, to the point that they need to be permanently revaluated in view of current, capitalist realities. Among these new, contemporary elements we can mention the ongoing debate regarding the nature of contemporary capitalism. Associated subjects include the command of financial capital and the speculative whirlwind (Bello, 2006; Harvey, 2007); the new US imperialism (Petras and Veltmeyer, 2001); the role played by the International Monetary Fund (IMF), the World Bank (WB), the World Trade Organization (WTO) and the Inter-American Development Bank (IDB) in the imposition of structural adjustment neoliberal policies (Bello, 2006); new forms of destruction and restructuring under modes of accumulation by dispossession (Harvey, 2003); and the relationship between capitalist restructuring and forced migration (Delgado Wise and Márquez, 2007a; Petras, 2007).

Going beyond the so-called paradigm crisis fostered by the current civilization crisis, which was in turn generated by the fall of real socialism and neoliberal capitalism, political economy constitutes a theoretical and methodological tool that provides the basic elements required for a historical, structural and strategic analysis of contemporary capitalism. The current systemic crisis and capitalist restructuring process (that is, globalization) can be examined in depth from this perspective, along with other related issues such as the formation of regional economic blocs; the internationalization of production under the aegis of the large, transnational corporations; the reconfiguration of the international division of labour and the emergence of new and more rapacious forms of unequal exchange; the transformation of labour processes under the expansion of a post-Fordist production regime; US political and military hegemony; the growing gap between developed and underdeveloped nations;[3] the transnationalization, differentiation and precariousness of labour markets; the growth of the informal econonomy; the increase in social inequality across the world; and the generation of a teeming overpopulation that feeds, propels and reconfigures migration processes.

In underdeveloped, peripheral or dependent countries – especially in Latin America – political economy has been used to analyse the conditions of underdevelopment as a concise form of capitalism applied in peripheral or postcolonial nations. This approach splits in two distinct theoretical branches: structuralism according to the Economic Commission for Latin America and the Caribbean (ECLAC) and dependency theory. In regards to the first one, during the 1950s and 1970s, Keynesian-influenced authors like Raúl Prebisch, Anibal Pinto, Osvaldo Sunkel and Celso Furtado examined the decline in terms of trade due to the centre/periphery scheme under which Latin America's insertion into the world economy operated. They proposed industrialization and the spread of technological progress as a solution that agreed with the interests of the national bourgeoisie. In contrast for the dependency theory, between the 1960s and 1970s and in the context of the Cold War, the limitations of Latin American structuralism and the recent success of the Cuban Revolution led researchers like Theotonio Dos Santos, Vania Bambirra, Fernando Henrique Cardoso, André Gunder Frank and Ruy Mauro Marini to posit that Latin America's real problem was its dependent insertion into the international economy. They endorsed a systemic rupture and envisioned socialism as a goal. Some, like Marini, used Marxist theory to characterize a type of dependency centred on the superexploitation of the labour force, while others took a more sociological and political approach. Additionally, there were some Marxist reinterpreters who, like Agustín Cueva, did not fully engage with dependency theories.

These approaches constitute an original system of thought established from the perspective of underdeveloped or dependent nations. However, they were displaced from academic and intellectual spheres with the imposition (often under the aegis of dictatorial regimes) of neoliberalism, which constituted a true counter-revolution in the theory and practice of development in Latin America and underdeveloped nations in general. Nowadays, given the socioeconomic damage caused by neoliberal processes, we are in need of theoretical, methodological and political alternatives that can lead to new development alternatives. While the alternative approach is characterized by a number of theoretical stances, they all reject the notion of the market as an agent of development. And this is where the political economy of development could play a central role.

5.2 THE POLITICAL ECONOMY OF MIGRATION

Marxist political economy addresses the phenomenon of migration at its highest level of abstraction. That is, in relation to the dynamics of capital in general and on the basis of the two following analytical categories: original accumulation and overpopulation.

Original accumulation is linked to the rise of capitalism out of the ruins of feudalism during the sixteenth century. The excision between the producer and the means of production turned direct producers into 'free' individuals lacking means of production and subsistence. Said individuals were then forced to sell their only possession, labour, to those in charge of the means of production (Marx, 1975). This way, the destruction of pre-capitalist forms of production yielded a source of labour for the capitalist entrepreneur and migration appeared as a phenomenon associated with the violent expropriation of peasant land or artisan tools (Meillassoux, 1981). In the context of contemporary capitalism (and particularly within the framework of neoliberal restructuring), this analytical category has been retrieved to characterize the liberalization of the labour force and the concentration of power and wealth among a reduced capitalist elite via what has been termed 'accumulation by dispossession' (Harvey, 2007). This involves the mercantilization of public resources, the progressive dismantling of the welfare state and, in general, a concerted attack on the living and working conditions of the majority of the population. These processes have driven many into unemployment, the informal economy and forced migration (Delgado Wise and Márquez, 2007a).

In regards to overpopulation, with the development of capitalism and the creation of a particular technical mode of production (the span from artisanal to industrial manufacture), the growth of capital and, consequently, accumulation ceased to depend on population growth.

Now, capital creates its own population dynamics and, unlike what Malthus posited, it is not population that determines economic growth and wealth: the dynamics of capitalist accumulation generate a supply of labourers that is always higher than actual demand. By creating a redundant population mass, capital permanently ensures access to exploitable human resources beyond the dynamics of demographic reproduction. This generates a relative surplus population, an industrial reserve army that, given its strategic importance for capital, 'becomes, conversely, the lever of capitalistic accumulation, nay, a condition of existence of the capitalist mode of production' (Marx, 1906, VII, XXV, p. 29). In order to address international migration we must first consider the geographical aspect and consider the asymmetrical relations that characterize processes of capital accumulation among regions, nations and areas within nations. The unequal geographical distribution of accumulation results in an also unequal distribution of overpopulation on the global scale. More developed regions and nations with a larger accumulation capacity tend to have less overpopulation, a feature that is compensated by labour immigration hailing from countries and areas with reduced accumulation capacity. Marx coined the term 'absolute surplus-population' in reference to the Irish case and this particular phenomenon (Marx, 1975, p. 880). This explains the existence of areas that serve as labour reserve sources and often suffer processes of depopulation, especially in underdeveloped nations. International labour migration not only manifests the nature of the international capital/labour relationship, it also evidences the subjection of surplus population to conditions of extreme labour exploitation and social exclusion in a context of growing labour market transnationalization, differentiation and precariousness.

As far as the concrete subject of global capitalist development is concerned (that is, that of regions and nations, and taking into account the asymmetries inherent to capitalist development), a number of theoretical, Marxist and heterodox approaches can be classified under the so-called historical-structural paradigm that runs against the functional-modernist one. The most important of these are dependency theories, world-system theory, cumulative causation and dual labour market theory.

Dependency theories tend to view migration as (a) the product of adverse conditions and the limitations of dependent or underdeveloped accumulation and (b) one of the causes behind deepening underdevelopment. Said theories were created during a time when underdeveloped nations were focused on the internal market and they therefore emphasize internal migration (Singer, 1974). World-system theory (Wallerstein, 2005) is derived from dependency theories but focuses on the global capitalist context rather than just Latin America, incorporating the concept of semi-periphery to the notions of centre and periphery. International migration is seen as the product of the growing (and asymmetrical) expansion and integration of world capitalism, along with the domination of central countries over the periphery and semi-periphery.

The theory of cumulative causation is based on the ideas of heterodox Swedish economist Gunnar Myrdal (1957). It maintains that capitalist development tends to deepen geographical and social inequalities in income and welfare. Migration is seen as a vicious circle that deprives communities of origin of their most valuable labour force, increasing dependency and stimulating subsequent emigration. Finally, dual labour market theory states that international migration is a response to a permanent demand for workforce in advanced industrial societies, leading to a segmentation of labour markets where foreign workers take the low profile jobs rejected by domestic workers (Piore, 1979).

It must be pointed out that the above-mentioned historical-structural approaches are primordially centred on the structural causes of the phenomenon and – most importantly and with the exception of the dual labour market theory – on the asymmetrical relationships produced across the north-south horizon. In contrast to functionalist, modernizing perspectives, they offer a more comprehensive approach to the phenomenon. Admittedly, they do have a limited view of the strategic phenomenon of agency, which is why they are often characterized as deterministic.

5.3 THE RELATIONSHIP BETWEEN MIGRATION AND DEVELOPMENT SEEN FROM THE PERSPECTIVE OF POLITICAL ECONOMY

The growing asymmetries and inequalities that characterize contemporary capitalism have led to a substantial increase in population movements, particularly labour migration from the southern hemisphere to the north, notwithstanding an important south-south flow. At the same time, there have been substantial transformations in internal migration circuits and the way these relate to international migration. North-south remittance flow has grown so much it has now surpassed foreign direct investment and foreign official aid in underdeveloped nations. This has encouraged the main international organizations in charge of neoliberal policy to support a *sui generis* development agenda that assumes migration can become a tool for development in countries with high emigration rates.

In view of this, political economy has been employed to provide a renewed, critical analysis of migration and development. While neoliberal stances exaggerate and obfuscate the nature and role of remittances, said approach expands the analytical field and drastically redefines concerns (Castles and Delgado Wise, 2008, introduction). Among these, the relationships between countries in a context of unequal development; growing imbalances and surplus transfers; labour migration and the precariousness of labour markets involving both qualified and unqualified labour force; and, generally speaking, the dialectics between accumulation and migration seen from a class perspective.

Political economy views international migration as a consequence of problems in development and denies this phenomenon can be studied in isolation. In order to examine migration's causes, effects and interactions with development and analyse the different stages in this dialectic, we must first consider the following analytical elements: strategic practices and structural dynamics.

Strategic practices involve confronting the divergent interests at the heart of the contemporary capitalist structure and its inherent development problems. There are two major projects. (1) The hegemonic project, promoted by large transnational corporations and the governments of developed countries led by the United States, in alliance with certain elites in underdeveloped countries, and under the umbrella of international organizations like the WB, the IMF and the WTO. Nowadays, given the loss of legitimacy suffered by neoliberal globalization, 'domination' is a more appropriate term than 'hegemony', since the project is no longer implemented through consensus but via military and financial imposition in the wake of the Washington Consensus and its post-consensus. (2) The alternative project, comprising a sociopolitical agglutination of social movements and classes, collective agents and subjects, and certain progressive governments and international organizations. All of these are aligned with a political project designed to transform the existing structural dynamics and eliminate political and institutional obstacles impeding the promotion of alternative development processes at the global, regional, national and local levels.

Structural dynamics refers to the unequal and asymmetric way in which contemporary capitalism is articulated across different planes and levels, including finance, commerce, production and the labour market. This also includes areas like technological innovation (a strategic control tool) and the use and allocation of natural resources. These demarcations shape the ways in which relationships between (a) developed nations, (b) developed and underdeveloped nations and (c) underdeveloped nations are established. Said demarcations determine the fields in which relationships between sectors, groups, movements and social classes are developed. All of these are expressed in unique ways at the global, regional, national and local levels.

ELEMENTS FOR THE ANALYSIS OF CONTEMPORARY MIGRATION: THE CONTEXT

In accordance with the tenets of political economy, migration cannot be analysed outside of the specific historical context in which it takes place. Therefore, it is essential that we examine the nature of neoliberal globalization, a process of capitalist restructuring led by large multinationals, the world's most powerful governments and the WB, the IMF and the WTO (Petras and Veltmeyer, 2000; Stiglitz, 2002). The following are some of its major features:

1. The internationalization of production, commerce, services and finance. This entails a profound restructuring of the global economic network via multinational subcontracting links extending throughout countries across the world. It is designed to reinsert peripheral nations into the global system and operates through production enclaves in underdeveloped nations with cheap natural and human resources. It is increasingly sustained by subcontracting mechanisms and implemented by large manufacturing, financial, agricultural, commercial and service sector transnational corporations (Robinson, 2008).

2. Financialization. Financial capital generates speculative strategies that foster the channelling of investment funds, sovereign funds and social-surplus toward new financial instruments that offer short-term high profit margins but can entail recurrent crises and massive fraud; the latter obstruct and affect the functioning of the so-called real economy (Bello, 2006; Foster and Magdof, 2009).

3. Environmental damage. Biodiversity, natural resources and communal and national wealth are now privatized for the benefit of large corporations that favour profits while ignoring social and environmental costs. This leads to increased environmental degradation, pollution, famines and disease. Resultant climate change (global warming and increasingly frequent extreme climatic events) threatens symbiotic relations between humans and the environment (Foladori and Pierri, 2005).

4. The restructuring of innovation systems. Advances in information technology (IT), telecommunications, biotechnology, new materials and nanotechnology cater to the needs of large corporations in search of profits. Scientific and technological research is restructured under mechanisms such as outsourcing and offshore-outsourcing, which allow corporations to have southern scientists at their service, transfer

risks and responsibilities, and capitalize on the benefits by amassing patents. This has led to an unprecedented mercantilization of scientific labour under a short-term approach and with little social concern (Lester and Piore, 2004).
5. Labour precariousness. The main engine behind the new capitalist machine has been the cheapening of labour. Massive labour supply in Africa, Latin America, Asia (mainly China and India) and the former Soviet Union supports this dynamic and has led to the growing transnationalization, differentiation and precariousness of labour markets. The result is a new set of divisions at the heart of the working class: labour, national, racial and cultural hierarchies allow large corporations to benefit from cheap and flexible labour sources (Harvey, 2007; Schierup et al., 2006).
6. The new migration dynamic. While migration is a historical process with a certain degree of continuity, it has undergone a dramatic transformation under neoliberal globalization. It is now characterized by (a) strong pressure to emigrate given the lack of labour opportunities in sending areas and (b) the growing vulnerability and extreme exploitation of migrants in origin, transit and destination countries. New migration waves primarily comprise south-north and south-south flows, as well as a significant volume of internal migration, turning this whole process into an essential element of the neoliberal restructuring strategy (Delgado Wise and Márquez, 2007a, 2009; UN, 2004, 2006).

At the end of the first decade of the twenty-first century, a capitalist crisis centred in the United States affected the whole global system on several levels (Márquez, 2009, 2010):

1. Financial. The overflowing of financial capital leads to speculative bubbles that start by affecting large conglomerates and developed nations and then devolve into global economic depressions (Bello, 2006; Foster and Magdof, 2009).
2. Overproduction. Overproduction crises emerge when the surplus capital available in the global economy is not channelled into production processes due to a fall in profit margins and a slump in effective demand, the latter usually a consequence of wage containment across all sectors of the population (Bello, 2006).
3. Environmental. The degradation of natural resources, climate change and the mercantilization of the environment severely affect the natural world, endangering the material bases for both human production and reproduction (Foladori and Pierri, 2005).

4. Social. Growing social inequalities and the dismantling of the welfare state and the subsistence system accentuate problems such as poverty, unemployment, violence, insecurity and labour precariousness, increasing pressure to emigrate (Harvey, 2007; Schierup et al., 2006).

This crisis in fact questions the dominant style of globalization and, in a deeper sense, the systemic global order, which has failed to acknowledge the value of our main sources of wealth – labour and nature – and has overexploited them to the extent that it has placed civilization itself at risk.

5.5 ELEMENTS FOR THE ANALYSIS OF CONTEMPORARY MIGRATION: KEY CONCEPTS

In order to analyse and understand the relationship between development and migration in the context of neoliberal globalization, we must first define two central concepts: unequal development and forced migration.

5.5.1 Unequal Development

The new architecture of neoliberal globalization has been promoted through the implementation of structural adjustment programmes in southern nations. These comprise privatization, deregulation and liberalization and have been the tools with which to insert underdeveloped economies into the dynamics of globalization. They dismantle the national productive apparatus, facilitate the penetration of foreign capital and create a massive labour force surplus (Delgado Wise and Márquez, 2007b). This process has led to deepening geo-economic and political asymmetries between countries and to growing social inequalities. The deepening geo-economic and political asymmetries between countries entail a growing gap between developed and underdeveloped countries. Capitalist development, however, is not a straightforward dichotomy but a complex system of power relations between regions, countries and localities. The growing social inequalities are expressed in the concentration of capital, power and wealth among an increasingly reduced elite while a growing part of the population suffers poverty, exploitation and exclusion.

The notion of unequal development encapsulates these dynamics of dominance and refers to the historical, economic, social and political processes of polarization among regions, countries and social classes, all of them derived from the dynamics of capitalist accumulation, the international division of labour, the new geopolitical map and class conflict across space and hierarchies.

5.5.2 Forced Migration

Although the concept of forced migration is not generalized, it does characterize, to a great extent, current migration flows. The term is habitually used to distinguish between voluntary and involuntary migration and, from a human rights perspective, refers to exiles or displaced populations. However, mechanisms of unequal development lead to the mass migration of dispossessed, marginalized and excluded populations. It is also an involuntary movement on the part of people who are literally expelled from their places of origin in an attempt to find subsistence opportunities in their country or abroad. This also applies to those who cannot find employment in accordance with their skills or capacities in their home country.

In the case of workers with low qualifications, migration entails substantial risks and dangers; it also implies permanent exposure to labour precariousness and social exclusion in receiving nations. As pointed out previously, international migrants are subjected to criminalization, racism and general discrimination, conditions that not only render them vulnerable and marginal but can also effectively imperil their lives. While qualified and highly qualified migrants have considerably more freedom of movement, they are still subjected to ethnic discrimination and labour degradation (Delgado Wise and Márquez, 2009).

Taking four criteria into account – unequal development, human rights, institutionalism and the labour market – we can identify four types of forced migration (Castles, 2003; Delgado Wise and Márquez, 2009; European Commission, 2004; Gzesh, 2008):

1. Migration due to violence, conflicts and catastrophes. Social, political and communal conflicts, natural disasters, infrastructure works and urbanization severely affect communities, families and individuals, to the point that they are forced to abandon their place of origin and even their own country. This is the case with refugees, asylum seekers and the displaced. These modalities, which tend to affect populations in underdeveloped nations, have been acknowledged in international law. Protection instruments are therefore in place.
2. Migration due to dispossession, exclusion and unemployment. Neoliberal globalization has led to permanent social tensions in underdeveloped nations, depriving large sectors of the population of production and subsistence means, forcing them to emigrate in search of better livelihoods. Most current labour migration falls in this category, which is characterized by extreme vulnerability and exploitation. While there are some protection measures in place for this type

of migration (for example, the 1990 International Convention on the Protection of the Rights of All Migrant Workers and Members of Their Families), these are limited and lack effective means of implementation. The category of 'economic migrants', who supposedly travel in a context of freedom and social mobility, ignores these issues and the risks incurred by migrants.

3. Human trafficking. This form of forced migration has increased alarmingly in recent years, becoming a highly lucrative business due to restrictive policies in receiving nations and sub-par living conditions in less developed countries. Human trafficking is associated with coercion, kidnapping and deceit, and includes sexual exploitation and illicit child adoption among other serious human rights violations. The global response to the sustained increase in this form of criminal activity is the United Nations' Convention against Transnational Organized Crime, signed in 2000 in Palermo, and the subsequent Protocol to prevent, suppress and punish trafficking in persons, especially women and children. The terms 'human trafficking' and 'illicit smuggling of migrants' have been erroneously used as synonyms, which is why this category is often included in one of the other groupings mentioned here.

4. Migration due to overqualification and lack of opportunities. Many highly qualified workers such as scientists, IT researchers, academics, artists and technicians who are unable to find jobs in line with their capacities at home may also decide to migrate to other nations. While some might have jobs and even enjoy decent salaries at home, they nevertheless lack basic resources such as access to project financing, infrastructure, equipment and human resources. They are attracted by the considerably more favourable conditions in developed countries, where they can enjoy better institutional support. While these migrants do not face serious problems when travelling, some will be subjected to labour and salary discrimination in countries of destination.

The first two categories of forced migration are defined in a 'strict sense', since they involve the inequalities fostered by development dynamics, human rights violations, institutional weaknesses and governmental failure to guarantee solutions to economic, political, social and environmental problems in nations of origin. They also imply imbalances in social relations produced in a climate of insecurity, exclusion and poverty (human trafficking is included in this grouping). The use of the term 'forced' in the fourth category is less strict, since this population is not seeking to cover basic necessities but fulfil their professional and intellectual roles. This is tied to imbalances in the labour market and institutional support in the home country.

In its diverse manifestations, forced migration is a cheap source of labour and thus plays a key role in unequal development and the new global architecture that promotes the 'free market' while restricting the free flow of people.

5.6 THE DIALECTIC BETWEEN UNEQUAL DEVELOPMENT AND FORCED MIGRATION

The following four postulates illustrate the dynamics of neoliberal globalization in relation to migration and development (Delgado Wise and Márquez, 2009):

1. Unequal development generates forced migration. In the current capitalist context, large corporations deploy a restructuring strategy that, on the one hand, internationalizes processes of production, commercialization and finance; on the other, it appropriates the natural resources, economic surplus and cheap labour of underdeveloped countries. Lagging development conditions are exacerbated with the implementation of structural adjustment policies by international bodies, leading to increased unemployment and the detonation of forced migration. The latter, in turn, leads to significant population losses and results in a negative net transference of the demographic bonus in countries of origin.
2. Migrants contribute to development in receiving countries in a context of increasing labour precariousness and social exclusion. Developed nations demand vast amounts of cheap, qualified and unqualified labour (including undocumented workers), which places migrants under conditions of increased vulnerability and diminished value. Less qualified migrants, the vast majority, contribute to devaluing labour costs across the board because they work in key sectors linked to the costs of labour reproduction. On the other hand, and in spite of being considered an elite labour segment, qualified migrant workers also constitute a cheap source of labour in relative terms: they earn less than equally qualified peers with legal citizenship. In both cases, the receiving country not only fulfils its labour needs but benefits greatly from the fact that it did not invest in the formation and reproduction costs of these migrants. In sum, migration constitutes a double transference from the sending to the receiving country: a cheap workforce along with formation and social reproduction costs.

3. Migrants contribute to their home country's precarious socioeconomic stability. A fraction of migrants' salaries is destined for remittances and ensures the subsistence of family members in places of origin. To a lesser extent, remittances are used to finance small businesses in a subsistence economy. Migrant organizations use collective remittances for the purpose of financing public works and social projects in places of origin. To a lesser extent, migrants with savings or entrepreneurial goals allocate their resources (productive remittances) to the financing of micro-projects in places of origin. The larger portion of remittances, however, is used for family consumption and has a limited multiplier effect, which means that these resources can hardly promote development processes. Moreover and in many cases, they contribute to dependency on foreign labour remuneration and the importing of consumer goods. From a macroeconomic point of view, remittances benefit neoliberal governments that, unwilling to generate development alternatives, use them as a source of currency that contributes to the nation's frail 'macroeconomic stability'. Some countries even use remittances as equity to warrant foreign debt. Given the absence of a real development strategy, migrants are now lauded as the 'heroes of development' and made responsible for a task that should belong to the government but, under the neoconservative precept of a minimal state, remains unfulfilled.
4. The promotion of alternative development as social transformation can prevent forced migration. Ideologically speaking, neoliberal globalization posits itself as inevitable. It is therefore crucial that we theoretically and practically endorse the feasibility of alternative strategies of development. Reverting the assymetrical power relationships between sending and receiving countries is paramount; this will allow us to identify and counter practices that submerge vast regions of the world into quagmires of inequality, marginalization, poverty, social exlcusion and forced migration. A project of genuine social transformation must focus on the root causes of forced migration by creating viable employment opportunities. This will make migration an option rather than a necessity.

5.7 CONCLUSION AND KEY ISSUES

The dynamics of contemporary migration flows pose an economic, political, social and geographical challenge. The following five issues are crucial to its analysis: (1) strategic indicators that demystify the relationship between migration and development; (2) human rights, development and migration; (3) environmental degradation, climate change, development and migration; (4) civil organizations, movements and networks; and (5) comprehensive, inclusive and humanistic public policies.

Given the premises of the alternative approach, we must expand the analytical horizon comprising migration and development in order to understand the context, processes and actors involved in it across countries of origin, transit and destination. The new theoretical perspective must focus on key problems and dynamics associated with the causes, costs and contributions of migration in its dialectical relationship with development. This requires a system of information involving new categories and indicators that can unequivocally reflect those costs and benefits, exposing the myths that underlie the dominant approach. It is also important to evince the role of internal migrations, their link to international flow, and create indicators that monitor compliance with human rights and evaluate migration policy. This will require joint efforts and coordination between civil society, governments and international organizations. The current crisis and growing anti-immigrant sentiment reinforce this need (Canales, 2008; Castles and Delgado Wise, 2008; Delgado Wise et al., 2009; Munck, 2010).

Neoliberal globalization undermines human rights by curtailing the right to development and subjecting the working class to conditions of extreme, life-threatening vulnerability. We must reassess the concept of forced migration and counteract migration policies that appeal to sovereignty and national security, criminalizing migrants and depriving them and their families of human rights. Many current temporary worker programmes exemplify the alleged humane treatment received by migrants, which masks both exploitation and human rights violations. Other relevant areas of inquiry include irregular migration, human trafficking, discrimination, and racist and gender-biased policies; the integrity and security of human rights defenders; new standards in labour rights and the implementation of a fair labour agenda; the applicability of international instruments for the protection of human rights as well as state-binding principles of progressive realization and non-retrogression. From a comprehensive viewpoint and in order to create an alternative approach to development that focuses on human rights, international law must be heeded and states must adhere to it. The dismantling of processes of labour flexibilization and precariousness is also crucial. Labour rights must be validated and include access to decent jobs, which must also encompass the recovery of the social security system and the promotion of human development in countries of origin and destination (Castles 2003; Gzesh, 2008; Munck, 2010; Wihtol de Wenden, 2000).

Climate change is only one aspect in the complex issue of environmental degradation and its impact on migration must be analysed in a wide-ranging context. This aspect involves two confronting approaches that, if taken to extremes, can lead to inappropriate public policies (Castles, 2002). On the one hand, we have an alarmist, almost Malthusian vision that anticipates massive influxes of 'environmental refugees' potentially perceived as a threat to receiving countries (Myers, 1995). This approach suggests large numbers of displaced persons (in the order of tens of millions), but these are clearly speculative given our inability to isolate environmental factors from other economic, social and political causes. The 'climate refugee' category is very difficult to pin down and define. It is also inappropriate insofar as it would expand the current definition of asylum, and this would create problems in the implementation of the United Nations' 1951 Convention Relating to the Status of Refugees. Last and perhaps most importantly, this approach fails to address the underlying causes of migration and has in fact been used by organizations seeking to promote anti-immigration policies in receiving countries (Lonergan and Swain, 1999).

On the other hand, a different approach denies the very concept of an 'environmental refugee' based on the weaknesses of the underlying assumptions it entails (Black, 2001). This approach minimizes the impact of environmental changes such as desertification, the loss of biodiversity and even global warming, with its wide array of consequences. It can also lead to inappropriate public policies.

The concept of forced migration presented in this chapter allows for a more fruitful analysis. By focusing on the phenomena and dynamics of unequal development as the factors underlying forced migration, including that caused by environmental degradation, this approach has two important advantages: it avoids numerical speculation and the trivialization of the negative impact of climate change. In contrast to the above-mentioned alternatives, this approach focuses on the most impoverished groups' capacity to adapt. It is these populations that are most vulnerable to environmental contingencies, both natural and human-made. The capacity to adapt (or lack thereof) is of course related to processes of unequal development and their impact on marginalized population groups (McAdam, 2010).

The construction of an agent of social transformation is crucial to the advancement of an alternative development, human rights and migration agenda. It requires overcoming the subjective, political, racial, national and local divisions at the heart of the migrant community and the eventual creation of a collective stakeholder, one that comprises migrants as well as other social sectors affected by neoliberal globalization. The transformative potential of this social agent depends on the organizational, institutional and financial capabilities of migrant and pro-immigrant movements, organizations and networks. The interaction of these groups with diverse civil society stakeholders that can make useful contributions (for example, unions and academia) is crucial (Gordon, 2009). The inclusion and empowerment of communities of origin is just as important.

Politically speaking, it is vital that these organizations, movements and networks move beyond reactive, defensive and short-term strategies and begin tackling transformative, long-term projects associated with the articulation of a collective, transnational agent for social transformation (Fox, 2005; Milkman, 2006; Munck, 2010).

In the current context of neoliberal globalization and unequal development, public policy processes have been dominated by an agenda and guidelines stemming from migrant-receiving countries. Forced migration, in its diverse forms, is subsumed under a context characterized by deepening geo-economic and political asymmetries and widening social inequalities. There are many complex factors in need of consideration for the design and implementation of policies aimed at promoting comprehensive, inclusive and humanistic development. While we cannot summarize them all here, they should include: (1) regional, mutually supportive and compensatory integration with fair commerce versus asymmetric integration and free commerce; (2) a human rights-based agenda versus a national security-based agenda; (3) free and voluntary mobility versus forced migration; and (4) fair labour standards versus superexploitation. An examination of these elements should be based on a critical appraisal of the requirements for a human rights-based, positive type of circular migration that exposes the human and labour rights violations of existing temporary worker programmes (Southern Poverty Law Center, 2007). Other issues requiring attention include the massive increase of irregular migration in excess of the demand for labour; the increasing incorporation of highly skilled migrant workers from underdeveloped countries and their contribution to the innovation processes of developed nations (Khadria, 2008; Lozano and Gandini, 2009; Xiang, 2007); and problems surrounding return policies and programmes that adversely affect migrants and their families.

The biggest remaining challenge in this regard is to shift attention from the type of migration policies implemented in receiving nations (that is, those based on a security agenda that criminalizes migrants and obscures the nature and causes of the phenomenon) to bilateral and multilateral negotiations based on an agenda of international cooperation and development.

NOTES

1. See Iosifides (Chapter 2, this volume) for further discussion of the reductionist nature of quantitative epistemology.
2. See Lozano and Steinberger (Chapter 8, this volume) for a review of traditional neoclassical economic approaches in migration studies.
3. It must be pointed out that the categorization of countries according to concepts of development and underdevelopment, centre and periphery is, to an extent, abstract and does not imply a strict dichotomy. Rather, it entails a complex system of power relationships established among regions, nations and localities. In this sense, unequal development appears as an inherent feature of the capitalist mode of production.

REFERENCES

Bello, W. (2006), 'The capitalist conjuncture: over-accumulation, financial crisis, and the retreat from globalization', *Third World Quarterly*, **27**, 8, 1345–67.

Black, R. (2001), 'Environmental refugees: myth or reality?', New Issues in Refugee Research, Working Paper No. 34, *Journal of Humanitarian Assistance*, available at http://www.jha.ac/articles/u034.pdf (accessed 5 July 2010).

Canales, A. (2008), *Vivir del Norte. Remesas, Desarrollo y Pobreza en México*, México: Conapo.

Castles, S. (2002), 'Environmental change and forced migration: making sense of the debate', New Issues in Refugee Research, Working Paper No. 70, Refugees Studies Centre, Oxford University.

Castles, S. (2003), 'Towards a sociology of forced migration and social transformation', *Sociology*, **37**, 13–34.

Castles, S. and Delgado Wise, R. (eds) (2008), *Migration and Development: Perspectives from the South*, Geneva: International Organization for Migrations.

Delgado Wise, R. and Márquez, H. (2007a), 'Teoría y práctica de la relación dialéctica entre desarrollo y migración', *Migración y Desarrollo*, **9**, 5–25.

Delgado Wise, R. and Márquez, H. (2007b), 'The reshaping of Mexican labor exports under NAFTA: paradoxes and challenges', *International Migration Review*, **41** (3), 656–79.

Delgado Wise, R. and Márquez, H. (2009), 'Understanding the relationship between migration and development: toward a new theoretical approach', *Social Analysis*, **53** (3), 85–105.

Delgado Wise, R., Márquez, H. and Rodríguez, H. (2009), 'Seis tesis para desmitificar el nexo entre migración y desarrollo', *Migración y Desarrollo*, **12**, 27–52.

Engels, F. (1859), 'Karl Marx: "A contribution to the critique of political economy"', reprinted in Karl Marx (1977), *A Contribution to the Critique of Political Economy*, Moscow: Progress Publishers, available at http://www.marxists.org/archive/marx/works/1859/critique-pol-economy/appx2.htm (accessed 21 August 2010).

European Commission (2004), *Report of the Experts Group on Trafficking of Human Beings*, Brussels: EU Directorate-General Justice, Freedom and Security.

Foladori, G. and Pierri, N. (2005), *Sustentabilidad? Desacuerdos Sobre el Desarrollo Sustentable*, Colection: América Latina y el Nuevo Orden Mundial, México: Miguel Ángel Porrúa.

Foster, J.B. and Magdof, F. (2009), *The Great Financial Crisis: Causes and Consequences*, New York: Monthly Review Press.

Fox, J. (2005), 'Repensar lo rural ante la globalización: la sociedad civil migrante', *Migración y desarrollo*, *Migración y Desarrollo*, **5**, 35–58.

Gordon, J. (2009), 'Towards transnational labor citizenship: restructuring labor migration to reinforce workers' rights', A Preliminary Report on Emerging Experiments, Fordham Law School, available at http://ssrn.com/abstract=1348064 (accessed 5 July 2010).

Gzesh, S. (2008), 'Redefining forced migration using human rights', *Migración y Desarrollo*, **10**, 87–113.
Harvey, D. (2007), 'Neoliberalism as creative destruction', *Annals of the American Academy of Political and Social Science*, **610**, 21–44.
Harvey, H. (2003), *The New Imperialism*, Oxford: Oxford University Press.
Khadria, B. (2008), 'India; skilled migration to developed countries, labour migration to the Gulf', in S. Castles and R. Delgado Wise (eds), *Migration and Development: Perspectives from the South*, Geneva: International Organization for Migration, pp. 4–37.
Lester, R. and Piore, M. (2004), *Innovation. The Missing Dimension*, Cambridge, MA: Harvard University Press.
Lonergan, S. and Swain, A. (1999), 'Environmental degradation and population displacement', *AVISO*, **2**, available at http://www.gechs.org/aviso/02/ (accessed 5 July 2010).
Lozano, F. and Gandini, L. (2009), 'La emigración de recursos humanos calificados desde países de América Latina y el Caribe', SELA, Caracas.
Márquez, H. (2009), 'Diez rostros de la crisis civilizatoria del sistema capitalista mundial', *Problemas del Desarrollo*, **40** (159), 191–210.
Márquez, H. (2010), 'La gran crisis del capitalismo neoliberal', *Andamios*, **13**, 57–84.
Marx, K. (1906), *Capital. A Critique of Political Economy*, Chicago, IL: Charles H. Kerr and Co., available at http://www.econlib.org/cgibin/searchbooks.pl?searchtype=BookSearchPara&id=mrxCpA&query=reserve+army (accessed 12 November 2010).
Marx, K. (1973), *Grundrisse. Outline of the Critique of Political Economy*, trans. M. Nicolaus, Harmondsworth: Penguin.
Marx, K. (1975), *Capital*, Oxford: Oxford University Press.
McAdam, J. (ed.) (2010), *Climate Change and Displacement: Multidisciplinary Perspectives*, Oxford: Hart Publishing.
Meillassoux, C. (1981), *Maidens, Meal, and Money: Capitalism and the Domestic Community*, Cambridge: Cambridge University Press.
Milkman, R. (2006), *LA Story: Immigrant Workers and the Future of the US Labor Movement*, New York: Russell Sage Foundation.
Munck, R. (2010), *Globalization and Social Exclusion: A Transformationalist Perspective*, New York: Kumarian Press.
Myers, N. (1995), *Environmental Exodus: An Emergent Crisis in the Global Arena*, Washington, DC: Climate Institute.
Myrdal, G. (1957), *Rich Lands and the Poor*, New York: Harper and Row.
Petras, J. (2007), *Rulers and Ruled in the US Empire: Bankers, Zionists and Militants*, Atlanta, GA: Clarity Press.
Petras, J. and Veltmeyer, H. (2000), 'Globalisation or imperialism?', *Cambridge Review of International Affairs*, **14** (1), 1–15.
Petras, J. and Veltmeyer, H. (2001), *Globalization Unmasked: Imperialism in the 21st Century*, London: Zed Books.
Piore, M. (1979), *Birds of Passage: Migrant Labour in Industrial Societies*, Cambridge: Cambridge University Press.
Robinson, W. (2008), *Latin America and Global Capitalism: A Critical Globalization Perspective*, Baltimore, MD: Johns Hopkins University Press.
Schierup, C.U., Hansen, P. and Castles, S. (2006), *Migration, Citizenship, and the European Welfare State: A European Dilemma*, London: Oxford University Press.
Singer, P. (1974), *Economía Política de la Urbanización*, México: Siglo Veintiuno Editores.
Southern Poverty Law Center (2007), 'Close to slavery: guestworker programs in the United States', Montgomery: Southern Poverty Law Center.
Stiglitz, J.E. (2002), *Globalization and its Discontents*, London: Penguin.
Tarbuck, K. (1991), 'Marx's method and political economy', *New Interventions*, **2** (3), available at http://www.whatnextjournal.co.uk/pages/newint/Method.html.
United Nations (UN) (2004), *World Economic and Social Survey 2004. International Migration*, New York: United Nations.

United Nations (UN) (2006), *World Population Monitoring, Focusing on International Migration and Development*, Report of the Secretary-General, E/CN.9/2006/3.

Wallerstein, E. (2005), *Análisis de Sistemas-mundo: una Introducción*, México: Siglo Veintiuno Editores.

Withol de Wenden, C. (2000), *Hay que Abrir las Fronteras?*, Barcelona: Bellaterra.

Xiang, B. (2007), *Global Body Shopping: An Indian Labor System in the Information Technology Industry*, Princeton, NJ: Princeton University Press.

PART II

INTRODUCTION TO DIFFERENT TECHNIQUES AND APPROACHES

6 Interviewing techniques for migrant minority groups
Luis Sánchez-Ayala

Any research attempt requires a serious engagement and the full comprehension of all the elements directly and indirectly related to the study. When the study involves human subjects, the research is a real challenge, more so if it involves interviewing members of minority migrant groups. This type of human subject represents a sensitive population and therefore special awareness is needed, not only because of the complexity related to human nature, but also because of the particularities of dealing with migrants who are considered, either by assertion or assignment, as minorities.[1]

Success in obtaining the necessary information when interviewing a migrant minority group depends on three factors. The first factor is the preparation that takes place prior to the interview process. The second factor is the application of the appropriate interview technique. The third factor is the proper analysis of the information. These factors can determine the interaction between the interviewer and the respondent, and the quality and richness of the data gathered.

The interview process of migrant populations and minority groups requires special attention. It is very important to keep open possibilities to fully engage in their everyday life, and to capture the complexity of social relations embedded in their daily experiences. However, the most important aspect when interviewing such groups is the way in which the interviewer identifies her- or himself and engages in the conversation with the potential interviewees. In other words, it is important to reflect on the ways in which the researcher could potentially influence the interview.

6.1 POSITIONALITY

The first step before conducting fieldwork, and also before engaging in any writing, is to consider our own positionality: the ways in which the values and subjectivity of the researcher are part of the construction of knowledge. This is perhaps the most difficult task to achieve during the interview process. A failure to do so can lead to misrepresentation of the potential results of the research. Considerations of positionality allow the researcher to be aware of its potential to influence the interviews and thus the end results. Therefore, positionality is a concept that requires close examination prior to engaging in research, and most certainly before conducting research dealing with qualitative methods.

Positionality is the notion that our location in the social structure and the institutions we belong to affect the ways in which we understand the world (Johnston et al., 2000, p. 604). Such a position acts on and reacts to our knowledge about things, both material and abstract. Therefore, there is no independent or objective position from which one can freely and fully observe the complexity of our world. Value-free research, if not impossible, is almost impossible to obtain. It is important to understand that research is shaped by the actions and values of the researcher (Limb and Dwyer, 2001, p. 8). No one has ever devised a method for detaching the scholar from the circumstances of life or from the fact of his involvement (conscious or unconscious) with a class, a set of beliefs, or a social position, or from the mere activity of being a member of a society (Said, 1979, p. 10).

Positionality is also a matter of representation, in other words, how the interviewer sees and perceives the interviewee. This can be described as an unequal relation of power where the interviewer is in the position of interpreting the lives of the interviewees. If the interviewer is not aware of such a relationship the results of the interviews could construct social reality instead of reflecting it. In that case the interviewer could be at risk of privileging certain points of view while silencing others. Therefore, how the interviewer constructs and represents 'others' through any judgment made for that matter responds in great part to their own personal situation and positionality. Failure to acknowledge this before engaging in the interviewing process represents an obstacle to full consideration of all the possible angles of observation. Such obstacles not only critically limit the construction of a proper interview instrument, but also affect its effective application in the field.

The subject of positionality requires self-reflexivity. When thinking about who to interview it is important to reflect on how the researcher's identity will shape the interactions that he or she will have with the interviewees. In this sense, the interviewee can treat the interviewer with either acceptance and trust, or skepticism and rejection. The interviewer can deal with this positioning as an insider or as an outsider with respect to the person or group being interviewed.

An insider position, or sharing the same background or similar identity with the informant, can have positive effects. It can facilitate the development of a rapport between interviewer and interviewee, thus producing rich, detailed conversation based on empathy and mutual respect and understanding (Valentine, 1997, p. 113). Similarly, the researcher may find it easier to build a bond with the research participants and conduct interviews if the project is linked to his or her own interests, or if he or she is interviewing people with whom he or she has something in common. In this sense, the researcher's personal position could allow her or him to have a much clearer understanding of the interviewee's position and problematic. This insider position can also situate the researcher in an advantageous position of having firsthand information, through life experiences, and even through common language, culture, background, and so on.

On the other hand, an outsider position can actually facilitate the progress of the interview. In this sense, the interviewer can be situated in a neutral position as an independent element. Such status can bring the necessary trust in the interviewer-interviewee relationship and thus create the proper environment for the development of a rich and detailed conversation. Similarly, an outsider can be perceived as a better position to preserve the interviewee's anonymity, and therefore the interviewee may find it easier to speak and answer questions freely.

However, it is possible to be positioned as an outsider and at the same time achieve an insider relationship with the interviewee. This is possible through an insider companion or co-researcher. In this sense, the insider companion or co-researcher is the link that can create the environment of familiarity and trust between the interviewer and the interviewees, and thus open the doors for a fluid conversation. Yet, as is the case of the main researcher, such an insider companion or co-researcher needs to be aware of her or his own biases and position.

Nevertheless, the interviewer needs to be very alert, as this insider/outsider border can be both beneficial and harmful to the research. An insider interviewer can also have the effect of making the researcher appear too close for comfort, making the people wary of sharing (Mohammad, 2001, p. 108). However, the danger lies in the possibility that the interviewer can get emotionally attached to the interviewee and thus unconsciously restrain her- or himself to see only one side, or to unconsciously not allow her- or himself to reflect upon views that are opposed to her or his own views. Moreover, an outsider position can be perceived as distant, and this can affect the development of the interview.

I will illustrate how this issue of positionality fits into a study involving interviews with migrant minority groups. During my research on Puerto Rican migration to Orlando, Florida, USA, I had to deal with my own positionality. In that research I was looking at the formation of a Puerto Rican community, as a migrant minority group in the Orlando area, and the perceived differences between being a Puerto Rican born in Puerto

Rico and being a Puerto Rican born in the mainland USA. In this context, the nature of my own identity as a Puerto Rican born in Puerto Rico made my case more complex.

As I came into contact with individuals and institutions, my own positionality became part of my research as some of my interviewees related to me and assumed I was part of the community. Since I am Puerto Rican, island-born, and lived in Florida, most of my interviewees assumed my research was an 'inside job,' a situation which they welcomed gratefully as something positive for the better of the 'community.' In this sense, both the topic of my research and my identity removed many obstacles in terms of my access to their lives. I ended up getting to know, in person, several important figures and elected officials in Central Florida, including officials representing the government of Puerto Rico in the Orlando metropolitan area. In most cases, these individuals offered me their help and support. Therefore, I took advantage of my own positionality as an insider sharing in their background and identity. As a result, I was able to endure a rich and detailed conversation that provided me with inside information about the community and its actors.

On the other hand, the same position that opened the doors of possibility among the Puerto Rican migrant community also introduced complications in the development of the interviews. On one occasion in which I failed to strike a balance between being a researcher and being one of 'them,' one of the interviewees did not perceive me as part of their community. The interview started well; the interviewee was supportive and gave me valuable information. However, after an hour of conversation the interviewee noticed a green wristband that I have on my left hand. The color green in Puerto Rico stands for independence for Puerto Rico. At the beginning of the interview, when I asked about the reason he migrated from the island to Florida, the interviewee made clear that he migrated in part due to political reasons, and since he was (and still is) part of the pro-statehood party in Puerto Rico, he was forced to migrate due to political 'persecution' from the pro-commonwealth government that had been in power at the time. After that point the interview started to fall apart. He became somewhat arrogant in his responses, attributing a political agenda to all my questions, and although he proceeded respectfully, he started to add comments about how pro-independence people should stay on the island. Since that experience I became more alert of any message that I could consciously or unconsciously send to my interviewees that could potentially affect the development of the interviews.

This is an example of the importance of why the interviewer needs to be aware of personal circumstances and constraints. Failure to engage the appropriate position could lead the interview and the study to misleading generalizations. In this sense, the researcher's own position can be both enabling and disabling. It all depends on the ability of the researcher to make visible the exact nature of her or his biases through a self-reflexive understanding of the researcher's social locatedness at the moment.

All these considerations are critical for the accuracy of the interview process, even more so when dealing with a sensitive population like a migrant minority group. This type of population requires careful attention due to the perception, either by assertion or assignment, of uniqueness, individuality, and sometimes rejection and marginalization. Yet these considerations alone are not enough; to fully understand migrants we need to understand their spatial context.

6.2 SPATIAL CONSIDERATIONS FOR INTERVIEWING MIGRANTS

Human mobility is a spatial phenomenon. Any serious attempt to understand migration must take into account the spatial setting and circumstances, in both the place of origin and the destination place, of the migrants to be interviewed. We must not forget that the causes of migration are not unrelated to the consequences of migration in the places of emigration (Samers, 2010). This includes socio-economic issues, but more importantly their sense or level of integration into the spatial setting. These factors will determine how these migrants construct their collective identity, in both their place of origin and their place of destination (for example, whether they perceive themselves as welcome, unwelcome, included, marginalized, empowered, discriminated against, insider, outsider, and so on), and in turn how receptive they are to sharing their stories and life experiences with another person. For instance, as Mitchell (1993, p. 277) puts it, individuals who have economic and/or cultural power are able to challenge and in some cases transform the notions of exclusion toward migrants, predominant in the host countries. Therefore, due to their particular spatial circumstances, such migrants are less likely to perceive themselves as a vulnerable minority group, and, thus, would be more receptive to share their stories and life experiences.

Therefore, to fully understand migrants we need to understand at least two basic spatial concepts. The first concept is place. Contrary to the concept of space, place is less abstract, as it is a site of meanings. In other words, what makes place are the social meanings that individuals and groups assign to any given space. Place signifies and is full of meanings that relate to lived experiences. In this sense, place can be viewed on a smaller scale than space (Cresswell, 2004).

It is critical to understand migrants' place-making process. Most of the time an interview is not enough to fully understand their stories. During an interview there are things that could be omitted, forgotten, hidden, or ignored. In this sense, the migrant's place-making process can help us put all the pieces together. In other words, we can understand their attitudes by looking at their constructed sites and their contextual meanings. Place and its symbolic contents play a central role in people's lives; people act and behave in great deal according to what they see. Therefore, places can be understood as our unwitting autobiography, reflecting our lives, our values and aspiration, in tangible, visible form (Lewis et al., 1973).

The other spatial concept relevant when looking at the life experiences of migrants is territory. Delaney (2005, p. 14) defines territory as a bounded social space that inscribes a certain sort of meanings onto defined segments of the material world. Therefore, territoriality is an important element of how cultures, societies, collectives, and institutions organize themselves in space (Delaney, 2005, p. 7). In other words, territoriality is a human strategy to affect, influence, and control (Sack, 1986, p. 2). The point is that when we look through territory what we will always see are constellations of social relations of power (Delaney, 2005, p. 16).

Therefore, to understand territory is to understand the boundaries and spatial extension of the social arrangement within the migrants' places. In this sense, we must be very much aware of the context of their territory before entering it. This knowledge not only will help the interview process itself by making the interviewer more aware of the 'hidden externalities' of the interview setting, but it will also provide some of the necessary tools to select and organize the interview instrument.

6.3 THE INTERVIEW TECHNIQUE

An interview does not consist of only asking questions; there are different techniques and ways in which to implement an interview in the field in order to properly obtain the necessary information. The first step the researcher must take is to reflect on how much interaction with the interviewees is required. In other words, the proper selection of an interview technique depends on the type of information desired, according to the research plan and goals. This consideration is particularly important when dealing with a sensitive population, such as is the specific case of migrant groups, that either by assertion or assignment is considered a minority population in a particular place. We must have in mind that not everyone migrates; therefore, those who migrate can be identified as a minority. Migration is a process which affects every dimension of social existence, and which develops its own complex dynamics (Castles and Miller, 2009, p. 21). In this sense, migrants, but more so those moving into a new social and cultural setting, could perceive themselves as being in a disadvantageous and vulnerable position, and thus would be reluctant to share their lived experiences. Therefore, getting too close could be interpreted as an intrusion, but, on the other hand, being too far could limit the quality of the research results.

In this sense, too much interaction with the interviewees can result in an excess of information. This can leave the researcher with too many irrelevant details, and thus hold back the progress of the research. The excess of information can make the process of data analysis and reflection a very complex one. Similarly, too much interaction can limit the total number of interviews conducted, affecting the findings of the research. On the other hand, the opposite can occur; insufficient interaction can limit the collection of valuable information, leaving the researcher with incomplete or inadequate data. This in turn can critically affect the outcome of the research as well.

The technique requiring the most interaction with research subjects is in-depth interviews. In investigating the different aspects related to minority migrant groups it is imperative to get the most information possible about their life experiences and perceptions, as well as their physical surroundings. In-depth interviews are sensitive and people-oriented, allowing interviewees to construct their own accounts of their experiences by describing and explaining their lives in their own words (Valentine, 1997, p. 111). In other words, this technique represents a window into the interviewees' consciousness. Such consciousness allows us to access the most complicated social issues because social issues are abstractions from concrete lived experiences (Limb and Dwyer, 2001; Seidman, 1998).

In-depth interviews can be structured, unstructured, or semi-structured. Structured interviews follow a predetermined plan. This plan includes a standardized list of questions which are asked in a strict order. On the contrary, unstructured interviews do not follow any standardized list of questions. In this technique the researcher starts the conversation and then allows the interviewee to direct the rest of the conversation. Finally, semi-structured interviews have elements of both structured and unstructured interviews. In this technique the interviewer establishes a general direction for the conversation but still ensures flexibility for the interviewee to direct part of the conversation.

Another technique that requires direct interaction between the researcher and the respondents is the group interview or focus group. Similar to in-depth interviews, focus groups can be structured, unstructured, or semi-structured. However, focus groups entail a collective interview process, and therefore individuals can be influenced by other participants of the focus group.

On the other hand, the technique requiring the least interaction between the researcher and the respondents is the use of questionnaires. The degree of interaction of this technique fluctuates depending on the method of administration of the questionnaire; the questionnaire can be self-administered or supervised. In self-administered questionnaires the respondents complete the form themselves with no or minimal interaction with the researcher, while supervised questionnaires involve more interaction between the researcher and the respondent, as the researcher interacts directly with the respondent. Nonetheless, questionnaires are a good tool to use in order to gain valuable information about the overall perceptions of the general populace. In this sense, the questionnaire can include specific questions that can provide a glimpse into individual patterns and collective behavior.

The appropriate selection of a technique depends on the goals of the research. A study interested in the full stories and experiences of the interviewee must keep possibilities open and not limit respondents' answers; the proper technique in that case would be in-depth interviews. Conversely, if the research seeks to explore collective behavior and patterns, the proper technique would be the use of questionnaires. However, if the research is interested in exploring the simultaneous reactions and divergences of various individuals, the proper technique would be the focus group. It is also important to know whether or not the researcher needs or wants to establish a general direction for the conversation and pursue specific topics raised by the respondent. This information is necessary in order to select a structured, unstructured, or semi-structured method of conducting the selected technique.

Once a technique had been selected it is crucial to decide what is going to be asked. Have in mind that selecting the right questions is as important as the selection of the interview technique itself. This in turn will ensure that the necessary information is collected in order to successfully meet the research plan. Therefore, the selection of the questions must take into account the specific circumstances and spatial situation of the respondent.

There are two types of questions, closed-ended questions and open-ended questions. The use of closed questions involves a predetermined set of answers provided by the researcher to the respondent to select one or more. Conversely, the questions that allow the respondent to provide her or his own answers are open-ended questions. Closed-ended questions are used more often in questionnaires because they provide more uniformity and are more easily processed, while in-depth interviews rely almost exclusively on open-ended questions because doing so keeps possibilities open for the respondents to fully share their life experiences.

Nonetheless, equally important in the process of selecting the proper interview technique is the use of other sources of complementary information and data to support the primary information gathered during the interview process. In this sense, participant and/or site observation and document analysis can be of great help.

Participant and site observation allows the researcher to study behavior in its natural setting and to fully understand the spatial context of the everyday life of those being researched. In other words, observing also means involvement in the migrant community and recurrent contact with the real actors, keeping in mind that the spatial setting of those being observed is an important factor in social and cultural relations. In this sense, social relations can be understood by actively examining such spaces. That space serves as a way to understand people's behavior. People do not just see the space; they read it and interpret what is in it. Symbols reflect values, aspirations, fears, biases in a tangible and visible form. Therefore, participant and site observation provides the researcher with the opportunity to engage in the web of immigrants' lives.

On the other hand, document analysis consists of the analysis of publications and documents such as newspapers, similar studies, census data, archive material, audiovisual material, and so on. Text analysis serves as a source of complementary information and data to support the information gathered through other primary data gathering techniques. In this sense, these secondary sources can be useful for the necessary theoretical and background data and information that is vital for a full and proper understanding of the results of the research. Therefore, document analysis can be a good source from which to draw a geographical portrait and a demographic and economic profile of the interviewees.

Nonetheless, all the previously mentioned techniques can provide valuable qualitative and quantitative information. Through each one of those techniques, regardless of its diverse forms of implementation, we can observe associations and trends that can be statistically compared, as well as stories and experiences that can be qualitatively analysed. Still, the richness of the data gathered, qualitative and/or quantitative, through these techniques ultimately depends on how they are implemented in the field.

6.4 THE INTERVIEW PROCESS

Once the issues of positionality and the selection of the technique have been properly addressed, the next step is to get started with the fieldwork. In this process the researcher/interviewer must give close attention to certain factors that are vital for the success of the research. Those factors are how to approach the respondents/interviewees, how to manage/interpret the body language during the interview, sample size, and sampling method.

Dealing with a population of migrant minorities the researcher must find the best mode to approach and formulate questions for the potential interviewees. This is critical for the success of the entire study. An inadequate first approach could have adverse consequences, being perceived as an intrusion or even as an insult, and thus jeopardizing the interview process. Within this context, we must have in mind that the current social arrangements of power are organized around conditions of membership. In most places there are groups who are denied full participation (Castles and Davidson, 2000). For individuals that translates into issues of inclusion and exclusion from society. This is critical in the case of migrant minority groups, as they are particularly aware of this. Non-members have no guaranteed place in the collective and are always liable to expulsion (Walzer, 1983, p. 32). In this sense, feelings of exclusion can be translated into distrust, and therefore block the rapport between the researcher and the interviewer, and in some instances even make difficult the process of finding potential interviewees. Therefore, any attempt to interview a migrant must deal with these issues. Ignoring this could have adverse consequences for the final results of the research. Therefore, in avoiding such consequences, participant and site observation could be of great help, as the researcher could acquire essential information beforehand regarding the interviewees' daily life and spatial circumstances.

However, on some occasions it is necessary to formulate questions in a rather indirect form. In other words, it can be the best choice to formulate questions that might involve a sensitive issue for the interviewee in a subtle way. In this sense, if the interviewer perceives that the interviewee might perceive that a specific question is too sensitive, or that the respondent may feel uncomfortable, or may think that the answer to the question could be self-incriminating, the interviewer can formulate the question using indefinite terms (for example, do you think someone, have you heard about, are you aware of). This issue needs close attention, even more so when interviewing a sensitive population such as migrant minority groups. In this case, it is essential to approach and formulate the questions to the interviewee subjects in an appropriate manner.

To provide a concrete example of such a situation, I will use my own experience conducting interviews with minority migrant groups in the Caribbean coastal regions of Nicaragua. On that occasion I was researching separatist movements among the minorities, migrants and descendants of migrants who had previously come to those regions of Nicaragua. I was very aware of the historical development of the region and the armed conflict with the government; therefore, I knew beforehand the sensitive nature that the separatism topic represents for the people of the region. Nevertheless, I was able to obtain the necessary information for my research by indirectly asking about the interviewees' separatist sentiments. In order to achieve this, I asked interviewees about their awareness of existing levels of separatist feelings instead of their actual separatist feelings. With this technique respondents openly expressed their feelings without the fear of being labeled as separatists. Consequently, I did not encounter major problems regarding the interviewees' reactions toward my presence in their community or their willingness to talk to me and answer my questions.

Similarly, a factor of critical importance is how to direct the conversation with the interviewees. It is vital to keep the conversation focused and directed toward the aims of the research. The researcher must have a clear idea of what is going to be asked and how it should be asked. In this sense, the proper conduct of the interview requires a balance between the researcher and the subject. Such balance is possible by adding some formality and emphasizing our position as researchers. This would keep away any potential situation that could mislead the development of the conversation, and, thus, the richness of the data gathered.

Nevertheless, knowledge of the potential messages that the body language of both the researcher and the respondent could send is crucial in the development of the interview process. In this sense, the researcher needs to be aware of existing dress codes, acceptable/unacceptable manners and gestures, and language usage. The oversight of any of these factors could seriously jeopardize the interview, and in extreme cases, it could even result in a dangerous or unpleasant situation for the interviewer.

For instance, let us refer to the previously mentioned interview I conducted with a Puerto Rican community leader in Orlando, Florida, USA. On that occasion I failed to adequately give the necessary attention to the issue of body language. As a result of my negligence the interviewee perceived some unspoken messages from me that he understood as being contradictory to his views, and, thus, threatening. This caused the deterioration of the conversation, and consequently the eventual termination of the interview.

However, the researcher not only needs to be alert to the possible messages she or he could be sending through his or her body language, but should also be aware of the body language of the interviewee. In this sense, the interviewer must interpret the body language of the interviewees. In other words, the interview process requires interpretation of what people mean based upon what they say, and also interpretation of what they say through the use of popular sayings and metaphors; more importantly, though, meaning can be communicated through gestures. Failure to correctly interpret such meanings can significantly affect and/or limit the results of the interview.

The last two important factors for the interview process are the size of the sample population and the sampling method that will be used. Usually only a segment of the people or the phenomena associated with a case is actually studied. This is why we talk about sample population and sampling method. The sample size will determine how many interviews are necessary or desired for the research. One of the most common questions when doing research is how big or how small the sample population should be. There is no absolute answer to this question. In other words, it depends on the goals of the research. In a study privileging quantitative information where representativeness is important, the question of the population size is more relevant. In that situation, the size of the sample population should be a number from which we can make generalizations with the smallest possible margin of error. Therefore, in this case, the sample size would depend on (1) the study's goals and (2) the size of the population itself.

On the other hand, in a study with emphasis upon an analysis of meanings in a specific context, where the sample is not intended to be representative, the question of the population size is less relevant. Thus, qualitatively speaking, there are no rules for sample size. In this sense, the size depends on what you want to know, why you want to know it, what information is useful, and the available time and resources.

Let me illustrate. During both of my research experiences, interviewing members of the immigrant Puerto Rican minority of Orlando, Florida and the migrant minorities of the Caribbean coastal areas of Nicaragua, I was interested in individual perceptions rather than collective behavior. In other words, I was more concerned with exploring the whole range of realistic responses from interviewees rather than achieving a specific number of interviews. Therefore, in both cases the actual size of the interview group was a secondary issue. Yet, that does not mean that I was not interested in acquiring quantitative data; rather it means that I was more interested in analysing the meanings of the interviewees' narratives than the representativeness of the sample size.

The next issue is how to select the potential participants, or the sampling method. As is the case with sample size, ultimately the sampling method also depends on the goals of the research. Nonetheless, there are two general types of sampling methods: (1) non-probability sampling and (2) probability sampling.

Non-probability sampling does not involve sampling based on a random selection. Among the more useful non-probability sampling methods are purposeful sampling, snowball sampling, and quota sampling. When using purposeful sampling the researcher must have a complete knowledge of the population. This is necessary because with this sampling method the researcher purposefully selects the subjects to be observed on the basis of which ones will be the most useful for the goals of the research. Snowball sampling, on the other hand, is appropriate when members of the target population are difficult to locate or the researcher does not have the information necessary to locate them. In this sense, the researcher interviews any member of the target population that she or he can locate, and then the interviewee suggests additional people to be interviewed or provides the information needed to locate more potential interviewees. Lastly, quota sampling, even though it is a non-probability method, has some elements of probability sampling. This is because quota sampling deals with the representativeness of the sample population. In this sense, when using quota sampling the researcher wants to maintain certain proportions representative of the target population; however, the respondents are not necessarily randomly selected.

The other set of sampling methods are the probability type. The principle behind this type of sampling is to construct a reliable description of the total target population. Therefore, probability sampling looks for a sample that maintains the same elements and variations that exist in the target population. Generally, the sample is selected using a random mechanism, and the data obtained are analysed using sophisticated statistical techniques. Some of the most useful probability sampling methods are simple random sampling, systematic sampling, and cluster sampling.

In simple random sampling the potential participants are selected randomly. The researcher does such selection by generating a list of the target population, and then assigning a number to each one of them. Then, a given table of random numbers is used to select the elements that will be part of the sample. That is, participating elements are determined by randomly selecting numbers on the table. That can be done in any way possible, for example, by pointing to numbers on the table with eyes closed, or choosing row X and column Y and selecting the number in that position. Those numbers then will be matched to the numbers given to each one of the members of the target population, and the individuals having those numbers will be included in the sample.

Nevertheless, an easier way of selecting the sample from the target population list is by using systematic sampling. In this type of sampling, instead of selecting numbers from a table of random numbers, you can select the sample directly from the target population list. That can be done by selecting individuals from the list at predetermined intervals. That is, for example, by systematically selecting every second (or fifth, or tenth, and so on) element in the total list to be included in the sample. Usually the researcher can start by randomly selecting the first individual and then selecting at systematic intervals. Ultimately, the interval will be determined by the total target population and/or the desired size of the sample.

However, in cases in which a list of the total target population is not available, or is somehow too difficult to generate, the research can systematically generate its sample on the field. In this sense, the presence of a list is not strictly necessary, as the researcher can interview every second or fifth person he or she encounters on the street, at the park, or in the mall, for example. In such a case, the researcher predetermines the sampling method but does not generate a sample prior to the interview process. The sample is rather generated throughout the development of the interviews themselves. In this sense, the systematic interval will be determined not as much by the total target population, but by the desired size of the sample.

On the other hand, cluster sampling involves the sampling of groups of elements or individuals that are part of the target population. Therefore, this type of sampling requires various stages of sampling. First, the researcher samples a group from the total target population. Second, the researcher samples subgroups from the previously sampled groups or clusters. This sampling method can be used when a list of the target population is impossible or too difficult to obtain or generate. Therefore, the researcher can select a sample from a known group or members of the target population.

All these sampling methods – simple random, systematic, and cluster – can be stratified, grouping individuals or the units that form a population into homogeneous groups. Such stratification is done before sampling to improve the representativeness of the sample in order to generate generalizations about the total target population with the least possible error.

A single study can use more than one sampling method. Remember that the selection of the sampling method depends on the goals of the study itself. In this sense, research involving migrant minority groups presents some complexity. To fully comprehend such complexity is essential for exploring the various aspects that affect, shape, and determine human behavior. Consequently, the wider the methods of analysis, the better chances we have of reaching a detailed understanding of such human agency. In this sense, the combination of various interview techniques with various sampling methods can generate richer results composed of both qualitative and quantitative elements.

I was able to prove the richness of these results through my research experiences, in which I combined several methods and techniques. That practice not only allowed me to gain a better understanding of the human agency behind the behavior and practices of the migrant minority groups of the Caribbean coastal areas of Nicaragua and the Puerto Rican diasporic community of Orlando, Florida, but it also provided me with better tools with which to critically analyse the information obtained through interviews. In the case of the Puerto Rican diasporic community I used purposeful criterion sampling to contact 'visible' key actors of the Orlando Puerto Rican diasporic community such as elected government officials, political leaders and policy-makers, religious leaders, civic and cultural leaders, and business owners. This practice was crucial to my data collection because I was interested in selecting participants with influence over public opinion. These participants reflected a wide range in the larger population that I intended to study, and therefore I purposefully selected different individuals with various political views and cultural and economic backgrounds. On the other hand, I was also interested in interviewing 'ordinary' members of the community. However, since I knew very few people in Orlando, it was difficult for me to locate my study population. Therefore I used snowball sampling to contact individuals and various Puerto Rican organizations in the area. In other words, I asked the respondents I was able to identify to recruit or locate other possible respondents.

The case of the minority groups in the Caribbean coastal areas of Nicaragua was similar. On that occasion I interviewed both 'decision makers' and 'ordinary people.' However, I did not have a list of the entire population of migrant minority groups in the area. Such a list, if it does not already exist, is almost impossible to generate. Therefore, the interviews with ordinary people were carried out following a systematic sampling procedure. In other words, I generated my sample not on the basis of the total population, but on the basis of a predetermined number that I decided was the adequate number of interviews I needed. Consequently, the sample was determined during the development of the interview process. In other words, interviews were conducted in the main street and marketplaces of each location I selected. The random selection method employed was that every third person that passed between 8:00 am and 5:00 pm was interviewed. In the case of the decision-makers, such as community, religious, and political leaders, both purposeful and snowball sampling were used. In this sense, I purposefully interviewed some of the 'visible' decision-makers of the region, and at the same time I asked the respondents to identify or locate other decision-makers.

Yet, there is a factor related to the selection of the interviewees that is worth emphasizing. In that regard, the selection of a sampling method should be made according to the research goals. In other words, the researcher must have a very clear idea of what she or he wants to know, and why she or he wants to know it. This will define then whom to look for and how to look for them, whether they be individuals or groups. Consequently, this will determine which sampling method, or methods, would be the most appropriate and how large or small the sample population should be. For instance, the information obtained from an interview with a person in a position or status of visibility will differ greatly from the information obtained from an interview with an ordinary person or member of the group.

Leaders and decision-makers (that is, elected governmental officials, political leaders and policy-makers, religious leaders, civic and cultural leaders, and business owners) have the power to influence public opinion and they are more aware of community and/or group matters than the everyday populace. They are visible figures, important personalities with followers who consider them to be leaders. Consequently, in their cases, processes of power relations are very much at play. These individuals occupy positions of power and have the authority to define knowledge and draw boundaries of affiliation. Contrary to ordinary people, their power to decide and influence provides the means to promote and institutionalize particular ways, forms, and norms in society.

6.5 ANALYSIS OF THE GATHERED INFORMATION

After the fieldwork has been successfully completed and all the interviews have been conducted comes the final step of the research: analysis of the information gathered. However, not all the data can be analysed using the same criteria. Therefore, for the purpose of an analysis, a distinction between quantitative and qualitative information must be made.

Qualitative information should be analysed by building several broad themes of analysis to address the research questions. Therefore, field notes, tape-recording of the interviews, and visual information such as photographs can be crucially important in extracting relevant details and salient themes of great relevance for the analysis. However, the construction of such themes of analysis needs to follow certain steps. First, transcribe the interviews and evaluate the information provided in them in order to develop a content analysis of each respondent's perceptions and behavior. Second, code the transcribed texts from the interviews, and organize that information into categories. By coding the transcribed texts the researcher can transform the raw data obtained from the interviews into a standardized form that facilitates its understanding and analysis. The exact coded concepts are determined recursively throughout the research process. In other words, the concepts to be coded and analysed are the most recurrent themes and concepts mentioned and/or discussed by the interviewees themselves. This method of analysis is designed to qualitatively examine textual, graphic, audio, and video data. It allows the researcher to use grounded theory to identify themes in the data not contained in the existing literature. In addition, codes reflecting concepts closely related to the theory contained in the existing literature can be used as well. Finally, a series of patterns among codes must be identified in order to delineate the most significant themes that in turn will allow the researcher to gain a broad and clear understanding of the interviewees' narratives, and, thus, of the problem being studied.

As is evident, a statistical approach with such qualitative information would seriously limit a meaningful analysis of people's stories and experiences. On the other hand, quantitative data must be analysed through the use of the proper statistical methods and techniques. Therefore, in the type of research that involves interviewing migrant minority groups we should pay special attention to social statistics. Such statistics allow the researcher to summarize data, measure associations, and make inferences.

Some of the most frequently used social statistics can be grouped into two categories: descriptive statistics and inferential statistics. Descriptive statistics help us summarize observations made about a sample and quantitatively describe the characteristics of a sample. In this sense, univariate data can be summarized through averages such as the mode, median, and mean and measures of dispersion such as the range and the standard deviation, whereas bivariate (two variables) and multivariate analysis can be done through tables and percentage distributions.

Likewise, descriptive statistics help describe the relationship among variables in a sample. Perhaps the most commonly used method for describing the association between two variables is regression analysis. However, there are many other ways to measure such associations. For example, for nominal variables (variables that are categorical and not numeric) some commonly used measures of association are Lambda, Percentage Difference, and Phi Coefficient. On the other hand, for ordinal variables (variables that permit a rank ordering of the objects) some commonly used measures of association are Gamma, Kendall's tau- (b and c), and Spearman's Rank-Order Correlation. Any introductory statistics textbook will give you a more comprehensive understanding of this subject.

At the other end of the spectrum, inferential statistics involve much more than just descriptions; rather they make inferences about the larger population to which the sample population belongs. Some inferential statistics estimate the single variable characteristics of the population through averages such as the mode, median, mean, and percentages, while other inferential statistics estimate the relationships between variables in the population. However, such inferences about the relationships between variables involve a test of statistical significance (for example, Chi Square test of statistical significance). Again, any introductory statistics textbook will give you a more comprehensive understanding of this subject.

Nonetheless, beyond statistics and content analysis, there is another tool of great value for the analysis of the gathered information. Geographic Information Systems (GIS) can open a door of possibilities in understanding patterns, tendencies, distributions, behavior, perceptions, and much more related to our interviewees. In other words, because everything happens in a space and/or has spatial consequences, we cannot ignore an event's spatial or geographical dimension. In that regard, GIS is a powerful tool that can integrate hardware, software, and data for capturing, managing, analysing, and displaying all forms of georeferenced information (information whose spatial location has been determined or established). Therefore, GIS allows us to view, understand, question, interpret, and visualize data (both qualitative and quantitative) in many ways that reveal relationships, patterns, and trends in the form of maps, globes, reports, and charts.

This kind of spatial analysis can complement in many ways not only the findings of our research, but also our own understanding of the phenomena being studied. In this sense, using GIS technologies can help us answer questions such as why migrants move where they moved, what relationships exist between their places of origin and their places of destination, whether or not they are clustered together in one place, and why or why not, whether migrants present the same characteristics and/or behavior in all locations, and whether there is any difference in a particular phenomenon dependent upon location. Therefore, GIS can help us to find features, patterns, and map quantities, see concentrations and the relationships between places, map where and how things move over a period of time, and map conditions before and after an action or event to see its impact. In conclusion, the spatial analysis of your data can provide an additional level of information to your research beyond simply producing graphs, tables, and interview transcripts.

Ultimately, the success of a study involving interviews of migrant minority groups depends on two factors. The first factor is the researcher's decision-making process regarding the applied method and techniques used in the study. The secret here is to keep a healthy balance between qualitative and quantitative information and methods. Remember that quantitative or numeric data alone is not enough; numbers alone cannot explain the complexity of real life. In the same way, qualitative data can be confirmed, clarified, and validated through quantitative data. The second factor is the researcher's sensitivity in understanding the human beings that she or he intends to study. However, and above all, the key element for the success of any study is to enjoy the research experience.

6.6 CONCLUSION

There is no doubt that human agency is extremely complex. However, it is not only the complexity of human behavior, but also its unpredictability that makes any research attempting to explore and understand the diversity of social and spatial arrangements a real challenge. In that sense, while the methods discussed in this chapter can be applied to any human population, we must emphasize and give particular attention to populations of migrant minority groups.

The particular situation of migrants, especially those who are considered either by assertion or assignment as minorities, presents even more complexity. On the one hand, the processes of human mobility in which they are involved add other issues and considerations that directly influence and impact forever not only their lives but the lives of their descendants. On the other hand, there is the issue of membership and belongingness; in other words, the perception of being a minority. Consequently, the lives of migrant minority groups, and thus their social behavior, are in great deal concurrent to the particularities of these circumstances.

These considerations are critical in the case of migrant minority groups, as they are particularly aware of the constraints that surround their lives. In this sense, success in obtaining the necessary information when interviewing a sensitive population, such as migrant minority groups, requires even more attention and dedication. This distinction could make the difference between the richness of the data and the impact that the research could have.

NOTE

1. See the van Liempt and Bilger (Chapter 21, this volume) for further discussion of the ethical challenges related to doing research with vulnerable migrants.

REFERENCES

Castles, S. and Davidson, A. (2000), *Citizenship and Migration: Globalization and the Politics of Belonging*, New York: Routledge.
Castles, S. and Miller, M. (2009), *The Age of Migration: International Population Movements in the Modern World*, Basingstoke and New York: Palgrave Macmillan and the Guilford Press.

Cresswell, T. (2004), *Place: A Short Introduction*, Oxford: Blackwell.
Delaney, D. (2005), *Territory: A Short Introduction*, Oxford: Blackwell.
Johnston, R.J., Gregory, D., Pratt, G. and Watts, M. (2000), *The Dictionary of Human Geography*, Malden, MA: Blackwell.
Lewis, P., Lowenthal, D. and Tuan, Y. (1973), *Visual Blight in America*, Washington, DC: Association of American Geographers, Commission on College Geography.
Limb, M. and Dwyer, C. (2001), 'Introduction: doing qualitative research in geography', in M. Limb and C. Dwyer (eds), *Qualitative Methodologies for Geographers: Issues and Debates*, London: Arnold, pp. 1–20.
Mitchell, K. (1993), 'Multiculturalism, or the united colors of capitalism?', *Antipode*, **25** (4), 263–94.
Mohammad, R. (2001), 'Insiders and/or outsiders: positionality, theory and praxis', in M. Limb and C. Dwyer (eds), *Qualitative Methodologies for Geographers: Issues and Debates*, London: Arnold, pp. 101–17.
Sack, R. (1986), *Human Territoriality: Its Theory and History*, Cambridge: Cambridge University Press.
Said, E. (1979), *Orientalism*, New York: Vintage.
Samers, M. (2010), *Migration*, New York: Routledge.
Seidman, I. (1998), *Interviewing as Qualitative Research: A Guide for Researchers in Education and the Social Sciences*, New York: Teachers College Press.
Valentine, G. (1997), 'Tell me about . . .: using interviews as a research methodology', in R. Flowerdew and D. Martin (eds), *Methods in Human Geography: A Guide for Students Doing a Research Project*, Harlow, Essex: Prentice Hall, pp. 110–26.
Walzer, M. (1983), *Spheres of Justice: A Defence of Pluralism and Equality*, New York: Basic Books.

7 Collecting, analysing and presenting migration histories
Jørgen Carling

'Migration' is often thought of as an aggregate flow of people from A to B. However, each individual in that flow has followed their own individual trajectory in time and space – possibly a rather complex one. Whether we are compiling information on a large number of people or trying to understand the experiences of a small group, we need to approach and digest those individual trajectories. This chapter addresses the collection, analysis and presentation of migration histories across different methodological approaches. The emphasis will be on the first of these steps: collecting information. However, I will show how information can be collected in different ways for different analytical purposes, and indicate how more specialized analysis might follow. Three forms of data collection will be addressed: conventional interviews, life history calendars and migration history charts. The presentation of migration histories in publications obviously depends on the analytical approach. What I will do here is to show how detailed family migration histories can be displayed and used as a complement to text, using either the migration history chart or the so-called Lexis diagram.

7.1 MIGRATION HISTORIES IN DIFFERENT METHODOLOGICAL APPROACHES

Migration research reflects the methodological diversity of the social sciences. The leading journals in the field publish a mixture of articles using qualitative and quantitative approaches, even if individual researchers are often methodologically specialized. Before going into the details of data collection, two hypothetical examples can serve to illustrate the different uses of migration histories. First, imagine a study of remittance-sending among Africans in Portugal, based on a large-scale survey. When and how they came to Portugal is likely to be important, but with hundreds of respondents, this information needs to be collected in a concise and standardized way. A common approach would be to reduce the migration histories to a couple of key questions such as 'when did you first come to Portugal?'. This is indeed a collection of migration history information, only in a highly condensed way. The data are straightforward and can easily be incorporated in quantitative analysis. However, a respondent who answered '1992' in response to the question might have left her country of origin a decade earlier and lived in another European country. Similarly, she might have come to Portugal in 1992 but left again in 1993 and not returned to Portugal until 2008. In a large-scale survey where migration histories can only take up a few moments of an interview, one might have to accept that nuances are missed, and hope that the deviations even out in the large material.

Second, imagine that the same topic is studied by a single researcher with a qualitative approach, doing in-depth interviews with 12 Africans over the course of a year. The possibilities for exploring the details of each person's migration history are now completely different. The first interview with each person could, for instance, be devoted entirely to how he or she came to Portugal, locating that move not only in a longer time span of personal mobility, but also in relation to the movement of other family members. Even with just 12 informants, we could then have information on the movements of 50–100 people over more than half a century. In the second or third interview, it will be challenging for the researcher to remember, for instance, when it was that the migration of a brother and the death of a grandmother decreased the informant's obligations to remit. Even more, two years later, when the researcher is writing, the scenario of browsing through piles of notes to find answers to such questions is disheartening. Efficiently recording intricate migration histories can therefore have implications for the quality of subsequent interviewing and analysis.

The emergence of transnational perspectives on migration illustrates the relevance of migration histories. In traditional studies of immigration and integration, one could more easily just see the arrival as 'year zero' and take it from there, while detailed histories of mobility were the concern of demographers. Transnationalism implies the continued relevance of people elsewhere in migrants' lives. Space and time both matter, since these relationships result from people's different migration trajectories over time and often involve reciprocity that can only be understood in light of interaction in the past. I will return to the relationship between transnationalism and migration histories when discussing migration history charts in a later section.

7.2 SETTING A THRESHOLD FOR MOVES

Migration histories consist of a series of moves. If histories are to be collected in a consistent manner, there must be a common temporal and spatial threshold for including a move or not. Even if this is most critical in large-scale quantitative data collection, reflecting on the spatial and temporal parameters of moves is also valuable in the context of qualitative research.

The 'spatial dimension' is generally straightforward in studies of international migration, where the defining element is whether or not the move was from one country to another. In studies of internal migration moves can be counted if they cross administrative boundaries (for example, from one province to another) or if they are between 'places' more loosely defined. One way of phrasing this is to ask about having lived in 'another place, such as another village, another town, or abroad' (Lucas, 2000b, p. 334). This allows for analysis of important moves within the same administrative unit (for example, from village to city), does not require awareness of administrative boundaries and is not affected by changes in administrative boundaries over time.

The 'temporal dimension' may be necessary to rule out short-term mobility such as travelling for social, business, religious or vacation purposes. One possible threshold is having lived somewhere 'for three or more months at one time' (Lucas, 2000b, p. 334). Thresholds of six months or a year are common in studies of international migration. However, some forms of migration might escape such a coarse measure. For instance, many of the relatively new migration flows in Europe such as those from Ukraine to Spain or Poland to Scandinavia involve high degrees of short-term mobility.

The spatial and temporal dimensions of mobility should be considered critically in relation to the specific context and the nature of the research. In my own research on children left behind by migrant parents, for instance, the intercontinental mobility of mothers interacted with local movements of children from caretakers in one household to another. Also, mothers' brief holidays were essential temporal landmarks in the long-term separation of families. Seeing these different forms of mobility in context was essential for understanding the practice and experience of transnational parenthood (Carling, 2008a).

7.3 WHAT DO INFORMANTS REMEMBER?

Researchers' need for information is only one starting point for compiling migration histories. Equally important is what information we can expect informants to provide. It is often impossible to determine the accuracy of information given to us by informants or survey respondents. In instances when, in some way or other, it is possible to verify retrospective information, the findings are often disheartening. In a widely cited article called

'The problem of informant accuracy: the validity of retrospective data' anthropologist Russell Bernard and his colleagues (1984, p. 504) conclude that 'informant accuracy remains both a fugitive problem and a well-kept open secret'. The fact that informants are inaccurate is not surprising, they say, since 'people everywhere get along quite well without being able to dredge up accurately the sort of information that social scientists ask them for' (1984, p. 513). One's exact pattern of past migration is precisely the type of information that might be of little practical value to informants, and which may, understandably, be difficult to recall. In migration histories, there is a possibility that moves are not reported at all, and that they are reported with the wrong timing. The latter can take two forms: irregular errors in which the dates recorded are just off the mark, and 'telescoping' which means that events are systematically reported either shorter or longer into the past than they actually occurred.

Two thought-provoking studies have connected different pieces of information to assess the accuracy of retrospective migration histories. Nadia Auriat (1991, 1993) examined migration histories of Belgian couples by comparing data from four sources: (1) interviews with the husband; (2) interviews with the wives; (3) joint interviews with the couple; and (4) the Belgian population register, where all moves were recorded within three months. Her findings provide valuable insight into how migration histories are remembered. First, the couple discussing together gave more accurate responses than either the husband or the wife alone. For instance, 73 per cent of couples were able to date their first move after marriage within a three-month error margin, compared to just 65 per cent of wives and 59 per cent of husbands interviewed on their own. Second, higher rates of mobility lead to a confusion in recall and increases the likelihood that a retrospective migration history will be incomplete. In particular, moves to a residence for less than one year and moves that are part of a series of more than three moves are easily forgotten. Third, recall errors can accumulate since respondents often rely on remembering one move for correctly reporting on another. If a move is forgotten or wrongly dated, this has a negative effect on the accuracy of the subsequent migration history. Fourth, when respondents are asked for the month of a move, errors tend to be heaped. Those who are not within three months of the correct date are most likely to be 10–13 months or 22–26 months wrong. In other words, respondents often report the correct season, but the wrong year. Fifth, moves that are more salient because they are linked to important transitions, such as the birth of a child, are more likely to be remembered correctly.

Some of these findings are echoed in a study by James Smith and Duncan Thomas (2003), who used two rounds of a survey in Malaysia to compare people's migration histories as they were reported in 1976–77 and in 1988–89 when the same people were re-interviewed. Their study differs from that of Auriat in Belgium, since it only examines the consistency in reporting over time, not the factual accuracy of reports. Of the pre-1977 moves reported in the first round of the survey, only about two thirds were also reported 12 years later. Multivariate analyses showed that the probability of consistent reporting was primarily affected by two sets of factors.

'Attributes of the respondent', in particular the level of education, significantly influences recall accuracy. A man with average educational attainment (6.5 years) was 40 per cent more likely to report a move in both interviews than a man with no education. This leads the authors to ask a pertinent question: is the common finding that mobility rises with schooling partly a result of more educated people's better ability to recall and report their migration histories? Smith and Thomas find that this is not the case in their own data, but point out the importance of understanding differences in reporting propensities before jumping to conclusions about mobility patters.

'Characteristics of the move' constitute the second set of factors that affect the likelihood of consistent reporting. The longer the period of residence in the new place, Smith and Thomas find, the higher the likelihood that the move is recalled. When there are many similar moves of short duration, they may merge in memory and be more difficult to recall. Moves that brought the respondent to the place he or she lived at the time of the first interview were particularly memorable. Like Auriat, Smith and Thomas also found that coincidence with other salient life events make moves more easily recalled. However, there were important gender differences: men recalled moves more easily if they coincided with the start of a new job; women's memory was better for moves that coincided with marriage or the birth of a child. Another gender difference in the findings was that men's memory was unaffected by whether or not origins and destinations were rural or urban. This was not the case for women, who had a better recall of moves that presumably involved greater adjustments for the household.

Not surprisingly, the likelihood that a move is consistently recalled decreases over time. Smith and Thomas's results echo others who have found that the so-called 'forgetting function' is particularly steep over the first few years into the past and then flattens out. In other words, there could be a big difference in what informants remember about their mobility one year ago versus five years ago, while moves that are remembered after ten years are likely to also be remembered after twenty years. Neither Auriat (1993) nor Smith and Thomas (2003) find consistent indications of telescoping. In other words, if moves in the past are remembered and reported at all, the timing may be inaccurate but is unlikely to be systematically skewed in one direction.

Smith and Thomas (2003) convincingly argue that 'survey characteristics' also affect the quality of recall. There were limited options for exploring this empirically in their own study of a single survey. However, they point to implications of their findings for survey practice. First, they suggest separating migration histories into two parts: a long-term history of the most salient moves (for example, those that led to a change of residence for at least six months) and a short-term history that had a lower threshold and thereby picked up circular or temporary mobility. Second, they suggest linking migration histories with other salient life course events (for example, marriage, childbirth and changes in employment) in order to improve recall. This recommendation is echoed by Auriat (1993) who suggests that data collection could benefit from structuring interviews 'in a transversal fashion', examining different spheres of life within one time period at a time rather than requesting longitudinal series of events to be reported in each sphere.

7.4 THREE DATA COLLECTION FORMATS

I will discuss three different formats for collecting migration history data: conventional questionnaires, the life history calendar and the migration history chart. Afterwards, I compare them systematically. Each approach has its strengths and limitations; researchers have to consider what is the best tool in a given research context.

7.4.1 Conventional Questionnaires

When migration histories are collected by means of a conventional questionnaire, there are two main approaches. First, it is possible to request 'complete migration histories' by tracing each move from the place of birth to the current place of residence. (A slightly simplified variant is to start with the place of residence at the time of reaching adulthood, for example, age fifteen or eighteen.) Table 7.1 exemplifies how such a migration history can be compiled, limited to international moves and a duration of at least six months.

Second, it is possible to ask a set of questions that will not yield a complete migration history, but still capture essential aspects of migration history. Simply comparing the place of birth with the current place of residence will identify 'lifetime migrants'. Another common question, for instance, in population censuses, is on the place of residence five or ten

Table 7.1 *Questionnaire grid for recording international migration history*

Country where you lived for at least 6 months	Date of departure	
	Month	*Year*
1. [*Country of birth*]		
2.		
3.		
...		
n. [*Country of current residence*]		

Source: Adapted from Bilsborrow et al. (1997).

years ago. This allows for identifying 'recent migrants'. Such comparisons of residence at two points in time say nothing about possible moves in the meantime, however. In surveys that deal more comprehensively with migration, questions may cover length of stay at the current place of residence, age at first migration from the place of birth and so on. Table 7.2 presents a short migration module for use in questionnaires (Lucas, 2000a, 2000b).

If the surveyed population consists of immigrants, other questions might be pertinent. As mentioned initially, this could be as brief as asking about the year of first arrival. An imminent danger is to assume that migration histories are more straightforward than they really are. Depending on the population being studied, multiple migrations to and from the country of origin, or trajectories involving third countries, could be common. Furthermore, saying when (or even whether) a move has taken place can be unexpectedly difficult. Highly mobile populations such as Senegalese traders in Italy or European expatriates in Brussels might not migrate in the sense of one day packing up their belongings and going to live in another country. Perhaps, after many years, they realize that 'home' is now the new place, but without being able to account for when they migrated. In a survey, this is partly related to setting the threshold for which moves to include: what is the relevant meaning of migration in this particular population and for this particular study? However, we cannot escape the fact that people's lives are often not as clear-cut as social scientists would want them to be.

7.4.2 The Life History Calendar

The second approach to collecting life history data is what may be called 'calendar interviewing'. It is based on the use of a calendar table, referred

Table 7.2 *Short migration module for surveys*

Question	Responses and routing
1. Have you ever lived in another place, such as another village, another town, or abroad, for three or more months at one time?	Yes No [→ *Next person*]
2. How long is it since you came to stay here, in this place?	Years and months [*If 5 years or more, leave months blank*]
3. When you were first born, did you live in [*current place of residence*]?	Yes [→ *Q 7*] No
4. In what province or country did you live when you were first born?	Province and country codes
5. During the time you lived there, was that place an urban area?	Yes No
6. Other than the place you were born and the place where you live now, have you ever lived anywhere else for more than 3 months?	Yes No [→ *Q 14*]
7. How old were you when you first left [*place of birth*]?	Age in years
8. In what province or country were you living before you moved to your current place of residence?	Province and country codes
9. Were you living in an urban area in that province/country?	Yes No
10. Besides the places you have mentioned so far, have you ever lived anywhere else?	Yes No [→ *Q 14*]
11. [*Check question 2. Has person been living here for 5 years or more?*]	Five years or more [→ *Q 14*] Less than five years
12. In what province or country were you living 5 years ago?	Province and country codes
13. Was this place you were living in 5 years ago an urban area?	Yes No
14. [*Check question 4 if the place of birth is a foreign country, ask:*] In what year did you first come to this country for more than three months?	Year

Source: Adapted from Lucas (2000b).

to as a Life History Calendar (LHC) or Event History Calendar (EHC) and deviates from the rigid question-response pattern of conventional questionnaire-based interviewing. In calendar interviewing, the interviewer and the respondent piece together the relevant aspects of the respondent's life history through a less standardized conversation. The

Collecting, analysing and presenting migration histories 145

	Year	2000	2001	2002	2003	2004	2005	2006	2007	2008	2009
Migration history	Where	Accra					Accra				
	When				X—	X—			—X		
	When					X—X			X—		
	Where					Apam				Takoradi	
[OTHER DOMAINS]											
Landmarks	National		Presidential elections	Stadium stampede; Floods in A.	Violence in the North		Presidential elections		Ghana 50 Floods in N.	Cup of African Nations	
	Personal					Death of mother		Car accident			

Source: Constructed by the author, inspired by Freedman et al. (1988) and Axinn et al. (1999).

Figure 7.1 Example Life History Calendar (LHC) segment on migration

rationale behind this is that a more flexible use of language and a more flexible sequencing of questions can help respondents remember the interrelationships of past events and thereby construct a more accurate and complete history (Belli and Callegaro, 2009).

The basic structure of a LHC is a grid with the columns representing a series of time units and the rows detailing various aspects of the respondent's life, such as employment, education and family events. The time units are typically either years or months, depending on the level of detail required and the length of the time period covered. Transitions such as starting or ending education are marked with an 'X' in the cells corresponding to the start and end date, with a line connecting the Xs to denote duration. The LHC approach has been documented in an instructive and widely cited article by Deborah Freedman and four of her colleagues at the University of Michigan (1988).

Figure 7.1 illustrates how migration histories can be collected in the LHC format. The 'when' rows are used to mark the beginning and end of residence and the 'where' rows are used to write the name of the place. The mirrored sets of lines ensure enough space for writing even with frequent moves. A typical LHC will contain other row segments for recording employment history, births of children and other transitions. Making connections between these domains can make it easier for respondents to remember their migration history (and vice versa). In addition, landmark events with known dates can help establish the timing of moves. National or local landmarks are events in the respondents' environment that they can be expected to remember. Relevant events depend on the nature of the target population and the research area, and could include natural disasters, elections, big national news events, changes in religious leadership and so on. If interviewing is constrained to a few local settings, events such as the provision of water or electricity or the building of new roads can be valuable supplements (Axinn et al., 1999). Personal landmarks can be filled in by the interviewer. These are important events in the respondent's life that are not addressed directly in the LHC. For instance, respondents might mention decisive events such as an accident that can later be used to establish the timing of transitions that are asked about in the LHC (Dijkstra et al., 2009).

The LHC can be used in various ways in an interview setting (Belli et al., 2001; Freedman et al., 1988; Harris and Parisi, 2007; Sayles et al., 2010). First, respondents may or may not be invited to look at the calendar together with the interviewer and use the visual display of information as a tool for remembering. Second, the completion of the LHC can be a separate section of the interview, or it may be interspersed with substantive questions about the various events and transitions. Third, the scripts for how the interviewer introduces the various segments of the LHC can be more or less standardized. Similarly there may be a predefined list of probes.

Using events as cues for other events is an essential aspect of LHC interviewing, reflecting the way in which our autobiographical memory appears to be structured (Belli, 1998; Dijkstra et al., 2009). Such cueing can take three forms: 'top-down cueing' makes connections from the more general to the more specific, for example, asking about domestic migration after establishing a period of residence in a specific country. 'Sequential cueing' connects events chronologically, for instance, retracing a migration history by thinking about how the moves followed or preceded each other. 'Parallel cueing' refers to associations across domains. Examples include connections between migration, family events and employment changes. It is this last form of cueing that reflects the greatest advantages of calendar interviewing in assisting recall.

Several studies have compared LHC interviewing with conventional interviewing (Belli et al., 2001; Belli et al., 2007; Dijkstra et al., 2009; Sayles et al., 2010). They have found that interviewer training is decisive to the success of data collection with LHCs and takes considerably longer than with conventional questionnaire interviewing. This reflects the more active role of the interviewers, and is related to the finding that interviewers prefer calendar-based interviewing. With detailed instructions and adequate training, however, there is only modestly more interviewer variance with LHC interviewing than with standard questionnaires. That is, the factual data that is collected about a person remains largely unaffected by which interviewer has done the interview. After interviews are completed, data entry typically takes considerably longer with LHC interviewing than with conventional questionnaires. This problem is eliminated with computer-assisted interviewing, which is becoming more common also for LHCs (Reimer and Matthes, 2007).

7.4.3 The Migration History Chart

Unlike the LHC, the migration history chart is not a well-established tool that is documented in the literature. The version I present here is developed through my own research and the term migration history chart (MHC) is one that I have coined.[1] It has clear antecedents, however, which will be discussed below. The migration history chart takes the graphical elements of the history calendar even further, by relying completely on a series of lines to record migration histories. It is particularly suited for combining factual data collection on migration histories with in-depth interviewing about the experiences and practices connected with mobility. Recording the migration history information visually rather than in writing has several advantages in an interview setting. First, it minimizes the time and effort spent on note-taking by the interviewer, and thereby makes it easier to sustain the interpersonal contact that is essential to a good qualitative interview. Second, visual recording makes it easier to use the family migration history as a frame of reference during the interview.

The MHC is inspired by the time-geographical models devised by the Swedish geographer Torsten Hägerstrand (for example, 1996). He used three-dimensional illustrations in which a vertical time dimension intersected a surface representing geographical space. Mobility in time and space could then be represented as three-dimensional paths. A major challenge with his models is that they are difficult to draw, and clearly not a feasible form for recording mobility information in an interview setting. The key question is: how can space be reduced to a single dimension in a chart? In their migration textbook, Paul Boyle and his colleagues (1998) simplified Hägerstrand's model by representing space as one dimension, namely, distance from Swansea, the city where the authors were based. They used such a figure to show the three authors' migration histories before coming to Swansea. This format requires a single target location, and has some limitations on its usefulness: it is difficult to represent short- and long-distance movements in a single diagram, and locations that are far from each other, but at the same distance from the target location appear adjacent in the figure. A more intuitive application of the

148   *Handbook of research methods in migration*

time-space surface is found in graphical timetables for railways, originally developed by Charles Ybry in France in the 1840s (Tufte, 1990). A railway line is represented as one dimension in the chart, calibrated with kilometres along the tracks. The other axis shows hours and minutes, and train schedules are displayed as lines running diagonally across the chart. The speed of the train determines the angle of the line, and one can easily see when or where trains travelling at different speeds pass each other. Ybry's original hope was that such charts would be used as timetables by the public. While this has not been realized, they have been widely used for planning by railway companies.

Instead of trying to reduce space to a single dimension, the spatial axis in a MHC is simply a subdivision of locations. This makes it easier to accommodate a range of places that are unknown at the start of the interview. There are also theoretical justifications for focusing on distinct spaces rather than on continuous space: transnational migrants typically navigate dispersed, highly localized attachments; they rarely roam expansive cosmopolitan spaces (Van Hear, 1998). The flexibility of the MHC also facilitates analysis of how internal and international migration are related to each other. For instance, Russell King and colleagues (2008) used a version of the MHC to explore Albanian trajectories between villages, regional centres, the capital and other countries.

Figure 7.2 shows the MHC with a simple family migration history recorded in it. The horizontal lines represent years, with the year of the interview at the top of the sheet. The divisions across the sheet are different locations, with a heading added for each one. Every individual is represented with a path through the chart, moving upwards from their year of birth to the year of the interview (or their death). Vertical segments indicate periods of residence in a specific place, and horizontal segments show migration between places.

The example shown in Figure 7.2 is the family migration history of the interviewee, Jandira, her parents and her two daughters.[2] The thick black curve shows her trajectory from birth in São Vicente (Cape Verde) in 1972, indicated with an asterisk, to her current residence in Palermo (Italy). The trajectories of her mother and father run from the 'M' and 'F' in their respective places and years of birth. The bottom lines on the chart have been left unlabelled to allow for registration of any event that occurred more than 50 years before the interview. The chart also includes Jandira's two daughters: Dóris born in São Vicente in 1988 and Nancy born in Palermo in 1994.

The chart reproduced here relies on solid and dashed lines for distinguishing individual trajectories. In an interview setting, coloured pens are useful. Quickly reading the chart is easier when colours are used

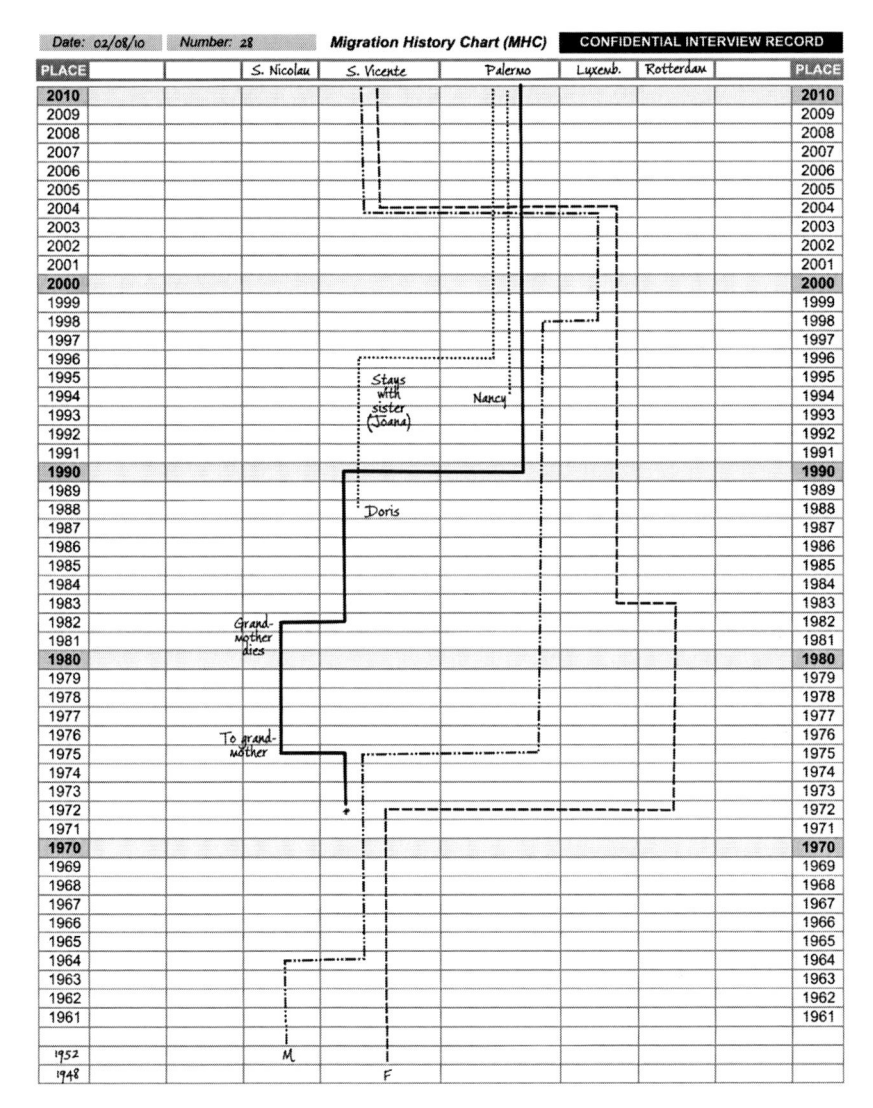

Collecting, analysing and presenting migration histories 149

Note: The asterisk marks the birth of the interviewee, Jandira. See text for additional explanations.

Figure 7.2   Example Migration History Chart (MHC)

consistently, for example, black for the interviewee, brown for the mother and grey for the father. In this example, first names are used for the two daughters. Depending on how confidentiality issues are handled and how the charts will be stored, an alternative would be to enter daughters as D1,

D2 and so on, with S1 and S2 indicating sons. How much of a disadvantage this is depends on the number of people included, the complexity of the family relationships and the ways in which the completed charts will be used during interviews.

When recording such a family migration history in an interview setting, it might not be clear from the outset which, or how many, locations will be included. It also depends on the research project and the migration patterns whether it is important to distinguish between separate locations within a country. In the example shown here, two separate locations in Cape Verde are included, and the overseas locations are identified as cities. When the chart is simply used for recording information, it does not matter which columns are used to represent the different locations. However, the chart can be adapted to typical migration patterns of the population under study. The chart shown in Figure 7.2 contains two wider columns at the centre, with three narrower columns on either side. The wide columns can be used for locations that are presumed to be important, that is, with many individual paths passing through. If the research is framed by a particular origin and destination (for example, migration from Somalia to the United Kingdom) the narrow columns to the left can be used for relevant locations in the region of origin (for example, Kenya and Djibouti) while the narrow columns to the right can be used for locations near the destination (for example, Denmark and the Netherlands). If more than six locations come up in the course of the interview based on this chart, some columns will have to be used for more than one location, with notes added to each vertical segment to identify the location.

Two other principles have guided the completion of the chart shown in Figure 7.2. First, the horizontal order of individual segments within a column is arbitrary. That is, if two people stay in the same place, it is irrelevant whose line is on the left and whose is on the right. Second, the vertical placement of a move within a year is arbitrary. In other words, one should not expect to read from the chart whether a move took part in the beginning, middle or end of a year. If migration is examined more in detail over a shorter period, a grid with months instead of years should be used.

One of the advantages of using the MHC in a retrospective interview is that it makes it easier to recall the timing of past events. There are essentially three ways of ascertaining when a migratory move took place: calendar years, age or relation to other events. With reference to Figure 7.2, Jandira might remember that she migrated to Italy in 1990. Alternatively, she could recall that she migrated when she was eighteen years old. Finally, she might remember that it was two years after her daughter Dóris was born. Making use of connections between events in this way is a parallel to the LHC. This is particularly pertinent to trying to establish the migration histories of family members. Referring to Figure 7.1 again, Jandira might not have been able to remember that her father moved from Rotterdam to Luxembourg in 1983, had it not been by knowing that it was the year after she, herself, moved from São Nicolau to São Vicente. The fact that this happened in 1982 she might have been able to deduce from knowing that she was ten years old at the time. Determining the age of the interviewee or her family members at different points in time requires some calculations by the interviewer, or quickly counting decades and years on the vertical axis from the time of birth. The shading of every tenth year in the chart makes this easier.

The three different approaches to timing – calendar year, age and relation to other events – can also be used for cross-checking and thus validating the information. If Jandira said, during the interview, that 'I think it was in 1996 that my daughter Dóris came to Italy', the chart can be used for follow-up questions such as 'So, she was eight years old at the time?' or 'So, Nancy must have been two years old at the time?'

The principal strength of the MHC is the possibility of recording the migration histories of several people. This raises the question of who to include. Like many other methodology issues, it depends on the context at hand. In studying Cape Verdean migration, it was useful to request information about the respondent's parents, children, siblings and spouse/partner.[3] While the household has become a widespread – if questionable – unit of analysis in migration studies, it is of limited use here. In general, long-term relationships that remain important despite separation are the most important to include. Siblings deserve particular mention, since they are easily left out by researchers who are used to thinking in terms of nuclear families. The sibling relationship is unique in its life-long importance but is understudied compared to other family relationships (Cicirelli, 1995). In the context of migration, the fact that siblings are age peers means that they influence each other's migration in very different ways than parents and children. Furthermore, relationships between adult siblings – including their geographical distribution – can also be essential to understanding transnational practices such as remittances to parents. Also in analysis of domestic migration in industrialized countries, the trajectories of siblings, parents and children play a significant role (Mulder, 2007).

Before starting data collection with MHCs, one should decide upon the importance of accuracy in the timing of events. This depends on the focus of the research project, the amount of interview time available and how the data will be used. An example can illustrate the issue: if Jandira (Figure 7.2) was born in the beginning of 1972 and migrated to Italy when she was eighteen years old, this probably happened in 1990 but could also have happened in early 1991, before her nineteenth birthday. Allowing for such

152 *Handbook of research methods in migration*

margins of error can drastically reduce interview time, especially when it concerns the migration histories of the respondent's family members. This is a matter of priorities: in my own research on migration of Cape Verdean women, for instance, there were many informants that I was only able to interview once. It was important to get the big picture of their family migration history, but also to save interview time for the substantive themes of the research. Consequently, I would not have spent much of Jandira's time trying to ascertain whether it was in 1983 or 1984 that her father moved from Rotterdam to Luxembourg. Having the approximate information, however, it was possible to see with a glance that for most of her teenage years, her relationship with her father was a transnational one between São Vicente and Luxembourg.

Like the LHC, the MHC can be used in different ways during an interview: as a separate section or interspersed with other questions. I have found the MHC a useful way of starting an interview; when I have had multiple interviews with the same informant, the first interview has been focused on the MHC. Completing the chart gives me an overview of the informant's migration history and transnational relationship, and the completed chart constitutes a useful reference for contextualizing questions during the remainder of the interview. It would typically take between ten minutes and an hour to complete the chart, depending on the informant's family migration history, the level of detail requested and the number of digressions. In the context of semi-structured interviews, some flexibility is valuable: selectively following up on issues that emerge as the informant recounts the family migration history is a variant of the attentive improvisation that is generally recommended in qualitative interviewing. When recording is possible, it is therefore recommendable to record the full interview, including the part devoted to the MHC. In Figure 7.2 notes are used to contextualize some of the migration: for instance, Jandira went to stay with her grandmother in São Nicolau when her mother emigrated, and returned to São Vicente when the grandmother died. Such notes would be more important without a recording.

MHCs for use in interviews can easily be produced in spreadsheet programs such as Excel. Like the LHC, the MHC can easily be adapted to the specific research contexts.

7.4.4 Comparison of Data Collection Methods

Table 7.3 summarizes key aspects of the three data collection methods, each of which has strengths and limitations. Conventional questionnaires are recommended when it is sufficient to record a few facts about a person's migration history, and when this information enters a quantitative

Table 7.3   Comparison of methods for recording migration histories

	Conventional Questionnaire	Life History Calendar (LHC)	Migration History Chart (MHC)
Interviewer training requirements	Low	High	High
Interview administration	Standardized	Flexible[a]	Flexible
Interview atmosphere	Mechanical	Collaborative	Collaborative
Amenability to integration with qualitative data collection	Low	Medium	High
Respondent-friendliness in assisting recall	Low	High	Medium
Ease of coding for quantitative analysis	High	Medium[b]	Medium
Amenability to seeing family members' migration in context	Low	Low	High
Amenability to connecting different domains of the interviewee's life	Low	High	Low
Data collection for which the method is recommended	Rapid recording of selected migration history facts	Recording of life histories with migration and other domains	Comprehensive recording of family migration histories

Notes:
a. Different degrees of standardization are possible.
b. High if the LHC is computerized.

dataset. The LHC is better suited for collecting complete migration histories. It is primarily established as a tool for collecting information on 'different domains of one person's life over time', with migration being one such domain. The MHC is most useful when the research focuses on 'relations between people in time and space'. Data from both LHCs and MHCs can be used to contextualize subsequent qualitative interviewing; the main difference, apart from the nature of information collected, is that the MHC's visual display can make it more easily used for reference in the middle of an interview. Data from LHCs and MHCs alike can also be coded for qualitative analysis.

154   *Handbook of research methods in migration*

All the data collection discussed so far has been about where and when a move occurred. Especially with LHCs and MHCs, where every move is recorded, data collection can easily be expanded to cover other aspects of the move: What motivated it? How was it financed? Who provided assistance? Such questions could be covered in subsequent qualitative interviewing, but it is also possible to amend LHCs and MHCs with a standardized set of questions concerning each move. The moves can be numbered in the LHC or MHC, and thereby matched with the corresponding contextual information.

7.5 ANALYSIS OF MIGRATION HISTORY DATA

If we follow the recommendations from the previous section, we can assume that conventional questionnaires are used for recording selected migration history facts, LHCs are used for recording complete migration histories alongside information on other domains in the interviewee's life and MHCs are used for recording the interviewee's migration history in relation to the migration histories of his or her family members. These differences have implications for analysis.

Migration history data from conventional questionnaires can primarily be used to 'classify or describe individuals' in statistical analyses. Basic examples are the distinction between foreign-born and native-born, between immigrants who arrived at different ages or between return migrants and non-migrants. Belonging to a specific migration history category can then be used as an independent variable in multivariate analyses (for example, Mulder and van Ham, 2005). Continuous variables such as time since migration can be used in similar ways.

Data from LHCs open up additional possibilities for analysis. Since every move is recorded, three types of dataset can be compiled from LHC data: datasets with 'individuals' as cases, with 'moves' as cases or with 'person-years' as cases. This level of detail also allows for using event history analysis, a form of logistic regression analysis that seeks to explain how events are affected by other events and states in the past (Wu, 2003). In the context of migration histories, such analyses would typically explore which circumstances trigger a move. For instance, Holly Reed and colleagues (2010) used LHC data in an event history analysis of migration in Ghana, estimating the probability of migration in the current year as a result of the previous year's characteristics.

If data MHCs are coded for quantitative analysis, they can be used much in the same way as LHC data. But how can they be used with a qualitative approach? Given the MHC's emphasis on recording migration

Collecting, analysing and presenting migration histories 155

histories of different people in relation to each other, two substantive areas of research stand out. First, 'chain migration dynamics' can be explored. In fact, MHCs can expose the shortcomings of the term 'chain migration' which implies that individuals migrate one after another to the same destination. What is often the case, by contrast, is that one person's migration is linked to the migration or permanence of several others, with multiple destinations involved. For instance, long-distance migration of one person can finance the regional migration of family members, such as when Somalis in Norway help relatives flee to Kenya or Pakistanis in Norway help relatives migrate for work in Saudi Arabia. The migration history presented in Figure 7.2, contained a different example: Jandira's move from São Vicente to her grandmother in São Nicolau was triggered by her mother's migration from São Vicente to Italy. In other words, departures in opposite directions linked to each other. The MHC can be a good tool for exploring such intricacies.

A related research topic that can benefit from the MHC is 'transnational practices' at the micro level, such as remittance-sending or long-distance parenting. The MHC allows for seeing the 'spaces' in which these practices take place. In Jandira's case (Figure 7.2), we can see how, in different phases of her life, she was the child of a migrant mother, a migrant mother who left a child behind in the country of origin and a migrant with an elderly mother in the country of origin. This framework is a good starting point for exploring her different experiences of transnational mothering (cf. Carling, 2008a). Similarly, with respect to remittances, the MHC can be used for exploring changes in remittance patterns. Was Jandira receiving any support from her father in Luxemburg when she was living with two children in Italy? Did she, herself, have to start remitting when her parents moved back to Cape Verde in 2004?

7.6 PRESENTING MIGRATION HISTORIES

There are four ways of using migration history data in publications: (1) as individual case studies; (2) as a basis for identifying and classifying patterns; (3) in aggregate analysis of quantitative data; and (4) as background information for the researcher that is not explicit in the text. I will discuss the first three in turn.

Individual case studies are frequently used in qualitative migration research. The story of a single migrant or family can sometimes serve well to illustrate more general dynamics, such as how transnational families deal with restrictive immigration regimes, or prioritize transnational and local obligations. Accounts of a detailed family history in prose can be hard to digest for the reader. Going back to Figure 7.2, many laborious paragraphs of text would have been needed to explain who moved where and when in Jandira's family. If these facts are presented graphically, the text can concentrate on more substantive themes, and contextualize them with reference to the chart.

A MHC used to present a case study on print could be quite different from the version used for recording information during an interview. Tidying up the information could mean reordering and resizing the columns and adjusting the individual trajectories to minimize clutter. As in all graphical displays of information, one should consider how the essential information can be conveyed most effectively to the reader (Tufte, 2001). In practical terms, the Excel printout and coloured pens from the field would need to be replaced with graphics software.[4]

The MHC allows for considering multiple locations. If this is not an essential aspect of the migration histories under study, the so-called Lexis diagram can be used to show family migration histories with an emphasis of how life courses interact. This is a two-dimensional chart with time on one axis and age on the other, where individual lives are represented as diagonal 'life lines' extending upwards from the year of birth (Vanderschrick, 1992). Migration can be introduced by distinguishing between dashed and solid segments of individual life lines (Carling, 2008b). Figure 7.3 exemplifies this type of display, showing migration of a family from Cape Verde to the Netherlands. What this diagram makes more explicit than the MHC is the age of family members at different points in time. In other words, we can see how old children were when their father migrated, and at what ages they followed together with their mother. The relationships displayed in the Lexis diagram are important in studies of intergenerational relations and in researching social change. The age and time dimensions of the diagram make it possible to demarcate life course thresholds such as adulthood and retirement, as well as historical thresholds such as changes in immigration policy.

Identifying and classifying patterns is the second way of displaying migration history data in publications. This could mean, for instance, presenting typical patterns of stepwise migration to subsequently more attractive destinations, or typical ways in which family members' trajectories are linked to each other. In Figure 7.4 the MHC is used to illustrate two of the migration patterns I found among Cape Verdean women (Carling, 2008a). In both cases, mother-child separation is unresolved: 'stepwise separation' occurs when a daughter joins her mother abroad and simultaneously leaves a child of her own behind; 'family bifurcation' occurs when the migrant mother leaves one or more children behind and gives birth to additional children abroad and there is no subsequent reunification. These

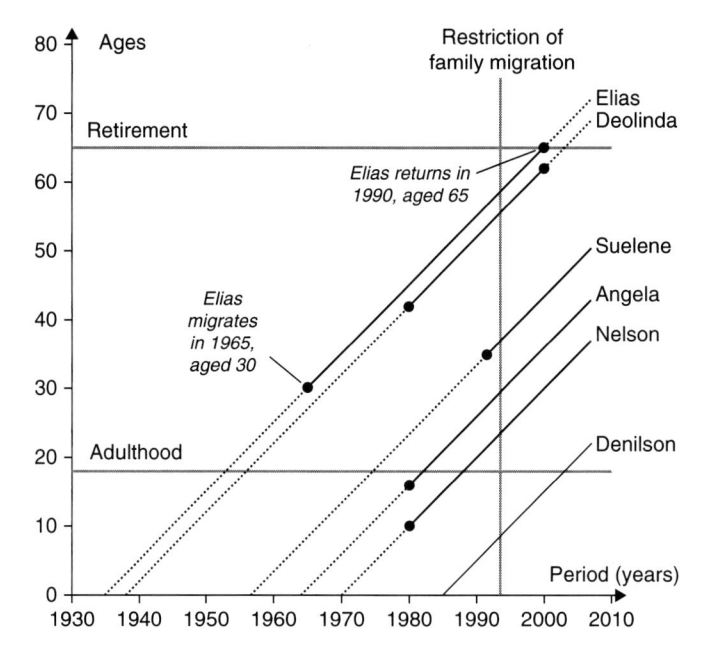

Collecting, analysing and presenting migration histories 157

Note: Dashed lines represent time in Cape Verde; solid lines represent time in the Netherlands.

Source: Based on Carling (2008b).

Figure 7.3 Example migration history in a Lexis diagram

MHCs present generalized patterns and are stripped to the bare essentials: only an approximate indication of the time scale rather than a precise grid, and with a single unnamed origin and destination. Similarly, King et al. (2008) use a simplified MHC to identify ten patterns of internal and international migration.

Aggregate analysis of quantitative data is the third, and most widespread, way of presenting family migration histories in publications. This would usually be in the form of tables that report descriptive statistics or regression results based on hundreds of cases. Possibilities for displaying these numbers graphically, in bar charts, for instance, are not specific to migration history data. But can the specialized diagrams for migration history data also be used to display aggregate statistics? The MHC is poorly suited for this purpose; it is difficult to imagine how hundreds of trajectories can meaningfully be synthesized in a visual display. The Lexis diagram, however, can be used for this purpose – as long as migration history data is limited to one move per person. As mentioned initially,

158 *Handbook of research methods in migration*

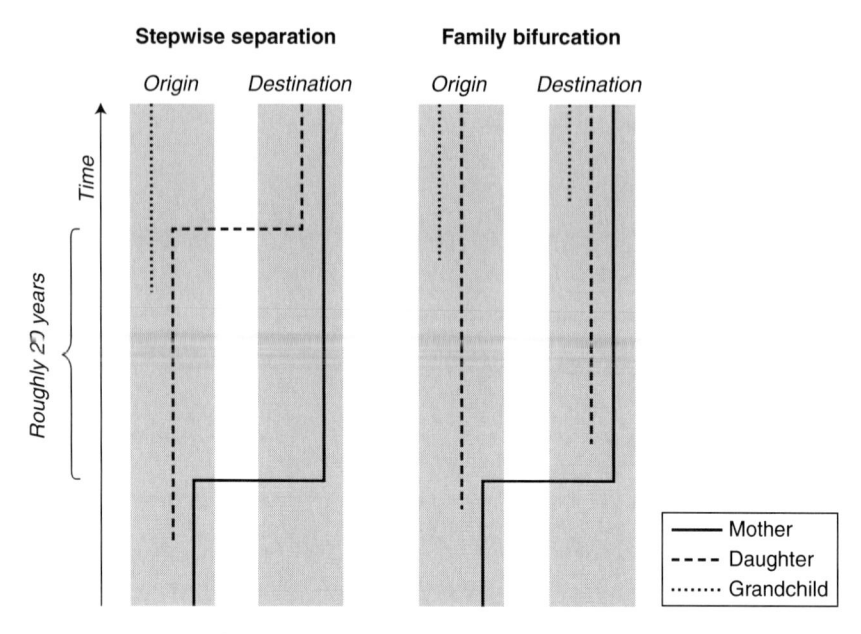

Figure 7.4 Family migration patterns displayed in migration history charts

large-scale surveys are often restricted in this way, for instance, by asking immigrants about the year of their first or most recent immigration. Such data can also be obtained from population registers. Figure 7.5 is the same kind of diagram as Figure 7.3, but displaying aggregate data for migration of Cape Verdeans to the Netherlands instead of a single family history. The connection between the two displays is illustrated by the migration of Elias, the father in the family case study. The aggregate data shows that few Cape Verdeans in the Netherlands arrived earlier than he did, and that most of the people who arrived around the same time were aged 25–45.[5] The analysis of such aggregate data in relation to policy changes is discussed in Carling (2008b).

While the Lexis diagram is not suited for collecting migration histories, it can be a useful tool in the data collection process, especially in qualitative studies among immigrants. Because 'time since arrival' and 'age at arrival' are essential aspects of variation in immigrant populations, the Lexis diagram can be used to get an overview of variation in the group of informants. Each person's immigration could be represented with a marker like the one for Elias's immigration in Figure 7.5. The underlying migration history information could stem from a MHC or from simple interview notes. Without assuming a quasi-quantitative approach and

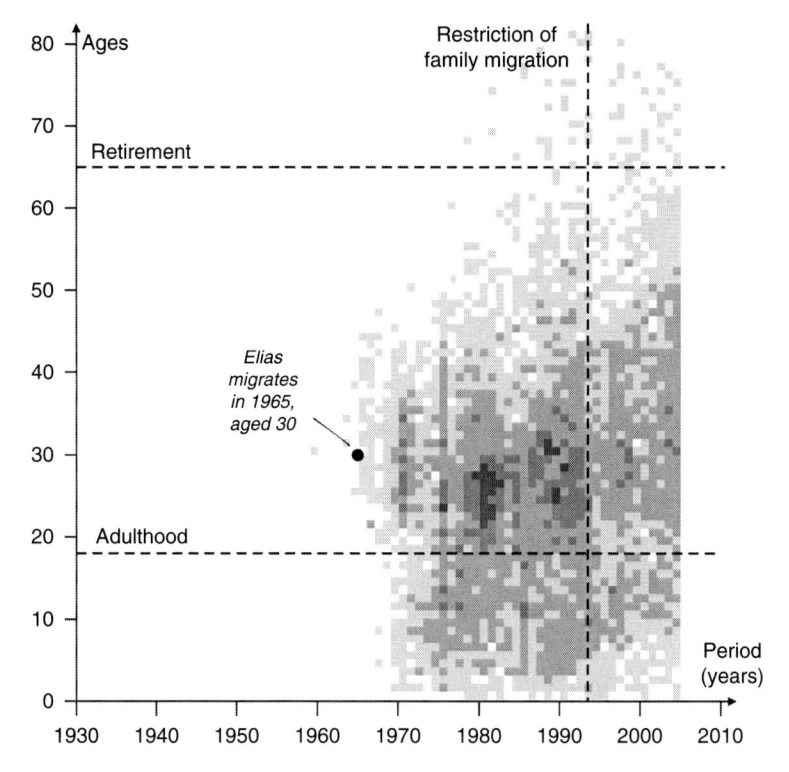

Collecting, analysing and presenting migration histories 159

Note: Shading reflects the frequency of different ages and periods of arrival among Cape Verdean-born persons resident in the Netherlands, January 2005.

Source: Compiled on the basis of data from Statistics Netherlands (CBS). Based on Carling (2008).

Figure 7.5   Aggregate migration history data in the Lexis diagram

looking for representativity, it could be pertinent to see whether most informants arrived at a certain age or in a certain period. If this is done continuously as informants are recruited, it can be a tool for ensuring the types of informant variation that is relevant to the study.

7.7   CONCLUSION

Migration histories are a rich source of information about migration processes and experiences. We should be realistic in terms of what informants can be expected to remember, and use the memory-assisting features of LHCs and MHCs when detailed accounts of the past are required.

Graphically displaying individual migration histories can be a way of bringing complex case studies into research texts without overburdening the reader.

NOTES

1. The term 'migration history chart' has been used once before, according to major search engines. Toney et al. (1985, p. 462) referred in passing to using a 'migration history chart' but described this simply as a record of 'duration of residence at each place of residence from birth'
2. All names are pseudonyms. The family migration history is a hypothetical one, inspired by real cases.
3. Conjugal relationships in Cape Verde are often instable – a fact that both affects and is affected by migration (Åkesson, 2004). As a result, there may be stepfathers and stepmothers that were important, as well as multiple partners of varying importance in the respondent's own life. The extent to which paternal half-siblings are important varies greatly. It would have been futile to adhere to biological facts in determining who to include, but, in retrospect, I should have had a better protocol for handling these ambiguities in a consistent manner.
4. Specialized vector graphics editors such as CorelDRAW or Adobe Illustrator are best suited. However, simple MCHs for print can also be produced with simple drawing tools such as those that are included in Microsoft Word and PowerPoint.
5. Note that the data displayed here is retrospective information about the stock of migrants residing in the Netherlands in 2005. The same type of display could also have been used with historical data on immigration flows.

REFERENCES

Åkesson, L. (2004), *Making a Life: Meanings of Migration in Cape Verde*, Gothenburg: Göteborg University.
Auriat, N. (1991), 'Who forgets?: an analysis of memory effects in a retrospective survey on migration history', *European Journal of Population*, **7** (4), 311–42.
Auriat, N. (1993), '"My wife knows best." A comparison of event dating accuracy between the wife, the husband, the couple, and the Belgium population register', *Public Opinion Quarterly*, **57** (2), 165–90.
Axinn, W.G., Pearce, L.D. and Ghimire, D. (1999), 'Innovations in life history calendar applications', *Social Science Research*, **28** (3), 243–64.
Belli, R.F. (1998), 'The structure of autobiographical memory and the event history calendar: potential improvements in the quality of retrospective reports in surveys', *Memory*, **6** (4), 383–406.
Belli, R.F. and Callegaro, M. (2009), 'The emergence of calendar interviewing: a theoretical and empirical rationale', in R.F. Belli, F. Stafford and D.F. Alwin (eds), *Calendar and Time Diary Methods in Life Course Research*, Thousand Oaks, CA: Sage, pp. 31–52.
Belli, R.F., Shay, W.L. and Stafford, F.P. (2001), 'Event history calendars and question list surveys. A direct comparison of interviewing methods', *Public Opinion Quarterly*, **65** (1), 45–74.
Belli, R.F., Smith, L.M., Andreski, P.M. and Agrawal, S. (2007), 'Methodological comparisons between CATI event history calendar and standardized conventional questionnaire instruments', *Public Opinion Quarterly*, **71** (4), 603–22.

Bernard, H.R., Killworth, P., Kronenfeld, D. and Sailer, L. (1984), 'The problem of informant accuracy. The validity of retrospective data', *Annual Review of Anthropology,* **13**, 495–517.

Bilsborrow, R.E., Hugo, G., Oberai, A.S. and Zlotnik, H. (1997), *International Migration Statistics. Guidelines for Improving Data Collection Systems*, Geneva: International Labour Office.

Boyle, P., Halfacree, K.H. and Robinson, V. (1998), *Exploring Contemporary Migration*, Harlow: Longman.

Carling, J. (2008a), 'Mother–child trajectories in Cape Verdean transnational families', Paper presented at Transnational Parenthood and Children-Left-Behind, Peace Research Institute Oslo (PRIO), Oslo, Norway, 20–21 November.

Carling, J. (2008b), 'Towards a demography of immigrant communities and their transnational potential', *International Migration Review,* **42** (2), 449–75.

Cicirelli, V.G. (1995), *Sibling Relationships Across the Life Span*, New York: Plenum Press.

Dijkstra, W., Smit, J.H. and Ongena, Y.P. (2009), 'An evaluation study of the event history calendar', in R.F. Belli, F. Stafford and D.F. Alwin (eds), *Calendar and Time Diary Methods in Life Course Research*, Thousand Oaks, CA: Sage, pp. 257–76.

Freedman, D., Thornton, A., Camburn, D., Alwin, D.F. and Young-DeMarco, L. (1988), 'The life history calendar: a technique for collecting retrospective data', *Sociological Methodology,* **18**, 37–68.

Hägerstrand, T. (1996), 'Diorama, path and project', in J. Agnew, D.N. Livingstone and A. Rogers (eds), *Human Geography. An Essential Anthology*, Oxford: Blackwell, pp. 650–74.

Harris, D.A. and Parisi, D. (2007), 'Adapting life history calendars for qualitative research on welfare transitions', *Field Methods,* **19** (1), 40–58.

King, R., Skeldon, R. and Vullnetari, J. (2008), 'Internal and international migration: Bridging the theoretical divide', Paper presented at Theories of Migration and Social Change, Oxford University, Oxford, 1–3 July.

Lucas, R.E.B. (2000a), 'Migration', in M. Grosh and P. Glewwe (eds), *Designing Household Survey Questionnaires for Developing Countries. Volume Two*, Washington, DC: The International Bank for Reconstruction and Development/The World Bank, pp. 49–81.

Lucas, R.E.B. (2000b), 'Migration (draft questionnaire modules)', in M. Grosh and P. Glewwe (eds), *Designing Household Survey Questionnaires for Developing Countries. Volume Three*, Washington, DC: The International Bank for Reconstruction and Development/The World Bank, pp. 333–48.

Mulder, C.H. (2007), 'The family context and residential choice: a challenge for new research', *Population, Space and Place,* **13** (4), 265–78.

Mulder, C.H. and van Ham, M. (2005), 'Migration histories and occupational achievement', *Population, Space and Place,* **11** (3), 173–86.

Reed, H.E., Andrzejewski, C.S. and White, M.J. (2010), 'Men's and women's migration in coastal Ghana: an event history analysis', *Demographic Research,* **22** (25), 771–812.

Reimer, M. and Matthes, B. (2007), 'Collecting event histories with TrueTales: techniques to improve autobiographical recall problems in standardized interviews', *Quality & Quantity,* **41** (5), 711–35.

Sayles, H., Belli, R.F. and Serrano, E. (2010), 'Interviewer variance between event history calendar and conventional questionnaire interviews', *Public Opinion Quarterly,* **74** (1), 140–53.

Smith, J. and Thomas, D. (2003), 'Remembrances of things past: test–retest reliability of retrospective migration histories', *Journal of the Royal Statistical Society: Series A,* **166** (1), 23–49.

Toney, M.B., Golesorkhi, B. and Stinner, W.F. (1985), 'Residence exposure and fertility expectations of young Mormon and non-Mormon women in Utah', *Journal of Marriage and Family,* **47** (2), 459–65.

Tufte, E.R. (1990), *Envisioning Information*, Chesire, CT: Graphics Press LLC.

Tufte, E.R. (2001), *The Visual Display of Quantitative Information*, Chesire, CT: Graphics Press LLC.

Van Hear, N. (1998), *New Diasporas. The Mass Exodus, Dispersal and Regrouping of Migrant Communities*, London: UCL Press.
Vanderschrick, C. (1992), 'Le diagramme de Lexis revisité', *Population*, **47** (5), 1241–62.
Wu, L.L. (2003), 'Event history models for life course analysis', in J.T. Mortimer and M.J. Shanahan (eds), *Handbook of the Life Course*, New York: Kluwer Academic Publishers, pp. 477–502.

8 Empirical methods in the economics of international immigration
Fernando A. Lozano and Michael D. Steinberger[*]

The United Nations reports that in 2010 more than 213 million people, or 5 percent of the world population, lived in a county in which they were not born. Not only is the stock of worldwide international immigrants significant in its own right, the net flow of immigrants has gradually increased over the last 20 years. During the decade of the 1990s, more than 23 million people moved to a different country; during the next decade this figure grew to 35 million people. As international migration increasingly prevails across different regions and countries it is natural to ask how do economists address the causes and consequences of these flows, and what are the strengths and shortcomings of the methodologies employed by economists?

The economics of immigration is a burgeoning field whose interest and research expands over many facets of immigration. The evolution of economists' interest on immigration is evidenced by the fact that general interest journals are increasingly publishing papers on this topic. Table 8.1 presents descriptive statistics about the recent research in nine top economic journals covering an immigration topic in the last 20 years. Among the issues economists address: (1) Why do people migrate to a different country, and who chooses to migrate? (2) What explains the labor market success of immigrants in the host country and their economic assimilation? (3) What is the effect of immigrants in the host economy, especially on the host country's most vulnerable populations? (4) What is the effect of emigration on the sending communities? (5) What are the public policy implications of migration? As Table 8.1 shows, research on immigration is becoming increasingly prevalent: growing from 23 papers on immigration between 1990–94 to 51 between 2005–09 in these nine top journals. In addition, while Ordinary Least Squares remains the most common econometric technique, more quantitatively sophisticated techniques like DiNardo et al.'s (1996) decomposition and other distributional techniques are becoming more popular. Finally, topics of interest for immigration economists are changing, possibly as a result of changing public perceptions of immigration; the most popular topic in 1990–94 was immigrant assimilation, yet in 2005–09

164   *Handbook of research methods in migration*

Table 8.1   Research in economics of immigration

	(1) 1990–94	(2) 1995–99	(3) 2000–04	(4) 2005–09
Number of papers	23	31	40	51
By Empirical Technique				
Ordinary Least Squares	11	14	11	20
MLE, Probit, Logit, Tobit	3	3	9	9
Difference-in-difference	3	1	2	0
Instrumental variables	2	4	12	8
Other	4	9	6	14
By Topic				
Assimilation	10	14	17	14
Immigrant selection	6	6	7	8
Natives outcomes	5	8	9	17
Other	2	3	7	12

Note: Papers on immigration in the following journals: *American Economic Review, Quarterly Journal of Economics, Journal of Political Economy, Review of Economic Studies, Economic Journal, Review of Economics and Statistics, Journal of Labor Economics, Journal of Human Resources, Industrial and Labor Relations Review.*

the most common topic was immigrants' effect on natives' labor market outcomes.

In this chapter, we explore four econometric methods commonly used by economists in the field of immigration.[1] We particularly highlight the strengths and potential pitfalls of each approach. We begin in the next section by exploring the various ways Ordinary Least Squares (OLS) regression techniques are used by immigration economists and comment on some of the inherent limitations of this approach. Building on that intellectual foundation, we turn our attention to other common econometric methods. In Section 8.2 we explore the use of difference-in-differences estimation on immigration. In Section 8.3 we address the use of instrumental variables techniques on immigration economics research, and the attempts to establish sound causal relationships between the outcomes highlighted above and immigration flows. In Section 8.4 we briefly explore two new econometric techniques we believe will become increasingly common in the future of empirical immigration economics, where interest will increasingly focus on distributional analysis of the influence of international immigration.

Empirical methods in the economics of international immigration 165

8.1 IDENTIFICATION STRATEGIES ON IMMIGRATION ECONOMICS

Economists are interested in analysing labor market or population outcomes across different counterfactual scenarios. For example, an economist may want to investigate whether the wages earned by natives in local labor markets are affected by a change in the number of immigrants. To properly analyse such a relationship, one needs to compare the outcome in the labor market with an exogenous shock in the number of immigrants, and the same labor market without the shock. Of course only one of these outcomes is observed, while the other remains unobserved. In order to correctly influence policy, and particularly immigration policy, it is important to identify any causal relationship between the outcome and the explanatory variables, and to understand the validity of any control group (explicit or implicit). This is true for other questions that economists are interested in exploring, for example: who chooses to migrate and the quality of immigrants, what explains the labor market success of immigrants in the host economy, or what determines immigrants' decision to invest or not in human capital?

8.1.1 Methodology to Study Immigrant Assimilation into the Host Economy

The first set of questions in the economics of immigration concerns how immigrants fare in the host economy, whether their labor market productivity or earnings differ from that of natives, and whether different cohorts of immigrants assimilate at different rates. For example, Chiswick (1978) and Borjas (1985, 1995) explore whether immigrant earnings assimilate to that of natives. Several empirical issues arise from estimating a model to answer this question. If the empirical model is:

$$\ln w_i = x_i' \theta + \gamma_1 I_i + \gamma_2 I_i \times Y_i + \gamma_3 I_i \times Y_i^2 + \varepsilon_i \qquad (8.1)$$

$\ln w$ is the natural log of earnings, I is an indicator variable whether the observation is an immigrant, and Y represents the observation's number of years in the source country. The vector x' includes different demographic characteristics. The parameters of interest are γ_1, γ_2 and γ_3, where γ_1 represents the earnings difference between native and immigrants and γ_2 and γ_3 represent how these earnings differences change as the immigrant's host country experience increases. Chiswick (1978) estimates an equation similar to (8.1) using the 1970 US Census with annual earnings (for self-employed and employed workers) as the response variable. He finds that $\gamma_2 > 0$ and $\gamma_3 < 0$ suggesting that as host country experience increases, immigrants' earnings increase at a decreasing rate. Importantly, these results imply that the earnings of immigrants overtake the earnings of demographically equivalent native workers in ten to fifteen years. This suggests that immigrants' rapid earnings acceleration is due to investments in host country human capital.

Although groundbreaking in the literature of immigration economics it does not account for out-migration and that different cohorts of immigrants may be of different quality in the labor market. Omitting these variables results in US experience-earnings profiles that are biased upward. Using the 1970 and 1980 Decennial Census, Borjas (1985) explores the nature of this bias by adjusting Equation (8.1) to include a variable for each immigrant cohort C_{it}. Borjas's empirical model is:

$$\ln w_{it} =$$

$$x_{it}'\theta + \gamma_1 I_{it} + \gamma_2 I_{it} \times Y_{it} + \gamma_3 I_{it} \times Y_{it}^2 + \delta_1 I_{it} \times C_{it} + \delta_2 I_{it} \times C_{it}^2 + \varepsilon_i \quad (8.2)$$

Note that if Equation (8.2) is estimated over a single cross-section for year T of data the vectors γ and δ are not identified because $T = C + Y$. Hence Equation (8.2) must be estimated over at least two-pooled cross-sections. In addition, the vector of characteristics x must include year controls as well as other demographic characteristics. The estimates from Equation (8.2) show that assimilation rates are much slower than those in Equation (8.1) (Borjas, 1985) and these results suggest that the years in host country profiles are confounded with the relative quality across different immigrant cohorts. Note that this approach has two important assumptions: the rate of immigrant assimilation is constant across different cohorts, and cohort labor market performance is independent from out-migration, death, or labor market separations from immigrants.

Figure 8.1 shows the predicted differences of log hourly wages between natives and immigrants. These estimates are constructed with and without controls for cohorts, representing Equations (8.2) and (8.1), respectively. The data is for all working males in the 1990 and 2000 US Census, and the 2006–07 American Community Survey. The vector of demographic characteristics x_{it}' includes age, age squared, and age cubed and includes indicator variables for education characteristics (all these variables are interacted with survey years). The dark line represents estimates from Equation (8.1) and the light lines represent estimates for three cohorts from equation (8.2). Figure 8.1 shows that Equation (8.1) predicts a much faster assimilation rate, yet as argued above, these estimates confound the years in the US effect with the cohort effect. Once controls for cohorts are

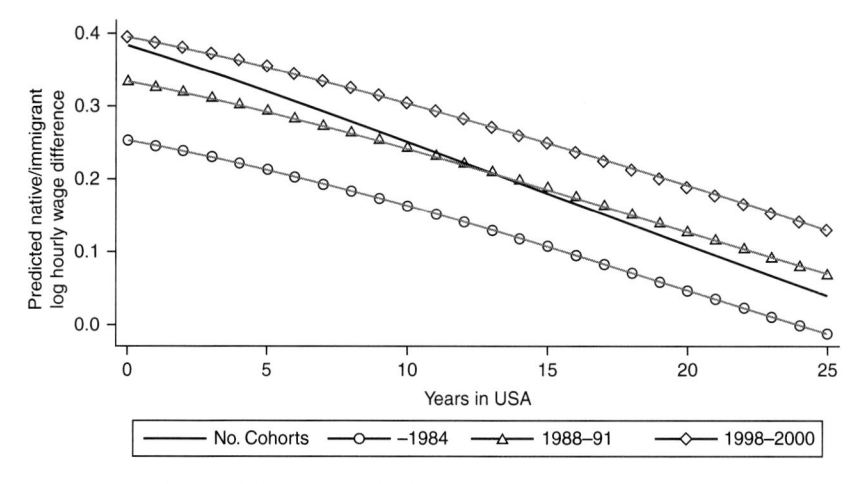

Figure 8.1 Native immigrant differences in predicted earnings: differences between estimates with and without cohorts controls

included, the assimilation rate is slower. Further, we see there are differences in the intercept for each cohort: differences are smallest with respect to earlier immigrants and greatest among the most recent ones.

There have been two recent significant developments in the assimilation literature. First, Antecol et al. (2006) extend the above methodology to estimate whether immigrants' earnings growth is due to returns to host country experience (wage assimilation) or whether they are due to employment assimilation. In particular, they use data from Australia, Canada, and the USA to determine what percentage of assimilation is due to changes in wages and what percentage is due to changes in employment. To do this they estimate Equation (8.2) using probability of employment as the dependent variable. Their results show that immigrant assimilation in Australia is mostly due to changes in the probability of employment, while immigrant assimilation in the USA is predominantly due to changes in earnings. Their results for immigrants in Canada are between those of immigrants to the USA and immigrants to Australia.

The second significant development in this literature is Lubotsky (2007) who uses administrative data to estimate immigrant assimilation in the USA. Lubotsky matches Social Security earnings records to the 1990 and 1991 Survey of Income and Program Participation and to the 1994 March Current Population Survey (CPS) Supplement to explore non-random out-migration of immigrants. His results show that out-migration (whether temporary or permanent) tends to be predominantly from low-earner immigrants, and therefore assimilation profiles using Decennial Census data which cannot control for out-migration tend to be overestimated. The result that temporary out-migration tends to be mostly by low-wage transient immigrants is similar to that of Lozano and Sorensen (2010) who show that assimilation estimates from the March CPS and the CPS Outgoing Rotations Groups (ORG) differ due to very recent immigrants being in the March CPS and not in the ORG.

8.1.2 Methodology to Study Immigrant Selection

A second issue that arises in the economics of immigration has to do with the fact that the decision of an immigrant to migrate or not is not random, and those immigrants who choose to migrate will have different observable and unobservable characteristics than potential immigrants who choose to stay in the source country. The concavity in the estimates of γ_2 and γ_3 in Equation (8.1) may suggest that immigrants' assimilation is a result of positive non-random immigrant selection. Consider first the selection of who chooses to migrate. It is clear that the selection of immigrants is non-random, as only the potential immigrants whose expected benefits from migration are greater than the expected costs from migration choose to migrate. Appropriately accounting for the selection of immigrants is still an ongoing issue for economists.

There are two ways to think about immigrant selection: one studies the quality of immigrants compared to the population of all potential immigrants (including those who do not wish to migrate) in the source country, the second compares immigrant characteristics across different source countries. This issue is widely examined by Borjas (1987), Cobb-Clark (1993), Antecol (2000), Blau et al. (2008), or Lozano and Lopez (forthcoming).[2] While the methodology differs across different papers, there is an underlying feature: including source country characteristics to account for immigrant's labor market success. The basic methodology, following Borjas (1987), includes two stages; the first stage estimates a measure of success of the immigrant across two different cross-sections, for example, Equation (8.2), and the second stage consists of recovering the cohort parameters $\hat{\delta}_{1,c}$ and $\hat{\delta}_{2,c}$ for immigrants from country c and uses them as a dependent variable regressed on different country characteristics:

$$(\hat{\delta}_{1,c} + \hat{\delta}_{2,c}) = w'_c \phi + \eta_c \tag{8.3}$$

where the parameter ϕ represents the correlation between the outcome of immigrants from country c and the characteristics of the country.

Cobb-Clark (1993) analyses women's immigrant characteristics using the host country's gross domestic product, income inequality, country's return to education, distance between country and the USA, among other characteristics.[3] The results in this literature show that immigrants from countries with high income inequality or high returns to education tend to have less desirable observable skills than immigrants from other countries.

One promising avenue for research relies on Chiswick's (1986) research that explores how the immigrant characteristics differ across different source countries. Chiswick compares the earnings of immigrants with the earnings of native-born workers who are of the same ethnicity as the immigrant. This is similar to Trejo (2003) who compares the outcomes of Mexican-American immigrants in the USA across different generations. Trejo expands Equation (8.2) into a fully interacted model that includes interactions between first- (foreign-born), second- (children of foreign-born), and third-generation immigrants and the other characteristics.

Finally, it is important to recognize that these results do not occur in a policy-less world. Indeed, economists are quite aware that different immigration policies may lead to different immigrant selection. This issue has been addressed by Miller (1999) or Antecol et al. (2003) among others. For example, Antecol et al. (2003) compare the selection of immigrants into the USA, Canada, and Australia by estimating a version of Equation (8.2) for immigrants in each country using education and earnings as the response variable. Their results suggest that after excluding Latin American immigrants, selection is not that different across these three countries, indicating that policy plays a small role in the selection of immigrants and that selection is predominantly driven by cultural and historical factors.

One final note must be made in the literature that explores the assimilation of immigrants; it is important to recognize that the analysis of outcomes of women differs to the analysis of outcomes of men. Noting the importance of separating outcomes between women and men, Blau et al. (2008) study the labor supply assimilation of immigrant women in the USA, and Antecol (2000) explores how labor market performance of immigrant women is determined by source country characteristics. Similarly, Lozano and Lopez (fothcoming) note that border enforcement policy in the USA generates a different selection of undocumented immigrant women than men.

8.1.3 Estimating the Effects of Immigration in Local Labor Markets

Next we explore what happens to the earnings of natives (and their welfare in general) when immigrants arrive into the local labor market. While some theoretical models argue that an increase in the supply of workers

170 *Handbook of research methods in migration*

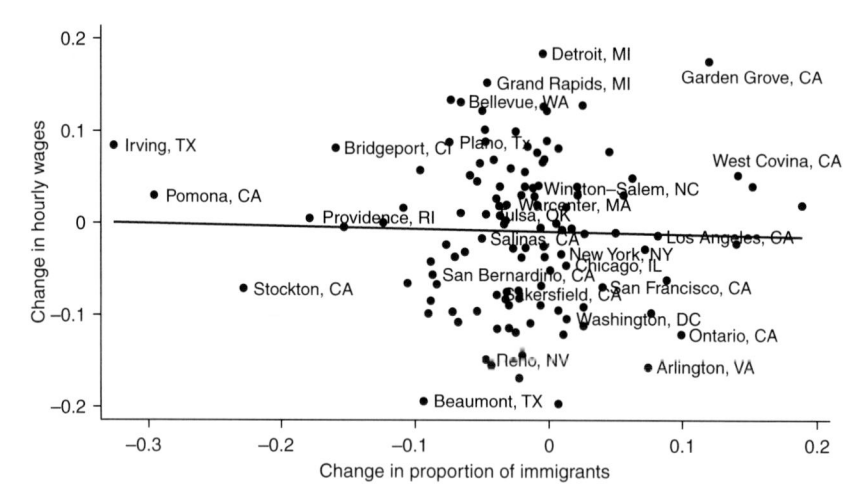

[Scatter plot with x-axis "Change in proportion of immigrants" ranging from −0.3 to 0.2, and y-axis "Change in hourly wages" ranging from −0.2 to 0.2. Labeled cities include: Detroit, MI; Grand Rapids, MI; Bellevue, WA; Garden Grove, CA; Irving, TX; Bridgeport, CT; Plano, TX; West Covina, CA; Pomona, CA; Winston-Salem, NC; Worcester, MA; Tulsa, OK; Providence, RI; Salinas, CA; Los Angeles, CA; New York, NY; Chicago, IL; San Bernardino, CA; Stockton, CA; Bakersfield, CA; San Francisco, CA; Washington, DC; Ontario, CA; Reno, NV; Arlington, VA; Beaumont, TX.]

Note: Sample is all workers in cities with at least 49 observations both years in the US Census and the 2006–07 American Community Survey.

Figure 8.2 Immigrants and earnings of native workers, 2000–07

will decrease wages because the demand for labor is downward sloping (Borjas, 2003), the empirical evidence is mixed. OLS models in this vein of the literature use cross-sections of data to evaluate whether local labor markets that receive a higher number of immigrants have depressed wages for native-born workers. There are two problems with this straightforward approach: first, mobility of native workers implies native workers will move out of areas with lower wages, hence muting the estimated effect. The second potential problem is that immigrants will self-select into labor markets where the demand for their skills is highest. Immigrant self-selection into these labor markets will result in a downward bias of the true effect of immigrants on natives' earnings.

A first generation of papers (see Goldin, 1994 or LaLonde and Topel, 1991) uses two cross-sections to look at changes in earnings of natives as a result of changes in the proportion of foreign-born workers. This methodology assumes that the idiosyncratic characteristics which may attract immigrants to each labor market are time invariant. Yet this approach cannot correct for any bias due to outflows in a local market when immigrants arrive. Figure 8.2 shows the change in the flow of immigrants in American cities between 2000 and 2007, and the change in natives' log hourly earnings during the same period. The association between these two variables is statistically almost zero, which suggests the fact that immigrants may self-select into markets where their earnings are higher.

To address this potential endogeneity problem economists have proposed using instrumental variable methods, which will be discussed in Section 8.3 below.

8.2 DIFFERENCE-IN-DIFFERENCE ESTIMATION

Having explored the three broad themes in the economic literature on international immigration in our overview of OLS methods, we now turn our attention specifically to other empirical tools used by economists that are perhaps lesser known in other disciplines' study of immigration. After OLS regression, one of the more popular econometric tools in the economics literature on immigration is the difference-in-difference (DD) estimator. In fact, the DD estimator itself can be obtained through OLS methods, as will be discussed below.[4]

The DD strategy is not completely unique to the field of economics, for instance, in psychology the technique is called 'non-equivalent control-group pretest-posttest design' (Campbell, 1969). The popularity of the DD technique stems from its intuitive simplicity and the fact that it can be employed using data from either panel data or from repeated cross-sections.

Following the logic of a randomized experimental design, the DD technique attempts to determine the effect of an intervention by comparing pre- and post-intervention group averages of a treatment group with a control group. However, unlike a true randomized experiment, the DD estimator must rely on an external shock that affects the treatment group and choose an appropriate control group not affected by the external shock. Because the DD estimator lacks true random assignment of observations into the treatment and control groups, it is referred to as a 'quasi-experimental' or 'natural experiment' design.[5]

To explore the DD strategy, we use the Mariel Boatlift example from Card (1990). If we are interested in the effect on natives' unemployment of an influx of immigrants, economists are seldom able to adjust immigration policy by region in randomized experiments. Instead, we must rely on real-world policy changes that provide discrete changes in immigration policy. One potential example began on 20 April 1980 when the Cuban government allowed Cuban citizens who wanted to emigrate to leave out of the port of Mariel, Cuba. Over the next six months roughly 125,000 Cubans entered the USA through Florida. Of the immigrants, nearly half settled permanently in Miami, raising the labor force there by 7 percent (Card, 1990).

To explore the effect of this large influx of immigrants on the unemployment rate of natives, we might first begin by comparing the unemployment rates in Miami before and after the Mariel Boatlift:

$$(U_{M,1981} - U_{M,1979}) \qquad (8.4)$$

where U stands for the unemployment rate, the first subscript denotes the city (that is, Miami), and the second subscript denotes the year. Before we ascribe the entire change in unemployment to the influx of immigrants associated with the Mariel Boatlift, we must consider if there were other factors that might have affected the unemployment rate in Miami during this time. Certainly there were, as the USA was then in the midst of a recession.

To adjust for other factors that would have led to a change in unemployment in Miami, Card derives the change in unemployment in four comparison cities, Atlanta, Los Angeles, Houston, and Tampa-St Petersburg,

$$(U_{M,1981} - U_{M,1979}) - (U_{C,1981} - U_{C,1979}) \qquad (8.5)$$

By taking the difference between the Miami difference and the difference in the control cities (C), the difference in differences, the DD estimator seeks to determine the effect on unemployment of the influx of immigrants in Miami, exclusive of other changes happening over time. Figure 8.3 shows the effect that the Mariel Boatlift may have had on Miami's labor market. This figure shows the employment rate of black males from January 1978 to December 1984, and Miami is represented with the squared markers. The data in the graph suggests that employment of black males in Miami fell compared to employment of black males in the control cities, and these differences only rose after the Mariel Boatlift.

This conceptual idea can be expressed in an OLS framework as:

$$lnw_{it} = \beta_0 + \beta_1 T + \beta_2 M + \beta_3 (M*T) + \varepsilon_{it} \qquad (8.6)$$

where T represents the year term(s) for the period after the intervention, in this case 1981, M again represents Miami, and $(M*T)$ represents the interaction of the period after the intervention in Miami.

If we want to control for changes in the underlying distribution of characteristics between control and treatment cities over time, we can add a vector of observable characteristics, x_{it}, to the regression:[6]

$$lnw_{it} = \beta_0 + \beta_1 T + \beta_2 M + \beta_3 (M*T) + x'_{it}\beta_4 + \varepsilon_{it} \qquad (8.7)$$

The critical assumption of the DD estimator is that conditional on the controlled characteristics, the unemployment rates for Miami and the

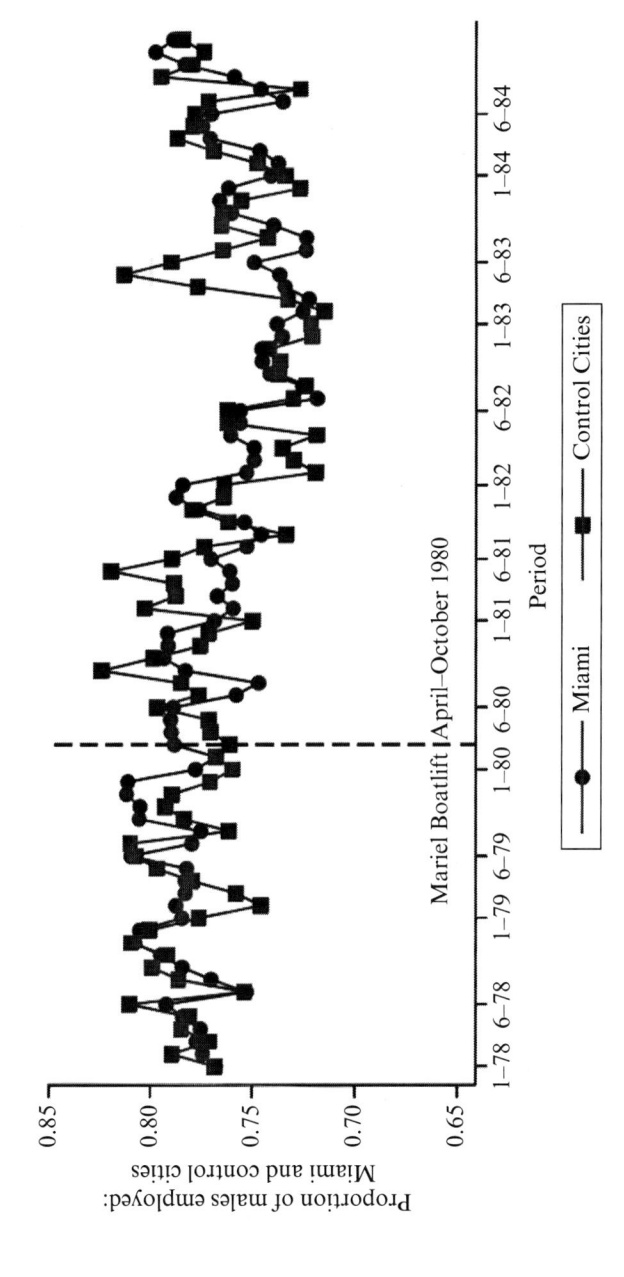

Note: Authors' calculations from the CPS monthly data. The sample includes all males 25–64 in the January 1978–December 1984 surveys. Excludes all observations of Cuban origin. Control cities are Atlanta, Houston, Los Angeles, and Tampa Bay.

Figure 8.3 The Mariel Boatlift

control cities would have followed parallel paths over time. Therefore studies that use DD estimators must explore the trends in the outcome variable of interest between the treatment and control groups before the treatment date to provide evidence that the chosen control group is appropriate. This is done by exploring the time series data before the treatment date to ensure that conditional on the other characteristics, the outcome variable of interest changes equally in the treatment and control groups over time.

The choice of an appropriate control group is of critical importance to immigration research utilizing the DD strategy. To ensure a proper control group, a researcher using the DD estimation strategy must be careful that the 'exogenous' treatment shock was not precipitated or caused by unique changes in the treatment group that were not mirrored in the control group (Ashenfelter and Card, 1985). For instance, if a majority of Mariel immigrants choose to relocate to Miami because of uncharacteristically low unemployment rates in 1979 relative to the other control cities, the DD estimator would be biased.

A second major consideration in DD estimators is correct estimation of the standard errors for the interaction term. Bertrand et al. (2004) show consistent estimation of the standard errors for the OLS regression (7) must correct for serial-correlation of the outcome variables over time for the treatment and control groups. They show that failure to properly account for serial-correlation can result in 45 percent of pseudo interventions being statistically significant at the 5 percent level. Incorrectly estimated standard errors will lead to misinterpretation of the statistical significance of results and incorrect inference of the immigration topic in question.

Angrist and Krueger (1999) provide an example of the problem of incorrectly matched control groups and improperly measured standard errors in a follow-up study to Card's Mariel Boatlift example. They track the changes in the unemployment rate in Miami and the four same control cities from 1993 to 1995. In 1994 a large group of potential Cuban immigrants were redirected from their intended destination of Miami to the US military base at Guantanamo Bay, Cuba. Since the immigrants did not arrive in Miami, they should not have affected the labor market conditions there. However, Angrist and Krueger show that if researchers would have naively utilized a DD strategy on the 1993–95 unemployment rates in the same five cities, they would have incorrectly found a statistically significant increase in the unemployment rate for blacks in Miami as a result of 'The Mariel Boatlift that Did not Happen.' This example serves as a warning to researchers of the importance of choosing the correct control cities and appropriately adjusting standard errors to adequately account for serial-correlation in the observations.

The DD model is a powerful tool for immigration economist researchers. The conventional DD estimator presented above can be expanded to include multiple time periods and control groups or combinations of control groups (synthetic control groups) (see Abadie et al., 2007). The strategy can also be generalized to include semi-parametric approaches (see Abadie, 2005; Athey and Imbens, 2006). While DD strategies are not true randomized experiments, and are hence subject to the weaknesses inherent in natural experiments (Meyer, 1995), they still represent a significant contribution for empirical immigration research.

8.3 INSTRUMENTAL VARIABLES TECHNIQUES

A second technique used by economists to simulate the causal interpretations possible with randomized experiments is instrumental variables (IV) regression. In several areas of international immigration research, it is unlikely that standard regressions will give correct estimates of the causal effect of an explanatory variable on the response variable because the assumptions of OLS regressions cannot be met. Using IV regression techniques, economists attempt to overcome the bias in OLS estimates by isolating a source of exogenous variation in order to estimate an explanatory variable's true effect on the dependent variable of interest. The IV technique utilizes a third variable called the instrument which is correlated with variation in the explanatory variable, but has no direct mechanism (except through the explanatory variable) to affect the response variable. While IV regressions are quite powerful and allow economists to address a much wider array of questions regarding immigration, difficulties in finding suitable instruments that can satisfy the significant restrictions of IV often limit application of this econometric tool.

Turning back to the question of the effect that immigrants have on the wages of natives, we use another article by Card (2001) to explain IV regression methods. We are interested in the effect that an increase in the share of immigrants in an area has on the wages of natives in that area. Economic theory predicts that an increase in the number of new immigrants in a local labor market will tend to depress wages if immigrants and natives compete for the same jobs, but can raise the wages of natives if immigrants take jobs that help make natives more productive.[7] So which is true, does international immigration lower or raise the wages of natives?

To explore this question, we might first attempt an OLS regression that looks at changes in average wages in areas of the country that have seen a large increase in new immigrants. We can model this as:

176   *Handbook of research methods in migration*

$$\ln \bar{w}_{jc} = x'_{jc}\theta + \alpha_{OLS}s_{jc} + \varepsilon_{jc} \tag{8.8}$$

where $\bar{w}_{jc}$ is the average wage in occupation j and city c, s_{jc} is the log population share of new immigrants in the city working in the occupation, x_{jc} is a vector of explanatory characteristics, and ε_{jc} is an error term with the usual properties. The estimated coefficient $\hat{\alpha}_1$ would be an estimate of the effect of an increase in the log share of immigrants on averages wages in occupations in the cities.

While OLS analysis would be straightforward in this case, it is unlikely to give unbiased estimates of the true parameter α. New immigrants likely do not randomly move to cities, nor do they randomly choose occupations once they arrive there. Instead, recent shocks that cause high wages in a particular city or occupation will likely induce new immigrants to take jobs in that area. This omitted variable, recent demand shocks, leads to bias in the standard regression estimates because it violates a necessary assumption of OLS, namely, that $E(\varepsilon|s) = 0$; all things equal, we would expect areas with positive wage shocks to pull a larger fraction of new immigrants.

Card uses an IV strategy to address the problem. In order to approximate the random experiment of adding more new immigrants to a particular area, he suggests as an instrument a variable that likely influences the share of new immigrants in an area, but has no direct effect on current local demand shocks to wages. Noting that new immigrants often tend to migrate to ethnic enclaves established by previous immigrants, Card suggests using the fraction of earlier immigrants from the same source country to an occupation in a given city as an instrument for new immigrants.

To employ the IV regression to eliminate the omitted variable bias, Card first creates an estimate for the share of new immigrants expected in each local area based only on the experience of previous immigrants:

$$s_{jc} = \eta_1 z_{jc} + \varepsilon_{jc} \tag{8.9}$$

In this first stage, the distribution of previous immigrants across occupations and cities, z_{jc}, is used to predict how current immigrants would distribute across the same occupations and cities. While the decisions of previous immigrants were likely based upon previous demand shocks to wages, it is unlikely that those decisions are correlated with current demand shocks. Therefore a prediction of how current immigrants will distribute across areas based only on the decisions of past immigrants will be free of the bias from the omitted variable (current demand shocks).

In the second stage of the IV process, Card takes the estimated values for the log share of immigrants, and uses those values instead of the actual values to estimate:

$$\ln \overline{w}_{jc} = x'_{jc}\theta + \alpha_{IV}\hat{s}_{jc} + \varepsilon_{jc} \qquad (8.10)$$

where $\hat{s}_{jc}$ is the log share of new immigrants in occupation j and city c predicted using OLS estimates from Equation (8.9). The difference between the actual log share of new immigrant, s_{jc}, and the predicted share, $\hat{s}_{jc}$, is that the actual share reflects decisions new immigrants made in response to recent local demand shocks, whereas the predicted share excludes any influence from this effect. Hence OLS regressions of Equation (8.10) using predicted values will not have the same omitted variable bias as the standard OLS regression on actual values (Equation 8.8). Using this IV approach, Card finds that immigration by new immigrants decreased wages and employment rates of natives in traditionally high immigrant cities by 1–3 percent.

Utilizing IV regression techniques places high requirements on the proposed instrument. If the instrument is not highly correlated with the explanatory variable, IV estimates will be unreliable. To avoid this 'Weak Instruments' problem usually requires a high t-statistics for proposed instrument(s) in the first stage regression which predicts the values for the endogenous explanatory variable (that is, Equation 8.8) (Staiger and Stock, 1997). A second consideration in IV regressions is called the Local Average Treatment Effect (LATE). For an instrument to be useful in estimating the true effect of the explanatory variable on the response variable, the subpopulation affected by the instrument cannot be dramatically dissimilar from the entire population; or else the IV estimate will not be true of the entire population, but only provide an estimate for the sub-, or 'local,' population. For instance, if new immigrants who settle in areas based on ethnic networks are radically different than all other immigrants, the Card estimate will not provide the true effect for an increase in the share of all new immigrants, but will instead only provide a LATE estimate for the effect of an increase in the subpopulation of immigrants affected by the instrument (Imbens and Angrist, 1994). Finally, IV regressions require relatively large samples for the estimates to be unbiased and hence are not appropriate for smaller data sets.

IV regressions allow estimation of the relationship between an explanatory variable and a response variable even when unobserved factors prohibit using standard OLS regression techniques. Given the power of IV techniques, there has been a number of econometric innovations which will likely become increasingly common in economic analysis of international immigration research. Limited Information Maximum

Likelihood (LIML) and Control Function techniques are alternative methods for dealing with endogenous explanatory variables which are closely related to IV methods. LIML analysis tends to perform better in situations with multiple instruments, and Control Function techniques tend to be more precise, while less robust, than IV methods (Wooldridge, 2002). While finding appropriate instruments remains difficult, the power of IV and related methods means they will continue to be a popular tool in the economics of international immigration research.

8.4 RECENT DEVELOPMENTS IN RESEARCH METHODS

Given the increasing levels of international migration in the past two decades, we predict that economic research of immigration will only continue to grow. While future analysis will continue to use OLS, DD, and IV methods, the literature is beginning to incorporate new econometric methods into the field. These new methods expand the research focus onto distributional analysis of the influence of international immigration.

The methods presented in the first sections of this chapter have focused on analyses of the mean. Researchers have assessed questions such as the average rate of wage assimilation of immigrants, or the average effect of immigrants on local labor markets. But are rates of wage assimilation different for low-wage and high-wage immigrants? Do immigrants have the same influence across the distribution of wages in the local labor market as they do on the average wage? To answer these research questions, economists have begun to use new econometric tools which shift the focus away from mean differences and instead focus on differences across the entire distribution. Most prominent among these new methods are quantile regressions (Koenker and Hallock, 2001) and DiNardo et al. (1996) reweighting analyses. These new methods represent a substantive addition to the economics of immigration literature, and we believe they will become increasingly common in the field as researchers seek to explore differences in the relationship between immigrants and labor market outcomes at various points along the distribution of earnings.

8.4.1 Quantile Regression

Since Chiswick's seminal work in 1978, economic research on immigration has focused on analysis at the mean of the distribution. Quantile regression is very similar to OLS regression methods in concept, but instead of focusing on associations at the mean, quantile regression presents

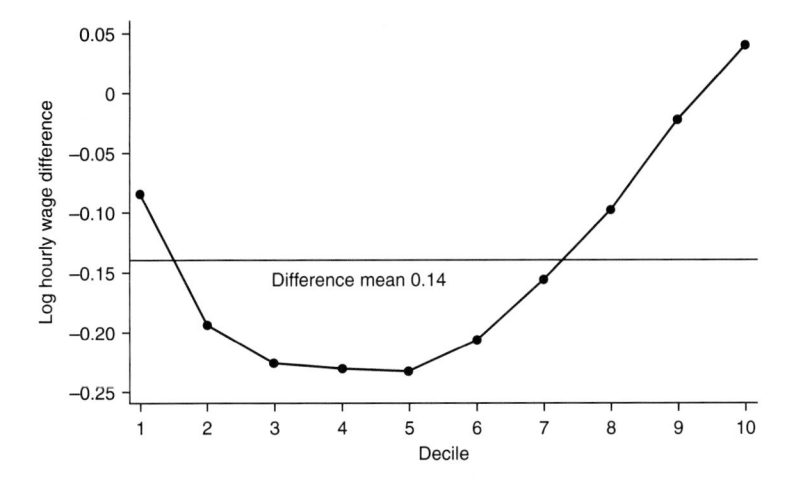

Figure 8.4 Immigrant–native log hourly wage differences

Note: Authors' calculation of male workers in the 2000 US Census.

associations at a specified quantile of the conditional dependent variable. Quantile regressions are essential when the relationship between the explanatory and response variables is not constant across the distribution.

To see the importance of quantile analysis we present the male native–immigrant wage gap from the 2000 US Census at each decile of wages in Figure 8.4. The figure is constructed by taking the difference between the given decile of log wage in the immigrant distribution minus the same decile of log wage in the native distribution. Whereas the average immigrant wage gap is –0.14, the wage gap actually goes from a low of –0.23 at the median to 0.04 in the 9th decile of wages. With such a large difference in the immigrant wage gap along the distribution, it is natural to ask if a given characteristic affects immigrants equally at all points in the wage distribution. For instance, we might wish to know if the change in the median wage for an extra year of education is the same as the change in the average wage for another year of schooling.

Referring back to Equation (8.1), which relates the wage of immigrants on a variety of variables, we remember that OLS regression coefficients denote the change in the response variable (wage) for a one unit change in the explanatory variable (for instance, years of education). Quantile regression is intuitively very similar to the standard OLS regression, but instead of estimating the conditional mean of the response variable, quantile regressions estimate the conditional specified quantile of the response variable.

In this section we follow Chiswick et al. (2008), who define $Q_\theta(w|x)$ as the θth quantile of the conditional log wage distribution given the vector of characteristics x ($0 < \theta < 1$). Quantile regression seeks to estimate a vector of coefficients $\beta(\theta)$ such that

$$Q_\theta(w|x) = x'\beta(\theta) \qquad (8.11)$$

Quantile regression estimates $\beta(\theta)$ by minimizing the weighted sum of the absolute value of the errors between the estimated conditional quantile function and the true log wage value. See Koenker and Hallock (2001) for more on estimation of quantile regression functions.

For example, the coefficient from a 0.5 quantile regression can be used to estimate the change in the median of the conditional wage distribution for immigrants for a one unit change in the education variable. Conceptually, the OLS coefficient is estimated by fitting a best fit line through the conditional means of log wage at each year of education. Similarly, a 0.5 (θ) quantile regression coefficient is estimated by fitting a best fit line through the conditional medians (or other quantiles) of log wage at each year of education. If the conditional medians increase at the same slope as the conditional means, the estimated coefficients of the quantile regression and the OLS regression will be the same. If the conditional medians rise at a different slope, the coefficients will not be the same, and quantile analysis has informed us of a potentially interesting deviance in the distributional analysis of our variable of interest.

In addition to addressing the problem of outliers, the real power of quantile regression for immigration researchers is that it allows analysis of multiple points along the wage distribution. Researchers can evaluate the relationship between the dependent variable and independent variables across the distribution of the dependent variable. An example from Chiswick et al. (2008) illustrates the usefulness of quantile analysis for researchers. They compare the quantile regression coefficient estimates for each decile with the OLS coefficients in assessing how immigrants compare to natives across the distribution of earning. They use the 2000 US Census to compare the log hourly wages of adult men. They find that while immigrants from non-English-speaking countries earn less than natives on average, using quantile analysis and controlling for differences in observable characteristics, immigrants from non-English-speaking countries in the bottom decile actually have a wage advantage relative to their native counterparts.[8]

Quantile regression analysis can be used to look at the same research questions as OLS analysis, and informs a more nuanced understanding of the relationship between the variables of interest. The OLS results are certainly a useful benchmark for understanding the relationship between the dependent and independent variables of interest. By further comparing the OLS conditional mean function results with the 0.1, 0.5 (median), and 0.9 conditional quantile function results, researchers can evaluate if the relationship is constant over the distribution of the response variable. Further, unlike OLS regression focused on the mean, quantile regressions are also robust to outlier log wage values.

8.4.2 Dinardo, Fortin, Lemieux (1996) Reweighting Analysis

A second recent econometric method that allows researchers to shift their focus beyond the mean and on other moments of the distribution is the DiNardo, Fortin, Lemieux (1996) (henceforth DFL) reweighting technique. Like quantile regression analysis, the DFL reweighting method allows researchers to explore the relationship of the explanatory and response variables at multiple points along the distribution. Using DFL reweighting methods, economists researching immigration can answer such questions as 'How has the widening of the distribution of wages in the USA and changes in source country of birth of recent immigrants affected the immigrant wage gap at median wages?' (Butcher and DiNardo, 2002), or 'If Mexican immigrants in the USA were paid according to the going rates they would receive in Mexico, where would they be in the distribution of Mexican wages?' (Chiquiar and Hanson, 2002). Analysis using DFL methods allows researchers to explore in greater detail the selection of immigrants across the distribution of skills in the source country, compare immigrant assimilation at wages above and below the median, and gain greater specificity on the effect of immigration on local labor markets.

The power of the DFL technique comes not only from its usefulness in distributional analysis, but also because it is semi-parametric and imposes fewer restrictive assumptions than the other methods discussed in this chapter. OLS, DD, IV, and quantile regression analyses all impose a polynomial functional form on the equation of interest. That is, they must estimate a linear relationship between an explanatory variable (including characteristics raised to a power) and the response variable. The DFL reweighting technique is advantageous over these methods because it does not need to estimate a functional form for the equation of interest. This allows the researchers to avoid biases if the explanatory and response variables of interest do not have a linear relationship. The DFL technique functions by reweighting one sample so that it has the same distribution of observable characteristics as a second sample. This is a powerful tool if a researcher wants to analyse how much of the differences between groups can be explained by differences in other observable characteristics.

The DFL method allows Butcher and DiNardo (2002) to explore the increase in the immigrant/native-born wage gap since 1970 without estimating a wage function. In 1970, 22 percent of immigrant men to the USA were Hispanic. By 1990, this number had risen to 45 percent. So, compared to 1970, male Hispanic immigrants were relatively more common in 1990, and immigrant men from other areas were relatively less common. To explore how much of the increase in the immigrant–native wage gap from 1970 to 1990 might be attributable to differences in the racial and ethnic composition of immigrants, the DFL technique would decrease the relative proportion of Hispanic immigrants in 1990, and increase the relative proportion of all other immigrants in that year. Specifically, the DFL technique would multiply the sample weight of each 1990 Hispanic immigrant male by 0.49 ($\approx$22/45) and would multiply the sample weight of each non-Hispanic immigrant male by 1.42 ($\approx$78/55). The resulting 'reweighted' sample of 1990 immigrant men would thus contain 22 percent Hispanic men and 78 percent men of other ethnicities. The wage distribution of this reweighted 1990 sample would be different than the actual 1990 sample. The difference between the reweighted 1990 sample and the actual 1990 sample is completely due to changes in the distribution of immigrant ethnicity over the period. If the only reason for the change in the immigrant/native-born wage gap was because of the change in the ethnicity of immigrants between the two periods, then the reweighted 1990 sample would be identical to the 1970 wage distribution. While Butcher and DiNardo (2002) find a large role for race and ethnicity changes, these variables do not explain all changes in the distribution of wages over the period.

This example is useful to highlight several advantages of the semiparametric aspect of the DFL reweighting approach. While previous research has focused on mean comparisons, the reweighted 1990 sample can be used to explore the effect of the change in ethnic composition of immigrants on the entire distribution of wages, including the median and each percentile of the distribution. Further, the analysis does not force the researcher to estimate the exact functional form of the relationship between ethnicity and wages in either period. Because the procedure only changes the sample weight of each observation, there is no need to estimate a wage function; each observation keeps their actual wage. The change in the wage structure comes from the change in the relative frequency of observations with particular characteristics, but it is not necessary to estimate the exact relationship between characteristics and the dependent variable of interest. This can be particularly useful when the researcher does not want to impose restrictions on the functional form of the relationship between the independent and dependent variables of interest. For a more detailed explanation of the DFL decomposition see DiNardo et al. (1996).

8.5 CONCLUSIONS

In this chapter we have highlighted the main empirical tools used by economists when studying international immigration. In particular we highlight four common methodologies that have made important headway in the literature. The fact that economists rely on large data sets and on identifying causal relationships gives us a unique perspective to contribute in the current immigration debate. Because of the relevance of population flows in the foreseeable future we argue that the field will continue to grow in the years to follow. Non-economists should take advantage of recent econometric developments to contribute to the current immigration debate.

NOTES

* We are grateful to Edward Funkhouser and Carlos Vargas-Silva for useful comments and Maria Zhu for providing excellent research assistance. All errors are our own.
1. While this chapter focuses on the economics of immigration, we do not explore the consequences of immigration on source countries or sender households. For a discussion in this topic see Funkhouser (Chapter 9, this volume).
2. A third way to think of immigrant selection compares immigrants with non-immigrants from the same country as in Chiquiar and Hanson (2002). The econometric methods used in their analysis are detailed in Subsection 8.4.2.
3. Unlike Borjas (1987), Cobb-Clark (1993) uses only one stage where the explanatory variables are both person-specific (education, age, family structure) and country characteristics.
4. See Funkhouser (Chapter 9, this volume) for further discussion.
5. See McKenzie and Yang (Chapter 12, this volume) for further discussion of experimental studies.
6. Meyer (1995) notes that if the treatment has an asymmetric effect on differential groups in the population, the OLS design may need to account for this by including an interaction term which interacts each included characteristic with the treatment effect.
7. One way immigrants may raise the wages of natives suggested in Peri and Sparber (2009) is that immigrants may take jobs that require a high degree of manual skills, like construction workers, which will increase the need for jobs with more management and complex skills, like construction supervisors.
8. To be precise, Chiswick et al. (2008) use a technique called quantile decomposition to obtain their results. Quantile decomposition, as introduced in Mata and Machado (2005), uses hundreds of vectors of quantile regression coefficient estimates to obtain a synthetic distribution of wages if the immigrant population was paid according to the same conditional wage functions as natives.

REFERENCES

Abadie, A. (2005), 'Semiparametric difference-in-difference estimators', *Review of Economic Studies*, **72** (1), 1–19.

Abadie, A., Diamond, A. and Hainmueller, J. (2007), 'Synthetic control methods for comparative case studies: estimating the effect of California's Tobacco Contol Program', NBER Working Papers 12831, National Bureau of Economic Research.
Athey, S. and Imbens, G. (2006), 'Identification and inference in nonlinear difference-in-differences models', *Econometrica*, **74** (2), March, 431–97.
Angrist, J.D. and Krueger, A.B. (1999), 'Empirical strategies in labor economics', *Handbook of Labor Economics*, **3** (1), 1277–366.
Antecol, H. (2000), 'An examination of cross-country differences in the gender gap in labor force participation rates', *Labour Economics*, **4** (4), July, 409–26.
Antecol, H., Cobb-Clark, D.A. and Trejo, S.J. (2003), 'Immigration policy and the skills of immigrants to Australia, Canada, and the United States', *Journal of Human Resources*, **38** (1), Winter, 192–218.
Antecol, H., Kuhn, P. and Trejo, S.J. (2006), 'Assimilation via prices or quantities? Sources of immigrant earnings growth in Australia, Canada, and the United States', *Journal of Human Resources*, **41** (4), Fall, 821–40.
Ashenfelter, O. and Card, D. (1985), 'Using the longitudinal structure of earnings to estimate the effect of training programs', *Review of Economics and Statistics*, **67** (4), November, 648–60.
Bertrand, M., Duflo, E. and Mullainathan, S. (2004), 'How much should we trust differences-in-differences estimates?', *Quarterly Journal of Economics*, **119** (1), February, 249–75.
Blau, F., Kahn, L.M. and Papps, K.L. (2008), 'Gender, source country characteristics and labor market assimilation among immigrants: 1980–2000', IZA Discussion Paper No. 3725, September.
Borjas, G.J. (1985), 'Assimilation, changes in cohort quality, and the earnings of immigrants', *Journal of Labor Economics*, **3** (4), October, 463–89.
Borjas, G.J. (1987), 'Self-selection and the earnings of immigrants', *American Economic Review*, **77** (4), September, 531–53.
Borjas, G.J. (1995), 'Assimilation and changes in Cohort quality revisited: what happened to immigrant earnings in the 1980s?', *Journal of Labor Economics*, **13** (2), April, 201–45.
Borjas, G.J. (2003), 'The labor demand curve is downward sloping: reexamining the impact of immigration on the labor market', *Quarterly Journal of Economics*, **118** (4), November, 1335–47.
Butcher, K.F. and DiNardo, J. (2002), 'The immigrant and native-born wage distributions: evidence from United States censuses', *Industrial and Labor Relations Review*, **56** (1), October, 97–121.
Campbell, D.T. (1969), 'Reforms as experiments', *American Psychologist*, **24**, 409–29.
Card, D. (1990), 'The impact of the mariel boatlift on the Miami labor market', *Industrial and Labor Relations Review*, **43** (2), January, 245–57.
Card, D. (2001), 'Immigrant inflows, native outflows and the local labor market impacts of higher immigration', *Journal of Labor Economics*, **19** (1), January, 22–64.
Chiquiar, D. and Hanson, G.H. (2002), 'International migration, self-selection, and the distribution of wages: evidence from Mexico and the United States', *Journal of Political Economy*, **113** (2), April, 239–81.
Chiswick, B.R. (1978), 'The effect of Americanization on the earnings of foreign-born men', *Journal of Political Economy*, **86** (5), October, 897–921.
Chiswick, B.R. (1986), 'Is the new immigration less skilled than the old?', *Journal of Labor Economics*, **4** (2), April, 168–92.
Chiswick, B.R., Le, A.T. and Miller, P.W. (2008), 'How immigrants fare across the earnings distribution in Australia and the United States', *Industrial and Labor Relations Review*, **61** (3), April, 353–73.
Cobb-Clark, D.A. (1993), 'Immigrant selectivity and wages: the evidence for women', *American Economic Review*, **83** (4), September, 986–93.
DiNardo, J., Fortin, N.M. and Lemieux, T. (1996), 'Labor market institutions and the distribution of wages, 1973–1992: a semiparametric approach', *Econometrica*, **64** (5), September, 1001–44.

Goldin, C. (1994), 'The political economy of immigration restriction in the United States, 1890–1921', in C. Goldin and G. Libecap (eds), *The Regulated Economy: A Historical Approach to Political Economy*, Chicago, IL: University of Chicago Press, pp. 223–57.

Imbens, G.W. and Angrist, J.D. (1994), 'Identification and estimation of local average treatment effects', *Econometrica*, **62** (2), March, 467–75.

Koenker, R. and Hallock, K.F. (2001), 'Quantile regression', *Journal of Economic Perspectives*, **15** (4), Fall, 143–56.

LaLonde, R. and Topel, R. (1991), 'Labor market adjustments to increased immigration', in J. Abowd and R. Freeman (eds), *Immigration, Trade and the Labor Market*, Chicago, IL: University of Chicago Press, pp. 167–200.

Lopez, M. and Lozano, F.A. (2009), 'The labor supply of immigrants in the United States: the role of changing source country characteristics', *American Economic Review*, **99** (2), May, 35–40.

Lozano, F. and Lopez, M.J. (forthcoming), 'Border enforcement, immigrant selection and the gender wage gap of Mexican immigrants in the United States', *Feminist Economics*.

Lozano, F. and Sorensen, T. (2010), 'Mexican immigrants, the labor market assimilation and the current population survey: the sensitivity of results across seeming equivalent surveys', *International Migration*, forthcoming.

Lubotsky, D. (2007), 'Chutes or ladders? A longitudinal analysis of immigrant earnings', *Journal of Political Economy*, **115** (5), October, 820–67.

Mata, J. and Machado, J.A.F. (2005), 'Counterfactual decomposition of changes in wage distributions using quantile regression', *Journal of Applied Econometrics*, **20** (4), March, 445–65.

Meyer, B.D. (1995), 'Lessons from the U.S. unemployment insurance experiments', *Journal of Economic Literature*, **33** (1), March, 91–131.

Miller, P.W. (1999), 'Immigration policy and immigrant quality: the Australian points system', *American Economic Review*, **89** (2), May, 192–7.

Peri, G. and Sparber, C. (2009), 'Task specialization, immigration, and wages', *American Economic Journal: Applied Economics*, **1** (3), 135–69.

Staiger, D. and Stock, J.H. (1997), 'Instrumental variables regression with weak instruments', *Econometrica*, **65** (3), May, 557–86.

Trejo, S.J. (2003), 'Intergenerational progress of Mexican-origin workers in the U.S. labor market', *Journal of Human Resources*, **38** (3), Summer, 467–89.

Woolridge, J.M. (2002), *Econometric Analysis of Cross Section and Panel Data*, Cambridge, MA: MIT Press.

9 Using longitudinal data to study migration and remittances
Edward Funkhouser

One of the most important recent developments in research on the effects of international migration and remittances is the availability of longitudinal data that allow researchers to follow individuals or households over time. Such data allow for before-and-after comparisons and the ability to control for unobserved characteristics that are constant over time. As a result, new directions in the literatures examining the motives to migrate and remit and the effects of migration and remittances on sender household outcomes have been developed that take advantage of these data.

This chapter will describe how longitudinal data can be used in research on the migration decision and the effects of migration and remittances. The first section will describe the advantages and disadvantages of longitudinal data compared with cross-sectional data. The second section will address some of the issues the researcher confronts when constructing a longitudinal data set. The chapter will then focus on two broad types of research questions for which longitudinal data provide a fresh approach compared to the existing literature. The third section will explore how longitudinal data allow the researcher to relate pre-migration outcomes to the subsequent migration decision. And the fourth section will describe recent approaches in the use of longitudinal data to examine the effects of emigration and remittances on sender-household outcomes.

9.1 CROSS-SECTIONAL VERSUS LONGITUDINAL DATA IN THE STUDY OF MIGRATION AND REMITTANCE OUTCOMES

Consider a migration process in which individuals or households choose to migrate based on some observable and some unobservable characteristics:

$$M_{i,h}^* = M(X_{i,h}, Z_h, \varphi_{i,h}) \qquad (9.1)$$

where $M_{i,h}^*$ is the latent variable determining migration $X_{i,h}$ are the observable characteristics of individual i in household h, Z_h are the observable characteristics of household h, and $\varphi_{i,h}$ are the unobservable characteristics of the individual (and household). The effect of migration on the outcome of interest – remittances, household income, labor market insertion, poverty, consumption, child health, and education – is estimated in the second stage in one of two forms:

$$E(Y_{ih} \mid M_{ih}^* > M) - E(Y_{ih} \mid M_{ih}^* < M) \qquad (9.2)$$

or

$$Y_{ih} = \alpha + X_{i,h}\beta + Z_h\delta + \gamma M_{ih} + \varepsilon_{i,h} \qquad (9.3)$$

The two main estimation issues in estimating Equation (9.3) are (1) self-selection in the migration decision leading to the possibility that the error term is truncated and (2) endogeneity between the migration decision and the outcome of interest. These issues, especially that of self-selection, are addressed differently with cross-sectional and with longitudinal data.

9.1.1 Approaches with Cross-sectional Data

With cross-sectional data, it is not possible to directly control for unobserved characteristics of individuals or households. When there is self-selection, the expected value of $\varepsilon_{i,h}$ is not zero and $\varepsilon_{i,h}$ may be correlated with X or Z. To address the issue of self-selection in the pool of households from which emigrants have left, previous authors have utilized two approaches. The first is inclusion of a self-selection correction estimated from a first-stage probit (or multinomial logit when there is more than one migration option), with the calculated inverse Mills ratio included in the second-stage equation for the outcome of interest:

$$Y_{ih} = \alpha + X_{i,h}\beta + Z_h\delta + \sigma_1 \lambda 1_{i,h} + \varepsilon_{i,h} \quad (M = 1) \qquad (9.4)$$

$$Y_{ih} = \alpha + X_{i,h}\beta + Z_h\delta + \sigma_2 \lambda 2_{i,h} + \varepsilon_{i,h} \quad (M = 0) \qquad (9.5)$$

where $\lambda 1_{i,h}$ and $\lambda 2_{i,h}$ are the expected value of the truncated error term (Inverse Mills ratio) and $\varepsilon_{i,h}$ now has mean zero and is uncorrelated with X and Z. While the non-linear relationship between the determinants of migrant status and λ allows inclusion of λ in the second-stage correction, in order to ensure that the second stage is not identified by functional form alone, it is necessary to include determinants of migration status that would not otherwise be included in the second-stage regression. Theory does not provide much guidance for such identifying variables, especially for economic outcomes related to the labor market, agricultural production, consumption, and poverty since the determinants of these outcomes are likely to also be determinants of migration.

In practice most authors that adopt this approach use variables that are designed to measure the extent to which households are integrated into migrant networks, either by including characteristics that are thought to be migration related (such as language or ethnicity) or by including characteristics of communities that are correlated with migration (proportion of emigrants, proportion of receiving remittances). In their study of the effects of remittances on consumption in Ghana, Adams et al. (2008) use ethno-religious dummy variables and the fraction of females in the community receiving remittances. Miluka et al. (2007), looking at the effects of migration on the adoption of new technologies in agriculture in Albania, used variables measuring knowledge of Greek and Italian prior to migration, the share of the community population that is male and aged 20–39, and the minimum distance to an international border crossing. Acosta et al. (2007) used a comparable methodology with cross-sectional data from 11 Latin American countries in which the first-stage regression was identified by an index of household assets, the percentage of households in the county of residence that receive remittances, and an interaction between the two. Mendola (2005) used data from Bangladesh to also look at the effect of migration on the adoption of agricultural technology, including education level of the highest educated household member and the proportion of households in the village with emigrants to identify the first stage. Brown and Leeves (2007), in their study of the effects of migration on income, identified their first-level regression with community-level migration rates. In a paper using data for Guatemala similar to the one cited earlier on Ghana, Adams (2006) identified the first stage with the value of housing in quadratic form and the age of the household head. And Barham and Boucher (1998) identified the first stage with wealth and household relationship measures.

A second approach to address self-selection is the separation of the sample according to exogenous variables that affect the decision to migrate, but which do not differentially affect individuals or households along the variables that lead to self-selection. The best of such variables lead to situations that are close to natural experiments, such as lotteries. Gibson et al. (2009) and Gibson et al. (2010) use the lottery process to select immigrants to New Zealand to assess the effects of emigration on remaining household members, finding that emigration has a negative effect on the sender household labor market outcomes (but a positive effect on poverty alleviation) and that studies that do not correct for self-selection mis-estimate the effects of emigration.[1] Slightly less attractive are natural phenomena such as drought or disasters, which are likely to be exogenous, but are likely to affect certain types of households and to affect other determinants of the migration decision, such as household income. Yang (2005), for example, uses households that were affected by a strong earthquake in El Salvador as an exogenous shock that leads to emigration.[2]

The use of exogenous variables that affect migration also addresses the potential endogeneity of the migration and remittance decision with other outcomes of interest. If the outcome of interest, say household income, is part of the vector X in Equation (9.1), then an appropriate instrument for the estimation of Equation (9.3) would be correlated with the probability that an individual or household member emigrates, but be uncorrelated with the outcome of interest.

The previous literature has been of two types. The first type uses own-household information on pre-migration behavior as an instrument for current behavior. The Miluka study mentioned above used pre-migration language skills. And Taylor and Mora (2006) used household migration in 1990, 13 years prior to their survey year of 2003, in their study of the effects of migration on consumption patterns in Mexico.

The second, more common, approach in the literature for finding instruments that correct for the endogeneity problem is based on the idea that previous migration patterns from a particular geographic area affect current migration through networks, but do not affect current economic outcomes of a household. Variables measuring previous migration patterns at the level of a geographic area larger than the household are one approach to address both the problem of self-selection and the problem of endogeneity. Several studies of the effects of emigration in Mexico have used state-level emigration rates from earlier decades, mainly rates from the 1920s (Hanson and Woodruff, 2003; Hildebrandt and McKenzie, 2005; McKenzie, 2006; McKenzie and Rapoport, 2007). Adams et al.(2008), in the paper mentioned above, adopt a similar approach, using emigration rates by ethno-religious groups calculated from a 1998/99 survey as instrument for the propensity to migrate in estimates from a 2005/06 survey in Ghana. Lokshin et al. (2007) use the proportion of migrants from wards in 2001 to capture the propensity to emigrate in 2004 for Nepal.

A less satisfactory approach uses geographic patterns in current, rather than historical, migration as instruments for household propensity to migrate. Current migration patterns are less likely to satisfy the conditions for a good instrument to address endogeneity though, since current migration patterns in a geographic area are likely to affect economic opportunities of all households, including the respondent households, in that area. Miluka et al. (2007) and McCarthy et al. (2006) use other variables correlated with current migration at the level of the geographic area, the proportion of males in the population which is thought to be inversely related to emigration rates, as the instrument for current emigration rates in their studies of adoption of agricultural technology in Albania.

A common feature of the previous research that has used an instrumental variables (IV) approach is that the effect of migration is much larger – almost implausibly larger – than the effect measured with Ordinary Least Squares (OLS) regession. Hanson and Woodruff (2003), for example, find that the impact of household migrant on the number of school grades completed increases from 0.16 to 0.83–1.26 for males aged 13–15 and from 0.04 to 1.6 for females aged 13–15. Similarly, Adams et al. (2008) find that the effect of receipt of remittances on expenditures increases substantially with an IV approach compared to OLS. For expenditures on food, the impact of each unit of remittances increases from 0.21 to 3.936. A third study that reports both OLS and IV results, Hildebrandt and McKenzie (2005), reports the coefficients of a probit regression for child health outcomes that are four to ten times higher with IV than for non-IV. None of the reviewed studies that report both OLS and IV estimates report IV estimates for the effects of migration or remittances that are similar in size or smaller than the OLS estimates.

A second concern is the performance of the instruments. Nearly all studies that adopted an IV approach show that instruments are significant in the first stage regressions.[3] But few of the studies test the over-identifying restrictions or the weakness of the instruments. Among those that did conduct such tests, there is no consensus on the appropriateness of previous migration as a valid instrument. Hanson and Woodruff (2003), for example, reject the over-identifying restrictions in one of the four gender-age groups that they use in their study of the effects of migrants on educational attainment. And Adams et al (2008) reject the over-identifying restrictions in all of their IV regressions.[4]

9.1.2 Approach with Longitudinal Data

The body of research using cross-sectional data has not provided completely satisfactory methods for dealing with self-selection and endogeneity when there is not a natural experiment. Use of longitudinal data, with appropriate assumptions, provides a potentially more attractive way to address some of these issues, especially those of unobserved characteristics and self-selection. The basic idea of the use of longitudinal data can be seen in Figure 9.1.

For a comparison in which there is data on households at two points in time – Year 1 and Year 2, households can be classified according to their

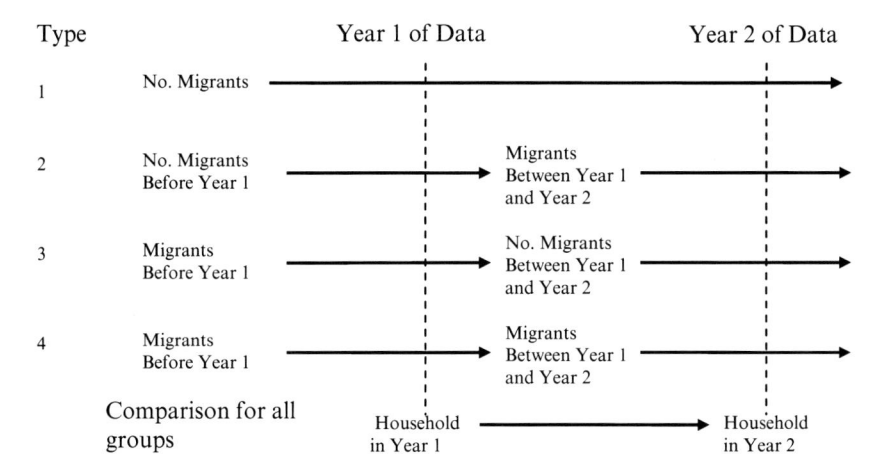

Using longitudinal data to study migration and remittances 191

Type		Year 1 of Data		Year 2 of Data
1	No. Migrants	──────────────────────────────────────►		
2	No. Migrants Before Year 1	──────────►	Migrants Between Year 1 and Year 2 ──────►	
3	Migrants Before Year 1	──────────►	No. Migrants Between Year 1 and Year 2 ──►	
4	Migrants Before Year 1	──────────►	Migrants Between Year 1 and Year 2 ──────►	
Comparison for all groups		Household in Year 1	──────────────►	Household in Year 2

Figure 9.1 The use of longitudinal data

migration or remittance status. For example, in Figure 9.1, Type 1 are households that have had no migrants; Type 2 are households from which there was no emigrant prior to the first survey year, but from which an emigrant left between the two survey years; Type 3 are households from which an emigrant had left prior to the first survey year, but no emigrant left between the two survey years; and Type 4 are households from which emigrants left both before the first survey year and between the two survey years.

The benefit of longitudinal data is best seen in the Type 2 households. The characteristics and outcomes of those households are seen prior to emigration in Year 1 and these characteristics can be used to estimate the determinants of emigration between the two years. In addition, the effect of emigration on the sender household can be estimated by a before-and-after comparison. It is tempting to merely calculate changes in outcomes for only Type 2 households, but the use of longitudinal data in a non-experimental setting introduces other potential biases. In particular, because other factors may have changed between the two years, it is necessary to control for these (unobserved to the researcher) other factors. However, if the unobserved factors affect households from which an emigrant left equally affect households from which no emigrant left, a difference-in-difference estimator can be used. For example, to estimate the effect of a recent emigrant on household outcomes can be seen by comparing the change in outcomes for households of Type 2 to the change in outcomes for households of Type 1. The change in outcomes for households of Type 1 from which no emigrant left captures the general changes that affect all households. Any deviation from this general change for households of Type 2 captures the specific effects of an emigrant having left the household. Similarly, the effects of adding a recent emigrant to a household with a prior emigrant can be seen by comparing outcomes for households of Type 4 with those of households of Type 2.

An important requirement for this estimate to truly capture the effects of emigration is that the two comparison groups – in this case households of Type 1 and households of Type 2 – must be otherwise comparable and equally affected by the general events. If, for example, severe weather caused household production to be low and this, in turn, caused household members to migrate, the researcher might conclude using the difference-in-difference estimates that migration caused household income to have low growth when, in fact, it was the weather that caused the change.

If the unobserved characteristics of the individual or household that lead to self-selection are constant over time, then the error term in Equation (9.3) can be rewritten:

$$\varepsilon_{i,h} = \mu_i + \mu_{i,h} + v_{i,h} \tag{9.6}$$

where μ_i is the time invariant individual component, $\mu_{i,h}$ is the time invariant household component, and $v_{i,h}$ is a random component that satisfies independence with the independent variables. Then:

$$Y_{iht} = \alpha + X_{i,ht}\beta + Z_{ht}\delta + \gamma M_{iht} + \mu_i + \mu_{i,h} + v_{i,ht} \tag{9.7}$$

and first-differencing leads to unbiased estimates of the coefficients of interest:

$$Y_{i,h,t} - Y_{i,h,t-1} = (\alpha - \alpha) + (X_{i,h,t} - X_{i,h,t-1})\beta + (Z_{h,t} - Z_{h,t-1})\delta$$
$$+ \gamma(M_{i,h,t} - M_{ih,t-1}) + (\mu_i - \mu_i) + (\mu_{i,h} - \mu_{i,h}) + (v_{i,h,t} - v_{i,h,t-1})$$
$$= (X_{i,h,t} - X_{i,h,t-1})\beta + (Z_{h,t} - Z_{h,t-1})\delta + \gamma(M_{i,h,t} - M_{ih,t-1})$$
$$+ (v_{i,h,t} - v_{i,h,t-1}) \tag{9.8}$$

since, by construction, $(v_{i,h,t} - v_{i,h,t-1})$ has mean zero and is uncorrelated with the vectors X or Z.[5]

Another possibility for the use of controls in Equation (9.8) is to include some of those variables in their levels:

$$Y_{i,h,t} - Y_{i,h,t-1} = (X1_{i,h,t} - X1_{i,h,t-1})\beta_1 + (Z1_{h,t} - Z1_{h,t-1})\delta_1$$
$$+ X2_{i,h,t}\beta_2 + Z2_{h,t}\delta_2 + \gamma(M_{i,h,t} - M_{ih,t-1}) + (v_{i,h,t} - v_{i,h,t-1}) \quad (9.9)$$

where $X1$ is a vector of individual variables included in differences, $Z1$ is a vector of household variables included in differences, $X2$ is a vector of individual variables included in levels, and $Z2$ is a vector of individual variables included in differences. The interpretation of the coefficients β_2 and δ_2 is in differences in the growth of the dependent variable according to the variables included in $X2$ and $Z2$. For example, including region controls in $Z2$ allows for differences in growth rates of the dependent variable by region (which, in turn, does allow for control for region-specific changes related to variables such as climate and weather).

And lastly, Equation (9.8) can also be estimated consistently by pooling the data (rather than calculating first-differences) and adding fixed or random effects:[6]

$$Y_{iht} = \alpha + X_{i,ht}\beta + Z_{ht}\delta + \gamma M_{iht} + \theta_{i,h} + v_{i,ht} \quad (9.10)$$

where $\theta_{i,h}$ is the combined time-invariant effect of $\mu_i + \mu_{i,h}$ in Equation (9.7). In this case, two (or more) years of data are used and, as in the first-difference approach, it is changes in the variables that contribute to the coefficient estimation. Random effects is the appropriate method when $\theta_{i,h}$ is uncorrelated with the within-household means of X, Z, and M. Fixed effects is appropriate when $\theta_{i,h}$ is correlated with the within household means of X, Z, and M. In either case, an additional benefit of using pooled data with more than two sample years is that it allows for estimates of time since emigration profiles net out cohort effects. This potential has been rarely explored in the existing literature.

Previous studies that have used longitudinal data to examine the effects of emigration and remittances are limited and have tended to use short time-periods. Lu and Treiman (2007) use fixed-effects and random-effects estimators to examine the effect of remittances on school attendance of children in South Africa, though their panel covers only 12 months from September 2002 to 2003. Duval and Wolff (2009) used data from the Living Standards Measurement Surveys (LSMS) surveys in Albania to look at the determinants of remittances.[7] Dimova and Wolff (2009) used data from LSMS-type surveys in Bosnia and Herzegovina in 2002 and 2004 to examine the impact that past remittances have on future migration plans. Using both fixed- and random-effects estimators, they find that remittances increase the likelihood of future emigration, especially for the young, healthy, and well educated.

Fewer studies have attempted to use longitudinal data to attempt before-and-after calculations of the effects of migration and remittances. Three studies, including the Funkhouser (2006) study discussed below, have approximated this, one using migrants, a second remittances, and a third both.[8] Alcaraz and Chiquiar (2007) use quarterly data from Mexico over the period 2000–04 in which households can be followed over five consecutive quarters in order to examine the effect of emigration on schooling of children age 12–15. They find that a change in household status from no emigrant to emigrant increases the probability that a child attends school and decreases the probability that a child works. More importantly for the present study, the effects of the panel estimates are stronger than those from a cross-section. They include IV estimates for endogeneity in the migration decision (using employment growth in the United States in the head's sector of employment as the main instrument), with imprecise results and insignificant coefficients on the migration variable. Also using panel data over a short time-period of 15 months, Yang (2005) used variation in exchange rate shocks by emigrant country of destination as an exogenous instrument for remittances in first-difference estimates. He found that positive income from exchange rate shocks leads to enhanced human capital formation and entrepreneurship.

In the use of cross-sectional data, the main issues are related to the difficulty in correcting for self-selection and endogeneity. With longitudinal data, the difference-in-difference method (or the inclusion of fixed or random effects) allows for controls for self-selection and the inclusion of pre-migration characteristics (or instruments for those characteristics) may be a good method for addressing endogeneity. With longitudinal data, the main research issues are related to the quality of the data and the appropriateness of treating observations as otherwise equal. The next section will address some aspects of the former issue. Methods for dealing with endogeneity within a panel data approach will not be addressed in this chapter.

9.2 CONSTRUCTING LONGITUDINAL DATA

Some of the sources for longitudinal data for the study of migration outcomes are shown in Table 9.1. Nearly all regularly conducted household surveys – demographic, labor market, or income and expenditure – in developing countries include some questions about migration and/or remittances. While many of those surveys include a longitudinal component that can either be less than 100 percent rotation of the sample over time or re-sampling of a sub-sample of a previous household survey, most

Table 9.1 Some longitudinal data sources

Name	Type of Data	Source
Living Standards Measurement Surveys	Comprehensive household survey including modules on demography, health, education, income	http://www.worldbank.org/lsms (World Bank)
Mexican Migration Project (MMP) Latin American Migration Project (LAMP)	Community-based surveys that follow migrants and their families over time	http://opr.princeton.edu/archive/mmp/ and http://opr.princeton.edu/archive/lamp/ (Princeton University Office of Population Research)
National Household Surveys	Regular labor market surveys	List of agencies available at http://www.census.gov/aboutus/stat_int.html

household surveys are conducted to extract current statistical information necessary for government policy. Because the primary purpose of most of these surveys is not the construction of longitudinal data, the statistical agencies usually do not conduct as many consistency checks for the longitudinal component as they do for the components that are of immediate interest to policy makers. As a result, additional care must be taken to ensure consistency across waves when using longitudinal data.

The first issue is the appropriateness of the available longitudinal data for the issue to be examined. As mentioned above, Equation (9.8) is an attractive form for estimating the effects of migration on outcome Y when there are fixed unobservable effects. It should be clear from Equation (9.6) that the ability to estimate Equation (9.8) depends on there being sufficient observations for which the values of a variable change between the two years. If all households either have a migrant in the two years or do not have a migrant in either year, then the value of $(M_{i,h,t} - M_{ih,t-1})$ would be zero for all observations and γ cannot be estimated. An important requirement necessary to use the difference-in-difference approach to examine the effects of emigration, therefore, is that there be a sufficient number of households that changed migration status between the two survey years. Similarly, questions which are answered with a binary dependent variable – such as whether a migrant left the household between the two survey years – are best estimated when the mean of the dependent variable is not in the tail of the distribution (because it relies more heavily on functional form).

A second issue is the matching of the data between waves. While statistical agencies in developing countries have increasingly included matched sampling techniques in data collection and often include identifiers that are intended to reference the same individual across survey years, they usually have not prepared the data to a sufficient level of reliability for the researcher. Therefore, construction of longitudinal data from matched cross-sectional data must include, in addition to usual data checking, the following:

- Programming that checks for consistency in age, gender, and relationship to other household members across survey years even when the longitudinal identifier indicates that the data corresponds to the same individual. Inconsistencies in any variable that should remain constant over time must be adjusted.
- Visual checking and matching of household members that are not given an identification number for the matched sample. This often includes persons who emigrated between the sample years or persons that were reported as emigrants in both survey years. For migrants, it is often a good idea to create a matching code that identifies those persons that were members of the household in the initial survey year and subsequently migrated prior to the second survey.

The reliability of the data is particularly important for longitudinal data because the impact of measurement error increases. As an example, consider a panel data set that includes 1000 observations on households of which 100 report an emigrant in the second year and 20 of the 100 report that the emigrant left the household between the first and second survey year. If a household that did not have an emigrant in either year is reported to have an emigrant in the second year, the impact on the estimated coefficients is greater when the panel approach is used. If the data from the second year are used as a cross-section, the one mis-reported household changes the number of households without an emigrant to 899 from 900 and the number of households with an emigrant to 101 from 100. With the assumption that the measurement error is random, these changes will bias the estimated coefficients slightly towards zero. But if a panel approach is used, this household will now be reported as a household that has switched from not having an emigrant in the first survey year to a household with an emigrant in the second survey year. Because only households that change status contribute to the estimation of the effect with longitudinal data, the measurement error for the one mis-reported household increases the number of such households to 21 from 20. The bias towards zero from the measurement error is increased when panel data are used.

The issue of measurement error turns out to be an important issue in the study of migration because one of the surprising patterns in the data is the inconsistency of reporting about migrants at the household level. While it is understandable that an emigrant's age or education is reported inconsistently across survey years, it presents a problem for the researcher using longitudinal data if the existence of an emigrant from the household or the receipt of remittances is reported inconsistently across survey years.

As an example of this phenomenon, consider data matched from the 2001 and 2005 LSMS for Nicaragua (available at the World Bank website listed in Table 9.1). Each survey included detailed modules on household activity, demographic, health, education, and labor market activity, consumption, and agricultural production. In addition, both surveys included a module on household members currently living abroad and included information on the amount of international remittances in a module on other sources of income.

The 2005 survey was designed to include a longitudinal sub-sample with the 2001 survey. Of the 4191 households in the 2001 survey, 3665 were part of the matched sample and 2889 households can be matched between the two years and have information for all variables. There are 897 emigrants reported in the 2001 survey and 1441 emigrants reported in the 2005 survey. In 2001 745 of the emigrants reported and in 2005 839 of the emigrants reported lived in households in which individuals can be matched between the two surveys. Despite this overlap, only 192 emigrants reported in the 2001 survey can be closely matched based on age, sex, and year of emigration with information on an emigrant reported in the 2005 survey.[9]

Even more surprisingly, the inability to match is based less on measurement error in individual information and more on whether or not a household reports an emigrant at all. Of the 565 households in the matched sample that report an emigrant that arrived prior to 2002 in either the 2001 LSMS or the 2005 LSMS (377 in 2001, 323 in 2005), only 172 report an emigrant in both 2001 and 2005. In 2001 252 report an emigrant, but not in 2005. In 2005 141 report an emigrant, but not in 2001. And 44 of the households that reported an emigrant in the 2001 survey only report an emigrant that left after 2001 in the 2005 survey.

There is much more consistency in the information reported about emigrants that left between the two surveys. Of the 360 emigrants that left following 2001 reported in the 2005 survey in households that can be matched to the 2001 survey, 283 can be matched to information on individuals reported in the 2001 survey. In addition, 27 of the 67 individuals in those households that are reported to have left in 2001 (with month not specified) can also be matched.

These observations on consistency in the reporting of emigrants suggest, not surprisingly, that household reporting of recent migrants is much more reliable than reporting of earlier emigrants. The latter reflects both changes in attachment over time and reporting bias with a change in respondent. Whether a household experienced a recent migrant is both a more reliable measure and indicates a change in household migration status. As a result, the main comparison of the empirical work that follows is between households from which an emigrant left between 2002 and 2005 and those that did not.

While this chapter is directed towards research methods using longitudinal data, the difficulties of constructing reliable data described above suggests one important way in which data collection in household surveys can be improved. The procedures of most surveys include extensive double-checking of the status of persons listed in the main household roster of the first survey in a panel, including those members that subsequently emigrate. Such efforts to link household member line numbers between panels should be extended to include those listed as emigrants at the time of the first survey so that they can be linked directly to the record for an emigrant listed in the later survey or a reason for absence from the second survey can be included. This is especially important when emigrant information on age or education is reported inconsistently across survey years.

9.3 USING LONGITUDINAL DATA – DETERMINANTS OF MIGRATION DECISION

One of the most promising, but not yet fully explored, aspects of using longitudinal data is the inclusion of pre-migration outcomes as determinants of the migration and remittance decision. Many of the distinguishing hypotheses of research that attempt to evaluate motives to migrate or remit – altruism, self-interest, enlightened self-interest, risk diversification – are based on the pre-migration or pre-remittance characteristics of the emigrant and the sender household. That is, for most theories of the migration decision, the components of the vectors X_i and Z_{hi} in Equation (9.1) are pre-migration characteristics of the individual or the household, not post-migration characteristics. Because cross-sectional data sets cannot identify migrants before they emigrate, studies that use cross-sectional data to study determinants of the migration decision must use post-migration characteristics or retrospective information on pre-migration characteristics. With longitudinal data and a sample large enough to include a sufficient number of persons that change migration status over the course of the panel, pre-migration outcomes can be related to subsequent migration decisions or the choice of migration destination.

The usual specification of these comparisons is of the form:

$$M_{iht} = \alpha + X_{i,ht-1} \beta + Z_{ht-1} \delta + \varepsilon_{i,ht} \qquad (9.11)$$

where the migration status is observed after migration at time t and the characteristics of the individual or household before migration at time $t-1$.

An example of this type of comparison can be found in Funkhouser (2009) in which the choice of migration destination – United States, Costa Rica, or non-emigration – for persons resident in Nicaragua in 1998. With a three-way choice, a multinomial logit can be used. The pre-migration outcomes include the economic status of the household (poverty) and labor market insertion of the migrant. The main finding related to the pre-migration characteristics is that emigrants that chose the United States as a destination between 1998 and 2001 were less likely to have been living in poverty before migration and individuals that emigrated to Costa Rica were more likely to have been unemployed. These patterns, and the inclusion of pre-migration economic characteristics of the individual and the household indicate that immediate economic motives play a larger role for emigrants to Costa Rica and accumulated economic success plays a larger role for emigrants to the United States.

9.4 USING LONGITUDINAL DATA – EFFECTS OF EMIGRATION ON SENDER HOUSEHOLD

The before-and-after approach is also naturally applied to research estimating the effect of emigration or remittances on the sender household. An example of estimates made with the difference-in-difference approach are taken from Funkhouser (2006) using data from the LSMA of Nicaragua in 1998 and 2001. That paper used the difference-in-difference approach and found that the change in the number of working household members and household labor income in households that have emigrants is lower than the change in households that do not have emigrants, but that the reduction in poverty is also greater.

To estimate these effects, the sample is divided into two groups – households from which an emigrant left between the two years and households from which no emigrant left. The basic idea of the difference-in-difference estimator can be seen in Table 9.2, in which mean values for the two groups in the two years are shown.

Table 9.2 All households, matched sample

	Households (HH) without emigrants 1998	2001	Households (HH) with emigrants 1998	2001
Average HH size	5.60	5.52	6.96	5.22
	(2.72)	(2.68)	(3.42)	(2.57)
Number working	1.94	2.13	2.26	2.13
	(1.33)	(1.38)	(1.47)	(1.57)
Average HH labor income	1778	3033	2547	2354
	(2664)	(4534)	(4442)	(2776)
Household consumption	2837	3472	4230	4912
	(2690)	(2720)	(4647)	(4987)
Proportion poverty	0.381	0.354	0.383	0.229
	(0.486)	(0.478)	(0.487)	(0.421)
N	2780		214	

Note: For further details see Funkhouser (2006, table 2, panel A).

9.4.1 Effect of an Emigrant Without Controls

Comparing the mean values for 2001, households from which an emigrant left between 1998 and 2001 were 0.3 smaller than households from which an emigrant did not leave. With an average of 1.64 emigrants per household, the cross-sectional estimate of the effect of emigration on household size (from 1.34 larger to 0.3 smaller) is not far off from actual change. However, when looking at other variables, the cross-sectional estimates overestimate or underestimate the effects of emigration, even looking just at the mean values. For example, in the next row of Table 9.2, the average number of household members working is shown. Looking at the comparison of mean values for 2001, households with emigrants have the same number of working members (2.13) as households without emigrants. However, this comparison masks the change between years in which households without emigrant members experienced an increase in the number of working members by .19 persons and households with emigrants experienced a decline of .13 persons. The difference-in-difference estimator of the effect of emigration on household members working with no controls is –0.32.

For the other variables included in Table 9.2, it can be seen that the cross-sectional comparisons in Columns 2 and 4 underestimate the relative change in household labor income – households with emigrants have average labor income 679 cordobas below those without emigrants, but the difference-in-difference estimator of 1448 cordobas overestimates the effect on household consumption, and underestimates slightly the effect on poverty.

9.4.2 Effect of an Emigrant from the Household With Controls

Table 9.3 introduces controls for the difference-in-difference comparison – consumption and labor income are reported with difference in natural logarithms. Row 1 includes cross-sectional estimates similar to those found in many studies of the effect of emigrants. Row 2 calculates the difference-in-difference estimator without any controls – this is equivalent to the difference-in-difference calculations based on the means in Table 9.3. Row 3 presents the difference-in-difference estimator with controls. For each of the regressions with controls – Rows 1 and 3 – each regression is estimated using a full range of controls, but only the coefficient on the migration variable is reported in the table. The controls include geographic controls (department dummy variables and rural dummy variable) and household controls (household members in 1998, age of household head in 1998, years of education of household head in 1998, and female headed in 1998).

The table demonstrates the importance of using the difference-in-difference approach. The cross-sectional estimates in Row 1 show that households that have had a member emigrate are of the same size, have the same number of working members but lower labor income, higher consumption, and lower poverty than households without emigrants. While these findings are consistent – even though the households with emigrants are the same size post-migration, they must have been larger and had more working members pre-migration, it is not possible to know how much of these differences are due to differences in unobserved characteristics between the two types of households. The difference-in-difference estimator with controls in Row 3 reveals that the reduction in household members is about one member as would be expected, all else equal, from the cross-sectional estimate. But it also reveals that the reduction in working members is about ¼ person, something that is not possible to know from the cross-section. In addition, statistically significant higher consumption of households with emigrants observed from the cross-section is revealed to be an equal change in consumption between the two years with the difference-in-difference estimator. Combined with the reduction in the number of household members, these patterns result in lower poverty for households that have experienced an emigrant. The cross-section shows that households with emigrants have lower poverty

Table 9.3   Household outcomes

	HH size	HH adult members	HH members working	Ln HH labor income	HH consumption	HH poverty
	(1)	(2)	(3)	(4)	(5)	(6)
Cross-Section: Regression 1 – All Controls						
Any Migrant	−0.050	−0.007	0.040	−0.254	0.127	−0.115
	(0.199)	(0.116)	(0.120)	(0.077)	(0.052)	(0.031)
Difference-in-Difference: Regression 2 – No Controls						
Any Migrant	−1.655	−0.998	−0.318	−0.339	−0.051	−0.127
No Controls	(0.191)	(0.139)	(0.131)	(0.091)	(0.039)	(0.037)
Difference-in-Difference: Regression 3 – All Controls						
Any Migrant	−1.105	−0.819	−0.252	−0.302	−0.031	−0.088
	(0.154)	(0.136)	(0.132)	(0.092)	(0.041)	(0.037)
Difference-in-Difference: Regression 4 – All Controls						
Migrant to CR	−1.177	−0.822	−0.381	−0.482	−0.010	−0.141
	(0.189)	(0.149)	(0.154)	(0.110)	(0.052)	(0.057)
Migrant to US	−0.875	−0.745	−0.233	0.091	−0.073	0.014
	(0.238)	(0.287)	(0.203)	(0.156)	(0.084)	(0.026)
Difference-in-Difference: Regression 5 – All Controls						
Only Pre-1998	−0.002	0.012	−0.060	−0.063	0.024	−0.061
migrants	(0.195)	(0.146)	(0.143)	(0.127)	(0.051)	(0.041)
Pre- and post-	−0.579	−0.396	0.200	−0.193	0.082	0.025
1998 migrants	(0.318)	(0.330)	(0.237)	(0.270)	(0.092)	(0.101)
Only post-1998	−1.262	−0.813	−0.301	−0.377	−0.064	−0.102
migrants	(0.142)	(0.180)	(0.182)	(0.111)	(0.058)	(0.046)

Note: Each entry in Regressions 0 to 3 is the coefficient and standard error from a separate regression. Each pair of coefficients in the rows for Regression 4 (within a column) are from a separate regression. Each set of coefficients in the rows for Regression 5 (within a column) are from a separate regression. Geographic controls include department dummy variables and rural dummy variable. Household controls include number of household members in 1998 (except column 0), age of household head in 1998, years of education of household head in 1998, and female headed in 1998. N for all regressions in Columns 1–3 and 5–6 is 2994. N for Column 4 is 2406.

post-migration, but the difference-in-difference estimator reveals that those households have had a reduction greater than that difference following the migration of a household member.

In the particular case of Nicaraguan emigrants, further evidence on the effects of emigration can be seen from the separate examination of emigrants to Costa Rica and those to the United States in Regression 4.

Nearly all of the effects of emigrants on sender households are those from emigration to Costa Rica and there is little effect on households from which an emigrant went to the United States. Cross-sectional estimates (not reported) suggest that emigration to the United States is associated with higher labor income, higher consumption, and lower poverty in the sender household. But the difference-in-difference estimator confirms that all of this association is due to differences pre-migration and households from which an emigrant went to the United States have changes similar to households from which no emigrant has left. In effect, consumption was high, the future emigrant was not a major contributor to income or poverty, and the emigration of the household member had little effect on either.

In contrast, migration to Costa Rica is associated with a statistically significant reduction in working household members, labor income, and poverty. This last effect is due to the similar consumption before and after migration event without the pre-migration labor income contributed by the emigrant through the receipt of remittances.

The comparisons that are most similar to those shown in Figure 9.1 are shown in Regression 5 at the bottom rows of Table 9.3. The first row includes the change in each dependent variable for households with only a migrant that emigrated prior to the first survey (Type 3 in Figure 9.1) relative to households with no emigrant (Type 1). The second row includes the relative change for households with an emigrant that left before the first survey and also had an emigrant leave between the two surveys (Type 4). And the third row includes the relative change for households from which there was no emigrant prior to the first survey, but from which an emigrant did leave between the two surveys (Type 2). The comparisons indicate that households from which an emigrant left prior to the first survey experienced changes between the two surveys that are similar to those of households without any emigrants. The changes for households that had earlier and more recent emigrants are larger, but still not statistically significant. But for households which only had emigrants that left between the two surveys, the changes in the household are large and statistically significant.

9.5 CONCLUSION AND LESSONS FOR FUTURE RESEARCH

Longitudinal data provide a rich source for future research on the determinants of migration and remittances and on the effect of emigration and remittances on sender household outcomes. There are two main advantages to the use of longitudinal data. First, when there are a sufficient number of persons that emigrated within the years of the data, before-and-after comparisons can be made. These comparisons can relate the characteristics of the individual or household before emigration occurs to the emigration status of the individual at the time of the second survey. They may also relate the outcomes of the household before emigration occurs (at the time of the earlier survey year) to the outcomes of the household after emigration occurs (at the time of the later survey year). Second, even if there are not new emigrants between the two survey years, the use of longitudinal data allows the researcher to control for fixed effects by differencing between the two years.

There are many directions that future research using longitudinal data to study migration outcomes can take. First, with the exception of studies using the Mexican Migration Project, there are few studies that use panel data sets that are longer than a few years. Over time though, as more household surveys with longitudinal data components are undertaken, longer panels can be constructed. Second, while there is now a large literature examining the motives to migration and remittances, very few of these studies have utilized information about the emigrant or the sender household prior to emigration. Third, the coverage of countries for which longitudinal data has been used to correct for self-selection in the migration and remittance process is still low.

NOTES

1. McKenzie et al. (2006) use the same lottery to assess the impacts of migration on earnings of migrants.
2. See McKenzie and Yang (Chapter 12, this volume) for further discussion of experimental approaches.
3. For example, Lokshin et al. (2007) and Taylor and Mora (2006) use t-statistics; Hildebrandt and McKenzie (2005) and McKenzie and Rapoport (2007) provide F-statistics for the instruments in the first stage.
4. Table 12.1. Also see the Lozano and Steinberger (Chapter 8, this volume) for further discussion of IV estimation.
5. Note also that the first-difference approach can also be applied when the migration variables are entered non-linearly. For example, for households that have an emigrant member in Year 1 and Year 2, there is no change in migration status. However, if the relationship between years since migration and the dependent variable includes both a linear and quadratic component, only the linear part will be differenced out when the first-difference is taken. The coefficient on the quadratic component can still be estimated.
6. See, for example, Greene (2007) for a more detailed discussion of fixed versus random effects.
7. Their main findings concerning the use of panel data are hard to interpret because it is not the focus of their paper.
8. The longitudinal approach can also be used to examine the determinants of remittance behavior using surveys of emigrants in the host country. For example, Dustman and

Mestres (2010) used data from the German Socioeconomic Panel from 1984–95 to examine remittance behavior of migrants from Turkey, Greece, Yugoslavia, Italy, and Spain. When they include individual fixed effects, they find that the coefficients of interest – whether the migrant is considered temporary – drops in magnitude with the inclusion of the fixed effects.
9. Of the 479 emigrants reported in the 2005 survey for which year of exit was before 2002 or missing, 208 can be matched to information on emigrants in the 2001 survey.

REFERENCES

Acosta, P., Calderon, C., Fajnzylber, P. and Lopez, H. (2007), 'What is the impact of international remittances on poverty and inequality in Latin America?', World Bank Poverty Research Working Paper No. 4249, World Bank, June.

Adams, R. (2006), 'Remittances, poverty and investment in Guatemala', in C. Ozden and M. Schiff (eds), *International Migration, Remittances, and the Brain Drain*, Washington, DC and New York: World Bank and Palgrave Macmillan, Chapter 2.

Adams, R., Cuecuecha, A. and Page, J. (2008), 'Remittances, consumption and investment in Ghana', World Bank Policy Research Working Paper No. 4515, World Bank, February.

Alcaraz, C. and Chiquiar, D. (2007), 'Emigration, schooling and child labor in rural Mexico', Banco de Mexico, Mexico City, November.

Barham, B. and Boucher, S. (1998), 'Migration, remittances and inequality: estimating the net effects of migration on income distribution', *Journal of Development Economics*, **55**, April, 307–31.

Brown, R. and Leeves, G. (2007), 'Impacts of international migration and remittances on source country household incomes in small island states: Fiji and Tonga', ESA Working Paper No. 07-13, Agricultural Development Economics Division, FAO, February.

Dimova, R. and Wolff, F.-C. (2009), 'Remittances and chain migration: longitudinal evidence from Bosnia and Herzegovina', IZA Discussion Paper No. 4083, Institute for Labor Study, Bonn, March.

Dustman, C. and Mestres, J. (2010), 'Remittances and temporary migration', *Journal of Development Economics*, **92** (1), May, 62–70.

Duval, L. and Wolff, F.-C. (2009), 'Remittances matter: longitudinal evidence from Albania', LEMNA 2009/20, University of Nantes, September.

Funkhouser, E. (2006), 'The effect of emigration on the labor market outcomes of the sender household: a longitudinal approach using data from Nicaragua', *Well Being and Social Policy*, **2**, 5–27.

Funkhouser, E. (2009), 'The choice of migration destination for Nicaraguans', *Review of Development Economics*, **13** (4), November, 626–40.

Gibson, J., McKenzie, D. and Stillman, S. (2009), 'The impact of international migration on remaining household members: omnibus results from a migration lottery program', World Bank Policy Research Working Paper No. 4956, World Bank, June.

Gibson, J., McKenzie, D. and Stillman, S. (2010), 'Accounting for selectivity and duration-dependent heterogeneity when estimating the impact of emigration on incomes and poverty in sending areas', World Bank Policy Research Working Paper No. 5268, World Bank, April.

Greene, W. (2007), *Econometric Analysis*, 6th edn, New Jersey: Prentice Hall.

Hanson, G. and Woodruff, C. (2003), 'Emigration and educational attainment in Mexico', UCSD, San Diego, April.

Hildebrandt, N. and McKenzie, D. (2005), 'The effects of migration on child health in Mexico', World Bank Policy Research Working Paper No. 3573, World Bank, April.

Lokshin, M., Bontch-Osmolovski, M. and Glinksaya, E. (2007), 'Work related migration and poverty reduction in Nepal', World Bank Policy Research Working Paper No. 4231, World Bank, May.

Lu, Y. and Treiman, D. (2007), 'The effect of labor migration and remittances on children's education among blacks in South Africa', CCPR 01-07, California Center for Population Research, UCLA, January.

McCarthy, N.G.C., Davis, B. and Maltsoglou, I. (2006), 'Assessing the impact of massive out-migration on agriculture', ESA Working Paper No. 06-14, FAO, Rome.

McKenzie, David (2006), 'Beyond remittances: the effects of migration on Mexican households,' in C. Ozden and M. Schiff (eds), *International Migration, Remittances and the Brain Drain*, Washington, DC and New York: World Bank and Palgrave Macmillan, Chapter 4.

McKenzie, D. and Rapoport, H. (2007), 'Self-selection patterns in Mexico–U.S. migration: the role of migration networks', World Bank Policy Research Working Paper No. 4118, World Bank, February.

McKenzie, D., Gibson, J. and Stillman, S. (2006), 'How important is selection? Experimental versus non-experimental measures of income gains from migration', World Bank Policy Research Working Paper No. 3906, World Bank, May.

Mendola, M. (2005), 'Migration and technological change in rural households: complements or substitutes?', University of Milan, March.

Miluka, J., Carletto, G., Davis, B. and Zezza, A. (2007), 'The vanishing farms? The impact of international migration on Albanian family farming', World Bank Policy Research Working Paper No. 4367, World Bank, September.

Taylor, J.E. and Mora, J. (2006), 'Does migration reshape expenditures in rural households? Evidence from Mexico', World Bank Policy Research Working Paper No. 3842, World Bank.

Yang, D. (2005), 'International migration, human capital, and entrepreneurship: evidence from Philippine migrants' exchange rate shocks', World Bank Policy Research Working Paper No. 3578, World Bank, April.

10 Measuring migration in multi-topic household surveys
Calogero Carletto, Alan de Brauw and Raka Banerjee

This chapter provides basic guidelines to researchers interested in studying migration for collecting migration information as part of a multi-topic household survey. Although migration has been an important phenomenon shaping the demographic profile of countries for centuries, the past decade has seen migration rapidly rise to become a prominent feature of the world economy. According to the United Nations (2009), the number of people living outside their country of birth is now increasing faster than world population growth. Since 1975, the global stock of migrants has more than doubled to more than 213 million, representing approximately 3.1 percent of the world's population. Corresponding to the increase in international migration, remittances from migrants residing in developed countries to households in developing countries have increased significantly. Formal remittance flows – which grossly underestimate total remittances – totaled $328 billion in 2008 and were second only to foreign direct investment (FDI) as a capital flow into developing countries (IFAD, 2007; Ratha et al., 2009). For many developing countries, remittance flows are larger than FDI and Official Development Asssistance (ODA) combined, and in at least 42 countries migrant remittances account for 10 percent or more of gross domestic product (GDP) (IFAD, 2007; World Bank, 2011).

As international migration and migrant remittances have increased, migration has once again emerged as a contentious policy issue in both developed and developing countries (Global Forum on Migration and Development, 2007; Massey, 1999). Policies to further liberalize migration flows into developed countries often face strident opposition from several fronts. Proponents of liberalization tend to argue that increased migration offers opportunities to advance the economic development of both sending and receiving countries. Meanwhile, critics emphasize economic, political, and social drawbacks to increased population movements. These issues are relevant with regards to both migration from the global south to the north, as well as migration within the global south itself. Despite the strongly held opinions on both sides of the migration policy debate, little solid empirical information exists on the ways in which various policies affect migration and migrant households.

The resultant need to better understand the determinants and impact of migration has generated a growing demand for better migration data, as reflected in the emergence of new data collection efforts. While existing data on migration and remittance flows is partial and imperfect, there are nonetheless a number of sources that currently produce data on these topics.[1] Formal international remittance flows are often reported by central banks, and the number of legal international immigrants in a given country is tracked by national governments through various sources, including border and other administrative records. Estimates of internal migration can often be obtained from population censuses. However, these sources are inadequate for a number of reasons. Aside from failing to distinguish and account for various types of migration (for example, international emigration, including long-term, circular, and seasonal migration), sources such as these do not typically include the types of variables that can be used to understand the determinants and impact of migration.

Labor force surveys and specialized migration surveys also fall short of including enough information to study the determinants and impact of migration. The International Labor Organization has recently developed specific modules focused on international migration to add to labor force surveys, such as the quarterly labor force survey conducted in Thailand (2007), which asks questions about the international origins of workers. Specialized migration surveys such as the Mexican Migration Project can also be used to analyse issues related to migration. However, both of these types of surveys are primarily limited to simply characterizing migrants and the driving forces behind migration. As minimal information on topics beyond migration is collected in these surveys, they often offer little insight into the relationship between migration, other sources of income, and welfare outcomes. Most significantly, these surveys seldom contain the information necessary to construct an acceptable welfare measure, thus precluding the use of the survey for any poverty or distributional analysis. Furthermore, the lack of information on other sources of income limits the analytical use of these surveys for understanding the role of migration in household livelihoods. Finally, specialized surveys are often too costly for most developing countries to be carried out on a large-scale and sustainable basis.

Collecting information about migration as part of a larger multi-purpose data collection effort represents a good opportunity to learn more about migration in a cost-effective manner. However, as discussed by Lucas (2000), collecting detailed information on migration has not traditionally been a priority for most household surveys, including the Living Standards Measurement Study (LSMS) surveys. However, in response to the strong demand for more high-quality migration data, an increasing number of LSMS surveys now include extensive modules on different types of migration, such as the latest LSMS surveys conducted in Albania and Tajikistan.

Although at irregular frequencies, most countries now implement nationally representative, multi-topic household surveys *à la* LSMS for poverty monitoring and analysis. LSMS surveys are based on multi-topic questionnaires designed to study numerous aspects of household welfare and behavior, and integrating migration information into this data collection effort can be an efficient way to collect migration data. The extent of this integration will depend on a number of factors, including the perceived importance of the subject by the survey implementers and policymakers, as well as the necessary trade-offs dictated by the multi-purpose nature of the instrument. Using LSMS surveys to study migration offers specific advantages; most importantly, one can analyse the relationship between migration and a number of variables to a far greater degree than would be possible with other types of surveys such as a Household Budget Survey (HBS) or a Labor Force Survey (LFS). The main drawback of using LSMS-style surveys to study migration is that migrant populations are often too small relative to the entire population and tend to be clustered. Consequently, a typical multi-stage cluster sample of a multi-topic LSMS-style survey may not be able to capture a sufficient number of migrants to enable analysts to make accurate statistical inferences about those sub-populations. Additionally, as mentioned, multi-topic surveys are designed to cover a large number of issues, resulting in potential compromises with regards to the level of depth with which these issues can be explored. Despite these limitations, the increased insight that multi-topic surveys can provide into the complex interactions of migration with issues of policy and welfare makes them a worthwhile method for the study of migration in developing country contexts.

The main objective of this chapter is therefore to provide basic guidelines to researchers interested in studying migration for collecting migration information as part of a multi-topic household survey. We begin with a brief discussion of definitional and measurement issues with regards to various types of migration. We then address key methodological considerations that should be taken into account, focusing particularly on overcoming the rare aspects of migration through alternative sampling designs. Lastly, we consider the measurement of migration and other variables of interest from the perspective of questionnaire design, acknowledging the necessary trade-offs between length, content, and accuracy inherent to the implementation of a multi-topic LSMS-style survey.[2]

10.1 DEFINING AND MEASURING MIGRATION

10.1.1 Who is a 'Migrant'?

Unlike mortality and fertility, migration is not related to a tangible biological occurrence, making it one of the more difficult demographic phenomena to measure. Quantifying this inherently subjective concept is further complicated by the fact that there are several modes of migration, and that these modes of migration can in turn be partially determined by the varying motivations for migration (Zlotnick, 1987a, 1987b). It is important to keep these issues in mind while making the definitional decisions that may have far-reaching effects on future migration policy.

In order to properly quantify migration within the context of a household survey, one must first resolve the specific characteristics that define a migrant. Although no consensus currently exists on the exact definition of a migrant in its many forms, five individual characteristics can help analysts to determine which individuals should be considered migrants. These characteristics are: (1) the place of birth; (2) whether or not the individual resides in the place of birth; (3) household membership; (4) the duration of any stays away from the residence; and (5) a time period of reference. From the perspective of a household survey, in some contexts it may be important to measure all five of these characteristics in order to be able to classify survey respondents accurately and consistently.

Depending upon their relationship with the community being surveyed, migrants can either be classified as 'immigrants' or 'emigrants.' Individuals who were originally located elsewhere but who now reside in the surveyed community are defined as immigrants. Individuals who originally resided in the surveyed community but are now located elsewhere are defined as emigrants. The concept of location in this case refers to the local geographic area, which can depend upon context, but might best be considered the primary sampling unit used for the survey. For example, with regards to international migration, individuals with citizenship in another country who were not born in the destination country are defined as immigrants. Emigrants who remain within the country where the survey is being conducted are defined as 'internal emigrants'; those who now reside elsewhere in the world are known as 'international emigrants.' Unsurprisingly, immigrants can be readily identifiable within household surveys and censuses simply by asking about the country of birth and/or citizenship, since these surveys typically enumerate all household members currently residing within the surveyed community. Meanwhile, emigrants associated with the household are more difficult to identify and are generally not enumerated.

As a result, although it is crucial to understanding the relationship between migration and policy and may even be a more important phenomenon to study from a developing country's perspective, emigration is generally more difficult than immigration to quantify using household survey data or censuses. Generally, households in surveys (and censuses) are defined on the basis of the individuals who eat together and sleep under the same roof on a regular basis.[3] For the purposes of measuring and analysing migration, this definition lends itself well to the study of migration experiences among the surveyed population, including the prevalence of immigration. However, in order to study the impact of emigration, the survey needs to ask a range of questions regarding a group of individuals who are not resident at the time of the survey. In this context, the standard definition of a household member is less useful, as it excludes individuals who maintain ties to the household but clearly do not eat with other household members nor sleep in the household regularly. Therefore, when emigration is a focus of the survey, it becomes necessary to expand the definition of household members to include information about additional individuals who do not fit into the primary definition of the household.

10.1.2 Types of Migration

There are several types of migration that must be accounted for when conducting a survey on the topic. More specifically, it is necessary to define the various forms that migration can take and to delineate the potential rules that can be used to differentiate them from one another.

Short-term ('temporary') and long-term ('permanent') migrants may have different motivations and as a result the impact of each type of migration may differ. Since temporary and permanent migration may have different determinants, each type of migration may also affect the households that migrants left behind (that is, the 'source households') differently. Beyond this, either type of decision to migrate is not irreversible. A temporary migrant may decide to overstay and remain permanently in the host country or, vice versa, a permanent or long-term migrant may decide to go back home. Migrants may also leave seasonally; 'seasonal' migrants are similar to temporary migrants, but a seasonal migrant leaves the household for a short period of time annually at the same time of year. The implications of seasonal migration for households can differ from temporary migration, and therefore it is worth studying separately in a number of contexts.

When migration has taken place for some time from a geographic area, it is also important to consider identifying 'return migrants,' who can potentially catalyse development at the origin through the use of skills they learned while migrants or capital obtained as migrants. Return migrants must in turn be distinguished from 'circular migrants,' who are similar in that they may be resident in the household at the time of the survey, but differ in that they either come and go seasonally or migrate repeatedly, leaving every few years.

In household surveys, these concepts can be difficult to measure clearly. Temporary migration and permanent migration are usually distinguished by what can be considered to be an arbitrary threshold. For example, the United Nations (1998) uses a threshold of 12 months to separate temporary from permanent migrants. Return migration, seasonal migration, and circular migration can also be difficult to distinguish from one another. Seasonal or circular migrants can be mistakenly categorized as return migrants if the survey form is not specifically designed to capture repeat instances of migration either within the calendar year, in the case of seasonal migrants, or over several previous years, which would be needed to study circular migrants. Still others who have recently returned from a long migration spell might not be truly circular migrants, but may have the intention or willingness to migrate again if the right opportunity arose. This distinction could eventually result in differing policy outcomes – for example, migrants who have returned temporarily or have not fully committed to their return might be less likely to make investments at home.

Differentiating migrant 'stocks,' or the population present or missing from a country or area at a given time, from migration 'flows,' or the number of individuals leaving or returning to a country or area in a given period of time, is also important for measurement purposes. There are complications in measuring both of these phenomena. With regards to migration stocks, if a multi-topic household survey is used to estimate the international emigrant stock, one might count all emigrants from households in the sample, yet some of these emigrants may already have returned home to live in a different household and/or an urban area. A survey that attempts to estimate the emigrant stocks in this manner is therefore likely to double count migrants, as the same out-migrant may be claimed by two or more households in the sample, leading to an overestimate of out-migration. Migration flows are equally difficult to measure accurately. Within a specific time period, there can be a difference between the gross migration flow (including multiple migration spells for one migrant) and the net migration flow. If care is not taken to measure coming and going during the time period in question, net migration flows can miss instances of migration by seasonal or temporary migrants.

Although our discussion of migration so far has implicitly assumed international migration, 'internal' migration is typically a more common phenomenon. As an economy develops, migration naturally occurs from rural to urban areas of a country. Urbanization has been an inevitable part of the development process ever since the Industrial Revolution (for example, Taylor and Martin, 2001; Williamson, 1988). Moreover, there is a distinct lack of high quality, nationally representative data on internal migration (Foster and Rosenzweig, 2008). One conceptual difficulty with measuring internal migration is that the concept of 'urban' can be difficult to define from the perspective of a survey designed to learn about internal migration. Its definition differs from country to country, and therefore defining rural-urban migration consistently across countries may well be impossible. Extending the classification to include peri-urban areas may be useful, as most rural migrants tend to concentrate in the outskirts of large cities where environmental conditions and access to services are often different than in an urban setting.[4]

Finally, a large number of international migrants are 'undocumented,' making them more difficult to identify in survey data, in part because proxy respondents may not want to discuss their whereabouts or any remittances they receive from undocumented migrants in fear of negative repercussions for the migrant (Heckmann, 2004; Massey and Capoferro, 2004). Similarly, surveys collecting information about immigrants may miss undocumented immigrants, either because undocumented immigrants are less likely to appear in the sampling frame or because they are less likely to accept being interviewed if they are selected. From the perspective of emigration, it is a worthwhile investment to train enumerators to first make respondents comfortable before asking sensitive questions about potential undocumented migration.[5]

10.1.3 Identifying Migration in Survey Data

An LSMS survey designed to study migration must gather information on past or current migration events for all household members as well as, even if only partially, for former household members and for some individuals who fail to qualify as household members based on the residency rule adopted by the survey. One potential problem for studying migration is that such residency rules are often too stringent, resulting in the exclusion of individuals of interest. Alternatively, collecting information about individuals who are away or are no longer members of the household may

214 *Handbook of research methods in migration*

be difficult and ultimately of little use, particularly for individuals who left the household a long time ago. The main trade-off faced by the analyst relates to collecting enough information about migrants to ensure that information about people who are connected to the household is included, while avoiding inaccurate information and significantly extending the length of the interview.

To determine individuals for whom additional information should be enumerated, a first step is to consider relaxing the residency rule, so as to include more individuals in the main questionnaire. For example, one may want to include all individuals who have lived in the household in the past 12 months in the roster, and gather information on the months of presence over that period. Collecting information on more individuals, including the months of residence, would then enable the analyst to adjust the definition *ex post* according to the specific objective of the analysis. Once a more exhaustive list has been created in the roster, a rule must be established regarding the individuals for whom the full questionnaire should be administered and the individuals for whom one should ask a limited number of questions through proxy respondents. In summary, the survey must strike a balance between attempting to ask for more information than can be accurately recalled by proxy respondents and asking for too little information, meaning that relationships with previous members or members temporarily away would be missing. The key is to achieve this balance while maintaining the ability to calculate household size based on the national criteria of household membership.

One must next decide how to broadly identify migrants, with an eye to identifying both migrants who are currently away and migrants who left the household in the past and have now returned. To categorize individuals either as migrants or non-migrants, one should use a residency rule specific to migration in order to distinguish the household members who are to be considered migrants for the purposes of the survey. For example, if the rule is an absence of three months, members of the household who have been absent for more than three months for reasons other than health or family visits would be considered migrant household members, whether or not they were considered household members by the residency rule. Meanwhile, individuals who were away for a shorter period of time might not be considered migrants.

For return migration, one would be interested in knowing about all current household members with past migration experience over a given period, and particular to international migration, all former household members with past international migration experience who now live in the source country. If migrants have returned to the household, it is also important to include a line of questioning to learn whether they intend to migrate again, or if they have migrated for short periods repeatedly in the past, in order to determine whether they would be better categorized as seasonal migrants or circular migrants. There are challenges in collecting information on each of these broader groups, since long recall periods can lead to errors in the memories of migration experience among return migrants, while information on current out-migrants or return migrants living elsewhere must be collected from a proxy respondent and is therefore subject to its own set of problems.

Individuals who can be considered migrants may have left the household 20 or 30 years earlier or, conversely, they may be a member of that sub-group of individuals who were excluded because they did not pass the residency restriction. The amount of time since an individual left the household can be a factor in determining which individuals are to be considered migrants from the perspective of the survey. In specifying criteria for individuals considered to be out-migrants, one must further decide whether all former household members should be included (that is, any individual who lived in the household at any point in time) or whether migrants should be restricted to nuclear family members (that is, referring exclusively to the sons, daughters, and spouse of the household head). Including all former household members may result in the aggregate double counting of migrants, and may lead to greater inaccuracies in respondents' self-reported definition of household membership. On the other hand, restricting attention to nuclear family members may improve accuracy, but could lead to underestimates of total migration.

10.2 MIGRATION AS A RARE EVENT

A methodological consideration that must be taken into account when incorporating a migration component into a multi-topic survey arises from the fact that migration is a 'rare event.' Rare events are defined as statistical occurrences that happen infrequently; in this case, we mean that in a random selection of any household for our sample in a particular country, the probability that the household has a migrant is close to zero.[6] As a result, in a normal clustered sample design typical of multi-topic surveys, the expected number of households associated with emigration may be very low. Furthermore, in light of the likely geographic clustering of migration, there is a high chance that the sample may miss these areas altogether. In order to counter this lack of prevalence, it is important to consider various strategies for alternative sampling frames and alternative sample designs that can account for this issue.

A standard LSMS survey produces data on the distribution of living standards within a country using a nationally representative sample. The typical sample design of an LSMS is a multi-stage cluster design, usually involving two or more stages, and possible stratification based on some administrative or location subdivision. In the case of a two-stage design, primary sampling units (PSUs) are selected in the first stage – also referred to as Enumeration Areas (EAs), these depend on the local context and may constitute villages, sub-villages, urban neighborhoods, or even partitions of neighborhoods that have well-marked boundaries, as established by the national statistical agency. Households are then randomly selected within each PSU in the second stage. If each PSU is assigned a non-zero probability of selection in the first stage and there is an accurate household listing of the selected PSUs, one can then use the sample to make inferences about the entire population. In the context of migration, however, the problem is that aside from a few countries with an extremely high prevalence of migration and/or a very large sample size, a sample drawn in this fashion is unlikely to contain a sufficiently large number of migrants. This prevalence will obviously be affected by the chosen migrant definition but, in most cases, irrespective of the definition adopted, a random cluster sample is unlikely to meet the demands of the research.[7] Theoretically, one could simply increase the planned sample size to ensure that there are enough migrants for statistical analysis by either increasing the number of PSUs, the number of households in each PSU, or both. However, it must be emphasized that in most cases, this is not a cost-effective option. Furthermore, beyond the increase in monetary costs, the implications in terms of data quality and measurement error can be extremely taxing. Given these issues, alternative sampling designs are a preferable method of ensuring sufficient variation in the characteristics of migrants (or impacts) to reach meaningful conclusions. One reasonable alternative is to use some other type of probability sampling when choosing PSUs for an LSMS survey with a focus on migration. With this option, households in each of the selected PSUs can be selected according to some pre-established stratification assigning migrant households a higher probability of being selected. Methods for oversampling migrant households in each stage of selection, if feasible and properly implemented, can provide an adequate probability sample to study migration within the context of a traditional multi-topic survey. Unfortunately, the sampling frames generally used for drawing the sample, primarily the most recent population census, do not contain any information to allow this type of disproportionate sampling. In the best case scenario, the population census may contain information for the identification of immigrants, but the collection of information on emigrants is extremely rare. Alternative probability sampling techniques must then be adopted to collect information on a sufficiently large number of migrants in a traditional LSMS.

While the literature suggests a number of techniques to better identify rare events such as migration (for example, Kish, 1965), two alternative sampling designs are particularly appropriate for the study of migration: (1) disproportionate sampling of high migration PSUs and (2) stratified random sampling within PSUs, also known as two-phase sampling. These two methods can either be used individually or in conjunction.

A disproportionate sampling design means that PSUs with higher migration rates are identified prior to the survey and oversampled. In other words, PSUs known to have a high rate of emigration would be allocated a higher probability of selection as compared to PSUs with lower rates of migration. Representativeness would be regained through weighting. The first challenge to implement such a technique is to obtain an adequate sampling frame allowing for stratification based on the incidence of migration. Unfortunately, as mentioned, this is notoriously difficult to accomplish, as population censuses do not collect this information. When the information is not readily available in the frame itself, alternative methods can be attempted in order to identify high migration areas (see below). In addition to, or in lieu of, adopting disproportionate stratified sampling in the first stage of PSU selection, one may also implement some form of disproportionate selection of households within each of the selected PSUs. Even in relatively high migration areas, the prevalence of migration is unlikely to be so high that a random draw of households will be an efficient way to select a sufficiently large number of migrant households. This method, commonly referred to as two-phase sampling, requires a full listing operation in each selected PSU, which must collect information on the migration variable of interest (as defined by the study) to enable the oversampling of migrant households. By carrying out a listing operation, in which information on migrant status is elicited either directly from the household or through proxy respondents, one can clearly identify migration households to select a sample with more migrant households. A household survey conducted in Guatemala used this approach, canvassing selected communities to identify migrant households with the help of a short census-like questionnaire. In this case, the listing operation was part of a broader community census used by a large regional food security project to identify and characterize areas at high risk of food insecurity (Covarrubias and Carletto, 2009). When using this method, it is crucial that the probability of selecting a migrant household is explicitly known, so that weights can be constructed and any econometric estimation of the determinants of migration remains consistent (see Cameron and Trivedi, 2005, chapter 24 for a discussion). Relative to an overall survey budget, listing operations are not very expensive and ultimately may be the most cost-effective way to identify migrant households (Muñoz, 2007). One could also use alternative methods of learning about the prevalence of migration among the population prior to using disproportionate sampling, such as respondent-driven sampling (Heckathorn, 1997, 2002) or the aggregation point intercept method (McKenzie and Mistiaen, 2009).

As noted, to use the alternative sampling methods described above, it is important to have information about the prevalence of migration either prior to sampling PSUs or within sampled PSUs after they have been sampled. Ideally, this information could come from a census or a similar large survey; however, if emigration is being studied, the existence of such information is unlikely, since censuses rarely include information about migration, as mentioned above.[8] Assuming that such information is not available, one can use alternative sources to learn about migration prevalence. These sources may include expert opinions, qualitative surveys, or surveys in destination areas that contain information about the specific location from which the migrant departed. However, there are a number of potential drawbacks to this method. First, without statistical information on migration to design the sampling frame, it is impossible to create correct sampling weights. Furthermore, if one uses destination surveys to learn about migration in source areas, one must be aware that unless all the migrants in the country migrated to the destinations for which one has data, migrants who migrated to other destinations will likely be poorly represented in the sampling frame. Lastly, by relying on anecdotal or qualitative information rather than on statistical information to choose a sample, one might be concerned that the resulting sample of migrants will not be representative of the target migrant population. A potential alternative could be to apply Small Area Estimation (SAE) techniques to estimate the prevalence of migration by combining survey and census information.[9]

Assuming that migrants can be properly identified in the sampling frame, a further decision must be made as to whether to select based on the proportion of migrants over the population in the reference area or, conversely, based on the proportion of households with migrants out of the total number of households. As much of the analysis on migration is done at the household level, the second option will likely be preferable.[10] A third option is to base selection on the proportion of households with household heads as a migrant (Bilsborrow et al., 1997).[11]

Finally, aside from using disproportionate sampling as part of the actual LSMS sample, the possibility of drawing a booster sample – that

> **BOX 10.1 ALTERNATIVE METHODS OF SETTING UP TWO-STAGE SAMPLING**
>
> To select rare events, other non-probability sampling techniques may be used; for example, multiplicity methods such as snowballing have been widely used in the migration literature. One use of snowballing gathers information on undocumented migrants, using as a starting point (or a 'seed') a list of members of a diaspora organization or a list of migrants assisted by a non-governmental organization (NGO) in destination countries. The 'seed' household is used to identify additional migrant households of the same country of origin, and so on until the necessary number of observations is reached. Since snowball sampling does not generally lead to a representative sample, it is useful primarily for description but not for statistical inference. A variant of snowball sampling is 'respondent driven sampling,' developed by Heckathorn (1997, 2002). The issue with respondent driven sampling is that something must be known about the population in order to properly weight it to mimic a representative sample. If the migrant population is not accurately represented in the secondary information source, then respondent driven sampling is not a panacea either.
>
> Techniques such as random walks using selected households in a community as starting points can also be used to identify additional rare events. A recent survey of the Nikkei population in Brazil used the aggregation point intercept method (McKenzie and Mistiaen, 2009). They found that although the method led to a higher estimated population than the stratified random sample, the estimates became close after reweighting to account for individuals who appear in the sample multiple times. In all cases when using these non-probabilistic methods, it is crucial to collect ancillary information on the implementation of the sample to be able to identify the reference population in an attempt to make 'educated inferences' about a larger population group.

is, an oversample – of migrants beyond the original sample households should also be considered. To save on fieldwork costs, the booster sample can consist of migrant households from the same or adjacent EAs that have previously been identified as high migration areas. An added advantage of the use of booster samples is that a large survey also provides a large control group of households for possible matching.

10.3 QUESTIONNAIRE DESIGN

A major advantage of collecting migration information in the context of an LSMS is that it can be analysed in combination with data from other parts of the LSMS questionnaire. Even if analysing the impact of migration on specific outcomes of interest is the primary goal of the survey, it is important to first ensure that the survey can identify all of the potential types of migration taking place either within or from the country or context being studied, as well as the determinants of migration. The analyst should also attempt to include information on as many potential determinants of migration as possible, as an omitted determinant of migration might bias the analyses of outcomes of interest.

In this chapter we will not describe the modules in a typical LSMS which are fully detailed in Grosh and Glewwe (2000) and on the LSMS website at www.worldbank.org/lsms. Here it will suffice to say that migration data collected in the context of an LSMS survey can be analysed in combination with data from these other modules of the questionnaire to yield a rich array of information on the interaction of migration with other key variables both as determinants or consequences of migration, including welfare and inequality, income sources and coping strategies, wage differentials at origin and destination, returns to education, access to services and infrastructures, as well as violence, disease, climate change, and environmental disasters.

The focus of this last section is to propose some basic principles in incorporating migration information into an LSMS-type survey to enable researchers to carry out this type of analysis and policymakers to benefit from it. As has been previously established, the trade-offs that must be made in order to keep the length of the questionnaires manageable are of key importance. Another important point is that migrants are a more mobile segment of the population and are therefore less likely to be found at the time of interview. As a result, one must assess to what extent certain questions can be administered through proxy respondents while still collecting reliable information.

Broadly speaking, information can be collected concerning the previous migration experiences of two sets of individuals: (1) current household members, or any household members who have been present at some point during the past 12 months and (2) individuals who are still associated with the household but may not have lived in the household over the past 12 months.

By definition, individuals in the latter group are absent and thus a proxy respondent must always be used. Furthermore, some of these individuals may now only have remote links to the households, as they may have left long ago. If studying these individuals is the primary objective of the study, then tracking and interviewing them at the new location would be the only other option. Short of tracking, asking a minimal set of questions as part of the survey through a proxy respondent is feasible. These questions should be included in a separate roster/module and must include the age, gender, and civil status of the migrant, as well as the year she or he left the household and some basic information about the new location. In addition, questions on the migrant's occupation in the month prior to migrating and the current occupation should also be asked, together with questions concerning the migrant's remittance behavior. As already mentioned, this group of individuals could include all former household members, but it is preferable to limit the list to the spouse of the household head and all children of the head of the household and/or his or her spouse.

With respect to the first group of individuals – that is, the current household members or people who lived in the household at any point during the previous 12 months – we recommend beginning by asking a short battery of questions as part of the household roster. These should describe the household members who were only present for part of the year as well as those who are present at the time of the interview(s). If a given individual is present in the household all year, full information should be collected as regards that individual. Full information should also be collected for individuals present for part of the year and in the household at the time of the interview, even if they fail the residency rule. However, a standard rule must be established regarding the proxy evidence that should be collected when the individual is not available. The basic household roster module asked at the beginning of the survey can be used to help determine the information that should be collected by proxy. We recommend initially asking about anyone who is considered a household member or has lived in the household over the past 12 months. In this way, limited demographic information is immediately collected about all individuals who have spent some time in the household, including any migrants who are away or who may have left during the course of the year. Using this method, the measure of household size relevant for measuring per capita consumption is clearly available, as information is captured that allows specific individuals to be excluded from the household definition for consumption purposes.

Some individuals who no longer live in the household may not be migrants. Specifically, some may have left to set up a household elsewhere in the village or community, while others may have left to set up a household in a nearby community – neither of these groups should be classified as migrant individuals. In order to restrict the collection of detailed

Muñoz, J. (2007), 'Sampling: what you don't know can hurt you', Presentation at the Multi-topic Household Survey course, The World Bank, January.
Ratha, D., Mohapatra, S. and Silwal, A. (2009), 'Outlook for remittance flows 2009–2011: remittances expected to fall by 7–10 percent in 2009', Migration and Development Brief No. 10, The World Bank.
Richter, S. and Taylor, J.E. (2005), 'Policy reforms and the gender dynamics of rural Mexico-to-U.S. migration', Working Paper 05-007, Department of Agricultural and Resource Economics, University of California at Davis.
Smith, J. and Thomas, D. (2003), 'Remembrances of things past: test-retest reliability of retrospective migration histories', *Journal of the Royal Statistical Society, Series A* (*Statistics in Society*), **166** (1), 23–49.
Taylor, J.E and Martin, P.L. (2001), 'Human capital: migration and rural population change', in G. Rausser and B. Gardner (eds), *Handbook of Agricultural Economics*, New York: Elsevier Science Publishers, pp. 458–511.
Thailand (2007), *The Labor Force Survey: Whole Kingdom, Quarter 4: October – December 2006. Report in Thai and English*, Bangkok: NSO, Ministry of Information and Communication Technology.
United Nations (1998), 'Recommendation on statistics of international migration: revision 1', Statistical Papers Series M, No. 58, Rev. 1, Department of Economic and Social Affairs, Statistics Division, New York.
United Nations (2009), 'International migration 2009', Population Division, New York.
Williamson, J.G. (1988), 'Migration and urbanization', in H. Chenery and T.N. Srinivisan (eds), *Handbook of Development Economics*, New York: Elsevier Science Publishers, pp. 426–46.
World Bank (2011), *Migration and Remittances Factbook 2011*, Washington, DC: The World Bank.
Zlotnick, H. (1987a), 'Introduction: measuring international migration: theory and practice', *International Migration Review*, **21** (4), v–vii.
Zlotnick, H. (1987b), 'The concept of international migration as defined in data collection systems', *International Migration Review*, **21** (4), 925–46.

11 Migration and its measurement: towards a more robust map of bilateral flows
Ronald Skeldon

The issue of data is central to the study of migration. In many ways, it is also its Achilles heel: weaknesses in the data have been identified in so many serious studies of migration, with calls for improvement in the quantity and quality of the information available for the study of the movement of population. However, one group of experts has drawn attention to 'a century of ignored recommendations' (Center for Global Development, 2009, p. 3). At the beginning of the twenty-first century, we seem to be uttering the very same pleas for better data on migration that we were making at the end of the nineteenth century, with little sign of progress across the intervening years. As robust data provide the evidence on which policy on migration is based, that same group of experts goes on to state categorically 'the nonexistence or inaccessibility of detailed, comparable, disaggregated data on migrant stocks and flows is the greatest obstacle to the formulation of evidence-based policies to maximize the benefits of migration for economic development around the world' (Center for Global Development, 2009, p. 5).

The reasons why little apparent progress has been achieved towards improving the quantity and quality of migration data are complex and the result not just of any lack of political will but also of the nature of migration itself. This chapter endorses the latest robust recommendations to improve migration data from the panel of experts but shifts the focus to review why the nature of migration makes it so difficult to measure. However, before going on to consider this substantive issue, it is perhaps worthwhile to venture a few thoughts on why governments find the collection of migration data so problematic. Migration is generally a highly sensitive topic where the debate tends to be dominated by opinion rather than evidence. Migration is rarely seen as a 'good thing' by governments where the electorate and public opinion are unlikely to favour further immigration. Not knowing the full details of certain issues can sometimes be advantageous. Be that as it may, rarely is migration a top priority for policy makers even if it sometimes seems to be a top political issue. Nevertheless, it is difficult to deny the significance of basic migration information for policy purposes: where immigrants come from; when they came; and their basic skills and characteristics. Certainly, in the United Kingdom, the 2011 population census is likely to deliver some of the most comprehensive information on migration yet available, together with considerable further detail on cognate issues such as citizenship and ethnicity.

This chapter will suggest ways in which the quantity and quality of data can be improved, with the aim of creating a more accurate global map of bilateral flows between countries rather than simply improving information on migration in general. A much more comprehensive discussion of methodologies to measure international migration is available in Bilsborrow et al. (1997). This chapter has the more limited objective to move towards an improved global database of origin and destination flows rather than reviewing all systems of relevant data-gathering. It assumes that an understanding of the spatial pattern of migration, the basic geography of the flows, is fundamental to informing any future policy designed to manage migration more effectively.

Migration is the third of the demographic variables but, unlike the other two, births and deaths, it is not a unique event but a continuous process across time and space. Thus, the number of migrants identified in any data-gathering exercise is essentially a function of how migration is defined and these definitions vary across countries but even within a country depending upon the objectives of those defining the migration. Fundamental to the study of migration is the question of numbers and, ideally, the types of people moving from A to B. Yet this simple question is not at all easy to answer. How is 'a migrant' to be defined? Any definition of migration must be in terms of time and space. That is, in order to be defined as 'a migrant', a person will have to have travelled a certain distance from their place of usual residence and be away for a certain period of time. It is at this early point in the discussion that the difference between international migration, on the one hand, and internal migration, on the other, needs to be drawn. The focus in this chapter will primarily be on the former but will incorporate internal migration as common issues do exist and students of international migration may be able to learn from the experiences of measuring internal migration.

In terms of international migration, the spatial dimension seems clear: if a person has moved from one independent state or territory to another, then he or she can be defined as an international migrant. The principal question is the length of residence a person has to have completed in order to be defined as 'a migrant'. Short-term visitors such as tourists are not considered as migrants as they, theoretically, have no intention to stay. However, with the revolution in relatively cheap air transportation and a globalization of economies, the numbers of short-term movers have proliferated to include those moving for business meetings or to attend conferences or training courses. Many industries have been outsourced from the developed to the developing world and a constant stream of staff within transnational firms move around the world to establish, expand and maintain these enterprises, as well as to train and rotate personnel. The number of international organizations and international non-governmental organizations has increased, adding to the numbers moving around the world. We are certainly in an 'age of mobility' even if not quite an 'age of migration' as the title of Castles and Miller's classic text might suggest (2009). This complexity of human movement makes its measurement and monitoring a challenging task indeed.

11.1 THE BASIC TOOLS TO MEASURE MIGRATION

11.1.1 Continuous Data-gathering Systems

Generally, people who cross an international border legally have to enter another country under a specific visa-entry category except in cases where agreements among states allow a waiver, as in the Schengen group of countries in Europe or between Australia and New Zealand, for example. Categories of entry include immigrants who are coming with the intention to settle. These cover principal applicants coming to live and work and various categories to allow family reunification after the principal applicant and his or her immediate family has immigrated. Other categories of permanent immigrants can include those whose entry is approved on the basis that they will establish businesses in the destination country. These immigrants enter as entrepreneurs or investors. Other immigrant categories can include those who wish to retire in a particular country. Non-immigrant categories are also important entry categories and include those coming to study and several categories requiring temporary employment visas ranging from the highly skilled to less skilled labour. A humanitarian category to cover refugees and asylum seekers is another important entry category in many countries. All these entry categories are for those who will be in the country either permanently or for an extended period, legally, at least.

Hence, the purpose of entry through the immigration procedure, which is itself the result of state immigration policy, is central to categorizing the number and type of migrants. Students of international migration focusing on the major destination countries, and principally the United States, Australia, Canada and New Zealand, have relied heavily on these continuous systems of data-gathering, which are normally published annually, in order to understand immigration to those countries. In the twenty-first century, useful though these sources remain for these particular countries, the demand for migration data has changed. The number of countries that have the capacity to collect and process continuous entry records is limited to the more highly developed countries with a relatively efficient bureaucratic apparatus. However, no matter how good the data-gathering capability of an individual country is, difficulties emerge if comparison between one country and another is attempted. Visa-entry categories can vary from country to country, definitions of student or the skilled vary, as does the length of time used to draw distinctions between long-term and short-term entrants. Periods for which the data are published vary, with some countries favouring the calendar year and others the (variously defined) fiscal year. International organizations such as the United Nations, and particularly its Population Division and its Statistics Division, as well as specialized agencies such as the International Labour Organization, are encouraging countries to move towards common definitions and procedures, although much still remains to be done. The annual SOPEMI reports of OECD, or the most developed economies of the world, provide the most useful summary of such data sources.

Quite apart from these questions of comparability, several other factors are encouraging us to extend our databases away from the continuous immigration registers. The first relates to the whole issue of categories of entry. These are becoming less useful as their boundaries erode. Many of those who enter as permanent settlers either move on or return home, and often quite quickly. See the examples that have been identified among Chinese migrants to Australasia or North America (Skeldon, 1994), although whether that particular group is any more or less mobile than other groups is less clear. Increasingly, many of those who enter as non-immigrants, students for example, become permanent settlers upon graduation. Hence, slippage among the entry categories exists. It is estimated that more than half of the one million immigrants accepted for permanent residence in the United States every year between 1996 and 2005 adjusted their status (Jasso et al., 2010, p. 478): that is, they had already been in the United States at the time they became permanent residents. Hence, the immigration records will have to be readjusted by year of arrival if a number for the annual flow of migrants into the United States is to be obtained. The published data are becoming less useful as a source for the study of actual migration.

Second, some of those admitted in a non-immigrant category, and perhaps particularly in a short-term visitor category as trainee or tourist, may decide to remain as an overstayer and become an irregular migrant.

Third, and most controversially, large numbers are entering countries without going through any formal channel at all, simply walking across the border or arriving by boat and landing on a beach. These illegal entrants are generally termed irregular migrants. Their migration is often hazardous and many have died in the attempt. Nevertheless, their numbers are substantial and almost certainly growing, with over 12 million estimated to be in the United States, the vast majority from Mexico, and between 1.9 and 3.8 million in the 27 states of the European Union.[1] These irregular migrants form the majority of immigrants in many developing countries such as Thailand or Malaysia. Clearly, these numbers do not appear in the continuous immigration records.

A fourth factor that undermines the usefulness of continuous migration registration systems is their partiality: they tend only to collect information on those arriving in a country and not on those leaving. Of highly developed economies, only Australia, New Zealand, Japan and Korea have detailed continuous records of those leaving, by category. We have no idea how many people leave the United States or the United Kingdom, for example. However, an uneasy feeling exists that large numbers of native-born as well as immigrants do leave, the former largely on a short-term basis for work and the latter either fairly soon after arrival or at the end of their working lives when they may return home to retire. A 'best-estimate' of the number of British nationals living abroad is 5.6 million, around 9 per cent of the UK resident population, with another half a million living abroad for part of the year (Finch et al., 2010; also Sriskandarajah and Drew, 2006). While this is a substantial number, the figure includes returning immigrants who had gained British citizenship while in the United Kingdom.

The above discussion suggests that the continuous migration data collection system is inadequate for the analysis of population migration in the modern world. This does not mean that these systems should be abandoned: far from it. Their advantage over the retrospective data-gathering systems to be discussed below is that they can generate information on a regular basis that can be much timelier than the data from population censuses, which may be taken only every ten years. Hence, continuous systems, from a policy point of view, are likely to be viewed favourably by governments and every effort needs to be made to extend and improve these systems, particularly to cover emigrant flows. Nevertheless, these systems are expensive and do omit important aspects of migrant flows, particularly in the developing world where these systems are partial at best. Even in developed countries, these systems can also be partial as it is logistically virtually impossible to cover all entry points adequately. Electronic visa records and cyberborders will only capture some of this some time to come. The birthplace data, if generated for small areas, may also provide the best source to create a sample frame for the design of later specialized surveys, discussed below.

11.2.3 The Issue of the System of Enumeration Applied

The third generic limitation of censuses for the study of migration relates to the nature of the enumeration system applied. Either one of two systems can be employed to record the population where it lives, de facto or de jure registration, although modifications can be introduced to blur the exact distinction between the two. De facto enumeration records the population where it is found at the time of the census: de jure enumeration records the population where it usually lives at the time of the census. It is often argued that the de jure method is the more appropriate for the study of migration as students of the subject are interested in longer-term shifts in residence. However, as emphasized earlier in this chapter, in our globalized world, non-immigration and short-term mobility are becoming increasingly a characteristic of the global migration system. De jure registration systems in Asia have been shown seriously to underenumerate circular and shorter-term internal migrants (Chamratrithirong et al., 1995; Skeldon, 1987) and no reason exists not to expect them to omit short-term international migrants too. De facto systems of enumeration, on the other hand, will, if correctly applied, capture a much higher number of these types of movers. Hence, the number and types of migrants captured by the census will vary by the system of enumeration adopted.

11.2.4 Towards a Global Inventory of Available Migration Data

The limitations identified above are raised not to undermine the quality of the existing migration data but to draw attention to potential weaknesses in the existing data. A global inventory of how countries have collected and coded their retrospective data needs to be compiled. Such an inventory should include for each country:

1. The migration questions included in the most recent census, if any.
2. The level to which international birthplace or previous place of residence data were coded.
3. Whether sampling was employed for the collection of the migration data.
4. The nature of the census enumeration system adopted.
5. The actual matrices of global origin-destination flows by:

- stocks
- flows.

The data contained in the inventory will help in the assessment of the types, quantity and quality of the migration-related data available around the world that are required for the creation of a global origin-destination database of both stocks and flows. It will also show where attention most needs to be directed in attempts to improve the quality and quantity of future data.

11.3 SAMPLE SURVEYS

Sample surveys form an important type of retrospective data-gathering instrument for the collection of data on migration.[7] These are various and vary from national surveys taken mainly by governments down to the thousands of local surveys taken by individual researchers. In terms of the creation of, or contribution to, global migration databases, attention in this chapter will only touch upon national surveys. These large-scale surveys too are various but the most relevant ones are the regular cycles of labour force surveys and demographic and health surveys. The former are mainly taken in developed economies on a regular, usually quarterly, basis and generate much useful data on migrant and non-migrant employment. The sample strategy is based on randomly selected households throughout a country rather than area sampling, allowing a much more reliable estimate of migrant populations.

The Organisation for Economic Co-operation and Development (OECD) compiles and publishes such data on an annual basis (for example, OECD, 2009). However, these data deal mainly with the flow data published from the immigration records and described earlier in the chapter, and stock data based on birthplace in the most developed countries of the world. This source is of lesser use in assessing global stocks and flows of migration even if the principal destinations of global migration, which do account for most migrants, are included within the OECD economies. Just over one third of the global migrant stock is accounted for by the United States, Canada, Australia, Germany, France and. the United Kingdom, for example.

The demographic and health surveys (DHS) have been taken in over 80 developing countries and although migration is rarely a specific objective of such surveys, they can be used to look at various dimensions of internal migration and health status and the use of health services. They have only limited use for the study of international migration flows. The University of Sussex has compiled an inventory of data from surveys, including from the DHS that can be used for the analysis of the migration of children but again these studies relate mainly to internal migrations. A further important multi-country national survey is the Living Standards Measurement Surveys (LSMS) of the World Bank. Like the DHS, these do not always include information of use to migration researchers, although for some countries such as Albania, a specialized module on migration was incorporated.[8]

Purpose-designed surveys on migration can be designed but again these are generally more relevant to the study of internal than international migration. In the early 1980s, for example, two comprehensive sets of guidelines were published for the design of national migration surveys (Bilsborrow et al., 1984; ESCAP, 1980–84). Nevertheless, data from the National Migration of Thailand, for example, did pick up a considerable number of households with members abroad. While the data from these surveys could not be used to estimate either the stock of Thais abroad or the flows of Thais leaving the country, they can provide much valuable information on the detail of specific migrations and the social and economic condition and context of these moves. The advantage of purpose-designed migration surveys is that they can collect very detailed information on the whole sequence of migrations over the lifetimes of individuals, showing just how complex the process actually is. Because the data are collected on a sample basis, only highly trained interviewers are used, thus ensuring the quality of the data collected. While such data can be collected through national migration surveys, they are perhaps best collected through community or local surveys. These surveys have a long tradition (Balán et al., 1973, for example) but perhaps reached their greatest significance in the Mexican Migration Project and its extension, the Latin American Migration Project, based at Princeton University and the University of Guadalajara. Based on ethnosurveys, the detailed data are posted online for public use and provide the insightful micro-data to the macro-data required for the construction of global origin-destination flows.[9]

11.4 ISSUES OF INTERPRETATION

Once a global origin-destination database has been constructed using the methods outlined above in, for example, a 226 x 226 matrix (Parsons et al., 2007), issues of interpretation emerge. Perhaps the greatest added value of the global database is to focus attention on migration in parts of the world other than the traditional destination countries in Australasia and North America and the newer destination countries in Europe. It draws attention to what has become known as South-South migration, or migrations within the less developed parts of the world. For example, in the existing global origin-destination database, South-South migration accounted for 24 per cent of global migration compared with 37 per cent for South-North and 16 per cent North-North (Parsons et al., 2007, p. 37). However, these broad regional and development categories have to be treated with great care. Much of the migration is to newly emerging developed areas in what was once considered to be 'the developing world' whose levels of development have come or are coming to rival the conditions in the developed world. This development is to be found not just in countries such as Singapore, Malaysia or Argentina but in parts of countries where huge numbers of poor still exist such as in China, India or Brazil. Globalization, while producing some clear trends towards homogeneity in economic, social and political systems, is also generating huge inequalities that are being reflected in the internal and international migrations observed today.

The information that X number of migrants left China for the United States or Y migrants left Bangladesh for the United Kingdom over a specific period of time is useful but raises more questions than it answers. A point raised under sampling above referred to the issue of the concentration of migrant origins as well as destinations. International migration is not just from China, Bangladesh, India, Mexico, Peru or Ghana to foreign destinations: it is from very specific parts of these countries to those foreign destinations. Ideally, we would like to know from which parts of the country migrants come and particularly whether they are from urban or rural origins. Given the issues of coding discussed above, it is quite clear that specific origins within countries cannot be included in national population census coding, illustrating the importance of sample survey or other data sources in augmenting the basic data derived from censuses.

A final issue that complicates interpretations of the data comes from boundary changes of the migrant-defining areas. This issue has plagued the analysis of internal migration as both administrative boundaries and urban-rural boundaries have changed over time in response to both political and developmental change. However, it is also relevant for the study of international migration as new states appear. The disintegration of the former Soviet Union and the former Yugoslavia created a number of new states when previous internal migrations became international. This not only complicates coding of places of birth or places of previous residence in subsequent censuses, where responses may relate to a prior political geography, but also any longitudinal assessment of the patterns of international migration. The principal solution to this issue is to be aware of the changes and to make adjustments as appropriate by returning to prior censuses if necessary and recreating internal migrations as if they were international. In this way, comparisons with the later period can be made in much the same way as adjustments for changes to the boundaries of internal migration-defining units often need to be made.

11.5 CONCLUSION

This chapter has examined the main means through which information relevant to the creation of a global migrant origin-destination matrix can be generated. It examined the strengths and limitations of the various approaches to the collection of the data, drawing attention to some issues that are often not well highlighted in the migration literature. The complexity of the migration process and the limitations of the several ways of measuring migration might give the impression that the task to improve the quality and quantity of migration-related data is futile. Perhaps, and in the context of the panel of experts cited at the outset of this chapter, we might still be bemoaning the weaknesses in the data in another 100 years. Nevertheless, progress has been made over the recent past. It was not so long ago that few direct questions existed for the measurement of internal migration. If we take the developed country of Canada, a major study of internal migration made from the 1961 census used indirect methods to calculate interprovincial net migration (George, 1970). Such methods would rarely be used today. Then, the direct question on migration was taken only on a sample basis and omitted parts of the sampled population. Great progress has been made in studying internal migration over the last 50 years. We can surely expect further improvements to be made over the next 50 years and particularly in the collection of information relevant to the study of international migration. This chapter has adopted an almost idealistic approach to the topic: what would be the ideal data required to produce a more robust database of global bilateral flows? If we can move only partially along the directions suggested in extending retrospective questions in censuses, improving coding and sampling strategies, then progress will gradually be made. However, as the discussions towards the end of the chapter emphasize, other data sources will always be required to reinforce the macro-level data. If these other approaches can be made more systematic in terms of being located within the framework of the macro-data and with adequate control between migrant and non-migrant populations, then progress will be further enhanced. It is currently an exciting time for students in migration studies, both internal and international, and a momentum and commitment appear to be building for real improvements in migration data and we can look forward to more extensive and robust sources in the future.

NOTES

1. Estimates of the number of irregular migrants in the United States come from the Pew Institute, see http://pewresearch.org and those for the European Union from the Clandestino project, see http://scoopproject.org.uk (accessed 6 May 2011).
2. I am indebted to the United Nations Statistics Division, New York, which responded efficiently to my requests for data. See also, 'Principles and recommendations for population and housing censuses' and their implementation in the 2010 census round, New York, United Nations Statistics Division, available at http://unstats.un.org/unsd/demographic/sources/census/2010_PHC/Census_Clock/CountriesPerTopic.pdf (accessed 6 May 2011).
3. The global migrant origin-destination database can be found on the website of the Development Research Centre on Migration, Globalisation and Poverty at the University of Sussex, available at http://www.migrationdrc.org/research/typesofmigration/global_migrant_origin_database.html (accessed 6 May 2011)..
4. In the 2000 round of censuses, some 109 countries took a clearly defined previous point in time against which to record a previous place of residence (for two countries, the dates, confusingly, were not clear). Fully 61 of those countries used five years previous to the census, 26 countries used one year prior to the census, five countries used two years and 17 countries used a date around ten years prior to the census. Some 19 of the 109 countries asked previous place of residence at two points in time and two countries asked questions at three different points in time. These figures were derived from information supplied by the United Nations Statistics Division, New York.
5. These data were presented in an Ipsos MORI report on a Migrant Survey Feasibility Study for the United Kingdom Border Agency, London, April 2010.
6. Data from the United Nations Statistics Division, New York.
7. See also Carletto et al. (Chapter 10, this volume).
8. See the website of the Child Migration Research Network at http://www.childmigration.net (accessed 6 May 2011). A further database is being prepared to incorporate migration-relevant information available in major national migration surveys to appear on the website of the migration DRC at the University of Sussex, available at http://www.migrationdrc.org.
9. See http://lamp.opr.princeton.edu (accessed 6 May 2011).

REFERENCES

Balán, J., Browning, H.L. and Jelín, E. (1973), *Men in a Developing Society: Geographic and Social Mobility in Monterrey, Mexico*, Austin, TX and London: University of Texas Press.

Bilsborrow, R.E., Oberai, A.S. and Standing, G. (1984), *Migration Surveys in Low-income Countries: Guidelines for Survey and Questionnaire Design*, London: Croom Helm (for the World Employment Programme of the International Labour Organization).

Bilsborrow, R.E., Hugo, G., Oberai, A.S. and Zlotnik, H. (1997), *International Migration Statistics: Guidelines for Improving Data Collection Systems*, Geneva: International Labour Organization.

Castles, S. and Miller, M. (2009), *The Age of Migration: International Population Movements in the Modern World*, 4th edn, London: Macmillan.

Center for Global Development (2009), *Migrants Count: Five Steps Toward Better Migration Data*, Report of the Commission on International Migration Data for Development Research and Policy, Washington, DC: Center for Global Development.

Chamratrithirong, A., Archavanitkul, K. and Richter, K. et al. (1995), *National Migration Survey of Thailand*, Bangkok: Institute for Population and Social Research, Mahidol University.

ESCAP (1980–84), *National Migration Surveys: Survey Manuals Volumes I–X*, New York: United Nations, Economic and Social Commission for Asia and the Pacific.
Finch, T., Andrew, H. and Latorre, M. (2010), *Global Brit: Making the Most of the British Diaspora*, London: Institute for Public Policy Research.
George, M.V. (1970), *Internal Migration in Canada: Demographic Analyses*, Ottawa: Dominion Bureau of Statistics.
Jasso, G., Wadhwa, V., Rissing, B. and Freeman, R. (2010), 'How many highly skilled foreign-born are waiting in line for U.S. legal permanent residence?', *International Migration Review*, **44** (2), 477–97.
OECD (2009), *International Migration Outlook: SOPEMI 2009. Special Focus: Managing Labour Migration Beyond the Crisis*, Paris: Organisation for Economic Co-operation and Development.
Parsons, C.R., Skeldon, R., Walmsley, T.L. and Winters, L.A. (2007), 'Quantifying international migration: a database of bilateral migrant stocks', in Ç. Özden and M. Schiff (eds), *International Migration, Economic Development and Policy*, Washington, DC: The World Bank, pp. 17–58.
Skeldon, R. (1987), 'Migration and the population census in Asia and the Pacific: issues, questions and debate', *International Migration Review*, **21** (4), 1074–100.
Skeldon, R. (1994), 'Hong Kong in an international migration system', in R. Skeldon (ed.), *Reluctant Exiles? Migration from Hong Kong and the New Overseas Chinese*, New York and Hong Kong: M.E. Sharpe and Hong Kong University Press, pp. 21–51.
Sriskandarajah, D. and Drew, C. (2006), *Brits Abroad: Mapping the Scale and Nature of British Emigration*, London: Institute for Public Policy Research.
United Nations (2009), *International Migration 2009*, New York: Department of Economic and Social Affairs, Population Division.

12 Experimental approaches in migration studies
David McKenzie and Dean Yang

Individuals and households decide whether or not to migrate – and whether or not to send remittances if they do migrate – with the outcome of these choices depending upon their skills, wealth, risk preferences, ambition, drive, family ties, and a myriad of other observable and unobservable characteristics. This self-selection of migrants poses a severe challenge for researchers attempting to ascertain the impacts of migration or remittances on individuals, families, and communities. For example, suppose we observe that children are more likely to attend school in households with a migrant than in households without a migrant. This may reflect the income effect of remittances, but could just as easily reflect that children in households with migrants have higher quality parental education, or better language skills, or that it is parents who care most about the education of their children who migrate to earn the money needed to pay for schooling costs. As a result, even if we condition on a wide array of observable characteristics, comparisons of migrants and non-migrants are unlikely to give convincing estimates of the impacts of migration.

Experimental approaches to migration studies aim to overcome this difficulty by exploiting situations where the reason one household engages in migration or remits and another does not is truly the result of random chance. This may occur as a result of policy experiments, such as visa lotteries; through natural experiments whereby 'nature' provides the source of exogenous variation; and through researcher-led field experiments which are explicitly designed to test specific theories of constraints to migration or remittance behavior. The purpose of this chapter is to introduce readers to the need for this approach, give examples of where it has been applied in practice, and draw out lessons for future work in this area. We begin with a short discussion to illustrate the perils and challenges of trying to estimate the causal impacts of migration or remittances using non-experimental approaches, and then discuss the different experimental approaches, before concluding with lessons for future work.

250 *Handbook of research methods in migration*

12.1 THE CHALLENGE OF ASSESSING THE CAUSAL IMPACT OF MIGRATION[1]

A large part of the development literature in migration attempts to answer questions of the form: 'what is the effect of migration or remittances on outcome Y?' One branch of this focuses on the migrants themselves, and is interested in how migration changes their incomes, health, stress levels, and life opportunities. A second branch focuses on remaining household members and communities in the sending areas, and is interested in the impact of having a household member migrate or of receiving remittances on the education and health of children, on levels of entrepreneurship and labor supply of adult members, and on poverty and inequality levels in the village. A common approach to answering such questions is to use survey data on migrants and non-migrants, and attempt to control for differences between them in a linear regression framework. We will set this out for the case of estimating the impact of migration, but the challenge is analogous for estimating the impact of remittances. For example, researchers may attempt to estimate an equation of the form:

$$Y_i = \alpha + \beta Migrant_i + \delta' X_i + \varepsilon_i \qquad (12.1)$$

where $Migrant_i$ is a dummy variable which takes the value 1 if the individual is a migrant, and zero if he or she is not, Y_i is the outcome of interest (for example, individual income), and X_i are a set of observed characteristics of the individual which are presumed not to have changed with migration (for example, age, sex and education level, location of birth, ethnicity, religion, parental education, and so on).[2] Then in order for the linear regression estimate of β to give the causal impact of migration on the outcome of interest, we require that:

$$E(Migrant_i \varepsilon_i | X_i) = 0 \qquad (12.2)$$

That is, we require the unobserved determinants of the outcome of interest (income in our example) to be uncorrelated with whether or not an individual migrates once we have conditioned on the observable characteristics of these individuals. But in the absence of experimental variation in migration, this assumption is unlikely to hold. Indeed, the seminal migration selectivity model of Borjas (1987) has migrants deciding whether or not to migrate in part on the basis of the ε_i they would expect to have at home versus abroad. It is easy to think of a whole range of typically unmeasured variables, such as entrepreneurial prowess, ambition, language proficiency, and health status which would both affect whether or not someone migrates, and also directly affect their income or other outcome of interest. Likewise liquidity constraints will likely determine both the pattern of self-selection of migrants (McKenzie and Rapoport, 2010), as well as the range of job opportunities and consumption-smoothing opportunities that individuals will have at home. As a result, Equation (12.2) will almost always be violated in practice, so that linear regression on Equation (12.1) will result in biased estimates of the impact of migration.

Equation (12.2) therefore says that we can only estimate the causal impact of migration if the only reason one person migrates and another does not is random (conditional on observed characteristics). That is, ideally we would randomly choose some people to migrate and others not to, and then by comparing these two groups, get the impact of migration. This is precisely what the experimental approach attempts to do.

12.2 POLICY EXPERIMENTS

Several countries use visa lotteries to choose among numerous applicants desiring to immigrate through a particular migration category that has a fixed quota. The most famous of these is the US Diversity Visa Lottery (commonly known as the Green Card Lottery), which each year makes available 50,000 visas, to be drawn randomly among eligible applications from countries with low rates of immigration to the United States. For the 2010 lottery, over 13.6 million qualified entries were received, with 102,800 applicants drawn as winners, under the assumption that half of these would migrate.[3] Whilst this is the most well-known example of a migration lottery, it has not been used for research yet.

Researchers have exploited smaller lottery programs. The first such set of studies considered the Pacific Access Category program for Tonga, which provides an opportunity for 250 individuals each year to move to New Zealand, with a random ballot used to select among all eligible applications received. McKenzie et al. (2010) collaborated with the New Zealand Department of Labour to draw a sample of individuals who had their names selected in this ballot, as well as a sample of those who applied but whose names were not drawn. They then surveyed the ballot winners in New Zealand, their remaining family members in Tonga, and the ballot losers in Tonga. As with the US diversity visa, not all those whose names were chosen in the lottery migrated, so the authors also had to survey in Tonga the ballot winners who did not migrate.

If everyone who applied for the migration lottery ended up migrating, and no one who lost the lottery migrated, then linear regression of Equation (12.1) (with or without the X controls) for the sample of lottery applicants would give a consistent estimate of the causal impact of migration for people who enter the migration lottery program. However, in practice, some of those who win the lottery may not move (they may change their mind, or fail an entry requirement), whilst a few of those who lose the lottery may find other ways of migrating. In such cases, the outcome of the lottery can be used as an instrumental variable for migration, and still be used to identify the impact of migration on the outcome of interest. If the impact of migration varies across individuals (is heterogeneous), then what will be identified is the local average treatment effect (LATE). Recently there has been debate as to whether the LATE is a parameter of interest in many experiments (for example, Deaton, 2010; Imbens, 2010). However, in the case of a migration lottery, it is easy to argue that the parameter is giving an effect of policy interest. The LATE tells us the impact of migrating for someone who would migrate if they won the lottery, and not migrate otherwise. This is precisely what we would be interested in when assessing the impacts of such policies on development outcomes.

McKenzie et al. (2010) use this migration lottery to estimate that Tongans moving to New Zealand have a 263 percent increase in income, within the first year of moving. The migrants also benefit in terms of improved mental health (Stillman et al., 2009). The authors then use a sample of non-applicants to the lottery and a large sample of the overall population and compare the experimental estimate to what one would obtain using non-experimental methods. They find that linear regression would overstate the income gain to migration by 27 to 35 percent, which is consistent with migrants being positively selected on unobservables (the authors find positive selection on observables). Using non-experimental methods like difference-in-differences or propensity score matching reduces this overstatement a little, but still results in an overstatement of around 20 percent in the income gain from migration. The only non-experimental method that gets close to the experimental estimate is a good instrumental variable.

Migration policies typically limit which other family members can migrate along with the principal migrant, often restricting this just to the spouse and dependent children of the migrant. This policy rule can be used alongside a migration lottery to deal with a second form of selectivity – selectivity into which household members move and which remain in the home country. Gibson et al. (forthcoming a) use the combination of the policy rule and the lottery to look at the impact of migration on remaining household members in Tonga, finding evidence that remaining household members appear worse off in the short term, with lower per capita incomes and consumption.

Experimental approaches in migration studies 253

The above studies relied on the use of administrative data to track winners and losers in the Pacific Access Category. It requires considerable effort and enlightened policymakers in order for researchers to obtain access to such data. An alternative approach would be to attempt to locate households with lottery winners and losers in a survey in the migrant-sending country. Gibson et al. (forthcoming b) provide an example of this approach, using a representative survey of Samoan households to identify households which entered the Samoan Quota lottery, which allows 1100 Samoans to migrate to New Zealand each year. Since Samoa's population is small, the lottery had been in place for several years, and there were 5000–7000 applications for the lottery each year, a random sample of households was able to identify sufficient numbers of lottery winners and losers for experimental analysis of the impact of migration through this category. In contrast to the Tongan results, the Samoan experiment finds migration to have reduced poverty and increased household incomes among remaining household members. However, there is suggestive evidence that this positive effect may be short-lived, with remittances and home production falling with time spent abroad of migrant members.

Clemens (2010) provides a final example of the use of a lottery provided by migration policy. He studies the H1-B visa, which is an admission channel for high-skilled workers who wish to work in the United States. There is a cap on the number of people who can annually enter through this category, and while applications are processed on a first-come, first-served basis, in 2007 and 2008 so many applications were received on the opening days that a lottery was used to select which applications to process. Rather than trying to get administrative data from the US Citizenship and Immigration Services, which would be incredibly difficult, Clemens obtained personnel records from a large Indian information technology/software firm that supplied a large number of applicants to this lottery. He is then able to use these records to determine the impact of migrating on the migration, job title, and earnings of the applicants in this Indian firm.

An underlying assumption of the experimental estimates is that the migration lottery influences the outcome of interest for an individual only through that individual's migration decision. In particular, we require the Stable Unit Treatment Value Assumption (Rubin, 1986), which means that the outcome of one individual should not be affected by the lottery outcome of another individual. Thus when we consider the case of measuring the income gain from migration, we would require that the income of lottery losers is not affected by whether other people in the sample win or lose the lottery. One potential way this assumption could be violated would be if the lottery winners send remittances to the lottery loser households. This is unlikely to be much of an issue in cases where the number of winners is small relative to the overall population, and can be directly checked through surveys. A more problematic concern would be if the employment prospects of the lottery losers change as a result of the winners migrating. Whilst there is some evidence to suggest that large-scale migration can increase the wages earned by non-migrants through less competition for jobs (Mishra, 2007), this is again likely to be at most a second-order concern when the number of winners is small relative to the overall population. But it is more of a concern in cases like that studied by Clemens (2010), where the entrants studied are all from the same company, and it is therefore harder to imagine that the job opportunities available to the non-migrants are not affected by having some company members abroad.

In addition to the lotteries discussed, the United States had a lottery for Cubans in the mid-1990s,[4] New Zealand's Pacific Access Category also has small lotteries for Kiribati and Tuvalu, and New Zealand also used a lottery to allocate places in its Family Quota and Refugee Family Quota Categories in the early 2000s.[5] Currently only a few studies to date have utilized migration policy experiments. However, given the massive excess demand for migration into many countries worldwide, a lottery system for choosing which applications to process provides one fair and equitable mechanism for countries to process such applications, and we see this as a rich area for both researchers and policymakers to work on in the future.

12.3 NATURAL EXPERIMENTS

In addition to exogenous variation generated by government policy, identification of causal effects in migration research can also take advantage of other sources of exogenous variation in right-hand-side variables of interest, or so-called 'natural experiments.' We review here recent studies that take advantage of two types of natural experiments: exchange rate shocks experienced by migrants and weather shocks to which migrants' origin households are exposed in the home country.

12.3.1 Impacts of Changes in Migrants' Economic Conditions

A question of general interest in migration studies is 'What is the impact of changes in a migrant's economic conditions on outcomes in their origin household?' Such questions help reveal the extent to which changes in migration host countries (such as economic conditions, exchange rates,

Experimental approaches in migration studies 255

job opportunities, restrictions on legal work, and so on) affect a migrant's willingness and ability to send resources home, as well as the ways in which migrant resources are used by recipient households. Impacts can be mediated by several channels, such as remittances sent home, the stock of savings held by migrants overseas, or return migration decisions.

A central difficulty in answering this type of question is that migrant earnings or migrant economic conditions are in general not randomly allocated, so that any observed relationship between migrant economic conditions and household outcomes may simply reflect the influence of unobserved third factors. For example, more ambitious households could have migrants who work for higher wages or in destinations with more attractive work opportunities, and also have higher entrepreneurial investment levels in the origin household. Alternately, households that recently experienced an adverse shock to existing investments (say, the failure of a small business) might send members overseas to make up lost income, and when migration decisions are made under duress migrants may accept going to less attractive destinations. In sum, simply observing a statistical correlation between migrant economic conditions overseas and outcomes in migrant origin households does not imply that migrant economic conditions cause the origin household outcomes in question.

An experimental approach to establishing the impact of migrant economic opportunities on household outcomes could start by identifying a set of households that already had one or more members working overseas, assigning each migrant a randomly sized economic shock, and then examining the relationship between changes in household outcomes and the size of the shock dealt to the household's migrants.

Yang and Martinez (2005) and Yang (2008b) take advantage of a real-world natural experiment that is analogous to the experiment just described. Many households in the Philippines have one or more members working overseas. These overseas Filipinos work in dozens of foreign countries, many of which experienced sudden changes in exchange rates due to the 1997 Asian financial crisis. Crucially for the analysis, the changes were unexpected and varied in magnitude across overseas Filipinos' locations. The net result was large variation in the size of the exchange rate shock experienced by migrants across source households. Between the year ending July 1997 and the year ending October 1998, the US dollar and currencies in the main Middle Eastern destinations of Filipino workers rose 50 percent in value against the Philippine peso. Over the same time period, by contrast, the currencies of Taiwan, Singapore, and Japan rose by only 26 percent, 29 percent, and 32 percent, respectively, while those of Malaysia and Korea actually fell slightly (by 1 percent and 4 percent, respectively) against the peso.

Taking advantage of this variation in the size of migrant exchange rate shocks, these papers examine the impact of the shocks on changes in outcomes in migrants' origin households, using detailed panel household survey data from before and after the Asian financial crisis.

Yang (2008b) shows that these exogenous increases in migrant resources are used primarily for investment in origin households, rather than for current consumption. Households experiencing more favorable exchange rate shocks see greater increases in child schooling and reductions in child labor (for children aged 10–17). They also raise their non-consumption expenditures in several areas likely to be investment-related (in particular in educational expenditures), and show enhanced entrepreneurship participation in entrepreneurial activities. Households raise hours worked in self-employment, and become more likely to start relatively capital-intensive household enterprises (transportation/communication services and manufacturing). By contrast, there is no large or statistically significant effect of the exchange rate shocks on current household consumption. Yang and Martinez (2005) extend the analysis and show that these positive migrant exchange rate shocks also lead these households to be more likely to exit poverty status.

Aside from impacts on migrant origin households, it is also of interest to examine how migrant return decisions changed in response to the exchange rate shocks accompanying the Asian financial crisis. In research on migration decision-making, a current debate is whether durations of migrants' stays overseas are determined primarily by straightforward life-cycle considerations, as opposed to being driven by the need to reach target-earnings levels. By 'life-cycle' considerations, one means simply that households choose the length of stay overseas that balances the marginal benefit from higher savings overseas (and thus higher lifetime consumption) against the marginal utility cost of overseas work (as in Dustmann, 2003 and Stark et al., 1997). On the other hand, when households face borrowing constraints and minimum investment levels, lengths of stay overseas can be determined by the amount of time needed to accumulate a 'target-earnings' level (as in Mesnard, 2004 and Piore, 1979).

Distinguishing between the two alternative motivations for return migration is important, because the return decisions of 'life-cycle' migrants and 'target-earners' can respond very differently to changes in overseas economic conditions. For 'life-cycle' migrants, improved economic conditions in host countries – say, increased wages – can lead to longer overseas stays (as long as substitution effects dominate any income effects). For 'target-earners,' on the other hand, improved economic conditions should lead to shorter overseas stays, as migrants reach their earnings goals more quickly.

Experimental approaches in migration studies 257

Empirically, attempts to distinguish between the two alternatives typically examine the correlation between return migration and migrants' overseas earnings. The evidence has been inconclusive. Borjas (1989) finds among the foreign-born in the United States that higher earnings are associated with less return migration. By contrast, Dustmann (2003) documents, among immigrants in Germany, that higher migrant wages (instrumented by parental education) are associated with more return migration (shorter overseas stays). Constant and Massey (2002) find no statistically significant relationship between earnings and migrant returns in the same German dataset, although migrants who are unemployed or marginally employed are more likely to return.

A key methodological concern with existing empirical work on this topic is that the independent variable of interest – foreign earnings – is not randomly assigned across migrants, so any observed relationship between foreign earnings and return migration may simply be caused by unobserved third factors. For example, a finding that migrants with higher earnings have shorter lengths of stay overseas need not imply that higher earnings cause shorter migration durations. Rather, higher-wage migrants could simply have other characteristics that make early return attractive (such as better job prospects at home, or stronger family ties).

Yang (2006) exploits the exchange rate shocks experienced by Filipino overseas migrants, making possible a causal estimate of the effect of migrant economic conditions on return migration. In so doing, he also sheds light on the relative importance of life-cycle versus target-earnings explanations for return migration. Overall, the paper finds that more favorable exchange rate shocks lead to fewer migrant returns, which supports the 'life-cycle' explanation for return migration. A positive exchange rate shock raises the marginal benefit of staying overseas (by raising the domestic-currency value of foreign wages), and leads to less return migration on the margin. However, the paper also finds that even though life-cycle considerations seem to dominate on the whole, migrants from a subset of households appear to be target-earners. In households with intermediate values of the foreign wage index, the exchange rate shocks lead to increases in variables associated with household investment, such as vehicle or real estate purchases and entrepreneurial income. These results are consistent with the theoretical prediction that the migrants most likely to be target-earners are those in the middle of the foreign wage distribution: positive exchange rate shocks make target-earners more likely to return home and to invest (because they become more likely to have reached the minimum investment threshold).

The general methodology used in these studies on Philippine migrants – examining the impact of an economic shock experienced by overseas migrants on remittances and the outcomes of family members left behind – can potentially be applied in a variety of different contexts. Studies using a similar methodology can be useful to ascertain whether the results in the Philippine case extend to other contexts, or, if not, what might account for the differences in impacts.

The key requirements for such a study are: (1) an origin country whose migrants are destined to a wide variety of overseas destinations; (2) large and heterogeneous economic shocks in destination areas; (3) data on migrant locations before the shocks; and (4) data on migrant and origin household outcomes after the shocks. Many situations satisfy elements 1 and 2: for example, migrants from India and the other countries of South Asia also are destined for a wide variety of overseas destinations, and regional or global country-level economic shocks (such as the 2008–09 global financial crisis) are often heterogeneous in magnitude across migrant destinations. Migrants from specific countries in Latin America are often destined for a variety of locations across the United States, and hence it can be possible to exploit state-level (and perhaps occupation- or industry-specific) economic shocks experienced by migrants to achieve identification. Antman (2010) provides one example of this approach.

A likely hindrance to future research along these lines among other migrant populations is that there are fewer situations where the requisite survey data (requirements 3 and 4) are available. The Philippine case is unusual, in that the National Statistics Office of the Philippines administers a linked set of high-quality surveys to a nationally representative household sample that includes a detailed module on migration which is administered if the household reports having one or more members overseas. Importantly, the migration module (called the Survey on Overseas Filipinos) includes questions on migration history that allows a researcher to track migration episodes up to five years in the past. Such a module turns out to be crucial for identifying households that had migrants in specific shock-exposed locations prior *to* the shock, because location after the shock could be endogenous and therefore introduce bias in estimation. A key implication for surveys of migrant-sending households in countries where migrants tend to only go to one or a few main destinations is to collect information not only on which country the migrant is in, but also the city or region to provide more scope for identifying local shocks.

12.3.2 Remittance Responses to Conditions in Migrant Origin Areas

An important potential benefit from international migration is that remittances may serve as insurance, rising in the wake of negative shocks in migrants' home countries. Rural households in many developing countries are highly exposed to weather risk, experiencing storms, flooding, and droughts with great frequency. Households therefore should benefit greatly from access to formal and informal insurance that alleviates their most important sources of weather risk. Potential benefits include the ability to maintain nutritional, health, and educational investments, to adopt new production technologies, and to start new entrepreneurial activities that weather risk made previously unattractive. A large literature has examined the mechanisms through which households cope with risk in developing countries, but until recently the insurance role of remittances has not been investigated.

Yang and Choi (2007) and Yang (2008a) explore whether migrant remittances serve as insurance in the wake of negative weather shocks. This is a mechanism for coping with shocks *ex post* on which previous micro-level studies have not focused. At the international level, it is commonly posited that remittance flows from overseas buffer economic shocks in the migrants' home countries (for example, Ratha, 2003), but there have been relatively few empirical tests of this claim with micro-level household data. Mishra (2005) examines remittances in 13 Caribbean countries from 1980 to 2002 and finds that every 1 percent decrease in gross domestic product (GDP) is associated with a 3 percent increase in remittances two years later. Related research on the role of internal (domestic) migration in pooling risk within extended families includes Lucas and Stark (1985), Rosenzweig and Stark (1989), and Paulson (2003).

Yang and Choi (2007) and Yang (2008a) emphasize credible identification of the effect of negative shocks on international remittances. Existing studies of the impact of household income on remittance receipts use cross-sectional data, and so are subject to potentially severe biases in directions that are not obvious a priori. Reverse causation is a major concern: productive investments funded by migrant remittances can raise household income, leading to positive correlations between household income and remittances. Alternately, remittances may reduce households' need to find alternative income sources, leading to a negative relationship between remittances and domestic-source income. Even if reverse causation from remittances to income in migrants' source households was not a problem, it would be difficult to separate the cross-sectional relationship between income and remittances from the influence of unobserved third factors affecting both income and remittances (for example, the entrepreneurial spirit of household members).

Yang and Choi (2007) resolve these identification problems by focusing on income changes for the migrant-sending family due to shocks – changes in local rainfall – that are credibly exogenous, so that bias due to reverse causation is not a concern. Among households in the Philippines with members who are overseas migrants, they find that changes in income from domestic sources lead to changes in remittances in the opposite direction of the income change: remittances fall when income rises, and remittances rise when income falls. In such households, the amount of insurance is large: roughly 60 percent of exogenous declines in income are replaced by remittance inflows from overseas. In a similar vein, Clarke and Wallsten (2004) find, using panel data from Jamaica, that remittances from overseas replaced 25 percent of damages from Hurricane Gilbert in 1992. Yang (2008a) examines the impact of hurricanes on international financial flows using country-level panel data and finds that, for the poorest developing countries, hurricane damage leads to large inflows of migrants' remittances, amounting to 20 percent of experienced damages. Strikingly, the remittance response to hurricanes for these countries is large in magnitude: roughly one quarter as large as the response of foreign aid.

12.3.3 General Thoughts on Natural Experiments

As these examples show, natural experiments offer the potential to provide a credible means of helping answer many important questions in migration studies. However, there are often clear limits to the types of questions such natural experiments can answer (see also Rosenzweig and Wolpin, 2000) and one needs to be cautious in interpreting the results. For example, work such as that by Yang (2008b) directly looks at the impact of the exchange rate shocks on outcomes for migrant-sending households. This does not reveal the average impact of remittances or of migration, but rather the response of these sending households to temporary shocks in the earnings their migrants earn abroad. A finding that households save or invest much of the additional amount remitted as a result should therefore not be used to infer that remittances in general are used for largely productive purposes – economic theory tells us we should expect households to save or invest more in response to temporary income shocks and temporary increases in remittances caused by exchange rate fluctuations than they would from regular income or their usual level of remittances.

This is not a concern for the Yang (2008b) study in which the question of interest is indeed the response of migrant households to temporary shocks in the conditions facing their migrants abroad. But it is more of a concern for studies which attempt to use these natural experiments to generate an instrumental variable for migration or remittances. When these natural experiments are used to instrument migration, the impact identified is the LATE for households affected by the instrument. For example, Antman (2010) instruments father's migration with economic conditions in the main US destinations in a study of the impact of paternal migration on child schooling. Assuming the instrument meets the other criteria required, the effect identified is only the impact of parental migration for children whose father's migration decisions are affected by temporary economic shocks in the US destinations. Given the large income differences between Mexico and the United States, the set of households likely to have their migration decisions change as a result of these temporary shocks may be small, and thus the impact identified not be one that applies to much of the overall migrant population.

An important warning about natural experiments is that they must be scrutinized carefully before they are used as instruments in instrumental variables (IV) estimation. When an exogenous source of variation in economic conditions is identified (for example, weather, exchange rates), it is often tempting to take the next step and use the shock as an IV. The concern is with the validity of the IV exclusion restriction, namely the requirement that the instrument only affect the second-stage variable of interest via the endogenous right-hand-side variable of interest (which is being instrumented).[6] It is actually quite rare for exogenous shocks to satisfy the exclusion restriction, because there are usually a number of different channels through which the shock can affect the second-stage outcome of interest. When this is the case, instrumenting for just one of several channels with the shock will generally lead to biased estimates. That said, it is generally acceptable to examine the 'reduced form' effect of the shock (for example, in a regression of the outcome of interest directly on the shock variables), and to interpret the effect of the shock as operating through multiple potential channels. For example, Yang (2008b) examines only the reduced form effect of the exchange rate shock on the dependent variables of interest precisely because the exchange rate shocks could operate through at least two channels: through remittances sent home as well through the Philippine peso value of savings and other assets held overseas. In this case using the exchange rate shock as an instrument for remittances would have led to biased estimates. This bias would probably have been in an upward direction because any effects of the exchange rate operating via changes in the value of unremitted overseas savings would have been 'loaded' onto the coefficient on remittances.

12.4 FIELD EXPERIMENTS

While governments should use them more often, policy experiments are rare. Natural experiments, while valuable and revealing when they occur, are difficult to find. When policy or natural experiments do not exist, a large set of questions can be answered via randomized control trials or field experiments. Well-designed field experiments can help us understand not only the impact of a particular program or intervention, but can also shed light on underlying causal mechanisms or test particular theories. While field experiments have become increasingly common in development economics research, they have only just begun to be attempted in research on migration.

In this section we provide overviews of a handful of recent or ongoing field experiments on migration: studies of savings among migrants in the United States and research on barriers to migration (for internal migrations in Bangladesh and international migrants from the Philippines).

12.4.1 Studies of Migrant Savings

While remittances bring numerous benefits to households in developing countries, to date we know very little about how migrants make their remittance-sending decisions. In particular, it is unknown whether migrants desire greater control over how family members back home use the remittances they receive. This question is relevant not only for migration studies but also for the large and active literature in development economics on intra-household resource allocation. What's more, a better understanding of these questions could have substantial impact on public policy, by suggesting policies to further stimulate remittance flows and potentially channel them towards more productive uses in migrant source countries.

Ashraf, Aycinena, Martinez, and Yang (2010), henceforth AAMY, address some of these questions via a randomized controlled trial among migrants from El Salvador who are living and working in the Washington, DC metropolitan area. The research aims to shed light on the extent to which migrants' lack of direct control over the use of remittances affects remittance flows, and on the impact of new financial products that could increase migrant control.

In particular, AAMY focus on improving the ability of migrants to ensure that remittances are deposited and accumulated in savings accounts in the home country. In survey data collected as part of the study, Washington, DC-based migrants from El Salvador report that they would like recipient households to save 21.2 percent of remittance receipts, while recipient households prefer to save only 2.6 percent of receipts. Migrants often intend the savings to be for the use of the recipient household in the future, but such savings also can be intended for the migrant's future use. In the latter case, migrants may send their own funds to be saved in El Salvador because they perceive savings held in the United

Experimental approaches in migration studies 263

States as relatively insecure (particularly for undocumented migrants who fear deportation and loss of their assets).

AAMY designed a field experiment that offered new facilities for Salvadoran migrants to directly channel some fraction of their remittances into savings accounts in El Salvador. Savings facilities were offered in conjunction with Banco Agricola, El Salvador's largest bank. To isolate the importance of migrant control over savings, AAMY test demand for different products that offer migrants varying levels of control. For example, they investigate differential demand for savings accounts that must be solely in the name of a remittance recipient in El Salvador versus accounts that are either jointly owned with the migrant or for which the migrant is the sole owner.

The impact evaluation uses a randomized treatment-control methodology. Migrants in the study are randomly assigned across treatment conditions, and so comparisons across the various treatment conditions reveal the causal impact of offering migrant control on the outcomes of interest (which include savings account take-up, savings balances, and remittances). The intervention studied is unusual among development economics field experiments in that it is conducted among migrants who are located in a developed country, while several primary outcomes of interest (savings) are those of individuals who remain behind in a developing country. Data on activity at the partner bank are available from the bank's administrative records. Baseline and follow-up surveys administered to both migrants in the United States and their corresponding remittance-receiving households in El Salvador provide data on a broader set of other outcomes.

AAMY's results provide evidence that a desire for control over remittance uses – in particular, control over the extent to which remittances are saved in formal savings accounts – is quantitatively large and has an important influence on financial decision-making by migrants. Across the experimental conditions in the sample, migrants were much more likely to open savings accounts when offered the option of greater control over the accounts. What's more, offering greater migrant control over El Salvador-based savings accounts led to higher savings accumulation in El Salvador.

A related randomized experiment on savings among immigrants was conducted by Chin et al. (2010). This study examines the impact of providing Mexican immigrants in the United States with assistance obtaining a form of ID (a *matricula consular*) that can be used as identification when opening a US bank account. Study participants were made aware of a collaborating US bank that had an ongoing savings promotion among Hispanic immigrants, but the *matriculas consulares* in principle could have been used at any number of US banks. Impacts of the treatment were assessed in an in-person follow-up survey. Assignment to the treatment is found to lead to increased opening of US bank accounts, higher savings in the United States, and reduced remittances to Mexico. Among migrants who report they have 'no control' over how remittances are used in Mexico, the above-mentioned effects are larger, and there is also a large, positive, and statistically significant treatment effect on migrant earnings.

Taken together with AAMY, the Chin et al. (2010) study reinforces the conclusion that migrants have a variety of types of demand for savings facilities. There is demand for savings in the United States, as well as demand for savings in the country of origin, and providing access to appropriate savings devices can have large impacts on savings. What's more, both studies underline the importance of migrant control over savings accounts in facilitating savings accumulation. We view such studies as just the tip of the proverbial iceberg. There is likely to be great potential for analogous future studies that partner with institutions to offer a variety of financial services to immigrants. Products that have yet to be investigated include credit, insurance, and direct payment facilities targeted towards the needs of migrants and their origin households.

12.4.2 Identifying Barriers to Migration

While international and internal migration flows are large in magnitude, even greater numbers of individuals do not migrate, even in the face of substantial wage differentials between less and more developed areas. There are likely to be a large number of potential migrants who are deterred from migrating by a variety of barriers, such as imperfect information on migrant wages and job conditions, imperfect information on one's own affinity for or returns from migrant work, lack of information on job-seeking procedures, and credit constraints (when migration or job search involves non-negligible fixed costs).

At the moment we know little as researchers about the relative importance of these various potential barriers to migration. Credible evidence on the importance of migration barriers has important policy implications as well. A number of developing countries – most prominently, the Philippines – have enacted policies intended to facilitate and regulate international migration and view such policies as integral components of their overall economic development strategies. If there is a desire to promote migration, it is crucial to understand which barriers are operative and the impact of interventions that are aimed at reducing these barriers. While no study has been completed so far, randomized control trials in Bangladesh and the Philippines are currently underway and seek to shed light on the relative importance of several potential barriers to migration.

Bryan et al. (2010) are currently analysing the results of an ongoing randomized field experiment in the northwestern region of Rangpur in Bangladesh. A relatively impoverished area, Rangpur experiences annual famines that lead to seasonal declines in household income and consumption. A key coping strategy for households in the face of the famine is internal labor migration to other parts of Bangladesh that are less affected or unaffected by the famine. The experiment involves 100 Rangpur villages that were randomly allocated to the following experimental conditions: a control group; a treatment group offered information on jobs available, typical wages, and the likelihood of finding migrant work in a set of migration destinations; and other treatment conditions that offered cash or credit to cover the initial fixed costs of migration. The experiment was implemented in 2008 and the endline survey of households in the 100 migrant origin villages were implemented in 2009. Preliminary results are revealing, suggesting that the information treatments had no effect but the cash and credit interventions had substantial effects on migration both in the year they were offered as well as in the next year's famine season (when the cash/credit were no longer offered by the research project). Treatments that had effects on migration also led to substantial increases in consumption in migrant households. Should they hold up, the results provide evidence of the importance of credit constraints as a migration barrier, and also – intriguingly – suggest that policies providing a small incentive to migrate in an initial period can have persistent effects in future periods even after the incentives are removed.

A field experiment seeking to shed light on barriers to international migration is being implemented by Beam et al. (2010) in Sorsogon province, the Philippines. International labor migration from the Philippines is very large in magnitude: the Philippine Overseas Employment Agency, with which all overseas labor contracts of Filipinos must be officially registered, has recorded over one million new contracts per year since 2006. Roughly one third of this number are 'new hires' or first deployments overseas, and the remaining two thirds are 'rehires' or new work contracts for workers who are already overseas or who have previously been overseas. Within the country, international labor migration rates are highest in areas closest to major cities like Manila (the capital) and Cebu. An open question is why individuals in some outlying provinces – such as Sorsogon, which is more than 12 hours by bus from the capital – typically have substantially lower rates of international labor migration despite facing larger income gaps between home and abroad.

The baseline survey and intervention for the Sorsogon experiment was completed in mid-2010, with roughly 5000 households in the sample. Randomization was at the household level. The experimental conditions

266 *Handbook of research methods in migration*

were as follows: a control group; a group offered information on typical wages in common overseas work destinations, on procedures for applying for overseas work, and on the typical fixed costs involved in overseas labor migration; and a group offered assistance in applying for overseas work (in addition to the information offered to the previous treatment group). Households in the 'assistance' treatment were offered access to and assistance with uploading information on themselves into a job-seekers' website that recruitment agencies in Manila could then use to search for suitable candidates to fill overseas job openings. These interventions are intended to test the relative importance of various types of information and transactions costs in explaining the low incidence of international labor migration from outlying areas of the Philippines.

Among the sample of individuals enrolled in the job-seekers' website database, a follow-on randomization will be implemented, in collaboration with a local microfinance institution, intended to shed light on the importance of credit constraints as a migration barrier. Prospective migrants in the database will be randomly allocated into the following groups: a group offered a small loan to cover the costs of job search (mainly costs of travel to and lodging in Manila to attend job interviews); a group offered a larger loan to cover costs of travel overseas once a job offer is obtained; a group offered both types of loans; and a control group offered no loan products. Estimated effects of these loan treatments should reveal the relative importance of credit constraints at two different stages of the international labor migration process (initial job search versus overseas travel once a job offer is obtained).

12.5 CONCLUSION

The decision of whether or not to migrate has far-reaching consequences for the lives of individuals and their families. But the very nature of this choice makes identifying the impacts of migration difficult, since it is hard to measure a credible counterfactual of what the person and their household would have been doing had migration not occurred. Migration experiments provide a clear and credible way for identifying this counterfactual, and thereby allowing causal estimation of the impacts of migration. Yet to date there have been relatively few such experiments, and we believe there are large gains from policymakers and researchers using experiments more frequently.

On the policy side, governments could use experiments more as a way of learning about the effectiveness of their policy initiatives. We have seen examples where migration lotteries have been used as a fair and equitable way of deciding among excess demand for quota-constrained immigration categories. A second natural place for such experiments is in piloting the introduction of new policies. For example, seasonal worker programs (such as those recently introduced in New Zealand and Australia) are seen as a way to enable less educated poor households to reap some of the gains possible with international migration. Yet there is debate about the optimal way to select such workers, and about the extent to which it will actually benefit sending communities. Randomly selecting among eligible workers in the pilot phase and experimenting with different recruitment mechanisms would provide a way for the design of such policies to be fine-tuned, alleviate potential concerns about political favoritism determining which individuals and villages participate, and provide a means for the development impacts to be identified. On the sending-country side, several developing countries have shown interest in providing premigration orientation seminars for potential migrants, in a similar way to the Philippines. But there is little evidence as to the effectiveness of such programs, or as to which components really matter. Before introducing such programs on a large scale, governments could experiment with offering different content to different groups of migrants, and measure which is most effective.

One argument governments might muster against randomly choosing among applicants for a given migration quota is a belief that they can get higher quality migrants by intensive screening of all applications. This argument is likely to be more important for policies to admit skilled migrants. Points systems for migration provide one such approach to screening, in which prospective migrants are scored on a basis of marketable skills and desirable characteristics, with only those individuals scoring above a certain threshold eligible to migrate. For example, Australia's points system scores applicants out of 170 based on their age, English skills, occupation, work experience, Australian qualifications, and other characteristics. The system had pass marks of 100 and 120 for different visa categories in 2010.[7] Whilst one can imagine the government being reasonably confident that someone with a score of 170 is a more desirable immigrant than someone with a score of 60, there is likely to be much more uncertainty about whether people getting a score of 95 are all that different from those getting a score of 105. Governments could therefore consider randomizing among excess applications within some range around the pass mark, in order to learn more about the impacts of such policies. This would be analogous to the approach used in some microfinance experiments, which have randomized access to credit for marginal applicants (Karlan and Zinman, 2010).

NOTES

1. See McKenzie (2005) and Gibson et al. (forthcoming b) for more detail on these challenges.
2. For simplicity we consider only the case of an individual-level outcome here, assuming that all migrants and non-migrants are observed. When the comparison involves households with and without migrants, a second form of selectivity is involved, since households can also choose whether all members migrate, or only some. Return migration also introduces a third form of selectivity. See Gibson et al. (forthcoming b) for discussion of this more complicated case.
3. http://travel.state.gov/visa/immigrants/types/types_4574.html (accessed 26 February 2010).
4. http://havana.usint.gov/media/pdfs/lottery.pdf (accessed 1 March 2010).
5. These categories have now been replaced, but New Zealand still uses a random ballot to fill residual places in its Refugee Family Support Category which provides a means for refugees to sponsor parents, adult siblings, or grandparents into New Zealand.
6. For a useful overview of this issue in IV estimation, see Angrist and Pischke (2009), section 4.1.
7. See http://www.immi.gov.au/skilled/general-skilled-migration/points-test.htm (accessed 11 October 2011).

REFERENCES

Angrist, J. and Pischke, J.-S. (2009), *Mostly Harmless Econometrics: An Empiricist's Companion*, Princeton, NJ: Princeton University Press.
Antman, F. (2010), 'The intergenerational effects of paternal migration on schooling and work: what can we learn from children's time allocations?', mimeo, University of Colorado, Boulder.
Ashraf, N., Aycinena, D., Martinez, C. and Yang, D. (2010), 'Remittances and the problem of control: a field experiment among migrants from El Salvador', mimeo, Department of Economics, University of Michigan.
Beam, E., McKenzie, D. and Yang, D. (2010), 'Financial and informational barriers to migration: a field experiment in the Philippines', ongoing study, University of Michigan and The World Bank.
Borjas, G. (1987), 'Self-selection and the earnings of migrants', *American Economic Review*, **77** (4), 531–53.
Borjas, G. (1989), 'Immigrant and emigrant earnings: a longitudinal study', *Economic Inquiry*, **27** (1), 21–37.
Bryan, G., Chowdhury, S. and Mobarak, A.M. (2010), 'The effect of seasonal migration on households during food shortages in Bangladesh', ongoing study, Yale University.
Chin, A., Karkoviata, L. and Wilcox, N. (2010), 'Impact of bank accounts on migrant savings and remittances: evidence from a field experiment', mimeo, University of Houston.
Clarke, G. and Wallsten, S. (2004), 'Do remittances act like insurance? Evidence from a natural disaster in Jamaica', Working Paper, The World Bank.
Clemens, M. (2010), 'How visas affect skilled labor: a randomized natural experiment', mimeo, Center for Global Development.
Constant, A. and Massey, D. (2002), 'Return migration by German guestworkers: neoclassical versus new economic theories', *International Migration*, **40** (4), 5–38.
Deaton, A. (2010), 'Instruments, randomization, and learning about development', *Journal of Economic Literature*, **48** (2), 424–55.
Dustmann, C. (2003), 'Return migration, wage differentials, and the optimal migration duration', *European Economic Review*, **47**, 353–69.
Gibson, J., McKenzie, D. and Stillman, S. (forthcoming a), 'The impacts of international

migration on remaining household members: omnibus results from a migration lottery program', *Review of Economics and Statistics*.
Gibson, J., McKenzie, D. and Stillman, S. (forthcoming b), 'Accounting for selectivity and duration-dependent heterogeneity when estimating the impact of emigration on incomes and poverty in sending areas', *Economic Development and Cultural Change*.
Imbens, G. (2010), 'Better LATE than nothing: some comments on Deaton (2009) and Heckman and Urzua (2009)', *Journal of Economic Literature*, **48** (2), 399–423.
Karlan, D. and Zinman, J. (2010), 'Expanding microenterprise credit access: using randomized supply decisions to estimate the impacts in Manila', mimeo, Yale University.
Lucas, R.E.B. and Stark, O. (1985), 'Motivations to remit: evidence from Botswana', *Journal of Political Economy*, **93** (5), 901–18.
McKenzie, D. (2005), 'Beyond remittances: the effects of migration on Mexican households', in C. Özden and M. Schiff (eds), *International Migration, Remittances and the Brain Drain*, Washington, DC: The World Bank, pp. 123–48.
McKenzie, D. and Rapoport, H. (2010), 'Self-selection patterns in Mexico–U.S. migration: the role of migrant networks', *Review of Economics and Statistics*, **92** (4), 811–21.
McKenzie, D., Gibson, J. and Stillman, S. (2010), 'How important is selection? Experimental vs non-experimental measures of the income gains from migration', *Journal of the European Economic Association*, **8** (4), 913–45.
Mesnard, A. (2004), 'Temporary migration and capital market imperfections', *Oxford Economic Papers*, **56**, 242–62.
Mishra, P. (2005), 'Macroeconomic impact of remittances in the Caribbean', Working Paper, International Monetary Fund.
Mishra, P. (2007), 'Emigration and wages in source countries: evidence from Mexico', *Journal of Development Economics*, **82**, 180–99.
Paulson, A. (2003), 'Insurance motives for migration: evidence from Thailand', mimeo, Kellogg Graduate School of Management, Northwestern University.
Piore, M. (1979), *Birds of Passage,* New York: Cambridge University Press.
Ratha, D. (2003), 'Workers' remittances: an important and stable source of external development finance', in *Global Development Finance 2003: Striving for Stability in Development Finance*, Washington, DC: International Monetary Fund.
Rosenzweig, M. and Stark, O. (1989), 'Consumption smoothing, migration, and marriage: evidence from rural India', *Journal of Political Economy*, **97** (4), 905–26.
Rosenzweig, M. and Wolpin, K. (2000), 'Natural "natural experiments" in economics', *Journal of Economic Literature*, **38**, 827–74.
Rubin, D. (1986), 'Which ifs have causal answers?', *Journal of the American Statistical Association*, **81**, 961–2.
Stark, O., Helmenstein, C. and Yegorov, Y. (1997), 'Migrants' savings, purchasing power parity, and the optimal duration of migration', *International Tax and Public Finance*, **4**, 307–24.
Stillman, S., McKenzie, D. and Gibson, J. (2009), 'Migration and mental health: evidence from a natural experiment', *Journal of Health Economics*, **28** (3), 677–87.
Yang, D. (2006), 'Why do migrants return to poor countries? Evidence from Philippine migrants' responses to exchange rate shocks', *Review of Economics and Statistics*, **88** (4), 715–35.
Yang, D. (2008a), 'Coping with disaster: the impact of hurricanes on international financial flows, 1970–2002', *B.E. Journal of Economic Analysis and Policy*, **8** (1) (Advances), Article 13.
Yang, D. (2008b), 'International migration, remittances, and household investment: evidence from Philippine migrants' exchange rate shocks', *Economic Journal*, **118**, 591–630.
Yang, D. and Choi, H.J. (2007), 'Are remittances insurance? Evidence from rainfall shocks in the Philippines', *World Bank Economic Review,* **21** (2), 219–48.
Yang, D. and Martinez, C.A. (2005), 'Remittances and poverty in migrants' home areas: evidence from the Philippines', in C. Özden and M. Schiff (eds), *International Migration, Remittances, and the Brain Drain*, Washington, DC: The World Bank.

PART III

INTERDISCIPLINARY APPROACHES AND MIXED METHODS

13 Mapping movements: interdisciplinary approaches to migration research
Pablo S. Bose

For those who are interested in the complex, multifaceted, and often contradictory lives of migrants – in their many variations and manifestations – understanding their histories, their motivations, their behaviors, and indeed even identifying and enumerating them at all poses many challenges. How do we begin to understand what motivates people to migrate? How do we interpret and analyse the patterns of movement, exodus, and return that characterize population flows across the globe? What sorts of data do we need to gather in order to examine this behavior and these practices? How do we analyse the information that we gather and what do we do with the results? What kinds of both practical and ethical issues must we keep in mind when conducting our research into migration?

There are of course many different traditions and disciplines that have engaged with such questions, many of them described in greater detail in other chapters of this handbook.[1] In this chapter I will focus on interdisciplinary approaches that borrow from and build upon a diverse range of methodologies and methods in order to carry out this inquiry into the movement of populations and individuals. For researchers interested in the intersections between culture, space, and power implicit in the study of migration, the nuances and complexities of transitional and transnational lives require triangulating research strategies. This means relying on multiple instruments and methods to conduct our inquiries into populations that are often difficult to define or demarcate, marked by hybrid or shifting identities, and frequently adaptive and flexible in the face of changing circumstances. Adopting an interdisciplinary approach to the study of population flows can potentially build a more holistic and comprehensive portrait of the migrant and the migration experience. The following chapter outlines such an interdisciplinary, multi-method approach to migration research, one that is primarily qualitative in nature and which is also framed by principles of community-based, participatory, and action-oriented inquiry.

I begin by considering in greater detail the question of interdisciplinary approaches – what are some of the benefits of this orientation? What distinguishes interdisciplinary research from more traditional approaches? How

274 *Handbook of research methods in migration*

might it be particularly appropriate for the study of migration? In particular I introduce the concept of 'diaspora' as an essentially interdisciplinary framework for investigating processes of movement across the globe. In the next section I examine some of the issues and challenges that lie in undertaking an interdisciplinary approach to this form of inquiry, particularly in terms of locating migration patterns, choosing appropriate sources of information, and some of the difficulties in determining the validity of data. The following section suggests ways of engaging with these challenges in an interdisciplinary fashion, as I emphasize tools and traditions for migration research that are drawn from diverse disciplines including geography, history, anthropology, sociology, political economy, and cultural studies and discuss the potential for each when used in concert. I also discuss several specific methods that can be employed for the purposes of interdisciplinary migration research using both primary and secondary forms of data collection. In particular I highlight several qualitative, fieldwork-based techniques including archival and documentary/textual analysis, key informant interviews, stakeholder focus groups, community surveys, case studies, and participant observation in order to undertake the research. The final part of the chapter focuses on research ethics and deals with issues such as the purpose and politics of migration research, critical views on data sources and collection, the process of building trust within communities, the use of information and negotiating the bureaucracy of institutional review boards, and finally, the importance of flexible and adaptive frameworks for situating our inquiry.

As a way of illustrating both the potential and the challenges of an interdisciplinary methodology, I present some brief examples from my own work throughout this chapter. These include my search for an Indian Bengali diaspora in North America as a way of trying to find the traces and the practices of a particular migration in both its 'new' and 'old' homes. As well, I draw on my work on the global phenomenon of development-induced displacement and internally displaced persons. A third example is drawn from my research on refugee resettlement in northeastern USA and within non-traditional immigrant locations.

13.1 WHY AN INTERDISCIPLINARY APPROACH?

What advantages might an interdisciplinary approach present for the migration researcher? Why not simply use the tools and methods that have emerged from disciplines such as geography, sociology, anthropology, or economics for studying populations and their movements? What need is there to look beyond census data, or formal, institutionally collected statistics? Indeed, what exactly does it mean to engage in an interdisciplinary approach? Is this any more than a buzzword – often used interchangeably with transdisciplinary, crossdisciplinary, or multidisciplinary[2] – to describe a practice that has been long familiar to those interested in migration, borrowing from multiple traditions in order to paint a more accurate picture?

One might argue that employing a pastiche of methods is a hallmark of such work, picking and choosing from the available tools to carry out the desired research. But an approach to migration research that moves beyond disciplinary boundaries and expectations offers more than mere convenience. For some scholars, the very phenomenon of migration itself is interdisciplinary – a practice that extends across diverse ways of being in the world and therefore requires diverse ways of capturing and understanding these activities and patterns. In this view migration stretches our ability to comprehend it through a singular, discipline-specific form of information gathering or source of data. As Murdock and Ellis suggest in their discussion of the subfields of applied demography and social demography, a broad range of academic disciplines stake a claim to the study of migration, yet 'practitioners have found that no single source exists to address their needs' (Murdock and Ellis, 1991, p. 2). In this view a decennial census, an annual community survey, or a novel detailing an immigrant's life story cannot provide more than a partial insight into what migration means. Indeed, the very complexities inherent in processes of migration and belonging have led to much confusion and debate as to how scholars should look at the varied phenomena of movement and mobility within and across borders, regions, and continents. Some of the most influential frameworks that have emerged as a means of engaging with migration are – though sometimes not explicitly named as such – fundamentally interdisciplinary.

One such framework is the idea of 'diaspora.' An older concept once associated primarily with the experiences of Jewish exile and African slavery, the field of diaspora studies has emerged in recent decades as a way of examining processes of global movement (Braziel and Mannur, 2003; Cohen, 1997; Hall, 1994; Jayaram and Atal, 2004). It has been especially concerned with both historical and contemporary periods of globalization, drawing on a wide range of sources and approaches to conduct its inquiry. For Brah, this is more than a collection of convenient methods; it is the idea of diaspora itself that is an interdisciplinary approach to understanding migration:

> The concept of diaspora then emerges as an ensemble of investigative technologies that historicise trajectories of different diasporas, map their relationality,

and interrogate, for example, what the search for origins signifies in the history of a particular diaspora; how and why originary absolutes are imagined; how the materiality of economic, political and signifying practices is experienced; what new subject positions are created and assumed; how particular fields of power articulate in the construction of hierarchies of domination and subordination in a given context; why certain conceptions of identity come into play in a given situation, and whether or not these conceptions are reinforced or challenged and contested by the play of identities. (Brah, 1996, p. 194)

Similarly, Gilroy has argued that 'the idea of diaspora offers a ready alternative to the stern discipline of primordial kinship and rooted belonging . . . [it] disrupts the fundamental power of territory to determine identity by breaking the simple sequence of explanatory links between place, location and consciousness' (Gilroy, 2000, p. 123).

Of course the use of diaspora – either applied as a term for migration or as an analytical and methodological framework as suggested above – is not without its own controversies. For writers like Gilroy, diaspora is a useful concept in opening up the question of identity beyond the particularities and atavisms of static, essentialized Selves, brought into clear definition by stark definition to the cultural practices and mores of ambiguous Others. Instead, diaspora can be a starting point, rather than end-point, a node of intersection between physical, cultural, and economic spaces. But for many critics, the concept of diaspora refers to only one form of migration – that of forced migration and displacement, as in the specific examples cited above. Ong, for example, argues that 'the terms 'transnational migration' and 'diaspora' are often used in the same breath, confusing changes in population flows occasioned by global market forces with earlier forms of permanent exile' (Ong, 2003, p. 86).

Such caveats are important but perhaps miss the point as to the potential that diaspora and the interdisciplinary approach it embodies offers to the scholar of migration. It is, in Gilroy's view, an elastic concept, one that helps us to understand better the multifaceted nature of movement. Moreover, the term does not take as its starting point the nation-state, something that transnationalism – the label preferred by many critics for non-exiled migrant individuals and communities – cannot claim. Transnationalism may transcend the state, but it is still concerned with activities across, beyond, and/or despite borders. Diaspora, on the other hand, could potentially be marshaled to examine the production of power and meaning across a variety of spaces and scales – though in most discussions it is still constrained by the spatial terms of the state. Yet despite such limitations the concept offers us a way of moving beyond essentialist notions of identity and instead captures the contradictions and idiosyncrasies that characterize flows of people, culture, and capital. The challenge in this sense may be not to define diaspora in terms of what it excludes, but rather in terms of what it allows to flourish – perhaps hybridity and indeterminacy (Bhabha, 2004), or to paraphrase Gilroy and Hall, the possibilities of concepts that travel (Gilroy, 2000; Hall, 1994). Basch et al. may prefer the concept of transnational migration to diaspora, but the description that they give of population movements seems to demand an interdisciplinary approach to their study:

> [Transnational migration] is the process by which transmigrants, through their daily activities, forge and sustain multi-stranded social, economic, and political relations that link together their societies of origin and settlement, and through which they create transnational social fields that cross national borders. (Basch et al., 1994, p. 6)

Any inquiry into the lives and practices of diasporas and global migration requires, in this view, an approach that can examine a collectivity of people living in multiple national/sub-national contexts who share a common set of narratives about their history, language, race, culture, religion, economic practices, and daily lives.

13.2 DIFFICULTIES IN LOCATING THE MIGRANT OR MIGRATION PATTERN

If they do indeed lead such multifaceted and often liminal lives, how then do we actually find the migrant communities and migration patterns that are the object of our study? In some cases and for certain forms of research, one can rely upon a census report, economic statistic or other formally collected data. Indeed, such sources – if available – are usually a crucial starting point for most inquiries, but to rely on these figures alone quite often is not enough. For one thing, the sheer complexities of what migration entails and what the migrant might look like means that information about them may not be easily accessible, or might be buried within other forms of data.

For example, my research into the material, cultural and ideological impacts of one-time emigrants from the Indian state of West Bengal in development processes within their original (or perhaps ancestral) homeland led to a significant challenge; namely, how was I to actually locate the objects of my study? The 'new homelands' in which I wished to examine the lives of Indian Bengali migrants – the USA, Canada, and the UK – all collect data on immigrants at the national level, represented as 'country of origin.' But how could I disaggregate this data in order to actually find Indian Bengalis abroad? Relying on national origin was only a starting point since census information is organized primarily in terms of categories such as the 'sending nation' of India, a nation-state, rather than the important sub-national culture of Bengal.[3] Religious or linguistic affiliation gave me no greater aid since West Bengal contains both a Hindu majority and a Muslim minority and the regional language of Bengali is spoken in both West Bengal and the nation-state of Bangladesh. This issue can in many ways be a central question for the study of migration – the affiliation that a migrant often feels with a 'home' may not be through association with the nation-state but rather in terms of other scales – the city, the region, a district, perhaps even a neighborhood or a single home. The difficulty then, in simply finding the migrant, is that one may not be looking for Germans in France, Lebanese in Nigeria, or Chinese in Indonesia, but rather sub-nationalities – Gujaratis living in New Jersey, Han Fujianese in Manila, Istanbulites in Berlin, Albertans in Ontario, Liverpudlians in London. Is such data even collected? In the course of my research I found such attempts by official authorities few and far between and of questionable verifiability.[4]

A similar challenge has arisen during the course of my research into those displaced by a plethora of development processes – those forced to relocate for projects and policies ranging from resource extraction and power generation to conservation and land reform to urbanization and privatization. Given that there is no internationally sanctioned category of 'developmental refugees,' those who are displaced by development fall within the nebulous and indeterminate category of the Internally Displaced Person (IDP). People who are displaced by development are most often migrants, forced from homes, livelihoods, cultural practices, and territorial homelands, yet often do not cross an international border and are not fleeing a conflict (UNHCR, 2006). They are therefore not recognized (nor afforded protections) under the rubric of 'refugee'; moreover, national governments and regional authorities – in many cases the very catalysts for the processes that have led to displacement – are often loathe to acknowledge their own responsibilities in this dynamic. At worst the displaced are not counted, at best, they show up as 'economic migrants' or are aggregated within the figures for internal migration of diverse populations within a country (Newbold, 2010).

Estimates of the numbers of IDPs (including conflict-, development-, and environmental change-related displaced) across the globe today are truly staggering – some suggest as many as 24.5 million people in 2006 alone (UNHCR, 2006). Yet these numbers are difficult to verify precisely because it is hard to find accurate measures of the displaced. Those displaced by development are often relocated more than once – not only by the building of a dam, for example, but by the construction of housing complexes for project managers, engineers, and workers, by compensatory afforestation projects, irrigation canals and pumping stations, or by upstream and downstream impacts on people's livelihoods (Vandergeest et al., 2007). If development agencies and planners do attempt to enumerate the numbers who will be affected by the building of a project, these estimates are often on the conservative side in order to keep costs manageable. What figures we do have are drawn primarily from field-based surveys of organizations such as the US Committee for Refugees and Immigrants, the office of the United Nations High Commissioner for Refugees (UNHCR), and the Internal Displacement Monitoring Centre (Centre and Council, 2006). Counting the displaced is therefore often dependent upon calculations such as the number of individuals accessing the relief services of aid or governmental organizations, plans and cost-benefit estimates by developers who estimate the numbers of 'project affected.'

In my work with a more formally recognized population flow – status refugees resettled in the northeastern USA – one might expect an easier time in locating the migrant. After all, unlike a sub-national diaspora or developmental refugees, groups and individuals who have been granted official refugee status in the USA are in many respects only too clearly counted. They must go through a lengthy process while abroad in a refugee camp, including interviews with the UNHCR and both the US State Department and Department of Homeland Security. Upon being granted refugee status, each individual and family is placed with a resettlement agency for transitioning to new homes. A case worker and volunteers then work closely with the newly arrived refugees who also receive direct financial assistance for up to eight months. All along the way, the refugees are counted – by both federal and state government agencies as well as by municipal and regional organizations, including religious institutions, school boards, housing authorities, employment agencies, and a host of others.

It is therefore often fairly straightforward to track the actions and the practices of refugees – at least for eight months. But after that period of direct support by the federal government, locating the refugee can be a more challenging task. In many cases refugee individuals and communities remain well connected to the institutions and organizations that have helped with their resettlement, many of whom offer support services for up to five years. There is, however, no official process in place to track refugees beyond the initial eight months. It is therefore often difficult to conduct longitudinal studies of their resettlement experience precisely because many groups continue the process of migration, especially that of moving from their initial resettlement site, to a larger clustering of their ethnic or national origin group. Eight months or even five years is simply far too short a time in which to make broader observations regarding the resettlement experience (except in a more limited sense).

In the case of Vermont, for example – the main focus of my research on refugee resettlement – while roughly 1700 individuals have been officially resettled from Bosnia, the entire Bosnian population of the state currently numbers closer to 3500 people (VRRP, 2010). Some of these individuals may have been born in Vermont to Bosnian parents, but many others relocated from their original resettlement sites in Michigan, New York, and even Canada. How then do we begin to understand what resettlement has meant for these individuals? Do we leave them out of our study of resettlement because they did not officially enter Vermont as refugees? Additionally, one might look to national origins in census data as a starting point for finding our migrants but such information once again aggregates a variety of different flows. One cannot assume, for example, that those of Somali, Bhutanese, or Burmese origin within Vermont are by definition refugees – there are many other forms of immigration that may have led these populations to the state. And as with the case of the Indian Bengali diaspora detailed above, language and religion are no clearer indicators of who or where the migrant might be. Finally, at what point does one stop being classified as a refugee? At the point of being cut off from direct federal aid? At the point of being cut off from broader resettlement support services by other agencies and organizations? When one gains citizenship? Or does this form of migration mark individuals and communities for the rest of their lives? How do such naming conventions affect our ability to research or even locate the migrant?

In all three of the examples cited above we see some similar problems and issues arising. Perhaps paramount amongst these is the lack of a clear set of sources upon which we can rely to identify and enumerate migrants and migration patterns. The unavailability or inaccessibility of the data may occur because of a number of different factors – authorities that are uninterested in counting migrants, the complexities of hybrid identities, or the time and scale of migration itself – but the end result is the same. We require more sophisticated and broadly conceived sets of methods – grounded in an interdisciplinary framework – in order to illuminate the lives and practices of migrants.

13.3 TRADITIONS AND TOOLS FOR INTERDISCIPLINARY MIGRATION RESEARCH

Just what kinds of methods, designs, and techniques can bring the migrant and migration patterns to light, if difficulties such as those mentioned above exist? The complexities of migrant lives and migration patterns require the use of multiple tools. But rather than use these methods in a random or ad hoc fashion, what interdisciplinary approaches can offer the researcher is a more systematic way of framing their usage. Indeed, the interdisciplinary approach highlighted in this chapter is not a new research methodology, though it has been gaining increasing acceptance and traction in recent years. But 'mixed-methods' – generally understood to be a combination of qualitative and quantitative techniques – and 'multi-methods' – generally understood to be multiple techniques within either tradition – research have long been utilized in a number of fields in order to deepen and broaden research projects (Bloor and Wood, 2006; Creswell, 1998; Denscombe, 2003). Creswell and Plano Clark define mixed-methods research and describe its potential thus:

> Mixed methods research is a research design with philosophical assumptions as well as methods of inquiry. As a methodology, it involves philosophical assumptions that guide the direction of the collection and analysis of data and the mixture of qualitative and quantitative approaches in many phases in the research process. As a method, it focuses on collecting, analyzing, and mixing qualitative and quantitative data in a single study or series of studies. Its central premise is that the use of quantitative and qualitative approaches in combination provides a better understanding of research problems than either approach alone. (Creswell and Plano Clark, 2007, p. 5)

What combining methods and methodologies – either within or across qualitative and quantitative traditions – offers is the opportunity to triangulate inquiries and results. The research may involve primary data collected by the principal researcher or it may use secondary data collected by an outside party or organization and then typically verified for publication or public consumption. Whatever the data source, method of collection, or approach to analysis, the overall value of using multiple or mixed methods in conducting research in general and migration research in particular cannot be underestimated. As Newbold points out in his discussion of data collection in the subfield of population geography:

> The widespread use and availability of census and other public data are due in large part to their validity and the degree of geographic, social and economic detail embedded in the files . . . This has not, of course, stopped researchers from constructing their own data sets or relying on qualitative data to understand demographic processes. In fact, these data sources should be seen as complementary rather than competitive, allowing different approaches and insights into population processes. (Newbold, 2010, p. 50)

Rather than simply throwing together these various methods as a hodge-podge or hoping that untested combinations will in fact work together, an interdisciplinary approach can help us provide a framework for placing appropriate research techniques together in a way that is adaptive, flexible, and holistic. It was precisely for such reasons that in order to resolve the difficulties in data collection and analysis described in the examples from my own research on diverse migration patterns that I turned to an interdisciplinary approach.

In my work on the Indian Bengali diaspora, globalization, and urban development in Kolkata, for example, I based my inquiry in the traditions of political economy, cultural studies, and urban geography, as related and overlapping yet still distinct fields. As befitting an interdisciplinary approach, I also borrowed liberally from other scholarly traditions where applicable for my research. Situating my work in this way meant, for example, utilizing political economy as an analytic lens to help me understand the complex interactions between institutions and individuals in material terms. Political economy informed the analysis of many interactions such as those between capital, the state, and both national as well as diasporic identities. It also allowed me to examine the constitution of the nation, the city, the diaspora, and of development itself as part of specific regimes of both discursive and material production. Political economy also provided me with a framework for understanding global economic flows, national accounting, development financing, political alliances, municipal land-use patterns, and a host of other activities.

The field of cultural studies, on the other hand, provided me with an effective way of analysing the regimes of meaning that were produced by these material practices. The cultural studies lens allowed me to see not only the function and ordering of power and knowledge, but the conditions of its constitution and reproduction. I was therefore able to read a variety of 'texts' as a way of examining the everyday life of diasporic experiences and desires, especially as they relate to development and displacement. These texts included discourses on identity in transnational communities, condominium advertisements on billboards in Kolkata, the recent emergence of the non-resident Indian (NRI) as a character in Indian film and literature, surveys of cultural associations, and transcripts of interviews and focus groups with the NRIs themselves.

Finally, for my examination of the transformations taking place in Kolkata, I applied theories drawn from urban geography – ideas such as colonial urban development, the world cities (or global cities) hypothesis, urbanization, primate cities and uneven development, as well as neoliberalism and gentrification. Thinking about diasporas and their behavior means considering their actions and influence across space, time, and their circulation within and between the various 'homes' and 'homelands' which they inhabit. In looking at the discourse of the global city and of the role of the migrant, for example, I used advertising campaigns, real-estate transactions, and land-use registries as ways of exploring the material and ideological manifestation of Kolkata as a 'world city.'

The specific tools I employed to carry out the research itself varied according to the traditions on which I was drawing and the research questions I sought to answer. They included extensive archival research, interviews, fieldwork in both India and North America, participant observation, focus group research, and surveys. Data sources included planning documents, policy statements, advertising campaigns, political party platforms, planning documents and government records, secondary literature and cultural texts including films, television, news media, and music. Other sources included a wide range of respondents with whom I conducted interviews and focus groups (including journalists, politicians, land developers, social activists, academics, civil servants, diasporic community members, banking officials, consular staff, property owners, and housing promoters) over 40 housing projects which I visited in person, and diasporic events that I attended. Finally, I also drew upon primary data collected through a survey of Indian Bengali cultural associations in North America designed to map and distinguish numbers and characteristics of their respective membership.

In the case of development-induced displacement, the research traditions I drew upon were international development studies, political philosophy, and economic geography. Development studies itself has roots as an interdisciplinary enterprise, drawing on numerous other fields including economics, political science, geography, and history. In the context of my work on displacement, development theory offered me insights into core-periphery relations as well as the role that nation building and modernization have played in the displacement of multiple populations across the world, especially marginalized and indigenous communities. Additionally, as a discipline it has been especially concerned with the issue of migration, with an especial focus on remittances, labor migration, postcolonialism, and uneven development (amongst many others).

Political philosophy, on the other hand, offered me the opportunity to examine forced migration in terms of the rationalizations and justifications offered in defense of displacement. It allowed me to understand the logic of eminent domain, the rhetoric of participation, and the difficult terrain of universalism, local interests, and rights-based frameworks. Of particular interest in this area for my work were the contested notions of the 'greater good' deployed by many actors including the state, opposition groups, corporate interests, and a variety of others. This analytic tradition suggested that I needed a much closer focus on the rhetoric of rights, responsibilities, and the interrelations between various stakeholders. As well, it encouraged me to widen my lens on who might be part of the migration flow – who was being displaced? How interrelated were local, regional, national, and international migration patterns and who did I need to consider as being affected by the projects?

Economic geography was another way of examining the issue of displacement with a special emphasis on such stakeholders. I looked in particular at such mechanisms as cost-benefit analyses in the planning and implementation of projects – what was counted and what was left out? How were compensation rates determined and negotiated, within local contexts, across particular sectors of displacement, and across the globe? What rights did the displaced assert and did they enlarge their concerns beyond their immediate self-interest? What spatial relations and impacts were implicit in the economic processes and projects that were causing the displacement? There are many overlaps between this tradition and development studies, especially in terms of core-periphery relations, globalization, gentrification, and the relationship between environment and economy, though in this sub-discipline the emphasis is on spatiality rather than human, economic, or cultural development per se.

The particular tools I have used to carry out this research on development-induced displacement have, as in my work with diasporic migration, fit the traditions in which the interdisciplinary framework is grounded. Beyond reviews of secondary literature and secondary data, the primary source materials have included interviews with project planners, project-affected persons, and activists. As well, a central feature of the research has been to rely on a series of project reports based on case studies of the impacts of development-induced displacement (Vandergeest et al., 2007). Over the course of ten years, these reports – produced out of a broader project on ethics and displacement – were the result of fieldwork-based, ethnographic analyses of the processes and practices of forced migration due to a variety of development-related factors in South and Southeast Asia, Latin and Central America, as well as parts of Africa. These case studies helped to create a more distinguishable sense of the internally displaced migrant than the rough estimates that we currently see discussed otherwise provide. Indeed, the specificity of each case and the systematic examination of issues in an in-depth and longitudinal manner provide a much sharper image of the displaced than we find elsewhere. As Bennett and Shurmer-Smith suggest:

> The strength of [case] study methods is that they put the real lives of real people right at the centre of explanation. Their stories dictate the form of the narrative,

their constructions of social relevance offer the context. Putting case studies at the centre of one's analysis allows the exceptional and the peculiar to shine through, but not eclipse, whatever passes for normality. (Bennett and Shurmer-Smith, 2002)

Finally, in my last example, for my research with refugee resettlement in northeastern USA I grounded my work primarily in the fields of demography, anthropology, and transportation geography, particularly in a project specifically looking at refugees, transportation equity, and mobility issues in Vermont. Sociology or some field of population studies and demography are those likely most familiar to scholars of migration. After all, the counting of populations and population change has long been considered the domain of those whose work explicitly deals with people, mobility, and change. Demography as a whole (usually as a subset of sociology) has tended to be quantitative in nature, primarily a statistical study of human populations and their behaviors, over time and space, and including migration as a key area of investigation. Formal demography in particular tends to limit its view to the measurement of population processes, while social or applied demography examines these processes in relation to economic, social, cultural, and political factors (Murdock and Ellis, 1991).

For the reasons outlined previously, however, relying on traditional demography alone was not going to be enough to build a complete picture of the refugee resettlement experience. Examining refugees through statistics alone was not enough to provide an accurate portrait, especially when time and scale were factored into the equation and the refugees came 'off the books' so to speak. To develop this deeper understanding and actually track the post-official resettlement experience of refugees I therefore turned to the anthropological tradition of ethnographic research (Clifford and Marcus, 1986) in order to conduct in-depth interviews with key informants and representatives of both the refugee and service-provider communities. As with case studies, ethnographic research is designed to develop a holistic understanding of individuals and societies, drawing on participant observation, genealogies, interviews, and a host of other methods in order to discover the large and small details of each life and life space (Fetterman, 2010). What an ethnographic approach offered was a broader and deeper glimpse into the lives of the refugee migrant – what other places and people they were connected to, both in the present moment and in the past. It allowed me to see the evolving relationships over time and distance, in terms of ethnicity, kinship, religion, and politics. It was more appropriate for longitudinal studies and a desire to build trust between the researcher and the researched (see more on this in the following section).

The last approach I drew upon for the project on refugees and mobility was the subfield of transportation geography, a branch of the discipline that focuses on spatial interactions, modes of traveling, and patterns of movement (Hanson, 1995). In particular I used the set of tools known as Geographic Information Systems (GIS) in order to show where refugees are located in relation to existing transportation infrastructure. Such a spatial representation was especially useful for illustrating issues of equity and access. Are refugee communities located near the services or workplaces that they need to access? GIS can help to illustrate the spatial relationship between refugees and destinations. As Nyerges suggests, '[a] major goal in using GIS for transportation analysis is to provide transportation planners, policy makers and the general public with easier access to important geographic relationships as part of the transportation decision-making process' (Nyerges, 1995, p. 166).

The tools provided by sociology (or population geography for that matter) gave me an excellent starting point for my research into refugees and transportation in Vermont. I was able to draw on some of the key measures used in sociology to begin my inquiry, including census data, community surveys (collected by others), vital or civil registrations, and statistics collected by government agencies as well as non-governmental organizations and service providers. Of particular use to me was data provided to me by the chief refugee resettlement agencies and government offices dealing with refugees in Vermont. Additionally I was able to draw upon information from the 2000 US Census as well as the 2006–09 American Community Survey. Further data was available from local school districts, housing authorities, and employment agencies, amongst others.

Turning to my ethnographic research, potential interviewees were identified using snowball-sampling or respondent-driven methods common in ethnographic research, especially with 'hidden' or potentially marginalized communities (Browne, 2005). Additionally, I developed and distributed a set of two community-based surveys of service providers and refugees, respectively. I also attended regular meetings of community associations and service providers in order to receive updates on their perspectives and interests. Finally, GIS methods were used to track the movements of representative refugee transportation users across four separate modes of travel – walking, cycling, bus, and car – and map their travel times as well as distances to various destinations (see Table 13.1 for a summary of the different projects).

Table 13.1   An interdisciplinary research approach matrix

Research question(s)	Research traditions	Data sources	Methods
Is there a relationship between Indian Bengali diasporas and urbanization in contemporary Kolkata?	Political economy Cultural studies Urban geography	Planning documents Housing developers City and regional planners Construction workers Diaspora members Government documents Advertising, television, film, news media, and literature Secondary literature Census information National and international financial statistics	Semi-structured interviews Key informant interviews Focus groups Surveys Critical textual analysis Participant observation
What is the impact of international development on population displacement?	Development studies Political philosophy Economic geography	Project planners Project-affected persons Government documents NGO publications Activists Project reports Secondary literature	Semi-structured interviews Key informant interviews Case studies
What is the experience of refugees with transportation in Vermont?	Sociology Anthropology Transportation geography	Census information Government documents Government statistics Refugees Service providers Newspaper reports	Key-informant interviews Surveys Focus groups Participant observation GIS

13.4 SEARCHING FOR THE MIGRANT: HOW DO WE LOOK AND FOR WHAT PURPOSE?

In the final section of this chapter I conclude by discussing one of the key issues framing migration research that many of us involved in such inquiry face – the broader politics and uses of these studies. After all, why is it that migration is such an important and growing field? What are the ethical and practical implications of tracking the movements of people, culture, and capital? How do the approaches and methods we use to engage in migration research depend upon developing and adhering to ethical principles of trust, reciprocity, and reflexivity? Ethics is, after all, more than simply receiving the requisite approvals from institutional review boards and signed consent forms. For migration researchers it is perhaps especially important to be clear regarding the objectives and the uses of their studies. For example, locating the precise dwellings of undocumented laborers might be an important intellectual project, but can one ignore the possible consequences for the migrants themselves – including potential legal ramifications – should such information become public? Similarly, while it might be of great interest to track the flow of informal remittances between foreign workers and homelands, if the migrants themselves are consciously avoiding official financial channels, does the researcher have any obligations to their research subjects to keep their confidences? In this section I describe three particular components of interdisciplinary approaches that can give us some guidance and assistance in building an ethical framework for our research into migration and the lives of migrants. These are:

1. Approaching data collection and analysis with a healthy skepticism.
2. Building trust with the subjects of study.
3. Designing a research process that is emergent and flexible.

The framing and organizing principle for the majority of my research related to migration has been that it is action-oriented, participatory in nature, uses qualitative tools, and is community-based in both design and execution. This has meant engaging with several community partners through their leadership and maintaining a dialogue with them on the research approach, including adjusting research strategies in order to refine both research questions and the appropriate methods of investigation, reporting back to communities, and making publicly available research findings. As is often the case with participatory projects, the researchers responded to the priorities and ideas articulated by the partner organizations and shifted some of its original focus and design throughout the course of the study.

Such an approach is grounded in what Reason calls 'participative inquiry' (Reason, 1998). This is an approach based on three particular elements: (1) co-operative inquiry; (2) participatory action research; and (3) action inquiry, in order to build a collaborative relationship between the researcher and the researched. The idea is that while a general outline of the research issue and key questions are initially determined by the principal investigator(s), the latter must be open to having his or her views and designs challenged, complicated, and even modified by the participants in the project. The goal is to leave the research itself as an emergent process, where issues become crystallized not as a top-down directive from the researcher, but as a dialogue and debate between discussants.

13.4.1 Avoiding Data Fetishism

Interdisciplinary research with its embrace of multi- and mixed-methods approaches values diverse forms of data, from vital statistics to community questionnaires to films and novels. It is often easy, however, to become infatuated with the form of the data itself. The sheer abundance of statistics, for example, on many different aspects of migrant lives and existence can tempt some researchers to rely overmuch on numbers alone. Figures on migration or economic activities then become more than mere representations, they become a stand-in for the migrant themselves. As this chapter has attempted to show, such a perspective can give a limited view of the complexities of migration.

On the other hand, one can just as easily become subsumed within an ethnographic minefield in examining the life space of the migrant. This is especially true when one engages in fieldwork, whether through interviews, surveys, participant observation, or any other of a number of qualitative methods. This is of course not a problem limited to migration research. Going into 'the field' is a requisite part of training in an increasing number of disciplines, often a rite of passage for academics in a range of disciplines. But both entering and exiting the field are complex and often difficult tasks (Scheyvens and Storey, 2003). Moreover, for the migration researcher employing ethnographic or other qualitative approaches, the temptation to represent their own particular case or set of studies as the definitive migration experience may often be strong. Resisting both of these urges – fetishing either quantitative or qualitative data (or perhaps even a combination of the two) – can be aided by adopting an interdisciplinary approach to migration research. The approach itself helps to remind us of the multifaceted and diverse nature of the subject and hopefully keeps the researcher focused on the fact that there is much more beyond their study in the universe of migration.

13.4.2 Building Trust

For migration research of the kind that I have conducted – primarily community-based, qualitative, and action-oriented – perhaps no greater ethical issue exists beyond building respectful, reciprocal, and trust-based relationships with diasporic groups and migrants.[5] At the heart of this belief lie those questions articulated above – for what purpose do we undertake our studies, whom do they affect, and what outcomes might they result in? In turn, such concerns raise important issues regarding power, representation, voice, privilege, and partiality (Mauthner, 2002; Scheyvens et al., 2003; Smith, 1999).

Developing reciprocal relationships with migrant communities and individuals requires a good deal of reflexivity by the researcher regarding their own positionality and relative power vis-à-vis their research subjects. It also needs considerable time and patience to nurture and a significant commitment to various forms of collaboration. In my work with refugee communities in Vermont, for example, this meant developing a multi-year working relationship with community organizations. It meant consulting service providers, community leaders, and individuals within the refugee population on various aspects of the research project and design, in order to define appropriate needs and methods. This included returning to the various involved parties with project updates, making both interim and final results available to all participants, and receiving feedback on various research tools and methods. In one instance, the members of a particular migrant community indicated that they were not comfortable with the research tool of the focus group. Rather than insisting upon using this method because it was part of the research plan or abandoning work with this group, having an interdisciplinary framework and approach to migration research meant that I was able to shift the data collection method (to in-depth interviews and surveys) and still include the population within my broader study. The purpose and concomitant result was, of course, to maintain the level of trust that the broader community had in me as well as their faith in the project.

Perhaps the most important step in setting the context for my research is in reflecting on my own positionality vis-à-vis my work. I do this not with the goal of using identity as a shorthand for intentionality and understanding; that is, there is nothing about a particular social category that can or should define my insight into or analysis of a given situation. The need for reflexivity in research does not require continued declarative statements about 'who the researcher is' if the only purpose is to thereby define the work according to predetermined labels. Indeed, as Nagar and Geiger argue:

> This demand needs to be challenged and resisted because uncovering ourselves in these terms contradicts our purpose of problematizing the dominant meanings attributed to pre-defined social categories – that is, social categories

that are not just essentialist or overly coherent, but a view of categories as existing prior to and isolated from specific interactions, rather than as created, enacted, transformed in and through those interactions. (Nagar and Geiger, 2007, p. 264)

Yet it remains important to recognize my own role and power as an academic and scholar when conducting my research with migrant communities.

13.4.3 An Emergent Research Process

Such efforts are part of a more general orientation toward an emergent research process. Interdisciplinary approaches are particularly well suited to such frameworks precisely because they are not rigid and narrow and are instead open to multiple possibilities. The migrant or migration pattern may not be easy to discern and therefore require interdisciplinary means to uncover. But equally apparent is the need to let the research take on different directions and utilize diverse methods, as necessary. As Hesse-Biber and Leavy suggest:

> Emergent methods often arise in order to answer research questions that traditional methods may not adequately answer . . . [and] are conscious of the link between epistemology (a view on how knowledge is constructed), methodology (the theoretical question[s] that informs our research and how it is carried out), and method (the specific tools used to carry out research). Emergent methods are particularly useful in getting at issues of power and authority in the research process, from question formulation to carrying out and writing up research findings. We can think of these methods as hybrid in the sense that they often borrow and adapt methods from their own disciplines or can cross disciplinary boundaries to create new tools and concepts or refashion tools or concepts that exist in order to answer complex and often novel questions. (Hesse-Biber and Leavy, 2006, p. xi)

For the migration researcher the potential that emergent research allows is to simultaneously draw on interdisciplinary approaches while remaining grounded within a firm ethical footing.

13.5 CONCLUSION

This chapter has suggested that researchers interested in the subjects and processes that comprise migration consider utilizing an interdisciplinary approach that triangulates research methods and draws from diverse scholarly traditions in order to frame their work. It is the very nature of the migration process and the often ephemeral and unstable data sources upon which we must draw that requires our flexibility and willingness to look creatively at the various practices in which migrants engage and the often hidden traces they leave across multiple landscapes. This chapter considers in particular the idea of diaspora as especially appropriate for this mode of inquiry. An interdisciplinary, multi-method approach to migration research, in this sense, offers a nuanced and potentially rich lens through which we can understand the flow of people, ideas, culture, and capital across the globe.

As important as this broad-based orientation to examining migration is, this chapter also argues that understanding the intricacies and politics of these processes means engaging with the ethics of our research. It also suggests that we need to ground migration research within principles of community-based, participatory, and action-oriented inquiry. Thus, it is the very complexity of migrant lives and migration patterns that require the use of multiple tools and approaches, in order to both understand these processes and to engage with them in an ethical fashion.

NOTES

1. See, for instance, Iosifides (Chapter 2), Delgado Wise and Márquez Covarrubias (Chapter 5), and Lozano and Steinberger (Chapter 8).
2. These terms are often used synonymously though scholars such as Fagin have broadly demarcated them by describing crossdisciplinarity as knowledge borrowed from one discipline to describe another, transdisciplinarity as knowledge that is not bound to any one field but rather exists in different disciplines, and multidisciplinarity as knowledge gathered from multiple sources and disciplinary traditions while retaining some form of distinctiveness. Such scholars differentiate interdisciplinarity as new knowledge that emerges out of these other fruitful collaborations (Fagin, 2003).
3. It is true that some sub-national regions with long histories of emigration – especially labor emigration and the concomitant remittances that such regions are often economically dependent upon – collect such statistics. The governments of the Indian states of Kerala and Gujarat are two such examples, keeping close tabs on their income and investment-remitting expatriates in the Persian Gulf, North America, and Western Europe in particular.
4. For example, if one looks in greater detail at the actual data collection on which the final report of the *Government of India's 2004 High Level Committee on the Indian Diaspora* is based, one finds that their country-by-country figures are a mixture of little more than census figures, rough estimates, anecdotes, and the occasional cultural association enumeration.
5. See Sánchez-Ayala (Chapter 6, this volume) for further discussion of building trust with the migrants and van Liempt and Bilger (Chapter 21, this volume) for further discussion of ethical issues in regards to migration research.

REFERENCES

Basch, L.G., Schiller, N.G. and Szanton Blanc, C. (1994), *Nations Unbound: Transnational Projects, Postcolonial Predicaments, and Deterritorialized Nation-states*, London and New York: Routledge.
Bennett, K. and Shurmer-Smith, P. (2002), 'Handling case studies', in P. Shurmer-Smith (ed.), *Doing Cultural Geography*, London: Sage, pp. 199–209.
Bhabha, H.K. (2004), *The Location of Culture*, London and New York: Routledge.
Bloor, M. and Wood, F. (2006), *Keywords in Qualitative Methods: A Vocabulary of Research Concepts*, London and Thousand Oaks, CA: Sage.
Brah, A. (1996), *Cartographies of Diaspora: Contesting Identities*, London and New York: Routledge.
Braziel, J.E. and Mannur, A. (2003), *Theorizing Diaspora: A Reader*, Malden, MA: Blackwell.
Browne, K. (2005), 'Snowball sampling: using social networks to research non-heterosexual women', *International Journal of Social Research Methodology*, **8** (47–60), 1464–5300.
Centre, I.D.M. and Council, N.R. (2006), *Internal Displacement; Global Overview of Trends and Developments in 2006*, Geneva: Internal Displacement Monitoring Centre.
Clifford, J. and Marcus, G. (1986), *Writing Culture: The Poetics and Politics of Ethnography*, Berkeley, CA: University of California Press.
Cohen, R. (1997), *Global Diasporas: An Introduction*, Seattle, WA: University of Washington Press.
Creswell, J.W. (1998), *Qualitative Inquiry and Research Design: Choosing among Five Traditions*, Thousand Oaks, CA: Sage.
Creswell, J.W. and Plano Clark, V.L. (2007), *Designing and Conducting Mixed Methods Research*, Thousand Oaks, CA: Sage.
Denscombe, M. (2003), *The Good Research Guide: For Small-scale Social Research Projects*, Maidenhead, Berkshire and New York: Open University Press.
Fagin, R. (2003), *Reasoning About Knowledge*, Cambridge, MA: MIT Press.
Fetterman, D.M. (2010), *Ethnography: Step-by-step*, Thousand Oaks, CA and London: Sage.
Gilroy, P. (2000), *Against Race: Imagining Political Culture Beyond the Color Line*, Cambridge, MA: Belknap Press of Harvard University Press.
Hall, S. (1994), 'Cultural identity and diaspora', in P. Williams and L. Chrisman (eds), *Colonial and Post-colonial Theory*, New York: Columbia University Press, pp. 392-403.
Hanson, S. (1995), *The Geography of Urban Transportation*, New York and London: Guilford Press.
Hesse-Biber, S.N. and Leavy, P. (2006), *Emergent Methods in Social Research*, Thousand Oaks, CA: Sage.
Jayaram, N. and Atal, Y. (2004), *The Indian Diaspora: Dynamics of Migration*, New Delhi and Thousand Oaks, CA: Sage.
Mauthner, M.L. (2002), *Ethics in Qualitative Research*, London and Thousand Oaks, CA: Sage.
Murdock, S.H. and Ellis, D.R. (1991), *Applied Demography: An Introduction to Basic Concepts, Methods, and Data*, Boulder, CO: Westview Press.
Nagar, R. and Geiger, S. (2007), 'Reflexivity and positionality in feminist fieldwork revisited', in A. Tickell, E. Sheppard, J. Peck and T. Barnes (eds), *Politics and Practice in Economic Geography*, London: Sage, pp. 267–78.
Newbold, K.B. (2010), *Population Geography: Tools and Issues*, Lanham, MD: Rowman & Littlefield Publishers.
Nyerges, T. (1995), 'GIS support for urban and regional transportation analysis' in S. Hanson (ed.), *The Geography of Urban Transportation*, New York: Guildford Press, pp. 240–65.
Ong, A. (2003), 'Cyberpublics and diaspora politics among transnational Chinese', *Interventions*, **5**, 82–100.

Reason, P. (1998), 'Three approaches to participative inquiry', in N.K. Denzin and Y.S. Lincoln (eds), *Strategies of Qualitative Inquiry*, Thousand Oaks, CA: Sage, pp. 261–91.
Scheyvens, R. and Storey, D. (2003), *Development Fieldwork: A Practical Guide*, London: Sage.
Scheyvens, R., Nowak, B. and Scheyvens, H. (2003), 'Ethical issues', in R. Scheyvens and D. Storey (eds), *Development Fieldwork: A Practical Guide*, London: Sage, pp. 139–66.
Smith, L.T. (1999), *Decolonizing Methodologies: Research and Indigenous Peoples*, London: Zed Books.
UNHCR (2006), *The State of the World's Refugees 2006: Human Displacement in the New Millennium*, Oxford: Oxford University Press.
Vandergeest, P., Bose, P.S. and Idahosa, P. (2007), *Development's Displacements: Ecologies, Economies, and Cultures at Risk*, Vancouver: UBC Press.
VRRP (2010), 'Summary of Vermont refugee arrivals to FFY10 07 31', Agency of Human Services, Montpelier, State of Vermont.

14 Even a transnational social field must have its boundaries: methodological options, potentials and dilemmas for researching transnationalism

Paolo Boccagni

This chapter explores the methodological bases of empirical research on migrant transnationalism. Most studies on the topic, as I will argue, show remarkably little concern with the import of the methodologies applied. Yet, studying transnationalism in empirical terms requires a peculiar emphasis on methodological issues – well beyond the criticism of 'methodological nationalism' – for many a reason: the integration of two different contexts at least, within one's analytical framework; the need to appreciate both the differences and the commonalities between them, as well as their evolving intersections in migrants' everyday lives; the need to delve into the variable degree and frequency of immigrants' transnational engagement in different life spheres and across their life courses.

Is it possible, and if so under which conditions, to translate the theoretical assumptions of transnationalism into circumscribed hypotheses to be empirically tested? How can researchers verify, and even measure, immigrants' interactions with their motherlands? The chapter will explore the main methodological options applied in linking the concept to empirical research, detecting the reach, distribution and intensity of transnational ties and weighing up their use and consequences in host and home societies.

After a theoretical review of the debate of transnationalism (Section 14.1), a case will be made for the peculiar relevance of its methodological implications (Section 14.2). The significance of a qualitative framework of research, with particular respect to multi-sited ethnography, will then be discussed, along with its typical limitations (Section 14.3). This will be followed by a review of the state of the art of quantitative research, in light of the scope for operationalizing transnational ties and activities into bounded indicators and variables (Section 14.4). The ensuing dilemmas, as well as the prospects of collaborative and multi-method research, will be analysed in Section 14.5. Given the lack of communal grounds for distinguishing specifically transnational phenomena, and the weak empirical status of constructs such as 'transnational social field', the conclusion will highlight the need for further methodological elaboration in Section 14.6. Enhancing the underpinnings of 'methodological transnationalism' (Levitt and Khagram, 2008), in order to make them more rigorous and self-reflective, is a worthwhile effort, if transnationalism is to be appreciated as a set of research tools rather than an over-used and 'trendy catch-all' (Pries, 2007).

14.1 LENS, PHENOMENON, BUZZWORD: THE CURRENT TERMS OF DEBATE ON TRANSNATIONALISM

The ties and activities that can connect migrants with their homelands have been approached, in the last two decades or so, by a burgeoning and multidisciplinary literature. An extended review is obviously out of the remit of this chapter;[1] suffice it to say that several 'mapping exercises' have been developed in this regard (for example, Østergaard-Nielsen, 2012; Vertovec, 2004). The inherent variability of cross-border practices and connections has been highlighted along a number of axes, including the following:

- The relevant domains of social action (that is, economic, sociocultural and political life spheres), and the distinctive implications on the institutions involved in host and home societies.
- The key actors (that is, individual migrants, households and families, broader networks and communities, organizations and enterprises, up to public authorities and national governments).
- The diverse configurations of transborder connections across time and space, in terms of breadth, reach, intensity, degree of institutionalization and durability.
- The contents of the transactions between 'here' and 'there', and the kind of resources thereby circulated and exchanged.
- The cross-border meso-level formations that may result, at an aggregate level, out of migrant transnational practices and network-building (that is, transnational communities, spaces and field).

Although there is broad agreement in regarding transnationalism as an optic, rather than a full-blown theory, the persisting ambivalence around this term is related not only to the variety of its definitions, not always consistent with each other. An even more critical point lies in the conflation of a practical, analytic and prescriptive dimension in one and the same word. 'Transnationalism' can indistinctly stand for a social phenomenon and a conceptual apparatus aiming to make sense of it, and even – especially in

Table 14.1   *A typology of the key forms of immigrant transnationalism, by analytical level and social action domain*

	Economic domain	**Political** domain	**Sociocultural** domain
Identitarian-attitudinal level ('bifocal' identifications and senses of belonging, pointing both to the home and the host society)	• Predilection for consuming goods from the country of origin	• Patriotism, long-distance nationalism • Attachment to the motherland's citizenship • Affiliation to the motherland's political parties or institutions • Interest to follow and keep systematically abreast of the current events in the motherland	• Long-term nostalgia • Prevailing social identification with co-nationals abroad or in the motherland • Self-identification with the culture, art, folklore, etc. of the motherland • 'Myth of return'
Relational-behavioural level (social relationships persisting at a distance; social practices creating systematic connections between origin and destination countries)	• Sending remittances (mostly to family members left behind) • Sending gifts or money supporting the motherland (and/or the origin community) • Investments (houses, estates, small businesses, etc.) in the motherland • Ethnic enterprises promoting exchanges with the motherland • Circular international labour migration	• Motherland-related political activism (enacted 'here' or 'there') • Distance voting • Exercise of dual citizenship	• Visits and/or systematic communication at a distance with kin and friends left behind • Participation in or support to civic, recreational, religious or solidarity initiatives or organizations – either in the motherland or promoted abroad, but addressed to the motherland

Source: Based on author's elaboration of Portes (2003), Snel et al. (2006) and Boccagni (2009).

the earlier elaborations – for an ideological subtext (as the final -ism suggests) celebrating the supposedly subversive and emancipatory potential of migrant transnational ties, against nation-state borders.

As a set of 'actually existing' social phenomena, migrant transnationalism can be classified according to the forms suggested in Table 14.1. A twofold heuristic distinction is used, by analytical level (attitudes versus behaviours) and by prevalent sphere of action. The cross-border ties and activities, thus classified, can be addressed to migrants' homelands or, more often, to their local communities of origin.

As a lens, transnationalism has contributed to the globalization-related claims for 'a reformulation of the concept of society', signalling a key step towards transnational studies as a distinctive disciplinary field (Levitt and Khagram, 2008). As far as migrants are concerned, the claim is grounded on the fact that at least some of them 'are embedded in multi-layered, multi-sited transnational social fields, encompassing those who move and those who stay behind' (Levitt and Glick Schiller, 2004, p. 1003). The notion of simultaneity specifically designates their potential for being 'incorporated into daily activities, routines and institutions located both in a destination country and transnationally' (Levitt and Glick Schiller, 2004, p. 1003).

Altogether, the systematic application of this lens has shed novel light on migration processes, by emphasizing 'the need to include non-migrants as well as migrants, consider the multiple sites and levels of transnational social fields beyond just the sending and receiving country, rethink assumptions about belonging, and trace the historical continuity of these processes' (Levitt and Jaworsky, 2007, p. 142). Nevertheless, the overall significance of the transnational perspective, and the epistemological status of its empirical findings, are contentious, and likely to remain so. The more common objections regard the actual novelty, durability and currency of transnational activities in strict terms (as qualified by Portes et al., 1999). Likewise, criticisms have addressed the extremely broad range of phenomena being covered under the same conceptual label, often on thin empirical bases.

That said, two more critical points deserve to be highlighted. On the one hand, very much at issue is the unprecedented, 'qualitative' difference marked by nowadays' transborder relations in migrants' life experience, as a result of the new communication and transportation technologies. In principle, the potential for them (indeed, for anybody) to participate in different life contexts is self-evident. However, the entity of the real disjuncture this would make with the past marks the most visible boundary between advocates and opponents of the transnational perspective.

On the other hand, the 'nature' of the border being crossed by migrant connections is by no means univocal. Despite the standard emphasis on a transnational dimension, migrant cross-border ties often rely on much more particularistic bases, related to family networks or specific local communities (Velayutham and Wise, 2005; Waldinger and Fitzgerald, 2004). Such ties may even be a-national, as they are fuelled by different kinds of affiliation such as religious or political ones. A more suitable, if less fashionable concept could thus be that of translocality, pointing to 'an individual's . . . ability not just to experience the social relations that are located in the place in which he or she is corporeally standing, but also . . . to experience social relations that are located in places elsewhere' (Gielis, 2009, p. 275).

In light of these objections, and of the variety of ways of defining migrant transnationalism, a few notes are worth making on the perspective informing this chapter. I will follow an 'actor-focused approach' centred, at a micro level, on the 'cross-border engagements of social actors', with particular respect to individual migrants and their families (Morawska, 2003, p. 619; see also Kivisto, 2001). My review will not specifically elaborate, instead, on the structural understandings of this phenomenon, such as those concerned with migrants' translocal communities and organizations (for example, Portes et al., 2008; Pries, 2007) or even with emigrant outreach policies (for example, Levitt and Dehesa, 2003). In methodological terms, this will result in a greater concern with multi-sited (Marcus, 1995) than with global ethnography (Burawoy, 2000).

At an actor-centred level, transnationalism stands for a multi-faceted range of interactions and transactions at a distance, having as a key sociological commonality the significant and reciprocal (if often asymmetrical) influence being exerted between migrants and those left behind. Quintessential to transnationalism is one's potential to (re-)establish social presence, despite physical absence (Boccagni, 2012; Carling et al., 2012). Migrant cross-border connectedness, in this perspective, is a matter of changing social attitudes and practices to be analysed in empirical terms, as to their actual prevalence and incidence, and to the social circumstances accounting for them. Hence, an in-depth revisit of the attendant methodological options provides a crucial *trait d'union* between theoretical elaboration and empirical research.

14.2 WHY METHODOLOGY MATTERS IN TRANSNATIONAL MIGRATION STUDIES

The relevance of the methodological question lies not only in the need to avoid an indiscriminate use of transnational as a catch-all category, ultimately as a mere (if more fashionable) synonym of international. As Peggy Levitt and Nina Glick Schiller (2004) contend, doing research on migrant transnationalism raises peculiar methodological challenges and dilemmas. The first of them lies in the need to focus, within a communal framework, on the changing intersections 'between the networks', and more broadly the life-worlds 'of those who move and those who stay behind'.

In the second place, the tools should be devised that 'capture migrants' simultaneous engagement in and orientation toward their home and host countries', as a basis for comparative analysis across time and space. The issue at stake, in other words, is accounting for a pluri-located social context, and for the simultaneous references and interactions occurring within it (Mazzucato, 2009). How can multi-sitedness and in-betweenness be approached in terms of distinctive methodological orientations, to be translated into systematic research designs and then in indicators, variables, or anyway specific issues of concern?

14.2.1 Beyond Methodological Nationalism: Searching for Appropriate Units of Research

A major commonality in transnational migration studies, as far as methodology is concerned, lies in the rejection of methodological nationalism. This oft-evoked concept can be basically understood as the 'assumption that the nation/state/society', constructed as an internally homogeneous unit, 'is the natural social and political form of the modern world' (Wimmer and Glick Schiller, 2002, p. 302). While not entirely new, the questioning of any naturally given equivalence between society and the nation-state, as the units of reference and the levels of analysis, has gained increasing consensus.[2] It also resonates with broader theoretical attempts at moving beyond the 'container theory of society', such as those developed by Beck (for example, Beck and Sznaider, 2006) and Urry (2000), amongst others.

Moreover, criticisms of a narrowly territorialized construction of society are consistent with another major contention of globalization theories: the lack of any necessary overlapping between territorial and social spaces, hence between the geographical and the social boundaries within which human interactions occur. Transnationalization, as 'the growing importance of plurilocal and transnational social relations, networks and practices' (Pries, 2009, p. 595), applies also, and crucially, to the primary space of social experience: the everyday constructed space, well theorized by authors such Berger and Luckmann (1967), which 'people use and in which they move, physically and mentally, in an unaware, unreflected way' (Pries, 2009, p. 590). Hence the interest for an understanding of the relevance displayed, in people's daily lives, by extra-local references, ties and practices – be it in affective or instrumental terms. This applies even more to migrants, whose biographic experience is inherently stretched between separate locales.

However, the methodological implications of this cognitive shift are less obvious. As a distinctive object of analysis, Pries (2007, p. 4) argues

Even a transnational social field must have its boundaries 301

for 'transnational societal units' to be understood 'as relatively dense and durable configurations of transnational social practices, symbols and artefacts'. Such configurations should be appreciated also in light of the interpersonal motivations and emotions, expectations and interests underlying them both 'here' and 'there'. Equally notable is Pries's (2007, p. 9) heuristic distinction, along a continuum of increasing specificity, between relevant units of reference, analysis and measurement (cf. also Amelina, 2010). The distinction, aiming to a stepwise operationalization of migrants' cross-border ties and activities, could be reformulated as follows:

- Units of reference: that is, the social and temporal settings to which research is related – relational, cross-border and plurilocal social spaces.
- Units of analysis: that is, the social entities about which data are collected, and findings obtained – social institutions, social networks, families, biographies, social and personal identities.
- Units of measurement: that is – depending on the specific phenomenon being studied – cross-border ties, activities and connections; feelings of belonging and identification; flows of material or immaterial resources through the relevant borders.

Empirically speaking, selecting the units of measurement is especially critical and contentious, due not only to the fact that some potential indicators of transnationalism cannot be reduced to ordinal, or even only categorical variables. While a quite diverse set of indicators has been employed in quantitative research, there is no agreed 'hierarchy' among them (cf. Section 14.4 below). This applies to individually relevant indicators at a behavioural level and, even more, at an attitudinal one, related to transnational and home-bound identifications and attachments.[3] After all, migrants may project their identities and cultural repositories towards their homelands, even without enacting transnational social practices (or indeed, displaying various degrees of engagement, related to several factors which should be analysed in their own right, as Waldinger (2008) suggests).

14.2.2 Coping with the Transnational Social Field: Metaphor, Heuristic Tool, Set of Observable Transactions?

Whatever the level of analysis, an oft-cited guiding notion is that of transnational social field. This can be broadly understood as 'a set of historical relations between actors that cross . . . geopolitical borders between nation-states', characterized by a 'relational configuration . . . endowed with a specific "gravity" imposed on objects and actors that enter it' (Cook, 2002, p. 53). Such a notion is pivotal to a distinctive, if contested, assumption of the transnational perspective: that migrant transborder connections, while by no means new, 'have not acquired until recently the critical mass and complexity' – and, we could add, the potential for simultaneity – 'necessary to speak of an emergent social field' (Portes et al., 1999, p. 217).

Albeit stimulating, this contention elicits further doubts. To begin with, how critical should the 'mass and complexity' be in order to warrant the use of a new theoretical construct? Does this imply, perhaps, that if transnational practices prove to be minority-bound – as, in fact, is often the case – they turn out to be irrelevant? Secondly, what features are suitable to distinguish what belongs to a transnational social field from what falls into the outside social environment? What is the ultimate commonality of the attributes, or the 'gravity', that qualifies a transnational social field as such?

While insisting on the 'empirical' relevance of this notion as a 'tool for conceptualizing the potential array of social relations' between migrants and non-migrants, Levitt and Glick Schiller (2004, p. 1009) conclude: '[I]n any given study, the researcher must operationalize the parameters of the field they are studying and the scope of the networks embedded within it, then empirically analyze the strength and impact of direct and indirect transnational relations'. Remarkably, this conclusion sounds less like a factual description than a future-oriented appeal (Soehl and Waldinger, 2010). Whether it has been followed so far, and – indeed – how far it can be followed, is the issue to be explored in the next sections.

How can one assess if a migrant (or for that matter, anybody) lives, interacts or even only feels to be within a distinctive transnational social field? A distinction, however schematic, between qualitative and quantitative methods will be instrumental in understanding the state of the art of empirical research against these challenges.

14.3 QUALITATIVE RESEARCH: MAKING PERSONAL SENSE OF CROSS-BORDER ENGAGEMENT

Each methodological approach has, of course, strengths and limitations of its own, depending also on the kind of transnational tie or activity analysed. Overall, most research on migrant transnationalism – particularly the earlier studies – has built on a qualitative framework. Ethnographical case studies are still the prevailing option, albeit by no means the only one.

Taken together, they have provided significant insights on the development of transnational social life, first in US-addressed labour migration flows and then, increasingly, on an almost worldwide scale.[4]

14.3.1 In-depth Interviews: Value and Limitations

In-depth narrative interviews with migrants, and even their extended biographic accounts, are the most obvious option to begin with – whether in the interview itself, or as a complement to different techniques, including participant observation. As Levitt and Khagram (2008, p. 18) remark, 'transnational dynamics can also be investigated by asking interviewees about the cross-border aspects of their identities, beliefs and activities, and those they are connected to, in a single setting'. After all, this is what any large-scale survey is expected to do, and often in far more superficial terms than a biographic interview would allow.

Personal interviews with migrants are also important to understand their changing processes of identity construction, at two levels: concerning (a) the ongoing relevance and the contents of their identification with the motherland and (b) the variety of the 'identity constructs and cultural repertoires' in which their life-worlds here and there can be intermingled, even in the absence of cross-border social practices or exchanges (Park, 2007, p. 201). Face-to-face interviews are a privileged choice for grasping migrants' cognitive and emotional border-crossings, which mirror their variable potential to 'organize multiple reference groups and sustain multi-layered allegiance' to their countries of origin and settlement (Park, 2007, p. 202).

That said, and apart from the ordinary risk of eliciting over-compliant and heavily prescriptive answers, a research design relying only on migrants' narratives – which, in fact, is not so infrequent (Mazzucato, 2009) – can be criticized in many respects. This highlights three major challenges ahead:

- Establishing an appropriate criterion for selecting interviewees – whether their (supposed) centrality in co-national networks, an expectation to maximize the heterogeneity of the ensuing 'sample' or even only as a matter of snowballing. This is particularly slippery when a researcher knows little, if anything, of the interviewees' social life context – that is, out of a significant ethnographic involvement. Although these efforts are typically driven by a grounded-theory orientation to understand emerging categories and meanings, they risk eliciting accounts disembedded from migrant daily life-worlds.
- Grasping, through a 'one-time snapshot', the dynamic dimension of transnational processes. Quoting Levitt and Khagram (2008) again,

migrants' homeward engagement often tends to 'ebb and flow over long periods', depending on major events in the motherland (for example, elections, environmental crises and so on) and, obviously, in their individual and family life cycles.
- Finding a suitable comparative term of reference, such as that provided by the non-migrant 'recipients' of transnational practices. While migrants' accounts may tell much, they still provide a unilateral picture. As this is intermingled with the views of the relevant non-migrants, one is faced with the inherent complexity of transnational family life (and of the broader migrants left behind nexus). If appreciated from both sides, 'long-distance proximity' practices may display strong asymmetries and inequalities, and sometimes overt conflicts, as part and parcel of the affective, moral and economic interdependencies between here and there (Boccagni, 2010a; Carling, 2008).

14.3.2 Ethnography and its Site(s)

As a broader set of methods based on extended co-presence and participation, ethnography is particularly effective in approaching transnational relationships and practices (Glick Schiller, 2003), with special regard to the everyday life dimension (for example, Olwig, 2003; Smith, 2006). As two decades of field research show, ethnography can hardly be replaced insofar as the focus is not only on transnational ties per se, but on the social dynamics through which they are constituted and transformed. It is simply the method whenever the epistemological aim is more ambitious than that, however important, of detecting the existence (and consequently the relevance, extent and so on) of transborder connections. Extended participant observation is crucial in understanding the grassroots social processes through which such connections are situationally reproduced and negotiated. Only an extended ethnographic involvement enables a researcher to make sense of 'transnational living', as an enacted 'set of crossborder relations and practices' stemming from migrants' 'drive to maintain and reproduce their social milieu of origin from afar' (Guarnizo, 2003, pp. 667–70).

An ethnographic perspective akin to transnational studies – although the nexus between the two domains has been relatively neglected (Boccagni, 2010b) – is the multi-sited one. More than a distinctive method, this is a distinctive agenda of research, specifically concerned with 'mobile and multiply situated' objects of study (Marcus, 1995, p. 102). The key argument is that ethnographers should find suitable ways to 'follow' – literally or symbolically – the mobility, or the multiple embeddedness and interconnectedness, inherent in a number of objects of research, including migration-related transnational flows. Central to this literature is an understanding of 'the field' not as a geographically bounded location, but as an interactive plurality of sites. Indeed, the field may even turn out to be a conceptual and deeply relational space, whose boundaries are negotiated and redefined by the actors' social practices and by the ethnographer's research questions. As Falzon sums up, building on Marcus's seminal contribution:

> The essence of multi-sited research is to follow people, connections, associations and relationships across space (because they are substantially continuous but spatially non-contiguous) . . . Multi-sitedness is still very much about partial choices, never about a 'fuller' picture by stacking site upon site. It is, however, a compromise worth making, especially in the case of research with transnational groups or phenomena. (Falzon, 2009, pp. 2–16)

Once ethnography is simultaneously conducted with migrants, their significant non-migrants and in the 'in-betweenness' of their transnational interactions, it does enable an appreciation of both the reach of transnational practices and the interpersonal meanings and expectations attached to them. It also provides, by the way, a peculiar degree of 'embodiment' within migrant life-worlds. Only an extended, multi-sited ethnographic involvement releases the potential to delve into migrants' transnational connections even in 'sensory' terms, well beyond their self-presentations in this regard. As a result of fieldwork co-presence with the relevant social actors, an ethnographer can tap, along with verbalized information, novel stimuli and insights from the complementary use of all his or her human senses (Buscher and Urry, 2009): sight and hearing, smell and taste, along with touch – not to mention the opportunity to grasp the emotions being expressed and circulated through the distance (cf. Baldassar, 2008). Remarkably, migrants' connectedness with the motherland is also displayed through a variety of expressive channels – in their ways of dressing, in their styles of consumption, in their ways of spending leisure time together – which can be hardly understood, unless through a 'multi-sensorial' ethnographic involvement. This, of course, gets more complex and demanding, as a multiplicity of settings is concerned (Matsutake Research Group, 2009).

Despite its global currency, indeed, the multi-sited discourse has by no means gone unchallenged. Interestingly, objections involve less the rationale of this approach than its actual viability (for example, Hage, 2005). Given the remarkable costs of a pluri-sited, extended fieldwork (as to time investment, field negotiation, collaboration with informants, linguistic and intercultural skills), a breadth versus depth dilemma may well apply:

the risk exists of providing thinner accounts – based on more superficial engagement in every site – than ethnography usually does. In the apt formulation of Fitzgerald (2006, p. 12), 'ethnography's capacity to show process in fine-grained detail and to open black boxes to show mechanism is an undisputed strength of the method. That same strength limits the ability of the ethnographer to study a wide range of cases intensively.'

Apart from that, the usual objections to ethnographic research, primarily involving representativeness and generalizability, can be equally addressed to transnational studies. Hardly can ethnography provide, even in a multi-sited fashion, extensive evidence – independent of the single contexts involved – about the diffusion, impact and prospects of transnational ties. Most of this research, moreover, is amenable to the charge of 'sampling on the dependent variable'. As a result of a researcher's peculiar concern with transnational issues only, the risk exists of arbitrarily selecting cases where transnational ties do matter, regardless of the broader social setting in which they are embedded.

That said, coping with multi-sitedness – by doing 'intensive research in several connected sites selected for their potential theoretical yield' (Fitzgerald, 2006) – remains a major, if elusive, challenge for any research method on transnationalism. Some potential, if partial solutions to it, such as collaboration and mixed methods, will be sketched out in Section 14.5, where the key issue of simultaneity will also be approached. Before that, a review should be made of quantitative research efforts – the typical answer, however non-exhaustive, to the drawbacks of qualitative fieldwork.

14.4 QUANTITATIVE RESEARCH: THE CHALLENGE OF MEASURING THE TRANSNATIONAL

Large-scale quantitative research on migrant transborder engagement has been a relatively new arrival, for several reasons. Among them, the typically anthropological imprinting of the earlier case studies (for example, Glick Schiller et al., 1992), and the need to build original datasets, since the pre-existing ones tended to neglect the transnational dimension of immigrants' lives (with some major exceptions, for example, Massey, 1987). Notably, quantitative findings share a major point, somewhat in contrast with the earlier accounts of the 1990s: except for remittances, transnational practices in strict and systematic terms involve only a self-selected and unrepresentative minority of immigrants. While their homewards engagement on occasional bases, in one life sphere or another, is often higher, a fact remains: migrant transnational ties and activities can by no means be taken for granted. They require careful empirical analysis in light of the background factors – demographic profile, social and economic resources, structure of opportunity overseas, geopolitical distance from the motherland – that make them more or less likely.

The first extended survey in this perspective has been conducted in the United States by Alejandro Portes (2003) and associates, resulting in a groundbreaking dataset on transnational activities in several public domains.[5] This has been often celebrated as a milestone in establishing the reach and the contents of migrant transnationalism, with an emphasis on the absence of any trade-off – and in some respects a positive correlation – with integration overseas. A major exception has come from Roger Waldinger (2008), who has argued for a more nuanced (indeed, sceptical) picture, based on different and more extensive datasets. This has ultimately resulted in a compelling argument for 'homeland connectivity', entailing the primacy of a multi-faceted range of intermittent and selective connections with the motherland, rather than of any sustained 'dual life' social pattern (Soehl and Waldinger, 2010).

An overview of some of the most remarkable surveys conducted so far is provided in Table 14.2. One of them is, in fact, only a component of a broader longitudinal survey on immigrant second generations (Portes and Rumbaut, 2005). A reference is also made to one of the relatively few quantitative analyses conducted outside the American context (the exploratory study of Snel et al., 2006).

As the table shows, operationalizing transborder ties, practices and feelings is still a quite thorny issue (Mazzucato, 2010). No clear-cut consensus exists on the most appropriate indicators, nor on the ways to operationalize them. While money remittances are a relatively straightforward indicator (Guarnizo, 2003), a number of other practices and connections can be equally employed in the same vein – with no self-evident hierarchy, however, as to their validity and reliability. In a sense, this somewhat loose set of indicators does reflect the mixed evidence on the actual reach and correlates of transnational ties. As Waldinger (2008, p. 24) remarks, most migrants seem to 'pick and choose' among a range of intermittent cross-border connections – be they remittances, travels or whatever – that 'do not cluster together' into a predictable and consistent whole, to be translated into univocal and well-bounded indicators. In the second place, their home-bound self-identification and loyalty – in a word, their symbolic ethnicity – may be relevant for a long period, even in the absence of sustained transnational practices, or of any real plan to return home. Whether the same theoretical rubric – that is, 'transnational engagement' – aptly applies at both levels, given the potential disjuncture between them, is an issue in need of further elaboration (Boccagni, 2012).

Table 14.2 *Operationalizing transnationalism: individual level indicators and units of measurement in some major surveys*

	Portes (2003) and associates	Rumbaut (2002)	Snel et al. (2006)	Waldinger (2008) and associates*
Survey	Comparative Immigrant Entrepreneurship Project (CIEP) on transnational activities in first-generation immigrant households of three Latino groups in the USA	A section of the Children of Immigrants Longitudinal Study (CILS), San Diego (USA) baseline sample, waves 1–3; seven national origins + separate interviews to respondents' parents (1 wave)	Survey on six immigrant groups (ethnic minorities, refugee countries, new labour migration) in the Netherlands	Pew Hispanic representative telephone survey on Hispanics, sub-sample of foreign-born Latino population (USA)
Sampling	Three-stage sampling strategy (62%) + referrals and snowball chains (38%) (key sites of residential concentration)	Representative samples of 1.5 and second-generation youth, about 15 years old (T1), 20 (T2), 25 (T3)	Snowballing	Stratified random digit dialing (RDD) sample
Vision of transnationalism	Occupations and activities based on regular, sustained cross-border contacts	Home-related perceptions, practices and identities	Transnational activities and identifications	Cross-border connections and attachments

	Research also in H	—	—	—
Operationalization	Preliminary interviews to key informants in H			Cross-border exchanges and activities
	Economic	*Perceptions* (to parents)	*Activities*	• Sending of remittances
	• Transnational entrepreneurs	• How proud of H	• Everyday economic (family remittances, sends goods to H, owns house in H, contributes to H NGOs)	• Travels to H
	• Transnational entrepreneurs as percentage of self-employed	• How important for child to know of H		• Voting in H
		• How often talks to child of H		*H attachments and loyalties*
	Political	• How often celebrates days connected to H	• Professional economic (invests in companies in H, conducts trade with H, visits H for business)	• Settlement plans
	• Member of H political party	• How important to keep in touch with others in H		• Self-identified 'real H'
	• Gives money to H political party		• Political (reads H's papers, keeps in touch with H's politics, member of H's political party, participates in H-related demonstrations	• Self-described identity
	• Participates in H political campaigns and rallies	*Perceptions and practices* (to immigrants' adult children)		
		• Knowledge of parents' H (out of 3 questions asked)		
	Socio-cultural	• Ethno-national self-identification		
	• Member of a hometown civic association	• Which feels most like 'home' (USA, H, both, neither)	• Socio-cultural (visits family/friends in H, frequent contacts with family in H, member of social organization in H, member of	
	• Gives money for community projects in H			

309

Table 14.2 (continued)

Portes (2003) and associates	Rumbaut (2002)	Snel et al. (2006)	Waldinger (2008) and associates*
• Member of a charity association in H • Travels to attend public festivities in H • Participates in local sports club with links to H	• How many times and for how long has visited H • How often sends money	H-related organization, attends meetings with primarily compatriots, visits cultural events *Identifications* (primarily with co-nationals in H or abroad) • Group id ('To whom do I belong?') • Normative id ('Whose norms and values are important to me?') • Feeling of proximity to relevant groups ('circle score' representation)	

Notes:
'H' stands for 'homeland'.
* While this is related to the 2002 database, further elaboration has then been made on the 2006 Pew Survey data, finally including telephone communication among the indicators of cross-border connectivity (Soehl and Waldinger, 2010).

Source: Based on the author's literature review.

Furthermore, most surveys have given little attention to the family-based dimension of cross-border engagement, apart from remittances. Although the complexity of transnational family life is reluctant to bluntly categorial variables, a fact remains: quantitative analyses have mostly approached transnationalism as a matter of migrant institutionalized engagement, addressed to the homeland public sphere. Quite overlooked has been the relevance of the emotional and affective ties which underlie their kinship (and broadly, sociability) at a distance: what one may regard as private transnationalism (Boccagni, 2010a). Survey-based data could fruitfully expand, for instance, the knowledge available on the following:

- The frequency, prevailing contents and perceived effects of transnational communication, against an extended physical detachment.
- The variety of channels through which migrants negotiate their affective relationships with their kin left behind.
- The reach of their capability to be informed about, to share emotionally and to affect the latter's everyday lives.
- The relevance, in emotional, affective and instrumental terms, of their long-distance social networks, against those based on geographical proximity, within the immigration life context.

These remarks can be connected to what is, arguably, the key challenge ahead, also and above all, for quantitative research: collecting extensive and, possibly, simultaneous datasets on the transnational engagement of immigrants and of their left behind counterparts, in a 'matched sample' logic (Horst, 2009; Mazzucato, 2009; see Section 14.5 below). Several practical reasons and constraints militate against this option. Chief amongst them, the attendant costs, the need for an extended and qualified network of research collaborators, and the adaptation of a communal research tool to a variety of linguistic, cultural and social contexts. Still, the ironic lack of a properly transnational research design is a major weakness. It affects the survey-based information on descriptive indicators of cross-border engagement, and, even more, on complex issues such as the faceted interdependence – at an economic, a moral and an affective level – between migrants and non-migrants.

Quantitative research on the US-Mexico migration system provides outstanding exceptions to the argument above, however independent from the transnationalism debate. The most renowned is the longitudinal, bi-national Mexican Migration Project (MPP) developed by Massey, Durand and associates through the multi-method ethnosurvey (Durand and Massey, 2004; Massey, 1987). This pioneer research design has resulted in a parallel sampling of a number of emigrant households, in several Mexican home communities, and of their family members in the USA. A key strength of this design lies in the systematic integration of quantitative and qualitative tools all across the research process – from site selection and survey designing, through the survey implementation, up to data analysis. This enables a continuous exchange of information and insights between different methods and researchers. Indeed, multi-method research deserves further remarks, along with the cognate topics of collaboration and simultaneity, as a final step of this review.

14.5 MIXED METHODS, COLLABORATION, SIMULTANEITY AND BEYOND

Setting qualitative and quantitative designs against each other is, of course, an oversimplification.[6] A variable 'methodological mix' (albeit with a clear dominance of qualitative tools) does inform several empirical studies on transnational ties, including some of the most compelling ones (such as Kyle, 2000; Levitt, 2001; Smith, 2006). After all, the need for a 'methodologically more diversified approach' – indeed, for 'a combination of methods ranging from the analysis of official and census data, to longitudinal surveys, to ethnographic work' – has been emphasized as a precondition for advancing research (Portes, 2003, p. 889; see also Bryman, 2006 for a review of mixed methods). Until now, however, single-method case studies have been by far predominant.

Against the typical limitations of the ensuing research findings, in terms of representativeness and generalizability, Fitzgerald (2006) argues for a range of integrated research agendas: using concomitant sources of statistical data, in order to establish how far a single case is representative of broader trends; promoting collaboration between ethnographers and survey researchers, in the vein of Massey et al. (1994); combining ethnography with statistical methods, in the framework of the same research; and last, and particularly relevant to transnational studies, multiplying the number of case studies. This may entail doing serial ethnographies on the same topic over time, and/or working simultaneously upon a communal concern in a multi-sited way, involving colleagues from different countries. In any of these respects, a collaborative and multi-method dimension is clearly vital. This equally applies to any future research effort, aiming for a better understanding of migrant transnational involvement in two crucial perspectives:

- Diachronic: concerning the evolution of transnational attributes over the life course of a migration flow, of specific networks

and households, or even at an individual level (both intra- and inter-generationally).
• Cross-country: promisingly entailing comparative analyses between distinct home/host societies in one migration system or, at a broader level, between different migration systems.

Two more issues, however, need to gain visibility in the methodological debate. The first is how to cope, if at all, with simultaneity. While transnational ties and activities display a potential for simultaneous social action – being started here and at the same time affecting life conditions there, or vice versa – research on them is typically developed stepwise, in one site after the other. A notable exception is the simultaneous matching sample (SMS) methodology, recently applied by Valentina Mazzucato (2009, 2010) and associates on the Netherlands-Ghana migration system. This is a peculiar case of simultaneous and matched-sample design, which entails 'studying the flows of information, money and goods from the sending and receiving countries while they occur' (Horst, 2009, p. 122). As a necessarily teamwork research, it aims to select and follow migrants' transnational social networks, kin-based or not, whose members interact at a distance from separate localities. Each of these local contexts turns into a fieldwork site, from which migrants' cross-border transactions can be simultaneously and systematically observed.[7] Besides enabling data triangulation, this methodology – however costly in terms of time and resources – can lead to innovative findings. Potentially, it enables researchers to appreciate the interactions between the reciprocal expectations, interests and representations which underlie cross-border transactions; to document the changing effects that transnational connections may have on both sides; and less obviously, to bridge the epistemological gap between migrants' self-accounts and their actual social practices.

The second issue leads us back to the need for clearer boundaries – once again, an ambivalence which applies to any technique of research on transnationalism, although it is particularly striking in quantitative analyses. On the one hand, as most researchers agree by now, cross-border engagement cannot just be reduced to a dichotomous, 'all or nothing' variable. It is rather a matter of differential and changing degrees, frequencies and intensities. That said, the distinctive grounds, if any, for qualifying any social phenomenon as transnational rather than simply international is still uncertain. Can some 'critical threshold' be found – numerical or otherwise – laying the foundations for a reasonably general distinction between the transnational and the rest? As Soehl and Waldinger (2010, p. 1490) put it, 'by drawing hard lines between the "transmigrants" and the much larger migrant rank and file, scholars also miss the pervasive nature of the everyday cross-border activities entailed in travel, communication and remittance-sending'. Yet, insofar as scholars draw no line (or just dismiss the point), they can hardly claim for cross-border connections as a distinctive and autonomous subject of study. Even less can they use the transnational social field as a proper research tool rather than a fascinating metaphor or, at most, a heuristic device.

14.6 CONCLUSION

Altogether, mixed methods, collaboration and – insofar as possible – simultaneity are promising prospects, with a view to making methodological progress in research on migrant transnationalism. Most of the work developed so far has been the result of individual or small group efforts, especially in qualitative research. However, more systematic resort to transdisciplinary and collective work is necessary for improving the breadth and depth of research findings, as well as their epistemic state. In this respect, representativeness and generalizability are issues that, whatever one's methodological preferences, can hardly be discarded as irrelevant (as the lack of specific reflections, apart from some exceptions, for example, Fitzgerald, 2006, may suggest).

A final remark can be made, by drawing from the 'cognitive turn' advocated by Rogers Brubaker in empirical studies on ethnicity and nationhood. In the author's contention, each of these heavily discussed concepts could be better understood less as a substantive entity than as 'a practical category, as classificatory scheme, as cognitive frame' (Brubaker, 1996, p. 16; cf. also Brubaker, 2009). In a similar vein, transnationalism could be reframed as something different from a noun that supposedly qualifies a distinctive group of people, along with the peculiar "condition of being" of the transmigrants: one 'so encompassing as to virtually erase the distinction between "here" and "there"' (Waldinger, 2008, p. 5). Cross-border connectedness could rather be understood as a set of potential and situated attributes which migrants can activate, depending on the structure of opportunities they face and on their social and family embeddedness, but also in light of their own needs, interests and life projects.

Approaching the transnational as a changing potentiality rather than a fixed property, however, requires further methodological elaboration, despite the plenitude of case studies that exist now. Under the current state of the art, the epistemological status of empirical research still seems to be a basically heuristic, more than explicatory one. While it does shed light on the ongoing connections between 'here' and 'there', it still needs progress in order to allow, arguably, for a general and empirically based delimitation – be it in terms of 'societal' or 'statistical' significance (Burawoy, 1991) – of the transnational social fields, which are assumed to concretize such connections.

NOTES

1. See, among the literature reviews on migrant transnationalism, Portes et al. (1999); Kivisto (2001); Levitt and Jaworsky (2007); Waldinger (2011). See also, on the theoretical traditions that have informed this perspective, Levitt and Glick Schiller (2004).
2. An alternative methodological trap, one less often discussed but not less insidious, can be labelled as 'groupism', after Brubaker's (2009, p. 28) criticism of the 'groupist social ontology'. This refers, here, to the framing of 'transnational communities as units that are stable over time, and are held to be of overriding importance for the individual identities and social practices of their members' (Faist, 2010, p. 28). As I will argue, the recognition of the selective and contingent relevance of transnational attributes, hence of the need to grasp their changing configurations, has marked a watershed between the earlier and the more recent studies on the topic.
3. Cf. Haller and Landolt (2005), as well as the distinction between migrants' 'ways of being' and 'ways of belonging' in Levitt and Glick Schiller (2004).
4. Cf. the reviews in Levitt and Jaworsky (2007) and Vertovec (2009).
5. Apart from the key findings in Portes (2003), cf. Guarnizo et al. (2003) on political transnationalism; Portes et al. (2003) on transnational entrepreneurs; Itzigsohn and Saucedo (2002) on social and cultural cross-border activities.
6. Several techniques potentially relevant to this research field, although scarcely tapped so far, do not sit easily in a single domain. Among them, network analysis (for example, Dahinden, 2009) and internet-based research (for example, Kissau and Hunger, 2010).
7. The relevant transactions – any cross-border sustained 'exchange of information . . ., goods, money or services' – have been classified into eight daily life domains: 'housing, business . . ., funerals, church, health care, education, remittances . . . and community development projects' (Mazzucato, 2009, p. 220).

REFERENCES

Amelina, A. (2010), 'Searching for an appropriate research strategy on transnational migration', *Forum: Qualitative Social Research*, **11** (1), 17.
Baldassar, L. (2008), 'Missing kin and longing to be together', *Journal of Intercultural Studies*, **29** (3), 247–66.
Beck, U. and Sznaider, N. (2006), 'Unpacking cosmopolitanism for the social sciences', *British Journal of Sociology*, **57** (1), 1–23.
Berger, P. and Luckmann, T. (1967), *The Social Construction of Reality*, New York: Anchor Books.
Boccagni, P. (2009), *Tracce transnazionali*, Milan: Angeli.
Boccagni, P. (2010a), 'Private, public or both? On the scope and impact of transnationalism in immigrants' everyday lives', in R. Baubӧck and T. Faist (eds), *Diaspora and Transnationalism*, Amsterdam: Amsterdam University Press, pp. 185–205.
Boccagni, P. (2010b), 'Exploring migrants' affective ties at a distance', COMCAD Working Paper No. 72/2010.
Boccagni, P. (2012), 'Rethinking transnational studies: transnational ties and the transnationalism of everyday life', *European Journal of Social Theory*, **15** (1), 117–32.

Brubaker, R. (1996), *Nationalism Reframed*, Cambridge: Cambridge University Press.
Brubaker, R. (2009), 'Ethnicity, race and nationalism', *Annual Review of Sociology*, **35**, 21–42.
Bryman, A. (2006), 'Integrating quantitative and qualitative research', *Qualitative Research*, **6** (1), 97–113.
Burawoy, M. (ed.) (1991), *Ethnography Unbound*, Berkeley, CA: University of California Press.
Burawoy, M. (ed.) (2000), *Global Ethnography*, Berkeley, CA: University of California Press.
Buscher, M. and Urry, J. (2009), 'Mobile methods and the empirical', *European Journal of Social Theory*, **12** (1), 99–116.
Carling, J. (2008), 'The human dynamics of migrant transnationalism', *Ethnic and Racial Studies*, **31** (8), 1452–77.
Carling, J., Menjívar, C. and Schmalzbauer, L. (2012), 'Central themes in the study of transnational parenthood', *Journal of Ethnic and Migration Studies*, **38** (2), forthcoming.
Cook, D.A. (2002), 'Forty years of religion across borders', in H.R. Ebaugh and J.A. Chafetz (eds), *Religion Across Borders*, Walnut Creek, CA: Altamira Press, pp. 51–74.
Dahinden, J. (2009), 'Network transnationalism and transnational subjectivity', *Ethnic and Racial Studies*, **32** (8), 1365–86.
Durand, J. and Massey, D. (eds) (2004), *Crossing the Border: Research from the Mexican Migration Project*, New York: Russell Sage Foundation.
Faist, T. (2010), 'Diaspora and transnationalism: what kind of dance partners?', in R. Bauböck and T. Faist (eds), *Diaspora and Transnationalism: Concepts, Theories and Methods*, Amsterdam: Amsterdam University Press, pp. 9–34.
Falzon, M.A. (2009), 'Multi-sited ethnography: theory, praxis and locality in contemporary research', in M.A. Falzon (ed.), *Multi-sited Ethnography*, Aldershot: Ashgate, pp. 1–24.
Fitzgerald, D. (2006), 'Towards a theoretical ethnography of migration', *Qualitative Sociology*, **29** (1), 1–24.
Gielis, R. (2009), 'A global sense of migrant places: towards a place perspective in the study of migrant transnationalism', *Global Networks*, **9** (2) 271–87.
Glick Schiller, N. (2003), 'The centrality of ethnography in the study of transnational migration', in N. Foner (ed.), *American Arrivals*, Santa Fe: School of American Research, pp. 99–128.
Glick Schiller, N., Szanton Blanc, C. and Bash, L. (eds) (1992), *Towards a Transnational Perspective on Migration*, New York: Annals of the New York Academy of Science.
Guarnizo, L. (2003), 'The economics of transnational living', *International Migration Review*, **37** (3), 666–99.
Guarnizo, L.E., Portes, A. and Haller, W. (2003), 'Assimilation and transnationalism', *American Journal of Sociology*, **108** (6), 1211–48.
Hage, G. (2005), 'A not so multi-sited ethnography of a not so imagined community', *Anthropological Theory*, **5** (4), 463–75.
Haller, W. and Landolt, P. (2005), 'The transnational dimensions of identity formation', *Ethnic and Racial Studies*, **28** (6), 1182–214.
Horst, C. (2009), 'Expanding sites: the question of "depth" explored', in M.A. Falzon (ed.), *Multi-sited Ethnography*, Aldershot: Ashgate, pp. 119–34.
Itzigsohn, J. and Saucedo, S.G. (2002), 'Immigrant incorporation and sociocultural transnationalism', *International Migration Review*, **36** (3), 767–98.
Kissau, K. and Hunger, U. (2010), 'The internet as a means of studying transnationalism and diaspora', in R. Bauböck and T. Faist (eds), *Diaspora and Transnationalism: Concepts, Theories and Methods*, Amsterdam: Amsterdam University Press, pp. 245–66.
Kivisto, P. (2001), 'Theorizing transnational migration', *Ethnic and Racial Studies*, **24** (4), 549–77.
Kyle, D. (2000), *Transnational Peasants*, Baltimore, MD: Johns Hopkins University Press.
Levitt, P. (2001), *The Transnational Villagers*, Los Angeles, CA: University of California Press.

Levitt, P. and de la Dehesa, R. (2003), 'Transnational migration and the redefinition of the state', *Ethnic and Racial Studies*, **26** (4), 587–611.
Levitt, P. and Glick Schiller, N. (2004), 'Conceptualizing simultaneity: a transnational social field perspective on society', *International Migration Review*, **37** (3), 1002–39.
Levitt, P. and Jaworsky, B. (2007), 'Transnational migration studies', *Annual Review of Sociology*, **33**, 129–56.
Levitt, P. and Khagram, S. (2008), 'Constructing transnational studies', in P. Levitt and S. Khagram (eds), *The Transnational Studies Reader*, New York: Routledge, pp. 1–28.
Marcus, G.E. (1995), 'Ethnography in/of the world system: the emergence of multi-sited ethnography', *Annual Review of Anthropology*, **24**, 95–117.
Massey, D. (1987), 'The ethnosurvey in theory and practice', *International Migration Review*, **21** (4), 1498–522.
Massey, D., Goldring, L. and Durand, J. (1994), 'Continuities in transnational migration', *American Journal of Sociology*, **99** (6), 1492–533.
Matsutake Research Group (2009), 'Strong collaboration as a method for multi-sited ethnography', in M.A. Falzon (ed.), *Multi-sited Ethnography*, Aldershot: Ashgate, pp. 197–214.
Mazzucato, V. (2009), 'Bridging boundaries with a transnational research approach', in M.A. Falzon (ed.), *Multi-sited Ethnography*, Aldershot: Ashgate, pp. 215–32.
Mazzucato, V. (2010), 'Operationalising transnational migrant networks through a simultaneous matched sample methodology', in R. Bauböck and T. Faist (eds), *Diaspora and Transnationalism: Concepts, Theories and Methods*, Amsterdam: Amsterdam University Press, pp. 202–26.
Morawska, E. (2003), 'Disciplinary agenda and analytic strategies of research on immigrant transnationalism', *International Migration Review*, **37** (3), 611–40.
Olwig, K.F. (2003), 'Researching global sociocultural fields', *International Migration Review*, **37** (3), 787–811.
Østergaard-Nielsen, E. (2012), 'Transnational migration: practices, policies and spaces', in M. Martiniello and J. Rath (eds), *International Migration and Immigrant Incorporation*, Amsterdam: Amsterdam University Press, forthcoming.
Park, K. (2007), 'Constructing transnational identities without leaving home', *Sociological Forum*, **22** (2), 200–18.
Portes, A. (2003), 'Conclusion: theoretical convergencies and empirical evidence', *International Migration Review*, **37** (3), 874–89.
Portes, A. and Rumbaut, R. (2005), 'The second generation and the Children of Immigrants Longitudinal Study', *Ethnic and Racial Studies*, **28** (6), 983–99.
Portes, A., Guarnizo, L.E. and Landolt, P. (1999), 'The study of transnationalism', *Ethnic and Racial Studies*, **22** (2), 217–37.
Portes, A., Escobar, E. and Araña, R. (2008), 'Bridging the gap: transnational and ethnic organizations in the political incorporation of immigrants in the United States', *Ethnic and Racial Studies*, **31** (6), 1056–90.
Pries, L. (2007), 'Transnationalism: trendy catch-all or specific research programme?', COMCAD Working Paper No. 34/07.
Pries, L. (2009), 'Transnationalisation and the challenge of differentiated concepts of space', *Tijdschrift voor Economische en Sociale Geografie*, **100** (5), 587–97.
Smith, R.C. (2006), *Mexican New York*, Berkeley, CA: University of California Press.
Snel, E., Engbergsen, G. and Leerkes, A. (2006), 'Transnational involvement and social integration', *Global Networks*, **3**, 285–308.
Soehl, T. and Waldinger, R. (2010), 'Making the connection: Latino immigrants and their cross border ties', *Ethnic and Racial Studies*, **33** (9), 1489–510.
Urry, J. (2000), *Sociology Beyond Societies*, London: Routledge.
Velayutham, S. and Wise, A. (2005), 'Moral economies of a transnational village', *Global Networks*, **5** (1), 27–47.
Vertovec, S. (2004), 'Migrant transnationalism and modes of transformation', *International Migration Review*, **38** (2), 970–1001.

Vertovec, S. (2009), *Transnationalism*, London: Routledge.
Waldinger, R. (2008), 'Between "here" and "there": immigrant cross-border activities and loyalties', *International Migration Review*, **42** (1), 3–29.
Waldinger, R. (2011), 'Immigrant transnationalism', Sociopedia.isa, http://www.isa-sociology.org/publ/sociopedia-isa/ (accessed October 2011).
Waldinger, R. and Fitzgerald, D. (2004), 'Transnationalism in question', *American Journal of Sociology*, **109** (5), 1177–95.
Wimmer, A. and Glick Schiller, N. (2002), 'Methodological nationalism and beyond', *Global Networks*, **2** (3), 301–34.

15 Mixing methods in research on diaspora policies
Alan Gamlen[1]

Research on migration and migration policy has, until recently, focused almost exclusively on immigration. Yet every immigrant is also an emigrant, with ties to a place of origin – ties which are often shaped by the policies of migrants' sending states. Thus, emigration states matter when it comes to migration policy, but they constitute a relatively new field of research. The main question here is: what types of methods are most appropriate for this kind of research?

The main purpose of this chapter is to put forward mixed methods as a feasible and useful approach to such research on new areas of migration policy. It discusses the methodology of a research project which aimed to examine how states relate to emigrants and their descendants, why they do so in different ways and how they should do so better. A major aim of the project was to analyse the full range of sending states' diaspora policies and investigate the hypothesis that various types of policy were much more widely spread than typically assumed. In order to do this, the research introduced the notion of an 'emigration state system', defined as a portion of the state system dedicated to the management of emigration and relations with emigrants and their descendants. This concept had the advantage of bringing together a fragmented case study literature on various aspects of state-diaspora relations under a single conceptual umbrella.

The research itself involved a deliberate mixture of quantitative and qualitative methods. The central components were an international survey of state-diaspora relations across more than 60 states, followed in sequence by in-depth analysis of two atypical case studies: New Zealand and Ireland. The remainder of this chapter discusses both the procedures followed and the principles behind the choice of these procedures. It falls into three main sections. The first section discusses the meaning and main features of mixed methods research, and explains why a specific mixed methods design was chosen for the project. The second section discusses the quantitative methods used in the research, and the final section discusses the qualitative methods used. The chapter concludes with a short summary.

15.1 MIXED METHODS

Because geography is concerned with the spatial dimension of a broad range of social, cultural, political and economic phenomena it is in a sense inherently interdisciplinary and has, since its inception, drawn on a wide variety of methodologies from both the social and physical sciences as well as the humanities, often used in combination. In that sense the discipline has a long tradition of 'mixed methods research' (McKendrick, 1999, p. 41). As Philip (1998, p. 271) puts it, 'Multiple-methods research is not a new approach to geographical inquiry. Indeed it may be argued that until recently multiple-method research was the norm, even if it was not reported as such.'

However, mixed methods as a distinct methodology unto itself is relatively new, and there are ongoing debates over the precise definition of the term (Tashakkori and Creswell, 2007). Some scholars still apply the term to works which combine writing styles or contrasting theoretical frameworks (see Philip, 1998, p. 263), and there are differences of opinion over the extent to which mixing methods requires comprehensive 'integration' of two approaches (and over what 'integration' means), or whether it merely requires the collection and analysis of two forms of data in a single project (Tashakkori and Creswell, 2007, pp. 3–4). However, there is now broad agreement on something resembling Tashakkori and Cresswell's (2007, p. 4) definition of mixed methods as 'research in which the investigator collects and analyzes data, integrates the findings, and draws inferences using both qualitative and quantitative approaches or methods in a single study or a program of inquiry'.

Creswell (2009) identifies four factors influencing the design of mixed methods studies: timing, weighting, mixing and theorizing. Quantitative and qualitative components can be 'timed' sequentially or concurrently (Philip, 1998, p. 264 reserves the term 'mixed methods' for concurrent designs only, referring to sequential designs as 'multiple methods'). In addition to the volume of each type of data and factors such as the researcher's philosophical approach (inductive or deductive), interests, aims and audience, timing will affect the relative 'weight' or emphasis on either quantitative or qualitative methods. 'Mixing' may take place during data collection, analysis or interpretation, and may involve 'connecting' (also see Philip, 1998, p. 271) data analysis at one stage to data collection at another (in sequential studies); 'integrating' or 'merging' data types (in concurrent designs) or 'embedding' one type of data type within a study weighted towards the other. Finally, the 'theoretical' purpose of mixing may be exploratory, explanatory or 'transformative' – for example, orientated towards changes in policy or institutional practice.

Mixing methods in research on diaspora policies 321

Based on combinations of different approaches to timing, weighting, mixing and theorizing, Cresswell identifies several types of mixed method research strategy. 'Sequential explanatory' designs tend to begin with and place greater weight on quantitative research, which is then 'connected' to the design of follow-up qualitative research. Phases are reversed in 'sequential exploratory' studies, for example, in order to develop a new quantitative research instrument to test or generalize qualitative results. In 'concurrent triangulation' designs, qualitative and quantitative data are collected simultaneously and then compared; this allows findings that converge to be presented more confidently as valid, whereas those which contradict can be interpreted more tentatively. Provided the necessary care is taken to align the two types of data collection methods in advance, this kind of 'triangulation' can significantly bolster the validity of findings. This may involve actually merging the two types of data at the stage of analysis and/or interpretation. 'Concurrent embedded' designs, by contrast, allow researchers to touch on tangential issues or other levels of analysis by nesting one kind of research within a study weighted towards the other. Policy and advocacy research often use both concurrent and sequential designs for a 'transformative' (rather than an exploratory or explanatory) purpose. These various designs are ideal types rather than prescriptions; in practice, mixed methods designs may draw on several of these models simultaneously, as was the case in this research project.

The overall structure of the research design described in this chapter most resembles the sequential explanatory model, where a quantitative overview is connected to qualitative case studies that 'drill down' into specific issues that arise. It began with an international survey of diaspora engagement policies in over 60 countries, which found relevant policies in an unexpectedly broad range of states. This unexpected finding was then examined up close through in-depth studies of two rarely examined cases – Ireland, which is well known as a migrant-sending state, and New Zealand, which is more surprising. However, within this overarching design the project also incorporated various other approaches to mixing. For example, the case studies themselves followed a concurrent embedded pattern, where a large-scale quantitative survey of New Zealand expatriates was embedded within a wider analysis of interviews, observation and archival sources. Although the main focus of the research was diaspora policy, this survey followed up on the important but in one sense slightly tangential topic of the 'diaspora' itself – what are its characteristics, how can these be explained and so on. There was also a sequential aspect to the case studies: findings from the survey generated research questions that fed back into the collection, analysis and interpretation of case study data. Specifically, the case studies were able to investigate the role of diaspora policies in explaining the surprising differences in expatriates' levels of transnational connection that were found during analysis of the survey. The research addressed exploratory, explanatory and transformative research questions: how do states relate to diasporas? Why do they do so in particular ways, and how can they do so better? Thus, the project drew on several different approaches to mixing rather than following a single prescribed model of mixed methods research.

McKendrick (1999, pp. 41–3) highlights a range of reasons for employing mixed research methods. One broad reason is that they provide a 'breadth of understanding' consistent with the 'traditional academic ideals of scholarship', which encourages exchange and cross-fertilization among different fields of knowledge (also see Philip, 1998, p. 271). In this respect mixed methods are particularly helpful for mapping out a field for more detailed future study, or providing an overarching model within which to situate existing but fragmented case studies. For example, sequential exploratory designs are particularly helpful when formulating new lines of inquiry for new fields of research, because they allow research questions to be sharpened in two stages and whittled down from more than one angle. More specifically, they are useful where no existing data or approach is ideal, but the strengths and weaknesses of some methods complement those of others. Similarly, using several methods may allow findings gleaned through each method to be independently verified, or 'triangulated'. Finally, and for all these reasons, mixed methods may be tactically useful in broadening the appeal of research to audiences – notably policy makers – that may be sceptical of one or other research method.

The appeal of mixed methods in policy research deserves further discussion. As Philip (1998) notes, conventions about what constitutes 'objectivity' differ among research communities. There is wide recognition in academic circles that objective research is where 'the author strives to produce work which is methodologically transparent, and free from overt bias and deliberate misinterpretation by the researcher' (p. 269), and that lack of self-reflexivity and transparency is as liable to undermine inferential statistics as interview or observation-based research. However, in policy circles quantitative research is usually viewed as 'standard' and 'acceptable', whereas qualitative research is often either not understood or deemed inappropriately 'subjective' because it is based on small samples that cannot be generalized, and is perceived as too in-depth and related to what are often seen as narrow academic theories (which may be seen as 'personal' interests) (Philip, 1998, pp. 272–3; also see McKendrick, 1999).

Several of these reasons were important in my choice of mixed methods for doctoral research on emigration state systems. The wider aims of scholarship, which include the pursuit of research training in addition to the pursuit of specialist knowledge (Pole, 2000), were furthered by gaining facility with a wide range of methodological techniques and approaches. Key findings (for example, concerning differences in transnational engagement between expatriates in different regions) were strengthened by having been 'triangulated' through several independent approaches with complementary strengths. Policy makers had indirectly funded the project via a scholarship, and were therefore a key intended audience of the research from the start – and they have indeed seemed more receptive to the quantitative aspects of the research (and, I infer, to the research as a whole by virtue of its including such an aspect). Most importantly, using a mixed methods design for the research allowed me to bring together a fragmented case study literature on 'diaspora engagement policies' under the umbrella concept of an 'emigration state system', and explore novel cases in a two-stage process. It also allowed for the refinement of research questions in an iterative fashion, and for 'drilling down' into questions raised at the previous iteration.

15.2 QUANTITATIVE METHODS

As outlined above, there were two main quantitative components to the research. The first was an international survey of emigration state systems across 64 countries, which formed the first component of the overall 'sequential explanatory' mixed methods research design. The second was an 18,002-response survey of the New Zealand diaspora, which was embedded concurrently within the qualitative second component of this sequential design. These two quantitative components are discussed in turn below.

15.2.1 Emigration State Systems: International Survey

Classifying and organizing comparative data into categories or 'typologies' is an important analytical stage in the development of social and political theories (see inter alia Peters, 1998, pp. 93–7). While several studies examine the diaspora engagement policies of migrant-sending states through comparative case studies and advance typologies (see inter alia Barry, 2006; Castles, 2008; Dufoix, 2008; Levitt and de la Dehesa, 2003; Østergaard-Nielsen, 2003b; Smith, 2003), a number of scholars highlight scope for further comparative work (see inter alia Bauböck, 2003, p. 700; Østergaard-Nielsen, 2003b, p. 4). In particular, typologies derived from comparisons involving a large number of case studies are relatively

324 *Handbook of research methods in migration*

rare (for a notable exception see Barry, 2006). Comparative studies are difficult without a common terminology and set of definitions, which was exactly what the research on state-diaspora relations lacked at the outset of the project.

The project addressed such concerns through a typology of emigration state systems. The typology drew on a thorough review of secondary literature covering over 60 states, in some cases supplemented by primary research. Diaspora policies framed differently across several smaller-scale in-depth studies were categorized, enumerated, tabulated and indexed. The strength of this method was that it brought together findings from fragmented studies, highlighting the existence of an overlooked phenomenon. Portes et al. (1999) proposes five necessary conditions for the establishment of a new phenomenon: establishing it, delimiting it, defining the unit of analysis, distinguishing types and identifying necessary conditions. The typology of diaspora policies fulfilled several of these aims. Firstly, it established the emigration state system as a durable, systematically overlooked phenomenon found in a large number of cases. Secondly, it delimited the phenomenon to a specific range of institutions and activities. Thirdly, it defined the unit of analysis as the migrant-sending state (in contrast to the bulk of studies which focus on the individual migrant and his or her support networks (Portes et al., 1999, p. 220)). And finally, it distinguished different types of policy.

The constraints of this method reflected the time and budgetary limitations of the research project. The limited availability of documentary sources made it impossible to look for all the target policies across all states. More time and resources would have permitted a review of more policies in more states. Similarly, the data were cross-sectional, though questions of historical development are crucial to a proper understanding of state-diaspora relations (Cano and Délano, 2007; Sherman, 1999; Smith, 2003; Thunø, 2001). The lack of historical perspective in the international survey was somewhat mitigated by the in-depth case studies of New Zealand and Ireland, as was the typology's limited use in identifying the necessary conditions for the emergence of emigration state systems. Notwithstanding these limitations, the method yielded the largest systematic comparison of diaspora engagement activities attempted to date, and provides a useful template for future comparative studies.[2]

15.2.2 The New Zealand Diaspora: Questionnaire Survey

Though the main thrust of the research concerned diaspora policies, the nature of the diaspora was an important tangential issue which the research design addressed through an embedded quantitative component:

Mixing methods in research on diaspora policies 325

a survey of New Zealand expatriates. The main dataset used in this analysis is the Every One Counts survey (EOC) of 'kiwi expatriates'. EOC was conducted over a period of 69 days between 1 March and 8 May 2006 by Kea New Zealand (short for Kiwi Expats Association). It was designed to coincide with the national census, and was supported with project funding from a range of New Zealand government departments. The questionnaire was disseminated by a 'viral email' initially sent to some 5,000 Kea members for onward referral, which contained hyperlinks to an online survey form fronted by a sophisticated marketing campaign.[3] The first half of the questionnaire asked respondents about their social and economic connections to New Zealand, and the second half largely duplicated the New Zealand Census. The survey drew a snowball sample of 18,002 responses in 155 countries, which were anonymized by Kea and supplied to me in an Excel spreadsheet, then transferred into STATA software for recoding and analysis. I was given full use of the data in return for helping to design parts of the questionnaire and analyse the results for media release.

Snowball surveys have been criticized extensively, including by researchers of transnationalism, so that it is sometimes difficult to be impartial about their strengths and weaknesses as sources of quantitative data. EOC has certain pros and cons as a source of data on the New Zealand diaspora. On the downside, it cannot necessarily be used to draw inferences for the New Zealand diaspora as a whole because the sampling was non-random (not all diasporic New Zealanders had the same probability of selection), and secondly, it cannot yield information about the differences between people who do and do not identify as part of the New Zealand diaspora, because the latter were excluded from the sample. These constraints placed clear limitations on the study's discussion of why people identify and behave as diasporic New Zealanders. Such limitations could be mitigated somewhat in future studies by more extensive comparison with national data in New Zealand and in receiving countries. However, only a limited amount of such comparison was feasible within the scope of the project.

On the upside, findings from EOC, which select on the basis of self-ascribed identity, are in some respects more generalizable than alternative data sources on the New Zealand diaspora, which are compiled from 2000-round censuses in countries where New Zealand-born expatriates live (Bryant and Law, 2004; Dumont and Lemaître, 2004; Migration DRC, 2007). There are two main aspects to generalizability: 'validity' and 'reliability'. A valid measure is one that measures the concept it is supposed to. Birthplace is neither a necessary nor a sufficient condition of diaspora membership: not all New Zealand-born people identify with or remain oriented towards New Zealand, and some foreign-born people do. In short, self-identification is the key feature of diaspora, birthplace is not, and because snowball samples only select those who self-identify they are a relatively valid measure of diaspora compared with birthplace samples.[4]

Census estimates trade off validity for a putative gain in reliability, which refers to the consistency and repeatability of a measure. However, on the one hand, it is important not to exaggerate the reliability of census-based counts of expatriates: as Hugo (2006) and others note, censuses systematically undercount immigrants for various reasons, and the definition of 'immigrant' is not consistent across all censuses.[5] On the other hand, consistent and repeatable measures of dynamic properties such as personal identity are by definition extremely difficult to achieve. In other words, the reliability gains of census estimates come at a high price in terms of validity, and in this sense snowball samples may represent the least worst alternative for diaspora researchers. In this sense, there are compelling reasons for using EOC data in addition to, if not instead of, alternative sources as baselines for comparisons between diaspora and non-diaspora groups.

EOC also has some strengths in terms of size, empirical richness and novelty. Firstly, EOC drew enough respondents to allow statistically robust comparison among groups within the sample. Thus, even though they do not on their own allow examination of why people are or are not diasporic, the EOC data can and do facilitate a discussion of why some groups in the sample are more diasporic than others. Secondly, EOC includes questions on transnational identity and connection which are not available elsewhere. And thirdly, EOC is the largest, most recent survey of New Zealanders abroad which has been conducted, and this project presented the first detailed analysis of the dataset. Thus, by embedding a quantitative component within the qualitative second phase of the research design, the project was able to address wider issues of indirect relevance.

15.3 QUALITATIVE METHODS

The second component of the sequential explanatory research design was a qualitative study of two underexamined cases discovered in the international survey that formed the quantitative first stage of the research: New Zealand and Ireland. Within this case study framework, the main research techniques used were elite interviewing, documentary research and (to a somewhat lesser extent) multi-sited fieldwork. The approach and the specific techniques are discussed below.

Following Yin (2003), Robson (2002, p. 179) defines case study as 'a strategy for doing research which involves an empirical investigation of a particular contemporary phenomenon within its real life context using multiple sources of evidence'. Expanding on this definition, he highlights that case study is a wider strategy rather than a specific method, and is associated with a broad range of types of empirical research. Case studies in general focus on a phenomenon 'within context', using multiple research methods. The emphasis on context is important; Robson stresses that case studies tend to be concerned with the particular, and so may not easily support generalization. This is particularly true of single case studies, which examine one event or one instance of a phenomenon, as opposed to comparative case studies which are typically chosen to allow the examination of key variables across a representative selection of instances. A particular use for single case studies is to examine a 'revelatory' instance (Yin, 2003), which Yin describes as one in which 'the investigator has the opportunity to observe a phenomenon previously inaccessible to scientific investigation'. Single case studies often use internal 'embedded units of analysis' – such as regions within a single country – in order to increase the units of observation available to the researcher and thereby the explanatory power of the analysis (see King et al., 1994).

The project drew on elements of single case study research design and comparative research design. The two cases were treated comparatively to a limited extent. The rationale for this limited comparison between New Zealand and Ireland was to contrast their approaches to diaspora policy, and to explain and evaluate these differences in light of controlled comparison across key variables of interest – particularly, the different migration histories of the two countries. The choice of cases made it possible to isolate this variable fairly effectively, because the two countries are very similar in many other respects. Both countries are insular territories on the semi-periphery of the former British Empire, with similar population sizes and distributions, and similar numbers of citizens abroad (although Ireland's non-citizen diaspora is massively larger than New Zealand's). Both migration systems are in transition (see Fields, 1994; Findlay et al., 2002): Ireland has been shifting from consistent net emigration to episodes of net immigration, whereas New Zealand has been shifting from consistent net receiving to periods of net sending. Immigration has brought unprecedented ethnic diversity to both societies, especially since the 1990s. Ireland is also a useful case to examine because it has sometimes been cited as a model for New Zealand policy makers (for example, see L.E.K. Consulting, 2001, pp. 84–5).

However, this comparison played a limited role in the research; Ireland was presented as an exemplar, and much more weight was given to the more unusual New Zealand case, which was treated in some respects like a single 'revelatory' case study. The New Zealand case study is revelatory in at least three respects. Firstly, it examines emigration policies whereas the vast bulk of existing migration research examines immigration policies (for exceptions see inter alia Green and Weil, 2007, p. 1; Martins, 1974, pp. 276–7; Østergaard-Nielsen, 2003a, p. 3). Secondly, it reveals diaspora policies in a developed liberal democratic state whereas the few existing studies of emigration and diaspora policies look almost exclusively at developing or somehow 'dysfunctional' states (for exceptions see Fullilove and Flutter, 2004; Larner, 2007; Sriskandarajah and Drew, 2006). And finally, it reveals New Zealand to be a migrant-sending state whereas it is conventionally thought of as a 'classical' settler society (Castles and Miller, 2003, p. 7).

The New Zealand case study employed several embedded units of analysis which were systematically compared in order to examine key variables of interest. The embedded units were different regions where New Zealand expatriates live, and the key variables of interest were regional New Zealand policies towards expatriates, and the relationship of these variations to regional differences in foreign policy, size and organization of the local expatriate community, availability of officials willing to spend time on diaspora communities and the cultural proximity of native populations. As well as studying diaspora policies at the 'centre' of policy formation in Wellington, the research examined them at the point of delivery in four locations: the UK, Australia, France and Japan. The locations fall into two pairs, chosen for comparability, contrast and convenience. Like New Zealand, the UK and Australia are newly multicultural nations with a shared colonial and Commonwealth history involving Anglo-Saxon domination. New Zealanders move among these locations with relative ease and in large numbers. By contrast, France and Japan are both Old-World societies characterized by less tolerance for ethnic diversity and more difference from the Anglo-Saxon world. New Zealanders in these locations are few and far between, and face greater cultural and linguistic challenges to integration. Feasibility was an important constraint on the research: budget and time limitations prevented visiting the other main emigrant destination (North America), while previous experience living in Japan and the fact that it is a stopover destination between Europe and the South Pacific made that a convenient choice for a contrasting location. Similarly, proximity to France while based in Oxford allowed affordable fieldtrips and easy contact.

In keeping with the overall mixed method approach of the project, the case studies employed four main research methods: documentary analysis, multi-sited fieldwork, interviews and survey research. These methods were concurrent and intertwined, not consecutive and separate. For example, interviewees were sometimes recruited during participant observation at events. During interviews, participants would suggest documents to analyse, which would lead to further documents, names of people to interview, places to visit and events to attend.

15.3.1 Elite Interviews in Principle and in Practice

One of the most important techniques used in the project was the 'elite interview'. Although the word 'elite' has connotations of superiority that are sometimes misleading, Dexter (2006, p. 19) defines an elite interview as any one in which the interviewee is given 'specialized and nonstandard treatment' in the sense that 'the investigator is willing, and often eager to let the interviewee teach him what the problem, the question, the situation is'. Elite interviews can be contrasted with 'focused interviews', where 'the investigator defines the question and the problem; he is only looking for answers within the bounds set by his presuppositions.' The term 'elite interview' is particularly associated with political scientists who have found them useful for interviews with 'people in important or exposed positions [who] may require VIP interviewing treatment on the topics which relate to their importance or exposure' (Dexter, 2006, p. 18). However, it is significant to note that the method may in principle be used with interviewees holding any status, and in this sense it is closely related to the ethnographic style of interviewing used, for example, by anthropologists, where it is more normal to take an inductive approach of allowing analysis to develop 'bottom up' from the concept and categories of the participants.

The types of sampling strategies used in elite interviewing are conditioned not only by statistical concerns but also more significantly by issues of convenience – or rather, of access – than those used in standardized interviewing. Although, as Berry (2002) notes, elite interviewing often uses a standardized instrument with a random sampling design, where 'elites in a particular institution are chosen at random and subjected to the same interview protocol composed of structured or semistructured questions', it is also frequently the case that the total population of interviewees is too small to sample from, and/or some of the most important members of the 'elite' are secluded behind a dense foliage of gated compounds, security guards, personal assistants and lawyers which is virtually impenetrable to the average academic researcher. For this reason, according to Goldstein (2002), with elite interviews – particularly where emphasis is on 'elite' in the sense of 'powerful' – everything 'depends on getting in the door, getting access to your subject'.

If one can penetrate this tough exterior and reveal a vulnerable individual submitting themselves to the gaze of the researcher, the question of power relations and informed consent inevitably emerge. The notion of informed consent is rooted in moral theories about autonomy, beneficence and justice (Faden et al., 1986). While personal autonomy and justice are more general moral principles which, respectively, emphasize the research participant's freedom 'to choose and act without controlling constraints imposed by others' (p. 8), and the researcher's obligation to treat the participant 'according to what is fair, due, or owed' (p.14), the concept of beneficence is rooted more specifically in medical ethics and is based around themes of 'promoting the welfare of others'. Problematic questions surrounding beneficence include the question of how much personal risk the benefactor must take, or harm they must suffer, as a requirement of the principle; the question of exactly 'to whom duties of beneficence are owed', and the related question of whether and when beneficence is a duty or merely an ideal (pp. 11–12).

The parallels between elite interviewing and anthropological research have already been drawn. The guidelines of the Association of Social Anthropologists (available at http://www.theasa.org.uk) enjoin researchers to protect research participants and honour trust, to anticipate harms, to avoid undue intrusion, to negotiate informed consent, to give fair returns for assistance and to observe participants' intellectual property rights. With respect specifically to informed consent, the guidelines are particularly clear that participants should be made aware of 'information likely to be material to [their] willingness to participate, such as: the purpose(s) of the study, and the anticipated consequences of the research; the identity of funders and sponsors; the anticipated uses of the data; possible benefits of the study and possible harm or discomfort that might affect participants; issues relating to data storage and security; and the degree of anonymity and confidentiality which may be afforded to informants and subjects'. The guidelines are equally clear that 'consent made after the research is completed is not meaningful consent at all'.[6]

Thus, to a great extent, informed consent fulfils the function of protection, under the assumption that the researcher holds or exercises power over the research subject (Pile, 1991). However, questions such as those surrounding beneficence can become particularly vexed in studies of elites, where the assumed power relations between the researcher and the participant of power are somewhat different. Lilleker (2003, pp. 211–13) cautions interviewers of elites to tiptoe carefully around the issue of recording, inquire deferentially about how much time the interviewee can spare, listen attentively and use flattering phrases when bringing the interview back to the questions at hand. As he puts it, with elites 'One must take whoever one can get, interview them at their convenience and just hope the results are useful.' Drawing on Linda McDowell's work (for example, McDowell, 1992), Cormode and Hughes (1999, p. 299) point out, 'When studying elites, the scholar is a supplicant . . ., dependent on the co-operation of a relatively small number of people with specialized knowledge, and not usually a potential emancipator or oppressor.'

Bound up with the issue of informed consent is the potential problem of exploitation, which raises the important question of compensation for research participants. Every researcher has to deal with the question of how to compensate participants. Institutional research-ethics guidelines for qualitative research often enjoin researchers to provide some form of compensation to research participants. For example, the guidelines of the Association of Social Anthropologists prescribe 'fair return for assistance'. This means that there 'should be no economic exploitation of individual informants, translators and research participants; fair return should be made for their help and services'. The obligation to 'give back' is interpreted differently across different fields of research. Some take a minimalist stance that compensation is a form of harm prevention, whereas others take a more proactive position, treating participant compensation as a way of providing benefits in return for those gained by the researcher (for discussion see Kopala and Suzuki, 1999, p. 7071). Compensation may be seen as the market price of a commodity demanded by the researcher and supplied by the participant; as a form of wage-payment for the participants' labour; as reimbursement for incurred expenses; or as a way of allocating a 'fair share' of research benefits to all the 'partners' in a research project – including the participants (Dickert and Grady, 1999). Some argue for financial compensation of the research participant, while others argue that financial compensation can bias participant selection, and that researchers should 'give back' in other ways. However, the issue of compensation is especially tricky for elite interviews, where the challenge of giving something of value to relatively wealthy and influential people can consume a great deal of energy and time – even to the extent of calling into question the independence of the researcher. In this context, compensation may be less like a reciprocal gift between equals in recognition of the subject's help, and more like the tribute of a supplicant in recognition of the subject's power over the researcher. This can be highly problematic: for example, if policy makers who participate in a research project are compensated with a report intended to assist and benefit policy making, it is a complicated matter to demonstrate that the findings of the report are independent.

Partly because of complications such as these, Dexter and others emphasize that elite interviews should be chosen when they seem likely to yield better or more data at less cost than other methods. As Aberbach and Rockman (2002, p. 673) put it, in elite interviewing as in all social science, 'the primary question one must ask before designing a study is, "What do I want to learn?"' – and the choice of methods will flow from this. Lilleker (2003, p. 208) advises that 'interviews are only necessitated when a researcher wishes to produce a work with textural depth as well as empirical strength'. When they are used, they must be used with caution: gaining access may be prohibitively difficult; fulfilling all the interviewees' needs may be costly and time-consuming; and the interviews may yield stories 'marred by hindsight' or restricted by fierce privacy conditions. However, they may also be the best way to fill in areas of research where no other more reliable sources are either available or can provide the necessary depth – not to mention that they may also be the most exhilarating drawcard for the research project as a whole.

15.3.2 Recruitment

In keeping with these various cautions, elite interviewing was selected as the central tool in this study for two main reasons. Firstly, much of the research was exploratory, and concerned a range of policies dispersed across many government departments. The form and content of policies varied widely across departments and typically only a few individuals in each department were involved in the relevant activity. More a priori knowledge about diaspora policies would have been needed in order to design a useful questionnaire survey, and more respondents would have been necessary for quantitative analysis of the resulting data. Secondly, I recognized that diaspora policy chiefly involved a limited number of policy makers interacting with a limited number of migrant associations, and that therefore it would be possible to speak with all or a large proportion of the key figures in the main regions of the study. This indeed turned out to be the case.

The participants were recruited from four main groups: policy makers involved in diaspora-related policy of some sort; business leaders involved in influential debates about the diaspora; migrant associations actively involved with diplomatic or consular posts to some extent; and independent migrants without strong ties to any migrant association. These groups were somewhat overlapping. Attempts were made to speak with all the key actors involved in state-diaspora relations in the regions under study; while this was not always possible, in the four main regions, a majority of the key people did take part in the study.

Some of the inherent limitations of snowball sampling – that is, a tendency for strong selection bias and especially for sampling on the

Mixing methods in research on diaspora policies 333

dependent variable – can be mitigated by snowballing from several starting points, dispersed as widely as possible in order to multiply the number of network pathways along which participant referrals will travel. For this reason, my New Zealand interviewees were recruited through snowballing from three different types of starting points. The first was the Kiwi Expats Association (Kea). In 2005 I posted an introduction to my research and an invitation to participate on the Kea website. In mid-2008 I included a notice in Kea's global newsletter to some 25,000 expatriates in around 155 countries, inviting 'second-generation kiwis' to contact me. A combined total of 78 people responded to these online invitations, around 20 of whom were eventually interviewed. (These 20 were essentially selected for convenience.)

A second starting point was to cold-call and email New Zealand diplomatic posts and government departments to identify key officials. These led to meetings where I presented my work and responded to questions before asking questions of my own. Various events constituted a third starting point. For example, I held two seminars in Wellington in February 2007: one at Victoria University of Wellington and the other in the Department of Labour. After presenting and discussing my work with the audience of academics and policy makers, I collected their business cards and followed up by phone or email to arrange interviews or get more referrals. I also met interviewees while on fieldwork at diaspora events that were not specifically organized for me. For example, a New Zealand networking event at the residence of Oxford University's then-Vice Chancellor John Hood led to a personal meeting and introductions to a number of senior businesspeople who, like Hood, had been important figures in New Zealand diaspora policy. These multiple starting points eventually reinforced each other: on the one hand, people began to contact me out of the blue having heard about my research, and, on the other hand, certain key people began to be referred by several others. Although there were significantly fewer of them, the interviewees for the Irish case study were recruited in a similar manner. I began with a focused review of the literature on Ireland's policies regarding emigrants, and then began cold-calling or emailing key figures to request interviews. These people then referred further interviewees and so on, until a sufficiently wide coverage was achieved.

15.3.3 Informed Consent and Compensation

My doctoral research was approved in accordance with the University of Oxford's ethical review requirements prior to my fieldwork commencing in 2006. The Central University Research Ethics Committee (CUREC) requires all researchers to complete a form indicating whether written informed consent will be obtained from their research subjects, and there is an expectation that researchers should answer in the affirmative. However, this requirement is deeply controversial among qualitative researchers. For example, the Anthropology Department takes the view that 'in many, if not most, of the contexts in which anthropologists work it would be inappropriate to produce a printed consent form every time one spoke to people or even every time one conducted a semi-formal interview. It would often lead to an immediate and complete loss of trust, since forms and signatures are liable to be used as tricks and to the disadvantage of the person signing. This simple ethnographic fact is simply not understood by many ethics committees.'[7] The department therefore recommends that students tick the CUREC box and provide a covering letter explaining that following the Association of Social Anthropologists' Guidelines are equivalent to obtaining informed consent in the circumstances in which the research is being done.[8] In most cases I chose to follow these guidelines instead of using release forms.

This doctoral research was founded on attempts to 'give something back' to the community of policy makers and migrants whom I was researching. My participants were not offered financial compensation because it was not financially feasible within the constraints of my project, and because in any case it would have seemed naïve and futile for a university student to offer token payments to senior public servants, ambassadors or business executives. However, I conceived the project with the explicit intention of finding policies that I judged would 'improve' relations between migrants and their home government. My initial thoughts on 'improvement' were that emigration constituted a form of social dislocation, and that policy in the sending country could help to remedy this. These thoughts were my instinctive reaction to New Zealand's prolonged debates over 'brain drain', which encompassed not only fear about loss of skilled and entrepreneurial young people, but about what mass exodus suggested about the viability of New Zealand society more generally. These thoughts were formed while I was living as an expatriate in Japan, and was struck by the way that simple provision of embassy space for workshops and rehearsals had facilitated the formation of a vibrant Māori performing arts group. On the one hand, the group kept a number of young, skilled migrants connected to New Zealand and provided a valuable cultural element to New Zealand diplomatic events. On the other hand, performances gave group members benefits like financial payment, free international travel for performances, access to diplomatic and business elites and, most importantly, the foundation of a support network to help them function better in an often challenging cultural environment. My sense was that a relatively small amount of effort from the embassy resulted in a substantial benefit for New Zealand, for the migrants themselves and for the host community. I hoped to see this model emulated in other contexts. My understanding of what constitutes 'improvement' and 'benefit' developed through the research, but this aim of giving back still informed one of the key questions of the project: how *should* states relate to their diasporas?

15.3.4 Interview Format

The nature of the 'elite interviews' varied in a number of important ways. In all, 194 participants were listed by name. The list did not include people met and spoken with informally, even though many such informal encounters did shape my understanding. Rather it included only those with whom I met formally or semi-formally, and who gave permission to be listed. These encounters ranged from 20 minutes to 1.5 hours in length, though most were around 40 minutes long. In several cases they involved groups – usually because the person initially contacted invited a colleague they thought would be as or more interested or expert than they were, and sometimes no doubt (although this was never explicit) because the participant felt more secure with a colleague present. In a few cases it was necessary to meet with several people at once due to time constraints in a location (Paris, Hong Kong).

These formal participants can be divided into two main groups. There were 140 'formal interviews' either with individuals or small groups. In these encounters there was a clear researcher/subject divide and the interview was typically recorded. There were also 121 'substantive exchanges', where the participant was made fully aware of my role as a researcher and explicitly agreed to answer substantive questions and to be named as a participant. These differed from formal interviews in several important respects. The encounters were often information exchanges with officials who wanted to 'pick my brain' (as several of them put it), about matters relating to the New Zealand diaspora and to diaspora policy. I provided detailed explanations of my work and answered questions as part of a formal conversation, where both I and my interlocutor took notes. Because these encounters often involved exchanges of personal opinions, they took place under variants of the 'Chatham House Rule',[9] where participants agreed to be named in the appendices of the research work and for information from the meeting to be used in the research, provided that it was not possible to link their name to their information. To protect the anonymity of research participants, I anonymized all interview references unless the interviewee was a prominent public figure *and* gave permission to be quoted personally. This is achieved by citing an interview code (for example, 'IV199') for anonymous quotes. Codes were not cited where the interviewee was named in the text, and the key for the code was not included in the written-up results.

15.3.5 Data Collection and Analysis

While most participants were encountered in person, almost 50 encounters took place by phone, and, in some cases, through detailed email correspondence, in order to reduce travel costs. Aural recordings were made of 120 encounters, using a range of electronic media (digital video, minidisk, analogue cassette and MP3). The remaining encounters were recorded in handwritten field notes. The notebooks and audio files were transcribed into MS Word files by myself and paid transcribers based in New Zealand. These files were then imported into NVivo software and analysed. The main analytical approach was thematic: sections of text were coded and grouped according to themes relating to the research problems. While 'narrative analysis' (see Wiles et al., 2005) was not a major feature of the research, interpretation and choice of quotes for use in the thesis was informed by efforts to interpret and understand the interview context, the participant's tone, tempo, style and body language – as well as what was not said explicitly – all added nuance to what was actually said.

15.3.6 Multi-sited Fieldwork and Documentary Research

Multi-sited fieldwork, chiefly participant-observation, was an important tool for contextualizing and refining the interviews conducted as part of this research. Dexter (2006, p. 27) notes that the utility of interview methods are constrained by the interviewer's understanding of context:

> no one should plan or finance an entire study in advance with the expectation of relying chiefly upon interviews for data *unless the interviewers have enough relevant background to be sure that they can make sense out of the interview conversations or unless there is a reasonable hope of being able to hang around or in some way observe so as to learn what it is meaningful and significant to ask.* (emphasis in original)

My own relative inexperience in policy circles made this particularly important for me, and I took a number of specific steps to achieve a better understanding of my subjects' 'frame of reference'.

Firstly, wherever feasible I conducted interviews in person in order to absorb as much contextual information as possible. This often allowed me to spend time in the participant's workplace, chat with their colleagues and get a sense for personal and professional relationships, look at documents that officials had on hand to illustrate what they were saying, read the participant's body language and interpret what this said about the significance of the topics being discussed and so on. These contextual clues were often very helpful in interpreting the explicit content of field notes and interview transcripts.

Secondly, outside of actual research encounters, I immersed myself as much as possible in my participants' environment. In-person interviewing necessitated trips to a number of different locations. In each location, I took accommodation as close as possible to my interviewees' offices, had morning tea in the same cafes, criss-crossed the same roads among departments, traipsed through the same subterranean passageways through security checks and looked down from the same high-rise offices. I met policy managers for interviews in street-side cafes, where other officials whispered conspiratorially in their own corners. Once, in New Zealand, I bumped into an MP on the street who helped me set up an interview with John Key, now the Prime Minister. Being immersed in those places for a time was an important step towards understanding the organizational culture of the local institutions whose members I was interviewing.

This kind of immersion was greatly facilitated by Visiting Status at local universities. In New Zealand I was based in the Institute of Policy Studies (IPS) at Victoria University of Wellington for a month between February and March 2007. I arranged Visiting Status at Sydney University for a month in April the same year. For interviews in Ireland during September, I was based at Trinity College, Dublin for a month.[10] These affiliations also enabled me to attend and present at policy-focused conferences and seminars. For example, my IPS affiliation enabled me to present my work to a group of policy makers, where I gained valuable feedback and was also able to recruit interviewees. In Dublin my Trinity College affiliation allowed me to attend a conference on migration where both academics and policy makers presented. In Sydney, being based at the centrally located University of Sydney put me in an environment surrounded by business and policy decision makers, at the same time as giving me the opportunity to share and test my ideas with a new set of academic colleagues.

Thirdly, I took every possible opportunity to be a participant-observer at events where my research subjects came together. Particularly important from this point of view were diaspora community events organized by or involving local diplomatic or consular officials. These ranged from informal gatherings, through meetings of migrant associations, to national events at New Zealand diplomatic posts. I was always open about my observer-researcher role, and wherever appropriate I obtained informed consent from organizers and/or participants before attending and taking notes. In total I filled 42 3B1 notebooks, which I selectively transcribed and analysed thematically using NVivo software at the same time as my formal interview transcript notes. Many of these were preceded or followed by less formal encounters – conversations on trains, in foyers, in pubs and the like – and often these serendipitous encounters provided valuable information or insights which shaped my thinking on particular issues. Wherever such encounters provided evidence used in the project, an agreement regarding use and attribution was reached with the individual concerned.

Finally, I attended a number of conferences on diaspora policies with policy makers, which gave me valuable insights into the policy process and fed back into my own research activities. I attended policy-oriented conferences and seminars on diaspora topics sponsored by the United Nations Educational, Scientific, and Cultural Organization (UNESCO) in Paris (2006), at the New Zealand Department of Labour (2007), at Mexico's Foreign Affairs Secretariat (2007), at the United Nations Economic Commission for Europe (UNECE) in Paris (2008) and at the National University of Ireland (2009). These conferences and seminars helped me to understand the migration policy world much better, to ask more pertinent questions of my interviewees and to interpret their responses more perceptively.

In order to 'triangulate' and fill out the findings of interview- and observation-based research, this project also drew on extensive documentary research. Primary documents consulted included electoral archives, newspapers, magazine and website articles, email newsletters and correspondence, as well as official documents and reports pertaining to aspects of diaspora policies in New Zealand and Ireland.

15.4 CONCLUSION AND SUMMARY

This chapter has presented mixed methods as a feasible and rigorous approach to studying new areas of migration policy, by detailing the methodology of a research project on the diaspora policies of emigration states.

The chapter has explained what mixed methods research entails, and has distinguished a range of different approaches; these include sequential and concurrent ways of connecting, merging and embedding quantitative and qualitative techniques at different stages of data collection, analysis and interpretation.

The chapter has also described how this specific project drew simultaneously on several different approaches to mixing methods: the overall structure of the project followed a 'sequential explanatory' design involving a quantitative overview followed by a 'drill-down' phase that was weighted towards qualitative data. This phase involved case studies – New Zealand

and Ireland – chosen for their 'revelatory' character: they revealed diaspora policies (which are themselves an understudied phenomenon) in countries where they would not conventionally be expected, thus demonstrating that diaspora policies are more widespread than is conventionally assumed. This drill-down, case study phase primarily involved interviews, observations and archival and documentary sources, but also included an embedded quantitative element in the form of a survey of expatriates. Issues associated with each of these techniques have been discussed in some detail.

This assortment of mixing techniques allowed the project to address exploratory, explanatory and transformative research questions, namely: how do states relate to diasporas, why do they do so in particular ways and how can they do so better?

NOTES

1. This is a revised version of a chapter in my doctoral thesis, 'The emigration state system: New Zealand and its diaspora in comparative context'. I am very grateful to Alisdair Rogers, Carlos Vargas-Silva and Alison Gamlen for their helpful comments.
2. Research based on the survey and using this framework has been published in several places (Gamlen, 2008, 2009a, 2009b).
3. Full details of the questionnaire schedule and summary results are downloadable in .pdf format from http://www.keanewzealand.com/sites/default/files/every-one-counts-survey-results-final.pdf.
4. For an example of a valuable contribution using this method see Inkson et al. (2004), who collect a sample of over 1000 expatriates by snowballing through various expatriate organizations. On the downside, in a sample of this size it is inevitable that some groups are too small for statistically robust comparison (Inkson et al., 2004).
5. See Skeldon (Chapter 11, this volume) for further discussion of the limitations of censuses for counting migrants.
6. http://www.theasa.org/ethics/guidelines.shtml (accessed 6 February 2012).
7. David Gellner, Email, 5 January 2007.
8. David Gellner, Email, 5 January 2007.
9. Under the Chatham House Rule 'participants are free to use the information received, but neither the identity nor the affiliation of the speaker(s), nor that of any other participant, may be revealed'. The Chatham House Rule, http://www.chathamhouse.org.uk/about/chathamhouserule (accessed 26 June 2009.
10. I am very grateful to Paul Callister, John Connell and Melissa Butcher for hosting these visits.

REFERENCES

Aberbach, J.D. and Rockman, B.A. (2002), 'Conducting and coding elite interviews', *Ps-Political Science & Politics*, **35** (4), 673–6.
Barry, K. (2006), 'Home and away: the construction of citizenship in an emigration context', *New York University Law Review*, **81** (1), 11–59.

Bauböck, R. (2003), 'Towards a political theory of migrant transnationalism', *International Migration Review*, **37** (3), 700–23.
Berry, J.M. (2002), 'Validity and reliability issues in elite interviewing', *Ps-Political Science & Politics*, **35** (4), 679–82.
Bryant, J. and Law, D. (2004), 'New Zealand's diaspora and overseas-born population', New Zealand Treasury Working Paper 04/13.
Cano, G. and Délano, A. (2007), 'The Mexican government and organised Mexican immigrants in the United States: a historical analysis of political transnationalism (1848–2005)', *Journal of Ethnic and Migration Studies*, **33** (5), 695–725.
Castles, S. (2008), 'Comparing the experience of five major emigration countries', in S. Castles and R. Delgado-Wise (eds), *Migration and Development: Perspectives from the South*, Geneva: IOM, pp. 255–84.
Castles, S. and Miller, M.L. (2003), *The Age of Migration*, 3rd edn, Basingstoke: Palgrave Macmillan
Cormode, L. and Hughes, A. (1999), 'The economic geographer as a situated researcher of elites', *Geoforum*, **30** (4), 299–300.
Creswell, J.W. (2009), *Research Design: Qualitative, Quantitative, and Mixed Methods Approaches*, 3rd edn, Los Angeles, CA and London: Sage.
Dexter, L.A. (2006), *Elite and Specialized Interviewing*, Colchester: ECPR.
Dickert, N. and Grady, C. (1999), 'What's the price of a research subject? Approaches to payment for research participation . . .', *New England Journal of Medicine*, **341** (3), 198–203.
Dufoix, S. (2008), *Diasporas*, Berkeley, CA and London: University of California Press.
Dumont, J.-C. and Lemaître, G. (2004), 'Counting immigrants and expatriates in OECD countries: a new perspective', OECD Social, Employment and Migration Working Paper.
Faden, R.R., Beauchamp, T.L. and King, N.M.P. (1986), *A History and Theory of Informed Consent*, New York: Oxford University Press.
Fields, G.S. (1994), 'The migration transition in Asia', *Asian and Pacific Migration Journal*, **3** (1), 7–30.
Findlay, A.M., Jones, H. and Davidson, G.M.M. (2002), 'Migration transition or migration transformation in the Asian dragon economies?', *International Journal of Urban and Regional Research*, **22** (4), 643–63.
Fullilove, M. and Flutter, C. (2004), *Diaspora: The World Wide Web of Australians*, New South Wales: Lowy Institute for International Policy, Longueville Media.
Gamlen, A. (2008), 'The emigration state and the modern geopolitical imagination', *Political Geography*, **27** (8), 840–56.
Gamlen, A. (2009a), 'Diaspora engagement policies: what are they, and what kinds of states use them?', in R.H.J. Adams, H. de Haas and U.O. Ukonkwo (eds), *Web Anthology on Migrant Remittances and Development: Research Perspectives. Topic 19 – Remittances, Diasporas, and States*, Brooklyn, NY: Social Science Research Council.
Gamlen, A. (2009b), 'el Estado de emigracion y los vinculos con la diaspora', in A. Escrivá, A. Bermudez and N. Moraes (eds), *Migracion y Participation Politica: Estados, Organizaciones y Migrantes Latinoamericanos en Perspectiva Local-transnacional*, Madrid: Consejo Superior de Investigaciones Científicas, pp. 237–64.
Goldstein, K. (2002), 'Getting in the door: sampling and completing elite interviews', *Ps-Political Science & Politics*, **35** (4), 669–72.
Green, N.L. and Weil, F. (2007), *Citizenship and Those who Leave: The Politics of Emigration and Expatriation*, Urbana, IL and Chesham: University of Illinois Press and Combined Academic (distributor).
Hugo, G. (2006), 'An Australian diaspora?', *International Migration*, **44** (1), 105–33.
Inkson, K., Carr, S., Edwards, M. et al. (2004), 'Brain drain to talent flow: views of Kiwi expatriates', *University of Auckland Business Review*, **6** (2), 29–39.
King, G., Keohane, R.O. and Verba, S. (1994), *Designing Social Inquiry: Scientific Inference in Qualitative Research*, Princeton, NJ: Princeton University Press.

Kopala, M. and Suzuki, L.A. (1999), *Using Qualitative Methods in Psychology*, Thousand Oaks, CA: Sage.
Larner, W. (2007), 'Expatriate experts and globalising governmentalities: the New Zealand diaspora strategy', *Transactions of the Institute of British Geographers*, **32** (3), 331–45.
L.E.K. Consulting (2001), *New Zealand Talent Initiative: Strategies for Building a Talented Nation*, Auckland: L.E.K Consulting.
Levitt, P. and de la Dehesa, R. (2003), 'Transnational migration and the redefinition of the state: variations and explanations', *Ethnic and Racial Studies*, **26** (4), 587–611.
Lilleker, D.G. (2003), 'Interviewing the political elite: navigating a potential minefield', *Politics*, **23** (3), 207–14.
Martins, H. (1974), 'Time and theory in sociology', in J. Rex (ed.), *Approaches to Sociology: An Introduction to Major Trends in British Sociology*, London: Routledge & Kegan Paul, pp. 246–94.
McDowell, L. (1992), 'Valid games? A response to Erica Schoenberger', *Professional Geographer*, **44** (2), 212–15.
McKendrick, J.H. (1999), 'Multi-method research: an introduction to its application in population geography', *Professional Geographer*, **51** (1), 40–50.
Migration DRC (2007), 'Global Migrant Origin Database', Development Research Centre on Migration, Globalisation and Poverty, University of Sussex, available at http://www.migrationdrc.org/research/typesofmigration/global_migrant_origin_database.html.
Østergaard-Nielsen, E. (2003a), 'International migration and sending countries: key issues and themes', in E. Østergaard-Nielsen (ed.), *International Migration and Sending Countries: Perceptions, Policies and Transnational Relations*, Basingstoke: Palgrave Macmillan, pp. 3–32.
Østergaard-Nielsen, E. (ed.) (2003b), *International Migration and Sending Countries: Perceptions, Policies and Transnational Relations*, Basingstoke: Palgrave Macmillan.
Peters, B.G. (1998), *Comparative Politics: Theory and Methods*, Basingstoke: Macmillan.
Philip, L.J. (1998), 'Combining quantitative and qualitative approaches to social research in human geography – an impossible mixture?', *Environment and Planning A*, **30**, 261–76.
Pile, S. (1991), 'Practicing interpretative geography', *Transactions of the Institute of British Geographers*, **16** (4), 458–69.
Pole, C. (2000), 'Technicians and scholars in pursuit of the PhD: some reflections on doctoral study', *Research Papers in Education*, **15** (1), 95–111.
Portes, A., Guarnizo, L.E. and Landolt, P. (1999), 'Introduction: pitfalls and promise of an emergent research field', *Ethnic and Racial Studies*, **22** (2), 217–37.
Robson, C. (2002), *Real World Research: A Resource for Social Scientists and Practitioner-researchers*, 2nd edn, Oxford: Blackwell.
Sherman, R. (1999), 'From state introversion to state extension in Mexico: modes of emigrant incorporation 1900–1997', *Theory and Society*, **28** (6), 835–78.
Smith, R.C. (2003), 'Diasporic memberships in historical perspective: comparative insights from the Mexican, Italian and Polish cases', *International Migration Review*, **37** (3), 724–59.
Sriskandarajah, D. and Drew, C. (2006), *Brits Abroad: Mapping the Scale and Nature of British Emigration*, London: Institute for Public Policy Research.
Tashakkori, A. and Creswell, J.W. (2007), 'The new era of mixed methods', *Journal of Mixed Methods Research*, **1** (1), 3–7.
Thunø, M. (2001), 'Reaching out and incorporating Chinese overseas: the Trans-territorial scope of the PRC by the end of the 20th century', *The China Quarterly*, **168**, 910–29.
Wiles, J.L., Rosenberg, M.W. and Kearns, R.A. (2005), 'Narrative analysis as a strategy for understanding interview talk in geographic research', *Area*, **37** (1), 89–99.
Yin, R. (2003), *Case Study Research: Design and Methods* 3rd edn, Thousand Oaks, CA: Sage.

PART IV

EXPLORING SPECIFIC MIGRATION TOPICS

16 Diasporas on the web: new networks, new methodologies

Jonathan Crush, Cassandra Eberhardt, Mary Caesar, Abel Chikanda, Wade Pendleton and Ashley Hill[1]

This chapter reviews new methodologies that embrace the connectivity of diasporas, the emergence of social media and the potential of online surveys for research purposes. The recent focus on diasporas by migration researchers has highlighted the rich potential of migrants as a force for shaping development activities in their countries of origin (Brinkerhoff, 2008; Cohen, 2008; Merz et al., 2008; Plaza and Ratha, 2011; Sorensen, 2007). The study of diasporas in development has also presented researchers with a number of significant conceptual and methodological challenges.[2] As Vertovec and Cohen (1999, p. xiii) suggest, 'one of the major changes in migration patterns is the growth of populations anchored (socially and culturally as well as physically) neither at their places of origin nor at their places of destination'. Further, as Lavie and Swedenburg (1996, p. 14) note: 'The phenomenon of diasporas calls for re-imagining the "areas" of area studies and developing units of analysis that enable us to understand the dynamics of transnational cultural and economic processes, as well as to challenge the conceptual limits imposed by national and ethnic/racial boundaries'. The fluid, multi-sited and multi-generational nature of diaspora groupings poses considerable methodological challenges of definition, identification, location, sampling, interviewing and data analysis and interpretation.

As the nature of global diasporas is constantly in flux, the methodologies we use to study them should likewise be fluid (Cohen, 2008). In practice, traditional approaches to research design, participant recruitment and data analysis repeatedly lead us to the same methodological roadblocks. Census and immigration data (particularly from destination countries) can provide an overall picture of diaspora stocks, flows and locations. However, privacy issues generally preclude these sources from providing disaggregated data at the level of the individual migrant or migrant household. Surveys of diaspora members have therefore become the standard means of collecting information on diaspora characteristics, identities, activities and linkages. This immediately raises a set of sampling problems and challenges. Census data can tell us the size of the population to sample but not who the individuals are, where they live and how to contact them. Without a sampling frame, researchers tend to rely instead on 'snowball', 'purposive' or 'convenience' sampling (Faye, 2007; IOM, 2010; Mosaic Institute, 2009; Pasura, 2006, 2010; Simich and Hamilton, 2004). This has produced a disproportionate number of studies that rely on key informant and focus group interviews in order to create a profile of diasporas and their development-related activities.

Diasporas are often geographically dispersed within a country and across different countries. Cost and time constraints and the spatial bias of snowball and convenience sampling lead to a focus on sub-sets. Studies of diaspora members in particular cities or regions are especially common, for example, Orozco (2005), Schmelz (2007), Schüttler (2007), Teo (2007), Makina (2010) and Warnecke (2010). While sample sizes vary considerably, there is a marked reliance in the diaspora research literature on very small samples, which raises obvious questions about the representativeness and generalizability of the findings (AHEAD, 2007; Arthur, 2000; Ndofor-Tah, 2000; Schlenzka, 2009).

The mail-out survey is still the preferred method of reaching members of a geographically dispersed diaspora, although response rates remain stubbornly low (Bloch, 2005; Nworah, 2005). To contact members of the diaspora, mailing lists are compiled from organizations that keep, and are willing to share, membership lists (such as diaspora organizations, embassies, alumni associations, immigrant service agencies and religious organizations). However, this means an inherent sampling bias since data collected from these individuals and groups has the potential to be skewed towards diaspora members actively engaged with their origin country. This method of 'accessing the diaspora through the diaspora' is also unlikely to provide much information on 'hidden' members of a diaspora whose immigration status may be undocumented or uncertain and who are wary of disclosing personal information to researchers (Bloch, 2007). Researchers have also noted that members of vulnerable populations such as asylum seekers and refugees might be reluctant to participate in studies due to fear and trust issues (Atkinson and Flint, 2001; Mosaic Institute, 2009; Warnecke, 2010).

In order to generate larger and more representative samples, different strategies need to be adopted. In this context, the potential of the internet has rarely been considered. Since the advent of the internet age, more than one billion people have become connected to the World Wide Web (WWW), creating seemingly limitless opportunities for communication (Weaver and Morrison, 2008; Wright, 2005). The past decade has also seen a major increase in the use of the internet by diaspora individuals and groupings. The internet has not only facilitated remittance transfers, but has increased communication among and between diasporas and influenced the formation of diasporic identities (Ackah and Newman, 2003; Bernal, 2004, 2006; Georgiou, 2006; Kissau and Hunger, 2008; Mano and Willems, 2010; Parham, 2004; Peel, 2010). In this context, the potential of web-based methodologies in diaspora research appears promising. The aim of this chapter is twofold. First, we argue for supplementing conventional approaches with new methodologies that embrace the connectivity of diasporas, the emergence of social media and the potential of online surveys. Second, we illustrate the potential of this approach through discussion of the methods adopted in our current research on the African diaspora in Canada.

16.1 DIASPORAS ONLINE

In the context of today's electronic media, there are opportunities for individuals using the internet to communicate in unprecedented ways (Weaver and Morrison, 2008). Online communication has become particularly valuable to transnational and diasporic communities as it creates a meeting place of the private and the public, the interpersonal and the communal (Georgiou, 2006; Karim, 2003). In and through the internet, diasporic communities have developed a space of (global) commons, a sense of 'imagined community' across borders (Georgiou, 2006). Several recent studies of African diasporas illustrate these points. Bernal (2006, p. 161), for example, argues that Eritreans abroad use the internet as a 'transnational public sphere' where they produce and debate narratives of history, culture, democracy and identity. Mano and Willems (2010) show that the growth of the Zimbabwean diaspora abroad has been accompanied by a corresponding rise in different types of media that aim to connect 'the homeland' and 'the diaspora' in multiple and imaginative ways. Their analysis focused on websites, chatrooms and discussion forums. Peel (2010) describes the 'online communities' within the Zimbabwean diaspora and their role in interrogating 'their own identities, their citizenship and sense of belonging, their politics, and their transnational aspirations'.

The recent explosion of social media is likely to provide further opportunities for diaspora connectivity, engagement, debate and identity-formation. Social Networking Sites (SNSs) have profoundly reshaped internet usage in the last decade (Table 16.1). The earliest SNSs had varying foci and success; however, it was not until the creation of MySpace in 2003 that the popularity of SNSs began to grow (Wink, 2010). SNSs

Table 16.1 Social networking sites

Social Networking Site (SNS)	Description	Founded	Membership founding year	Membership 2010
Facebook	Facebook is a social utility that helps people communicate with friends, family and co-workers.	2004	1,000,000	400,000,000
LinkedIn	LinkedIn was created to connect the world's professionals	2003	81,000	75,000,000
MySpace	MySpace is an online service that allows its members to set up personal profiles that can be linked together through networks of friends	2003	Data unavailable	76,000,000
Twitter	Twitter is a real-time information network	2007	1,000,000	75,000,000

have since become a way for users to connect and interact with family, friends and colleagues globally. They have also opened up opportunities to make contact with new individuals, both personal and professional, and with other members of diasporas (Wink, 2010).

Facebook.com is now the most trafficked SNS in the world with over 400 million active users (Facebook, 2010). Launched by Harvard student Mark Zuckerberg in February 2004, Facebook is a peer relationship-based SNS that allows users to create personal profiles and to establish 'friendships' with other users. In addition to basic demographic information, profiles also include information on personal interests, political views, group affiliations and cultural tastes (Facebook, 2010). Lewis et al. (2008) show how Facebook data can be used to define sub-groups by gender, race/ethnicity and socioeconomic status with distinct network behaviours and cultural preferences. In addition, Facebook users have the ability to form and to become members of formal 'groups'. Groups are based around shared interests and activities, and provide members with the ability to network with other members and to share information relevant to the group description. Diaspora Facebook groups have grown rapidly in number and size since 2004. Many diaspora-related groups are nationally based – for example, Zimbabweans in Canada, Nigerians in the UK – while others link diaspora members across countries and even globally.

As Lewis et al. (2008, p. 330) note, SNSs are 'historically unique in the amount and detail of personal information that users regularly provide; the explicit articulation of relational data as a central part of these sites' functioning; and the staggering rate of their adoption'. SNSs, like other internet tools, also provide 'remarkable new research opportunities' (Lewis et al., 2008, p. 340; see also Boyd and Ellison, 2007). In this context, the question addressed in this chapter is not what diaspora social networking tells us about diasporas (an important but separate issue) but how the use of social networking and other internet tools by diaspora members can be used by the researcher to collect data from and about diasporas. The internet, and SNSs in particular, are potentially very valuable as they open up a space for reaching widely dispersed diaspora populations.

The remainder of this chapter focuses on a case study of the Southern African diaspora in Canada. The discussion focuses on the use of the internet, and SNSs in particular, to identify and recruit a large national sample of diaspora individuals. The chapter also discusses the use of online surveying to collect information on the diaspora and its linkage with countries of origin. By way of background, the next section provides an overview of African migration patterns and trends to Canada.

16.2 LOCATING THE AFRICAN DIASPORA IN CANADA

Over the last decade, Canada became an increasingly important destination for migrants from Africa. According to the United Nations, the African-born migrant stock of Canada is 307,505. Of these, 246,000 (80 per cent) are from only twelve countries (Table 16.2). In terms of migrant flows, between 1980 and 2009, a total of 277,620 African immigrants officially landed in Canada. Figure 16.1 shows that the volume of annual migration to Canada steadily increased over time with two peak periods (1990–93 and 2004–09). In both of these periods, the number of refugees entering Canada increased sharply. In 1991, for example, nearly 50 per cent of African immigrants were refugees. Of 128,000 African migrants to Canada since 2000, 42 per cent entered as refugees.

The migrant stock in Canada from the Southern African Development Community (SADC) is 88,820 (or 29 per cent of the total African migrant stock). Three countries – South Africa, Tanzania and the Democratic Republic of Congo (DRC) – make up nearly 80 per cent of the SADC

350 *Handbook of research methods in migration*

Table 16.2   African migrant stock in Canada, top twelve countries of origin

Country	No.	% of total African migrant stock
South Africa	37,681	12.2
Egypt	36,924	12.0
Morocco	26,050	8.5
Algeria	20,894	6.8
Kenya	20,821	6.8
Somalia	20,376	6.6
Tanzania	19,960	6.5
Ghana	17,072	5.6
Ethiopia	14,486	4.7
Uganda	11,085	3.6
Nigeria	10,652	3.5
DRC	10,201	3.3
Total	246,202	79.9

Source: United Nations (2007).

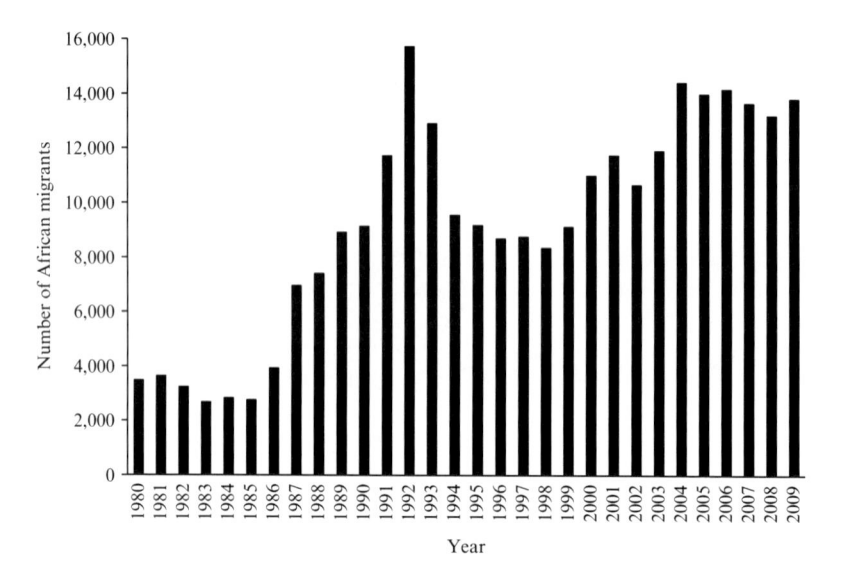

Figure 16.1   African immigration to Canada, 1980–2009

Table 16.3 Southern African Development Community migrant stock in Canada

Country	No.	%
South Africa	37,681	42.5
Tanzania	19,960	22.5
DRC	10,201	11.5
Mauritius	6,720	7.6
Zimbabwe	4,186	4.7
Angola	2,501	2.8
Zambia	2,380	2.7
Madagascar	1,950	2.3
Seychelles	1,035	1.2
Mozambique	911	1.0
Malawi	430	0.5
Namibia	305	0.3
Botswana	200	0.2
Swaziland	195	0.1
Lesotho	165	0.1
Total	88,820	100.0

Source: United Nations (2007).

migrant stock in Canada (Table 16.3). The flow of immigrants from Southern Africa has increased gradually over time (Figure 16.2) and is currently around 4–5000 per annum. The proportion of refugees is much lower than for Africa as a whole (at around 22 per cent). Economic migrants make up 55 per cent of the total migrant inflow since 1980 (compared to 36 per cent for Africa as a whole).

Southern Africa's major source of migrants to Canada is South Africa with over 40 per cent of the total SADC migrant stock (Table 16.3). Contrary to established wisdom that there has been a growing brain drain from South Africa to Canada since the end of apartheid, immigration has not risen markedly since the mid-1990s (Figure 16.3). The peak year was 1994 but thereafter there has been an overall annual decline in the flow to Canada, particularly since 2000. For example, more South Africans emigrated to Canada in 1980 than in 2009. The vast majority of South African immigrants entered in the economic migrant class (80 per cent between 1980 and 2009).

In 2009, the Southern African Migration Project (SAMP) initiated a research project on the 90,000-strong Southern African diaspora in Canada. The objectives were (a) to examine migration numbers, patterns and trends from Southern Africa to Canada after 1990; (b) to construct a socioeconomic and demographic profile of the SADC diaspora in Canada;

352 *Handbook of research methods in migration*

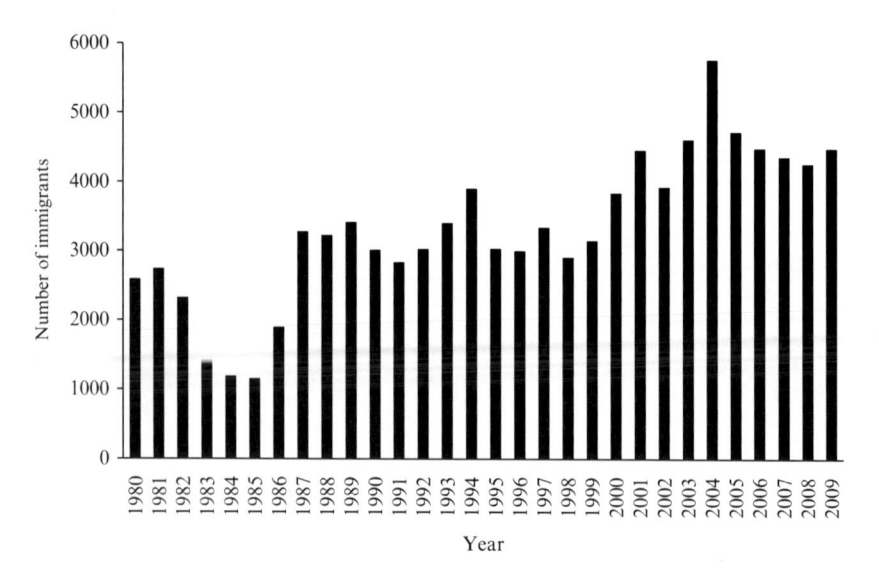

Figure 16.2 Immigration from the Southern African Development Community to Canada, 1980–2009

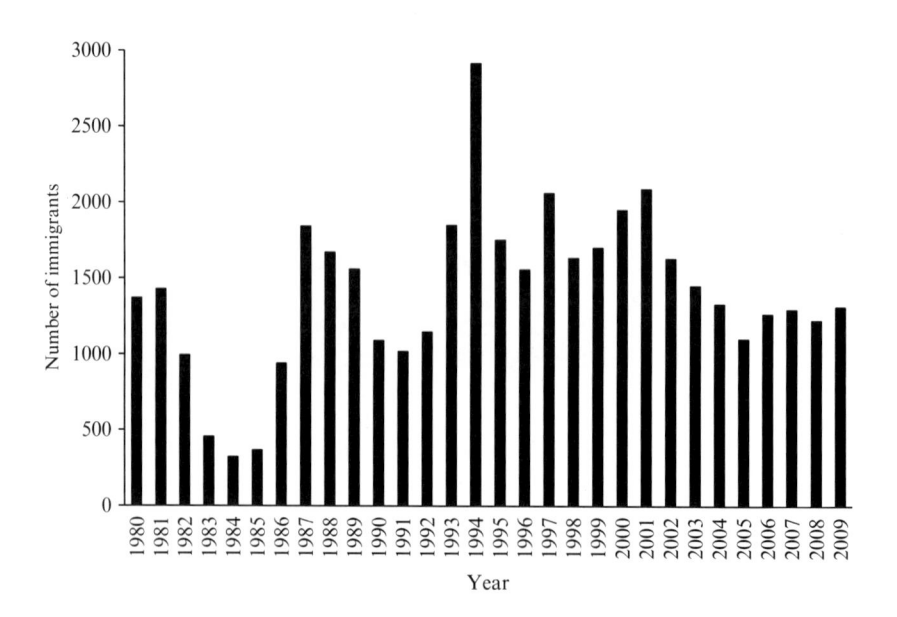

Source: Data from Citizenship and Immigration Canada (2009).

Figure 16.3 South African immigration to Canada, 1980–2009

(c) to explore the migration experience of Southern African migrants including their reasons for leaving Africa, their attitudes towards Canada and Africa and their attitudes towards African development; (d) to uncover the social, cultural, material and transnational ties that migrants in Canada maintain with Africa; and (e) to examine the potential for return migration and for involvement in individual or group development-related activity.

16.3 E-RECRUITING

The question of how to locate diaspora individuals for interview preoccupied the research team throughout the study. Apart from global migrant stocks and a general idea of diaspora distributions around the country, there was no sample population nor was it possible to develop a sampling frame. Census and immigration data provide a general picture of the size and spatial distribution of the diaspora but do not, by law, identify individuals by name or provide their contact details. Initially, in a variation on the 'snowball' and 'convenience' sampling methods beloved of diaspora researchers, each member of the research team made a list of names and email addresses of people they knew who were from Southern Africa. They invited them to come to the SAMP website and complete an online survey and pass information about the survey and link on to their friends and acquaintances. This strategy proved largely unsuccessful as did efforts to ask diaspora organizations to publicize the survey. Six weeks in, only 80 people had completed the survey and these were disproportionately from the two towns in which the team members lived (Kingston and London, Ontario).

A multi-faceted e-recruitment strategy was therefore developed using social media and diaspora websites to identify potential diaspora individuals. These included the use of:

- Facebook
- LinkedIn
- Academia.edu
- University websites
- Diaspora websites (for example, South Africans in Ontario, Jewish South Africans in Canada)
- Professional websites.

The relative importance of each medium in identifying diaspora members is shown in Figure 16.4.

Facebook proved to be the key to accessing large numbers of diaspora members. In total, 97 diaspora-related Facebook groups were located

354 *Handbook of research methods in migration*

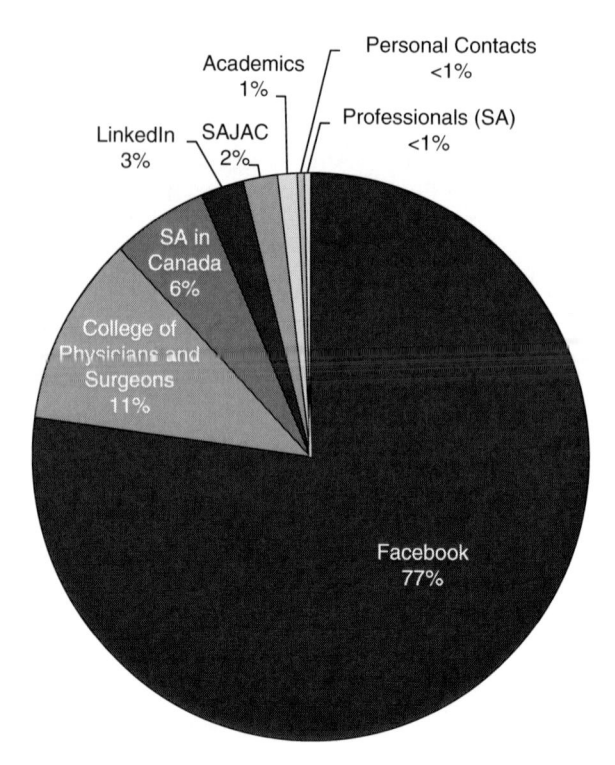

Figure 16.4 Southern African Development Community online recruitment strategies

(the majority relating to South Africa (36), Mauritius (15) and Zimbabwe (11)). Each member of a group was sent a personalized message explaining the purpose of the survey and inviting participation. Many people belonged to more than one group but each individual was only messaged once. Despite fears that messaging might lead to charges of spamming from recipients, the overall response was both positive and overwhelming. Numerous supportive messages were received (not to mention invitations to become Facebook 'friends' with respondents). From the moment that the Facebook e-recruitment campaign began, the overall numbers of respondents escalated dramatically (Figure 16.5) reaching over 2000 within a matter of weeks. A total of 5621 people were eventually messaged on Facebook with an overall response rate of over 40 per cent.

The country coverage achieved via Facebook varied considerably (Figure 16.6). In total, around 6 per cent of the diaspora was sent an individualized message. Most countries were in the 5–15 per cent range although over 20 per cent of migrants in Canada from Botswana, Madagascar and Zimbabwe

Diasporas on the web 355

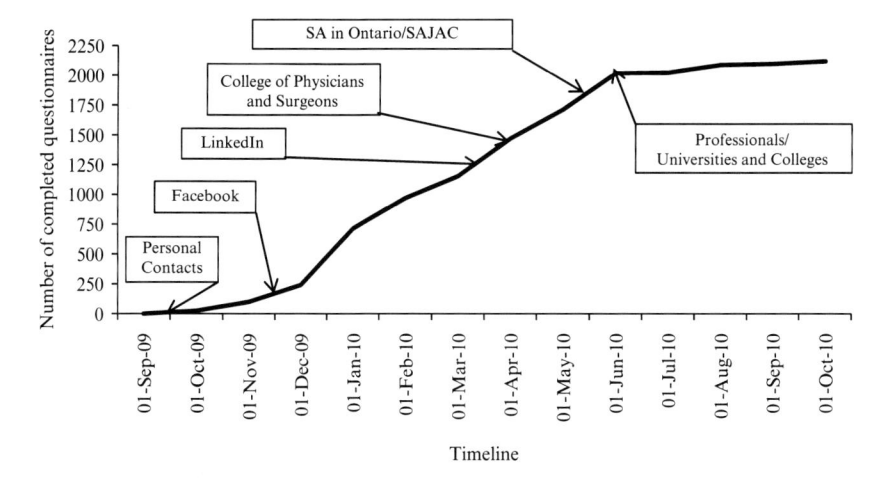

[Figure: line graph with y-axis "Number of completed questionnaires" (0–2250) and x-axis "Timeline" from 01-Sep-09 to 01-Oct-10. Labeled events: Personal Contacts, Facebook, LinkedIn, College of Physicians and Surgeons, SA in Ontario/SAJAC, Professionals/Universities and Colleges.]

Note: The graph shows the date on which various different e-recruiting strategies commenced and their impact.

Figure 16.5 Southern African Development Community questionnaire respondents over time

were located and messaged. Concerns that Facebook e-recruitment would produce a predominantly young (even student) cohort proved unfounded. A few years ago this would have undoubtedly been the case. However, the demographics of Facebook users in general have changed dramatically in the last 2–3 years and diaspora users are no different.

Some SNSs deliberately target particular sub-groups. LinkedIn and Academia.edu, for example, target professionals and academics, respectively. LinkedIn proved a useful tool for identifying and messaging professionals (primarily from the business, banking, legal and IT sectors). Academia.edu proved less useful for e-recruiting diaspora academics, necessitating a rather tedious search of Canadian university websites using keywords to identify people to email who had trained in Southern Africa.

Another professional sub-group in which the study was interested was physicians, given the considerable amount of attention and controversy which surrounds the 'brain drain' of health professionals from South Africa to Canada (Labonte et al., 2006). Some physicians were recruited during the Facebook campaign but this was clearly insufficient to undertake any general analysis of the medical diaspora in Canada. The website of the College of Physicians and Surgeons provides the names and addresses of all physicians in the country. Using the language and degree granting institution, it was possible to construct a large physician database. In the

356 *Handbook of research methods in migration*

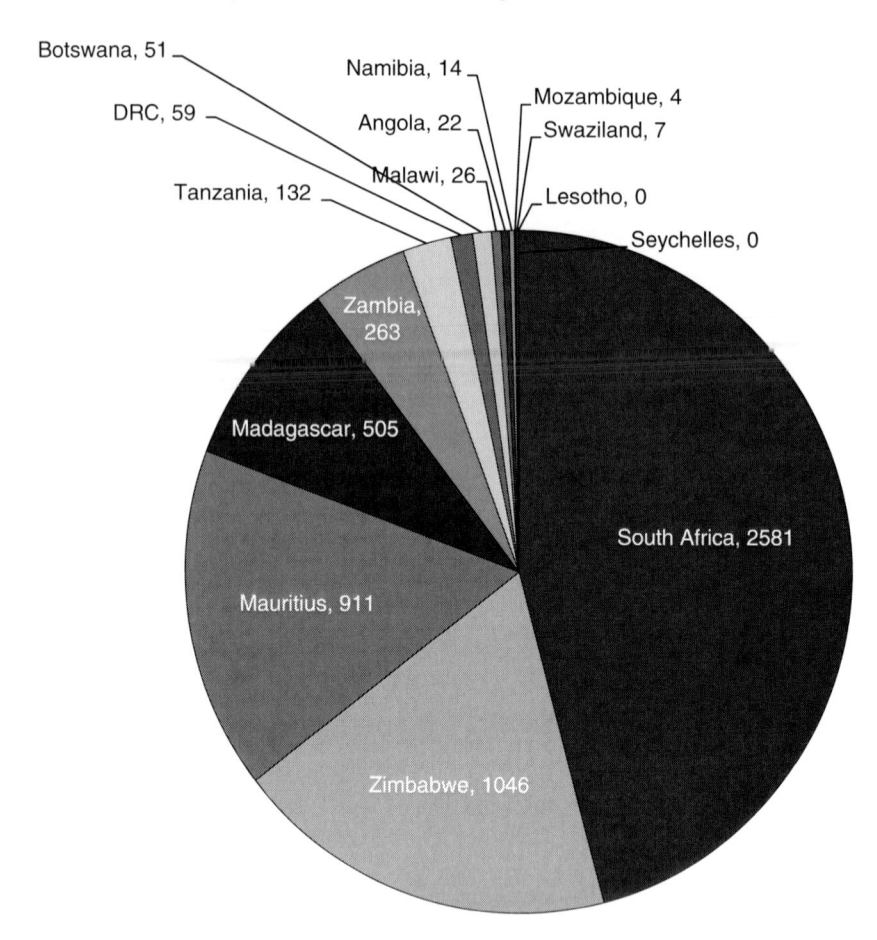

Figure 16.6 Number of Facebook messages sent by Southern African Development Community country

case of South Africans, for example, a total of 791 physicians were identified. The questionnaire was mailed out to all physicians identified and 554 responded (a response rate of 70 per cent). This far exceeds the 32 per cent response rate reported for the National Physician Survey conducted in 2007 by the College of Family Physicians of Canada (Grava-Gubins and Scott, 2008). Two other diaspora websites – South Africans in Ontario and the South African Jewish Association of Canada (SAJAC) – also contain names and addresses (but no emails) of members in the public domain. Again, hard copies of the survey were mailed out to 554 addresses with a response rate of over 40 per cent. Data from the returned hard copies was entered online and seamlessly integrated into the overall database.

Table 16.4 Southern African Development Community diasporic Facebook presence

Country	Number of Facebook groups	Number of Facebook group members	Number of individuals messaged*	% of migrant stock messaged
Angola	3	34	22	0.9
Botswana	3	54	51	26.0
DRC	5	130	59	0.6
Lesotho	0	0	0	0.0
Madagascar	7	663	505	26.0
Malawi	1	26	26	6.0
Mauritius	15	1639	911	14.0
Mozambique	1	27	4	0.4
Namibia	3	68	14	5.0
Seychelles	0	0	0	0.0
South Africa	36	5371	2581	7.0
Swaziland	2	506	7	4.0
Tanzania	4	201	132	7.0
Zambia	6	366	263	11.0
Zimbabwe	11	477	1046**	25.0
Totals	97	9562	5621	6.0

Note:
* The number of individuals messaged may not correspond with the total number of individuals in a Facebook group for one or a combination of the following reasons: Facebook profile prohibited sending a message, individual was not currently living in Canada, duplicate profiles, individual was under the age of 18. As some groups were 'global' in nature, only individuals who appeared to be living in Canada were sent a message.
** Figure is higher than the total group membership as a member of the research team identified individuals on Facebook by a 'six-degrees-of-separation' technique that yielded more potential respondents.

The overall importance and potential of the Facebook e-recruitment strategy for many (but not all) countries is clear (Table 16.4). Without the use of this SNS, the study would have been far less effective in accessing the diaspora in Canada. The other online methods of e-recruitment provided significant additional numbers of South Africans but not many individuals from other countries (Figure 16.7).

At the time of writing (mid-2010), the total number of respondents had reached 2119. Response rates varied considerably from country to country (Table 16.5). In the case of a number of countries (such as Lesotho, Swaziland and Mozambique) the (small) numbers who completed the survey were greater than the number messaged. However, with

358 *Handbook of research methods in migration*

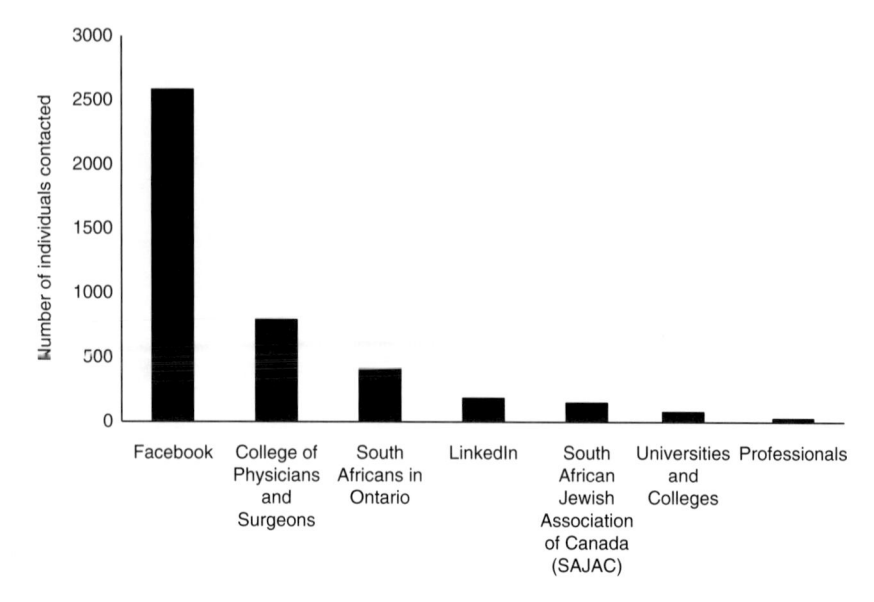

Figure 16.7   Online recruitment of South Africans in Canada

Table 16.5   Southern African Development Community questionnaire respondents by country of birth

Country of birth	Total individuals contacted	Total responses	Response rate (%)	Proportion of migrant stock (%)
Angola	22	10	45.5	0.4
Botswana	51	7	13.7	3.5
DRC	59	12	20.3	0.1
Lesotho	0	2	200.0	1.2
Madagascar	505	30	5.9	1.5
Malawi	28	10	34.7	2.3
Mauritius	925	53	5.7	0.8
Mozambique	5	8	160.0	0.9
Namibia	14	26	185.7	8.5
Seychelles	0	2	200.0	0.2
South Africa	3839	1653	43.1	4.4
Swaziland	7	9	128.6	4.6
Tanzania	135	37	27.4	0.2
Zambia	264	40	15.2	1.7
Zimbabwe	1050	220	21.0	5.3
Total	6904	2119	30.7	2.4

the exception of a few countries, response rates were generally over 20 per cent and in some cases (Angola, South Africa) were over 40 per cent. In total 2.4 per cent of the migrant stock completed the survey.

16.4 SURVEYING THE ONLINE DIASPORA

The Southern African diaspora in Canada is widely dispersed. Although diasporas do cluster in particular provinces, the major provinces are also extremely large (Table 16.6). Cost and time constraints prohibited face-to-face interviews with individuals identified in the e-recruitment campaign. As a result, the preferred interviewing methodology was the online survey. The internet has opened up new opportunities to study geographically dispersed populations with a strong online presence and there has been increased usage of online questionnaires (Berrens et al., 2003; Schmidt, 1997; Wright, 2005). By moving from a paper or telephone format to an electronic medium costs are significantly reduced (Schmidt, 1997; Wright, 2005). The online survey potentially allows researchers to reach much larger numbers of individuals with common characteristics in a short period of time, despite their being separated by sometimes vast distances (Schmidt, 1997; Wright, 2005). The primary disadvantage, of course, is that individuals without an online presence are overlooked.

Other general advantages of online surveying include the ability to post adverts and invitations on websites and to send invitations to list-serve members. Self-administered surveys mean that fieldworker costs are minimized. If the data is automatically collected and written to an online database file, the costs of data entry are also eliminated (Wright, 2005). There are many low-cost, or even free, online survey providers who provide technical and administrative support in research design, data collection and data analysis. This eliminates the need to hire individuals who are experienced in IT and survey design to assist in the research project. In sum, the costs in terms of both time and money for publishing a survey on the web are low compared with the costs associated with conventional surveying methods. The data entry stage is eliminated for the survey administrator, and software can ensure that data acquired from the participants is free of common entry errors (Schmidt, 1997).

This project used an online survey instrument accessible through the SAMP website (http://www.queensu.ca/samp). This was a methodology with which SAMP had prior experience (and success) in interviewing medical professionals in South Africa (Crush and Pendleton, 2007). In SAMP's study of health professionals, the online survey was supplemented by a mail-out survey to capture nursing professionals who did not

Table 16.6 Distribution of Southern African Development Community migrants in Canada

Province or Territory of Original Landing

Country of previous residence	NL	PE	NS	NB	QC	ON	MB	SK	AB	BC	YT	NT	PNS
Angola	5	0	0	0	607	1,317	0	0	68	26	0	0	0
Botswana	0	0	0	0	8	640	11	7	81	78	0	0	0
DRC	12	14	65	255	10,610	5,090	689	189	631	470	0	0	0
Lesotho	0	0	0	0	0	71	0	0	0	0	0	0	0
Madagascar	0	0	0	0	1,666	62	0	0	6	0	0	0	0
Malawi	6	0	5	5	32	333	13	5	45	37	0	0	0
Mauritius	0	0	0	0	3,465	5,417	125	39	452	695	0	32	0
Namibia	12	0	0	0	11	156	0	8	62	24	0	0	0
Seychelles	0	0	0	0	1,013	122	0	0	11	16	0	0	0
South Africa	398	22	244	115	864	19,984	1444	2089	4950	12,083	20	13	17
Swaziland	7	0	0	0	11	75	0	0	6	48	0	0	0
Tanzania	7	6	22	15	478	6,841	63	64	2157	813	0	0	0
Zambia	0	0	10	26	174	2,288	108	103	194	304	0	6	0
Zimbabwe	12	0	44	35	728	4,425	133	49	947	867	5	16	0
Total	459	42	390	451	19,667	46,821	2586	2553	9610	15,461	25	67	17

Note: NL – Newfoundland and Labrador; PE – Prince Edward Island; NS – Nova Scotia; NB – New Brunswick; QC – Quebec; ON – Ontario; MB – Manitoba; SK – Saskatchewan; AB – Alberta; BC – British Columbia; YT – Yukon Territory; NT – Northwest Territories; PNS – Province not stated. Table shows province of original residence on arrival in country. Data for Mozambique not available

Source: Citizenship and Immigration Canada (2009).

have internet access (Crush and Pendleton, 2007). In other words, internet surveys are not a complete substitute for more conventional methods, which suggests that a mixed methodology approach is preferable.

One significant advantage of online surveys for diaspora research is that it takes advantage of the internet's ability to provide access to groups and individuals who would be difficult, if not impossible, to reach through other channels (Schmidt, 1997). Not only are diaspora members easier to access but online surveys are easily accessible to users irrespective of geographical location and can be completed at their convenience. Furthermore, online surveys ensure a high degree of anonymity which has the potential to increase response rates by participants (Bloch, 2005). As with any study, there are a number of potential pitfalls to carrying out online survey research including the validity of data and sampling issues, design and implementation issues, and the question of access (Schmidt, 1997; Wright, 2005).

The advanced nature of some online survey providers allows researchers to export data to a variety of data analysis programs further saving time. Some providers allow researchers to conduct preliminary analyses on data while the survey is in progress (Wright, 2005). With the rapid advances in online survey technology over the past ten years, collecting and storing data online is now more secure than ever before. Through the use of encryption, survey data can be stored without the possibility of sensitive and confidential data being accessed by the public. Another significant advantage of online surveying is the convenience of automated data collection which reduces any opportunities for input errors by individuals entering the data manually (Schmidt, 1997; Wright, 2005).

After testing and reviewing numerous online survey tools, StudentVoice© Canada was selected. StudentVoice© provides free services to university subscribers, which makes it an attractive option. All team members have access to the same 'dashboard' where project information can be posted, data can be obtained in real-time and where data can be exported, analysed and reported. Data collected by the program is encrypted and stored on a Canadian (rather than US) server. The company offered unlimited and free IT support. IT team members assisted the research team in questionnaire design, putting the survey online, and rectified any technical difficulties that arose while the survey was live.

StudentVoice© also offered unlimited questionnaires with an unlimited number of responses for no additional cost. In total, the SADC project required the design and hosting of 14 country questionnaires in both official languages, English and French (28 in total). The Tracking Program allowed members of the research team to monitor the project in real-time which facilitated the monitoring and success of various survey recruitment strategies as members of the team were able to export and analyse data at various stages throughout the project. Furthermore, the program provided several basic reporting tools such as frequency tables, filters, graphs and cross-tabulations. Once a survey was completed the data set was easily downloaded and manipulated with SPSS.

The questionnaire also invited respondents to comment on their migration and diaspora experience, which has proved a rich source of qualitative information. Every individual who completed the survey was also invited to supply their contact details for a follow-up telephone interview. Of the 2119 respondents who completed the survey 334 were willing to be personally interviewed, a process now in progress.

16.5 CONCLUSION

This chapter has described and discussed the potential of the internet for identifying and interviewing individuals as part of a research project on diaspora engagement with their countries of origin. Its original methodological contribution lies in the e-recruitment strategies used to access a widely dispersed diaspora. Initial attempts to pursue an internet version of snowball sampling were not especially successful. The turn to social media proved decisive. Diasporas are spontaneously using SNSs for all kinds of online networking activity. In doing so, they provide contact details on public sites which can be readily accessed by the researcher. Mass mailings are inadvisable since they contravene the spamming controls on many SNS sites. However, there is no obstacle to messaging individuals with personalized messages and invitations to participate in a survey. SNSs thus provide a powerful new tool for diaspora research to supplement other methods (Brickman-Bhutta, 2009; Redmond, 2010). Abandonment of other methods (such as the mail-out survey) is inadvisable since, as this study found, there are diaspora members who are not accessible through SNSs. However, as we show, the internet can also be used in combination with the mail-out survey to identify and interview various professional and cultural group members.

Online surveys have been around for some time (Evans and Mathur, 2005), although their use in diaspora research has been limited. There is a general sense of user fatigue surrounding the online survey, since most people's exposure to this methodology is restricted to intrusive assessments of their consumer behaviour. In the case study discussed here, potential participants were given a full description of the aims and objectives of the survey, various ethical guarantees and the opportunity to find out more about the project on the SAMP website. The survey took at least

20–25 minutes to complete (and even longer for the 771 individuals – over one third – who also provided additional verbatim comments and commentary). Not only were high response rates achieved but the researchers received numerous queries and positive comments on the survey by email. Some 334 respondents (16 per cent) made themselves available for a follow-up in-depth interview and 835 (40 per cent) requested copies of the final report. All of this indicates that the degree of interest in the survey amongst diaspora individuals in Canada was extremely high. More generally, it indicates that the study of diasporas may be particularly amenable to the use of web-based methodologies.

NOTES

1. We wish to thank the IDRC for funding the SAMP research project on the Southern African Diaspora in Canada.
2. See Gamlen (Chapter 15, this volume) for some further discussion of this topic.

REFERENCES

Ackah, W. and Newman, J. (2003), 'Ghanaian Seventh Day Adventists on and offline: problematising the virtual communities discourse', in K.H. Karim (ed.), *The Media of Diaspora*, London: Routledge, pp. 203–14.
AHEAD (2007), 'Enabling diaspora engagement in Africa: resources, mechanisms and gaps. Case study: Ethiopia', Ottawa: AHEAD.
Arthur, J.A. (2000), *Invisible Sojourners: African Immigrant Diaspora in the United States*, Westport, CT: Praeger.
Atkinson, R. and Flint, J. (2001), 'Accessing hidden and hard-to-reach populations: snowball research strategies', *Social Research Update*, 33.
Bernal, V. (2004), 'Eritrea goes global: reflections on nationalism in a transnational era', *Cultural Anthropology*, 19, 3–25.
Bernal, V. (2006), 'Diaspora, cyberspace and political imagination: the Eritrean diaspora online', *Global Networks*, 6 (2), 161–79.
Berrens, R., Bohara, A., Jenkins-Smith, H., Silva, C. and Weimer, D. (2003), 'The advent of internet surveys for political research', *Political Analysis*, 11 (1), 1–22.
Bloch, A. (2005), 'The development potential of Zimbabweans in the diaspora: a survey of Zimbabweans living in the UK and South Africa', IOM Migration Research Series No. 17, London: International Organization for Migration (IOM).
Bloch, A. (2007), 'Methodological challenges for national and multi-sited comparative survey research', *Journal of Refugee Studies*, 20 (2), 230–47.
Boyd, D.M. and Ellison, N.B. (2007), 'Social network sites: definition, history, and scholarship', *Journal of Computer-Mediated Communication*, 13 (1), article 11.
Brickman-Bhutta, C. (2009), 'Not by the book: Facebook as sampling frame', ASREC/ ARDA Working Paper, Pennsylvania State University, University Park, Pennsylvania.
Brinkerhoff, J. (ed.) (2008), *Diasporas and Development: Exploring the Potential*, Boulder, CO: Lynne Rienner.
Citizenship and Immigration Canada (2009), 'RDM facts and figures 2009', Ottawa: Citizenship and Immigration Canada.

Cohen, R. (2008), *Global Diasporas: An Introduction*, 2nd edn, New York: Routledge.
Crush, J. and Pendleton, W. (2007), 'The haemorrhage of health professionals from South Africa: medical opinions', Migration Policy Series No. 47, Kingston: Southern African Migration Programme (SAMP).
Evans, J. and Mathur, A. (2005), 'The value of online surveys', *Internet Research*, 15 (2), 195–219.
Facebook (2010), 'Statistics', available at http://www.facebook.com/press/info.php?statistics (accessed 7 September 2010).
Faye, M. (2007), 'The Senegalese diaspora in Germany: its contributions to development in Senegal', Deutsche Gesellschaft für Technische Zusammenarbeit (GTZ), available at http://www.gtz.de/en/dokumente/en-senegalese-diaspora-2007.pdf (accessed 7 September 2010).
Georgiou, M. (2006), 'Diasporic communities on-line: a bottom up experience of transnationalism', in K. Sarikakis and D. Thussu (eds), *Ideologies of the Internet*, Cresskill, NJ: Hampton Press, pp. 131–45.
Grava-Gubins, I. and Scott, S. (2008), 'Effects of various methodologic strategies: survey response rates among Canadian physicians and physicians-in-training', *Canadian Family Physician*, 54 (10), 1424–30.
International Organization for Migration (IOM) (2010), 'A study on the dynamics of the Egyptian diaspora: strengthening development linkages', Cairo: IOM.
Karim, K. (ed.) (2003), *The Media of Diaspora: Mapping the Globe*, London: Routledge.
Kissau, K. and Hunger, U. (2008), 'Political online participation of migrants in Germany', *German Policy Studies*, 4 (4), 5–31.
Labonte, R., Packer, C., Klassen, N. et al. (2006), 'The brain drain of health professionals from Sub-Saharan Africa to Canada', African Migration and Development Series No. 2, Cape Town: Idasa.
Lavie, S. and Swedenburg, T. (eds) (1996), *Displacement, Diaspora and Geographies of Identity*, Durham, NC: Duke University Press.
Lewis, K., Kaufman, J., Gonzalez, M., Wimmer, A. and Christakis, N. (2008), 'Tastes, ties, and time: a new social network dataset using Facebook.com', *Social Networks*, 30 (4), 330–42.
Makina, D. (2010), 'Zimbabwe in Johannesburg', in J. Crush and D. Tevera (eds), *Zimbabwe's Exodus: Crisis, Migration, Survival*, Cape Town and Ottawa: Southern African Migration Programme (SAMP) and International Development Research Centre (IDRC), pp. 225–43.
Mano, W. and Willems, W. (2010), 'Debating "Zimbabweanness" in diasporic internet forums: technologies of freedom?', in J. McGregor and R. Primorc (eds), *Zimbabwe's New Diaspora: Displacement and the Cultural Politics of Survival*, New York: Berghahn Books, pp. 183–201.
Merz, B., Chen, L. and Geithner, P. (2008), *Diasporas and Development*, Cambridge, MA: Harvard University Press.
Mosaic Institute, The (2009), 'Profile of a community: a "smart map" of the Sudanese diaspora in Canada', Mosaic Institute, Toronto, available at http://www.mosaicinstitute.ca/uploaded/tiny_mce/File/Sudanese_Report.pdf (accessed 7 September 2010).
Ndofor-Tah, C. (2000), *Diaspora and Development: Contributions by African Organisations in the UK to Africa's Development*, Report commissioned by the African Foundation for Development (AFFORD) as part of the Africa21 project, 'Target Africa 2015: Development Awareness, Networking and Lifelong Learning among African Organisations in London'.
Nworah, U. (2005), 'Study on Nigerian diaspora', Global Politician, available at http://www.globalpolitician.com/2682-nigeria (accessed 7 September 2010).
Orozco, M. (2005), *Diasporas, Development and Transnational Integration: Ghanaians in the U.S., U.K. and Germany*, Report commissioned by Citizen International through the US Agency for International Development, Institute for the Study of International Migration and Inter-American Dialogue.

Parham, A. (2004), 'Diaspora, community and communication: internet use in transnational Haiti', *Global Networks*, **4**, 199–217.
Pasura, D. (2006), *Mapping Exercise: Zimbabwe*, London: International Organization for Migration (IOM).
Pasura, D. (2010), 'Competing meanings of the diaspora: the case of Zimbabweans in Britain', *Journal of Ethnic and Migration Studies*, **36** (9), 1445–61.
Peel, C. (2010), 'Exile and the internet: Ndebele and mixed-race online diaspora homes', in J. McGregor and R. Primorc (eds), *Zimbabwe's New Diaspora: Displacement and the Cultural Politics of Survival*, New York: Berghahn Books, pp. 229–54.
Plaza, S. and Ratha, D. (eds) (2011), *Diaspora for Development in Africa*, Washington, DC: The World Bank.
Redmond, F. (2010), 'Social networking sites: evaluating and investigating their use in academic research' MSc Thesis, Dublin Institute of Technology, Dublin.
Schlenzka, N. (2009), 'The Ethiopian diaspora in Germany: its contribution to development in Ethiopia', Deutsche Gesellschaft für Technische Zusammenarbeit (GTZ), available at http://www.gtz.de/en/dokumente/en-Ethiopian-Diaspora-2009.pdf (accessed 6 February 2012).
Schmelz, A. (2007), 'The Cameroonian diaspora in Germany: its contribution to development in Cameroon', Deutsche Gesellschaft für Technische Zusammenarbeit (GTZ), available at http://www.gtz.de/de/dokumente/en-cameroonian-diaspora-2008.pdf (accessed 7 September 2010).
Schmidt, W.C. (1997), 'World-wide web survey research: benefits, potential problems, and solutions', *Behavior Research Methods, Instruments & Computers*, **29** (2), 274–9.
Schüttler, K. (2007), 'The Moroccan diaspora in Germany: its contributions to development in Morocco', Deutsche Gesellschaft für Technische Zusammenarbeit (GTZ), available at http://www.gtz.de/de/dokumente/en-moroccan-diaspora-2007.pdf (accessed 7 September 2010).
Simich, L. and Hamilton, H. (2004), *The Study of Sudanese Settlement in Ontario – Final Report*, Toronto: University of Toronto.
Sorensen, N. (2007), *Living Across Worlds: Diaspora, Development and Transnational Engagement*, Geneva: International Organization for Migration (IOM).
Teo, P. (2007), 'Vancouver's newest Chinese diaspora: settlers or "immigrant prisoners"?', *GeoJournal*, **68**, 211–22.
United Nations (2007), 'Global Migrant Origins Database', United Nations, available at http://www.migrationdrc.org/research/typesofmigration/global_migrant_origin_database.html (accessed 1 May 2010).
Vertovec, S. and Cohen, R. (eds) (1999), *Migration, Diasporas and Transnationalism*, Cheltenham, UK and Northampton, MA, USA: Edward Elgar Publishing.
Warnecke, A. (ed.) (2010), 'Diasporas and peace: a comparative assessment of Somali and Ethiopian communities in Europe', Brief 42, Bonn International Center for Conversion (BICC), Bonn.
Weaver, A. and Morrison, B. (2008), 'Social networking', *Computer*, **41** (2), 97–100.
Wink, D. (2010), 'Social networking sites', *Nurse Educator*, **35** (2), 49–51.
Wright, K. (2005), 'Researching internet-based populations: advantages and disadvantages of online survey research, online questionnaire authoring software packages, and web survey services, *Journal of Computer-Mediated Communication*, **10** (3), article 11.

17 Approaches to researching environmental change and migration: methodological considerations and field experiences from a global comparative survey project

Koko Warner

This chapter addresses current experience identifying the impact of environmental change on human mobility, migration and displacement with an emphasis on methodological issues. Scientific findings about anthropogenic climate change and its actual and potential dramatic impacts on human societies have spurred discussions about the impact of environmental change on human mobility, migration and displacement (IPCC, 2007). This has included recent discussion in many forums about the impact of environmental change including climate change on human mobility, migration and displacement (Warner et al., 2009a). It is important to understand the role of environmental change among other variables in contributing to human mobility, migration and displacement. Beyond scientific understanding, the role of environmental change may have highly differentiated impacts on migration, and requires a variety of policy responses ranging from identifying adaptation strategies that allow people to remain where they currently live and work to identifying resettlement strategies that protect people's lives and livelihoods when they are unable to remain (Martin and Warner, 2010).

The central research question has revolved around what happens to the dependent variable of human mobility, migration and displacement when the independent variable (environmental change) changes. The general hypothesis has been formed that changes in the environment in the future will drive migration in significant, possibly new patterns. The hypothesis draws on observations that forms of environmental change have already affected human movements. These examples are drawn from two sets of observations: marginal environmental impacts along with other factors such as historic cases of cultural decline and associated migration in cases of extended drought or environmental degradation; or as a main driving factor where migration may not have occurred without the environmental impact (such as Hurricane Katrina, relocation of communities from the

Cataret Islands and coastal Alaska, and the eruption of the Montserrat volcano in the Caribbean).

This chapter describes some of the central methodological issues in undertaking research on environmental change and migration. Three of these challenges include, first, general lack of data and definitions of environmentally induced migration (what is or could be the scale of environmentally induced migration, and can a correlation between independent and dependent variables be observed?). Second, methodological approaches in this topic area are challenged to isolate the independent variable and establish counterfactuals (would migration have occurred in the absence of environmental change? Would migration have occurred in the same way in the absence of environmental change?). Third, methods in current use may be prone to selection bias and are challenged to define the population of interest, in part because the mechanisms that contribute to migration are not well defined. As environmental change, particularly anthropogenic climate change, progresses in different areas of the world, research methods will be increasingly needed that can address these three challenges and yield plausible and solid results upon which policy discussions can be based.

17.1 SCOPE AND ORGANIZATION OF CHAPTER

This chapter shares the methods and fieldwork experiences of a first-time, multi-continent survey of environmental change and migration from the recently completed research project supported by the European Commission: Environmental Change and Forced Migration Scenarios (EACH-FOR, Contract Number 044468, http://www.each-for.eu).[1] This chapter has three purposes. First, the author explores issues related to how EACH-FOR designed its methodological approach for the first global survey of environmental change and migration in Section 17.2. Section 17.3 then describes how the project attempted to create a method that would produce comparable results in a challenging context of multiple scientific challenges and trade-offs for research design. The second purpose of this chapter is to examine how field researchers implemented and used this methodology in the EACH-FOR project. This chapter takes a closer look at the fieldwork approach applied in investigating the 23 EACH-FOR project case studies. These case studies presented diverse local conditions and social contexts, and with different types of environmental change. Next, Section 17.4 discusses some of the practical considerations and shortcomings of the method in practice, and illustrates how local researchers from selected case studies managed the challenges of their complex assignment.

The third purpose of this chapter is to explore lessons learned from the initial fieldwork experience and fruitful directions for future research. Section 17.5 therefore draws lessons from the EACH-FOR project experience and examines how future empirical research attempts could build and improve on these experiences. Section 17.6 concludes the chapter with the hope that this discussion will facilitate future research efforts on the topic.

17.2 ENVIRONMENTAL CHANGE AND FORCED MIGRATION SCENARIOS

In 2006, under the 6th Framework Programme, the European Commission issued a call for proposals to support comparative research of factors underlying migration and refugee flows, including illegal immigration and trafficking in human beings. In response, seven organizations formed a consortium to investigate whether and how environmental change affects human migration. The overarching purpose of the EACH-FOR project was to enhance understanding of the role of environmental change in forced migration (both internal and international) and its related societal consequences.

17.2.1 Theoretical Background

The EACH-FOR project was conceived as a multidisciplinary study that aimed to undertake original empirical research through deskwork and case study research, complemented by statistical and other information sources. The research consortium created a set of broadly comparable studies using a unified methodological research approach. It was hoped that using one common approach across almost two dozen case studies would create a set of internally valid results, with some degree of external validity as well. At the time, this type of investigation had not been done, so researchers first conducted an analysis of literature and methodologies (see Vag et al., 2007). This review revealed a number of individual case studies that mentioned migration or environmental change (Vag et al., 2007). Yet existing studies lacked consistent and comparable data on migration related to environmental change (Black, 2001; Castles, 2002).

Terms and concepts such as environmental or climate change migration, environmentally induced or forced migration, ecological or environmental refugees, and climate change refugees are used throughout the emerging literature, with no general agreement on precise definition(s) (Dun and Gemenne, 2008; El-Hinnawi, 1985).

The lack of definitions for migration caused in part by environmental change and degradation is linked to two issues. First, scholars have pointed out the challenge of isolating environmental factors from other migration drivers (Black, 2001; Boano et al., 2008; Castles, 2002). Because environmental factors are in most cases not solely responsible for driving migration, defining the phenomena becomes a complicated task of defining causes and consequences of environmentally induced migration. Lonergan described migration as 'an extremely varied and complex manifestation and component of equally complex economic, social, cultural, demographic, and political processes operating at the local, regional, national, and international levels' (Lonergan, 1998, p. 6). Research on environmentally induced migration falls into the realm of complex interactions of human and natural systems, including outcomes such as livelihood impacts, conflict and a variety of human-induced environmental change including climate change (Gunderson and Holling, 2002; Homer-Dixon, 1994; Hussein and Nelson, 1998).

Multiple factors contribute to migration, as widely stated in the literature. It remains difficult to isolate these contributing factors from one another to determine which factor had the more important role in contributing to migration (Castles, 2002; Biermann, 2007; Black, 2001; Boano et al., 2008). Environmental experts from the project noted that environmental change is not monolithic: diverse patterns and complex processes are involved in changing environments. This is also a reason why quantifying the numbers of environmentally induced migration is problematic. Expert estimates range widely in part because no measurable definition exists (Döös, 1997).

Second, it has been difficult to define the range of environmentally related migration because of the institutional and governance implications of doing so. Definitions of the 'problem' allow an assignment of authority to address related policy and practical action (Bogardi and Warner, 2008; Conisbee and Simms, 2003). Thus the definition of the concept also strongly influences what institutions bear responsibility for action. Without a definition or range of definitions for the phenomena, institutions have not gathered systematic and comparable time series data about migration, with the exception of international migration (measured as stocks in national censuses, although migration processes are flows in reality).

EACH-FOR used the working definition of environmentally induced migrants proposed by the International Organization for Migration (IOM): 'Environmentally induced migrants are persons or groups of persons who, for compelling reasons of sudden or progressive changes in the environment that adversely affect their lives or living conditions, are obliged to leave their habitual homes, or choose to do so, either temporarily or permanently, and who move either within their country or abroad'

(IOM, 2007, p. 1). This working definition is comprehensive, and identifies environmental degradation as an important push factor triggering migration. Its limitations include that it does not distinguish between temporal or permanent migration, nor does it identify the destination of migrants. This definition does not address the circumstances under which people have migrated (voluntary, forced, was return possible?), and does not indicate how institutions and policies might help environmentally induced migrants.

The project recognized the difficulty of attempting to explain the patterns and trends of migration, both international and internal, using only one approach or academic discipline. For example, push factors were frequently mentioned in fieldwork, as migrants sometimes mentioned declining livelihoods from farming at home, due to land degradation or erosion, and the sense that a combination of environmental and economic factors contributed to migration. It was recognized from the beginning that it might be difficult to interpret research results, as the literature has established that migration outcomes have multiple causal factors. Also, the existing data on migration are uneven, with much of the information based on international migration figures from census data that do not necessarily capture temporal or geographic dynamics of human movement (Afifi and Warner, 2008; Kniveton et al., 2009). This presented a situation in which it would be challenging to measure any difference between migration in the absence of the independent variable and migration in the presence of the independent variable (environmental change).

This suggested that a qualitative approach to first describe and then analyse the diversity of migration patterns would be useful, given the parameters of the project that was in development in the autumn of 2006. Subsequent synthesis reports supported this approach (Boano et al., 2008; Brown, 2008; Kniveton et al., 2009; Piguet, 2008; McLeman and Smit, 2006).

17.2.2 The Project at a Glance

A major component of the EACH-FOR project was to conduct empirical research on the ground with individuals and communities who are migrating or may migrate due in part to environmental reasons. The project aims were:

- To discover and describe in detail the causes of forced migration in relation to environmental degradation/change and their association with other social, political and economic phenomena in Europe and in the main countries of migration origin.

Approaches to researching environmental change and migration 371

- To provide plausible future scenarios of environmentally induced forced migration.

After a literature review on the topic (UNIBI, 2008), the project undertook general overview studies to provide a basis for case study selection. The general overview studies examined the overall characteristics of the region in question, including information about the demographic and socio-economic trends, political context and relevant socio-cultural factors. The overview studies described the main types of environmental degradation, emphasizing 'hot spots' of degradation in the regions and countries considered. The overview studies considered the migration processes in the region including historical context, main patterns and policies, trends and migration networks.

Figure 17.1 indicates the countries which were selected as case studies, focusing on developing and transition countries because of their particular exposure to extreme events and climate change-related stressors (IPCC, 2007).

The EACH-FOR case studies explore a cross-section of climate-related environmental impacts and migration, illustrating the impacts of desertification and sea level rise, flooding and sea level rise, and desertification and drought. For readers interested in the findings of the project, Jäger et al. (2009) report on results for all of the case studies, and individual case studies can be downloaded at the EACH-FOR project website http://www.each-for.eu.

17.2.3 Case Study Selection

The project aimed to study environmental change effects on migration, but could not in any way manipulate the independent variable in fieldwork. To address this challenge, the project carefully selected case study countries to ensure the presence of several different types of environmental processes and migration processes. The project design aimed to observe cases where both independent and dependent variables were present, in order to determine whether there was a discernible environmental signal in migration patterns (that is, whether the independent variable affected migration). The case studies were conducted in areas within countries where it was thought that both independent and dependent variables were present. Although EACH-FOR refers to 'case study countries' the results are not exhaustive and do not necessarily reflect conditions in the entire country. Rather, 'hotspot' locations within each country were examined and analysed. The reports by Jäger at al. (2009) and Warner et al. (2008, 2009a) more specifically delineate the areas

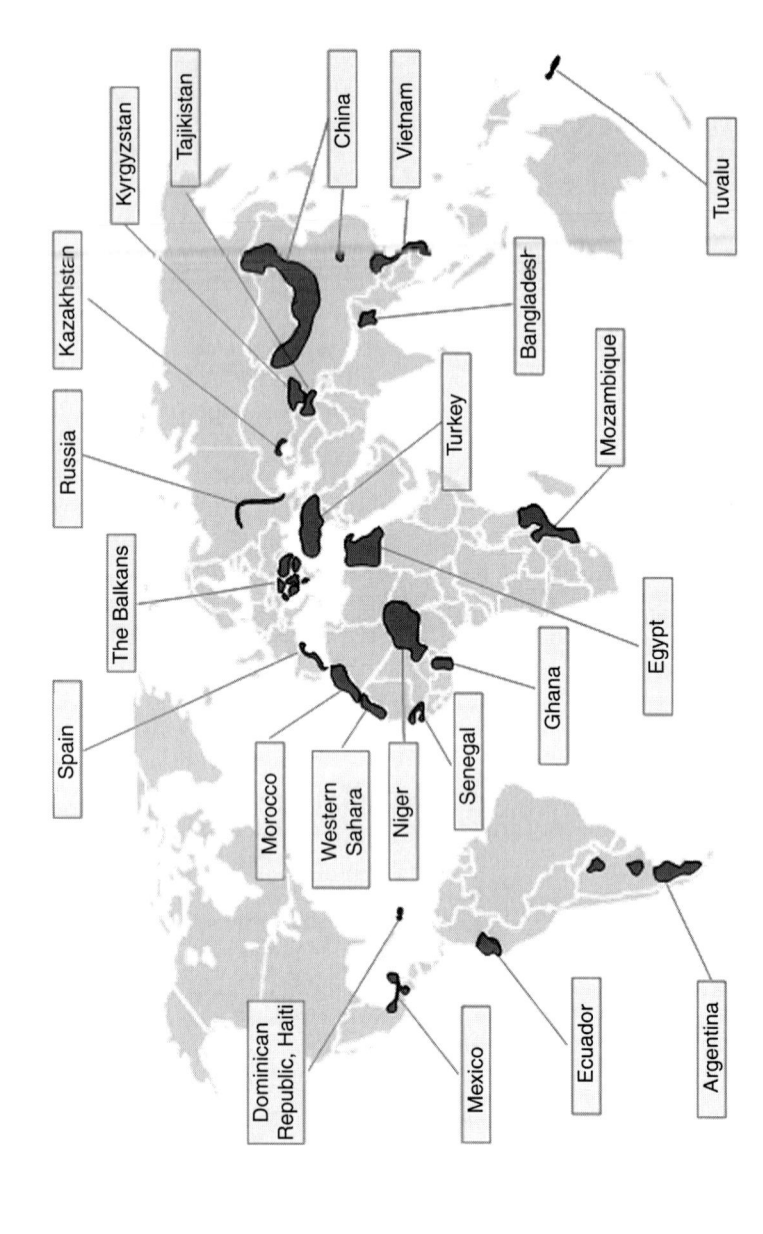

Figure 17.1 Environmental change and forced migration scenarios case study locations

within countries (based on provincial boundaries) where fieldwork was conducted.

Case study areas were selected to create a snapshot of environmental processes and their possible interactions with migration (Table 17.1). For example, case study areas with documented environmental problems of one or more of the following types were selected:

- extreme flooding
- desertification
- land degradation
- water shortages and drought
- the potential of sea level rise
- industrial pollution.

This approach allowed the project to identify 'hotspot' countries with potentially high descriptive value, but it was noted that multiple environmental processes, as well as complex migration processes, could be going on in each country. The fieldwork was not able to cover the entire country exhaustively and some processes were cross-border. Some areas with under-reporting of migration (especially internal migration), or areas with environmental degradation of a creeping nature that is not reflected in international databases, were possibly passed over in the case country selection.

The chapter now looks briefly at some of the major observations from the EACH-FOR project, followed by a more extensive discussion of methodological issues in Sections 17.3 and 17.4.

Now the reader has been introduced broadly to the EACH-FOR project, its approach and its general findings, the chapter turns its attention to an analysis of research design and experiences with the method in fieldwork.

17.3 PROJECT DESIGN FOR INVESTIGATING ENVIRONMENTAL CHANGES AND HUMAN MIGRATION

The EACH-FOR project faced several considerations about how to design the research approach. These considerations stemmed from the multidisciplinary nature of the research question, but especially the omnipresence and characteristics of the independent variable, environmental change. Table 17.2 outlines the research design process of the EACH-FOR project. Table 17.2 touches on some of the methodological design issues

Table 17.1 *Environmental change and forced migration scenarios case studies overview (regions/countries, environmental issues addressed and case study sites)*

Case study region/ countries	Environmental issues addressed	Case study sites
Asia-Pacific		
Bangladesh	Sea level rise; cyclones	Coastal regions of Bangladesh (south-west), chars (moving islands) on Jamuna River (north-west), Dhaka
China	(a) Dam construction (b) Desertification	(a) Three Gorges Dam affected regions: Shangdong Province, Jiangsu Province, Chongming Island of Shanghai, Zhejiang Province (b) Erenhot, Inner Mongolia Autonomous Region
Tuvalu	Sea level rise, erosion, waste disposal, water stress	Funafuti Atoll, Tuvalu and Auckland, New Zealand
Viet Nam	Flooding	Mekong Delta, particularly An Giang Province
Central Asia		
Kazakhstan	(a) Desertification and water stress (b) Nuclear testing	(a) Aral Sea region, Almaty (b) Semipalatinsk
Kyrgyzstan	Soil pollution, waste disposal, landslides, earthquakes	Whole country, with particular focus on the Ferghana Valley
Tajikistan	Soil pollution, degradation and erosion, mud flow, landslides, floods, earthquakes	Whole country, with particular focus on the Ferghana Valley

Europe and Russia

Spain	Water shortage and desertification	South-eastern regions of Spain – Murcia and Almeria
Turkey	(a) Dam construction (b) Water destruction	(a) South-east Turkey (Adiyaman – Samsat District; Urfa city centre); west of Turkey (Didim-Yalikoy village; Izmir – Torbali) (b) South-east Turkey (Urfa – Suruc District); Istanbul
Balkans	Unavailable at time of writing	Danube Basin
Russia	Unavailable at time of writing	Unavailable at time of writing

Latin America and Caribbean

Argentina	(a) Floods, increase of rain – water excesses with periods of abnormal droughts (b) Droughts – decrease in water availability, melting of glaciers (c) Droughts – decrease in water availability.	(a) Pampa Arenosa and Depresión del Salado north-west of the Province of Buenos Aires (b) Pre-Andean region (Comahue and the city of Jáchal, San Juan) (c) Yungas in the Salta Province
Dominican Republic, Haiti	Deforestation (and its consequences during tropical storms)	Province of Independencia, Dominican Republic; Port-au-Prince, Haiti
Ecuador	Water quality and availability; soil degradation; climate issues (El Nino Southern Oscillation (ENSO) and its consequences)	Guayas, El Oro, Pichincha, Manabi, Imbabura, Bolívar, Tunguruha, Azuay eta Quevedo provinces
Mexico	(a) Tropical storms, landslides, flooding; (b) Desertification, soil degradation	(a) Soconusco/Chiapas, south-eastern Mexico; (b) Western Tlaxcala (approx. 60 km east of Mexico City)

Table 17.1 (continued)

Case study region/ countries	Environmental issues addressed	Case study sites
Middle East and North Africa		
Egypt	Water shortage	Newly reclaimed desert lands (Western Cairo), Cairo slums, Nile Valley and Nile Delta, Upper Egypt (Southern Egypt)
Morocco	Water shortage, desertification and the impact of other environmental challenges on rural villages in arid areas	Desert fringe villages in south-east Morocco: the two most southern Oases of the Drâa River Valley: Mhamid and Tagounite (Province of Zagora)
Western Sahara	Desertification and water shortage	Algeria: Interviews with refugees from Western Sahara in refugee camps in Algeria (Tindouf region) under the control of the *Frente Polisario* government-in-exile
Sub-Saharan Africa		
Ghana	Unreliable rainfall, poor soil fertility	Source area: Upper West Region; Destination area: Brong Ahafo Region
Mozambique	Flooding, droughts	Central Mozambique – Zambezi River Valley
Niger	Droughts, deforestation, overgrazing, land degradation, Niger River problems and Lake Chad drying out	Niamey, Tilabéri
Senegal	Desertification, drought and water management	Fatick and Kaolack (the Peanut Basin) in Central Senegal and the Sénégal River Valley in Northern Senegal

Approaches to researching environmental change and migration 377

Table 17.2 The environmental change and forced migration scenarios project research steps and design issues

Step	Description	Design issue
1. Hypothesis	• Discernable environmental signal in migration today. Null hypothesis: no discernible environmental signal in migration today	• How to establish whether the environmental signal is discernible in migration patterns? • How to assess or measure environmental signals?
2. Variables	• Independent variable of interest: environmental change • Dependent variable: migration	• How to isolate the independent variable of environmental change? • How to determine that the presence of the independent variable caused a dependent variable?
3. Intervention group and control group	• Intervention group is made up of people that will experience environmental change • Control group is made up of people that will not experience environmental change	• How to isolate the control group that does not experience environmental change (independent variable)?
4. Introduce intervention	• Environmental change	• Impossible to control environmental change; need to carefully select case study countries
5. Measure dependent variables in intervention group and control group	• Did migration occur when the environment changed?	• How to prove that migration would not have occurred in the absence of environmental change?

Source: Based on Warner et al. (2009b, p. 206).

encountered at each step of the process. This section describes and analyses how the project addressed the challenges involved in investigating links between environmental change and migration.

The next sub-section discusses some of the key design issues for the project, such as how to address intervention and control groups,

378 *Handbook of research methods in migration*

controlling the intervention and measuring the dependent variable after the independent variable had been introduced.

17.3.1 Research Questions about Environmental Change and Migration

EACH-FOR was conceived as an initial study, at the community level, upon which further extensive research would be built. EACH-FOR came up with a set of questions to help gather observations in the field that could test the central hypothesis of the project. The EACH-FOR project started its scientific inquiry by forming a hypothesis to test in desk and field research: there is a discernible environmental signal in human migration patterns today. The project considered this general hypothesis to hold true if fieldwork found empirical qualitative and quantitative evidence that migration occurred, in part, due to environmental factors. The failure to find migrants in whose mobility pattern environmental causes were negligible or played no role would negate the central hypothesis. The weakness of this hypothesis is in the difficulty of determining a measure for 'discernible' and environmental 'signals' and in defining a null hypothesis. The latter would require sufficiently isolating variables so as to be able to establish that the environment played no role in migration.

The questions below guided the collection of data in desk study and fieldwork activities. These questions tried to avoid drawing a deterministic relationship between environmental degradation and migration, which was considered inappropriate for the topic area. The questions helped identify cases where environment plays an important role as a contributor to population movement. The following questions served as the basis for all research efforts in the global survey, and were intended to create a comparable set of descriptions of how environmental factors interact with migration pressures in the 23 field studies.

1. Who is migrating away from situations of environmental degradation/change?
2. Where are environmentally induced migrants coming from and where are they going to?
3. Why have people migrated (that is, what role has environmental degradation or change played)?
4. How does environmental degradation interplay with other social, economic and political factors in decisions relating to migration?
5. What might prevent people from migrating when they are faced with environmental degradation (that is, what assistance was needed, what was lacking)?
6. Why do some people remain in areas of environmental degradation/

Approaches to researching environmental change and migration 379

change while others migrate (that is, what are their coping/adaptation strategies and capacities)?
7. How does environmentally induced migration occur (for example, choice of destination, networks used)?
8. What is the role of people's perception of environmental degradation in triggering them to move?

These eight questions provided a basis upon which individual case studies could build additional falsifiable hypotheses about the particular relationships between environmental factors in specific areas and migration trends there. Its case studies were intended to provide insights into the many possible hypotheses that could subsequently be formulated and tested.

The EACH-FOR project worked at the community level, interviewing experts and affected people or households. As indicated in Section 17.2.3, EACH-FOR worked in specific countries, but only in particular provinces expected to be more affected by both (documented) environmental change and migration. It was assumed that the household was the migration decision-making unit, and questions about the household unit are reflected in the questionnaires (understanding that migration decisions are made in combination with other risk management/resource management decisions). Because the EACH-FOR project needed some documentation that a particular environmental change was occurring in a country for case study selection, the scale of environmental change considered was usually at a significant scale or intensity. For example, flooding in Mozambique has reached international attention in recent years, and displaced tens of thousands of people. Similarly, desertification in countries such as Egypt and Niger are documented and widespread phenomena there.

17.3.2 Variables: Environmental Change and Migration

The project chose the dependent variable migration (including a range from internal to international migration). The EACH-FOR project defined a broad set of independent variables (including a range of complex phenomena from sudden to gradual and creeping processes). The project's case studies investigated a wide range of environmental change variables, from natural hazards of a sudden and gradual nature, to longer-term processes. The EACH-FOR project treated the independent variable as certain types of environmental change: it employed a multi-case study approach to examine major types of environmental change and how these environmental factors might affect migration.

Taking environmental change as an independent variable was associated with at least three issues from the outset. First, the set of environmental variables that make up 'environmental change' are difficult, if not impossible, to isolate from other factors driving migration. Similarly, it is not possible to control the independent variable in this kind of research attempt: there are likely few cases of migration where it is possible to fully exclude the environmental variables of interest. Environmental processes are ongoing and omnipresent in all migration or non-migration situations, making it quite challenging to devise a methodology that can accurately test the impact of environmental change on migration. The project relied on the relative importance that interviewees placed on environmental factors to begin to isolate the relevance of environmental change variables in the migration choice. Second, 'environmental change' is comprised of many different phenomena, spanning different geographical and temporal scales. Third, because the EACH-FOR project placed such importance on an *ex post* methodology, the ability of subjects to perceive change required them to be at a boundary where change could be observed – either a physical boundary, such as the desert noticeably advancing onto a subject's field, for example, or a noticeable time boundary, such as a violent storm or an exceptionally dry period (in a time scale relevant to human memory).

The project foresaw the challenges of attempting to explain the patterns and trends of migration, both international and internal, using only one approach or academic discipline. For example, push factors were frequently mentioned in fieldwork, as migrants sometimes mentioned declining livelihoods from farming at home due to land degradation or erosion, and the sense that a combination of environmental and economic factors contributed to migration. Indeed, Lonergan described migration as 'an extremely varied and complex manifestation and component of equally complex economic, social, cultural, demographic, and political processes operating at the local, regional, national, and international levels' (Lonergan, 1998, p. 6).

It was recognized from the beginning that it might be difficult to interpret research results, as the literature has established that migration outcomes have multiple causal factors. Also, the existing data on migration are uneven, with much of the information based on international migration figures from census data that do not necessarily capture temporal or geographic dynamics of human movement (Afifi and Warner, 2008; Kniveton et al., 2009). This presented a situation in which it would be challenging to measure any difference between migration in the absence of the independent variable and migration in the presence of the independent variable (environmental change). The central method design issue was how to isolate the independent variable in a way that would provide a meaningful statement about the degree to which it (environmental change)

Approaches to researching environmental change and migration 381

affects human mobility. The project examined a wide range of environmental factors across the 23 case studies, further challenging its ability to assess the role of the independent variable in human mobility. The next generation of research, which is explored below in Section 17.5, will find additional ways to isolate the independent variable, assess its change and link those changes to potential or actual changes in the dependent variable. As noted above, pragmatic budgetary and time constraints limited the ability of the project to undertake long-term observations to assess environmental change processes, and how these might affect migration through time.

These facts posed a frame of limitations within which the EACH-FOR project needed to work to produce results. From the outset, the project sought a set of methodologies that would allow for an *ex post* observation (observation after the fact) of whether or not environmental variables affected migration and, if so, how this occurred. One implication of this was that an important part of the EACH-FOR project's work was to gather information about how people perceive the influence of environmental factors on their decision to migrate.

Given these methodological limitations, some scholars recommend not attempting this kind of research, or at least not this 'driver-focused' framing of environmental factors and migration (Black, 2001). However, the EACH-FOR consortium recognized the need to address the knowledge gaps, particularly in light of findings from the Intergovernmental Panel on Climate Change (IPCC) fourth assessment report indicating that the impacts of climate change are expected to increase in the future (IPCC, 2007) which coincided with the project's start. The EACH-FOR project was given the timely opportunity to gather information from the field and report its findings back to a wider academic and policy-centred community. The EACH-FOR project accepted these limitations and shaped itself as a scoping study that would contribute to the building of a basis upon which more rigorous scientific studies could be undertaken. The EACH-FOR project also had several assets it utilized to address some of the practical limitations of completing an ambitious two-year project on a complex research topic. The project had access to good statistical data sources and geo-information, as well as a partnership with numerous local partners, research organizations and international organizations.

17.3.3 Challenge of Defining a Control Group

Both the literature and experts consulted in the methodology design phase emphasized that it would not be surprising to find that the environment was one of many factors that contributed to migration (Castles, 2002;

Faist, 2007). The project struggled to find ways to isolate the independent variable(s) in order to create a research design that would develop comparable, internally valid results. The ideal design would have allowed for the isolation of intervention groups and control groups in every case study area, so that the hypothesis could be established or rejected in each case. Two practical difficulties arose. First, the researcher could not randomly assign individuals into the two groups. Second, it was unclear as to how to isolate a control group in each case that does not experience environmental change. Some case studies offered conditions in which some parts of the country experienced a particular kind of environmental change, while other areas remained intact. Examples of these will be offered below in the context of specific case studies. A pre-test (assessment of the migration situation before environmental change was introduced) was not possible, due to limited time and budget, and the more important fact that it is impossible to control the independent variable.

This left the project with a significant design limitation: could it attempt to define a control group against which the intervention group could be compared? Without a control group in each case, how would the project know whether migration would or would not have happened, even in the absence of environmental change without a control group? In other words, without a control group that was sure not to have experienced environmental change, how could the project establish whether there was an environmental signal in migration patterns?

Faced with the challenge of defining meaningful control groups, the project instead defined eight central questions to guide interviews during fieldwork (listed in Section 17.3.1). It was hoped that the answers to these questions would aid researchers in determining the validity of the hypothesis in the absence of true control groups.

17.3.4 Measuring the Intervention and Control Group

EACH-FOR researchers tried to find ways to establish whether migration would not have occurred in the absence of environmental change. To test whether there was indeed an impact on migration when the environment became less hospitable, the project had a three-step procedure: first, desk research was undertaken to examine historical patterns of both environmental change and migration; second, expert interviews were conducted to help capture the dynamics of environmental change and how this might have affected human mobility in the past and current situation in a given case study; and, finally, a questionnaire was given to migrants and non-migrants who had stayed behind in areas with documented cases of environmental degradation.

Approaches to researching environmental change and migration 383

This latter comparison of migrants and non-migrants was hoped to reveal answers to the central question of the project: what role has environmental degradation or change played in people's decision to migrate or not migrate? For those individuals that remained behind, the project was keen to understand what factors intervened to keep people from migrating, even when they faced environmental problems. It was hoped that this set of answers would help researchers verify or reject the hypothesis, and also help measure the environmental signal in migration patterns (especially in relation to other factors).

17.3.5 Controlling for Threats to Validity of Project Findings

The project considered several designs to help control for threats to validity and increase the internal and external validity of results. An *ex post facto* design and a 'static group comparison design' were particularly considered. In the end the *ex post facto* design was chosen. The reasons for this choice are discussed below.

The *ex post facto* design is used when a single group of people is measured on some dependent variable (migration) after an intervention (environmental change) has taken place. This research design is often used when it is impossible to manipulate the dependent variable (migration). The researcher tries to evaluate the experiment by interviewing people (observation) and assessing the impact of the intervention. This design involves no pre-test or control group – two characteristics that fit the situation of the EACH-FOR project. Yet this research design makes it difficult to be sure that the observations from fieldwork are the result of some particular intervention (environmental change). In spite of this weakness, the *ex post facto* design has the potential to produce powerful intuitive results based on numerous migrant responses about environmental factors that contributed to household migration decisions.

The project considered an alternative research design: the two-group post-test design. In this design, the researcher has no control over assignment of participants. This leaves the static group comparison design open to irresolvable validity threat. There is no way of telling whether the two groups were comparable at time 1, before the intervention, even with a comparison of observations 1 and 3. The researchers can only guess whether the intervention caused any differences in the groups in time 2. The short nature of the project (24 months) weighed against the nature of the independent variable (environmental change, which may happen abruptly or gradually or not at all in a discernible way in 24 months) and did not offer significant advantages over the *ex post facto* research design.

384 *Handbook of research methods in migration*

17.4 CHALLENGES ENCOUNTERED IN APPLYING THE PROJECT APPROACH IN FIELDWORK

Following the design stage, the EACH-FOR project undertook fieldwork in 23 areas across the world to try and apply the methods described above. The aim was, to the extent possible, to produce a set of globally comparable case studies. This section examines some of the fieldwork experiences using this methodology in the case study countries portrayed in Figure 17.1.

17.4.1 Fieldwork Approach

To explore the questions outlined in Section 17.3.1 of this chapter, the EACH-FOR project asked experts, migrants and non-migrants about their perceptions of environmental factors and whether these factors had any relationship with the decision to migrate or not to migrate. Where participants answered positively, this was considered as evidence that environmental factors were perceived as having played a role in migration (discernible).

At the outset of each field study, field researchers visited experts and institutions in the case study country (usually in capital cities). It was hoped that these experts could assist in 'ground truthing' background preparation and offer more specific insights about the overall country situation, the kinds of policies that affect environmental degradation and migration, and feedback about identification of locations where migrant questionnaires could be conducted fruitfully within the countries. The experts sought were usually in government ministries of agriculture, environment, justice (dealing with border issues, migration), and disaster risk management and humanitarian assistance. Non-governmental organizations (NGOs), international organizations and local academics provided further inputs at this stage of field research. In many of the field studies, the IOM played a critical role in linking EACH-FOR researchers with these local experts. Where possible and appropriate, the IOM accompanied researchers in several case studies and helped provide input about the local context about some of the facts that were gathered. Field researchers used sampling techniques such as the snowball method to identify migrants who had departed a situation of 'sudden' or 'gradual' environmental change. Field researchers also tried to assess the situation of potential migration, by looking for contacts with people or groups who had not departed the same situation of sudden or gradual environmental change (control) for particular reasons but who might migrate in the future.

Even in the preparation phase for fieldwork, the project identified several limitations of field questionnaires (one developed for migrants and one for non-migrants) and interviews. These general limitations of the EACH-FOR project in establishing the relationship between the independent variables (types of environmental degradation) and the dependent variable (migration) included limits in fieldwork budgets. This constrained time spent in case study areas and placed constraints on gathering extensive field observations. Ultimately each case study gathered 30 or more migrant and non-migrant interviews per case study, in addition to 15 or more expert interviews. On average, field researchers gathered about 65 observations per case study area, and some case studies gathered substantially more observations. Over the full project, about 1500 observations/surveys were gathered from migrants and non-migrants who indicated that environmental factors had played some role in their decision to migrate. As the number of questionnaires in each case study area was limited and sampling techniques not exhaustive, EACH-FOR results do not lend themselves to robust statistical analysis. The general trends do provide insights, however, about decisions to migrate (or not) related to environmental processes.

17.4.2 Confounding Factors in Fieldwork

The project managed several confounding factors that could threaten the validity of project findings. The general purpose of the methodology design activity in EACH-FOR was to provide guidelines that would help produce comparable data from fieldwork, while taking into account the diverse field conditions in the 23 case study areas. It was considered advantageous for the project to define the eight research questions, and then use a few standard methods complemented by methods tailored to local conditions.

The EACH-FOR project involved multiple case studies, research teams and field workers, and it created a comparable questionnaire for both migrants and non-migrants, as well as guidelines for semi-structured expert interviews.[2] The questionnaires were pre-tested in an early case study and then adjusted and revised before all other case study work began. All investigators received field guidelines about how to work with participants/interviewees, record their results and interpret the results (to ensure interpreter reliability). Yet the reality of fieldwork inevitably led some researchers to change wording to meet local conditions. Language translation further exacerbated the instrumentation confound, and complicated the interpretation and comparison of results from one case study to another. This created locally specific and useful case studies with a moderate degree of comparability.

To address language and local context challenges, EACH-FOR worked in many case study countries with the IOM in local in-country offices, and in all case study countries with local researchers and experts. IOM and local experts, to the extent possible, were engaged as partners prior to the fieldwork commencing. They played a crucial role as locally based partners in identifying and establishing initial contact with relevant experts, arranging logistics and assisting with translation and implementation of the EACH-FOR questionnaire. A key contact point within the IOM was established as the main interpreter and assistant for the duration of the field research in all three locations.

17.4.3 Non-probability Sampling Technique

One of the most significant confounding factors was the possibility of selection bias (that is, no control group, no random assignment and no control over assignment of participants to groups). The project limitations did not allow for a random sample of a large population of people. Field researchers were looking for people exposed to environmental problems in order to ask whether those problems affected the participants' decisions about whether or not to migrate. In most cases, researchers were only able to interview people from a limited number of areas, due to time and budget constraints. Expert interviews and desk studies were used to help balance the sampling biases that would emerge in migrant and non-migrant questionnaires.

A non-probability sampling method was chosen because it was suitable for research during which the population of interest is not fully visible and where accurately defining the population of interest is problematic. This sampling method is used frequently in sociological studies in hidden populations involved in sensitive issues, and in the study of human systems where factors with the most influence in a system are not necessarily those whose exact characteristics are known. This method fitted the nature of the problem: to better understand the impact of a little-understood variable (environmental change) on decisions relating to migration.

The snowball, or chain-referral, sampling method was used in the project. Researchers identified an initial set of relevant respondents in pre-fieldwork preparations. During field interviews, researchers requested that participants suggest other potential subjects who shared similar characteristics or had relevance in some way to the object of study. This second set of subjects was then interviewed, and also requested to supply names of other potential interview subjects. The process continued until the individual researcher felt that the sample was large enough for the purposes of the study (a minimum of 15 expert interviews and 30 migrant and 30 non-migrant interviews was performed in each case study). The limited amount of time for each case study – an average of seven weeks – prevented an exhaustive sampling.

The researcher for each case study was directly involved in developing and managing the initiation and progress of the sample. Each researcher sought to ensure that the chain of referrals remained within boundaries that were relevant to the study. Researchers were instructed to ensure that the initial set of respondents was sufficiently diverse so that the sample was not skewed excessively in any one particular direction (Tansey, 2006, p. 12).

17.4.4 Multiple Field Objectives and Tasks[3]

While there was one overall field research goal (that of investigating whether there were linkages between the environment and migration), there were several field research objectives, as mentioned above in Section 17.2. The focus on whether there was a link between environment and migration meant that the field research did not strike a balance in terms of exploring the range of other reasons why people migrated. The project attempted to address each objective with the questionnaire, semi-structured migrant and non-migrant interviews and interviews with experts. Yet each of the field objectives could require a specific type of methodology.

The fieldwork was a scoping exercise, but one that did not allow for repeat visits to follow up on information gathered. Researchers also had the difficult task of conducting both expert interviews, migrant and non-migrant interviews and questionnaires within the field research phase. There was little time for analysis of expert interviews before the researchers interviewed migrants and non-migrants. At times, for example, the researchers obtained crucial pieces of information from experts, following interviews with migrants – information that would have been useful to know before interviewing migrants.

17.4.5 Timing Issues: Gap(s) between Environmental Events and Site Visits[4]

Researchers found that the more recently a particular locality had experienced the environmental problem or issue under investigation, the more people in that locality were aware of the situation. Therefore, they were able to discuss their recent experience as a factor leading to livelihood impacts and possible migration or resettlement. For example, in the EACH-FOR Mozambique case study, communities in flood-prone areas had experienced the 2007 flooding event six months prior to the researcher's visit (Stal, 2009). On the other hand, in the Viet Nam case study, the last major disaster flood in the Mekong Delta occurred in 2000 (Dun, 2009). Considering that the research was conducted seven years later, it was more difficult to pinpoint the exact migratory impacts of that particular event, despite the fact that people could clearly remember the event.

In addition, the personal experience of a migrant or non-migrant with the environmental event in the past also played a significant role in shaping research findings. For example, in Mozambique, interviews were carried out with people who had experienced multiple flooding events. This revealed a change in attitude towards migration or resettlement from temporary evacuation to permanent resettlement. The affected people accepted the fact that they should not move back to their places of origin. Similarly, in Viet Nam, the researcher found that the impacts of repeated flooding (as opposed to a unique flooding event) could play a crucial role in prompting people to migrate.

Since gradual environmental change is a constant part of life in Niger, the time gap between environmental events and the site visit did not play a significant role in influencing the results of migrant interviews (Afifi, 2009). Even in the cases of the severe droughts of 1973 and 1984, farmers and cattle herders have continued to suffer from the cumulative impacts of those events.

Another timing issue that had to be taken into account was the daytime and seasonal timing, especially for rapid research, for interviewing migrants/non-migrants in the field location. For example, the researchers in Mozambique and Niger found that the farmers and cattle herders were only available in the villages at certain times of the day and the year (Afifi, 2009; Stal, 2009). Likewise, when the farmers living along the Zambezi River Valley were busy seeding their almost inaccessible fields, it was mainly the elders and the children who were interviewed. In the case of Niger, the researcher visited the country in the dry season (January/February 2008), during which time many farmers wander with their cattle to other regions that were not covered in the field visit. Therefore, the researcher had to rely on interviews with people who stayed in the Tilabéri region, as well as people in the capital.

17.5 CONSIDERATIONS FOR FURTHER ENVIRONMENT–MIGRATION RESEARCH

EACH-FOR gathered empirical observations and contributed to the building of a research agenda for investigating the complex relationships between environmental factors and migration (Stal and Warner, 2009; Warner and Laczko, 2008). Future research will certainly improve on these efforts and increase the level and quality of information available about these relationships. Some considerations may help guide the design of research methodologies for further investigation.

A spectrum of emerging tools for further research is available – from macro-level to micro-level approaches. We have identified several possible approaches from recent literature, although many more exist. To gain a global or regional overview, Perch-Nielson et al. (2008) and others illustrate the possibility of linking climate and environmental models with migration models. Other researchers have begun introducing environmental variables into geographic regression models (Afifi and Warner, 2008; Barrios et al., 2006; Neumayer, 2005), including a multi-level approach that simultaneously uses area and individual data (Henry et al., 2004). A particularly promising area appears to be simulation with agent-based modelling (Kniveton et al., 2009).

There are gaps in the general understanding about the migration and environment nexus due to gaps in methods and lack of data. Research on environmental triggers and drivers that affect human mobility should focus on the following research questions:

- How to characterize/analyse/quantify the sensitivity of multiple interacting drivers of migration to environmental changes?
- Under what conditions do environmental drivers trigger migration?
- How to develop a menu of interventions to deal with people sensitive to environmental changes and who have the potential to become environmentally induced migrants?

17.5.1 Research Questions and Hypotheses

Methods and approaches that find ways to isolate the role of environmental variables in the migration decision are needed. For example, it is widely accepted in the literature that environmental factors usually accompany other factors (particularly economic) that contribute to the ability of poor people to sustain their livelihoods. Environmental problems often accompany economic factors that affect migration, but economic factors do not necessarily accompany environmental problems in affecting migration. The results from the EACH-FOR project point in one direction. Future research may find effective ways to begin isolating environmental variables in certain cases from others, particularly economic. A case study in which environmental variables were present, but economic variables were not clearly present as drivers of migration, would be a starting point in developing methods for better isolating the role of environmental variables in migration. This type of research would also strengthen the ability to create falsifiable hypotheses.

Another way to help isolate environmental variables in the migration decision would be to test different typologies of environmentally induced migration (see, for example, Renaud et al., 2007; Renaud et al., 2009). It would be useful to have a clearer understanding of the role of sudden and gradual or creeping environmental processes in migration processes. Defining the parameters for environmental change (natural catastrophes, output of the land, desertification and so on) would increase the comparative strength of empirical research. For instance, a research project that looked at comparable areas with desertification and without desertification could form hypotheses about whether or not migration would occur in both locations to the same extent, and then test the hypothesis through empirical study. Use of objective information sources, such as satellite imagery, may provide an additional means of improving the validity of research results from subjective sources, such as migrant interviews.

17.5.2 Satellite Imagery and Participatory Fieldwork Methods to Combine Qualitative and Quantitative Approaches

Qualitative and quantitative data need to be combined and should feed into different methodological approaches, such as multi-level statistical analysis, agent based modelling, micro simulations or systems dynamic models. The research on environmental triggers and drivers that affect human mobility should improve the interpretation/understanding of the results through ethnographic/qualitative work, working closely with local communities, collecting and sharing the gathered information.

In order to characterize, analyse and quantify the sensitivity of multiple interacting drivers of migration, future research needs to answer these research questions with a certain degree of generality. Experts recommend that research should further develop case studies, using approaches that focus on quantitative and qualitative data collection and continuing methodological development. Another focus for future research should be to develop new methods for assessing the current situation and understanding the impacts on social development, conflicts and security. Case studies will also help to highlight best practice solutions and exchange experience.

17.5.3 Census, Combined Use of Socio-economic and Environmental Data

Census data has to be used and analysed with respect to the research question(s). In addition, multi-level data based on specific areas have to be gathered. Ethnographically informed large samples of individual data should be assembled, such as social demographic, capital bases, or data based on migration history. In addition, improved local indicators of the environmental, climatic and economic situation in the area are needed. An integrated assessment of environmental impacts on migration behaviour could be attempted in scale-dependent and context-dependent monitoring mechanisms.

To gain more comparable and geographically specific insights, longitudinal research needs to be undertaken with panel studies of the evolution of the environment and of the migration behaviour (Massey et al., 2007). Looking back, historical analogues can provide insights into coping mechanisms and tipping points beyond which coupled human-ecological systems began to break down (McLeman and Smit, 2006; Piguet, 2008). Other authors have, with reasonable success, developed indices of vulnerability to localize 'hotspots' of environmental change and migration (Dasgupta et al., 2007; Kuriakose et al., 2009; Thow and de Blois, 2008). Finally, empirical fieldwork such as that performed by EACH-FOR, particularly using a combination of survey and ethnographic study methods, will provide detail and help build hypotheses about the relationships between the multiple factors affecting migration.These indicators of potential drivers of migration and their interactions with other factors would help in answering questions related to environmental triggers, drivers and migration behaviour.

The collection of this data and indicators could be approached within a panel study including migration observatories monitoring a sub-sample of people at regular intervals. Additionally, more empirical studies on the basis of existing work will help to fill the data gaps. As a starting point for future empirical evidence, a meta-analysis of existing literature could serve as a basis and be used to scale up good practice. Additional empirical evidence could also be used to develop and expand the treatment of environmental factors into new or existing migration theories (Lazcko and Warner, 2008).

Methods and project design are rarely free from considerations of funding. Ideally, funding will become available for longer-term longitudinal studies that would allow for the establishment of a globally comparable set of data on environmental change and migration. Case studies could continue to provide rich localized insights that may be aggregated and compared in meta-analyses.

17.6 CONCLUSIONS

This chapter has described the attempt of the first global survey of environmental change and human migration/mobility to design and use a comparable method across 23 case studies worldwide. The benefits of the approach were to gather qualitative feedback and observations about the many ways that environmental factors can influence human mobility. This work has contributed to understanding current as well as potential trends in environmentally induced migration. The project faced significant method design issues, of which the isolation of the independent variable and understanding the complex interactions between the independent and dependent variable beyond the local scale were the two most prominent challenges.

Future research will combine Earth observation techniques that help build more robust time series on various kinds of environmental change with qualitative case studies. Such approaches can provide more precise insights about the relationships between factors such as rainfall variability over time, crop yields and livelihood management strategies that include migration. This new generation of methodological tools will add to the emerging and rich literature about the interaction of the many factors that affect human migration.

NOTES

1. See Siegel (Chapter 22, this volume) for further discussion about coordinating major migration research projects.
2. The migrant and non-migrant questionnaires can be found online at http://www.each-for.eu/index.php?module=project_outline.
3. Parts of Section 17.4.4 come from Warner et al. (2009b, p. 219).
4. Parts of Section 17.4.5 come from Warner et al. (2009b, pp. 226–7).

REFERENCES

Afifi, T. (2009), 'Niger Case Study Report for the Environmental Change and Forced Migration Scenarios project', available at http://www.each-for.eu (accessed 16 July 2011).
Afifi, T. and Warner, K. (2008), 'The impact of environmental degradation on migration flows across countries', UNU-EHS Working Paper No. 1.
Barrios, S., Bertinelli, L. and Strobl, E. (2006), 'Climatic change and rural–urban migration: the case of sub-Saharan Africa', *Journal of Urban Economics,* **60** (3), 357–71.
Biermann, F. (2007), 'Earth system governance as a crosscutting theme of global change research', *Global Environmental Change,* **17**, 326–37.
Black, R. (2001), 'Environmental refugees: myth or reality?', New Issues in Refugee

Research, Working Paper No. 34, University of Sussex, Brighton, available at http://www.unhcr.org/3ae6a0d00.html (accessed 6 February 2012).

Boano, C., Zetter, R. and Morris, T. (2008), 'Environmentally displaced people: understanding the linkages between environmental change, livelihoods and forced migration', Forced Migration Policy Briefing 1, Refugee Studies Centre, Department of International Development, University of Oxford.

Bogardi, J. and Warner, K. (2008), 'Here comes the flood. Nature. Nature reports climate change', 11 December, doi:10.1038/climate.2008.138.

Brown, O. (2008), 'Migration and climate change', IOM Migration Research Series No. 31, International Organization for Migration, Geneva.

Castles, S. (2002), 'Environmental change and forced migration: making sense of the debate', New Issues in Refugee Research, Working Paper No. 70, United Nations High Commissioner for Refugees (UNHCR), Geneva.

Conisbee, M. and Simms, A. (2003), *Environmental Refugees. The Case for Recognition*, London: New Economics Foundation.

Dasgupta, S., Laplante, B., Meisner, C., Wheeler, D. and Yan, J. (2007), 'The impact of sea level rise on developing countries: a comparative analysis', World Bank Policy Research Working Paper No. 4136, The World Bank, Washington, DC.

Döös, B. (1997), 'Can large-scale environmental migrations be predicted?', *Global Environmental Change*, 7 (1), 41–61.

Dun, O. (2009), 'Linkages between flooding, migration and resettlement, Vietnam case study report for the Environmental Change and Forced Migration Scenarios project', available at http://www.each-for.eu (accessed 16 July 2011).

Dun, O. and Gemenne, F. (2008), 'Defining environmental migration', *Forced Migration Review*, 31, 10–11.

El-Hinnawi, E. (1985), *Environmental Refugees*, Nairobi: United Nations Environment Programme.

Faist, T. (2007), Personal communication on the validity of EACH-FOR methodology and field questionnaire, 14 August.

Gunderson, L.H. and Holling, C.S. (2002), *Panarch – Understanding Transformations in Systems of Humans and Nature*, Washington, DC: Island Press.

Henry, S., Shoumaker, B. and Beauchemin, C. (2004), 'The impact of rainfall on the first out-migration: a multi-level event-history analysis in Burkina Faso', *Population and Environment*, 25, 423–60.

Homer-Dixon, T.F. (1994), 'Environmental scarcities and violent conflict', *International Security*, 19, 1–40.

Hussein, K. and Nelson, J. (1998), 'Sustainable livelihoods and livelihood desertification', Working Paper No. 69, Institute of Development Studies, Brighton, UK.

International Organization for Migration (IOM) (2007), 'Discussion note: migration and the environment (MC/INF/288 – 1 November 2007 – 94th Session)', International Organization for Migration, Geneva, 14 February.

Intergovernmental Panel on Climate Change (IPCC) (2007), *Working Group II Contribution to the Intergovernmental Panel on Climate Change Fourth Assessment Report Climate Change 2007: Climate Change Impacts, Adaptation and Vulnerability Summary for Policymakers*, Cambridge: Cambridge University Press.

Jäger, J., Frühmann, J., Günberger, S. and Vag, A. (2009), *Environmental Change and Forced Migration Scenarios Project Synthesis Report*, Deliverable D.3.4 for the European Commission.

Kniveton, D., Schmidt-Verkerk, K., Smith, C. and Black, R. (2009), 'Climate change and migration: improving methodologies to estimate flows', IOM Migration Research Series No. 33, International Organization for Migration, Geneva.

Kuriakose, A.T., Bizikova, L. and Bachofen, C.A. (2009), 'Assessing vulnerability and adaptive capacity to climate risks: methods for investigation at local and national levels', World Bank Social Development Papers, Social Dimensions of Climate Change, No. 116, May.

Lazcko, F. and Warner, K. (2008), 'Migration, environment and development: new directions for research', in J. Chamie and L. Dall'Oglio (eds), *International Migration and Development, Continuing the Dialogue: Legal and Policy Perspectives*, New York and Geneva: International Organization for Migration and Center for Migration Studies (CMS), pp 59–60.
Lonergan, S. (1998), *The Role of Environmental Degradation in Population Displacement. Global Environmental Change and Security Project Report*, Research Report 1, July, 2nd edn, British Columbia, Canada: University of Victoria.
Martin, S. and Warner, K. (2010), 'Climate change and migration: findings of the transatlantic study team', German Marshall Fund Study Team on Climate Change and Migration, German Marshall Fund, September, available at http://www.ehs.unu.edu/article/read/gmf.
Massey, D., Axinn, W. and Ghimire, D. (2007), *Environmental Change and Out-migration: Evidence from Nepal*, Population Studies Center Research Report 07-615, January.
McLeman, R. and Smit, B. (2006), 'Migration as an adaptation to climate change', *Climatic Change*, **76**, 31–53.
Neumayer, E. (2005), 'Bogus refugees? The determinants of asylum migration to Western Europe', *International Studies Quarterly*, **49**, 389–410.
Perch-Nielsen, S.L., Bättig, M.B. and Imboden, D. (2008), 'Exploring the link between climate change and migration', *Climatic Change*, **91**, 375–93.
Piguet, E. (2008), *Climate Change and Forced Migration: How can International Policy Respond to Climate-induced Displacement?*, Geneva: UNHCR Evaluation and Policy Analysis Unit.
Renaud, F.G., Bogardi, J.J., Dun, O. and Warner, K. (2007), *Control, Adapt or Flee: How to Face Environmental Migration?*, Bonn: United Nations University Institute for Environment and Human Security.
Renaud, F.G., Dun, O., Warner, K. and Bogardi, J.J. (2009), 'Deciphering the importance of environmental factors in human migration', Paper submitted to *International Migration*.
Stal, M. (2009), 'Mozambique case study report for the Environmental Change and Forced Migration Scenarios Project', available at http://www.each-for.eu (accessed 16 July 2011).
Stal, M. and Warner, K. (2009), 'The way forward researching the environment and migration nexus', UNU-EHS Research Brief based on the Outcomes of the 2nd Expert Workshop on Climate Change, Environment, and Migration, 23–24 July, United Nations University, Munich, October.
Tansey, O. (2006), 'Process tracing and elite interviewing: a case for non-probability sampling', available at http://www.nuff.ox.ac.uk/politics/papers/2006/tansey.pdf (accessed 16 July 2011).
Thow, A. and de Blois, M. (2008), *Climate Change and Human Vulnerability: Mapping Emerging Trends and Risk Hotspots for Humanitarian Actors*, Report to the UN Office for Coordination of Humanitarian Affairs (OCHA), Geneva: Maplecroft, OCHA, CARE.
UNIBI (2008), 'D.2.7.1 state of the art report. EACH-FOR project', available at http://www.each-for.eu/documents/EACH-FOR_D.2.7.1_State_of_the_Art_Report.pdf (accessed 16 July 2011).
Vag, A., Faist, T., Enzinger, H, Jäger, J. and Bogardi, J. (2007), *Research Guidelines Book 1, Version 3*, Working document, EACH-FOR Work Package 3: Methodology & Synthesis, available at http://www.each-for.eu (accessed 16 July 2011).
Warner, K. and Laczko, F. (2008), 'A global research agenda. Climate change and displacement', *Forced Migration Review*, **31**, 59–60.
Warner, K., Dun, O. and Stal, M. (2008), 'Field observations and empirical research. Climate change and displacement', *Forced Migration Review*, **31**, 13–14.
Warner, K., Erhart, C., de Sherbinin, A., Adamo, S.B. and Onn, T.C. (2009a), 'In search of shelter: mapping the effects of climate change on human migration and displacement,' Policy paper prepared for the 2009 Climate Negotiations, Bonn, United Nations University, CARE and CIESIN-Columbia University and in close collaboration with

the European Commission's 'Environmental Change and Forced Migration Scenarios Project', the UNHCR and The World Bank.
Warner, K., Afifi, T, Stal, M. and Dun, O. (2009b), 'Researching environmental change and migration: evaluation of EACH-FOR methodology and application in 23 case studies worldwide', in F. Laczko and C. Aghazarm (eds), *Migration, Environment and Climate Change: Assessing the Evidence*, Geneva: IOM, pp. 197–241.

18 Chasing ghosts: researching illegality in migrant labour markets
Bridget Anderson, Ben Rogaly and Martin Ruhs

The issue of migrant 'illegality' and labour markets is the subject of intense policy concern and public debate in Britain and many other high-income countries. Fears of migrants working illegally and thereby undercutting domestic workers (and legally resident migrants), or concerns about exploitation of vulnerable workers by unscrupulous employers have been given fresh impetus by economic recession. Yet the evidence for these concerns is limited. Data is poor, and the analysis of the impacts of migrants on labour markets is highly complex, even without introducing the additional element of legal status. It is clearly an area where research is needed, but it is also one which is dogged with complexity, theoretically and in practice. Thus the methodological challenges are not simply logistical, but reflect broader theoretical and political issues.

Academics from a wide range of disciplines have been engaging in research on illegality and immigration. Their contributions (geographers, sociologists, economists, anthropologists, political scientists, philosophers, to name but a few), have tended towards a qualitative/quantitative division. There is an interest in estimating the size and economic impact of the population of illegally resident migrants, often using standard sources of demographic data though, particularly in the USA, also by generating new data. There are particular interests from policy actors in this kind of quantitative research. There have also been small-scale qualitative studies, principally with migrants, but occasionally with employers. As yet the mixed method approach advocated by prominent migration scholar Douglas Massey has been relatively undeveloped with the exception of research around trafficking, which has tended to combine numerical estimates – often rather unreliable (United States Government Accountability Office, 2006) – with a case study approach.

This chapter makes the case for a mixed methods approach to the study of illegality in migrant labour markets. It focuses on two core challenges for research into the connection between migrants' legal status and labour markets: (1) defining illegal status (and immigration status more generally) and (2) analysis and interpretation. We discuss these challenges and how mixed methods can respond to these challenges by way of a case study, using a research project on the effect of European Union (EU) Enlargement on the living and working conditions of East European migrants in the UK, conducted at the University of Oxford research centre, the Centre on Migration, Policy and Society (COMPAS) during 2004–06.

18.1 THE CHALLENGES

What, exactly, is meant by 'illegal immigration'? Is it a policy problem to be solved, or an inevitable phenomenon characterizing territorially bounded states in the global economy? Is it an end state, a category or a process? And what terminology is appropriate to use? The contested nature of the adjectives attached to migrants who are the subject of these studies and policies – undocumented, irregular, clandestine, unauthorized, trafficked, *sans papières* and so on – is an indication of the intensely politicized nature of claims to knowledge and analysis. The terms used may in themselves indicate a particular political position. For states, 'illegality' is often regarded as a problem to be solved through stronger borders (internal and external), strict enforcement of immigration controls and increasing co-operation between the state and civil society. However, there is also a strong current in civil society that is more sympathetic to the vulnerability of 'undocumented migrants'. While recognizing its political limitations and controversies, for the purposes of this chapter we have chosen to use the term 'illegal'. This is not meant to reflect a value judgement on our part, but it is useful as a reminder that '(il)legality' is a status constituted through the operation of law (de Genova, 2002). We have, however, refrained from the use of quotation marks, for ease of reading.

Terminological debates risk obscuring the issue of definitions, which are a key challenge in research, policy and activism on illegality. There are serious definitional issues even with the terminology of '(im)migrant' in national datasets. These typically use definitions such as 'foreign born' or 'foreign national' which often do not match the policy tools that governments have to manage migration. For example, some foreign-born people are citizens of the host country, and, in the case of EU member states, some foreign nationals are EU citizens, and so not affected by immigration legislation.[1] The question of who counts as a migrant is not susceptible to a simple answer and those who are working illegally is a troubled subset of an already vague category.

The research project, Changing Status, Changing Lives?, focused on particular foreign nationals who, at the time we started our research, were subject (as a group) to immigration controls (this changed with EU

Enlargement when some of our interviewees became EU nationals and hence not subject to immigration controls). One of the advantages of limiting the study to people who were 'subject to immigration controls' at a particular period was that it indicated the importance of legal status, and more particularly that the interest was in people who have 'immigration status'. Immigration status indicates the absence, presence and/or conditions of legal residence including any associated employment restrictions. It is a key factor determining rights and responsibilities in the immigration state, including employment and social rights. Most high-income countries are characterized by a multitude of different immigration statuses, each associated with different employment restrictions, and economic and social rights. When researching illegality in migrant labour markets a researcher is concerned with a group of people who are subject to immigration controls. Importantly for the purposes of research into labour markets, the range of these restrictions means that legality of residence does not equate to legality of employment: a migrant may be legally resident but not entitled to access to labour markets; or they may be entitled to work in one sector, but not in another.

Importantly, recognizing the importance of the restrictions attached to being subject to immigration controls means that one cannot ignore the passing of time. Restrictions on legal residence and/or employment may change their nature, or even be lifted, and (il)legal status is not static but changes over time. The state may change the legal status of an individual or group. This could be done, for example, by creating new immigration statuses or by moving people within existing statuses, as was the case when the EU enlarged in May 2004 or, more generally, under any regularization of illegally resident migrants. A migrant's immigration status and legality of employment may also change because of the individual's actions or inactions. Most obviously, migrants can enter legally and overstay, they may regularize their status through marriage, gain citizenship and so on. Research on illegality can take the form of either a 'snapshot' or 'trajectory' and researchers may choose to engage with migrants who are currently working illegally, or with those who have been doing so in the past (Cvajner and Sciortino, 2010). The fundamental point is that illegality has an important temporal component that is all too often ignored in research.

However well defined and instrumentalized, it can be difficult for researchers seeking face-to-face interviews to access those working illegally – even more so, perhaps, those employing illegally – though this is likely to be sectorally and nationality dependent as will be discussed below. Snowball sampling is common, but this limits generalizability. Practical issues such as interviewees' limited time and availability can impoverish data and raise issues of interviewer as well as interviewee physical safety.

Indeed, ethical issues are inescapable (Black, 2003). There are obvious issues to do with the security of the migrants themselves, their anonymity and protection from self-incrimination and deportation, but there are also more difficult matters: for example, what if an interviewee is physically abusing a child or an older person? Or how to handle requests for advice and support when it may be illegal to provide them?

Finally of course there are issues pertaining to analysis and interpretation. Having defined and instrumentalized illegality, how helpful is it as an analytical tool? Can illegality be isolated as a variable? Is the term commensurable when used by different actors (migrants, state actors, employers) even if it has been firmly defined in the research design and practice? And is it possible to capture migrants' subjective experiences of illegality?

Having touched on some of the key challenges associated with researching illegality and labour markets, we will now consider them with reference to a particular research project, with a particular focus on definitions and analysis.

18.2 RESEARCHING LEGAL STATUS: CHANGING STATUS, CHANGING LIVES?

The research project Changing Status, Changing Lives? was motivated by the accession of ten new countries to the EU on 1 May 2004. The ten accession states included the 'A8' countries – Czech Republic, Estonia, Hungary, Latvia, Lithuania, Poland, Slovakia and Slovenia – plus Cyprus and Malta. EU Enlargement enabled A8 workers to migrate and take up employment in the UK without restrictions (as long as they registered in the 'Worker Registration Scheme'). It also meant that overnight A8 nationals who were already working in the UK before 1 May 2004 experienced a 'change of status', acquiring most of the rights of an EU national. For A8 nationals residing in the UK illegally, 1 May 2004 was, in effect, an amnesty. EU Enlargement thus provided an ideal opportunity for us to study the role of illegality in the employment of Central and East European migrants in the UK (for detailed findings see Anderson et al., 2006).

Changing Status, Changing Lives? set out to study the consequences of granting most of the economic and social rights of an EU national to A8 nationals who were already working in the UK before 1 May 2004 – with legal or 'illegal' status. A total of 576 face-to-face survey interviews and 93 separate in-depth interviews with Central and East European workers and au pairs in the UK were carried out in two waves, just before EU Enlargement on 1 May 2004 and 6–8 months after. All of the migrants who participated in this study were already working in the UK before EU enlargement. The sample was non-representative and non-randomly selected and had very particular characteristics: they were predominantly young, without dependants, with fluent or adequate English and white. A third were from Bulgaria and the Ukraine, both of which remained outside the EU during the period of our study (Bulgaria joined the EU in 2007) and thus served as a control group of individuals whose immigration status was unaffected by EU Enlargement in May 2004. The other two thirds of our sample of migrants were nationals of Lithuania, Czech Republic, Republic of Slovakia and Poland. All were working in one of four sectors: agriculture, au pairing, construction and hospitality. (More details on the project, including all research instruments, can be found at: http://www.compas.ox.ac.uk/publications/reports/changingstatus/.)

The exploration of some of the research questions, such as the relation between demand for migrant labour and their legal status, clearly lent themselves to quantitative approaches. Moreover, we were interested in having a policy impact, and policymakers, whether government or those more broadly concerned with migrant workers, are more convinced by an analysis and recommendations that contain numbers and statistics than quotations from individuals without the possibility of generalizing from their opinions and experiences.

Research on 'impacts', however, also requires consideration of personal experiences, aspirations, feelings and responses which are more suited to a qualitative approach. Issues that trouble policymakers are not necessarily the same as those that trouble migrants or indeed employers. A survey can provide data on whether or not workers changed employment following a change in immigration status, but in-depth interviews can explore how this change affects whether workers might want to change employment. Both kinds of impact are related to each other, and for a full picture it is important to capture both. The simple responses required by quantitative approaches can iron out some of the uncertainties and complexities of real life that are part of what a research project like this one aims to capture. The complex social lives of individuals, and the power-laden sets of relations within which we all work, cannot be captured in surveys. In particular we anticipated that we would be dealing with particularly complex employment relations that shade into personal relations, overtly with au pairs and through the myriad subcontracting arrangements that are a feature of the other sectors. Exploration of these issues required a qualitative approach.

For these reasons, we attempted to formulate a truly interactive methodology for this project, drawing on quantitative (survey) and qualitative (in-depth interviews and diaries) methods.[2] Both survey and in-depth worker interviews were exploratory and contemporaneous. One did not 'lead' the other but rather some questions were explored predominantly through survey and others chiefly through interview methodology, but both sets of data were drawn on for analysis. In-depth interviews had a quantitative component to enable us to match our qualitative data with our quantitative data when necessary. We also decided on administering the survey interviews face to face and in the first language of the interviewee, rather than using self-completion questionnaires. Survey interviews were therefore a social interaction, which we believe alleviated anxieties about confidentiality when it came to asking questions about legal status, for example. In sum, we chose a flexible, issue-led model, in which we selected our method depending on whether it was the most appropriate for the questions we were exploring, so quantitative and qualitative approaches were combined, not only in the fieldwork, but also during the conceptual design and analysis.

18.3 DEFINITIONS AND ACCESS

Many of the challenges discussed above only became apparent to us as we were doing the research. In the original research design we intended that 50 per cent of survey and in-depth interviews with workers be conducted with those working with permits and 50 per cent with those working illegally. This was to be evenly spread across sectors, so we imagined half of our sample working in construction, for example, would be on permits (in this case, self-employed visas), and half would be working illegally. We recognized from the outset that there would in this case be a problem with classifying student visa holders, who do not have a permit to work, but who, at the time of the research, could work for 20 hours a week in term time, and 40 hours a week out of term. We therefore decided to include student visa holders with those working with permits. Moreover, on reflection it became apparent that there were both methodological and theoretical issues implicated in instrumentalizing who would 'count' as an illegal au pair. Is an illegal au pair the same as being an illegal 'domestic worker'? This might be so in terms of tasks, but having the immigration status of an 'au pair' indicates a particular type of relationship (being treated as a family member) and not simply a task performed. For this reason we decided to interview as au pairs only those who were working with host families and who had not overstayed their au pair visas.

The same access methods were used for both quantitative and qualitative interviewees. Where possible we wanted to avoid accessing workers through their employer for ethical and methodological reasons.[3] We therefore negotiated access with community groups and other gatekeepers. Our interviewers were obvious points of contact with same nationals. Their role in accessing interviewees who trusted them from prior knowledge, and snowballing from these initial contacts was crucial to the success of the project – though we anticipated 'interviewer effects' on the composition of our sample. Many (though not all) of our interviewers were students: realizing that this might lead to an over-sampling of students if interviewers relied on their immediate networks, we placed a limit on the number of those on student visas to be interviewed. These were the easiest migrants for this group of interviewers to find, in contrast to au pairs, who seemed to have little social contact with students. Moreover, this approach did not work for agriculture, a sector in which workers' housing can be relatively remote and can change across the year, and hence where our urban-based interviewers had few contacts. Time constraints (the importance of completing our first interviews by 1 May in spite of the project having begun just two months earlier) meant that we therefore had no option but to approach workers through their employers for the agricultural sector. Partly as a consequence we were not able to interview agricultural workers working outside the terms of their immigration status or without any such status. In contrast to the difficulties in the agricultural sector, in the hospitality sector it proved difficult to find migrants who were working legally. While there was a Sector-Based Scheme visa which enabled migrants to work in low-waged jobs in hospitality, it proved very difficult for us to locate them.

The 'balanced' sample that we had originally envisaged in practice, even though non-random, would have required considerably more time with more varied means of access. This was not possible given the 'natural experiment' model of our research design.

18.3.1 Popping the Question: Asking about Status

A key methodological issue in researching illegality is being able to ask the interviewee or respondent about their immigration status, and having confidence in the validity of response. One cannot assume legal status simply on the grounds of citizenship or type of work. Of course, given that our interviewers were looking for particular groups of workers, and legal status was a key element in this, it was usually something they had informally ascertained before the interview or survey, but this is not sufficiently robust. How one deals with this problem varies between qualitative and quantitative methodologies, however both must be sensitive to the issues of language and translation. On an individual basis, a person might describe themselves as 'irregular' rather than 'undocumented', for instance, but more generally the connotations of terminology might be different when translated. These issues were discussed at some length between native speakers of the relevant languages in the process of translating research instruments.

The fact that the survey instrument was designed to be conducted face to face alleviated some of the difficulties that might be associated with asking about status in surveys, in particular non-response. We had six questions directly addressing immigration status in our survey, three concerned with status on entry, or channel of immigration; and three with current status. We carefully formulated and sequenced the relevant questions in order to encourage 'matter of fact' answers, rather than trying to induce blunt 'admissions' of illegality. The final question of the sequence however asked: What is your immigration status?, and included, as one of its 11 options, 'visa expired'. Eighty-nine out of 548 respondents classified themselves in this way. It was possible to triangulate data on this question with other responses (date of entry, visa held, whether they had since left the UK and so on) and when we did so we found the data on self-reported status to be internally consistent. This, together with the high response rate (548 out of 576) arguably suggests that our approach worked reasonably well.

For in-depth interviews, immigration status was ascertained more indirectly, with interviewers instructed to probe when appropriate within an exploration of the migratory process how people came to be working in the UK. For example:

Interviewer: Did you choose any particular kind of visa or did you come as a tourist?
Interviewee: As a tourist.
Interviewer: Why did you choose to come this way?
Interviewee: Because I thought that it was the easiest one. Because generally I wasn't thinking about paying the school here. Because if I had paid for some language course or I don't know how it looks, I could apply for a student visa and I would have it and I would be able to work legally part-time. But I thought this was the simplest way.

The interviewer later ascertained that the interviewee had not left the country or married, nor made any efforts to change his status. It could therefore be deduced that he was continuing to work on a tourist visa (in this case in construction).

Both approaches required that the people administering the instruments underwent training in relevant immigration matters. This was particularly true for the qualitative interviewers, as they had to be aware of the ramifications of the responses that they were getting and if they were likely to impact on immigration status.

18.4 DATA ANALYSIS

18.4.1 Quantitative Approaches and Counting Illegality

A further factor making it difficult to implement our initial plan of interviewing regular and irregular migrants in roughly equal numbers became clear only after the data had been collected and we had started to analyse it. Although used in many academic and public debates, the classification of migrants into a simple binary of legal/illegal is extremely difficult. This is a particular issue for us as researchers interested in the impact of legal status on experiences and conditions of the labour market. While most existing data defines illegality in terms of illegal residency, this is not sufficient to delineate our target group. As mentioned above, legality of residence is not sufficient to ensure legality of employment. A person who has a non-expired visitor's visa, for example, may be working illegally even though they are legally resident.[4]

Take the example of student visa holders. We had already ascertained that these posed a sampling issue for us and had opted to include them as 'legally working' migrants. However, the data revealed a far more complex situation. They were only permitted to work 20 hours a week in term time, yet the majority were working for longer, sometimes far longer, than that. How then could one characterize a student visa holder who is working 25 hours a week? Or 40 hours a week? This kind of problem was not restricted to student visa holders. Almost all the au pairs surveyed and interviewed did part-time cleaning or babysitting in other households, or sometimes bar and hospitality work. This is not permitted under the conditions pertaining to au pair visas, and despite its widespread nature would technically mean that the au pair visa holders could be removed from the UK. It was clear from our data that a significant proportion of our sample, while legally resident, was working in breach of their conditions of entry.

To account for this contested space of (il)legality, we distinguished between three levels of compliance with immigration controls. 'Compliant' migrants were legally resident and working in full compliance with the employment restrictions attached to their immigration status. 'Non-compliant' migrants were those without the rights to reside in the UK (that is, those 'illegally resident'). 'Semi-compliance' indicated a situation where a migrant was legally resident but working in violation of some or all of the employment restrictions attached to their immigration status

Chasing ghosts: researching illegality in migrant labour markets 405

Table 18.1 Respondents' imputed compliance by self-reported immigration status in April 2004

		Total	Compliance in April 2004			
			Compliant	Semi-compliant	Non-compliant	Compliance unknown
Immigration status in April 2004	Self-employed	129		39		90
	Au pair	100	20	66	8	6
	Student	91	22	67		2
	Visa expired	89			89	
	SAWS permit[a]	49	43		6	
	Don't know	46			12	34
	Other	37			8	29
	Dependant	17				17
	SBS permit[b]	9	5		4	
	Asylum seeker	5				5
	Illegal	2			2	
	No answer	2				2
	Total	576	90	172	129	185
	(%)	(100)	(16)	(30)	(22)	(32)

Notes:
a. The Seasonal Agriculture Worker Scheme (SAWS) was a programme for employing non-EU nationals in agriculture for up to six months.
b. The Sector-Based Scheme (SBS) was a programme for employing non-European Economic Area (EAA) migrants in selected low-skilled jobs in the hospitality sector and food processing sector (maximum one year).

Source: Survey interviews with migrants, April 2004 and 6–8 months later.

(Ruhs and Anderson, 2010). The term 'compliance' does not reflect the usage of this term in law or other disciplines. We used 'compliance', 'semi-compliance' and 'non-compliance' to denote three different types of situations pertaining to immigration status that we thought important but overlooked in theory and practice. We used it to nuance the discussion about illegality in the employment of migrants, and move away from the oversimplified legal/illegal binary without creating a multiplicity of further categories and distinctions. Table 18.1 shows respondents' self-reported immigration status and our evaluation of respondents' level of 'compliance' in April 2004, that is, just before EU Enlargement.

In contrast to the strictly defined situations of 'compliance' and 'non-compliance', the category of semi-compliance is extremely broad and captures a range of violations – with varying degrees of severity – of the conditions of employment attached to immigration status. Consider the case of four full-time students all of whom have the right to reside in the UK and are legally allowed to work 20 hours a week in term time, and full time in the holidays. They are working 20, 21, 25 and 40 hours per week, respectively. Based on our definition of compliance, we would describe the first student as compliant and the other three as semi-compliant. Clearly, there is a substantial difference – in terms of the degree of violations – between the student who works 21 hours and the student who works 40 hours. The discussion of where and how the line should be drawn between semi-compliance and non-compliance – or indeed between compliance and semi-compliance – is highly politicized and often rests on personal judgement. Different actors may draw the line in different places, an example of how illegality is 'socially constructed' (Engbersen and van der Leun, 2001).

Abandoning the legal/illegal dichotomy meant that as researchers we had to challenge assumptions of research users, and it forced a greater transparency in our analysis. It is interesting to observe the difference in initial response to this approach between government policymakers, who regarded all semi-compliant migrants as obviously illegal, and employers who felt that it captured an important distinction. As one employer put it: 'It's like driving 32 miles an hour in a 30 mile an hour zone.' Unfortunately we did not have the opportunity to ask enforcement officers for their response.

The complexity of conditions attached to immigration status means that a significant amount of information – and, in some cases, more information than was possible to collect – is required to assess whether a migrant complies with all the regulations governing his or her status or not. Given these challenges, our empirical discussion of the concept of compliance using the survey data came with a strong health warning about potential misclassifications (Ruhs and Anderson, 2010). Compliance levels are a reflection of our best assessments based on the interview data rather than the result of a comprehensive evaluation of respondents' positions (Table 18.1). Whenever we were unable to make a decision, we assigned the category 'compliance unknown'. This included many migrants who reported their immigration status as dependent, asylum seeker or who did not provide any information at all when asked about their immigration status.

18.4.2 Qualitative Approaches: Migrants' Experiences of Illegality

While the quantitative data enabled us to identify this substantial grey area, the qualitative data indicated the differences in subjective experiences of these statuses. Research shows that the impacts and experiences of illegality for migrants can be very varied (for a review see, for example, Schonwalder et al., 2004), and these characteristics and motivations are likely to affect migrants' perceptions and experiences of risks associated with illegality. Crucially, because the majority of migrants interviewed in April 2004 were from 'A8 countries', they expected to become EU citizens with easier access to the labour market and some social protection. This is likely to be a factor in understanding why a small number of A8 nationals interviewed professed themselves unconcerned with immigration status. This suggested the space for A8 nationals to take strategic decisions about their immigration status was greater than the space for the comparison group of Ukrainians and Bulgarians who could not anticipate any state facilitation of change in status in the short term.

As interviewees pointed out, there are differences in the extent to which individuals can tolerate illegality which are partly to do with personal assessments and implications of risk, but also with more complicated feelings: 'I could have lied, maybe to buy other passport like others do it now, but I can not lie like this' (Ukrainian male construction worker, aged 28).

Some migrants clearly felt less deportable than others. In particular certain types of (non-employment) visa were perceived as less risky to work on. More specifically, the degree to which achieving economic objectives was perceived as risking security of residence was affected by the 'particularities' of immigration status. Qualitative data found that migrants (and employers) differentiated between 'types' of illegality, and perceived there to be more subtle differences of degree than are captured by a sharp legal/illegal dichotomy. Working on false/fraudulent documents or on a visitor's visa, illegal entry or overstaying were generally perceived to be unambiguously illegal, including by those who were in this situation. However beyond this, the picture becomes more complicated. While 'law on the books' deems migrants who breach these conditions as deportable, when it comes to migrants the 'law in their minds' (that is, migrants' perceptions of the law) clearly is more flexible. This slippage also suggests that certain groups felt relatively secure in their balancing of residence and employment choices. For example, a Czech au pair who took on additional cleaning work described this as 'slightly illegal but tolerated', while a Polish waitress working 47 hours a week described herself as 'employed legally – maybe for a little bit more than the law on students' employment allows'.

Many of the migrants interviewed engaged with immigration laws in order to work and maximize security of status. It was clear from the quantitative data that switching status while in the UK was common among our sample. With the exception of Ukrainians, all of the nationalities studied could move from visitors' to self-employed visas. Thirty-nine per cent of the survey respondents on self-employed visas in April 2004 had switched to self-employed status after entering the UK on visitors' visas. What the in-depth interviews revealed was that this was for many a deliberate trajectory: they described themselves as entering on visitors' visas with the intention of applying for a visa as self-employed once in the UK. Most seemed to view this as in effect a relatively easy means of 'self-legalisation'. More generally a widespread concern with ease of entry and legal residence was given for the take-up of certain types of visa including au pair and self-employment. It was this concern with status that motivated many of our interviewees, rather than an interest in 'being' an au pair or self-employed per se.

Attempts were thus made to be in a position which migrants interpreted as 'bending' rather than breaking the immigration rules. Some people actively engaged with immigration frameworks from the start: they did not want to 'be' an au pair or student, when they chose that mode of entry, but they selected these visas as the most desirable of possible visa (rather than employment or life) options, typically because they enabled relatively easy entry to the UK, and some restricted form of working.

Most of the migrants interviewed did not perceive illegality in employment as directly leading to labour market outcomes worse than those of legally employed migrants.[5] Two people suggested that lack of enforceability of contracts meant that settlements about non-payment, for example, had to be made 'in your own way', and there was some suggestion that illegal residency meant that migrants could only go to particular agencies or had more limited job options. This does not mean that interviewees did not feel exploited, but rather that this was not simply felt to be a function of illegal immigration status. Having work experience, education, English language skills and 'get up and go' were perceived as important in combating the difficulties of being a migrant, of whatever status.

Similarly, most migrants we interviewed did not perceive illegality as leading to an unacceptably low level of social integration. It was their economic priorities, long hours and low pay, rather than concern with security of residence that was perceived to have a significant impact on this aspect of their lives.

18.5 CONCLUSION

As we suggested at the outset, seeking a greater understanding of how illegality works in migrant labour markets is a politically fraught endeavour. There is a high-profile public and media battleground over data on this topic and its interpretation, which has been sharpened by the current

Chasing ghosts: researching illegality in migrant labour markets 409

economic crisis. Engaging in such research thus requires a very careful and sensitive approach in order not to simply expose to greater control those migrants whose limited agency may rely on being able to bend immigration rules. At the same time, to be effective in contributing to evidence-based policy, such research needs to be methodologically robust. As this chapter has shown, this requires a plurality of methods. Policy actors can too easily dismiss studies based on relatively small numbers of qualitative interviews on their own, and tend to give greater weight to studies involving larger numbers of participants. Given the cost and the available analytical tools, information from large samples of people can only be accessed through survey questionnaires (whether face to face, online, or canvassed by mail or phone). At the same time, studies which rely on surveys alone too often lack texture and insight into the subjectivities of research participants. In the case study we have drawn on in the present chapter, in-depth face-to-face interviews in participants' own languages led us to a more nuanced understanding of how Central and East European work migrants in the early twenty-first century viewed the available array of visa rules, and how, in some cases, they made use of or worked around them.

Careful engagement with the design of a multi-method study like this one brings researchers face to face with conceptual conundrums partly because of the sensitive nature of the topic, and partly because of the need to ensure consistency across research tools. Emerging out of the work of designing the study and analysing the emerging data – and only possible because of the multiplicity of methods – was a new understanding of illegality no longer as a binary (legal versus illegal) but rather as something subject to semi- as well as full and non-compliance. Also coming out of this work was a greater appreciation of ways in which migrant workers – and their employers – could act as knowing agents in response to a complex visa regime.

NOTES

1. This has implications for secondary data analysis, and indicates the importance of attention to the definitions, as well as the methodology, that has been used.
2. Changing Status, Changing Lives? also conducted research with employers (both in-depth interview and survey based). Discussion of this part of the research is beyond the scope of the present chapter (for details see Ruhs et al., 2006).
3. See van Liempt and Bilger (Chapter 21, this volume) for further discussion of ethical considerations in migration studies.
4. Of course this is somewhat oversimplified as they would be forfeiting their legality of residence because of their working.
5. Although elsewhere we have drawn on data which suggests that regularization of the kind experienced by some Central and East European migrants on 1 May 2004 did improve the terms and conditions of their employment (see, for example, Rogaly, 2008).

REFERENCES

Anderson, B., Ruhs, M., Rogaly, B. and Spencer, S. (2006), 'Fair enough? Central and East European migrants in low-waged employment in the UK', Centre on Migration, Policy and Society (COMPAS), Oxford, available at http://www.compas.ox.ac.uk/publications/reports/changingstatus/fair-enough/ (accessed 6 February 2012).

Black, R. (2003), 'Breaking the convention: researching the "illegal" migration of refugees to Europe', *Antipode*, **35**, 34–54.

Cvajner, M. and Sciortino, G. (2010), 'A tale of networks and policies: prolegomena to an analysis of irregular migration careers and their developmental paths', *Population, Space and Place*, **16** (3), 213–25.

de Genova, N. (2002), 'Migrant "illegality" and deportability in everyday life', *Annual Review of Anthropology*, **31**, 419–47.

Engbersen, G. and van der Leun, J. (2001), 'The social construction of illegality and criminality', *European Journal on Criminal Policy and Research*, **9**, 51–70.

Rogaly, B. (2008), 'Intensification of workplace regimes in British horticulture: the role of migrant workers', *Population, Space and Place*, **14** (6), 497–510.

Ruhs, M. and Anderson, B. (2010), 'Semi-compliance and illegality in migrant labour markets: an analysis of migrants, employers and the state in the UK', *Population, Space and Place*, **16** (3), 195–211.

Ruhs, M., Anderson, B., Rogaly, B. and Spencer, S. (2006), 'Changing status, changing lives? Methods, participants and lessons learnt', Centre on Migration, Policy and Society (COMPAS), Oxford, available at http://www.compas.ox.ac.uk/publications/reports/changingstatus/changing-status-changing-lives/ (accessed 6 February 2012).

Schonwalder, K., Vogel, D. and Sciortino, G. (2004), *Migration und Illegalitaet in Deutschland. AKI-Forschungsbilanzl, Arbeitsstelle Interkulturelle Konflikte und Gesellschaftliche Integration*, Berlin: Wissenschaftszentrum Berlin Fuer Sozialforschung.

United States Government Accountability Office (2006), *Human Trafficking: Better Data, Strategy and Reporting Needed to Enhance U.S. Anti-trafficking Efforts Abroad*, Washington, DC: US GAO.

19 Using qualitative research methods in migration studies: a case study of asylum seekers fleeing gender-based persecution
Connie Oxford

This chapter outlines the strengths and limitations of using qualitative research methods in migration studies. Its focus is a case study of asylum seekers who sought refuge in the United States from gender-based persecution. Gender-based persecution includes harm such as female circumcision, domestic violence, rape, coercive family planning, forced marriage, honor killings, and repressive social norms. In this chapter, I draw from my fieldwork experiences. I discuss the research design and how the research questions were formed, entrée into the field, which qualitative methods were used in various settings and which ones were not and why, and the challenges of working with vulnerable populations.[1]

The research for this project was done in Los Angeles, California from 2001–03 and in New York City, New York from 2009–10. The qualitative methods used in this study were in-depth interviews with asylees, immigration officials, such as asylum officers and immigration judges, immigration attorneys, immigrant service providers, and human rights organization employees and activists; observations of immigration court asylum hearings; participant observation with immigrant service organizations and human rights groups; and content analysis of documents such as asylum applications. The interviews and observations of immigration court hearings from New York City provide comparative data, a valuable feature for understanding migration that is uncommon in qualitative studies in general. In this chapter, I discuss how qualitative methods reveal the nuances of how geographic location affects the process of seeking asylum in the United States from gender-based harm.

The culmination of the research is a book manuscript in progress titled *Fleeing Gendered Harm: Seeking Asylum in America*. This manuscript is the first study to examine how gender affects the policies and practices of seeking asylum in the United States. It interrogates how claims of gendered harm are different from other types of asylum claims because they are overwhelmingly made by women, tend to involve some type of sexual

411

violence, and immigration officials did not consider them to be a valid justification for asylum until the mid-1990s. The ethnographic methods used illuminate how gender-based asylum laws and policies are implemented in the United States.[2]

19.1 GENDER-BASED PERSECUTION AND ASYLUM IN THE UNITED STATES

Similar to many nation-states, the United States treats asylum seekers as a distinct type of immigrant. The 1980 US Refugee Act, which is derived from the 1951 United Nations Convention and 1967 Protocol relating to the Status of Refugees, differentiates asylum seekers from other types of immigrants based on their fear of persecution. This Act defines a refugee or asylum seeker as an individual who has either been persecuted or fears persecution based on his or her race, religion, nationality, membership in a particular social group, or political opinion. Gender is absent as a category (or a ground, the terminology used in asylum law and studies) that confers asylee status. One consequence of this omission is that asylum seekers cannot claim that they were persecuted or that they fear persecution based on their gender. While the inability to claim persecution based on one's gender potentially affects all asylum seekers, it has had a particularly devastating effect on women.

For example, in 1989, the US Fifth Circuit Court of Appeals upheld a denial of asylum to Sofia Campos-Guardado, a Salvadoran woman who was raped by members of the political opposition (guerrillas) as she witnessed the brutal deaths of her uncle and male cousins. Her family managed a local agricultural cooperative that the Salvadoran state considered radical regarding its agrarian land and food reform rhetoric. When Sofia's uncle refused to meet the guerrillas' demands for money in exchange for protection, Sofia was bound and raped while her cousins and uncle were hacked with machetes and ultimately shot. During the rape, torture, and killing of Sofia's relatives, the guerrillas shouted political slogans that connected the attack with the political opinion of the perpetrators. After the attack, her attackers and other members of the guerilla militia threatened and harassed Sofia. She fled to the United States and sought asylum based on the claim that the political slogans linked her persecution to the category of political opinion. Members of the Fifth Circuit upheld a lower court's ruling that her case was personal and that her claims of persecution based on political opinion were unfounded and unrelated to her attack (*Campos-Guardado v. Immigration and Naturalization Service*, 1987; Ericson, 1998; Kelly, 1993).

Using qualitative research methods in migration studies 413

The widespread denial of asylum to women with claims of sexual violence, such as Sofia Campos-Guardado, prompted a movement of scholars and human rights activists who sought to change immigration laws to facilitate women's ability to gain asylum. In 1995, the United States became the second country, after Canada in 1993, to recognize gender-based persecution as a legally acceptable way of gaining asylum. On 26 May 1995, Phyllis Coven, Director of the International Affairs Office of the Immigration and Naturalization Service (INS), issued a memorandum that provided asylum officers with 'guidance and background on adjudicating cases of women having asylum claims based wholly or in part on their gender' (Coven, 1995).[3] This policy memo, along with growing case law, created legal recourse for women claiming persecution based on gendered forms of harm, such as female circumcision, coercive population control, honor killing, domestic violence, rape, forced marriage, and repressive social norms. The passage of gender-based persecution laws and policies allowed immigrant women the ability to claim asylum based on forms of harm that historically were not considered persecution. Consequently, these laws created new patterns of migration to the United States that facilitated women's mobility.

19.2 USING QUALITATIVE RESEARCH METHODS

I became interested in this topic when I was completing the coursework for my doctoral degree in sociology in 2000. I had taken a class with an anthropology professor who had served as an expert witness on an asylum case. She encouraged me to write a research paper on gender-based persecution, which served as the basis for my dissertation project. At that time (and even today, a decade later), academic scholarship on gender-based persecution was nearly exclusive to legal studies (Anker, 2001; Crawley, 2001; Goldberg, 1993). Legal scholars understand gender-based persecution within the context of US case law, international law, and United Nations' policy regulations, making the law – not people – the subject of inquiry. Such a focus ignores the social relations and networks of people who make, implement, and rely upon the law.

My training as a qualitative social scientist led me to ask different questions about gender-based persecution than those asked by legal scholars. Unlike legal scholars, who focus on the outcome of a case, I privileged process over outcome in my research questions and design. By this, I mean that I was less interested in laws and policies per se and more interested in how human beings who created, implemented, and relied upon these laws and policies understood gender-based persecution. The growing field of feminist theory and gender studies provided me with a conceptual framework for designing a research project on gender-based persecution. A mainstay of feminist theory is a critique of how gender often serves as a synonym for women (Lorber, 1995). According to feminist scholarship, the conflation of gender (a relational concept) to women (a descriptive category) is present in much nonfeminist scholarship. Based on my initial reading of the INS policy that allowed women to claim asylum for gender-based persecution, three preliminary questions guided my review of the legal scholarship on asylum. What is gender? What does it mean to be persecuted? What does it mean to be persecuted on account of one's gender? These questions served as my original research questions as I canvassed the academic literature on asylum.

As I learned about the process of seeking asylum, I became interested in how what I later termed 'differently situated participants' (asylees, immigrant service providers, immigration attorneys, immigration judges, asylum officers and supervisors, and human rights activists and organization employees) interpret gender-based persecution. Three questions in particular provided specificity to my general questions on gender and persecution: How and why were gender-based asylum policies and laws in the United States created? How are gender-based asylum laws and policies applied? How do differently situated participants interpret ideas about gender-based persecution?

In addition to feminist studies, sociological qualitative research informed how I would go about designing this study. Sociologists have contributed a wealth of scholarship that supports the value and contribution of qualitative research (Denzin and Lincoln, 1994; Lofland and Lofland, 1995; Reinharz, 1992). One criticism that sociologists pose regarding qualitative research design is that social scientists tend to choose such methods – interviewing, participant observation, and ethnography – only when they encounter a paucity of available quantitative data (Ragin, 2004). Sociologists are likewise critical of how scholars who favor quantitative methods often view qualitative research as supplemental to quantitative research or inferior to the 'theory → hypotheses → data collection → analysis → conclusion' model used in quantitative studies (Blee, 2004, p. 55).

I was convinced that qualitative research had value not as supplemental data or as an inferior alternative to quantitative methods; its value was its ability to answer the research questions.

19.2.1 Designing a Qualitative Migration Study

Qualitative methods – ethnography in particular – has joined historical and quantitative research as a widely used approach for studying migration

Using qualitative research methods in migration studies 415

(Fitzgerald, 2006). The growing ethnographic literature on migration coupled with the longstanding scholarship on female immigrants provided a springboard for how I would conceptualize a study of gender-based persecution (Hondagneu-Sotelo, 2001). Designing and implementing a research project on a topic that has not been explored by social scientists is a daunting task. Migration scholars have studied various aspects of gender and forced migration that include violence in refugee camps (Martin, 2004), changing status during resettlement (McSpadden and Moussa, 1993), and economic adaptation (Montgomery, 1996). Yet none have examined gender-based persecution and asylum claims. My dissertation was the first qualitative study of gender-based asylum in the United States.

In order to answer my research questions, I chose qualitative research methods because to question the interpretation of concepts such as gender and persecution requires dynamic data. Quantitative data such as that found in statistical yearbooks are limited.

Many studies of asylum rely on available data such as those marshaled by the US Citizenship and Immigration Service (USCIS), the office that supervises affirmative asylum applications in eight asylum offices across the United States, and the US Executive Office for Immigration Review (USEOIR), the office that oversees defensive asylum claims that take place in the 52 immigration courts across the country. Data such as those found in USCIS and USEOIR statistical yearbooks provide information on how many women and men apply for and either gain or are denied asylum, but not on how gender-based persecution laws and polices emerge, how they are implemented, or how law and policy makers, immigrant service providers, human rights activists, and asylees respond to them.

I had to decide where to locate the fieldwork site, what types of data were accessible, and which qualitative methods were appropriate to answering my research question. While researching asylum and immigration, I learned that there are eight INS asylum offices in the United States. I chose Los Angeles as the fieldwork site because its immigration court and asylum office have the greatest number and diversity of applications in the United States (US Executive Office for Immigration Review, 2002; US Immigration and Naturalization Service, 2002). Upon arriving in Los Angeles in August 2001, I e-mailed the district director of the San Francisco INS asylum office, whom I met during a summer program on refugee studies at York University. The director put me in touch with Michael, a supervisor at the Anaheim office, who facilitated my interviews with asylum supervisors.[4] Michael made arrangements for me to receive copies of the INS asylum officer training materials as well as memos and letters regarding gender-based asylum claims. I contacted four refugee resettlement organizations, one organization that serves torture survivors, and two human rights organizations. These organizations served as initial sampling points from which I was able to locate interviewees. I met with personnel from these organizations and made arrangements to work as a volunteer and with immigration attorneys who agreed to facilitate my access to asylum applications and contact with asylees.

Based on my initial contacts, I surmised that I would be able to collect the following data: interviews with asylees (persons with a grant of asylum), immigration attorneys, immigrant service providers, INS asylum supervisors, and human rights activists; document analysis of asylum applications and INS asylum officer training manuals; and – through volunteer work with the organizations mentioned above – observation of participants in immigration court hearings and of interactions with asylees, immigrant service providers, and attorneys. I developed an interview guide and divided it by category of interviewee. For example, I did not ask all immigration attorneys and human rights activists the same questions, but I did ask similar questions of all attorneys and all activists. With the exception of asylees, nearly everyone I interviewed was involved in asylum through their employment. Therefore, I designed a guide that asked questions such as 'When did you begin working with the INS?' or 'How long have you practiced immigration law?' as a way of getting respondents to speak about their experiences with asylum. I did not ask all participants in a particular category the same questions. For example, not all asylum seekers are detained when they arrive in the United States. Questions regarding experiences in INS processing facilities are only relevant if the interviewee was in detention.

I situated this study in what sociologists Barry Glaser and Anselm Strauss termed 'grounded theory,' a mode of inductive inquiry (Glaser and Strauss, 1967). This method of inquiry begins with observations and then seeks to discover patterns based on those observations. There are no dependent or operationalized variables. I did not define gender or persecution, the two most salient concepts in this project, prior to data collection. Instead, I created an interview guide with open-ended questions that would allow participants in the asylum process to describe how they engaged in practices that define gender and persecution. The sampling method was purposive, with the sample size determined by availability of subjects, sampling of legally recognized gender-based claims, and multiple sites of snowball sampling.[5] Nonprobability sampling is limited in its generalizability, but probability sampling was impossible. Because of how the INS and USEOIR collect data, there is no way to know how many or what types of gender-based claims are received. No list of all gender-based asylum claims is available in the United States to serve as a sampling frame. During my interview with Michael, the asylum supervisor

Using qualitative research methods in migration studies 417

at the Anaheim office, he explained how: in our database, asylum officers have to mark which grounds the person claimed. If you want to know how many gender persecution cases were granted or denied, you are not going to get any usable figures out of this system, because it only says race or nationality. I granted a domestic violence case once for religious reasons. If you searched the database for that application, it would show religious persecution, not domestic violence.

By 'marking the grounds,' Michael referred to the five legally accepted grounds of persecution that include race, religion, nationality, political opinion, and membership in a social group. His example of domestic violence demonstrates that type of harm is not recorded, only the ground on which that harm is based. This means that the INS and USEIOR have no official (or at least publicly available) data on how many types of gender-based asylum claims – such as female circumcision, honor killings, or domestic violence – are adjudicated. One of the strengths of my methodological design is that the information gleaned from my research serves as the only available empirical data of how gender-based laws and policies are applied and interpreted in the United States.

19.2.2 Data Collection and Data Analysis: Interactive Stages

The linear model that structures quantitative methods dictates that research happens in stages. The researcher begins with a theoretical framework, formulates a hypothesis, collects data, analyses the data, and then draws conclusions that either support or refute the theory. Qualitative methodology eschews the linear model of research through its simultaneous data collection and analysis (Becker, 2004). One of the strengths of qualitative research is its ability to refine the research question during and after data collection and analysis. In this section, I outline the challenges and rewards of treating data collection and data analysis as simultaneous research steps and the ways in which I refined my research questions through method choices of participant observation, interviewing, and document analysis. In an effort to understand the patterns that structure everyday social exchanges, sociologist Harold Garfinkle (1967) advanced ethnomethodology as a reflective method of data collection. Garfinkle demonstrated how assumed understandings of concepts operate in verbal exchanges among friends, students and parents, and consumers and store clerks. Throughout this study, my exchanges with INS and USCIS supervisors, immigration judges, attorneys, service providers, and activists took the form of Garfinkle's questioning techniques regarding the meaning of gender. The following example shows how a telephone discussion with an immigration attorney served as an opportunity to collect and analyse

418   *Handbook of research methods in migration*

conversation data about the meanings of gender-based persecution. An exchange with one attorney over the telephone was as follows:

Oxford: I was given your name by ___ because I am writing a dissertation on gender-based asylum. He/she mentioned that you've represented these types of cases.
Attorney: What do you mean by gender-based claims?
Oxford: I mean cases like honor killings, female circumcision, or domestic violence.
Attorney: I've never had a domestic violence case.
Oxford: What about other types of gender claims?
Attorney: I've never had any of those cases.
Oxford: Do you know other attorneys who have had those types of cases who you could put me in touch with?
Attorney: [Pauses before responding.] I've had clients who were raped, is that what you mean?
Oxford: Yes, I'm interested in rape cases.
Attorney: I don't know if I would call that a gender case; most of my clients have been raped.

This exchange supports Garfinkle's contention that familiar social interactions are structured by assumptions that merit a 'sociological inquiry in its own right' (Garfinkle, 1967, p. 136). While my contacts with attorneys and service providers were for the purpose of gaining access to asylees with gender-based claims, these exchanges also provided data by answering my research question regarding what 'constitutes' gender-based harm. This example reveals a paradox about gender-based claims by showing how rape, a legally recognized form of gender-based harm, is not initially understood as such because of its pervasiveness across all asylum claims. Moreover, in my insistence that rape cases be included, this exchange reveals my preconceived notions about what types of acts are considered gender-based harm. By treating data collection and data analysis as simultaneous stages, I was able to incorporate my analysis of how gender-based harm is interpreted into future conversations with immigration attorneys. I did this by asking attorneys whether they had represented cases that included specific types of harm (such as those mentioned in the above exchange: rape, domestic violence, female circumcision, and so on) instead of using the legal term 'gender-based persecution' with no examples of what types of harm those cases might include.

A second example of how data collection and analysis occurred in simultaneous stages during my research is the following interaction between an asylum seeker and her attorney. In order to gain access to asylees, I volunteered with organizations that assist asylum seekers. Volunteering afforded me the opportunity to observe extensive interactions between asylum seekers and their service providers. In the spirit of client advocacy, I was occasionally drawn into disagreements between clients and their service providers and attorneys. While organizations expect employees and volunteers to support their clients, I was sometimes presented with situations in which I was expected to concur with service providers and attorneys concerning the assumed best interests of their clients. While volunteering for one such organization, I was drawn into a conflict between an asylum seeker and her attorney.

During a master calendar hearing for a woman seeking asylum from Cameroon whom I accompanied to court, her attorney requested a continuance in anticipation of arriving documentation that her client had been working in Nigeria just before she fled to the United States. This documentation was important as evidence that the woman had filed her asylum claim within the legally accepted time frame. The Illegal Immigration and Reform Act of 1996 legislated the 'one-year rule' that requires all asylum seekers to file an application within one year of their arrival in the United States. The judge offered a hearing date three days from the calendar hearing, advising that the documentation might not matter, since the greater issue was one of resettlement in Nigeria, not of timeliness in filing the application. However, at the attorney's insistence, the judge issued a continuance for three months, and the applicant, attorney, and I retreated to a waiting area outside the courtroom.

The applicant became angry with her attorney and yelled for her to 'go back in there and tell the judge I want to be heard in three days. I am tired of waiting.' The attorney responded in similar fashion, yanked her cell phone from her briefcase, and began dialing the number for the asylum seeker's psychologist, curtly telling the applicant that it was her responsibility to make sure her therapist was available to testify, that her testimony was ready, and that all documentation was available. I witnessed this exchange with the assumed gaze of invisible researcher until the attorney turned to me and exclaimed: 'Tell her. Tell her that there is no way I can prepare her case in three days with all that I would have to do. I don't even have her work papers from Nigeria and I still have to prepare her testimony. If we go forward in three days we will lose. Tell her it is better to wait. You have been to court. You know how asylum works.'

I turned to the Cameroonian woman who stood in silence with tears pouring down her face and told her that I knew that she was frustrated for having to wait, but that whereas postponing a hearing could not hurt her case, a premature hearing could prove problematic.

In this exchange, I became a pawn in a struggle for authority by the attorney. My expertise in having 'been to court' was invoked in an effort to persuade the applicant to continue her hearing in three months rather than three days. I tacitly agreed with the attorney because I was fearful that her client's defiance would invoke negative repercussions such as poor legal representation, resulting in a denial of her claim. Prior to this day, the questions from my interview guide assumed a benign relationship between attorneys and clients. Questions such as 'Did you have a lawyer?' or 'How did you locate your attorney?' were the limits of how I probed asylees about their relationship with their legal representatives. After this observation, I altered the interview guide to include questions regarding conflicts between asylees and their attorneys or service providers. This exchange occurred in June 2002, nine months into my 19 months of fieldwork. At the time of this exchange, I had interviewed six of the 21 asylees included in this project. Although altering the interview guide strengthened the project in that I was able to capture data about negative exchanges between asylees and attorneys, a corresponding weakness was that I had no data on this subject for approximately one third of my sample.

A third example of how data collection and analysis occurred in simultaneous stages was through the acquisition of asylum applications. Through the assistance of immigration attorneys, I was able to procure a total of 19 asylum applications, four of which were from asylees I was able to interview. Because I gained access to asylees through their attorneys and service providers, I was often given extensive information about their asylum applications prior to meeting them. Some attorneys and service providers revealed that their clients had been raped, circumcised, kidnapped, and detained (in their country of origin and in the United States). Sometimes asylees would discuss the same information with me in our interview, but, overwhelmingly, interviewees did not discuss instances of rape documented in their applications. For example, Mary, an asylee from Congo, did not mention a gang rape that her attorney discussed with me in detail and instead focused during our interview on the two assassinations carried out against her family. Conversely, asylees also gave me information during our interview that they did not discuss with their attorney. Miriam, an asylee from Iran, discussed how she was raped repeatedly while detained after a protest for women's rights. During our interview she told me that she did not discuss the rapes with her attorney, an Iranian man, because she 'knew what men from my country would think about such things.'

These examples presented a challenge of data recording in ethnographic research. If an attorney or service provider reveals that a client was raped but the asylee does not mention the rape during the interview, should the researcher record 'rape' as an example of gender-based persecution in the data? Instead of regarding this seeming conflict as a discrepancy in the data, I included both accounts as data. Because I was interested in knowing ways in which differently situated participants understand and articulate gender-based harm, I consider both the attorney's discussion and the client's silence about her rape data. By treating data collection and analysis as interactive – not linear – stages of research, I was attuned to how differently situated participants are willing to divulge stories about gendered harm, such as rape. After hearing varying accounts from asylees, their service providers, and attorneys about the same case, I was convinced that I needed a question that tapped the multiplicity of accounts of persecution in asylum claims. These examples persuaded me to include another research question: How are narratives of persecution created in gender-based asylum claims?

19.2.3 Comparative Qualitative Research

After completing the dissertation, I extended the study to include research from New York City for a book manuscript. I was specifically interested in knowing how the immigration courts and asylum offices, immigrant advocacy networks, and asylum seeking communities are different in New York City than those in Los Angeles. New York City is an ideal location for comparative research because it receives the second largest number of asylum claims in the United States (Los Angeles receives the largest number), the immigration court and asylum office are in a different US Circuit Court of Appeals from California, and the national and racial characteristics of the asylum seeking population are different than those in Los Angeles. Much of the Los Angeles study was duplicated in New York City. I observed immigration court hearings and interviewed the same types of participants (asylees, immigration attorneys, former asylum officers, and so on). While there are many distinctions in the asylum process in Los Angeles and New York City, I discuss two significant differences in the research below that circumscribe the comparative data for this study.

The first difference is the time frame in which the data was collected. The Los Angeles study was done on the heels of the 9/11 terrorist attack. I witnessed changes in US immigration laws and policies in 'real time' as the Bush administration announced edicts that suddenly and profoundly altered immigrants' ability to seek asylum. For example, in Los Angeles, prior to 9/11, detained asylum seekers were regularly released on bail until their court hearing. This practice ceased making detention in Los Angeles similar to the experiences of immigrants in New York City who were not released on bail, even before the 9/11 terrorist attacks.

In terms of gender-based persecution, one significant difference was a change in immigration laws. While I was doing the research in Los Angeles from 2001–03, immigration law regarding female circumcision was settled in that it constituted past persecution and therefore made it an acceptable means of gaining asylum (*Matter of Kasinga*, 1996).[6] In 2007, the Board of Immigration Appeals (BIA), the appellate board for all immigration courts in the United States, began overturning lower court decisions that granted asylum and upholding lower court decisions that denied asylum for applicants claiming persecution based on female genital cutting that reverberated throughout the country. In a case involving a woman from Mali who had been circumcised as a young girl (so young that she has no memory of being cut), the BIA found that because the harm is 'inflicted only once' that asylum seekers cannot demonstrate a well-founded fear of persecution because they will not be subjected to it again (*Matter of A-T*, 2007). The BIA compared genital cutting to cases of forced sterilization and argued that while both are done only once, they are fundamentally different because female genital mutilation 'has not been specifically identified as a basis for asylum within the definition of a "refugee" in the Immigration and Naturalization Act in the way that forced sterilization has' (*Matter of A-T*, 2007). The BIA argued that persecution based on coercive family planning is because of one's political opinion, or opposition to the Chinese government. Conversely, there are no laws that define the reason (that is, one of the five grounds of asylum) that female genital cutting is done. In another case, the BIA found that seeking asylum based solely on the fear that one's daughter would be circumcised is not a legitimate argument for immigrants who fear for their daughter's lives (*Matter of A-K*, 2007).

The BIA's actions seem contradictory toward the issue of female genital cutting. This same judicial body that was denying asylum to women who experienced female genital cutting in 2007 was responsible for the precedent setting case that prepared the way for women to gain asylum based on female genital cutting less than a decade earlier. The most famous case of a woman fleeing a forced circumcision is *Matter of Kasinga* (1996) and is based on the story of Fauziya Kassindja, a Togan woman who arrived in the United States in 1994 and filed an asylum claim the next year.[7] For over a decade, immigrants rights advocates thought that the debate over whether female genital cutting constituted persecution was settled. The case *Matter of Kasinga* allowed women who were fleeing a forced circumcision and women who had been circumcised to be eligible for asylum. Moreover, it justified the claims of those who sought protection from genital cutting for their daughters. Then in 2007, the BIA began issuing decisions such as *Matter of A-T* and *Matter of A-K* that for all intents and purposes reversed *Matter of Kasinga* which provided the basis for women gaining asylum because of genital cutting in the United States.

In the aftermath of *Matter of A-T* and *Matter of A-K*, some cases that had been denied by immigration judges were appealed to the US Circuit Court of Appeals. One such case that originated in the New York City immigration court was *Bah v. Mukasey* (2008). This Second Circuit case found that female circumcision does indeed constitute past persecution which superseded the BIA's decisions, but only for asylum seekers in the geographical boundaries of the Second Circuit because the Second Circuit Court of Appeals is a higher court than the BIA. The BIA did eventually reverse its finding in the *Matter of A-T* in 2009. However, the outcome for asylum seekers is that those who were circumcised were able to gain asylum in New York City while women with similar claims in other areas of the United States would have been denied between 2008 and 2009. These new cases show how the law is never completely settled but instead shifts and changes over time. Asylum law in particular is modified and sometimes drastically altered based on the current political landscape that governs who may gain entry into the United States and under what circumstances.

A second difference between the Los Angeles and New York City data is the ways in which immigration officials demarcate 'real' stories of persecution from ostensibly fraudulent claims. Nation is inextricably linked to how immigration officials construct truth telling subjects. In Los Angeles, Mexican applicants (and some Central American ones) are nearly summarily assumed to be ineligible for asylum because Mexican migration is based on 'economic' rather than 'political' motivations, according to some immigration officials. In New York City, a parallel suspicion of Chinese immigrants exists who some immigration officials believe are only in America 'to work' rather than seek refuge from persecution. Immigration officials' discourses regarding fraudulent claims by Mexicans in Los Angeles and Chinese in New York City may be explained in part by the large volume of asylum applications from these nationals. Between 2001 and 2006, there were a total of 32,236 asylum cases by Chinese nationals adjudicated in immigration court in the United States. Of these, 24,164 or 75 percent were decided in New York City (TRAC Immigration, 2007). Below are two excerpts from my observations of the New York City immigration court of a Honduran woman fleeing domestic violence and a Chinese man who sought relief based on the forced sterilization practices his wife endured.

In June 2009, a judge in the New York City immigration court granted asylum to Lupe, a 22-year-old Honduran woman who had fled an abusive boyfriend. As the judge read aloud the basis for her decision to approve the asylum application, she stated that Lupe was involved with a man who had become a member of a gang and subsequently became violent toward her when she too would not join the gang. Lupe had sought refuge at her mother's and grandmother's homes, only to be found repeatedly by her boyfriend. After the boyfriend threatened to kill Lupe, along with her mother and grandmother, she fled Honduras for the United States and applied for asylum. The judge pronounced that Lupe was a member of the social group of 'Honduran women who refuse to submit to Honduran men' and that the government of Honduras did not provide protection, therefore, leaving Lupe with no choice but to leave her country or face continued violence and possibly death.

Like all asylum seekers, Lupe had many obstacles to overcome before she could gain asylum. Among two important criteria she had to meet were persuading an immigration official that the harm she feared was indeed grave enough to constitute persecution and that the harm was based on at least one of the following factors: race, religion, nationality, political opinion, or membership in a social group. The immigration judge who determined Lupe's fate accepted that the beatings she endured constituted persecution and that the persecutor, her boyfriend, was committing acts of violence against Lupe because she would not acquiesce to his demands to join the gang; hence the somewhat awkward wording of how her refusal to submit to the boyfriend made her a member of a social group. In addition to finding Lupe's testimony about the harm and the reasoning for why her boyfriend was beating her legally acceptable, the judge affirmed her position that Lupe deserved asylum because her testimony was credible, as it was consistent with her application, detailed, and her demeanor indicated that her story was believable.

The Assistant District Counsel (ADC) for this case did not reserve the right to appeal and therefore Lupe was not only granted asylum but the judge's decision was final. The ADC is the attorney who works for the Department of Homeland Security (DHS) and whose role in immigration court is somewhat like a prosecutor in that an ADC argues why immigrants should not receive asylum on behalf of the government. Unlike many asylum seekers who are granted asylum but are subjected to a drawn out process of appeals that often takes years and depletes what little resources undocumented immigrants are able to cull from family and community members because their case is contested by the ADC, Lupe was fortunate in that her struggle to gain asylum came to a close in immigration court.

Just one month after Lupe was granted asylum, I observed a hearing in a different courtroom of Li, a man who was seeking asylum based on China's coercive family planning policies. Li's wife became pregnant

Using qualitative research methods in migration studies

before they were married and even though the neighborhood medical unit had demanded she have an abortion, they were able to keep the child by paying a fine. Soon after her son's birth she became pregnant with their second child. According to Li's testimony during the hearing, when local officials learned of her pregnancy they forced their way into the couple's home, 'dragged' her to the family planning clinic, and coerced her into having an abortion and wearing an Intrauterine Device (IUD). The couple paid a private doctor to remove the IUD and when the family planning officials came for a routine check to ensure that the IUD was still in place, Li's wife went into hiding with relatives. On multiple occasions during the visits from the family planning officials, Li was arrested and beaten because he would not disclose his wife's whereabouts.

During the hearing, the ADC's tone (that was nearly sarcastic at times) while he questioned Li indicated that he did not believe Li's story. The ADC asked questions such as: Why can your wife live in China safely and you cannot? To which Li replied that *he* was the one who had been arrested, detained, and beaten, not his wife. During the ADC's closing arguments he affirmed that he did not find Li credible, in part, because of Li's demeanor during his testimony. The ADC noted that Li was 'monotone and looked ahead, even when he talked about his wife's abortion and being beaten.' Although the judge granted Li asylum, the ADC reserved the right to appeal the case. The next step for Li and his attorney would be to submit Li's application for asylum to the BIA, the appellate board for all immigration courts in the United States in the hope that the BIA upholds the judge's decision and DHS officials choose not to continue with the appeal process to the Second Circuit Court of Appeals and then possibly the Supreme Court, if they are dissatisfied with the BIA's ruling.

Li's hearing demonstrates the power that immigration officials who are not the arbitrator have in asylum cases. The ADC reserved the right to appeal Li's case because Li did not display the emotions the ADC deemed credible while testifying about his wife's forced abortion and his arrest and beatings during detention. The harm itself or potential harm is not enough to secure asylum. Asylum seekers must persuade multiple immigration officials that they experienced persecution or will experience persecution in such a way that is convincing.

19.2.4 Research Findings and Limitations of the Data

In my study of gender-based asylum claims in Los Angeles and New York City, I show that asylum is gendered because asylum laws and policies are applied by asylum officers and immigration judges differently in three ways: the treatment of applicants by sex; when the substance of the claim is gender-based, such as cases of rape; and types of gendered harm such as how honor killings are adjudicated differently than domestic violence claims, for example. Yet there are significant distinctions between seeking asylum in Los Angeles and New York City such as immigration officials' obligation to follow laws in different Circuit Court of Appeals and the ways in which immigrants' nationality may determine whether they gain asylum. This comparative data is paramount for migration studies because it shows how regional differences within a country affect asylum in the United States.

I found that, while gender-based persecution laws and policies laid the groundwork for gender equality in asylum adjudication, asylum officers, immigration attorneys, judges, and service providers participate in what I term a 'gender regime' of asylum practices that exacerbates inequality for some migrant women. For example, I found that a differentiation emerges in gender-based asylum claims between what I term 'ethnocentric' and what I term 'exotic' harm. While asylum officers and judges are more reluctant to consider cases of ethnocentric harm (harm that American women experience, such as domestic violence) as persecution, they overwhelmingly consider exotic claims (harm that non-Americans experience, such as female circumcision and honor killings) as persecution. Moreover, immigration attorneys and service providers encourage female asylum seekers who are circumcised to claim persecution based on female circumcision regardless of the actual reason they left their country. None of the five interviewees who gained asylum because of female circumcision left their country because they considered their own circumcision to be persecution. Instead, they migrated to the United States and sought asylum because they had been detained, tortured, or had lived with threats of torture of a spouse.

My high school English teacher was famous for her advice to students regarding their behavioral decisions: 'Choices cause consequences' was her steadfast motto. Her directive reaches beyond the scope of personal decisions and is pertinent to research design and methodology. Throughout this project, I was confronted with choices about my three types of research methods: participant observation, interviewing, and document analysis. My goal was to collect data across sources; ideally, I would observe an asylum seeker's hearing, interview her after she gains asylum, obtain her application, and interview her attorney, service providers, and the judge who adjudicated the case. Unfortunately, this was not possible for at least three reasons. First, the time span between filing an asylum application and its adjudication in immigration court can take years, and the data collection was limited to 18 months. Second, all subjects in the project were willing participants, and some asylees, attorneys, and judges whom I approached refused an interview. Third, I was unable to locate some participants for interviews. Attorneys lost contact with clients, asylees couldn't remember their judges' names, and human rights activists were no longer in touch with the detainees they assisted. A shortcoming of this project was incomplete data with regard to comparability across sources.

19.3 CONCLUSION

The greatest strength of my research is that it is the first (and to date only) empirical study of gender-based asylum in the United States. My findings are the only data available that address how gender-based asylum laws and policies are applied and interpreted. The greatest methodological strength of my research was its multi-method approach: extensive data collection; its qualitative approach that allowed me to collect and analyse data simultaneously; and its methodological design that allowed me to refine my research questions throughout the project. While the decision to change research questions and data instruments is problematic in regard to issues of comparability across data sources and reliability across interviews, I chose this approach because it best answered my research questions about gender-based persecution.

NOTES

1. See van Liempt and Bilger (Chapter 21, this volume) for further discussion of research with vulnerable populations.
2. This chapter is a revised and updated version of 'Changing the research question: lessons from qualitative research' in Louis DeSipio, Manuel Garcia y Griego and Sherri Kossoudji (eds), *Researching Migration: Stories from the Field* (2007), New York: The Social Science Research Council, pp. 116–30.
3. On 1 March 2003, the INS was divided into three agencies – the United States Citizenship and Immigration Services (CIS), the United States Immigration and Custom Enforcement (ICE), and the Bureau of Customs and Border Protection (CBP) – and moved from the Department of Justice to the newly created Department of Homeland Security. I refer to the federal office that oversees immigration as the INS until its dissolution in March 2003. Thereafter, I refer to the asylum office as USCIS.
4. All interviewee names are pseudonyms.
5. Snowball sampling refers to recruiting research subjects from existing participants.
6. Although asylum law uses the term 'female genital mutilation,' I refer to the practice as female circumcision. I discuss the implications of using terms such as mutilation in 'Protectors and victims in the gender regime of asylum', *National Women's Studies Association Journal* (2005), Fall, **17** (3), 18–38.
7. The spelling of Kassindja and Kasinga are incongruent. The asylum seeker's last name is spelled Kassindja and the legal case is spelled Kasinga because the INS airport inspector who processed Fauziya's application spelled her last name incorrectly when she arrived

in the United States. See Fauziya Kassindja and Layli Miller Bashir's (1998), *Do They Hear You When You Cry?* for details of Fauziya's interactions with the INS that led to this discrepancy.

REFERENCES

Anker, D. (2001), 'Refugee status and violence against women in the "domestic" sphere: the non-state actor question', *Georgetown Immigration Law Journal*, **15**, 391–402.
Bah v. Mukasey, Diallo v. Department of Homeland Security, Diallo v. Department of Homeland Security, 529 F.3d 99, 103 (2d Cir. 2008).
Becker, H. (2004), 'The problems of analysis', in C.C. Ragin (ed.), *Workshop on Scientific Foundations of Qualitative Research*, Washington, DC: National Science Foundation, pp. 45–7.
Blee, K. (2004), 'Evaluating qualitative research', in C.C. Ragin (ed.), *Workshop on Scientific Foundations of Qualitative Research*, Washington, DC: National Science Foundation, pp. 55–7.
Campos-Guardado v. Immigration and Naturalization Service, 809 F.2d 285 (5th Cir. 1987).
Coven, P. (1995), 'Considerations for asylum officers adjudicating claims from women', US Department of Justice, reproduced in *Interpreter Releases*, **72**.
Crawley, H. (2001), *Refugees and Gender: Law and Process*, Bristol: Jordans Publishing.
Denzin, N.K. and Lincoln, Y.S. (1994), *Handbook of Qualitative Research*, Thousand Oaks, CA: Sage.
Ericson, C.M. (1998), 'In Re Kasinga: an expansion of the grounds for asylum for women', *Houston Journal of International Law*, **20** (2), 671–94.
Fitzgerald, D. (2006), 'Towards a theoretical ethnography of migration', *Qualitative Sociology*, **29** (1), 1–24.
Garfinkle, H. (1967), *Studies in Ethnomethodology*, Cambridge: Polity Press.
Glaser, B. and Strauss, A. (1967), *The Discovery of Grounded Theory: Strategies of Qualitative Research*, Chicago, IL: Aldine Press.
Goldberg, P. (1993), 'Anyplace but home: asylum in the U.S. for women fleeing intimate violence', *Cornell International Law Journal*, **26**, 565–604.
Hondagneu-Sotelo, P. (2001), *Domestica: Immigrant Workers Cleaning and Caring in the Shadows of Affluence*, Berkeley, CA: University of California Press.
Kassindja, F. and Bashir, L.M. (1998), *Do They Hear You When You Cry?*, New York: Delta.
Kelly, N. (1993), 'Gender-related persecution: assessing the asylum claims of women', *Cornell International Law Journal*, **26**, 625–74.
Lofland, J. and Lofland, L.H. (1995), *Analyzing Social Settings: A Guide to Qualitative Observation and Analysis*, 3rd edn, Belmont, CA: Wadsworth.
Lorber, J. (1995), *The Paradoxes of Gender*, New Haven, CT: Yale University Press.
Martin, S.F. (2004), *Refugee Women*, 2nd edn, Lanham, MD: Lexington Books.
Matter of A-K, 24 I&N Dec. 296 (BIA 2007).
Matter of A-T, 24 I&N Dec. 275 (BIA 2007).
Matter of Kasinga, 21 I. & N. Dec. 357 (BIA 1996).
McSpadden, L.A. and Moussa, H. (1993), '"I have a name": the gender dynamics in asylum and resettlement of Ethiopian and Eritrean refugees in North America', *Journal of Refugee Studies*, **6**, 203–5.
Montgomery, J.R. (1996), 'Components of refugee adaptation', *International Migration Review*, **30**, 679–702.
Oxford, C.G. (2005), 'Protectors and victims in the gender regime of asylum', *National Women's Studies Association Journal*, Fall, **17** (3), 18–38.
Oxford, C.G. (2007), 'Changing the research question: lessons from qualitative research', in L. DeSipio, M. Garcia y Griego and S. Kossoudji (eds), *Researching Migration: Stories from the Field*, New York City: The Social Science Research Council, pp. 116–30.

Ragin, C.C. (2004), *Workshop on Scientific Foundations of Qualitative Research*, Washington, DC: National Science Foundation.
Reinharz, S. (1992), *Feminist Methods in Social Research*, New York: Oxford University Press.
TRAC Immigration (2007), 'Asylum disparities persist, regardless of court location and nationality' Table Seven 'Nationality and court-by-court disparity in asylum decisions', available at http://trac.syr.edu/immigration/reports/183/ (accessed 30 July 2010).
US Executive Office for Immigration Review (2002), *2001 Statistical Yearbook*, Washington, DC: US Government Printing Office.
US Immigration and Naturalization Service (2002), *2001 Statistical Yearbook*, Washington, DC: US Government Printing Office.

20 The importance of accounting for variability in remittance income
Catalina Amuedo-Dorantes and Susan Pozo[1]

A great deal of research has examined remittances to developing economies detailing the size and influence of these money flows. Are the poorest or the better-off households the primary recipients and are the flows sufficient to lift households out of poverty (for example, Lucas, 2007; Terry and Wilson, 2005)? Is labor force participation influenced and changed on account of remittance transfers (for example, Amuedo-Dorantes and Pozo, 2006; Cox-Edwards and Rodríguez-Oreggia, 2009; Funkhouser, 1992)? Is investment in schooling increased or decreased with the receipt of remittances (for example, Amuedo-Dorantes and Pozo, 2010; Borraz, 2005; Cox Edwards and Ureta, 2003; Kandel and Kao, 2001)? While much of this work is valuable and has the potential to increase our understanding of remittance flows and their implications, we are interested in yet another aspect of these flows that has not been researched to any great degree, as is the case with the 'regularity' and 'predictability' of remittance flows and how they can influence the economic behavior of recipient households.

Before embarking on an extensive study of this nature, one might question the need to study how remittances behave and influence economic behavior. Aren't remittances simply a transfer payment similar in nature to unemployment insurance payments, to welfare payments, and to old age security transfers? Why not simply resort to the vast literature on transfer payments to answer questions about the likely impact of remittances on household behavior? Our view is that remittances are significantly different from government transfer payments and need to be studied in their own light for at least two reasons. First, remittance inflows are often, but not always, accompanied by family migration.[2] Someone in the family may have migrated (the remitter) and that, in itself, is likely to impact household behavior. In that regard, remittance-receiving families are a 'selected' sample of households. While households who receive government transfer payments are also selected with regards to a variety of characteristics, such as age, employment status, or illness, there exist well-known program rules that clearly state program participation requirements. Therefore, we can foresee which households will receive such

430

transfers, control for those characteristics, and accurately assess how the transfers impact household behavior. However, in most cases, surveys that include information on remittances do not include information on the migration of household members. The inability to account for this variable creates an omitted variable bias that can make it difficult to assess the impact of remittances on the behavior of the recipient households.[3]

The second way in which remittances differ from government transfer payments is in the uncertainty surrounding their receipt. If one is unemployed and qualifies for unemployment insurance, the stream of unemployment insurance payments is likely to be fairly stable and predictable. This predictability is a major component of social insurance programs. But remittances are not so formalized. The receipt of payments from a family member living in another country may vary and be less predictable for a variety of reasons. The ability to obtain employment in the foreign country, the exchange rate, the cost of living in the foreign country, and the altruistic sentiment on the part of the migrant are all factors that can influence the regularity and predictability of the payments sent by the remitter and, hence, on the recipient's expectation regarding future receipts. This, in itself, is likely to influence the behavior of the recipient. It is this aspect of remittances that we wish to further explore in this chapter. Is the stream of remittance inflows steady and predictable? Or are remittances fairly predictable for some households and less predictable for other households? If so, their receipt will influence household behavior in ways that differ from government transfers. Furthermore, as with migration, failure to account for the volatility of remittance flows can bias the estimated impact of remittance flows if (a) the variability with which remittance flows are received affects household behavior and (b) the level and volatility of remittance flows are correlated. Because both (a) and (b) can often occur, the inability to account for the volatility of remittance flows can seriously bias the estimated impact of remittance flows on the household behavior being examined.

This chapter makes a first excursion into measuring and understanding the regularity and predictability of remittances using Mexican households as a case study. Our intent is to demonstrate that there is great diversity in the time pattern and apparent predictability of remittance receipts by households in Mexico. Therefore, it is only natural for the behavior of remittance-receiving households to be influenced not only by the amount of the remittance inflow, but also by its regularity and predictability. That the level and predictability of receipts matter is well documented in the literature detailing the impact of the level and predictability of income on saving behavior. While saving is surely related to income 'levels,' it is well

432 *Handbook of research methods in migration*

known that the 'predictability' of future income flows is also an important determinant of savings (Ando and Modigliani, 1957; Friedman, 1957). For example, it is well accepted that uncertainty about future income inflows causes individuals to engage in precautionary saving and to raise their saving rates. Hence, both the level of income and its uncertainty determine the level of saving.

Because remittances are an important and significant source of income for many households in developing countries, variation in the pattern of remittance inflows is likely to impact spending and other household behavior (see Amuedo-Dorantes and Pozo, 2009). Hence, it is important for the literature to take into account remittance income predictability when assessing the impact of remittance flows on the behavior of recipient households.

20.1 THE DATA

We use data from the harmonized 2000, 2002, 2004, 2005, 2006, and 2008 waves of the Mexican *Encuesta Nacional de Ingresos y Gastos de los Hogares* (ENIGH) – a nationally representative survey carried out by the Mexican Statistical Institute (Instituto Nacional de Estadística, Geografía e Informática – INEGI at http://www.inegi.gob.mx) with the purpose of providing information on the size, structure, and distribution of Mexican households' income and expenditures. The survey was first administered in 1983–84, re-administered in 1989, and carried out on a biennial or annual basis from 1992 onwards. Its population coverage includes all national and foreign households living in private dwellings.

The ENIGH queried households about all income sources during each of the past six months. This feature is of particular interest to us as it provides information that can be used to gain insights into the regularity or predictability of remittance (along with income) receipts by the household. Data detailing the time pattern of remittance receipts (in particular for such a large sample) are rare.[4] In this chapter, we show that there are significant differences in the regularity and predictability with which remittances are received by households. Therefore, one cannot make generalizations about the pattern of these inflows and, instead, such patterns should be taken into account when gauging the impact of remittances on household behavior.

A total of 125,807 households are surveyed in the six waves of the ENIGH used for this chapter. Of these households, a little more than 6 percent (7692/125,806 = 0.061) receive remittances. This percentage is

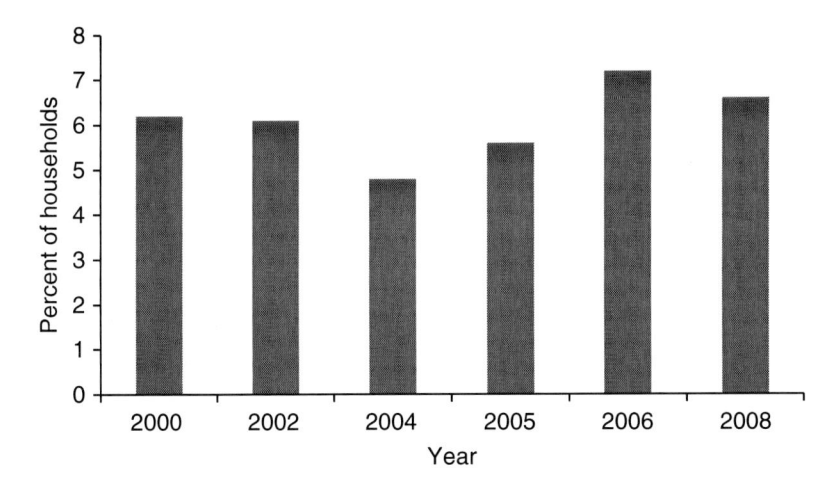

Figure 20.1 Percent of households claiming to receive remittances

Source: ENIGH 2000–08 waves.

fairly consistent with other microeconomic studies that have surveyed the Mexican population. However, it is interesting to note that examination of remittance receipts by year (Figure 20.1) reveals year-to-year variation in the share of households that receive remittances. While a little over 6 percent of Mexican households claimed to receive remittances in 2000, only 4.8 percent did in 2004. Two years later, however, 7.2 percent of households enjoyed remittances. Hence, there is some variation in the proportion of households that receive remittances over time.

It is interesting that the household-level data do not mirror macroeconomic data on remittances flows to Mexico. The World Bank publishes yearly data on remittances as a percent of Mexican gross domestic product (GDP). These are displayed in Figure 20.2. Remittances inflows in US dollars as reported by the Mexican Central Bank are another source of aggregate data on remittances. These are reproduced in Figure 20.3. While both statistics indicate that remittances have continually risen in value and in importance (at least until 2006), the microeconomic data displayed in Figure 20.1 show greater variation in the percentage of households enjoying remittance inflows over time. For example, the total inflow of remittances as a percentage of GDP (Figure 20.2), as well as remittances in US dollar terms (Figure 20.3), increased substantially from 2002 to 2004. But the percentage of households receiving remittance inflows decreased from 6.1 percent of the population to

434 *Handbook of research methods in migration*

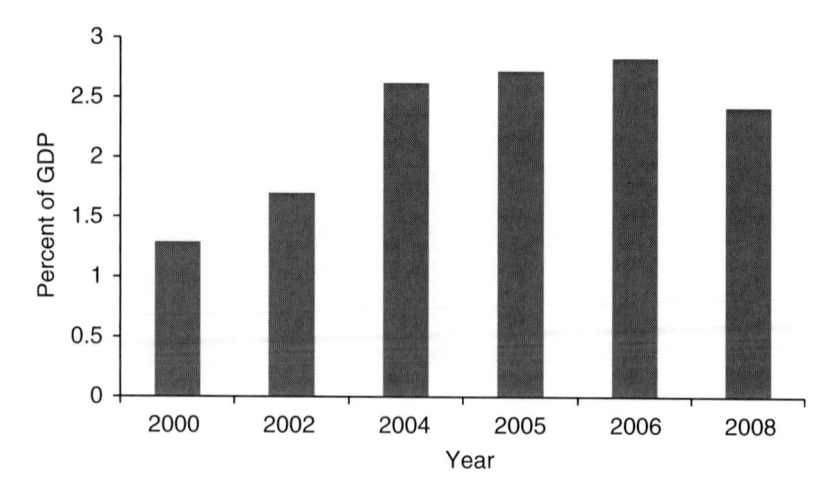

Note: Remittances are defined as workers' remittances plus compensation of employees.
Source: World Development (2009).

Figure 20.2   Remittances as a percentage of Mexican GDP

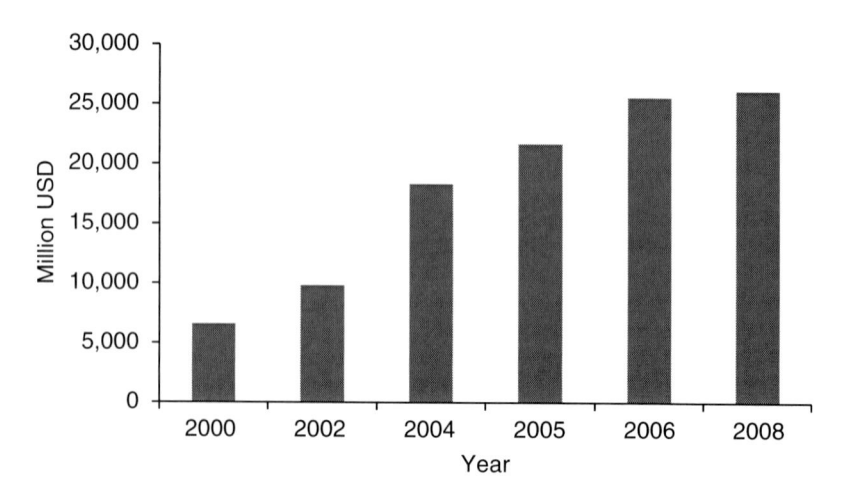

Source: Banco de Mexico (2009).

Figure 20.3   Remittances inflows by year

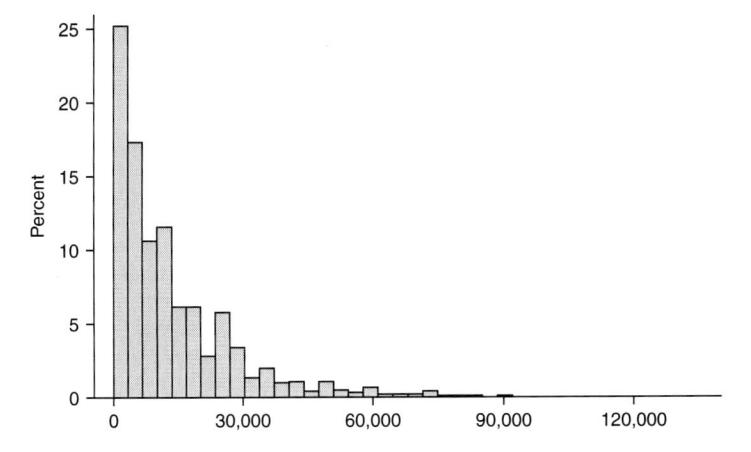

The importance of accounting for variability in remittance income 435

Note: The far right tail of the distribution (values in excess of 130,000) has been truncated. Less than 1.5 percent of remittance-receiving households report inflows in excess of 100,000 pesos for the six-month period.

Figure 20.4   Histogram of remittance receipts over the past six months

4.8 percent of the population (a 21 percent decline) according to the household data. While the microeconomic and macroeconomic series are not necessarily inconsistent with one another (for example, fewer households might be receiving remittances, but each household might be receiving larger inflows), they demonstrate that we may gain some insights from examining the data from various angles and from exploring different sources of data.

Using the ENIGH data, Figure 20.4 displays a histogram of the peso amount received by households over the past six-month period. We have truncated the far right of the tail (74 observations in total) in order to visualize more clearly the bulk of the distribution of remittance receipts. Despite being truncated, the plot displays considerable skewness. Data with this degree of skewness are often transformed into a logarithmic form for a variety of reasons, including better visualization. Figure 20.5 displays the transformed data. Summary descriptive statistics for the untransformed and the transformed data series (including outliers) are reported in Table 20.1. Over this time period, remittance receipts from receiving households average about 18,000 pesos over a six-month period. The median receipt, however, is half of that amount (that is, 9000 pesos over six months), which corresponds to approximately 136 USD per month.[5] What can we say about household remittance-receiving patterns? We address this question in what follows.

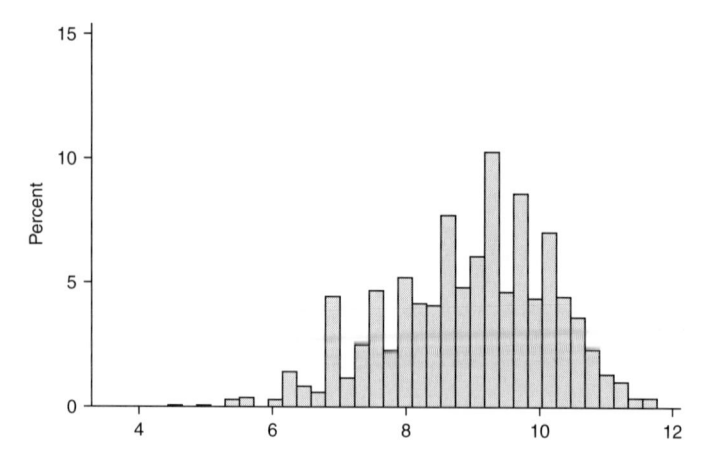

Figure 20.5 Histogram of log (remittance receipts) over the past six months

Table 20.1 Simple descriptive statistics for total (log) remittance receipts over the six-month period

Descriptive statistics	Remittances	Log (remittances)
Mean	18,043	8.98
Median	9,000	9.10
Standard Deviation	87,750	1.28
Skewness	57.78	–0.34
Kurtosis	4,162	3.63
Minimum	2	0.69
Maximum	6,600,000	15.70
N	7,693	7,693

20.2 REMITTANCE INFLOWS: HOUSEHOLD-LEVEL RECEIPT PATTERNS

In addition to gaining a better understanding of the overall incidence of remittance inflows and of the distribution of receipt levels, it is useful to describe the time series pattern of remittance inflows. We first focus on the 'frequency' of receipts at the household level. Next, we look at both the level and frequency of receipts at the household level in order to categorize the time-series pattern of receipts as either 'regular' or 'irregular.' Finally,

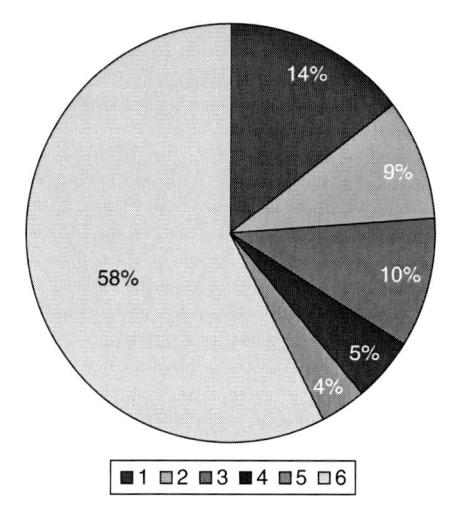

The importance of accounting for variability in remittance income 437

Figure 20.6 Number of months out of six household receives remittances

we resort to using a continuous measure of remittance income variability to discuss the 'predictability' of the inflows.

20.2.1 Frequency of Remittance Receipts

Some remittance-receiving households receive transfers on a relatively frequent basis, while others receive them less often. To appreciate the diversity in the frequency of remittance receipts, we explore how often households receive remittances over the past six-month period. A pie chart in Figure 20.6 details our findings. Over half of remittance-receiving households (57.4 percent) receive remittances each and every month. About 10 percent of remittance-receiving households receive transfers every other month, and a similar percentage receive them every third month. Nearly one sixth of remittance-receiving households enjoy transfers only once every six months. The final 9 percent of households receive transfers in four or five of the six months recorded by the survey. Clearly, households differ in the frequency of remittance receipts.

20.2.2 Regular Versus Irregular Remittance Receipts

While Figure 20.6 informs on the frequency of remittance receipts, it does not account for changes in the level of receipts. A household might receive remittances each and every month. However, the receipt of 150 pesos in month one, 2000 pesos in month two, and 850 pesos in month three will

438   *Handbook of research methods in migration*

Table 20.2   Patterns of remittance receipt

Variables	Observations	Percent of total
Remittance-receiving household	7693	–
Households receiving equivalent amounts each month	2765	35.9
Household receiving equivalent amounts every other month	213	2.8
Households receiving equivalent amounts every third month	122	1.6
Household receiving amounts on an irregular basis	4593	59.7

likely have a different impact on household behavior than the receipt of 1000 pesos on a monthly basis. Therefore, we explore the regularity of remittance flows in our sample. As shown in Table 20.2, approximately 40 percent of remittance-receiving households receive remittances in equivalent amounts at equally spaced intervals. Specifically, about 36 percent of remittance recipients claim to receive equivalent remittance amounts every month, 2.8 percent receive equivalent amounts every other month, and 1.6 percent receive equivalent amounts every third month. The other 60 percent of remittance-receiving households receive remittances on an irregular basis. They may receive remittances of differing amounts in each of the six months, or receive remittances only once over the entire six-month period.

20.2.3   Predictability of Remittance Receipts According to their Variability

Classifying the pattern of remittance receipt as 'regular' or 'irregular' is useful. However, a continuous measure of the variability of remittance inflows may reflect better on the predictability of such money transfers. Consider the following pattern of remittance receipts: 999 pesos in month one, 1001 pesos in month two, and 1000 pesos in month three. Then, compare that remittance-receiving pattern to the following one: 50 pesos in month one, 2500 pesos in month two, and 450 pesos in month three. While 3000 pesos are transferred in total in both examples, the second series is much more variable and, as a result, we probably would have a hard time guessing what the fourth value in the series would be. In contrast, the first series is fairly stable and, if we were to infer the fourth value in the series, we would be much more willing to wager that it is in the order of 1000 pesos. The first series is more predictable than the second one.

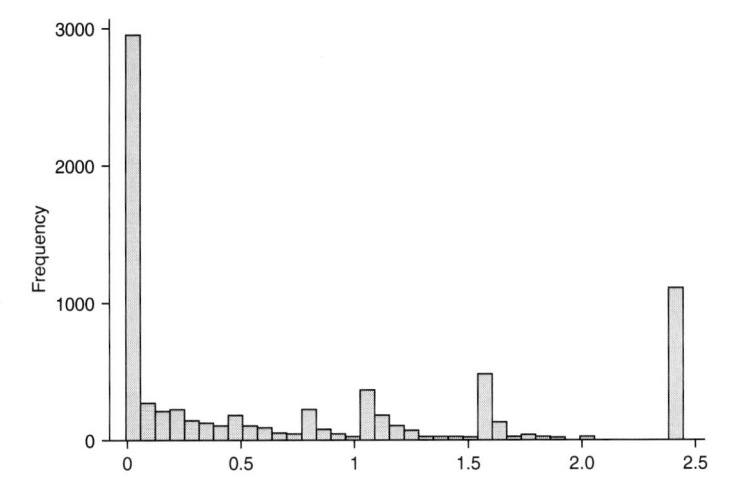

The importance of accounting for variability in remittance income 439

Note: $N = 7693$.

Figure 20.7 Histogram of the coefficient of variation of remittance receipts for remittance-receiving households

Figure 20.7 displays the histogram of the 'variability' of remittance inflows for each household in the ENIGH that received remittances at least once in the six-month period. We use the coefficient of variation of the past six months to measure such variability. The coefficient of variation is computed as the standard deviation of the six-month series of receipts divided by its mean.[6] The histogram reveals the large range of values for the coefficient of variation, that is, from 0 to about 2.5. The average value is 0.77 and its standard deviation 0.89. Thus, remittance-receiving households differ in the level of remittance income variability that they face. A relatively large number of households face no variability in their receipts (nearly 3000 households out of 7693), while others seem to be receiving inflows from abroad in a seemingly less predictable pattern.

In sum, there is a wide range of remittance-receiving patterns that, in turn, are likely to influence household behavior, even more so if such patterns fluctuate over time, as we shall show in what follows.

20.3 REMITTANCE RECEIPT PATTERNS OVER TIME

After learning about the various patterns of remittance receipt by households, we look at how the latter may have changed over time. Specifically,

440 *Handbook of research methods in migration*

Table 20.3 Number of months the household received remittances in the past six months

Year	Number of months					
	One	Two	Three	Four	Five	Six
2000	17.7	11.4	9.4	5.8	5.0	51.0
2002	14.6	11.3	9.3	5.6	4.9	54.3
2004	14.0	8.7	9.6	5.1	3.4	59.2
2005	12.8	8.9	10.4	5.0	3.5	59.4
2006	11.3	8.8	10.7	4.2	4.0	61.1
2008	17.3	8.9	10.2	5.1	2.5	56.0

we ask: have there been changes in the pattern of receipts over time? Has the frequency of receipts risen, fallen, or remained unchanged over time? Are more households receiving remittances on a regular basis in 2008 relative to the year 2000? Has the predictability of remittance flows varied over time? Can households feel more or less secure about the amounts they will receive on a month to month basis?

Table 20.3 reports on the 'frequency' of receipts by year. In the 2000 survey, 51 percent of remittance-receiving households reported receiving remittances each and every month, while 17 percent reported receipts only once during the six-month period. The proportion of households receiving remittances each and every month seems to have increased over time. However, there is some variation in this trend, which reversed in the 2008 survey.

Next, we ask whether we observe changes in the proportion of households who receive remittances on a 'regular' basis and those that receive remittances on an 'irregular' basis. That is, has the proportion of households receiving remittances in equal amounts and at equal intervals (what we term 'regular' receipts) varied over the eight years of data? According to the figures in Table 20.4, the proportion of households receiving remittance 'regularly' has been increasing over time. In 2000, only 25 percent of households could count on receipts of equal amounts at regular intervals, while in 2005, 47 percent could count on equal receipts at equal intervals of time. But, in 2008, that percentage reversed somewhat suggesting that more households may count on a steady inflow but with some variation over time.

Finally, we also check to see how the 'predictability' of remittance inflows as captured by the coefficient of variation of inflows at the household level has behaved over time. The results are reported in the far right column of Table 20.4 and show that the variability of inflows decreased up until 2006. As with the other two measures, the reliability of inflows did reverse from a peak amount around 2005 or 2006.

The importance of accounting for variability in remittance income 441

Table 20.4 *Patterns of remittance receipt over time*

Year	Percent of households with regular receipts*	Coefficient of variation of receipts
2000	25.4	0.89
2002	34.5	0.81
2004	43.3	0.73
2005	47.2	0.70
2006	41.4	0.69
2008	40.9	0.82

Note: * Regular receipts refer to receiving remittances in equal amounts at equal intervals.

Overall, there have been changes in the frequency, regularity, and variability of remittance receipts that is suggestive of changes in the predictability of the flows over time. Remittance inflows to households are overall steadier, perhaps due to reductions in the cost of remitting. However, this trend is not uninterrupted, as we observe a reversal around 2005 in this trend. Because of its change over time, accounting for the remittance-receiving pattern when modeling the impact of remittances on household behavior may be particularly important.

20.4 HOUSEHOLD CHARACTERISTICS AND REMITTANCE RECEIPT PATTERNS

Once we have learned about differences in the pattern of remittance receipt by households and on how they may have changed over time, we look at households to learn whether there are differences in the characteristics of remittance-receiving households according to the pattern of remittance inflows. Are households that receive inflows at equal intervals and in equivalent amounts different from households that receive remittances on a more sporadic basis? Table 20.5 compares households with 'regular' versus 'irregular' remittance receipts along various demographic characteristics. It is interesting to note that regular remittance-receivers enjoy larger transfers. Their remittance inflows average 22.5 thousand pesos over a six-month period (about 350 USD a month), while those of households receiving remittances irregularly average 13.5 thousand pesos (about 200 USD a month). Additionally, we note that households that regularly receive remittances are more likely to be female-headed. They also have fewer children (under the age of 6), have more elderly members (over the age of 65), and, on average, are more educated. These differences are significant at the

Table 20.5 Household characteristics conditioned on the regularity of remittance receipts

Variable	Regular receipts	Irregular receipts	t
Remittance amount	22,517	13,592	8.31***
Male headed household	0.53	0.61	7.11***
No. young kids in household	0.58	0.65	3.43***
No. elderly in household	0.44	0.36	45.46***
No. household members with higher education	0.28	0.20	5.60***
No. household members with middle education	1.04	1.08	1.65*
No. household members with low education	2.26	2.64	6.73***
Married	0.65	0.69	2.91***
No. household members with insurance coverage	0.78	0.89	2.87***
Household size	3.91	4.20	5.62***
Rural	0.42	0.52	8.30***

Note: ***signifies significant at the 1 percent level or better and *signifies significant at the 10 percent level or better.

1 percent level or better. Households with irregular inflows tend to report having a married household head, a larger number of less educated adults, a larger number of uninsured members, and rural residency.

In sum, there are significant differences in the demographic characteristics of households that receive remittances on a regular as opposed to an irregular manner. These differences hint at the importance of accounting for the ongoing selectivity that lies under the regularity of the remittance receipts by households when evaluating the impact of remittance flows on their behavior. Neglecting to do so may seriously bias the estimated impact of remittances on the behavior of remittance-receiving households being examined.

20.5 REMITTANCE INCOME AND THE VARIABILITY OF HOUSEHOLD INCOME

In addition to its potential impact on household behavior, knowledge of the variability of remittance inflows is also important to improve our understanding of migration and remitting motives. For instance, we may ask ourselves: Do remittances reduce total income variability otherwise experienced by remittance-receiving households? Does remittance income compensate for decreases or increases in other sources of household income? The New Economics of Labor Migration (NELM) paradigm claims that migration is a household strategy used to reduce income variations over time by getting households to spread its labor efforts spatially (see Sana and Massey, 2005). Geographic dispersion helps families cope with income shortfalls in one region, by permitting a family member living elsewhere to compensate for that shortfall (assuming that the shock is not global). Remittances are thought, therefore, to be the transfers that stabilize income for the household.

In order to roughly gauge whether indeed remittances are stabilizing household incomes, we compare the income distributions over various groups of households. For remittance-receiving households, we compare the distribution of income without remittances to the distribution of income with remittances. This information is summarized in Figure 20.8. The histogram of values for average monthly household income without remittances is plotted in panel A, whereas the histogram of values for average monthly household income with remittances is plotted in panel B.[7] By comparing the two histograms, we observe that the income distribution (including remittance income) is shifted to the right. In other words, the mean is higher, as we would expect from adding remittance payments. However, we also note that the two income distributions vary in several ways. For example, the left tail of the income distribution is modified by the addition of remittance income. The 'no-income' portion of the distribution is gone. There are a total of 724 households (about 10 percent in total) claiming no other sources of income for the sample period but remittances. Those households depend exclusively on remittances. Hence, in these cases, it seems unlikely that household migration has taken place to diversify income risk by spreading geographically. Rather, migration may have occurred to, for instance, collect an overall higher income stream as suggested by the neoclassical theory of migration, which views migration as a means to reap higher returns from human capital (for example, Sjaastad, 1962).

We further compare the income distribution of households in our sample according to whether they receive remittances or not. Panel B in Figure 20.8 displays the histogram for remittance-receiving households, while Figure 20.9 does the same for non-remittance-receiving households. The distributions look very similar. This similarity is borne out in Table 20.6, which presents summary descriptive statistics for the two groups. Recipient and non-recipient households are similar

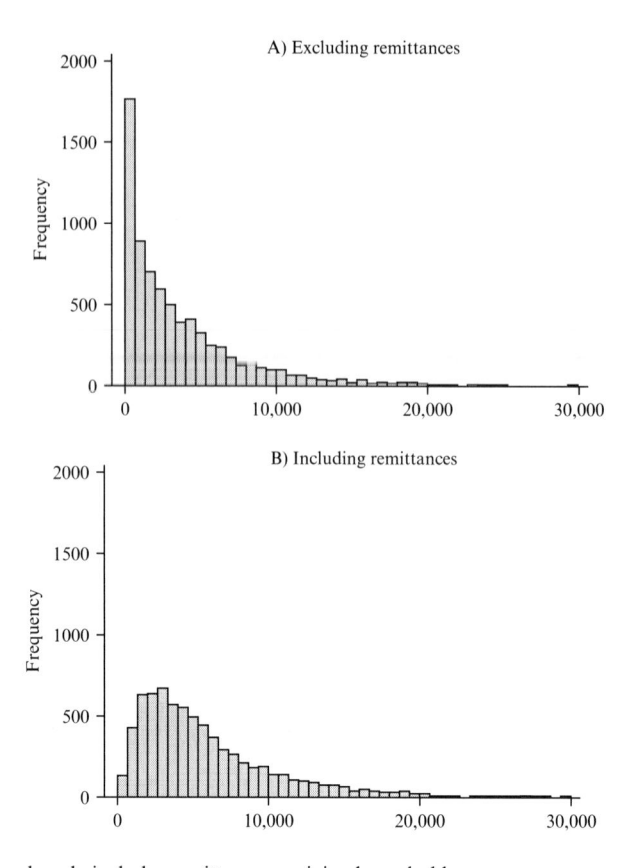

Note: Sample only includes remittance-receiving households.

Figure 20.8 Distribution of average monthly household income by remittance receipt

with regards to monthly mean total incomes – 6761 pesos (about 600 USD) for recipient households and 7162 pesos for households that do not receive remittances. Thus, remittances either pull up total income to the average or, alternatively, we can think of Mexican households as replacing domestic income with foreign income. The two sets of households do, however, vary in the standard deviation of their total incomes. Remittance-receiving households experience more volatility in the stream of total income receipts as measured by the standard deviation (7693 versus 5969) and by the coefficient of variation (0.37 versus 0.24).

The importance of accounting for variability in remittance income 445

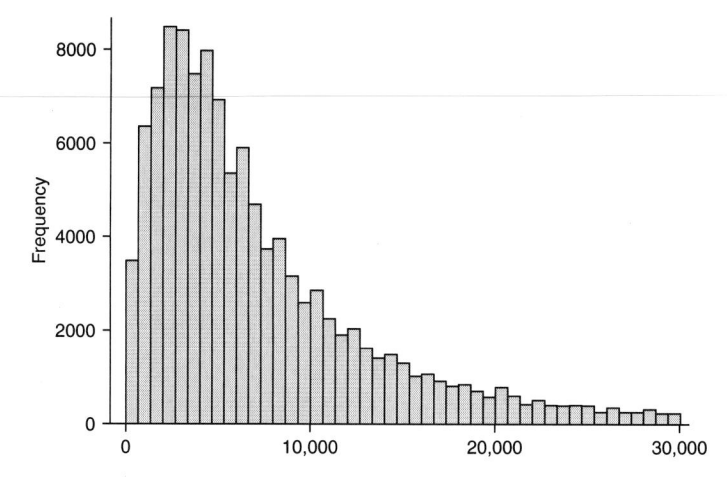

Note: Sample is those households that do not receive remittances.

Figure 20.9 Distribution of average monthly household income

Table 20.6 Summary descriptive statistics for average monthly household income

Household type	N	Mean	Standard deviation	Average coefficient of variation
Recipients				
Income without remittances	7,574	4066	4827	0.49
Income with remittances	7,574	6761	7693	0.37
Non-recipients				
Income	112,833	7167	5969	0.24

20.6 CONCLUSIONS

Using the 2000, 2002, 2004, 2005, 2006, and 2008 waves of the Mexican ENIGH, we examine the pattern of remittance receipt of Mexican households. We find that there is great diversity in the pattern of remittance receipt by households that enjoy these international money transfers. Some households receive remittances on a regular, and predictable, basis, while other households seem to receive these transfers on a more irregular or erratic basis as judged by both the level and frequency of remittance receipts. Additionally, there have been changes in the 'frequency,' 'regularity,' and 'variability' of remittance receipts that are suggestive of changes in the 'predictability' of the flows over time. Such changes emphasize the need to account for variability in remittance-receiving patterns by households when examining the impact of remittance income on their behavior.

We also note that demographic characteristics of households that receive remittances on a regular basis significantly differ from those of households that receive remittances on an irregular basis. The former tend to be female-headed, have more elderly inhabitants, and higher levels of education. Neglecting to account for these differences and for the variability in the remittance-receiving pattern may seriously bias the estimated impact of remittances on household behavior, from labor supply to educational, health and business investments. Although remittance levels and remittance income volatility tend to be inversely related for Mexican households, we cannot forecast what the sign of the bias on the estimated coefficient of remittances on household behavior will be. The direction of the bias depends also on the correlation of remittance income volatility with the outcome being examined. In some instances, increased remittance income variability may result in greater asset accumulation or labor supply, but perhaps in reduced investments in children's educational attainment. Nevertheless, we can forecast that if the correlation between remittance income volatility and the household behavior being examined is non-negligible, we may run into a considerable bias in the estimated impact of remittance income on household behavior. After all, we already know that remittance levels and remittance income volatility at the household level are significantly and non-negligibly correlated.[8] Therefore, it is important that statistical studies take into account both the level and the variability in remittance flows when assessing the impact of remittances on the behavior of households in remittance-receiving economies.

Finally, our analysis of the data also suggests that remittance-receiving households endure greater variability in household income than non-remittance-receiving households. This is not to say that remittances increase household income volatility. Household income variability may have been even greater without the transfers from abroad. But it certainly is the case that, on average, these households experience greater volatility in their month-to-month income receipts. The latter may impact household spending and investing patterns in ways that may be important to consider when learning about the motives for migrating and remitting – a first step in trying to forecast migration and remittance flows and gauging their impact on household behavior.

In sum, there is great variability in the pattern with which remittances are received by households that surely needs to be taken into account when modeling migration, remittance flows, and the impact that both may have on the behavior of recipient households in the developing migrant-sending world.

NOTES

1. We are grateful to the Fundación Banco Bilbao Vizcaya Argentaria for supporting this research.
2. See Amuedo-Dorantes, Georges and Pozo (2010) and Amuedo-Dorantes and Pozo (2010) on the incidence of remittances with migration in Haiti and in the Dominican Republic. They provide evidence that remittances and migration often occur simultaneously. Yet, in a non-trivial number of cases, remittances do not follow migration and, in other instances, remittances are enjoyed by families even if they do not have a close family member abroad.
3. For example, if we wish to understand the impact of remittances on educational attainment, it is important to be able to control for migration of a family member since migration may impact educational efforts on the part of the child. For instance, children living in households that have sent a member abroad may need to devote more effort to family tasks, leaving the child with less time to devote to scholarly tasks. If we do not have information on family migration, the coefficient detailing the impact of remittances on the children's educational attainment will be biased downwards.
4. Other Mexican surveys containing nationally representative information on household income and expenditures, such as the Mexican Life Family Survey, do not allow us to (1) distinguish between national and international remittance transfers and (2) do not contain detailed month-to-month income information required to construct measures of remittance income predictability, as we do here. Similarly, the Mexican census only reports last month's receipts, making it impossible to construct a variable that can measure the predictability of remittance income.
5. This is computed using an exchange rate of 11 pesos per US dollar, the average exchange rate over the time period.
6. The rationale for using the coefficient of variation instead of simply the standard deviation of the series, is to make the summary measure for each household unit-less.
7. One hundred and eighty-seven outlier values have been truncated.
8. In this data, the correlation is –0.123.

REFERENCES

Amuedo-Dorantes, C. and Pozo, S. (2006), 'Migration, remittances and male and female employment patterns', *American Economic Review Papers and Proceedings*, **96** (2), 222–6.
Amuedo-Dorantes, C. and Pozo, S. (2009), 'When do remittances facilitate asset accumulation? The importance of remittance income uncertainty,' mimeo.
Amuedo-Dorantes, C. and Pozo, S. (2010), 'Accounting for migration and remittance effects', *World Development*, **38** (12), 1747–59.
Amuedo-Dorantes, C., Georges, A. and Pozo, S. (2010), 'Migration, remittances, and children's schooling in Haiti', *The Annals of the American Academy of Political and Social Science*, Issue 'Continental Divides: International Migration in the Americas', ed. K.M. Donato, J. Hiskey, J. Durand and D.S. Massey, **630** (1), 224–44.
Ando, A. and Modigliani, F. (1957), 'Tests of the life cycle hypothesis of saving: comments and suggestions', *Oxford Institute of Statistics Bulletin*, **19**, 99–124.

Banco de Mexico (2009), 'Balansa de pagos', available at http://www.banxico.org.mx (accessed 17 October 2011).
Borraz, F. (2005), 'Assessing the impact of remittances on schooling: the Mexican experience', *Global Economy Journal*, **5** (1), 1–30.
Cox-Edwards, A. and Rodríguez-Oreggia, E. (2009), 'Remittances and labor force participation in Mexico: an analysis using propensity score matching', *World Development*, **37** (5), May, 1004–14.
Cox Edwards, A. and Ureta, M. (2003), 'International migration, remittances, and schooling: evidence from El Salvador', *Journal of Development Economics*, Special Issue, **72** (2), 429–61.
Friedman, M. (1957), *A Theory of the Consumption Function*, Princeton, NJ: Princeton University Press.
Funkhouser, E. (1992), 'Migration from Nicaragua: some recent evidence', *World Development*, **20** (8), 1209–18.
Kandel, W. and Kao, G. (2001), 'The impact of temporary labor migration on Mexican children's educational aspirations and performance', *International Migration Review*, **35** (4), 1205–31.
Lucas, R.E.B. (2007), 'International migration and economic development in low income countries: lessons from recent data', in S. Pozo (ed.), *International Migrants and their International Money Flows*, Kalamazoo: Upjohn Institute for Employment Research, pp. 11–32.
Sana, M. and Massey, D.S. (2005), 'Household composition, family migration, and community context: migrant remittances in four countries', *Social Science Quarterly*, **86** (2), 509–28.
Sjaastad, L.A. (1962), 'The costs and returns of human migration', *Journal of Political Economy*, **70**, October, 80–93.
Terry, D. and Wilson, S. (2005), *Beyond Small Change: Making Migrant Remittances Count*, Washington, DC: Inter-American Development Bank.
World Bank (2009), 'World Development Indicators online', Washington, DC: The World Bank.

PART V

PRACTICAL ISSUES IN MIGRATION RESEARCH

21 Ethical challenges in research with vulnerable migrants
Ilse van Liempt and Veronika Bilger

In this chapter we present some of the challenges and issues that resulted out of several research projects involving migrants in vulnerable situations. We believe that the 'lessons learned' are suited to contribute to the design of new research that will have to deal with similar challenges. Over the last decade international migration has become much more complex than in previous years. It is no longer predominantly a movement between selected states, like, for example, during the guest worker period, but is becoming increasingly global and complex. More persons from more diverse countries of origin migrate over longer distances, in a shorter period of time and with more interruptions along the route. At the same time, and accompanied by increasingly restrictive approaches towards specific forms of immigration, a clear trend emerges towards a selective approach towards international migration. States seek to promote 'desirable' migration and to reduce what is considered 'unwanted' migration. This approach is reflected in restrictive measures in regard to admission, residence, access to the labour market, social benefits and so on. The (unintended) consequences of these immigration policies are reflected in a considerable increase in irregular migration in the last decades (Arango, 2000; Castles and Miller, 2003) and an increasing number of migrants in precarious situations connected to illegal residence, exploitative labour conditions, social and economic marginalisation and so on.[1] These changes in migration processes have resulted in the emergence of important new fields for the study of migration in the 1990s, like irregular migration, human smuggling, human trafficking and transit migration. In these early studies on irregular migration processes the economic and the criminal discourse were most of all dominant with a lot of attention on the causes of the 'problem' and on questions like how human smuggling and trafficking functions as a 'business' (Salt and Stein, 1997).

The fact that these irregular migration processes often result in precarious situations for migrants has not been studied much, in contrast to the United States where many more studies on irregular migrants' lives have been conducted (Duvell et al., 2010). Recently research interests in Europe in the field of irregular migration, however, have started to diversify and other aspects of irregular migration such as the implications of migration policies on 'illegal' migration or the conditions of these 'vulnerable' migrants are given much more attention.

An increase in research where migrants in vulnerable situations are at the centre of attention asks for subsequent methodological discussions and ethical considerations. As the concept of 'the vulnerable' is socially constructed a precise definition is problematic. Moore and Miller (1999) contend that 'vulnerable persons include persons who are, individually or as part of a group, stigmatised, excluded or have limited control over their lives, to maintain independence and to self-determine' (Moore and Miller, 1999, p. 1034). This includes, for example, low status populations, minors, members of excluded groups, unemployed or impoverished persons, people in emergency situations, prisoners or detainees, homeless, minorities and refugees, traumatized, persons with mental illnesses and mentally incompetent people.

Research involving vulnerable persons or groups, sensitive topics (for example, 'illegal' or political behaviour, the experience of violence, abuse or exploitation); groups very difficult to access (for example, 'ethnic or cultural groups'); and, in particular, research involving 'access to records of personal or confidential information' is generally considered as involving more than minimal risk (ESRC, 2005, cited in Duvell et al., 2010, p. 228). However, in our view the increased attention given to research involving vulnerable migrants has still not yet been adequately translated into corresponding publications on methodological and ethical challenges in the study of migration (van Liempt and Bilger, 2009). There are very few books that document and provide advice on how to go about performing sensitive research with vulnerable persons. And while reading about research results of others we rarely get information on the design of the research or the research process such as how participants were selected, identified and accessed. Even less insight is provided in regard to difficulties experienced, possible biases, the researcher's positioning and how confidential information was dealt with. Qualitative research often results in face to face interactions, observations and participating in research participants' lives which imposes particular ethical challenges (Dench et al., 2004, p. 31) that are also hardly ever discussed.

On the one hand, this gap in the literature reflects the dilemma of the multidisciplinary nature of the study of migration which requires comprehensive knowledge and understanding of the methodological approaches of various disciplines (Agozino, 2000). Outside the migration field there is excellent work addressing methodological and ethical issues which are often overlooked or cannot be easily translated to issues of migration

(Bilger and van Liempt, 2009). On the other hand, the limited amount of publications on this topic also reflects the reservation towards handling the fact that there are particular difficulties related to empirical research with vulnerable migrants (Bilger and van Liempt, 2009).

21.1 THE ETHICAL CONTEXT

There is consensus across the literature that qualitative research imposes more ethical challenges than quantitative research. Quantitative research applies more formal interview situations of a hierarchical nature between interviewer and interviewee whereas qualitative research asks for a relationship between the researcher and the research subjects (Dench et al., 2004, p. 31). Face to face interactions, observations and participating in research participants' lives create particular tensions when considering research ethics.

For a long time ethical issues relating to research involving human subjects were limited to the field of medical studies and related to subjects such as human anthropology. Ethical standards in social science are much more recent. The first international code of ethics to protect the right of people from research abuse was conducted in 1949 in the Nuremberg Code. Other Codes of Ethics are the 'Declaration of Helsinki' (1964) and the 'Belmont Report' (1978). Today, in many countries social science research is routinely assessed in respect to its ethical implications. Ethical principles are integrated in a variety of national guidelines and regulations and especially in the Anglo-Saxon countries and ethic committees are set up to which researchers should hand in their research ideas for approval. Ethical standards in social science are generally based on three basic principles: respect for human dignity, justice and beneficence. These standards also emphasize four guidelines through which these principles should be applied: informed consent, non-deception, privacy and confidentiality, and accuracy (Christians, 2005, p. 144).

These standards and ethical assessment procedures, however, still bear the hallmarks of medical research and life science and are not always easily applicable in qualitative research. Rather than searching for neutral principles to which all parties can appeal social ethics in human relations are much more complex and influenced by all sorts of moral judgements and beliefs and feelings that go beyond rigid sets of rules and guidelines. Feelings of shame and approval, empathy and intuition may, for example, have effects on human interactions. Besides, interview settings are always influenced by power-relations. Paradoxically, when research strives for a more reciprocal relation between the 'researcher' and the 'researched' the criteria of informed consent, non-deception, privacy and confidentiality are more difficult to deal with.

21.2 PLANNING THE RESEARCH

21.2.1 Understanding the Institutional Framework

Migrants' lives in general but particularly those shaped by irregular migration, exploitation or other aspects of 'illegality' are very much influenced by a specific political and institutional framework that poses very concrete methodological and ethical challenges. The legal framework surrounding migration is rooted in a political context that is currently most of all restrictive and selective towards certain types of immigrants. This has an intrusive impact on immigrants' lives, especially on irregular migrants' lives. Under the jurisdiction of immigration legislation the framework in which these migrants move and organize their lives is, in many ways, fundamentally different from the majority population's. Immigrants are subjected to a different realm of legal and administrative procedures at all levels and in many cases of a discretionary nature (see Barsky, 2009).

However, not every aspect in a migrant's life is to be explained by migration alone. In reality various dimensions my overlap, influence or determine one another. Important observations in the field may equally apply to non-migrants. Thus, researchers need to carefully weigh different factors according to their actual significance in order to avoid, what we call, a 'migration bias' (Bilger and van Liempt, 2009, p. 3).

Acknowledging a possible 'migration bias' is particularly important when taking into consideration that most research in the field of migration has its origin in policy concerns (Black, 2001). Migration research has increasingly developed into a policy supporting research field and shows an increase in the number of commissioned research where the topics and directions of research are already predefined by stakeholders. This kind of research is likely to bring more significant changes to the lives of migrants because certain questions derived from policy priorities may produce results that would, positively or negatively, directly affect the community (Minnery and Greenhalgh, 2007). This situation has, however, also encouraged researchers to take the categories, concepts and priorities of policymakers at the core of their research design (Bakewell, 2008) and thus privileges the worldview of the policymakers in constructing the research, constraining the research questions asked, the subjects of study and the methodologies and analysis adopted.

21.2.2 Framing the 'Right' Research Questions and Methodological Approach

The fact that the lives of 'vulnerable' migrants is very much shaped by particular institutional settings and legislation has a number of basic ethical and methodological implications specific to migration research and particularly to research involving migrants in precarious situations. Understanding the institutional framework and the informed positioning of the envisaged research within this particular framework is a first important ethical challenge. The framing of research questions and methodological approaches include fundamental ethical decisions which shape the orientation of the research, but also the nature and level of involvement of participating persons. Moreover, if the research is not carefully designed and potential negative effects are not assessed research results may have severe negative impacts on migrants' current and future lives.

We think there are three important questions to ask right at the beginning of framing the research:

- What should be researched?
- Why should it be researched?
- How should it be researched?

The framing of the subjects of study, the research question(s), and subsequent methodological approaches determines what type of information can and will be acquired. Researchers are often asked by interviewees to explain why they are doing what they are doing and although this may seem a question with an easy answer in terms of acquiring knowledge or in academic terms 'empirical evidence', it may not always be obvious from an ethical point of view why the research should be conducted or why it should be conducted in a particular way.

Researchers should be more critical about the fact that they often have a detective's urge to know 'everything' without reflecting on the need to collect all that data. An important ethical consideration is how to deal with collected data that is not of direct use for the research project. In her work on Hutu refugees in a refugee camp in Tanzania Malkki states that: 'the success of the fieldwork hinged not so much on a determination to ferret out "the facts" as on a willingness to leave some stones unturned, to listen to what my informants deemed important, and to demonstrate my trustworthiness by not prying where I was not wanted' (Malkki, 1995, p. 51). Our own experience with interviewing irregular migrants is that there is a fine line between what participants consider appropriate behaviour for a researcher and when they start to see you as a journalist who is interested in the 'juicy details'.

21.3 CONDUCTING THE RESEARCH

21.3.1 The Ethical Rule of Informed Consent

In the case of research with 'vulnerable' migrants the 'why do you want to know this' question often determines to what extent people are ready to participate in research and is linked to the ethical question of how research can benefit or harm respondents. There is no need to participate in research if participation might have negative consequences on people's lives and research participants have the right to know what type of information will be collected by researchers and how this is going to be used. Important questions to ask at the start of a research project therefore are:

- Who should benefit from the research?
- What might be the outcome of the research?
- Could the research harm anybody?
- Who is or might be interested in the results?

Positioning the research project is vital, not only to reassure participants about how personal information provided by them is used, but also to give them an idea of the overall purpose of the research project. It is important to be aware of the wider effects research might have for participants. When irregular migration is, for example, the subject of research it is important to make clear to participants whether research results will be shared with the police or immigration officers and if so why this is done. In most cases respondents will ask researchers about this at the start of the interview. There are, however, also situations in which it can be difficult for researchers to know beforehand how participation in research may exactly impact respondents. Therefore it is very important to inform respondents about the goal of research and to give them the opportunity to calculate the risks and decide for themselves whether they want to participate or not. The ethical rule of voluntary participation or 'informed consent' requires the 'provision of information to participants about the purpose of the research, its procedures, potential risks, benefits and alternatives' (Christians, 2005, p. 144).

This rule of informed consent normally requires a written or verbal agreement between researcher and research subject. This is sometimes, however, very impracticable, for example, when groups of people are researched, or when researchers spent a lot of time with participants and do not want to emphasize the fact that they are part of an academic research project over and over again. The principle of informed consent also bears particular difficulties when there are big differences between the researcher and the participants in regard to legal and socio-economic status, culture or education. For a researcher it may in that case be difficult to know exactly what possible risks and harms will be for participants simply because he or she is not familiar with the circumstances respondents find themselves in. Too often, researchers ignore the values, the lifestyle and the cognitive and affective world of the participants but are guided by their own worldviews and ignorance about the participants' realities (Augustin, 2008), which aggravates the difficulties in assessing possible harms of the research for persons participating in the research.

An unequal relationship between researcher and researched may also result in people participating in research against their will. It may be difficult for 'vulnerable' migrants to refuse to participate in research because they feel a social pressure to do so. This was, for example, clearly visible on occasions where respondents anxiously enquired after having been interviewed for an hour or so whether the information that they had provided would suffice. This situation may lead to unethical situations where participants are somehow forced to share information they would rather not share. Moreover, the laws and regulations which shape migrants' lives are often not fully transparent to both the researcher and the potential participants. As such, possible consequences of participating in research may not always easily be appraised by either side.

21.3.2 The Ethical Rule of Guaranteeing Anonymity

Researchers working with vulnerable migrants usually write about the strong privacy concern and the ethical rule of guaranteeing anonymity. In most qualitative methodological approaches it is a standard not to reveal names of participants and the reason why this is done is usually thoroughly explained in methods sections of articles or book chapters. Guaranteeing anonymity, however, is much more complex than just hiding or changing someone's name. It is often not enough to simply change someone's name when the sample is very small and persons may be identified already by the fact of being part of a certain group such as a Hutu refugee living in a small village where no other Hutu refugees are. Rather than applying the rule of guaranteeing anonymity as a standard thing to do it is important to think about how the person could be identified (also within their own group).

Again, it is important to understand the situation respondents find n to be able to realize what the effects can be if one's identity lements of their life story are concealed. Particularly, when research with persons navigating at the margins of the law, researchers may be put in the position of a 'secret holder' sometimes without even being aware of it. It can be very difficult for a researcher to know whether the 'secret' if brought to the public could lead to any harm. This places extra demands on the researchers for accuracy and sensitivity and asks for active involvement of the researcher.

Within methodological paragraphs attention is often put on the reasons why people refuse to participate in research, the so-called non-response. Within our own research it turned out important to know as well why migrants wanted to participate in research because they had specific expectations towards participation in terms of benefits. It is thus equally important to ask why people want to participate in research. The political climate may, for example, deter, but at the same time encourage migrants to participate in research. Some of our participants, for example, were reluctant to make themselves visible through research, even when their anonymity was guaranteed because they felt discouraged by the anti-immigrant attitudes in society whereas others explicitly participated because they wanted to bring their private story to the public to influence public opinion. Research participants may also expect or hope for legal or economic help from the researchers' side. Moreover, networking and making friends can be essential for survival when being in a precarious situation and that may impact the interview setting considerably. Interviewees may, for example, try to present themselves in a particular way in order to increase the chances of becoming friends/lovers. It is important to acknowledge that interviewees may have their own reasons for participating in research and are able to set limits on what information they provide (Glazer, 1982). Being overprotective and focusing on the reasons for refusal and the dangers involved in participating in research can be interpreted as a lack of respect for dignity on the participants' side.

21.3.3 How to Build Up Trust in a Context of Mistrust?

In methodological textbooks we find much attention on how to build up trust with respondents (see also Sánchez-Ayala, Chapter 6, this volume). Authors often let us believe that after having build up trust the research process went smooth and quickly. We do not want to deny that building up trust is very important. It is even of particular importance in the specific context of researching vulnerable immigrants. However, when dealing with vulnerable migrants our experience is that it is more about taking away mistrust than about building up trust. Similar findings are reported in research with asylum seekers where mistrust is often considered a key factor in asylum seekers' survival strategies.[2] As Robinson, for example, makes clear 'many asylum seekers have had to learn *not* to trust people to survive. Their persecutions in the country of origin may have been sparked by a casual comment made by a neighbour, a colleague, a friend or even someone who wished them ill' (Robinson, 2002, p. 64, emphasis added). Undocumented immigrants, persons who engage in 'illegal' activities or who suffer from any kind of violence or dependency such as, for example, victims of trafficking are often sworn to secrecy about their current situation, status or activities (see, for example, Atkinson and Flint, 2001; Cornelius, 1982; Duncan et al., 2003; Ellis and MacGaffey, 1996). This particular situation calls for research approaches different from those commonly used in terms of building up trust. In a continuous balancing act these persons time and again have to decide whether to trust a person or not and sometimes even find themselves fully at the mercy of strangers. Unfortunately, understanding why and how individuals develop mistrust but also to what extent respondents are mistrusted is only rarely taken into consideration in research involving vulnerable migrants.

21.3.4 Deconstructing Constructed Identities

'Mistrust' and 'suspicion' do not only play an important role in migrants' survival strategies. Migrants themselves are also often mistrusted and intensively questioned from many sides (Hynes, 2003). Upon arrival, or if in contact with institutions, they are exposed to rather unpleasant interview situations on their person and biography such as the asylum authorities, police, medical doctors, journalists, persons from their own community and so on. These kinds of conversations usually follow the logic of an interrogation rather than the nature of a conversation driven by genuine interest. Talking about one's life is exclusively about finding inconsistencies in a life story, about testing the life story for legally relevant information and for rational logic. Providing a 'wrong answer' can have drastic effects on the person's current and future life, for example, a negative decision on the asylum claim, detention or imprisonment, deportation, losing a job and so on. Immigrants, who run the risk of being detected or interviewed by officials at any time, might be biased and suspicious when approached by a researcher and may try to fit their story to their expectations in order to minimize possible damage done to them.

In this context it is important to ask oneself how the situation respondents find themselves in influences the life stories told to a researcher. Narrations are always adapted to the circumstances one finds oneself in at the moment of revealing them, but in case of 'vulnerable' migrants this is even more the case. The fact that vulnerable migrants live in an environment of suspicion produces a high level of pressure on how best to present themselves and to be cautious on what aspects should be presented to whom. Migrants learn how to present themselves in different settings over time; this is particularly the case for asylum seekers who are constantly questioned and tested to find out whether they are 'genuine' or 'bogus'. These conditions influence the way migrants present themselves and may lead to a constant adaptation of narrations according to the requirements imposed on them in a given situation.

This situation not only has an impact on how people present their life stories to researchers or to the authorities, but also on the personal perception of certain periods of life and how one comes to terms with this new situation. If the personal past must be adjusted consistently and memory has to shift from an unofficial to an official identity, from a very personal biography to a safer and public version, it creates stress. Khosravi (2010) in this regard writes about the embodiment of being an 'illegal' immigrant and how being seen by others as 'illegal' may have huge implications for one's wellbeing and self-image. This specific situation asks for a very accurate and ethically sound approach from the researchers' side because it could destroy the trust that was built up with respondents.

One strategy of responding to repeated interrogative questioning is to convey one's life story according to the needs of the person listening. In this context respondents are likely to provide information about themselves in accordance with their own needs and with the needs of the listener. They may thus (consciously or unconsciously) be reluctant or afraid to inform the researcher about their true views, tell what they think the researcher expects or wants to hear, wish to promote a particular vision of their situation or hope for any kind of benefit by participating. What information will be disclosed to researchers very much depends on how participants assess the researchers' role vis-à-vis the respondent. For example, information that could lead to benefits might be particularly elaborated upon, highlighted or upgraded while providing insight and information that would possibly have negative effects will either be presented in such a way that it will not cause any harm (for example, by a partial construction of specific events or by leaving out certain details) or simply not be elaborated upon at all.

The Dublin regulations may serve as a good example of how a certain legal regulation may have an influence on a narrated biography. Without some modifications or secrecy in descriptions of the route or on specific countries a person had transited through the person will not be allowed to stay in the country of arrival, but will be sent back to the 'safe-third-country' he or she passed through. This may explain why often only little or no detailed information is to be found on the final part of the migration trajectory towards Europe. One major challenge for the researcher in this regard is that she or he requests a behaviour from the respondents' side which is not only atypical with regard to the interview situations the respondents normally find themselves in, but she or he creates a situation where the respondents have to act contrary to their general survival strategy, namely, by revealing private details. This opens a new field of attention, namely, the need for placing oneself as a researcher into context.

21.4 THE ROLE OF THE RESEARCHER IN RESEARCH WITH VULNERABLE MIGRANTS

Researchers always hope to establish trustworthy relationships with their respondents in order to obtain reliable, truthful answers to produce as credible a research as possible. Establishing trust with respondents is, however, context-bound and 'usually has something to do with dynamics of "giving" and "receiving"' (Lammers, 2005, p. 8). Given this situation it is important to understand participants' perceptions and expectations towards the researcher. This requires a serious reflection on:

- Who am I, the researcher, in the eyes of the respondents?
- What are the expectations from the participants' side of research?

Feminist research has been extremely helpful in reciprocal understanding of research processes and has found its way into the broader theoretical and methodological frameworks especially when it comes to questions on how societal structures and institutions shape and impact migrants' lives and their strategies to cope with it. This is maybe also why feminist research has contributed a lot to refugee and asylum research (see, for example, Temple and Moran, 2006). In terms of research ethics the reciprocal relation can make it difficult for researchers to follow rigid guidelines and ethical codes. By strict ethical standards it is, for example, unethical to become deeply involved and familiar with your informants. This will contribute to a 'distorted' research process, produce biased information and compromise findings (Jacobsen and Landau, 2003). Apparently, it is considered 'unethical' to give in a context defined by power differences because giving further exacerbates these differences. Whether to help respondents or not is an ethical challenge that is open for debate and strongly influenced by one's personal views. Lammers (2007), for example, found herself paying for a variety of things for her respondents, from passport size photos to letters of recommendations, appeals, requests and complaints to be typed and posted, to blood tests, hospital bills, monthly rents and even school fees. She was also engaged in hands-on advocacy work. She argues that it is rather unethical not to help respondents in need (see also Markova, 2009).

Next to ethical questions around inequalities researchers also need to have a certain readiness to deal with unexpected, traumatic or just different views, experiences and opinions that cannot always be evaluated beforehand or are not always mentioned in ethical guidelines. Differences between the researcher and the participants in regard to legal and socioeconomic status, culture or education may have a strong effect on the nature of interaction in an interview setting and can go beyond ethical rules on paper. An open attitude and reflection on methodological and ethical decisions during the research process that allow for transparency reduces tensions 'because typically, marginalised persons rarely express their view towards outsiders and "experts" often only have selective knowledge about their lives' (Achermann, 2009, p. 57).

21.5 POST FIELDWORK ETHICS

As research participants may follow a particular strategy when revealing details of their life in order not to further jeopardize their future plans, the interpretation of information collected constitutes again a very delicate exercise. Researchers might, for example, realize that certain aspects of the information collected seem unrealistic. It is an ethical choice on how to deal with 'inconsistencies' in collected data. In order to assess research insights in a responsible way researchers not only need to reflect on what was disclosed but also what aspects were possibly not disclosed to the researcher and why this was done. Putting information in context also requires reflections on how participants have presented themselves and their situation and when and particularly why participants could possibly have kept certain details back or have 'adapted' their story. Analysing collected information thus again asks for sensitivity and intuition with regard to harms and benefits of research especially when taking into account that information revealed could be used against the participants and researchers might be 'bearers of secrets' which are not meant to be publicly known.

Once a study is finished the next step will be the dissemination of findings. Such dissemination may potentially reach different audiences, academics, policymakers, non-governmental organization (NGO) workers, the media and the wider public. When placing information in the public arena in a responsible way, researchers would, interestingly enough, need to follow the same strategic patterns for balancing harms and benefits as respondents apply for providing information. They would also need to distinguish between:

- Information that could lead to benefits for participants.
- Information that would possibly have negative effects on participants' lives (or the group participants belong to).
- Information that could be considered 'neutral' by participants.

While balancing the final harms and benefits of research, researchers are subject to a set of complex responsibilities. They not only have responsibilities towards individual informants, but also towards social groups, their co-academics, their funding body and society at large. As such, researchers need to take various levels into account: the individual as well as the group level, the research field and the wider societal level. This places extra demands on the researchers for accuracy and sensitivity in assessing what possible effects of certain portrayals might have on all these various levels.

21.6 CONCLUSION

Ethics is about taking responsibility and 'responsibility entails thinking about the consequences of one's actions on others, and the establishment of clear lines of accountability and the redress of grievance' (Dench et al., 2004, p. 3). 'Good' quality research takes into account its responsibility towards the individual, the group, the research field and towards society. It also addresses concerns over power which is of specific relevance when researching migration and even more so when involving migrants in a vulnerable position. Who decides on who has a say and who has not, who decides over the relevance of research for society? Thus, besides methodological considerations, the questions of why the research is conducted and why it is conducted in a specific way are particularly important to ask. 'Good' research also addresses the need to balance the potential for harm against the need for research. Why do we actually need this type of research and is it necessary to collect data on every single aspect? These questions will, if carefully thought through, mitigate ethical tension throughout the research process.

Taking into consideration that migration research has increasingly developed into a policy supporting research field where the topics and directions of research are already predefined by stakeholders also asks for a critical approach towards the concepts used and the questions asked in (commissioned) research. Understanding the migratory context and the institutional context in which participants move are of vital importance for conducting good quality research in an ethically sound way. At the same time it is important to avoid a 'migration bias' and to recognize that participants are not only part of a specific group. Researchers need to take into consideration what in (vulnerable) migrants' lives is determined by the specific institutional and social framework and what is actually not.

Finally, it is important to acknowledge that ethical questions are not static. They need to be raised and reflected from the very start of a project when conceptualizing the research until placing the results in the public arena and need to be balanced against methodological and practical issues. General ethical guidelines are a good start for discussion but often it is up to the individual researcher to make a decision and to decide on a case-by-case basis what is best. Sharing considerations and experiences with other researchers will contribute to a much needed discussion on methodological and ethical developments in the field of migration and a step forwards on our way to better understand 'how to do it right'.

NOTES

1. See Anderson et al. (Chapter 18, this volume) for an example of research on illegal migration.
2. See Oxford (Chapter 19, this volume) for an example of research on asylum seekers.

REFERENCES

Achermann, C. (2009), 'Multi-perspective research on foreigners in prisons in Switzerland', in I. van Liempt and V. Bilger (eds), *The Ethics of Migration Research Methodology: Dealing with Vulnerable Migrants*, Brighton: Sussex Academic Press, pp. 49–82.
Agozino, B. (2000), *Theoretical and Methodological Issues in Migration Research: Interdisciplinary, Intergenerational and International Perspectives*, Aldershot: Ashgate.
Arango, J. (2000), 'Becoming a country of immigration at the end of the twentieth century: the case of Spain', in R. King, G. Lazaridis and C. Tsardanidis (eds), *Eldorado or Fortress? Migration in Southern Europe*, Basingstoke: Macmillan, pp. 253–76.
Atkinson, R. and Flint, J. (2001), 'Accessing hidden and hard-to-reach populations: snowball research strategies', *Social Research Update*, 33, available at http://sru.soc.surrey.ac.uk/SRU33.pdf (accessed October 2011).
Augustin, L. (2008), 'Border thinking on migration, culture, economy and sex', available at http://www.lauraagustin.com/border-thinking (accessed 6 February 2012).
Bakewell, O. (2008), 'Research beyond the categories: the importance of policy irrelevant research into forced migration', *Journal for Refugee Studies*, 21 (4), 432–53.
Barsky, R (2009), 'Methodological issues for the study of migrant incarceration in an era of discretion in law in the southern USA', in I. van Liempt and V. Bilger (eds), *The Ethics of Migration Research Methodology: Dealing with Vulnerable Migrants*, Brighton: Sussex Academic Press, pp. 25–48.

Belmont Report (1978), *Ethical Principles and Guidelines for the Protection of Human Subjects of Research*, The National Commission for the Protection of Human Subjects of Biomedical and Behavorial Research, DHEW Publication No. OS, 78-0012.

Bilger, V. and van Liempt, I. (2009), 'Introduction', in I. van Liempt and V. Bilger (eds), *The Ethics of Migration Research Methodology: Dealing with Vulnerable Migrants*, Brighton: Sussex Academic Press, pp. 1–24.

Black, R. (2001), 'Fifty years of refugee studies: from theory to policy', *International Migration Review*, **35** (1), 57–78.

Castles, S. and Miller, M.J. (2003), *The Age of Migration. International Population Movements in the Modern World*, London: Macmillan.

Christians, C.G. (2005), 'Ethics and politics in qualitative research', in N.K. Denzin and Y.S. Lincoln (eds), *Handbook of Qualitative Research*, 3rd edn, Thousand Oaks, CA: Sage, pp. 139–64.

Cornelius, W. (1982), 'Interviewing undocumented migrants: methodological reflections based on fieldwork in Mexico and the US', *International Migration Review*, **16** (2), 378–411.

Dench, S., Iphofen, R. and Huws, U. (2004), 'An EU code of ethics for socio-economic research', Brighton: Institute for Employment Studies, available at http://www.respect-project.org/ethics/412ethics.pdf#page=33 (accessed 1 October 2010).

Duncan, D.F., White, J.B. and Nicholson, T. (2003), 'Using internet-based surveys to reach hidden populations: case of non-abusive illicit drug users', *American Journal of Health Behaviour*, **27** (3), 208–18.

Duvell, F., Triandafyllidou, A. and Volmer, B. (2010), 'Ethical issues in irregular migration research in Europe', *Population, Space and Place*, **16** (3), 227–39.

Ellis, S. and MacGaffey, J. (1996), 'Research on sub-Saharan Africa's unrecorded international trade. Some methodological and conceptual problems', *African Studies Review*, **39** (2), 19–41.

Glazer, M. (1982), 'The threat of the stranger: vulnerability, reciprocity and fieldwork', in J. Sieber (ed.), *The Ethics of Social Research: Fieldwork, Regulation and Publication*, New York: Springer-Verlag, pp. 49–70.

Hynes, T. (2003), 'The issue of "trust" or "mistrust" in research with refugees: choices, caveats, and considerations for researcher', UNHCR Working Paper, New Issues of Refugee Studies No. 98, November.

Jacobsen, K. and Landau, L. (2003), 'Researching refugees: some methodological and ethical considerations', UNHCR Working Paper, New Issues of Refugee Studies No. 90, June.

Khosravi, S (2010), *Illegal Traveller: An Auto-ethnography of Borders*, Global Ethics Series, Houndmills, Basingstoke: Palgrave Macmillan.

Lammers, E. (2005), 'Refugees, asylum seekers and anthropologists: the taboo on giving', *Global Migration Perspectives*, **29**, April, GCIM, Geneva.

Lammers, E (2007), 'Researching refugees: preoccupations with power and questions of giving', *Refugee Survey Quarterly*, **26** (3), 72–81.

Malkki, L. (1995), *Purity and Exile. Violence, Memory and National Cosmology among Hutu Refugees in Tanzania*, Chicago, IL: University of Chicago Press.

Markova, E. (2009), 'The "insider" position: ethical dilemmas and methodological concerns in researching undocumented migrants with the same ethnic background', in I. van Liempt and V. Bilger (eds), *The Ethics of Migration Research Methodology: Dealing with Vulnerable Migrants*, Brighton: Sussex Academic Press, pp. 141–54.

Minnery, J. and Greenhalgh, E. (2007), 'Approaches to homelessness policy in Europe, the United States and Australia', *Journal of Social Issues*, **63** (3), 641–55.

Moore, L.W and Miller, M. (1999), 'Initiating with doubly vulnerable populations', *Journal of Advanced Nursing*, **30** (5), 1034–40.

Robinson, V. (2002), 'Doing research with refugees and asylum seekers', *Swansea Geographer*, **37**, 61–7.

Salt, J. and Stein, J. (1997), 'Migration as a business: the case of trafficking', *International Migration*, **35** (4), 467–89.

Temple, B. and Moran, R. (2006), *Doing Research with Refugees. Issues and Guidelines*, Bristol: The Policy Press.
van Liempt, I. and Bilger, V. (eds) (2009), *The Ethics of Migration Research Methodology: Dealing with Vulnerable Migrants*, Brighton: Sussex Academic Press.
WMA Declaration of Helsinki (1964), *Ethical Principles for Medical Research Involving Human Subjects*.

22 A guide to managing large-scale migration research projects
Melissa Siegel

Migration research projects come in all shapes and sizes and individuals, groups (teams) and organizations are running them all over the world. However, there is a lack of guides on project management particularly for migration projects, which often run across countries. This chapter hopes to provide some guidance on this subject, particularly for younger researchers starting out in project management. This chapter is meant to be a general guide that you can tailor to your own specific and different project needs.

While winning the projects from the beginning is a very important aspect of project management, this is beyond the scope of this particular chapter. In this chapter, I assume that the project has already been granted and you are now at the stage in which you must implement it.

Project management is defined here as the planning, organizing and managing of resources to bring about the successful completion of specific project goals and objectives. The main difficulty of project management is to achieve all of the project goals and objectives while honouring the preconceived project constraints (Ireland, 2006; Phillips, 2003) which are typically described as a triangle of constraints consisting of scope, time and money (budget) (Microsoft, 2010). While migration research project management falls under this general definition, it differs from many other typical forms of project management. Already, research project management is different from traditional business project management (for which most of the project management literature is written). For example, the University of Melbourne's School of Enterprise (2010) explains how research project management is different in the following:

> Unlike traditional project management, research project management has to deal with different degrees of uncertainty ranging from using known approaches in different ways and using new approaches in existing areas through to developing new approaches and technologies in new areas. Whilst many traditional project management techniques can be adapted to better known technologies and fields of application, assumption management (and therefore risk management) is a more significant factor in achieving successful research project outcomes. Add to this the way in which research teams are formed and funded and you have highly complex and uncertain organizational continuity supporting projects with unknown outcomes.

468 *Handbook of research methods in migration*

The management of research projects and migration research projects more specifically becomes even more complex due to the nature of migration studies in which research is usually done on individuals and communities which are difficult to reach and across countries (both developed and developing) making the risk factors in project management increase dramatically.

The project manager is the main focal point for liaison between the different parts of the project and different team members. It is the job of the project manager to ensure the success of a particular project and the project manager is the main responsible person. In this chapter we discuss migration project management on a larger scale but migration projects come in different shapes and sizes from one-person projects to large-scale projects with more than 50 team members.

We will go through some of the most important aspects of migration project management but this is not an exhaustive list. We will discuss getting organized at the beginning of the project and hiring the necessary staff. The chapter then goes on to discuss the marketing of the project, dealing with different funders, dealing with partners and choosing any additional partners or consultants. This follows with sections on the supervision and management of young researchers, budgeting and reporting. The chapter then concludes with a guide to working in different countries.

22.1 GETTING YOURSELF ORGANIZED

22.1.2 Hiring Additional Team Members Needed

In a large-scale project, you will often receive funding for your project and still need to hire more people to help implement it. This is often the case when the research will fund PhD or postdoctoral positions. Besides PhD researchers and postdoctoral positions, you will often also have to hire research assistants and interns. There are also different types of other jobs for which you may have to hire more people, especially on a short-term basis, such as translators.

Since I assume that most people reading this chapter have not had to hire many people in the past, this can be a daunting task in a large project where many people need to be hired and it takes time unless you already had particular people in mind for your positions. First, you must decide what positions you need, what tasks they will have to perform and what kind of person or qualifications you need. Then you will have to write the job announcements and circulate them as widely as possible. It is generally not needed to pay for an advertisement. As long as you have a good

A guide to managing large-scale migration research projects 469

network that can disseminate the call, paying for an ad is really unnecessary, especially if you are on a tight budget. Preferably, give at least one month from the time you disseminate the announcement until the deadline for applicants to make sure that you can saturate the market enough with the announcement and to ensure that the kind of people you want will be able to apply. When marketing the call, send it out as widely as possible. Send it to groups and distribution lists that will find your target audience.[1] Also, send the call for applicants to trusted people in the field whose opinions you trust, who can then send appropriate people your way. These trusted people will also play a key role later when you actually have to decide on who you want to hire.

Once you have saturated the market with the call for applicants, then it is time to wait for applications to come rolling in. While it can be extremely exciting to see many applications coming in, it can also be a daunting task to begin sifting through them for the appropriate candidates. To help manage this load, especially when you receive more than 100 applications for a position, it is best to make initial criteria that are clear-cut for the first cuts. For this, I suggest making a points list where you list all of the criteria you want in a specific candidate and the weight you give to that characteristic. Then set a cut-off point at which applications are discarded. For instance, see the example form in Figure 22.1. Here you have an example of an initial list of qualifications and characteristics that may be important in an applicant with possible value scores. Characteristics that you consider more important to the position should have a higher possible score. Then you must decide what your cut-off point is for which you will take a closer look at the applications and throw out the others. In this case, a total score of 20 may be a good indication.

After the initial cut, it is time to go more in-depth with those who qualified to go on to the next round. At this point you will take a more detailed look at their applications and call their listed references. I suggest that you talk to references personally instead of only relying on written letters. It may not be necessary to have written letters of reference at all and, instead, you can just ask for a list of references and contact details. Another good way to screen a candidate is to call people who you know they have worked with even if they are not on the reference list to ask about their qualifications for a specific position. Then, narrow your list down to the top (perhaps five) people and arrange interviews. These interviews do not have to be in person, but this is preferable. Given our age of technology, it is quite easy to have conference call interviews through programs like Skype or other specific conference call technology.

Once you have decided on your top applicant, offer them the position. Most universities and public institutions have set salary scales that can

470 *Handbook of research methods in migration*

Name: _____		Number: _____
Subject	**Maximum score**	**Score**
Age < 35	0–1	
Mathematics and statistics (courses, grades)	0–3	
Economics, social science, law (courses, grades)	0–3	
Degree (relevance, success)	0–3	
Work and/or research experience (relevance, time, responsibilities)	0–3	
English level (test results, experience)	0–2	
Motivation (question, overall appearance)	0–2	
Research proposal (innovative, reasoning)	0–3	
Letters of recommendation	0–3	
CV format and content	0–3	
Relevant languages other than English	0–2	
	Total score: 28	
Completed by: _____		

Figure 22.1   Example of application ranking form (for PhD position)

be offered to applicants. However, there may be times when the salary is negotiable. Then it is important to stay within your budget while accommodating the best applicant. You can try to negotiate on other terms than salary because you must make sure to keep your project resources intact to be able to implement the rest of the project. Only let the others know that they were not accepted for the position once the preferred candidate has accepted. The reason for doing this is that your preferred candidate may turn down the position in the end and then you will need to choose the next best person from your top five and so on. It is important to let the other candidates know that their application is still under review, without making it clear that they are the second choice, as this may affect their future motivation.

When deciding and doing the hiring for several positions at once (for instance, 20 interviewers to be enumerators for a survey or interns) it is

A guide to managing large-scale migration research projects 471

very important to take leakage into account. With more junior positions, there is a higher tendency for people to leave a project early (perhaps due to getting another job or deciding that this particular job is not for them). This means that you have to take account of this possible leakage or turnover in staff and plan for it, by perhaps hiring more people or doing a second round of hiring.

After hiring the necessary people, then it is important to train and manage the new employees. A more in-depth discussion of this aspect, especially with regard to junior positions, will be dealt with in a later section on managing young researchers.

22.2 MARKETING THE PROJECT

It seems strange to start talking about marketing a project before you even start properly implementing, but this is a very important aspect of the project that should take place from the very beginning and along the entire duration of the project. While this is good for the project as a whole, it will also keep your funders happy to see that the project which they are putting money into is being promoted and is good for future funding opportunities. That being said, you need to make sure that the logos of all partners and funders of the project are on all of the work that you put out (unless there is a good reason for not doing so) and you may want to even come up with a special project logo.

At the beginning of a large project, it is a good idea to set up a website for the project, either independently or as a section of the institute or implementing body's website. This is extremely important for efficient (and cost-effective) dissemination of project material. Project materials, brochures and output should be placed there. It is also advisable to set up a unique e-mail account for the project and a news list-serve where people can sign up to have regular updates on the project if they would like. At the same time, it is important to develop public relations materials such as brochures and flyers for your project to be able to easily hand out to those interested. If your budget allows for it, a launching conference is also a great way to kick off a project.

As the project progresses, for proper dissemination of output, it is imperative that as much material as possible is posted on your website and regularly disseminated information through networks, conferences, workshops and other forums.

At the end of a project, having a closing conference is a nice way to wrap up and publicize findings. Make sure all reports are posted on-line and easily accessible and that the website for the project stays live for people to access all of the information you have collected. Keep everything as open source as possible.

22.3 DEALING WITH DIFFERENT TYPES OF FUNDERS/DONORS

All projects are funded one way or another and some come with more strings attached than others. Either way, you will almost always have to deal with the funder once a commitment is made to do a particular project. You should do your best to make sure that the research stays as independent and objective as possible no matter who is the funder or donor. There are very different relationships that you can have with a benefactor depending on the nature of the project and funder. This differs between large bureaucratic institutions without a particular responsible person and those in which you deal mainly with one person or group.

There is not a 'one-size-fits-all' way to deal with funders. When dealing with a large institution, for instance, the European Union, European Commission or Europe Aid, you will usually not be dealing with one responsible person. There will be a list of guidelines for reporting and deliverables and you will have to follow this guide as best as possible. There will probably be a different contact point for budget reporting and content reporting. Often, there is not much to be discussed here in the way of content and not much room for manoeuvre with the donor and the specified deliverables must be met. This is in contrast to a more involved or engaged funder that has a specific stake in the research conducted. This could be the case, for example, with a specific department of a ministry or a part of the International Organization for Migration (IOM). Here, you will generally have a specific contact point and the donor will be regularly engaged in the content of the research. You will want to do your best to get to know the contact point and understand how they work. It is important to feel comfortable with the people at the organization for which you are working and to keep a good working relationship and open lines of communication. Don't be afraid to ask questions when things are not clear to you and keep the contact points regularly updated so that they feel like they are a part of the process and so that misunderstandings are minimized.

From the beginning, stakeholder or donor interests should be made clear and matched with possible deliverables/activities/output. Particularly with more 'hands on' funders, make sure that the output is defined in advance to prevent expansion of a 'wish-list' as the project proceeds. It is never a bad idea to give more deliverables than previously agreed upon if you wish but you do not want to be forced to continuously give more output than was agreed upon from the beginning.

22.4 DEALING WITH PARTNERS: KEEPING EVERYONE HAPPY

Many large-scale projects will include a group of partners which are responsible for the project and it is extremely important to keep a good working relationship with all partners throughout the project as this will help the project to run smoothly. In this context, regular communication is extremely important. The ideal situation would be for you to have regular update meetings with a representative from each of the partners. In reality, it can be very difficult to find one time and place when everyone is available, especially when partners are spread out across large distances or countries.

To keep everyone up-to-date regularly, an internal newsletter could be a possible solution and/or the project manager could send out regular e-mail updates to all partners. It will, however, still be important to meet as a group at different points in the project. Internet communication technologies can be a very useful way to hold meetings across countries and time zones (for example, using Skype).

Because of the nature of migration research, partners will often be spread out over several countries and not only will you have to worry about time differences, visas and practical matters, but you will also often be working with cultural differences that are important to understand to ensure a minimal amount of misunderstandings and cultural mistakes.

22.5 CHOOSING IMPLEMENTING PARTNERS

There will often be certain parts of the project (particularly to do with data collection) where you will need more partners or external consultants to complete the project. At this stage, it is extremely vital to choose these consultants or partners well. This is again where it is a good idea to do some scoping in the country in which you need the work to be done and to collect information from trusted colleagues on whom to work with in that particular setting.

Once you have a list of possible partners, you should not only gather information about them from colleagues but it is also important to consult possible partners' previous work or contact commissioning agents or groups. Then you must contact the partner with which you would like to

474 *Handbook of research methods in migration*

work to discuss the nature of the work and their possible interest. Here, it is a good idea to send a 'warm-up' e-mail about your project and intentions to possibly work with them. Give a few days for the institution or responsible person to reply. If there is no response after a few days, it is then best to follow up with a phone call. If the party is interested, suggest a meeting either in person or via a conference call. It is much easier to sort things out this way and you can get a much better feel for the partner than with a long string of e-mails. It is imperative that you clearly specify expectations and make clear (contractual) agreements *ex ante* (for example, liabilities in case of non-delivery and so on). There are some clear signs when not to work with a specific partner. If they are not reliable in the beginning stages of your cooperation, it is better to go with another partner and if other respected colleagues doubt their ability and competency to complete the needed tasks, it is best to go with another partner.

22.6 DEALING WITH YOUNG RESEARCHERS ON THE PROJECT

Besides dealing with funders, partners and consultants, you will often have PhD researchers, research assistants and/or interns involved in your project that you will also have to direct. It is extremely important to manage these researchers properly to both get the most out of the project and to help them build their skills and experience. Often, when a person doesn't perform as you would want, it is a matter of bad management.

First of all, and most importantly, it is extremely important to make sure the young researcher knows what is expected of him or her and that guidelines are made clear from the beginning. If this isn't made clear right from the start, there will be a great deal of room for wasted time and mistakes. While you want to be clear and firm about what you expect from your young researchers, it is important to make sure that your people feel appreciated and are praised for a job well done. It is imperative to keep everyone motivated to give their best to the project.

In a large project, there will be times when you will have to ask a lot from your team. This is normal of any project, but the important point here is to lead by example. If you ask your team to work late then you should also do so. If you need or expect your team to give 125 per cent, you should give 150 per cent and make sure that they always know their work is appreciated. Make sure you verbally and in actions acknowledge the extra work and effort they are putting in.

Also always remember that young researchers are not just there to work for you but also to learn. It is your job to facilitate this learning process. Make sure your researchers are challenged. Make time for them and answer their questions. Make sure they know they can come to you for advice, questions or concerns. This will create a creative, interactive and trusting work environment in which everyone can thrive. In many projects, young researchers will be working on their PhD dissertations next to the research project. This fits best when they can use the work they are doing for the project also for their dissertation work. If the project manager or leader is different from the PhD supervisor or promoter, it is also important that these two 'bosses' coordinate their efforts with regard to the particular young researcher.

22.7 BUDGETING AND MONEY MANAGEMENT

Like it or not, a very important aspect of project management is money or budget management. One of the points on the triangle that was discussed earlier was managing the money you have for a project while still getting everything accomplished. This can be a daunting task, especially for someone who is used to the academic or content side of project work. As the project manager, though, you are responsible for knowing your budget and managing it. It is likely that you will have a central controller or person at your institute who is in charge of fund management and you will have to work closely with that person to make sure that everyone who needs to be paid is paid accordingly and that you are not overspending. It is best to check your budget regularly to make sure you have a good grasp of the current financial situation.

22.8 REPORTING REQUIREMENTS AND PROJECT TIME-LINE

For many projects, especially longer-term projects, there are periodic reporting requirements. This reporting is usually a mix of financial and content reporting. Reporting usually happens at the end of a year and/or beginning of a year, with many possibilities in between. Make sure that all reporting is done on time. The requirements of reporting are different for every institution and guidelines can be opaque. Do not be afraid to ask for clarification of requirements to make sure you give the necessary information in the format in which it is needed. Just make sure you give yourself enough time to work on the reporting requirements. Begin early enough so that all questions you might have can be answered and necessary provisions made before turning in the final product.

476   *Handbook of research methods in migration*

In every project, you will have a time-line of activities and it is important to both stick to deadlines, on the one hand, and to be flexible, on the other. The project must move along and you will have to make sure that you can deliver output in the time that is needed. That being said, do not sacrifice quality for time. Make sure you have ample time to finish what needs to be done. There are many unknowns in a project and time-lines sometimes need to be adjusted. Just make sure you discuss these changes with your donor and get permission to adjust the time-line to avoid problems later.

22.9   WORKING IN DIFFERENT COUNTRIES

Due to the nature of migration research, it is often necessary to run projects across countries, which means that there are many more practicalities to take care of from visas, to safety and language issues. There can also be plenty of cultural dimensions to be aware of. You should make yourself aware of the culture and way of working in the particular country before embarking on a project there. The Dutch organizational psychologist Geert Hofstede (who studied the interactions between national cultures and organizational cultures) has put together a list of cultural dimensions for many countries around the world (Hofstede, 2001; Hofstede and Hofstede, 2004). This index can be a good starting point for beginning to understand how to work in a specific culture or country.

22.9.1   Practicalities

Particularly when you have a project in a developing country, there are several extra things to deal with, not least of which is a visa. Perhaps you will also need to get permission from the government to run your particular project. This is, for example, the case in Morocco. You will need to do your research beforehand on the best way to go about accomplishing this. There are many other things to consider also like travel, accommodation, familiarity with local network (gatekeepers/informants, experts), safety (particularly when working in conflict areas), language, vaccinations, access to technology, food and dietary requirements (you do not want to be sick during your field work) and so on. Women should also be particularly aware of appropriate behaviour when working in Muslim countries (see more on this below). Make sure you are aware of all of these before embarking on work in the particular country.

There are some specific types of areas that you should make sure to become particularly familiarized with before embarking on project work. Some of these areas include working in conflict or post-conflict countries,

A guide to managing large-scale migration research projects 477

working in Muslim countries, working in rural areas and in desert areas. In conflict or post-conflict areas security will be a clear issue. In many official post-conflict countries, there are still security issues and possibilities for new conflict eruptions. You should make sure that you and your team take all of the necessary precautions. Make sure to register with your embassy in the country so that you can be evacuated in case of emergency. It is probably a good idea to take a security course (usually offered by private companies on how to deal with first aid, hostage situations and so on) before venturing to these countries.

In Muslim countries there are also particular things to be aware of, especially with regard to female researchers. This does not necessarily hold for all Muslim countries but I will describe some of the most strict cases (as in Afghanistan or Iran, for instance). There are two main things to be aware of in these countries and that is your attire and interactions between men and women. Men and women should dress conservatively but often women will also need to cover their heads. It is best for both men and women to wear clothes that cover as much skin as possible and that are loose. Interaction between the sexes is another tricky issue. Often it is not appropriate for men and women to touch, so you should never initiate the shaking of hands with the opposite sex. There could be other issues depending on the country so make sure you do your homework in this respect.

Working in rural areas can also bring challenges of its own. Infrastructure is usually a main concern in rural areas. In some countries you will not have proper roads (especially in the rainy season), no running water, no electricity (or internet for that matter), and toilet facilities will be non-existent or leave much to be desired. You should be aware of the infrastructure issues before you go and plan accordingly. Rural areas are also usually the more conservative areas in a country so make sure you understand local customs to avoid unnecessary offences. Working in desert areas can also be challenging because of infrastructure issues, lack of water and extreme temperatures, just to name a few, so make sure you are ready for these challenges.

22.9.2 Familiarizing Yourself and Your Team

Like many of the things being discussed in this chapter, familiarizing yourself and your team with the country will be dependent on your particular country or countries you are working in. It also may be a country that you already know well but in which you are working in a new way.

Scoping visits to the country are very important. Besides making yourself and your project known, you should identify all of the different institutions or organizations that can be helpful for you to get information from, to work together with or to just make sure you share information. This will also help with marketing your research, which was discussed previously. For instance, when working on migration research, some of these could be local universities, research institutes or non-Governmental organizations (NGOs), the IOM, United Nations Development Programme (UNDP), United Nations International Children's (Emergency) Fund (UNICEF) and so on. More broadly, it is a good idea to have meetings with the embassy of the country in which you are working, in the country where you are based and then to be in touch with the appropriate ministries in the country where you are implementing the field work. Of course, this all depends on the nature of the work that you will conduct.

22.10 CONCLUSION

While there is no 'one-size-fits-all' guide to managing large-scale migration projects, this chapter aims to give a flexible guide that you can use for your own needs. Migration research projects have specific elements that make them more complicated and more unique than other types of project management. Mainly, there are many more risk factors in migration research project management due to working with (sometimes) hard-to-reach populations, working across countries and cultural boundaries. This chapter has touched upon the most important aspects of a project to keep in mind: getting organized at the beginning of a project, hiring everyone that is needed and managing them; keeping funders and partners happy, organized and efficient; marketing your project, budgeting and reporting; and perhaps most specific to migration research management, knowing how to work in other countries on a practical level and a cultural level.

NOTE

1. For instance, the International Migration, Integration and Social Cohesion in Europe (IMISCOE) network and the Forced Migration Network, Harvard Migration and Immigrant Incorporation Workshop list-serve and the Network on Migration History (LISTSERV@H-NET.MSU.EDU). University departments that have migration centres like Oxford University, the University of Sussex, Maastricht University School of Governance, Institute for Migration and Ethnic Studies (IMES) at the University of Amsterdam, Princeton University, University of California at San Diego and so on are also good places to send calls. Other institutes such as the Migration Policy Institute, the International Migration Team at the World Bank (migrationteam@worldbank.org) and the International Center for Migration Policy Development are also helpful to keep in mind. This is not an exhaustive list but just a way to get started.

REFERENCES

Hofstede, G. (2001), *Culture's Consequences, Comparing Values, Behaviours, Institutions, and Organizations Across Nations*, Thousand Oaks, CA: Sage.

Hofstede, G. and Hofstede, G.-J. (2004), *Cultures and Organizations: Software of the Mind*, New York: McGraw-Hill.

Ireland, L.R. (2006), *Project Management*, New York: McGraw-Hill Professional, 2006, p. 110.

Microsoft (2010), 'Every project plan is a triangle', Microsoft, available at http://office.microsoft.com/en-us/project-help/every-project-plan-is-a-triangle-HA001021180.aspx?CTT=3 (accessed 30 July 2010).

Phillips, J. (2003), *PMP Project Management Professional Study Guide*, Emeryville, CA: McGraw-Hill Professional, 2003, p. 354.

University of Melbourne School of Enterprise (2010), 'Research project management', available at http://www.soe.unimelb.edu.au/Content.aspx?topicID=480 (accessed 30 July 2010).

PART VI

MOVING FROM RESEARCH TO PUBLISHED WORK

23 From dissertation to published research: so close, yet so far
Anna O. Law

When are you actually 'finished' with a research product? While the completion of a Master's thesis or dissertation are major milestones in your career, these events should be conceived of as the beginning, not the end of a research project if your aim is to actually publish the research piece as a journal article or academic book. Elsewhere I have written about the search for a research question and about finding the appropriate methodology and research design to match your research question (Law, 2007). In this chapter I draw upon my own experiences from the field, particularly how to transition from a dissertation into an academic publication.[1] This chapter also addresses questions of how to enhance and build on existing research by identifying and shoring up weaknesses. In revising an existing work for publication, two general themes apply: you must remain 'flexible' and 'humble.' Flexibility will be necessary because in going from existing research to publishable research, the transition may require continuing your education beyond the attainment of a degree and the learning of new and unfamiliar skills and methodologies. Humility will be required because the move from existing research to publishable research will entail receiving sometimes harsh critiques of your work and then later, it may require massive and extensive revisions to an existing project. The discussions in this chapter will also have implications for anyone revising any existing project, including conference or seminar papers, into a publishable piece in an academic journal.

You breathe a sigh of relief upon finishing a long project like a dissertation or Master's thesis, and the event should be marked by celebration because it is a great achievement. But after the rejoicing is passed and the champagne drunken, the question that you should ask yourself is 'What next?' You have to fight the natural urge to file the project away as 'done,' never to lay eyes on it again. A common refrain I hear from newly minted PhDs is 'I'm so sick of the dissertation. I don't ever want to see it again.' Indeed many MA theses and doctoral dissertations are never published, but if you have any ambition to put it in print, you have to work past the initial fatigue of the project and the urge to never look at it again. For that reason, it is highly advisable to take a few months break and set the project aside, and to start other projects. But if your goal is to turn the thesis or dissertation into an academic publication, the files eventually will need to be dusted off and re-examined, this time with a new set of considerations in mind than from the initial ones that came with the dissertation or Master's thesis. The good news is that the second round, in which you revise a project to turn into a publication, is easier than the original thesis or dissertation. You do not feel as blind and lost because you have been through the process before; you have already defined the research question, fashioned the research design, and chosen a research method/methodologies to answer the research question. The bad news is that just because you have undergone the process before does not mean you do not have to do it yet again by revisiting those initial choices you previously made about research design and methodology.

23.1 REVISING FOR A GENERAL AUDIENCE

After you have made the affirmative decision to work on turning existing research into an academic publication, the first question to ask yourself is: what venue do you want to publish the piece in? As a book at an academic press? As a series of articles in refereed journals? Even if you choose to try to publish the manuscript at a trade press, many trade presses have a vetting procedure in which the manuscript is sent out to a third party for peer review. Once you have identified the target venue, some revision is in order before you even begin shopping the manuscript around or even shipping it out as individual journal articles.

Research decisions that were acceptable in a dissertation or thesis may not be appropriate for a journal or academic press. One reason for this situation is because the objectives behind a dissertation/thesis are dissimilar from the objectives for publishing an academic article or book. The purpose for completing a doctoral dissertation is because it is a required element toward earning not just a degree, but for all intents and purposes, a union card that will allow you entry into academia. In contrast, the publication of academic articles and books are the building blocks of your academic reputation and an illustration of your expertise, your field of specialization. Of course one is linked to the other: the quality of your dissertation or thesis dictates also the quality of your future publications, and your dissertation is the thing that launches your career.

You must undertake some basic revisions of any existing work before even sending it to any publication outlet because the thesis/dissertation and academic articles/academic books represent entirely different genres of writing. These preliminary revisions generally involve editing of the text as well as framing of the research question. Take the time to clean up the manuscript before you send it to a publisher or journal. It is never a good idea to send an unedited, unrevised dissertation or thesis or a portion of these to a publication outlet without editing – even if your professor, adviser, or committee raved about it. Editors can smell unrevised dissertation or theses from miles away; they seem to have a sixth sense for it. They do not look upon these sorts of projects favorably because it has not been correctly calibrated for the target audience of general readers.

The audiences for your dissertation or thesis and the audience for an academic publication or book are different. Presumably when you seek to publish in an academic journal or university press, you wish to reach as wide an audience as you can; that means a likely audience of educated academics, including ones that may or may not be in your field of study. The difference between writing for a dissertation committee and writing for a general audience must be taken into consideration; the imperatives of each are dissimilar. In the first round of revisions, I strongly suggest two basic revisions. First, remove all unnecessary jargon and obscure 'inside baseball' type references. To the extent that you need to use terms of art, make sure you explain them in plain language that is understandable even to a layperson. Second, consider removing or drastically streamlining the literature review. It is common in dissertations and theses to have extensive literature reviews to demonstrate your competence and mastery of the literature to your committee, but in a book or article, the audience is no longer your committee members who read every chapter of your dissertation or theses and are persons completely up to date on your research area because indeed, you selected them to be on your committee because of their particular expertise that was related to your own project.

In revising your manuscript for a more general audience, the framing of the research question must be sharpened. While working on the dissertation, a common mantra is 'A good dissertation is a done dissertation.' That is true, but once the dissertation is complete, and you have decided to try to publish it, a whole other set of considerations come into play. Why would other scholars beyond the three that do work in your narrow area want to read your book or article? What implications and lessons can be drawn from the findings of your project and applied to broader social science? While the purpose of the literature review for your dissertation or thesis was mainly to demonstrate your mastery over the subject, the literature review in the book or article should not be as extensive or detailed. It should instead highlight the particular contribution of your manuscript, the point of intervention of your study, within the broader existing literature. Explain to the audience what is value added for your study, why they should be interested in your study, and why you are not reinventing the wheel.

In the transition from my own dissertation to book manuscript, the framing of the question changed quite significantly. My dissertation was about how the two highest federal courts decide immigration cases (Law, 2003). The focus in my dissertation was on the influence of intuitional norms, the formal and informal rules, practices, and structures that constitute the Supreme Court and US Courts of Appeals. I argued that just as the rules of the game in baseball and football shape the way the players strategize and play the game, similarly the rules and norms of the Supreme Court and US Courts of Appeals (which are dissimilar) shape how judges and justices conceive of what they should be doing in their jobs and also how they should be doing it.

In the dissertation, my literature review was centered on engaging in a conversation with the American political development literature, a subfield within American politics that my theoretical framework was derived from. Political development or American Political Development (APD) is a recognized subfield and organized section within the American Political Science Association. While scholars interested in political development employ an array of quantitative and qualitative methodologies, one common set of theoretical concerns bind political development scholars together, regardless of their subfield home. It would be inaccurate to characterize political development scholars as political historians, or even to say political development scholars use history as a source of data for testing non-historically grounded theories (Orren and Skowronek, 2004). Rather, APD scholars are interested in the timing, sequencing, and ordering of political arrangements, macro-historical analysis. Their research begins with the premise that a polity, and all its different parts is constructed over time. Therefore, 'the nature and the prospects of any single part will be best understood in the process of political formation,' in other words, some aspects of institutions can only be understood as they unfold over time (Orren and Skowronek, 2004). The identification of patterns across time is a primary endeavor of this type of research. Given my own great interest in political development most of the dissertation's literature review was about the political development literature, but I did recognize that not everyone is interested in all the minutiae and sub-debates within that field.

The marketing of your book is a consideration that enters the picture, a consideration that was not present in the dissertation and thesis project in which the main imperative was to finish and get the thumbs up from your committee. In the revision of the book manuscript, and particularly in the writing of the prospectus, the proposal in which you pitch your manuscript to academic presses, I was forced to think about how to broaden the audience for the book and what other scholars might be interested in the book beyond the political development folks. After all, what press was going to publish a book that was only of interest to a narrow group of scholars? Given that my book was a comparison between the Supreme Court and the US Courts of Appeals' treatment of immigration cases over time, I had many more framing options than I had considered when writing the dissertation. The book could be cast as one that might appeal to Courts of Appeals' scholars, immigration scholars, and constitutional interpretation scholars, in addition to the political development scholars. But to appeal to these other groups of scholars, the literature review section, which also is used to frame your own research question, had to be drastically reshaped to situate the manuscript in these separate streams of literature in addition to the political development literature. In reconstructing the literature review to illustrate your point of intervention, you also have to indicate how the different streams of literature relate to each other, which is easily done by showing how they intersect and come together in your own project. This is a good time to consult your favorite books and articles to see how other authors accomplished this task.

In the framing of your book or article, you might also give some thought to what type of scholar you consider yourself to be and which group of scholars you see your work as being in conversation with. What subfield do you regard as your intellectual home base? Within political science, I consider my home base to be in APD and Law and Courts, both are organized sections in the American Political Science Association. My other options were to cast myself, through my publications, as a topical specialist in immigration, as Supreme Court scholar, a Courts of Appeals' scholar, or APD scholar. You do not have to pick only one of course, but think of which is the dominant note or theme in your body of research.

Although my book project addresses the Courts of Appeals' literature, my decision to align myself with the APD scholars had to do with my methodological predilections. The vast majority of scholars who study the Courts of Appeals in political science are behavioralists, who study legal decision making by focusing on the effect of individual characteristics of the judges (their race, sex, religion, and so on), or attitudinalists, scholars who study legal decision making by focusing on the influence of a judges' ideology on their decision making. I was the first to wade into that substantive area and study the subject with a set of theories that had not previously been used before. Although I was substantively studying a subject that is dominated by quantitative scholars, I was using political development theories to frame the analysis (even as I learned to use some quantitative methods). My alignment with and the decision to pitch the book as primarily, although not exclusively, in conversation with other political development was made in part with regard for my own preferred epistemological worldview of research methodologies. I do not regard any research methodology as invalid, but I do favor the theoretical assumptions of political development methods over other types of methods and APD methods tend to favor qualitative methodologies. Regardless of the group of scholars you wish to be a part of, if your work overlaps with subfields that are dominated by other approaches, you are still required to master that literature and to situate your work within that literature.

23.2 GETTING INITIAL FEEDBACK, BUILDING NETWORKS, APPLYING FOR FUNDING

Once all the jargon is removed and the literature review shortened and sharpened, and any weaknesses or errors pointed out by your thesis or dissertation readers rectified, it is time to send out some chapters to get some initial feedback. Sometimes, the more you look at something, the more you cannot see it. Of course if you chose to carve up the thesis or dissertation into several articles, you will have to rewrite and reframe the chapter into article format. To learn how to structure an article, re-read your favorite journal articles, paying close attention to how the argument is structured and laid out. For example, note how short or long the literature review section is, how the data is presented, and of what length is the discussion of the findings. Replicate the structure and organization of these articles in your revisions. It is also worth reading multiple volumes of the journal you hope to publish in to get a sense of the style and conventions of a particular journal.

Whatever form you have revised your manuscript to, whether article or book manuscript, do not send it out to a publication outlet without first getting some initial feedback from a third party. It is infinitely better to have your friends critique your writing and research rather than have a journal reviewer or manuscript reviewer rip apart your work and ultimately reject the manuscript, thereby costing you time and emotional investment. A fresh pair of eyes reading your draft will save you from unnecessary errors of the factual, substantive, as well as grammatical and organizational variety. If you have not already done so during the course of graduate school, the post dissertation/thesis period is a time to start building a network of friends and colleagues to read your work because you will need this network later. My experience has been that using graduate school friends and colleagues you met at conference for this purpose has worked better than trying to prevail upon your committee members or dissertation adviser after you have graduated and your degree is already completed. I suspect this is the case because my friends and I were all in the same boat, trying to publish to achieve tenure, and we understood each other's pressures and need to publish and therefore were willing to help. Other people have successfully persuaded their committee members or dissertation adviser to read revised drafts after graduation; it depends on your relationships.

Bringing a publication into being, whether it is in the form of a journal article or academic book, sometimes requires acquiring a set of skills beyond the skills and training necessary for completing the dissertation or thesis. One of the main skills you will need to learn as early as possible in your academic career is how to write grant proposals to apply for funding. It is a useful skill that will serve you well even if you end up choosing a non-academic career route. Many graduate programs offer dissertation fellowships that may or may not require a proposal. These are fine if you are sure you are going to land one; in my graduate program, these awards were very limited in number and competitive. Indeed any dissertation fellowship, whether internally granted from your university or externally granted from outside sources, that releases you from teaching or teaching assistant duties will dramatically speed up your progress in the degree.

From my own experience, what was more preferable than relying on internal funding was to apply for external funding. Although these external grant sources were far more competitive than internal fellowships, with many of these being national, international, and multidisciplinary competitions, their proposal application required far more detail and rigor than any internal grant based at your home university. Also, obtaining funding from a very competitive grant source like the National Science Foundation (which has dissertation improvement grants for graduate students), the Social Science Research Council, and so on are additional confirmation of the quality of your research by an external group of scholars not related to or based at your own graduate program. These external awards carry more prestige than internal grants from your home institution.

External grants add luster to your curriculum vitae and will be noted by future employers. For the purposes of furthering research, learning how to write a grant proposal is not only about the money the grant will bring in to fund your research, but the proposal writing forces you to lay out your research question clearly, justify and defend your choice of methodology by explaining why it is an appropriate methodology to answer the question you wish to attack, and stipulate how and why your findings are applicable to other phenomena in broader political science. In other words, the rigors of grant writing force you to clarify your thinking on your research project.

Another added side benefit of applying for external grants, even when you are unsuccessful in obtaining the funding, is the feedback you receive. In my case, I applied for a National Science Foundation research grant in my second year as an Assistant Professor. Although I did not successfully receive the funding, each reviewer sent back detailed feedback. One reviewer in particular sent back a roadmap of how to fix many of the major flaws in the project, indications of why certain aspects of the project were not working, but more importantly, also provided concrete and clear suggestions about what I could do to rectify the situation. It was a transformative review and a turning point in the intellectual development of my book project. I was enormously grateful and humbled that some scholar out there (who I am sure did not know me because it was early in my career) had taken the time to engage my ideas by very carefully reading my research and writing up a blueprint of how I should proceed. It took three months to write up the National Science Foundation grant proposal and I did not obtain the funds, but the payoff was that I was forced to clarify and justify my research methods and design and I received invaluable and very high quality feedback that helped enormously in future revisions of what was eventually my published book.

If you are nearing the end of your dissertation and intend to seek a tenure track position somewhere, it is also time to be searching for post-doc programs. These programs are also a good idea if you are biding your time and are waiting out a bad economy that has negatively affected the academic job market. A post-doc has multiple benefits in furthering your research and setting you up for a tenure track job. Again, you should not think of a post-doc as just a source of funding. Before tenure, your time is more valuable than money, and you need time to revise your dissertation before it is turned into articles or a book manuscript suitable for submission to a press for publication. The post-doc year will buy you that time without taking time off of your tenure clock, which begins running immediately when you arrive at a tenure track job.

Among the important benefits of a post-doc fellowship (or a pre-doctoral program like I did) are the intangibles: the networking opportunities and being a part of an intellectual community for a year. A post-doc program provides a year in which you will meet other young scholars working on similar subjects and they are excellent sounding boards for your ideas. It is an ideal time for forming a reading group to read and provide feedback on each other's work. Such reading groups also create structure by providing deadlines for the completion of work and keep you accountable to others. Otherwise, the writing and revision process can be lonely and isolating, and an amorphous period, with no clear deadlines.

I was lucky enough to be awarded a pre-doctoral dissertation fellowship at the University of California's Center for Comparative Immigration Studies. The fellowship gave me an office and a salary for a year as I sat in sunny San Diego to finish my dissertation. The fellowship program brought together social sciences scholars from many disciplines including sociology, psychology, history, economics, and Latin American studies. What we all had in common was an interest in migration issues. The reading group we formed was strengthened by the benefit of interdisciplinary input. From my year in San Diego, I formed life long friendships and a support network that I continue to lean on. Although the pay for most post-docs is not high, you cannot place a price tag on the intellectual fellowship and the luxury of sitting around talking about ideas with like-minded scholars for a year as you work on your own research before your serious teaching and service obligations kick in at a tenure track position.

23.3 TESTING THE WATERS

Once all the initial rounds of revisions have been made, and you have vetted the piece with at least a few friends and colleagues, you can try sending out a few articles to journals. This advice is true equally for those who intend to publish a book; carve out at least a chapter or two as articles first to test the waters. Send those off to journals to get some initial feedback as a way of assessing how reviewers will receive the lengthier book manuscript. Realize also that you can only submit to one social science peer-reviewed journal at a time and that some journals have a faster turnaround time than others. Ask more established scholars at conferences which journals have a faster turnaround time and submit to those first. Be aware also that many academic book publishers will decline to publish a manuscript from which more than two chapters have previously been published as articles.

My experience at this stage was that I spent my third year of a tenure track job sending out a revised chapter that I had turned into an article to various academic journals only to have it unceremoniously rejected from different journals, three rejections in total within the same year. Those rejections occurred even though I did revisions between submissions based on the previous reviewers' critiques. It was a bruising experience for my self-esteem, but the experience, however painful, taught me some valuable lessons. Sometimes journal reviewers' feedback is hard to decipher, especially when three reviewers give you three different and conflicting sets of critiques. But when multiple reviewers at different journals have the same critiques, they have identified problems that you must address before sending the book manuscript to a publisher. It is not a good idea under those circumstances to cross your fingers and hope that those critiques will not come up again with the book manuscript reviewers. Academia is a small world and it is likely your journal reviewers might end up also as one of your manuscript reviewers again. If you are lucky enough to get a revision and resubmit, it will provide you with the experience in addressing the reviewers' concerns, which includes explaining why there are some changes they wanted you to make that you will not be making. Simply stating that you refuse to make the change because the reviewer is simply wrong or the reviewer does not understand what you are doing is insufficient and will not get you published. Hubris and defensiveness will not get you very far in this process at all. It is true that not all reviewers will like or even 'get' what you are trying to do. It is still incumbent upon you to explain it to them. You must explain in the revised and resubmitted version why the reviewer is wrong and how making the change they ask for would negatively affect what you are trying to accomplish with your study. You need not undertake to do all the revisions the reviewers have asked for, but you must explain clearly why you are not doing those revisions.

In my case, all the critiques centered on the issues of research design and methodology, reviewers were not convinced that either one was helping to get to the research question I had posed. My dissertation had looked at the Supreme Court and US Courts of Appeals' treatment of immigration in two ten-year time periods that were about 100 years apart. The inevitable question by reviewers had been: 'What happened in the intervening years between the two ten-year periods?' The original two ten-year time periods sufficed for the dissertation because I was able to illustrate distinctive ways in which the Supreme Court and US Courts of Appeals treated immigration cases in those time periods, but the journal reviewers had raised the legitimate concern that I might have missed important phenomena that were happening in the intervening period that were not studied. It was clear that one of the major changes I would have to make was to collect data to bridge those two original ten-year periods, which would be no small feat given that the two blocks of time were over 100 years apart. But the journal reviewers had correctly identified that point as a major weakness of the study, and I knew I had to address that critique if I hoped to publish the research in any outlet.

During meditation, Buddhists teach that you should not endeavor to clear your mind completely, because it is not possible to do so. Instead, they suggest that when a negative or distracting thought enters your consciousness, you should experience the feeling and just let it be instead of fighting it. But afterwards, let it go (Blackmore, 2009). A similar process must be undertaken when doing revisions. You are working from an existing document, either a thesis or dissertation. You should enjoy the accomplishment, but you must also learn to let it go. In my transition from my dissertation to the eventual book, I not only rewrote the entire work, I redid all the data and added three new methodologies. If you are to publish successfully, you simply must learn to let go and not to get too attached to any draft. In the case of my transition from dissertation to the book, it was a complete overhaul and rebuilding, not minor tweaking. The process taught me a few lessons about humility. I was faced with the question of what was more important to me, my pride or my wish to get published.

One lesson I learned in addressing the journal reviewers' critiques is that your choice of methodology and research design does not have to be perfect, but they must be justifiable and defensible. My lack of success at publishing journal articles was due to the mismatch between my research and the research design and methods. The reviewers simply were not convinced that the research design and methods that I had chosen could in fact answer my research question. Throughout the revisions process, I consulted with graduate school friends who were more adept than me at questions of research design and methodology. Growing from those discussions, I formulated a new justification for the extended time period that now spanned 1881–2002, namely, that it would capture periods of exclusion/restrictionism and also periods of openness in US immigration history, certainly a consideration that is relevant to any study on how federal courts decide immigration cases over time. Unfortunately, the decision to expand the time period of the study was one of the easier choices I made in the process of converting the dissertation into a book manuscript.

The decision to change the methodology was far more difficult. In my dissertation, I had collected information on thousands of Courts of Appeals' cases, but I had put that information into a MS Word chart instead of an Excel spreadsheet. What this meant is that while I had information from a lot of cases, it was not in a format that could be statistically analysed or manipulated; I could not do a count of frequencies, or cross tabulations. The patterns I was picking up for the dissertation were therefore impressionistic rather than concrete quantifications and measurements of patterns. I had never been comfortable with quantitative methodology mainly due to my own math phobia and my weakness in quantitative reasoning. I also had epistemological reservations about quantitative methodology. However, as I learned through multiple journal rejections, it is increasingly unacceptable to use as an excuse for not learning a particular methodology, 'I do not know how to use that method.' The factor dictating which methodology should be used is the research question – not which research methods you have and have not mastered. What is the best method to answer the research question you have posed?

In my case, because I was studying the Courts of Appeals that generate thousands of cases every year, the required methodology was to use a large N dataset. Given the number of cases coming out of these courts this year, quantitative analysis is absolutely necessary to the studying of the Courts of Appeals. Of course qualitative analysis can be used, but quantitative assessment must be part of the analysis as well to chart trends and patterns across the many cases.

It was evident that if I wanted to produce a credible study that included the Courts of Appeals, I would have to learn to use a dataset and learn at least basic quantitative methods, like how to do multi-variable cross tabulations. From consulting with friends well versed in quantitative methods, I learned I had two options: use an existing dataset of Courts of Appeals' cases or create my own dataset. After my dissertation was completed, I did a broader and far more systematic survey of the research on the Courts of Appeals, all of which was quantitative. It appeared that the vast majority of those studies used two existing datasets, one dataset created by Zuk et al. (2009) contained Courts of Appeals' cases information focusing on the individual attributes of the judges themselves, the other more commonly used dataset is created by Songer (1998), consisting of randomly sampled Courts of Appeals' cases spanning the years 1925–96. The reason why scholarship in the Courts of Appeals relies so heavily on these two datasets is because the creation of a new dataset is extremely time consuming and requires, ideally, a small army of graduate research assistants. In fact the creation of the Songer dataset led to a boon in research on the Courts of Appeals.

As I was undertaking the massive changes that needed to be done, I discovered that any and every research choice you make will have consequences and tradeoffs. There was a problem though with me using these two databases, which was that neither one worked very well in answering my research question of what mode of legal reasoning, or legal justification, did Courts of Appeals' judges use in immigration decisions. Because the Courts of Appeals are generalist courts and hear all sorts of cases, not just immigration ones, both existing datasets consisted of all types of federal litigation and were not limited to immigration cases. More serious a problem than that was that the existing datasets did not code variables that were relevant for my analysis, not just a variable for the modes of legal reasoning, but variables about the immigrants in the immigration cases, such as their sex, country of origin, and the kind of immigration case it was (deportation, exclusion, asylum, naturalization, and so on). Using an existing dataset will save you a tremendous amount of time, but you will be constrained by the variables the existing dataset has as well as the time period of the dataset. I did not want to subject myself to those constraints especially because these datasets would not help me answer my research question. I soon realized that using existing datasets for my project was not a good option; I would instead have to create my own dataset.

When revising existing research, one very necessary trait is to maintain flexibility. You are never too old to learn not just knowledge but skills, including computer programs, but also never too old to confront old fears, math phobia in my case. Of course the decision to use an original dataset meant I had to learn an entirely new set of skills and also new ways of thinking about research. I would have to learn how to construct a dataset and to learn related skills like how to draw a true random sample of cases, how to code data, and what to do with all the data once you have collected it.

Although I was well versed in qualitative methodologies, I was completely new to quantitative ones. It was very much like learning a new language and indeed an entirely new way altogether of looking at and approaching research. I was adept at qualitative methodologies that call for thick description analysis, archival work, and close readings of the text. The data I was most comfortable working with were historical documents, and legal opinions that I approached as rich texts that could be unpacked. But this was a new kind of data I was working with and the creation of the dataset required me to re-vision what constitutes data and to approach the legal opinions to extract important variables that would be helpful in answering my research question. As well I had to think about what variables I should collect that would help me answer the research question.

The first step was to re-read(!) the over 1900 legal opinions from the Courts of Appeals to systematically extract and record variables such as individual characteristics of the immigrants in those cases, the mode of legal reasoning used, and some of the characteristics of the judges who sat on the three-judge panels that heard the cases, including who authored the opinion and who, if anyone, dissented. These variables were assigned codes and placed into an Excel spreadsheet. Thus, my new dataset was a collection of three clusters of variables: about the immigrants, the judges, and the circuits that heard the cases, variables that were not found in pre-existing datasets.

The commitment to use certain types of methodology will sometimes not just involve a great investment of time to learn new methods and skills, but also the need to apply for funding to facilitate the execution of the chosen methodology. Sometimes in conducting research, ignorance is truly bliss. Having never before undertaken the kind of work that required the construction of an original dataset, I had no idea what to expect. I started coding the cases and realized how slow and tedious the work was. Had I known in advance how much work this process would entail,

I might not have undertaken it. I immediately came to understand why most people use existing datasets instead of trying to create their own. But having made the decision to create my own dataset, I now looked for ways to speed up the construction of a large *N* dataset since I had about 1900 Courts of Appeals' cases and 200 Supreme Court cases to code. Professor Donald Songer, for example, the creator of the famous Courts of Appeals' dataset, had a large National Science Foundation grant and legions of graduate students work on the dataset. Since I was at a teaching institution and the political science department did not even have Master's students, the army of graduate research assistants would not be an option for me. But most teaching schools have some sort of grant for professors to integrate their undergraduate students into their research. DePaul had such a fellowship called the Undergraduate Research Assistants Program. The faculty member and student jointly submit an application and the student is paid by the university while working on the faculty member's research project. The dataset had an array of variables, some that were easy to code like the immigrant's sex, their country of origin, the name of the judges that decided the case, the opinion writers' names. I trained a series of five undergraduate research assistants to help me collect those variables and place them into an Excel spreadsheet.

The most difficult variable to extract and code from these legal opinions was the mode of legal reasoning, the justification for how the judges decided what they decided. It is not a piece of information that is as cut and dried as which judges sat on the panel or what the country of origin of the immigrant was. The coding of this variable required knowledge of both US constitutional law and immigration law, which my undergraduates did not have. I coded that variable myself in the 2000 plus cases. The construction of the dataset alone, one methodology for my book, took 1.5 years and required five internal grant proposals for the research assistants.

In coding that variable, I had the option of using keyword search software like NUDIST and NVivo, which would have greatly speeded up the coding. But every research choice includes tradeoffs. In my assessment would be trading speed for accuracy. One of the key terms I was looking for was 'congressional plenary power,' or the idea that Congress has full, complete, and absolute power over immigration, which I knew would be a recurring theme in immigration opinions. Keyword search software would only pick up the literal words, 'plenary power,' whereas if I read the opinions, I would pick up references such as those in which the judge indicates that she believes immigration to be the province of the elected branch of government rather than the judiciary. That idea is plenary power, although those words are not actually used. Using keyword search software would have missed those cases entirely.

Also, since the mode of legal reasoning is the most crucial variable to my argument, I needed to pinpoint exactly what was the primary mode of legal reasoning in each opinion. Often, the opinion writer would run through a series of possible justifications for reaching a legal outcome, discussing the merits and demerits of each, before finally settling upon one rationale. Keyword software would have distorted these findings, and picked up references to modes of legal reasoning that judges were only pondering instead of actually using as the actual justification for their decisions. Of course, if you choose to use keyword search software, it would allow you to study many more cases than the approximately 2000 cases I studied.

There is no right or wrong methodology; it all depends on what your research question is and which methodology will best help you answer that question. The construction of the two datasets, one of Supreme Court cases, and the other of Courts of Appeals' cases, took quite a bit of time. I had made the calculation that the very costly investment of time and resources was worth it, including the time spent writing grants to hire research assistants and to train those assistants. Friends had advised that since I was going to spend the time reading all the cases that I should also collect and record additional variables beyond just the mode of legal reasoning variable that I needed for the book. I therefore collected an array of data about the four courts I was studying (Supreme Court, Third Circuit, Fifth Circuit, and Ninth Circuit), which judges or justices heard the case and how they voted, and also characteristics of the immigrants themselves. The side benefit is that now I have an original dataset and a wealth of data that can be used to generate other articles beyond the book project.

Of course the completion of the dataset was a day of celebration for me, but the work had only just begun. Having a dataset meant that I also had to learn how to analyse and manipulate the data by using statistical analysis software. Again, in consultation with my more experienced quantitative friends, I decided that STATA was the way to go, especially if I was later going to work with a coauthor. It took me several months to learn to do even basic commands on STATA, software that is not particularly intuitive, or perhaps just not intuitive to me because I was unaccustomed to doing quantitative research. I was not doing any sophisticated analysis like regressions; I was simply using STATA to run cross tabulations. Still, the time investment was well worth it because it means that in acquiring the skill to construct a dataset and to use a dataset with STATA, even if to do just basic cross tabulations, I had added to my research arsenal of skills that can be used for other projects beyond the book. I had also greatly added to my methodological range and these new skills added to the arrows in my quiver that could be used for other projects.

23.4 THE BENEFITS AND IMPORTANCE OF MULTIPLE METHODOLOGIES

In another article, I have written about my long search for an appropriate methodology to answer the research question I was interested in (Law, 2007). Specifically, I was looking for some way to empirically document and assess the effect of institutional settings and norms on the decision-making process of the US Courts of Appeals and Supreme Court. Just as the formal and informal rules and norms in a game like football or baseball can shape the way players play and strategize about the game, so too can the formal and informal rules and norms of the Supreme Court and Courts of Appeals circumscribe how these justices and judges approach their job. I eventually discovered the concept of 'modes of legal reasoning,' which is the rationale presented by the judges for why they have decided the way that they have. I took this concept, which had previously only been discussed in theory, and operationalized it for empirical purposes. No scholar had ever used this variable in empirical research before and so no one had seen such an approach. Because it was a novel approach and bound to be controversial since it was unfamiliar, I wanted to shore up the project by using multiple methodologies. To rely on one methodology alone, and a new and unfamiliar one at that, would have been risky. If critics and reviewers found my modes of legal reasoning approach flawed or illegitimate, they could dismiss my whole argument in the book if that was the only methodology.

To strengthen the overall argument in my book that the Supreme Court and US Courts of Appeals operate in decidedly distinct institutional settings that lead them to decide cases differently, I added several other methodologies to supplement and complement the cross tabulation data of the modes of legal reasoning. Since I was writing a book that used immigration cases as a case study to assess judicial decision making in the US Courts of Appeals and Supreme Court, I needed to incorporate the analysis of the development of legal doctrine in this area of law. In assessing the effect of institutional norms on the federal courts, that process is mediated by legal doctrine. Unlike other political actors like Members of Congress, judges and justices are not free to decide cases based on their own political or policy preferences. Even if judges and justices wish to act upon their preferences to reach a desired legal outcome, they are still bound by the legal doctrine governing that area of law. My overall argument about institutional development was made with regard also to the constraining influence of legal doctrine.

I also conducted in-person interviews with some of the judges and central staff from the Courts of Appeals for the Ninth Circuit, the appeals court that handles the largest volume of immigration cases nationally. These interviews took a year to set up. It was worth the extra effort; federal judges do not often give interviews to researchers and before my book, there were only two works of social science that I knew of that had included interviews with Courts of Appeals' judges.[2] The addition of the interviews to my study added color and texture to what could have been a dry discussion of legalese. The rare interviews also added novelty to the study. More importantly, the interviews allowed me to confirm and disconfirm some understandings of judicial decision making that I had found in reading the legal opinions.

In addition to those methodologies, I dug in the archives of the US Citizenship and Naturalization Services to unearth historical documents about the history of the immigration bureaucracy to better understand the growth of the administrative capacity. I also conducted close, interpretative readings of the texts of many of the legal opinions of some of the opinions that were in my database. These close readings allowed me to pick up rhetorical moves and indications of strategy that quantitative analysis would not have picked up. While the quantitative analysis of the longitudinal data from my two datasets allowed me to assess and chart aggregate trends across time, close readings of individual opinions shed light on the way judges and justices thought about these cases, and their logic in considering and dispensing with some modes of legal reasoning while settling on others. Each of the multiple methodologies I used provided additional leverage on the research question and another layer of analysis.

I do not recommend in this book chapter that everyone must or even should carry out a research project by using five methodologies in one project: cross tabulations from an original dataset, archival work, and interviews with judges, close readings of the text, and doctrinal analysis. I relay my own experience here only as an illustration of the way the addition of multiple methods can strengthen and shore up an existing study. In the field of comparative politics, the stronger studies are those that utilize multiple methodologies. This situation is true for scholarship in any social science subfield. You can, and indeed many studies do, only rely on one methodology. But since you are revising existing work for publication, it is a good time and opportunity to at least reconsider and reassess whether adding another methodology, and finding another way to answer your research question, might be a good move.

Of course the commitment to undertake multiple methods requires a huge investment of time and funds, but consider the payoff: the addition of multiple methodologies beyond the two (doctrinal research and close readings of the text) used in my dissertation allowed me to cross check my findings and triangulate the results in a manner that was far more rigorous than using one methodology. Each methodology on its own has its weaknesses. It was my hope that the addition of an array of methodologies would allow the weaknesses of each methodology to be balanced out and offset by the strengths of other kinds of methodologies.

23.5 CONCLUSION

Admittedly my own experience from the field of transitioning from dissertation to academic book was an epic struggle (at least it felt like it), and I certainly do not anticipate that everyone will have to undergo the sort of extreme and massive overhaul and rebuilding from the ground up that I had to do. Others' dissertations and existing work will probably be in a better condition than my dissertation, thereby requiring far less revisions. Still others at research universities will have the resources that I did not have and will not be required to stitch together nine internal grant proposals to fund one long project. Certainly, you should use the types of methodologies that best answer your research question and not undertake multiple methods if it will not help you answer your research question. In my case, it made sense to me to use the five methodologies that I used; I wanted to show that on multiple dimensions the Supreme Court and US Courts of Appeals function differently even though both courts are technically appellate courts and both courts are looking at the same statutes and same bodies of law. Still, I believe that others can learn from my experiences and realize that revisions are a matter of degree. My hope is that someone can learn from my worse case scenario as to what the process of transitioning from existing work to a publication will entail instead of going into the process blindly.

NOTES

1. From my dissertation (Law, 2003) to my book (Law, 2010).
2. Klein (2002) and Cohen (2002).

REFERENCES

Blackmore, S. (2009), *Ten Zen Questions*, Oxford: Oneworld Publications, pp. 3–13.
Cohen, J. (2002), *Inside Appellate Courts: The Impact of Court Organization on Judicial Decision Making in the United States Courts of Appeals*, Ann Arbor, MI: University of Michigan Press.
Klein, D. (2002), *Making Law in the U.S. Courts of Appeals*, New York: Cambridge University Press.

Law, A.O. (2003), 'Who's minding the gates: the effects of institutional norms on judicial decision making in immigration', Doctoral Dissertation, completed in the Department of Government, University of Texas at Austin, ProQuest, Ann Arbor, Michigan.

Law, A.O. (2007), 'In search of a methodology and other tales from the academic crypt', in S. Kossoudji, L. DeSipio and M. Garcia y Griego (eds), *Researching Migration: Stories from the Field*, New York: Social Science Research Council publications, available at http://www.ssrc.org/publications/view/42451838-264A-DE11-AFAC-001CC477EC70/ (accessed 23 August 2010).

Law, A.O. (2010), *The Immigration Battle in American Courts*, New York: Cambridge University Press.

Orren, K. and Skowronek, S. (2004), *The Search for American Political Development*, New York: Cambridge University Press.

Songer, D.R. United States Courts Of Appeals Database Phase 1, 1925–1996 (computer file), ICPSR version, Columbia, SC: D.R. Songer (producer), 1990, Ann Arbor, MI: Inter-university Consortium for Political and Social Research (distributor), 1998.

Zuk, G., Barrow, D.J. and Gryski, G.S. (2009), Multi-User Database on the Attributes of United States Appeals Court Judges, 1801–2000 (computer file), ICPSR06796-v2, Ann Arbor, MI: Inter-university Consortium for Political and Social Research (distributor), 2009-02-03, doi:10.3886/ICPSR06796.

24 What the textbooks don't tell you: moving from a research puzzle to publishing findings
Irene Bloemraad

During my undergraduate degree, I was a consumer of academic research. I read books and articles that my professors assigned, and I searched for more books and articles when asked to write a 'research paper.' My papers were analyses of other people's scholarship: I compared, contrasted, and criticized theory and research, but I did not carry out my own studies.

One of the harder parts of being a graduate student was becoming a producer of research. I had become so well trained in criticizing other people's work that the thought of producing my own was unnerving. How do you map out a solid research plan when you had never done research before? The dissertation felt like a mountain of Everest-like heights, and all I had were hiking boots, but no other climbing gear.

The methods textbooks, which were supposed to be the 'how-to' guides for this journey, tended to increase my anxiety rather than alleviate it. They invariably made the research process sound easy: identify a research question, review the relevant literature, pick an appropriate methodology, collect data, analyse the data, and then write up the results. The academic articles I read in class all seemed to follow the textbook format, describing a logical and orderly process that unfolded effortlessly.

Over the seven years of my PhD, I learned that these templates, while accurate about the parts of a research project, obscure the messy reality of putting it all together and carrying out the project. In this chapter, I describe my own journey, focusing on articulating a research question, building comparisons into research design, and using mixed methodologies. There is much that textbooks, and polished academic articles, don't tell you about the research process.

24.1 FINDING A PUZZLE: THE RESEARCH QUESTION

In my first year of doctoral studies at Harvard University, I had an unnerving experience that made me question whether I should be in graduate school. I had managed to get an appointment with my advisor – which meant signing up for a 15-minute time slot weeks in advance – and I was trying to outline a dissertation project. As my advisor listened, tapping a stack of yellow 'While you were out' message slips against her chair, I felt more and more foolish. With my vast knowledge of US society – I had lived in the United States for six months at that point – I was convinced that the dynamics of immigrant integration differed significantly in the United States compared to Canada. I was having trouble, however, articulating the difference, much less how I was going to study it.

I had lived in Canada for 14 years before moving to Massachusetts for graduate school, and I believed the Canadian cliché contrasting Canada's multicultural mosaic with the melting pot to the south. According to Canadian conventional wisdom, immigrants in Canada could be themselves – a unique tile in a vast mosaic – and still be Canadian; in the United States, assimilatory pressures forced immigrants to pledge exclusive loyalty to an American identity and way of life. I suspected that the Canadian government's support for official multiculturalism affected immigrants' integration, especially their incorporation into the political system. I thought it would make them feel more included, and thus participate more in the political and civic life of their adopted country. I was aware that the opposite argument could be made – by promoting diversity and pluralism, official multiculturalism might divide Canadian residents and ghettoize newcomers, thereby marginalizing immigrants from politics – but I thought this perspective was wrong. Now I wanted to write a dissertation to support my claim.

An obvious problem, of which I became more and more aware as I spoke, was that I was starting my research project at its conclusion: I had an argument, and now I seemed to be looking for evidence to back it up. My advisor quickly showed me that I faced an even more fundamental problem. She put the message slips down and asked a single question: 'What is the puzzle?' I didn't have an answer. After a short silence, she asked a second question: 'Do you have any evidence that there are differences?' I shook my head. I had lots of ideas, but not an iota of data. I left her office as soon as I could, convinced that my career as a political sociologist was over before it had begun.

While not particularly good for my self-esteem, this meeting was critical to the success of my dissertation. It forced me to think about what, exactly, I wanted to study. What was the outcome that I wanted to explain? What were the hypothesized dynamics, the mechanisms, by which differences in Canadian and American society and public policy, as epitomized in the mosaic/melting pot distinction, influenced immigrants' political behaviors?

My advisor's challenge – What is the puzzle? – demanded a clear statement of the research problem. As a new graduate student, I viewed social science research as a quest for answers. I had not realized that an equally difficult task was finding and asking the right question. Before I could develop an argument about Canadian and American societies' affect on immigrants, I needed to establish that there was some US-Canada difference worth explaining. In the language of hypothesis testing, I needed a dependent variable. This sounds obvious now, but specifying the research question became a project in itself.

24.1.1 Research Questions and 'the Literature'. From Books to Real Life

According to the literature, my assumption about a significant US-Canada difference was wrong. As a political science undergraduate I had reviewed research on naturalization, the process by which immigrants acquire citizenship. While variation in citizenship acquisition in Europe was explained by contrasting different state structures and national ideologies, research on the United States and Canada suggested that the two countries were interchangeable: both are traditional immigrant-receiving societies with liberal welfare states and low obstacles to political participation. Given few structural barriers, differences in citizenship acquisition must stem from immigrants' attributes – differences in skills, resources, and interests – not from differences in the context of reception. As one long-time observer of American immigration put it, 'the settlement, adaptation, and progress, or lack of it, of immigrants is largely, in the US context, up to them' (Glazer, 1998, p. 60).

Most North American naturalization research consequently replicated standard voting models in political science using statistical models. Variables such as immigrants' length of residence, income, and level of education were regressed on an individual's propensity to acquire citizenship. These studies were helpful in identifying individual-level variation in naturalization, but I found the exclusive focus on newcomers' attributes problematic. This approach invited the seductive conclusion that if some immigrants, or some immigrant groups, did not integrate into the political system, there must be something wrong with them, rather than with the reception provided by the receiving society.

For my graduate training, I turned to sociology, drawn to sociologists' attention to structure and institutions. I thought that interpersonal ties, immigrant organizations, and the symbolism of public policies, such as multiculturalism, must affect political incorporation. Even here, however, existing research challenged my presumptions. One book published by two sociologists a few years earlier questioned the mosaic/melting pot duality, showing little difference in Canadians' and Americans' attitudes on diversity and cultural retention (Reitz and Breton, 1994). The authors were cautious in generalizing from their data, but based on results cobbled together from a variety of surveys and opinion polls, they argued that US-Canada distinctions were overblown. Their thesis did not auger well for my project.

My hunch about US-Canada differences in immigrants' political incorporation went against prevailing academic models, but I could not shake the sense that the two societies felt different, and that these differences mattered for immigrant integration. Method textbooks usually suggest that research projects come from literature reviews. In my case, knowing the literature was important, but mostly because it seemed to contradict my own observations. Only a few textbooks talk about using personal experience to generate research questions, but now that I have worked with many students on their research, I think all textbooks should point out that many – perhaps most – research projects flow from the personal interests and individual experiences of the researcher. The lab coat model of the social scientist is wrong; most of us build projects from ideas that come from our own lives and our interaction with the society around us. Articulating a theoretically informed research question becomes a conversation between literature and personal observations.

24.1.2 Comparing Numbers is Harder than You Think

My first step in identifying a research puzzle was to define 'political incorporation.' I read a variety of theoretical literatures and developed a conceptual understanding of political incorporation, but I kept getting stuck when it came to specifying observable, empirical indicators of my phenomenon. What could I measure to see whether a US-Canada difference in political incorporation actually existed? More problematic: what could I measure that was 'comparable' in the two countries?

I started with naturalization.[1] Immigrants acquire citizenship for myriad reasons, from feelings of belonging and a desire to vote to more practical concerns such as wanting to sponsor a relative to the United States or wanting a Canadian passport for travel. Indeed, when I casually asked acquaintances about acquiring citizenship, most stressed the mundane rather than the political. Nevertheless, citizenship is a prerequisite for political acts such as voting and running for office, and it is a symbol of political membership. I felt it would be a good measure of political integration.

I then had to move from conceptualization to measurement. I assumed that collecting and comparing data on naturalization would be simple: A person either was or was not an American or Canadian citizen. However, I soon learned that gathering and comparing statistical data was much more complex than a neat column of numbers lets on. A naturalization statistic could be calculated in diverse ways, but I found myself constrained by the data available.

I first had to figure out how I should measure citizenship acquisition. I assumed that this would be easy: I would find out how many immigrants held the citizenship of their country of residence, and I would compare these numbers for various immigrant groups living in the two countries. However, naturalization could be measured as a flow (how many people became citizens in any particular year?), as a level (what proportion of the total immigrant population in the country were naturalized?), or as a rate (how many years did it take the average immigrant to naturalize, or what proportion of all immigrants who entered a country ten years earlier had naturalized?). Which should I use?

Working from the assumption that the agencies in charge of naturalization, the (then) US Immigration and Naturalization Service (INS) and Citizenship and Immigration Canada (CIC), would have good data on immigrants' citizenship, I poured over their publications and asked about public use datasets. The INS published the number of naturalizations annually, but it did not put this number in relation to the number of immigrants eligible for naturalization. The INS figures thus had limited value: if the number of naturalizations in one decade exceeds that of a previous decade, but the number of immigrants increases more rapidly, political incorporation is slowing down, despite the increasing number of new citizens. I decided that it made more sense to talk about the level of naturalization – the total number of naturalized immigrants divided by all immigrants eligible for naturalization – but neither the INS nor CIC could furnish the denominator for these calculations. They didn't know how many immigrants eligible for citizenship lived in the country.[2] I needed another data source.

Luckily national census enumerations in each country ask residents where they were born, whether they are citizens, and how they acquired citizenship, by birth or by naturalization. Using these pieces of information, I could calculate the total foreign-born population and the population of naturalized citizens, producing an estimate of each country's level of naturalization. Unfortunately, the foreign-born population is not the same thing as the population of immigrants eligible for citizenship. The former category includes those without legal residence status and temporary residents who cannot apply for citizenship. My inability to separate those eligible for citizenship from all foreign-born individuals was problematic since the United States has a bigger undocumented migrant population than Canada. However, an alternative measure, calculating a rate of naturalization, was impossible; the INS and CIC rarely published these data and when they did, the calculation was done differently in the two countries.

And so it went. What I thought would be a simple exercise in gathering readily available numbers turned into a significant undertaking. I kept confronting comparability challenges, not just in measuring citizenship, but in measuring all sorts of information that I initially thought was self-evident. Instead, I learned that statistics are rarely self-evident. How do you compare people's level of education across two countries (and multiple states and provinces) when education systems vary? How do you compare immigrants' ability to speak English when the Canadian and US Census questions have slightly different wording? I nevertheless opted to use census data despite their limitations, as these data were the most reliable and extensive available. They also included important information on immigrants' socio-demographic characteristics such as age, gender, level of education, and length of residence. All told, it took months to evaluate the available data, learn how to work with public use census data, and resolve issues of comparability. All this to establish a 'puzzle' for my advisor!

I was thus thrilled – and relieved – when my citizenship calculations were transformed into a striking bar graph. The graph showed that naturalization in the United States and Canada rose and fell in tandem throughout most of the twentieth century, but after 1970, the patterns diverged. In 1970, 64 percent of the foreign-born in the United States were Americans, a figure close to the 60 percent of naturalized immigrants in Canada. By the 2000 US Census, the level of naturalization had fallen to 40 percent, but north of the border, 72 percent of the foreign-born living in Canada held Canadian citizenship. I had a puzzle!

Or so I thought.

24.2 RESEARCH DESIGN: SELECTING CASES AS A CREATIVE ENDEAVOR

I shared my research puzzle with all and sundry – I finally had a question! – but I was quickly confronted by doubters. Sure, maybe aggregate citizenship levels differed, but getting citizenship was probably easier in Canada. Or, some suggested, the benefits of citizenship were more attractive in Canada than the United States. Perhaps, others said, the naturalization gap was just due to differences in the sorts of immigrants who moved to the two countries. Finding a puzzle was not enough. I had to convince people that it was a true research problem, a surprising difference that could not be easily explained by common sense.

Those who questioned the significance of the citizenship gap frequently pointed out that immigration flows to Canada and the United States differ in important ways. About two thirds to three quarters of legal newcomers arrive in the United States through family sponsorship. In Canada, the percentage is smaller, about a third to a half, while a substantial proportion of migrants instead enter as 'independent immigrants,' selected on factors such as education, language skills, and age. The national origins of immigrants also vary. Most migrants to the United States come from Mexico and Spanish-speaking countries in Latin America, South America, and the Caribbean. In contrast, a majority of contemporary migrants to Canada come from Asia. Skeptics objected that the gap in naturalization levels stemmed from differences in immigration, not from the two societies' reception of immigrants. I needed to find a way to respond to these doubters.

24.2.1 The Portuguese as Quasi-experiment

Many introductory research methods courses, including one I took as a master's student at McGill University, introduce novice researchers to social science by holding up experimental design as the golden yardstick. Students are told that a well-designed experiment isolates causal forces in a way that observational data cannot. Most observational data suffer from selection bias: if you compare the educational outcomes of children in public and private schools, you cannot necessarily conclude that one type of school is better than another. Families that send their children to private schools are inherently different from those who enroll their children in public schools, and this difference cannot be captured completely through statistical controls for income, religious background, and parents' education. Thus, if you find a statistically significant difference in public and private students' test scores, you cannot be sure whether this is because of the school, or because of the factors that led parents to enroll their children in one system or another. In contrast, experimenters randomly assign participants to a 'treatment' or a 'control' group. Since placement in one group or the other occurs by chance, variations in the outcome can be attributed to the treatment, not selection.[3]

It is usually unethical or impractical to do random assignment in social science. Ideally, to see whether the context of reception in one immigrant-receiving society facilitates naturalization more than in another, we should randomly place foreigners in one country or another and compare outcomes. But we cannot travel the world arbitrarily sending some people to certain countries and forcing others to stay where they are. We can, however, try to minimize selection biases by comparing immigrants with very similar origins and comparable patterns of migration.

To deal with the doubters, I thus learned of the importance of carefully selecting the cases you study. Case selection – from the immigrant groups examined, to the research sites compared – is a creative endeavor of research design. Studying particular groups or sites can have value because the group or place hasn't been studied before, but it is even better when case selection advances a project's theoretical focus or the ability to test a hypothesis.

For my research, I set up a 'quasi-experiment' by studying Portuguese immigrants. Early in my doctoral program, a summer research job introduced me to the glories of salted cod, Holy Ghost festivals, and the spirit of migration that many Portuguese trace back to Henry the Navigator and Vasco da Gama. For this job, I had to write up a migration history of Portuguese migrants to the United States. I knew little about Portugal prior to my PhD studies and, embarrassingly, I had never heard of the Azores, Portuguese islands home to the majority of Portuguese immigrants in North America. Coincidentally, I lived in an area with a heavy concentration of Portuguese Americans, so I struck up conversations at the grocery store that sold *linguiça*, Portuguese sausage, and at a local tailor shop where I went to get a zipper replaced. These conversations provided a human face and direct testimony to what I was reading in books and scholarly articles, and they encouraged my interest in in-depth interviews as a method of gathering data. Equally intriguing, when I told people that I was from Canada, they would invariably mention that they had a Portuguese-born cousin, aunt, or brother who lived in the Toronto area.

These casual conversations pushed me to systematically investigate Portuguese migration to Canada and the United States. Using my new familiarity with census data, I created a statistical portrait of Portuguese-born individuals in Ontario and Massachusetts. The two groups were strikingly alike. Indeed, when later I conducted interviews in Toronto, one Portuguese Canadian man told of being selected for agricultural work by Canadian immigration officials the same week that his brother stepped on a plane for New England. Portuguese migration became my quasi-experiment.

Given the substantial similarities between the Portuguese communities of Ontario and Massachusetts, we would expect little variation in citizenship levels if the US-Canada naturalization gap is purely a function of immigrants' characteristics, rather than the context of reception. I used the power of statistics to model the probability that a Portuguese immigrant who lived in Ontario or Massachusetts was a naturalized citizen. My model included variables identified by prior research as consequential to explaining naturalization, such as length of residence, English ability, and educational attainment. Even after introducing these statistical controls, the odds that the average Portuguese immigrant in Ontario was a naturalized citizen were significantly higher, a three out of five chance, than a similarly situated compatriot in Massachusetts, whose odds were just two out of five. The research puzzle remained.

Dealing with the skeptics took a significant amount of time, but it paid off in an article published in *International Migration Review* (Bloemraad, 2002). The article shows that citizenship regulations in Canada and the United States are remarkably similar, so European research that identifies legal differences in citizenship law as a source of variation does not apply in North America. Further, the benefits of citizenship are higher in the United States than in Canada. For example, American citizens can more easily sponsor a broader range of relatives than permanent residents; Canadian citizenship provides no sponsorship benefits. Finally, the article breaks down aggregate naturalization data by country of origin, revealing that in every case proportionally more immigrants hold citizenship in Canada than in the United States. I had a solid, intriguing puzzle.

24.2.2 Using Comparative Logic to Deal with the 'Small *N*' Problem

During my time at Harvard University, the sociology faculty included Theda Skocpol and Stanley Lieberson, two leading scholars of social science methodology. I purposely took courses from both of them because they hold opposing approaches to comparative research. I wanted to be exposed to this diversity in outlook to better determine my own approach to research design and epistemology. Both fundamentally influenced my overall project, as did conversations with other students who took these classes.

Skocpol helped instigate a revival in comparative-historical studies in sociology and political science by insisting that a small number of case studies, carefully compared for their differences and similarities, can produce causal theories (Skocpol, 1979,1984; Skocpol and Somers, 1980). Critics such as Lieberson question such 'small *N*' studies. According to Lieberson, such studies imply deterministic theories in a world that can be better understood using probabilistic causality (Lieberson, 1991). Furthermore, given numerous possible explanations – or independent variables – for an outcome, a researcher cannot dismiss all alternative hypotheses if the number of cases is smaller than the number of potential explanations. Studies with a large number of cases – that is, with a 'large *N*' – should be preferred.

Case-oriented researchers respond to these criticisms by arguing for the power of process tracing: researchers who study a limited number of cases can use their in-depth knowledge to follow the sequence of behaviors and events that led to a particular outcome. Comparative-historical research, according to proponents, gets much closer to robust explanation of social phenomena than the correlation analysis conducted in 'large *N*' studies precisely because of the careful selection and examination of cases.

In the spirit of true open-mindedness, or indecisiveness, I saw merit in both sets of arguments. My overarching project was a 'small *N*' comparison of just two countries, the United States and Canada. As I had already seen, each time I suggested that government multiculturalism or integration policies might explain cross-national differences in immigrants' political incorporation, people came up with alternative explanations. I was thus faced with many potential explanations, but only two country cases.

I could have increased the number of countries studied to make my project a traditional statistical analysis, but the data requirements were insurmountable – countries just did not have similar data on immigrants and their political behaviors. More fundamentally, however, I agreed with the critics of variable-oriented comparisons that causal mechanisms could be better understood through in-depth comparison than statistical correlation. If differences in the social and political contexts of Canada and the United States influenced immigrants, the effects would occur through a complex conjunction of causal dynamics, not the additive effects of variables understood to be independent of each other.

Yet I felt very vulnerable to the 'small *N*' criticisms. The United States and Canada might be quite similar relative to most countries in the world, but they clearly differ in many ways. The United States is founded on a republican Presidential system; Canada has a parliamentary constitutional monarchy. The United States must contend with a legacy of slavery, while Canada has repeatedly overcome secession threats by its French-speaking minority. The United States is a country almost ten times more populous than Canada, and it is a world superpower. Canada has a slightly more generous welfare state and more income redistribution through its tax system. The list could go on. If I identified a reason for the divergent pattern of political incorporation over the past 30 years, how could I be sure that it was the right one, rather than a product of one of the other numerous US-Canada differences?

The short answer was that I could not be sure, but as I audited a course on research methods with Lieberson and read more about research design, I began to consider the power of multiple comparisons. Could I extend the logic of my argument to another comparison, within the overarching US-Canada study? By this time I had started doing interviews with Portuguese immigrants and community leaders in the Toronto and Boston areas. Based on these interviews, I began to develop an explanation centered on the ways that government policy could foster immigrants' political participation. Many of the local advocacy organizations and social service providers, which often spoke up in the media on behalf of immigrants and which occasionally organized citizenship drives or voter registration campaigns, relied heavily on government grants and contracts to stay alive. In Canada, governments provide more money to such organizations through settlement assistance and multiculturalism programs than similar groups receive in the United States. Was there a way to test the general applicability of this argument using another comparison?

I found that there was, thanks to an inspired idea from a fellow graduate student. Discussing my 'small N' problem in the research methods seminar, a classmate noted that refugees in the United States also receive significant government assistance, unlike migrants who come to the United States as workers or through family reunification. Indeed, the US government has a long history of working with refugee settlement organizations and mutual assistance associations to help this special category of migrant. According to the logic of my argument, I should see less variation in the political incorporation of refugees in Canada and the United States since they are supported by governments in both places. I should see more variation between non-refugee immigrants given broader Canadian support to all migrants. And I should see significant differences in political incorporation between similarly situated refugees and non-refugees within the United States. By carrying out this third comparison within the United States, I could hold constant all the alternative explanations suggested by the Canada-US comparison.

My colleague's observation led me to expand my project to include the Vietnamese communities living in the Boston and Toronto areas. The Vietnamese also constitute something of a quasi-experiment. Vietnamese populations in the two metropolitan areas differ more than the Portuguese, but the resettlement decisions made for many refugees in Thai, Indonesian, or Filipino refugee camps at times felt like the random assignment of a lab experiment. My dissertation project was thus built on multiple comparisons specifically chosen to rule out alternative theories and to provide further evidence for my emerging argument. This argument would also lead me to go beyond statistical analyses to conduct in-depth interviews and documentary analysis.

24.3 MIXED METHODS: COMBINING STATISTICS AND IN-DEPTH INTERVIEWS

Many research method textbooks, if they mention mixed methods at all, outline a division of labor between quantitative- and qualitative-oriented social science. In-depth interviews and ethnography, we are told, help generate ideas and provide fertile ground for the germination of new theories. For these ideas and theories to put down roots, however, they must be tested using rigorous statistical methods that evaluate their credibility and generalizability.[4]

My research did not follow this conventional wisdom. Quantitative data and statistical modeling laid the groundwork for the project. I needed numbers to establish the citizenship puzzle and, later, that representation by the foreign-born in national legislative office is more prevalent in Canada than in the United States. Statistical modeling also helped eliminate some alternative hypotheses. In this way, quantification set the stage. It was ill-equipped, however, to explain the players' actions.

24.3.1 In-depth Interviews and Process Tracing

I turned to in-depth interviewing to uncover the mechanisms structuring political incorporation. Whether quantitative or qualitative, the purpose of an interview is to collect information from those with direct knowledge of or experiences with something. The census data I used were based on survey-style interviews. These follow a predetermined interview schedule with carefully chosen question wording. Survey questionnaires assume that people understand questions in a similar manner so that the researcher can compare answers and identify patterns.

In contrast, in-depth interviews are guided conversations where respondents are encouraged to tell stories or elaborate on answers rather than checking a box or giving an answer of a few words (Rubin and Rubin, 1995; Weiss, 1995).[5] In-depth interviewing assumes that respondents might have different understandings of key concepts, and that the researcher does not necessarily know the right questions to ask. Instead, during the interview, the researcher probes respondents' answers specifically for unanticipated discoveries. This type of interviewing is especially helpful for process tracing and to better understand the meaning people give to particular words, experiences, identities, and so forth.

For my dissertation, I conducted 151 in-depth interviews with ordinary immigrants and refugees, community leaders, government officials, and others involved in newcomer settlement. I started my interviews with immigrants by asking how the person came to North America. This open-ended question usually led them to tell their migration story. Many of those I interviewed were nervous, never having been asked questions for a research project before, and some were intimidated, uncomfortable with my status as a university student when they had not completed elementary school in their homeland. More than once, after the interview was finished, a person would ask worriedly, 'Did I pass?' Since everyone is an expert on their own migration journey, this question usually broke the ice and encouraged people to talk freely.

I would follow up with questions about their early experiences finding work or going to school in North America, experiences with discrimination, and their sense of identity and awareness of multiculturalism. I then asked a series of questions about political incorporation: whether they had naturalized, whether they voted, what type of civic groups they belonged to, and so on. I had a complementary set of questions for community leaders, government officials, and others involved in immigrant settlement.

I faced a number of challenges. First, I speak neither Portuguese nor Vietnamese, so at times I turned to interpreters to help me understand migrants' narratives of political activity. This was not ideal – I literally lost some of the richness of their stories in translation – but the loss was similar in the United States and Canada, thereby avoiding bias in my overall comparison.[6]

I also had unanticipated emotional challenges. For a number of immigrants, recounting their trip to North America and discussing what they had gained – and lost – in migrating provoked tears. Ilda told of how an American teacher humiliated her when, in the eighth grade, she did long division as she had been taught in Portugal rather than the 'American way.' This led her to drop out of school, killing her dream of becoming a nurse. The first time a man cried during an interview, he told of leaving his family by boat after a nighttime dash across a Vietnamese beach. My cultural background left me ill-prepared to see a man cry, and I didn't know what to do, other than listen. I often came home exhausted from my interviews. Asking questions and listening carefully, with empathy, is much more difficult than textbooks let on.

A third intellectual challenge was trying to link individuals' personal stories to the larger institutional factors that I thought influenced political incorporation. In-depth interviews were invaluable here, since they helped get at the process tracing I found so powerful. Instead of 'yes' or 'no' questions, like those used in surveys, I asked my respondents how they became citizens or learned about voting. I asked questions such as 'When did you first hear about citizenship? From whom? Where? Did anyone help you file for citizenship? Who? Was this person affiliated with any organization?

Did someone else help? In what way? What was the process like?' Using these types of questions, I had respondents reconstruct the thoughts and events that led to a successful citizenship application, or their first experience voting, or the respondent's most recent electoral campaign.

The answers to these questions helped show that political incorporation is a 'social' process: immigrants received assistance from friends and family, from employers and coworkers, from teachers at school and from fellow students. Community organizations played a significant role. Immigrants with limited English language skills often received help from a local social service agency with co-ethnic staff, or from the agency that first helped them resettle, even though naturalization came many years later. From my respondents' narratives, it was clear that political incorporation was not the atomized, individual process implicit in many statistical models of naturalization and voting.[7]

I then took process tracing to the next level. While personal ties facilitated political incorporation, the institutional location of various 'helpers' was also important. A number of these helpers worked for non-profit organizations or government agencies, so I wanted to know more about the establishment and maintenance of immigrant community-based organizations. I visited most of the major organizations and agencies serving Portuguese and Vietnamese migrants in the Toronto and Boston areas, interviewed key informants in these organizations, and, where possible, collected copies of annual reports and financial statements. The financial statements allowed me to trace funding streams; in almost all cases, government played a significant role. Given what I knew about greater government funding for immigrants in Canada, and relatively more support for refugees in the United States as compared to others, I speculated that the organizational capacity of a migrant community – that is, the number and diversity of its community organizations – should vary with public financial support. This was indeed the case (Bloemraad, 2005).

By tracing immigrants' stories of their political incorporation upward, to the assistance provided by community organizations, and government funding downward, to the financial backing given to these organizations, I linked micro-level dynamics with my larger structural argument about institutional differences. I call this process of political incorporation 'structured mobilization': immigrants acquire citizenship, learn about politics, and, in numerous cases, participate due to localized social relations and personal mobilization efforts. These efforts lie nested in, and are structured by, the level of public and symbolic support afforded to the newcomer community.

24.3.2 In-depth Interviews and Meaning

In-depth interviewing also offered an advantage over standard survey questions by allowing me to probe respondents' feelings about their new home and their understanding of what citizenship was and what it entailed. To incorporate feelings and beliefs in quantitative studies, a researcher must classify responses into a relatively small number of mutually exclusive categories, thereby losing much of the richness, and contradictoriness, of people's emotions. In the United States and Canada, for instance, the Census Bureaus ask respondents' race and provide a set of specific options. Respondents can check one of these predetermined categories, 'other' (and write in an alternative category), or refuse to answer the question. This allows researchers to provide statistics based on racial self-identification, but we learn very little about people's understandings of these race categories as a salient identity, or how context might alter the label someone adopts at any particular time.

In-depth interviewing allows for more of this nuance. For example, Ann, who I interviewed in Toronto, repeatedly said that she loved Canada and that she felt at home in her new country. Asked why she had applied for Canadian citizenship only three years after arriving, she told me, 'Because I love my country! This I look at like my country. I feel it's my country.' She had arrived in Canada as an adult from Vietnam with few job skills, but she took courses at a local community college and eventually became the owner of a successful beauty salon. She claimed to have experienced no discrimination in Toronto, be it at school, work, or in public places.[8] I expected, when I asked her how she would identify herself, to say Canadian or Vietnamese Canadian. But when I asked whether she felt Canadian, she looked surprised and answered, 'I still Vietnamese . . . I never think I'm Canadian, right? Because I live here, I from Vietnam, I still Vietnamese. Maybe my son will think differently . . . because he born here. But for me, I think I still Vietnamese.' Ann was not the only one who claimed strong attachment to her new country, but who found it incomprehensible to say that she was just Canadian, or even Vietnamese Canadian.

These responses forced me to rethink my simplistic assumptions about the Canadian mosaic versus the American melting pot, or any automatic association between citizenship and ethnic identity. Immigrants and refugees in Canada usually felt accepted in their new home, but this did not necessarily translate into a clear preference for a Canadian or hyphenated Canadian identity. Some could not imagine themselves as Canadian while others bristled at being anything but 'only' Canadian; they believed that hyphenation ghettoizes minorities by underscoring their otherness. In the

United States, some immigrants who had migrated decades earlier, like Ilda, recounted stories of unforgiving Americanization, but many recent newcomers experienced American society as tolerant and welcoming of diversity. In the eyes of many, Americans accepted multiculturalism, so immigrants could easily be American and identify with their cultural origins. As Reitz and Breton (1994) had argued, the Canadian mosaic/US melting pot distinction was overblown.

Yet official multiculturalism does matter for notions of 'political' inclusion, rather than personal or ethnic identity. I found that the political expression of multiculturalism, especially as a discourse that legitimizes immigrants' place in the country, sends a strong message to immigrants that they are rightful citizens. Participation in the political system – both as a right and a responsibility – is normalized. Government programs that include or explicitly serve immigrants reinforce this sentiment. Ann, for example, took part in a new mothers' program hosted in a municipal community center soon after arriving in Toronto. Sensitive to local demographics, the program was offered in a variety of languages, including Vietnamese. The more universal nature of social programs in Canada also fosters a sense of engagement with government. Since government programs affect people's lives, participating in the selection of government matters.

In the United States, immigrants had more ambiguous views of political inclusion. Social benefits, a link between people and government in Canada, are more prone to stigmatization in the United States, and are often overlaid with the politics of race (Lieberman, 1998; Quadagno, 1994). Multiculturalism in the United States also centers on groups distinguished by race, with a greater focus on native-born minorities than immigrant newcomers. These dynamics affect immigrants' notions of citizenship. Migrants in the United States were grateful for the rule of law and economic opportunity, but they did not feel the same sense of engagement or invitation to participate in a common political space (Bloemraad, 2006). My in-depth interviews consequently showed not only the social processes behind citizenship and political engagement, but also how government policy affected the very meaning people attributed to citizenship and political engagement.

24.4 CONCLUSIONS AND LESSONS LEARNED

I regularly show the graph of divergent citizenship levels when I give talks about my dissertation research, published in 2006 as a book called *Becoming a Citizen*. The graph is a striking visual representation of my research question and it immediately invites the audience to speculate about what is going on. Having others puzzle with you engages them in your research enterprise. Not everyone will agree with the conclusions, but most will be sufficiently curious to listen and become absorbed in the work. Not all research requires a neat puzzle, but a crisply worded question certainly helps the researcher, and her audience.

Working through this project also taught me not to see research design as a dry methodological enterprise, but rather as a creative venture. We are all limited in what we can do – how many countries we can study, how many groups we can include, whether we can find the right data for our topic. But every project contains multiple observations, as ethnographic field notes, interview responses, or cases considered. Creative comparisons can leverage the available data by testing the logical implications of an emerging or hypothesized relationship. Maximizing such comparisons increases confidence in your conclusions.

I also found mixing methods to be particularly helpful in building my argument. Some are suspicious of mixed methods – I was told by one professor while on the job market that those who mix quantitative and qualitative research tend to do neither very well – but I find my results much more convincing after I triangulate data sources and data types. In my case, statistics described the generalized nature of the problem and helped cast doubt on alternative hypotheses. Qualitative interviews and documentary data uncovered the mechanisms linking the structuring forces of governmental policy to the individual actions, decisions, and understandings of immigrants and refugees. Without one or the other, the story would have been incomplete.

Finally, ego considerations aside, I learned to be thankful for the hard questions of a dissertation advisor that forced me to rethink my entire project and to get serious about research design.

NOTES

1. I also considered voting as an outcome measure, but voting surveys included too few immigrants to allow for sustained statistical analysis, especially when the category of 'immigrant' was broken down by country of origin. In addition, most surveys are conducted in a single receiving society. It is rare to find a survey conducted in multiple countries or using wording that is similar across countries. I had more success with a second outcome measure, immigrants' election to national office. I found a pattern similar to the citizenship data.
2. The INS and CIC compile data on inflows of legal migrants, but they do not keep track of who leaves the country or passes away. They consequently do not publish figures for the stock of legal immigrants in the country at any given time.
3. I leave aside the question of whether experiments actually help determine the 'mechanisms'

of causality. Even if we could conduct an experiment on public versus private school education, random assignment would only tell us that the absence or presence of a certain factor leads to a specific outcome (for example, low teacher:student ratios produce better test scores), but it would not necessarily tell us how this happened (for example, by providing each student with more time with the teacher and more personalized instruction, or by creating fewer distractions from a smaller number of peers, allowing students to better concentrate on the material).

4. See also Bose (Chapter 13, this volume) and Boccagni (Chapter 14, this volume) for further discussion of mixed methods and interdisciplinary approaches.
5. See Sánchez-Ayala (Chapter 6, this volume) for further discussion of interviewing techniques.
6. People often study communities that they know well: the adult child of Hmong refugees might study the Hmong in California, or a researcher born in India who grew up in Canada might study transnationalism among Indian migrants. This approach offers clear advantages: you often have easier access to people because of past interactions, you likely speak the language better than someone outside the community, you better understand cultural codes and taken-for-granted norms alien to an outsider, and so forth. My background – someone born in Spain to Dutch parents and who migrated to North America as a young child – was very different from those I interviewed. This sometimes made it more difficult to understand my respondents' lives. However, being an outsider also had advantages: I was seen as more neutral when it came to internal community divisions, I was better able to identify what was unique or different about community practices than someone who takes such practices for granted, and I found that people wanted to speak to me as an outsider, to tell a broader audience about their experiences. Not being Portuguese or Vietnamese sometimes made my work more difficult, but researchers should not assume they need to be of a particular immigrant community in order to study it.
7. Of course, not all the literature takes this tack. The qualitative naturalization study by Alvarez (1987) first alerted me to the role of non-profit organizations in citizenship acquisition. I also found the social and institutional approaches of Rosenstone and Hansen (1993) and Sidney Verba and colleagues (Verba et al., 1995) useful; both books rely on statistical data.
8. Since I am of European origin, it is likely that my respondents under-reported instances of racial or ethnic discrimination. In addition to such interviewer effects, the Vietnamese appear to report far fewer experiences with discrimination than other Asian groups (Lien et al., 2001). It is unclear whether this is because the Vietnamese experience fewer problems or, more likely, because they are more reluctant to report problems.

REFERENCES

Alvarez, R.R. (1987), 'A profile of the citizenship process among Hispanics in the United States', *International Migration Review*, **21** (2), 327–51.
Bloemraad, I. (2002), 'The North American naturalization gap: an institutional approach to citizenship acquisition in the United States and Canada', *International Migration Review*, **36** (1), 193–228.
Bloemraad, I. (2005), 'The limits of de Tocqueville: how government facilitates organizational capacity in newcomer communities', *Journal of Ethnic and Migration Studies*, **31** (5), 865–87.
Bloemraad, I. (2006), *Becoming a Citizen: Incorporating Immigrants and Refugees in the United States and Canada*, Berkeley, CA: University of California Press.
Glazer, N. (1998), 'Governmental and nongovernmental roles in the absorption of immigrants in the United States', in P.H. Schuck and R. Münz (eds), *Paths to Inclusion: The Integration of Migrants in the United States and Germany*, New York: Berghahn Books, pp. 59–82.

Lieberman, R. (1998), *Shifting the Color Line: Race and the American Welfare State*, Cambridge, MA: Harvard University Press.
Lieberson, S. (1991), 'Small Ns and big conclusions: an examination of the reasoning in comparative studies based on a small number of cases', *Social Forces*, **70** (2), 307-20.
Lien, P., Conway, M.M., Lee, T. and Wong, J. (2001), 'Summary report of the pilot study of the National Asian American Political Survey', 2 March, available at http://www.apapolitics.org/ (accessed 21 January 2002).
Quadagno, J. (1994), *The Color of Welfare: How Racism Undermined the War on Poverty*, New York: Oxford University Press.
Reitz, J.G. and Breton, R. (1994), *The Illusion of Difference: Realities of Ethnicity in Canada and the United States*, Toronto: C.D. Howe Institute.
Rosenstone, S.J. and Hansen, J.M. (1993), *Mobilization, Participation, and Democracy in America*, New York: Macmillan.
Rubin, H.J. and Rubin, I.S. (1995), *Qualitative Interviewing, The Art of Hearing Data*, Thousand Oaks, CA: Sage.
Skocpol, T. (1979), *States and Social Revolutions: A Comparative Analysis of France, Russia and China*, New York: Cambridge University Press.
Skocpol, T. (1984), 'Emerging agendas and recurrent strategies in historical sociology', in T. Skocpol (ed.), *Vision and Method in Historical Sociology*, Cambridge: Cambridge University Press, pp. 256-391.
Skocpol, T. and Somers, M. (1980), 'The uses of comparative history in macrosocial inquiry', *Comparative Studies in Society and History*, **22** (2), 174-97.
Verba, S., Schlozman, K.L. and Brady, H.E. (1995), *Voice and Equality: Civic Voluntarism in American Politics*, Cambridge, MA: Harvard University Press.
Weiss, R. (1995), *Learning from Strangers: The Art and Method of Qualitative Interview Studies*, New York: Free Press.

PART VII

EXPERIENCES FROM THE FIELD

25 Immigrants and 'American' franchises: experiences from the field
Jennifer Parker Talwar

In an earlier paper I discussed my accidental entrance into the study of immigrant labor while I was a graduate student working at a Burger King and studying poverty at the bottom rungs of the growing service economy. As I explained then it had not occurred to me to study immigrant workers until my on-the-job experience provoked this interest. During my three months of employment I witnessed this workforce transform from a predominately African-American staff to a diverse group of immigrants from all over the world with seeming effects on the chances for mobility for different groups of workers, including immigrants and the native born.

My paper focused on some of the theoretical quandaries I faced trying to develop a framework for a topic that had not been studied before and how my research methodology (including fieldwork) evolved out of my theoretical questions. On an applied level I discussed issues of access and rapport; two methodological concerns I struggled with attempting to implement an interview-based research design in a giant corporate franchise organization characterized by low-wage, low-status, temporary, and part-time employment. I also provided examples of 'unintended' research findings that evolved directly from my choices in methodological approach in order to illustrate the inextricable link between research methods and results.

This research culminated in a book titled *Fast Food Fast Track: Immigrants, Big Business, and the American Dream* (Westview Press, 2002) and provided a foundation for a postdoctoral fellowship with the Social Science Research Council (SSRC), International Migration Program on ethnic entrepreneurs and American franchises. In this updated version it stands to reason that I share work from my postdoctoral research because it evolved from this initial research. This study examined the relationship between ethnic resource mobilization and the development of ethnic ownership niches in this same industry. Since the methodological approaches of both of these studies are tied to the same theoretical framework it is useful to retrace the theoretical and methodological challenges I faced in defining a research question in the earlier study.

25.1 DEFINING A RESEARCH QUESTION: THEORETICAL AND METHODOLOGICAL CHALLENGES

As I had stated in my earlier paper, had I been interested in the study of immigration I do not think I would have chosen to study fast food restaurant chains. First of all, the fast food literature, and modern corporate organizational studies, in general, lacked a focus on immigrant employment or capital. Second, studies involving immigrant workers who relied on low-level jobs in the host society or immigrant entrepreneurs, in general, tended to focus on traditional 'ethnic economies' – where immigrants and employers share the same ethnicity (co-ethnicity) and are relatively segregated from the mainstream economy such as in Chinese garment factories and ethnic restaurants (Light, 1973; Portes and Bach, 1985; Waldinger and Bozorgmehr, 1996; Zhou, 1995).

The most relevant literature in respect to the theoretical questions I was thinking about then was the ethnic enclave literature. The ethnic enclave was conceptualized as the geographical concentration of 'ethnic economies' in immigrant neighborhoods. It was argued that the geographical concentration of ethnic business and employment activity provided the economic foundation for the preservation of cultural traditions from homelands, including language, religious customs, and family practices (Portes and Bach, 1985). I thought it was interesting that at the same time this literature was channeling students into studies of these traditional ethnic sectors the globalization literature was growing in influence. Globalization studies, and particularly the homogenization thesis, was envisioning a 'McDonaldized' world culture in which Western-type corporate institutions were devouring local culture and institutions (Ritzer, 1993).

My preliminary research including working at a Burger King restaurant and talking to over 100 fast food restaurant participants in all five boroughs of New York City made it clear to me that the big fast food chains were, indeed, making deliberately planned inroads into immigrant neighborhoods, often with specific strategies to attract a new immigrant clientele and new immigrant workers. It seemed that immigrant neighborhoods having strong cash flows and a workforce eager to 'Americanize' were ideal targets for the fast food industry.

But it was not so clear the extent to which the industry was drawing on an immigrant labor force and how this was related to consumer strategies to attract new immigrant groups to fast food. This led to a series of questions: Was the industry drawing on the same people who worked in traditional 'ethnic economies'? Or was it drawing on different groups altogether? Were immigrants carving out occupational niches in American fast food restaurants, an industry long perceived as the quintessential employer of American teenagers? Were immigrants using jobs that the American public considered dead-end and last-resort as a stepping-stone into the American mainstream culture and economy? Did fast food restaurants in the immigrant neighborhood provide the same opportunities as traditional ethnic enterprises or different ones? Or were fast food jobs in the immigrant neighborhood simply dead-end opportunities reflecting the already polarizing forces of the American city and the economy at large. In the long run, did the fast food restaurant help reinforce or break down the traditional norms of ethnic community in the immigrant neighborhood?

It seemed that answering these questions and developing an appropriate methodology to study them required moving beyond the homogenization thesis as well as the image of immigrant communities as homogeneous and immigrant workers who depend on low-level jobs as socially and culturally isolated. James Watson, in his work on the global expansion of American-style fast food restaurants in East Asia, had argued that the spread of global cultural institutions is not a unilateral process, as the homogenization thesis tends to proclaim; nor are local cultures immune from these processes, as the ethnic enclave literature was seeming to suggest. Rather, it is a two-way street. This idea of the linking of the global with the local among immigrant communities in American cities came to frame my methodological approach to the study of immigrant fast food workers (Portes and Bach, 1985; Watson, 1998 [2006]).

25.2 DEVELOPING A METHODOLOGICAL FRAMEWORK

Most studies of the immigrant enclave or ethnic economy, as I learned, relied on fieldwork; either survey data or face-to-face interviews with immigrant employees and owners. Likewise, my methods were primarily qualitatively based with a heavy emphasis on semi-structured, face-to-face interviews with restaurant participants at all levels of the hierarchy – from entry-level crew members and managers to owners. I conducted in-depth, face-to-face interviews with 52 people including crewmembers, managers, and owners. They came from over a dozen different countries in Asia, Africa, Europe, and, Latin America.

The nature of my questions, being open-ended , rather than hypothesis-oriented, were best treated through a kind of grounded theory approach that would allow me to move back and forth between empirical findings and theoretical framework to continually redirect the orientation of my research questions. I thought that a survey method, usually more associated with a positivist methodology, would not give me this kind of flexibility. Semi-structured interviews (what I referred to as an 'interview guide') would give me the freedom to orient and develop an interview design that would revolve around respondents' experiences and knowledge, enabling me to capture that which I could not have anticipated during the interview interaction.[1]

In order to capture local variations (including the ways in which ethnic relations play a role in labor market processes) I used a neighborhood comparative approach. I focused on two fast food chains/brands and seven restaurants located in three different immigrant neighborhoods. The criteria for choosing the immigrant neighborhoods I studied (Manhattan's Chinatown, 'Little Dominican Republic' in Inwood/Washington Heights, and Downtown Brooklyn) were based on a number of criteria: (1) the size of the immigrant community – it had to be relatively large; (2) the presence of both a traditional ethnic enclave and the big fast food chains; and (3) convenience and personal access were important – I lived in Inwood, my research job as a graduate student was in Downtown Brooklyn, and Chinatown was in between these neighborhoods. I decided to focus on the two biggest hamburger chains – McDonald's and Burger King, simply because they seemed to have the biggest and most aggressive marketing strategies among the big fast food chains and they were similar in organizational structure. It was also because I was familiar with both of these chains. I had worked in both of them – at Burger King as a participant observer and at McDonald's when I was a teenager.

In retrospect, I could have chosen virtually any immigrant neighborhood or any fast food chain(s). I wanted to understand how local neighborhoods and giant corporate franchises interacted to create specific global-local patterns, rather than understand how a specific immigrant group or company functioned within it. It was this, I thought, that would tell a larger story about the cultural strategies and operations of modern corporate organizations in the global economy and how they interacted with immigrants' strategies of survival and mobility in American society.

Therefore, what was important was limiting the number of variables I studied, while being careful to not make it a study about a particular company, immigrant group, or neighborhood. For example, if I had focused on only one company, say McDonald's, it could have been interpreted as a study about a specific company. If I had broadened my focus to include several different chains, then there would have been too many structural variances related to the work process to make reasonable comparisons within and between restaurants and neighborhoods.

A central theoretical finding of my research came from my methodological approach and helped to inform subsequent theoretical questions. Given the standardized nature of the industry I had assumed that a uniform approach could be applied across the entire industry. But as you will see this was not the case. I found the industry to be enormously complex with immense organizational diversity at the local level, not simply in terms of the diversity of people they hire, but also structurally. The decentralized nature of the social organization of this industry, in fact, formed the basis of my critique of the rationalization thesis (McDonaldization), a critique that emphasized the significance of local agency and variation in globalization processes (Ritzer, 1993).

On a structural level, for instance, I was surprised to find an absence of social linkages (both formal and informal) between restaurants which meant that each of my seven restaurants had to be approached entirely anew. A snowball approach (which I assumed would be an effective approach in this industry) would be limited to connections that existed within each restaurant. Second, the local autonomy accorded to restaurant owners meant that each restaurant could have its own organizational culture and I would likely need to negotiate access to respondents in each restaurant differently which was certainly the case.

In the case of my subsequent study on owners I was interested in a very different question: how ethnic niches had been formed in a giant franchise organization. If, in fact, the industry was decentralized and as locally varied as it seemed on a neighborhood by neighborhood level how was it that certain ethnic groups seemed to be creating their own large-scale social organizations in the industry by developing ethnic ownership niches that appeared to cover entire regions of the country?

The methodological design, then, was turned on its head – where the unit of analysis was not the industry itself or a single franchise unit but rather of particular ethnic groups, similar to group-level studies of entrepreneurs in the traditional ethnic economies field. But it was premised on a decentralization hypothesis – that the nature of how the industry was structured is what provided ethnic groups endowed with 'entrepreneurial capacity'[2] the opportunity to make large-scale inroads into it in an ownership capacity. Therefore, I was moving from an understanding of how local neighborhoods and giant corporate franchises interacted to the relationship between ethnic resource mobilization (at the entrepreneurial level) and giant corporate restructuring. To what extent, I wondered, were ethnic social structures/ethnic resource mobilization (at the ownership level) integral to giant franchise organizations' expansion and reorganization, particularly in the transition from the 'mom and pop' model of franchising to the big business model (multiple franchising) and its accompanying changing cost structure (profit squeeze) and heightening operational demands.

I relied on fieldwork (like in my first study). My methods were primarily qualitatively based with a heavy emphasis on semi-structured, face-to-face interviews with franchisees. I chose three among the largest metropolitan immigrant-receiving areas of the country: New York, Los Angeles, and Miami. I spoke with over 100 representatives of the most visible chains in these cities in order to identify some of the most significant ethnic ownership niches in the country: (1) Asian Indian Punjabis who had formed sizable niches in SUBWAYS and 7 Elevens in Southern California and (2) Asian Indian Gujaratis who had formed an enormous niche in Dunkin Donuts restaurants in the New York area. Focusing on these two groups, I thought, could provide substantial qualitative insight into the significance of ethnic ownership niches in giant franchise organizations.

25.3 ISSUES OF ACCESS IN AMERICAN CORPORATE FRANCHISES

Accessing respondents is always a concern in qualitative research. There were issues that were particular to the giant corporate restaurant chains. One of my first concerns that goes back to my earlier work was whether or not I would need to seek authorization to interview workers or even if it would be required at all. Originally I thought that I would be required to gain permission from the corporate headquarters of each chain in order to interview on-site restaurant participants. Given this, I was apprehensive about what this would imply – from flat out rejection to a research design controlled and/or limited by corporate headquarters. This turned out not to be the case. Franchise owners, as I was told by headquarters representatives, are not restricted by corporate headquarters in what they can say as spokespeople of their restaurant. Likewise, managers can consent to their own interviews and authorize their employees to give interviews 'on the job' if they choose to.

Second, I wondered if fast food workers would even talk to me given the hectic and low status nature of fast food jobs. How much would the national stigma against McDonald's employment affect their willingness to be identified with their job status?

Third, I worried about where and how I should approach potential respondents. Since my unit of analysis was the restaurant (rather than a specific ethnic group) it seemed appropriate to seek out respondents where they worked (at the restaurant). But thinking in the context of political economic thought, or more generally, labor studies, I also thought I should talk to employees independently, away from the restaurant setting and the managers' purview. I wanted respondents to talk freely and honestly without their job status being threatened. But how would I do that? Being a part of the flexible-based global corporate labor market jobs were defined as temporary, part-time, with individualized work hours. Because of this there would be no consistency in workers' schedules and it could be a nightmare trying to make effective contacts across seven different restaurants. There could be hours between when employees arrived or left the restaurant. Also, even if an employee would agree to an interview then there would be a host of other challenges. I could be negotiating for an interview in another context, the employee's family. But more importantly, it was obviously difficult for employees to find time outside of work. They were either students balancing school and work schedules, parents balancing the demands of work and children, and/or people struggling with two or more jobs.

Fourth, the nature of the industry itself would prevent me from using strategies scholars have used to interview workers in traditional ethnic economies – the use of employee networks. Being a mainstream franchise organization the composition of the fast food workforce was diverse (globally, ethnically, and socioeconomically) rather than dominated by co-ethnic networks.

Given the constraints to approaching workers independently I aimed to gain the support of franchisees. This came with its own methodological nightmares; because of the decentralized nature of the industry each restaurant had a unique social organization, it came with its own rules and dynamics. Some restaurants were ruled by a strong top-down authority structure where issues of access were more formalized, requiring permission from the franchisee (local owner). For example, one restaurant franchisee among my respondents was the biggest restaurant corporation in New York City. I was required to submit a formal letter of request to the central corporate administration. It took several weeks and numerous phone calls to get a response. In cases like this where a lot of persistence was required I felt that permission was finally granted just so I would stop bothering them. It would have been easy (even reasonable) to give up after a series of unreturned phone calls. In this industry, though, and especially when dealing with a large local ownership structure, persistence is crucial.

Some restaurants had a looser, flatter chain of command that gave managers and crewmembers more flexibility in their interactions with outsiders. In one restaurant, for instance, a manager gave me an interview as soon as I walked in off the street. As I later learned, the franchise owner of this restaurant, also an owner of a small retail shop in the Vietnamese ethnic economy (within Chinatown), had no involvement with the restaurant because of his limited language skills. He did not speak either language (Spanish or English) spoken by the Colombian-born general manager and the predominately pan-Latino workforce.

While the structure of the social organization determined how I gained access to respondents, it also affected how interviews were conducted. Spontaneously given interviews, such as with the Colombian-born general manager, seemed ideal at first. But like any relationship, the immediate pace of involvement and intimacy had its own drawbacks. This manager, for instance, sat with me for over two hours providing me with very rich material about his perceptions and experiences in the industry over the past years. But when I returned the next day to finish the interview with him and to interview members of his staff (as he had committed to) he seemed much less engaged, as if he had rethought his involvement. While he kept his word to allow me to interview his staff, he seemed to do so with a different attitude. Had he not expected me to come back? Did I do something wrong? Was he suddenly uncomfortable about what he had disclosed to me so readily the day before? Or, was he simply too busy that day to want to deal with me? In the spontaneous interview the establishment of formal boundaries and expectations are often sidestepped to make way for receiving the immediate and unfiltered thoughts of an eager respondent. But this comes at a risk with the possibility of leaving the researcher without an established formalized context in which to negotiate further research needs in the organization.

While the organizational culture and owner-management relations helped determine how and if I would gain access to restaurant staff (as well as written material, memos, and so on) it was also impossible to know what this structure was like until I interacted with it – face to face. Ironically, it seemed that the more formal the process of gaining access, the greater the ease I had in conducting interviews and gathering data. Authorization from the top worked not only as a license for restaurant staff to talk to me (and, usually, in the absence of this top-level authority) but also to afford the time during working hours for interviews. In retrospect, the informality of the spontaneous interview provided a unique opportunity to gather 'off the cuff' data, data that almost always probed into new territory. On the other hand, the more formalized the interview context, the greater the ease in which people talked and the greater consistency there was in my respondent sample.

My approach was entirely different in the franchisee study because I was focused on a particular ethnic group rather than a geographical space (restaurant/neighborhood). Also, I was focused on a different level of the organization – owners versus employees. But this earlier work helped prepare me for accessing franchisees. Knowing that franchisees were autonomous from the parent company meant that I could approach them directly. And having experienced the social dynamics of hierarchy in the restaurant workplace I understood that it would be ineffective to try to gain access to franchisees through cold in-store visits (the approach I took in the earlier study). On-site managers were accustomed to playing the role of 'gatekeeper'; they would pass on information but would rarely give out their supervisors' contact information. My approach then utilized two strategies: (1) I repeatedly phoned restaurants/stores until I was able to speak directly to the franchisee and (2) I snowballed further contacts.

25.4 THE INTERVIEW: ESTABLISHING TRUST AND RAPPORT IN CORPORATE RETAIL FRANCHISES

In-depth interviews seem to provide one of the most important contexts where data is collected among immigration scholars. But as I wrote in my earlier paper little has been written about the interview process itself. This is still true. Data seems to rely heavily on 'personal encounters,' yet investigators of the immigrant economy tend to remain 'silent' and ' hidden' in the literature (Goodwin and Horowitz, 2002) with little reporting of 'reflexive processes' (Bourdieu, 1993; Wacquant, 1999). The relative absence of writing about 'personal encounters' may be related to the fact that the interview situation itself is so highly personal, relying heavily on personality or ethnic affinity, rather than learned traits.

In my earlier paper I discussed particular challenges I came across in establishing rapport in the giant corporate retail sector. Part of the challenge in this industry pertains to the diversity and multi-situational identities of the people it hires; rapport had to be negotiated differently depending on the situational identity of each respondent and raised questions about how identity is produced in the research process (Robb, 2004). I referred to two types of respondents (common to the giant corporate retail sector at large) to illustrate the strategies I developed to overcome particular challenges to establishing rapport: (1) teenagers who tend to be resistant to being identified with the brand names and companies they work for and (2) authority figures (including managers) who have a tendency to frame their responses in the context of corporate rhetoric rather than their own experiences. But I first discussed the concept of rapport, and particularly two elements of rapport that I found helpful to distinguish in this industry: (1) trust and (2) getting respondents to buy into the research project. I will now discuss these again while referencing the uniquely different challenges I faced in my interviews with franchisees.

I referred to 'trust' as that which gives your respondents confidence that the information they provide to you is everything you say it is – important, confidential, and so on. This is partly based on building a relationship based on the interactive elements of the interview, finding a balance between the roles of listening and probing (Tusini, 2004). I discussed how 'trust,' in some cases, became a kind of secondary concern for me over how to get respondents to buy into the interview goals. A respondent, as I learned, may trust your scholarly motives, but be completely uninterested in your project or not take it seriously. Likewise, a respondent may be completely interested in your project, but be suspicious, and therefore withholding, or even, misleading. In some cases, a respondent may be both trusting and interested in your project, but to such an extreme level that you are forced to establish boundaries around your professional interests. Given the diversity of my respondents, not simply their ethnic backgrounds, but also their socioeconomic backgrounds, age/maturity levels, and gender (in the earlier study), these three elements of rapport were important to distinguish.

They were also important to distinguish because issues related to trust need to be thought of differently in the fast food industry than in traditional ethnic sectors of the low-wage economy. In many studies of the traditional immigrant economy researchers need to be cautious about their respondents' vulnerable and often undocumented status. Issues of 'trust' significantly revolve around ensuring confidentiality so that employees do not perceive their job status and lives in the new country to be threatened. Since the most vulnerable immigrants tend to rely on co-ethnic relations within their own immigrant communities as a means of survival, then establishing 'trust' in the interview situation has tended to revolve around establishing 'indigenous identity' or 'ethnic insider' status. Recent studies have shown that about 'half of immigration scholars in the United States are themselves of immigrant stock' (Gans, 1999; Kusow, 2003; Rumbault, 1999). It occurred to me that the importance placed on 'indigenous authenticity' and ethnic insider status may have influenced a methodological tendency within US immigration studies to focus on immigrant group (rather than organization) as an analytical starting point.

I had found that establishing trust among respondents in a fast food chain restaurant required a different kind of thinking than in traditional co-ethnic establishments. There were two relevant issues to consider. First, the ethnic diversity of the fast food staff meant that a particular ethnic background of a researcher may not necessarily be advantageous for approaching a diverse population. Second, immigrants who work in fast food sectors are different from those who work in traditional 'co-ethnic' sectors, most notably because they do not necessarily attach their ethnic identity to their job position or the organization they work for, at least not as a primary status. Immigrants in fast food sectors tend to be a step above their counterparts who rely on 'co-ethnic' employment. They are employed on a legal basis. And they are socioeconomically diverse, ranging from the poor to the middle class. Many are upwardly mobile and few plan on lingering in the industry for very long. Those who do, plan on becoming managers. In fact, their fast food job status is not typically a primary status at all.

Their more privileged status in an ethnically diverse environment allows them to step beyond both 'ethnicity' and job position as primary statuses in an American organization. The American fast food restaurant for many of my immigrant respondents represented a kind of 'in between' or 'transitional' space between their own immigrant communities and mainstream America. Moreover, they occupied a whole 'set of social statuses' not simply an ethnic status (Kusow, 2003; Merton, 1972, p. 24). Other social statuses, such as socioeconomic status, student, future career, age, and gender, play central roles in their identity as 'American' employees.

25.4.1 Immigrant Teenagers and the Fast Food Social Stigma

Rapport, then, was negotiated in light of these multiple situational identities. I, as an interviewer, played on my own multiple identities, as a student, a former fast food crewmember, an 'American,' a woman, a young person, and so on, in accordance with who I was interviewing. For instance, there were a set of issues that particularly concerned the younger, especially teenage employees. One of these pertained to the social stigma attached to fast food work. Being a fast food worker carried so much social stigma that employees usually chose to work in fast food restaurants outside of their own neighborhoods to avoid being taunted, embarrassed, or pressured into breaking rules and giving away food. Even though employees did not believe their jobs deserved the low social status they were associated with they were acutely aware that the rest of society did. Establishing trust as an interviewer usually depended on being able to convey, first of all, that I did not share in the societal stigma and that I recognized their more 'primary status' as a future doctor, basketball player, or teacher, or simply someone who was trying or wished to do better. My status as a former fast food worker and a current student helped convey the degree to which I could communicate an understanding that their fast food status was not really what they were all about.

In my initial interviews, without being attentive to this, my youngest respondents seemed defensive. This defensiveness, as I interpreted it, stemmed from my respondents feeling subjugated to an inferior status, perceiving me as an outsider who was interested in fast food workers as 'losers' or illustrations of failure. As one teenager asked me, 'Why would you want to study fast food workers? There are a lot better jobs out there.' By emphasizing my own experiences as having had jobs in the industry and starting out the interview by talking about respondents' 'primary status' and future goals I was better able to reconfigure status distinctions between interviewer and respondent, elevate the respondents' status, and negotiate a more even playing field. Asking respondents for 'help' also contributed to elevating their status to informant versus object of research.

These strategies affected the degree to which employees bought into the project. For example, without reconfiguring status distinctions in the interview relationship, these young respondents viewed the project differently – as a study about them, in the objective, rather than informant sense. Once they realized that their thoughts and experiences could actually shape the study's story, rather than feel like their lives were being interpreted by it, they were more apt to express what seemed like genuine interest.

Still, it was a challenge to get some of the teenagers to talk, especially 14- and 15-year-old boys of the lowest socioeconomic status. With some it felt like I was prying information out of them, getting only one-word responses. My gender, I believe, helped mediate this kind of social distance among my female respondents of equivalent socioeconomic status and age (Hall, 2004). On the other hand, respondents' young age and temporary and part-time attachment to the industry also seemed to reflect the fact that many people who work in this industry (and giant corporate retail chains, in general) simply do not have the depth of experience or conscience investment in their jobs to be able talk about workplace dynamics. In these cases, the interview focused more heavily on personal issues; respondents' relationship to the industry rather than particular roles within it.

In hindsight, I believe it would have been productive to conduct focus group sessions among the teenagers, rather than rely exclusively on one-on-one interviews. Given the complex issues surrounding struggles over identity and social stigma in the industry, as well as temporary attachment to the industry, focus groups (involving both male and female teenagers) may have been an effective strategy for capturing both individual and interactive dynamics in the workplace and illuminating issues that were difficult (or simply uninteresting) to express for respondents on an individual level. On the other hand, it may have been difficult, on a methodological level, to orchestrate focus group sessions. It is unlikely that managers would have allowed more than one or two crewmembers at a time to be taken away from their job tasks while 'on the clock.' Furthermore, given the individual staggering of work schedules and the fact that employees do not live in the neighborhoods where they work it would have been difficult to get enough crewmembers together outside of work hours to conduct focus group sessions.

25.4.2 Getting Beyond Corporate Rhetoric: Interviews with Fast Food Managers and Franchisees

Another concern when doing research in corporate organizations is how to get beyond corporate rhetoric when interviewing authority figures, in my case, fast food managers and franchisees. Among managers and franchisees establishing trust was factored on different grounds and inspiring interest in the study was usually not necessary. Becoming a manager, first of all, already implied having some investment (including time and interest) in the industry. Though most managers did not feel comfortable being interviewed until they fully understood what the study was about, what it would be used for, that they were assured of confidentiality, and so on. At first, managers' frame of mind was typically situated in the context of corporate rhetoric, using it as a shield from personalizing the issues or simply interpreting my interests in this context – that I was there to find out how the organization is supposed to work. In nearly every interview with managers I needed to shift the framework of conversation away from the corporate philosophy, or rhetoric, in general, to managers' personal perceptions and experiences in the industry.

In doing this, it was helpful to draw on my own experiences as a fast food worker, or to recount what other respondents had told me. This served a number of purposes. First, it allowed me to negotiate an insider status as a former crewmember and someone familiar with the nuts and bolts of the industry. Second, it elevated my respondents to a consultant or informant status, rather than an object of analysis, or mere interpreter of corporate codes.

For example, consider the following exchange in an interview with a general manager:

Parker Talwar: Do you tend to hire certain kinds of people for particular jobs in the restaurant? For example, do you need a certain kind of person to work on the front-line?
Manager: That person would need to have a cheerful personality and communicate well.
Parker Talwar: Are there certain kinds of people, say men or women, who are better in these roles?

Manager: No, anyone can be given the opportunity to be on the front-line.

Parker Talwar: Last week, a manager in another restaurant explained to me that he prefers to have women on the front-line because of . . . [elaboration] . . . Also, in my experience working at a Burger King, none of the guys wanted to work on the front-line because they said it was a 'girls' job' . . .

Manager: Yes, yes, it is like that here too. While the opportunity is there for everyone, I notice that the girls do a better job, they are more friendly with the customers, are more attentive to their appearance, see the guys, they don't pay attention to things, they will come to work with their hair uncombed, their finger nails dirty, things like that . . . I just don't put the guys on the front-line . . .

It seemed easier for managers to verify and elaborate on a trend rather than explain how things worked in contradiction to the corporate philosophy, partly because their job responsibilities were defined in the context of corporate manuals even though their day to day activity was completely different. Presenting a trend was also a way for me (the interviewer) to communicate what I was really interested in without posing a direct question such as: 'Are there ever any exceptions to the corporate organizational philosophy?' Once the framework of conversation shifted away from corporate rhetoric, managers usually seemed highly motivated to talk. Managers, as I learned, are true middlemen, caught between corporate rules and local realities; standardized policies and diverse immigrant cultures. Several told me that they had not had an outlet for these concerns and had rarely had the chance to place their everyday experiences into real thoughts. The interview, then, was an outlet for many of the manager respondents to voice the everyday contradictions inherent in this middleman position.

The large degree of negativity voiced by many managers, especially concerning the nature of their jobs and company expectations, led me to believe that they did not feel particularly constrained or self-conscious while being interviewed 'on the job.' An interview with a manager from India at a Burger King at 5:00 am one Sunday morning became one of the saddest personal critiques I had ever heard about the industry. In a three-and-a-half hour interview beginning at 5:30 in the morning this manager explained how his life was a pathetic, pathetic story and his position shameful, located at the bottom rung of the US socioeconomic ladder. He discussed the 'despicable' nature of pay hierarchy in the United States, the unfairness of the minimum wage, the grueling nature of fast food work, and so on. Managers, I came to understand, held positions of power, but felt powerless to change the structural conditions of the industry. This was why they could sympathize with the employees who complained about their conditions and at the same time be the object of blame on the part of these same employees. (This was also why employees did not feel particularly constrained when complaining about their work conditions – because the real authority structure was amorphous to the local organization.) Interviewing both managers and employees provided a lens in which to view social interactions in the restaurant and how they played out in structuring ethnic divisions of labor and opportunities for employment. This interplay between managers' and crewmembers' voices led to an article entitled 'Contradictory assumptions in the minimum wage workforce' in the *Journal of Contemporary Ethnography*.

25.4.3 Establishing Professional Boundaries: When Interview Relations Become Too Personal

In some cases, both trust and interest levels (on the part of the respondents) became personalized, and I found myself in the awkward situation of having to establish my own personal and professional boundaries. In one particular case, an immigrant from Cuba, a former military officer, and Burger King crewmember, asked to meet at a restaurant where he would give me an interview. It was apparent that he was financially and emotionally 'down and out' and represented the dire situations of about 10 percent of my respondents. The interview lasted well into the night and he asked for more time for the interview the next day. The second day he asked to meet me again. The relationship began to feel awkward. I decided that as long as our discussions continued to be of relevance to the research project that I would continue to meet with him. We met for three consecutive days after which I explained to him that he had made a valuable contribution and that I needed to move on to other industry participants. He had shared his life history, the trajectory of his financial decline (Burger King representing the rock bottom of his career), his divorce, the days he spent with his son, his one-room living conditions, his fallen childhood dreams, his nightmares, the details of his current work life, and so on. He had given me a lot, a glimpse into some of the misery that exists in this industry, a misery that works to entrap people in what one manager referred to as 'the cycle that never ends.' I felt guilty taking his story when he went right back into this cycle of poverty and misery. Moving between my graduate student life and the lives lived by many of my respondents magnified for me the social distance between the profession and workers in poverty and the greater need for sociology to emphasize practical application to improving people's lives.

538 *Handbook of research methods in migration*

25.4.4 Rapport with Immigrant Owners: 'Ethnic Insider' Versus 'American Informant'

Establishing rapport with franchisees came with its own set of challenges quite different from what I experienced with workers and managers in the industry and also fundamentally different from what researchers have encountered with business owners in traditional ethnic enterprises. The differences are related to both differences in status as well as the nature of the study's inquiry. On the one hand, establishing rapport came with greater ease because of the perceived non-threatening and positive nature of the study's goals (focusing on ethnic groups' ascension in the industry).

Their circumstances as franchisees in an American mainstream enterprise also meant that I did not face some of the hurdles researchers have encountered when trying to establish rapport with business owners in traditional ethnic sectors. Co-ethnic worker exploitation and exploitation of undocumented workers (such as what many researchers have often come across in low-end ethnic sectors) were not factors of concern in this industry. Franchisees, under the guise of a corporate parent, are not likely to risk employing workers illegally. Many public critics have argued that the fast food industry exploits workers by paying them the minimum wage (albeit not a 'living wage') but this was not an issue that preyed on franchisees' consciousness or one that could have threatened legal disclosure. Franchisees seemed to have nothing to hide that could have threatened their legal status. In fact, they spoke frankly about both the constraints and motivations for elevating workers' conditions.

On the other hand, interviewing owners was a more challenging process than that I experienced with workers and managers. The social relationship was more complicated; most were wealthy, highly educated, many had professional backgrounds. Many described their migration experiences as a kind of 'rags to riches' story. Most were men and many were substantially older. In my earlier research I tended to downplay my social status, including educational attainment, in order to lessen the social distance with respondents. But with owners, I tended to 'play up' my socio-economic status for the same reason.

Moreover, considering that my unit of analysis was ethnic group (rather than organization like in my earlier study) I anticipated possible drawbacks related to being an 'ethnic outsider.' But, similar to what I found with fast food employees, identity seemed to be situational, not uniform. Ethnic identity is only one status among several franchisees related to; they were also business people in the American mainstream economy, many had become leaders in their community, most had become American citizens. Ethnicity, in other words, could not be assumed a significant status in a mainstream American industry. It seemed apparent that they had bought into my study, in part, not because they carried great significance to their Indian identity as much as the fact that I was interested in their success and insight (as immigrants) into an American industry. Rapport, in this sense, was primarily built around emphasizing their status as informants in an American industry rather than seeking mutual understanding through ethnic insider status. In this way I found myself assuming a tendency to overcompensate their informant status at the expense of adhering to previously defined research objectives.

25.5 THE RELATIONSHIP BETWEEN METHODOLOGY AND RESEARCH FINDINGS: THREE EXAMPLES OF UNINTENDED FINDINGS

The inextricable relationship between research methodology and research findings is made most prevalent in the case of unintended research findings. In my earlier paper I provided two examples to illustrate this. I am providing an additional example in reference to my later study of franchisees. The first example refers to how 'interactive elements of the interview,' often elements that go beyond the control of the interviewer, can affect the content of discussion, and hence, the nature of the data that is collected. The second example refers to how a 'comparative approach' can work to illuminate unanticipated findings through what I call a 'reflective experience' – or what a grounded theory approach would refer to as 'conceptual re-examination' – looking back on previous observations and noticing what previously went unnoticed or passed as insignificant. The third example refers to how the process of establishing rapport in the interview process can sometimes lead to alterations in approach and therefore affect the nature of the data that is collected. An emphasis on 'informant led dialogue' at the expense of adhering to a preconceptualized interview guide resulted in a new angle of inquiry.

25.5.1 First Example

The first example, referring to the relationship between interactive elements of the interview and the nature of the interview discussion, is made most clear in a particular situation I found myself in when attempting to interview a recent immigrant from China in a Chinatown restaurant. The languages spoken by most of the Chinese immigrant employees at that time were Mandarin and Cantonese. I did not speak a Chinese language

540　*Handbook of research methods in migration*

and the interviewee did not speak enough English to warrant a legitimate interview. The general manager, who was fluent in four languages, including Cantonese, Mandarin, Taiwanese, and English, offered to translate. I suggested that someone of the interviewee's own status (another crewmember) may be better and he obliged, although he hovered over the interview, often interjecting his own views and insights.

At first, the manager's presence seemed like an annoying intrusion, stifling the voice of the crewmember, sometimes even interrupting and offering his own interpretation of the respondent's answers. I felt stuck between trying to conform to my methodological principles and displaying tolerance for the general manager's 'helpfulness' because he held the reigns to my access to future respondents and company memos. But as it became clear that these were the dynamics that would characterize this interview I decided to politely finish the interview but not include the material among my data. After writing it off and simply letting the conversation go on between the general manager, the crewmember translator, and the respondent, I realized how interesting the conversation had become. It became a kind of focus group session, discussing matters that relate to relationships that had evolved between Chinese managers, crewmembers, and their parents, particularly the role that Chinese McDonald's managers were playing in socializing Chinese families into the norms of American teenage jobs and culture. (The topic was approached when I asked one of the questions on the interview guide: 'How do your parents feel about your job here?' The manager responded by pointing out how the interviewee's and the translator's parents had different perspectives on their children's fast food jobs and how he (the manager) dealt with these parents.)

Up to this point the role fast food managers were playing in socializing new immigrant families into American teenage work culture was not even an issue I had thought about. But it was extremely significant for understanding the way multinational chains successfully incorporate themselves into ethnic communities. In this way, it became apparent that the interactive elements of the interview itself can often determine the content of discussion and, hence, the nature of the data collected. It is a good example of how analytical categories can be derived directly from the methodological approach, reflecting the interaction between and among the observer (investigator) and the observed (respondent), even when transcending the methodological 'rules' (Charmaz, 2006).

25.5.2　Second Example

Another example of how analytical categories can be derived directly from the methodological approach pertains to how a 'comparative approach'

Immigrants and 'American' franchises 541

can work to illuminate unanticipated findings, through what I call a 'reflective experience' – or what a grounded theory approach would refer to as 'conceptual re-examination' – looking back on previous observations and noticing what previously went unnoticed or passed as insignificant. It was through a reflective experience that I discovered specific ways in which technologies play a role in facilitating and shaping a multiethnic workforce in this industry. Because the literature on modern technology and work relations stressed tendencies toward homogenization I assumed that workforce diversity was correlated with rationalization processes, or what Ritzer described as the 'robotization' of the workforce. In other words, various language groups could work together precisely because their individuality was irrelevant to the functioning of the modern workplace. But what I found was quite the opposite. While it was true that advanced technologies facilitated diversity, it was also true that diversity and ethnic identity played a proactive, rather than an irrelevant role. A comparative approach where restaurants had different levels of technology made this apparent.

When I studied a Burger King restaurant in Chinatown I made a presumption that the absence of Chinese employees had to do with a combination of factors that I had observed and that had been explained to me by the general manager. These included a lack of an existing Chinese network in the restaurant, the general manager's expressed bias against the Chinese (including stereotypical views that they were not friendly with the customers and emphasized studying over jobs), and the lack of a local marketing strategy aimed at attracting Chinese residents to fast food.

It was only when I went across the street to study a McDonald's restaurant that it became apparent that technology also played a highly significant role in the fast food restaurant's hiring practices concerning Chinese immigrants. New computer technologies had altered modes of communication in the fast food restaurant, affecting the kinds of people who could be hired, the jobs they could do, and the diversity of the people who could work together. Restaurants that still had the old microphone technology (like the Burger King) required front-line workers to verbally call out customer orders on a microphone to the food preparers in the back. Therefore, a common language spoken among all employees was required and had obviously prevented the restaurant from hiring non-English speaking job seekers, and hence, recent Chinese immigrants.

With the advanced technology, verbal communication was not necessary between the front-line and back-food preparation area. Front-line workers simply press the required code button on their register which is then transmitted to a computer screen in the back. This technology significantly affected the fast food organizational culture. It has helped to place a greater emphasis on face-to-face communication between front-line workers and customers, enabling the organization to hire foreign language speakers who can communicate with customers in their same language. In the McDonald's in Chinatown, Mandarin and Cantonese speaking workers were placed on the front-line to help Chinese customers who were new to the McDonald's system order their food. In the meantime, these employees did not have to verbally communicate with the Spanish, Russian, and African workers who were preparing the food in the back, and could instead concentrate on their customers. It was through comparative methodology and resulting 'reflective experience' that the significance of technology and its interactive effects on hiring policies, ethnic divisions of labor, and marketing strategies, became apparent.

25.5.3 Third Example

The final example is relatively simple and became apparent in my interviews with franchisees where I inadvertently found myself playing up my respondents' informant status at the expense of adhering to my predefined interview guide (as a strategy for establishing rapport). I had begun my research with the aim of understanding the relationship between ethnic resource mobilization and the development of ethnic ownership niches in the industry. In other words, I intended to examine how immigrant entrepreneurs were using ethnic resources to make inroads into the industry. I had assumed, of course, a positive relationship. What I had not anticipated, however, was how the very nature/structure of ethnic relationships in certain immigrant communities might have an influence on industry reorganization, particularly the movement away from the 'mom and pop' model that characterized the industry into the 1970s/1980s to the multiple franchising model of today. In other words, the extended family business economies of Asian Indian groups were helping to shape the big business model of corporate franchising, its accompanying changing cost structure, and heightening operational demands. In this way, by playing up informant led dialogue, and allowing my respondents to take the lead in the interview process I stumbled upon my most significant finding and what became the framework for my whole analysis.

25.6 CONCLUSION

Studying immigrant economies in expanding sectors of the American mainstream may require us to move beyond traditional conceptual boundaries. As I have shown conducting fieldwork in just one industry – American franchise organizations – poses new challenges related to the diversity and multi-situational identities of those it hires and those who invest as owners. The organization and structure of the industry itself is complex, both socially and geographically; it is not homogeneous as the rationalization thesis would have us assume. In this way, qualitative fieldwork needs to progress and our approaches need to be open to reflect this growing complexity.

NOTES

1. See Sánchez-Ayala (Chapter 6, this volume) for further discussion of interviewing techniques.
2. This is what Light and Gold (2000) define as the 'ability to open and operate numerous, large, and lucrative business firms.'

REFERENCES

Bourdieu, P. (1993), *La Misere du Monde*, Paris: Seuil.
Charmaz, K. (2006), *Constructing Grounded Theory: A Practical Guide through Qualitative Analysis*, Thousand Oaks, CA: Sage.
Gans, H. (1999), 'Filling in some holes: six areas of needed immigration research', American Behavioral Scientist, **42** (9), June–July, 1302–13.
Goodwin, J. and Horowitz, R. (2002), 'Introduction: the methodological strengths and dilemmas of qualitative sociology', *Qualitative Sociology*, **25** (1), Spring, 33–47.
Hall, R.A. (2004), 'Inside out: some notes on carrying out feminist research in cross-cultural interviews with South Asian women immigration applicants', *Social Research Methodology*, **7** (2), 127–41.
Kusow, A. (2003), 'Beyond indigenous authenticity: reflections on the insider/outsider debate in immigration research', *Symbolic Interaction*, Fall, **26** (4), 591–9.
Light, I. (1973), *Ethnic Enterprise in America*, Berkeley, CA: University of California Press.
Light, I. and Bonacich, E. (1988), *Immigrant Entrepreneurs: Koreans in Los Angeles, 1965–1982*, Berkeley and Los Angeles, CA: University of California Press.
Light, I. and Gold, S. (2000), *Ethnic Economies*, San Diego, CA: Academic Press.
Merton, R. (1972), 'Insiders and outsiders: a chapter in the sociology of knowledge', *American Journal of Sociology*, **77**, July, 9–47.
Portes, A. and Bach, R. (1985), *Latin Journey: Cuban and Mexican Immigrants in the United States*, Berkeley, CA: University of California Press.
Ritzer, G. (1993), *McDonaldization of Society*, Thousand Oaks, CA: Pine Forge Press.
Robb, M. (2004), 'Exploring fatherhood: masculinity and intersubjectivity in the research process', *Journal of Social Work Practice*, **18** (3), November, 395–406.
Rumbault, R. (1999), 'Immigration research in the United States: social origins and future orientations', *American Behavioral Scientist*, **42** (9), 1285–301.
Tusini, S. (2004), 'The role of the interviewer in in-depth interviews: sociologist or mermaid?', *Sociologia e Ricerca Sociale*, **25** (74), 75–94.
Wacquant, L. (1999), 'The double-edged sword of reason: the scholar's predicament and the sociologist's mission', *European Journal of Social Theory*, **2** (3), 275–81.

Waldinger, R. and Bozorgmehr, M. (1996), *Ethnic Los Angeles*, New York: Russell Sage Foundation.
Watson, J. (1998 [2006]), *Golden Arches East: McDonald's in East Asia*, Stanford, CA: Stanford University Press.
Zhou, M. (1995), *Chinatown: The Socioeconomic Potential of an Urban Enclave*, Philadelphia, PA: Temple University Press.

26 In the factories and on the streets: studying Asian and Latino garment workers in New York City
Margaret M. Chin

This chapter examines how trust develops between respondents and researcher in a study of two types of garment shops and the women garment workers in New York City. Specifically, the research examined the Chinese who hire co-ethnics, and the Koreans who hire Mexicans, Ecuadorians, and Dominicans. The project explored immigrant garment shop owners' and women workers' views on who they worked with and why they worked. The study also looked at how immigrants fared in employment and how ethnicity was invoked as a resource. In the end, immigrant women workers looked for jobs that complemented their household roles as parents, providers, or overseas kin rather than just jobs with wages. Ethnic relations mattered, although not all of the time.

26.1 THE RESEARCH

Although the New York City garment industry itself has been studied extensively, no comparisons exist of the Chinese, Korean, and Latino groups within the industry. Methodologically, by choosing different immigrant groups in the same industry, I was able to draw inferences about economic adaptation, the use of social ties to attain jobs, and the benefit of those jobs to the workers.

My initial premise was to study the garment industry in New York City's Chinatown. I was very interested in ethnicity and how ethnic groups and ethnic enclaves seemed to support one another. Studying just the Chinese and garment work in depth would surely have led me to interesting findings, but would the study help me understand ethnicity any better? I was intrigued and for a while tried to understand the Chinese community in the Chinatowns of Manhattan and Brooklyn. I did fieldwork and a number of interviews in both communities and found that the two communities had many links to the garment industry. For example, Chinese employers often ran shops in both neighborhoods simultaneously; however, the shops in Brooklyn were nonunionized and paid lower wages. This framework allowed me to understand how businesses expand and how an ethnic 'enclave' can expand across noncontiguous sites. These visits also allowed me to see the different kinds of workers attracted to these shops. The neighborhood affected the wages, the benefits, and the workers' expectations.

At the same time, I was also exploring shops in Manhattan's garment district a few miles north of Chinatown. Surprisingly, I found few Chinese shops; the majority were run by Korean employers who hired a mix of Mexicans, Ecuadorians, and Dominicans. In fact, there were many more of these Korean enterprises in Manhattan than there were Chinese enterprises in Brooklyn.

Shortly after my preliminary fieldwork, I realized that a comparative study of different immigrant ethnic groups in the same industry would yield much more information about how ethnicity is used and defined. One of the most important decisions that I made was to conduct this research as a comparative study of different ethnic and immigrant groups.

In doing a comparison, I thought I would be able to show that the ethnicity of the owner or employer in a garment shop mattered little. Initially, I thought both the Chinese who hired co-ethnics and the Koreans who hired Latinos used similar methods in recruiting workers. Chinese co-ethnics shared information about jobs in the industry and sent friends and family to the industry. This is exactly what Latinos told me in preliminary interviews. They sent other co-ethnic Latinos to look for jobs with the Korean employers. If both sectors worked similarly, then what previous researchers thought of as 'ethnicity' in examining a single group would in fact just be immigrant ways of finding jobs, regardless of ethnicity.

In comparing the two groups, I discovered that the hiring and work practices were different and much more nuanced than I had expected. Ethnicity was invoked at different times and under different conditions. Ethnicity was appealed to differently in both these sites such that there was a very positive effect on hiring for the Chinese, while the use of ethnicity was limited among the Latino workers. For example, ethnicity and relationships were hidden from the Korean employers because the Korean owners did not want workers who knew of the conditions in the garment factories. Koreans preferred Latinos who could sew but had little knowledge of the acceptable wages. Latino workers did not or could not reveal any prior knowledge of a friend or family member in the New York City industry – revealing that information would hurt their chances of getting a job. Ethnicity and the information shared between co-ethnics was optional, and, in fact, workers or employers learned to use or hide that information for their own benefit.

In deciding against a study only on Chinese garment workers, I was able to gather information that would develop a richer, more intricate description of the two cases. My current research has been shaped by this experience. Whether I am writing or doing fieldwork on one or more groups, I go back to this first study in order to inform and develop my ideas by using a comparative perspective.

26.2 THE SITES

Although these groups work in the same industry, the sites are entirely different. The Chinese work on the northern edge of Chinatown, surrounded by the ethnic shops and services in the neighborhood. The Latinos work in midtown, surrounded by other ethnic groups. No one ethnic group dominates the midtown area.

At the time of my research, from 1994 to 1999, there were more than 400 Chinese shops in Chinatown, with an average of 40 employees each. Thus, more than 16,000 garment workers populated Chinatown. In midtown, Mexicans, Ecuadorians, and Dominicans come pouring out from the subways to work in the shops of the garment district. The majority of these shops are on the side streets between 35th and 41st Streets between 7th and 9th Avenues. Within this neighborhood, more than 300 shops clustered with 12,000 mostly Latino workers. The only visible hint of a garment industry were the trucks double-parked to load and unload clothing and other materials. There was no specific ethnic feel to this neighborhood, while Chinatown is clearly an ethnic enclave with specialty shops and Chinese language signs everywhere.

26.3 THE TOPIC

The comparison of the sites intrigued me. The subject matter of my book, *Sewing Women* (Chin, 2005b), and much of my subsequent work on the garment workers has been a reflection of personal concerns. The research topic, the research questions, the way I collected and the data, and how I interpreted the data were all deeply connected to who I am.

Moreover, since ethnicity mattered, how would I gain access to both sites – where the ethnic groups were so different? Ethnicity mattered to the workers and owners. How would that contribute to my access to the two different sites? I am Chinese and a daughter of a garment worker and a restaurant worker. Moreover, during five months of my fieldwork at the sites, I was visibly pregnant. How would these factors facilitate or detract from my entry into these two sites and the work I had to do?

548 *Handbook of research methods in migration*

As a child, I used to spend much time in Chinatown garment factories with my mother. I remember very clearly playing with dolls and putting them to sleep in boxes filled with fabric. I grew up listening to my mother and her friends discussing their lives as garment workers and I followed their search for better jobs that eventually took them out of the factories. As my mother left to pursue other jobs, her brothers' wives, all recent immigrants, entered the industry. My aunts worked in the garment industry until just after 9/11.

In addition, as a sociologist, I always had questions about immigrant ethnic enclaves and how immigrant workers and entrepreneurs were portrayed in the literature. I often wondered how the findings would differ if two different immigrant groups were contrasted. I felt that a comparison would yield an excellent study since it could reveal nuances between the different immigrant groups. Thus, the research questions grew out of my personal interest in immigrant groups and the working poor, and in my sociological belief that there was much more operating in these industries than economic laws of supply and demand or ethnic collaboration.

The sectors described above are just two of many in the garment manufacturing industry in New York City. These sectors are just three miles apart in the borough of Manhattan. They are very different from each other; however, there are enough similarities to compare. Both the Korean- and Chinese-owned shops produced moderately priced women's clothing with a 'Made in the USA' label and were able to produce short runs of fashionable items. They differed in that the Chinese shops were most often unionized and hired documented co-ethnic workers, whereas the Korean shops were not unionized and often hired undocumented Latino workers.

The comparison was extremely important. If I had looked at each of the cases individually, I would have found that the Chinese followed the patron-client ethnic enclave paradigm in which the Chinese do well enough by taking care of their own. If I had looked at the Korean factories only, I would have found that they followed a strict Fordist model, always looking for the cheapest employees and exploiting undocumented workers as much as possible. This would have been the easiest and simplest characterization of the two sectors. My fieldwork indicated that more was going on.

Underlying these two types of industries is a whole host of social factors that challenged the images I mentioned above. It seemed as if the Chinese workers had a patron-client relationship within the shop, such that existing employees often trained newer workers for the owners. However, whilst the owners gave workers somewhat flexible hours, and health benefits, the workers were more often exploited. These workers rarely earned more than four dollars per hour on average, and they often worked late and extra hours just to get the extra pieces finished. At the same time, these Chinese women went into this industry because they were young mothers who wanted the flexible hours and family health benefits. So while they knew they were being exploited, this industry also offered what they needed to maintain their life in the United States. The Chinese women workers were able to combine their household and childcare needs with the hours required in the garment industry and took what little wages they were offered.

In the Korean/Latino sites, while these workers were in very structured assembly-line workplaces, they were often paid more than the Chinese and were able to gain even higher wages, especially if they were willing to change jobs. This was wholly unexpected, because these workers were undocumented. In the end, the experienced, undocumented workers could command higher wages. The Latino workers did not feel any loyalty to their employer. If given the chance, they would leave for the highest paid job.

A major difference between these two groups was how their ethnic social networks operated. I found that one way to understand this was to examine how ethnic groups might be utilized in getting jobs. I had already observed Chinese garment workers in their factories and was more familiar with them. I had read research on the Mexicans in New York City and their working relationship with Korean grocery owners and was fascinated by the Latinos' kin-like relationship with their Korean employers.[1] This finding in the literature indicated to me that the kinds of information shared in these relationships are not limited to ethnic networks. Therefore, ethnicity may not be the defining factor of job networks. There were structural factors as opposed to cultural factors that led these groups to share job information. To show this, one cannot just look at the inner workings in the Chinese sector; the process also had to be compared with the Latinos who worked for Koreans.

After looking closer at the two sites together and doing some preliminary comparisons, the most 'obvious' was no longer obvious. Deciding to do a comparative study was simple. It was apparent that the only way to answer questions of how people use ethnic networks was to compare them. When people use ethnic networks, is it a cultural or structural phenomenon? The literature pointed the way to this study. Moreover, a comparative study offered a logic and a plan in how I constructed questions. From the broader questions of whether ethnicity mattered at work to looking at the particular situations of why Chinese and Latino garment workers immigrated, the comparison helped frame the study. The Chinese worker exploited every single ethnic connection

550 Handbook of research methods in migration

they had among friends and family to gain a seat in the factory. On the other hand, the ethnic relationship that the Mexicans, Ecuadorians, or Dominicans had with their co-ethnics was hidden from the Korean employers. If those relationships were revealed, workers had a more difficult time in getting hired.

26.4 RECRUITMENT (ENTRY)

26.4.1 Workers

To locate workers for the study, I used a variety of techniques at various sites. For the Chinese workers, I recruited at garment shops and at English as a Second Language (ESL) classes. At most places, I was able to make announcements about my study and I would just arrange a time and place for an interview. Another source of interviewees came from the Chinese workers' referrals. The referral interviewees were always eager and ready to arrange an interview appointment immediately. They expressed their interest and relayed information about the positive experiences that others had. They were much easier to talk to than the interviewees that I contacted via the classes or the shops. Their friends had a huge influence on them. The social networks that brought the Chinese women to the shops were also useful in recruiting interviewees.

In the case of the Latino workers, I also recruited using a variety of techniques. For the most part, a Spanish-speaking graduate student and I stood on what I call the 'for hire' corner in midtown Manhattan and canvassed for participants. We were able to take our time in explaining the study to many of the folks at the street corner. We visited on a regular basis two to three times each week for over six months. Many of the workers recognized us as the graduate students. Some overheard our interview questions; others knew we offered a fee for participating. It was difficult at the start of the interviewing process, but recruitment became much easier over time. For the follow-up, we relied more on worker referrals. As with the Chinese, worker referrals provided much better interviewees. They were more relaxed and understood our study better. In general, I had more luck in recontacting the Chinese workers than the Latino workers. Nevertheless, the follow-up interviews with both groups were much more thorough.

Moreover, as my pregnancy became very obvious, both the Latinos and the Chinese workers recognized me as a peer. I was less threatening and was much more like them – a future mother. In fact, many more workers agreed to be interviewed because their impression of me was more favorable. My pregnancy became the subject of the first ten minutes of every interview. Discussing pregnancy and motherhood allowed the workers to become at ease with the interview process and allowed me to build a rapport with them. It seemed quite natural to discuss my concerns in becoming a working mother. In fact, just about all the interviewees were willing to offer advice on pregnancy, childcare, motherhood, and even spousal relationships. Since I was a first-time mother, they were the experts in the area. I also told them that they were the experts on the garment factories as well.

It was quite remarkable that my pregnancy helped me gain entry into the garment shops. My condition surprised me; for in my role as a graduate student, my pregnancy more often caused anxiety. Professors who were confident in my research skills were also worried that my pregnancy would delay my finishing the PhD.

26.4.2 Owners

The Chinese owners I interviewed were recruited from the two shops I visited, through contacts via the business association, and garment owners' friends. Gaining interviews through the Chinese contractors' business association seemed by far the simplest, but it really was not. After meeting with officials from the organization and explaining my project, they agreed to give me a few names of owners for me to interview. After I called and mentioned that the association gave me their names, they seemed more than happy to oblige. In the end, I only interviewed one Chinese owner through the association. The second person and I could never find an appropriate time to meet; I believe that he really did not want to be interviewed, and avoided setting up a meeting. After I already found my fifth interviewee, I told this owner that it was all right not to meet and I would not contact him again.

Although I gained entry to two Chinese garment shops via worker contacts, it was hard for me to initially speak with the owners. Even though they allowed me to witness illicit activity at their shops, they were not ready to be interviewed. In the beginning, they were somewhat skeptical of what I was doing, even though they trusted the workers who brought me in. After I had become a semi-regular figure in their shop – I often offered services such as advice on high schools for their children, help with their children's homework, translation services, and occasional errands – they began to trust me. The other two owners I interviewed were friends of these two owners.

The Chinese owners of the shops I visited did not complain to me about my visits. I think my being Chinese, and therefore an insider, helped allay any distrust they had of me. The owners assumed that I had seen or knew everything that happened in a garment shop because my mother had been a garment worker. I tried not to interfere with any of their regular operations. I was just an observer and the slow approach I took to gain their confidence helped me attain interviews that were more thorough. I had a somewhat different experience with the Korean owners. The owners I met while observing shops proved to be reluctant interviewees. Although I did interview them, both were hesitant to introduce me to others.

They told me that they did not want others to know that they had an outside visitor in their shops observing their work, and they especially did not want others to know that they were interviewed for a study. First, I believe that they felt this way because they did not give me permission to observe the shop; instead, it was their foreman who granted me access. Because of the excellent relationship the Ecuadorian foreman had with the owners and the extra favors he had given to them, he convinced them that it was all right for me to observe. Second, I witnessed many 'violations' that they thought were completely new to me.[2] The Korean owners of shops I visited felt uncomfortable with my presence. They did not ask me to leave, but they felt like they had lost control. They told me that my visits had to be confidential, and that no one should know about my presence. I believe they did not want to appear to their peers as violating secrets of their trade to an outsider, or a Chinese, or someone who could report their labor violations. All of these issues were conflated. On the other hand, the owners who were introduced to me via the Korean Contractors' Association (KCA) were very friendly and forthcoming. The president of the KCA was impressed with my background, mostly my educational background, and how I started as the daughter of a garment worker. He was also very helpful in securing Korean owners for my interviews.[3] The owners he introduced me to were more willing to speak and to find others for me to interview. I interviewed three owners who were friends of officers of the association. Although I only visited these owners' shops briefly, it seemed that they were not only doing this interview for me, but for the association. I believe these owners were more open because the KCA had validated my study. Thus, when I approached these owners, they were not fearful or apprehensive

During the first study, I interviewed only ten owners (five Chinese and five Korean). I had remained friendly with both the Chinese and Korean owners I interviewed before.[4] They also kept in contact with me because many of them wanted me to advise them on their children's schooling. I told them that I needed to interview them again and wanted them to help me find more employers to interview for the follow-up study. I asked additional questions: What did they think was going to happen to their workers? Will there be another group that comes to replace them? Will the Chinese women work shorter hours because their parents will no longer be able to get Supplemental Security Income to support themselves while babysitting for them? Will the Dominican women leave to get other jobs by retraining, or will they compete for jobs with Mexican and Ecuadorian workers because there are few jobs for which they are qualified?

I convinced six of the ten original owners (eight of them agreed to be interviewed for the follow-up) to agree to contact other owner friends for me to interview. Basically, I asked if they could each come up with three others. I figured that if they could get at least one person for me I could continue with a 'snowball' sample by asking each of the new participants to recruit as well.

I was convinced that the owners would be my best recruiters. They had known me for at least three to four years and they understood the study. However, the owners really had to be pushed to call other interviewees, and even to give me names. Like everyone, they were reluctant because they were wary about revealing too many illegal practices in the industry. I did not think it was because it was a closed community, but was, in fact, a real decision that they thought could have an impact on their livelihood. They knew many owners who were willing, but they were reluctant to make that call for me. They thought it was fine that they themselves were involved in these discussions with me, but they did not want to get others involved. I had to reaffirm my study once again, convincing them that the information I was gathering concerned how these women lived and how they needed more money to live on. The owners saw that other support allowed these women to work for them. I was not interested in a study on illegal activities. These owners each found at least one other recruit for me, and I followed up with snowball sampling.

The owners were quite open and many of them did tell me that they knew that their workers were receiving other types of government support. The Chinese owners were quite accurate in describing the benefits that their workers received. However, the Korean owners were less likely to know that many of their Dominican workers were actually permanent residents or citizens who received welfare, food stamps, or Medicaid. Most of the owners assumed they were undocumented like the Mexicans and Ecuadorians. For a few, it was a revelation that many of their workers were hard-working public assistance mothers. However, most of the Korean owners were not surprised to hear that women worked while getting benefits on the side. They admitted that their wages were not enough to support a family.

My pregnancy also helped to enhance my rapport with the garment shop owners. Even though the owners seemed more sophisticated than the workers, it was the owners who needed the assurance that I was harmless to them and their industry. Just seeing me pregnant allayed their fears. Like the garment workers, my pregnancy was a frequent topic of discussion with the garment shop owners and they too offered me advice. The opportunity for them to give advice automatically changed the roles we had. They became the expert. And I emphasized that I also thought that they were the experts on the garment industry as well. Many times, I could tell that they wanted me to be the expert.

26.5 COLLECTING THE DATA

26.5.1 Insider/Outsider Status

Most studies depend on access to data. In a comparative study, one needs to gain entry to at least two sites. For this study, I had to find four groups of people willing to be interviewed. I needed to understand what the Korean and Chinese owners thought about their employees, how they hired them, what favors, if any, were offered on the job floor, and what they thought about workers receiving outside funds (I discuss interviewee compensation in a later section). At the same time, I wanted to understand the hiring process from the viewpoint of the Chinese workers and various Latino workers who were employed by the Koreans. I also wanted to understand the family lives of the individuals in the garment industry, including those who had children and spouses and those who were alone.

As you can imagine, my identity was deeply intertwined with the subject matter. As a researcher, I drew upon the most obvious identity – a Chinese immigrant garment worker's daughter. There are many works that discuss the impact that a researcher's social identity can have on subjects and their projects (Reich, 2003; Rosaldo,1989; Stanfield, 1994; Warren and Hackney, 2000). These studies state that researchers need to learn how the relationships between the subject and researcher can affect, both positively and negatively, the ability to gather information and to interpret the data. My main concern at the start was whether I could access the data.

I did preliminary fieldwork in a graduate research class, and I thought I would be able to gain access to at least one of the communities – that of the Chinese who hired Chinese workers. While it would be a challenge to enter the Korean shops that employed Latinos, I thought I would be able to overcome any obstacles. I had some reasonable success visiting the Korean garment shops in the midtown area. In the early stages, I realized that I needed a translator. Since I had reasonable success myself in access to the Chinese garment shops, I searched for someone like me, that is, who might have had parents who worked in the industry. During the course of the research, I learned that there were other social identities that I needed to draw upon or to distance myself from. I could gain access to the Korean owners if I stressed that I was an Ivy League college graduate. They were impressed with my social mobility from being a garment worker's daughter and wanted advice for their children. Latinos trusted me more if I made sure to explain that I was not Korean, even though I was also Asian. I had to explain that my mother was a worker, not an owner, and that I could relate to their work conditions. My pregnancy was another way for me to get closer to the workers and owners.

After getting into the sites, I started to wonder if my data were trustworthy. I found that having access to many subjects and the ability to do long-term fieldwork allayed many of my concerns regarding the validity of the data. In each of the two sites, I was able to interview more than 100 individual workers and more than 30 owners. I was also able to observe the workers' and owners' interactions in the factories on a long-term basis. I was able to use both sources of data to cross-check the information. When what I observed did not agree with what people told me, I could follow up and make an inquiry.

In collecting data from two separate sites, I found myself inquiring more deeply. Some of the information I took for granted initially was questioned by the data I found in the other site. I inquired more. I interviewed more. I did more background research. I kept resorting the data as I analysed the information. I had confidence in my findings when the various data from the different sites started to repeat and to make sense as a whole.

26.5.2 The Process

For *Sewing Women* (Chin, 2005b) and subsequent follow-up work, I used the following multifaceted qualitative approach in collecting data: (1) nonparticipant observation at four garment shops; (2) informal, in-depth interviews with 72 Chinese workers and 68 Latino (Mexican, Ecuadorian, Dominican) workers, 15 Chinese garment shop owners, and 15 Korean garment shop owners; and (3) various interviews with union officials, Department of Labor employees, and ethnic business association officers and support staff.

Because of the nature of my population – mostly new and undocumented immigrants – and the fact that all the owners were participating in some kind of off-the-books unregulated activity, I did not think it was appropriate to tape-record their interviews. I felt that introducing a recording device would have discouraged many of the informants from discussing sensitive matters that were crucial to my study. Thus only handwritten notes were used to aid my memory for the later reconstruction and transcription of the interviews. Because of this limitation, I could not do more than two interviews at a time. In fact, I preferred to do one interview at a time, type up the field notes, and then start another, even if the interviews were on the same day.[5]

Although garment factories were too noisy and workers in them were too busy to take time away from their work for extensive interviews, I chose to observe in garment shops because I was interested in the interactions between workers and owners and wanted to be able to discuss on-the-job interactions readily. The workplace was the only setting where I could observe this. Thus observation was necessary for my data gathering.

For *Sewing Women* (Chin, 2005b), I interviewed everyone personally.[6] For the follow-up study, I hired interviewers who were fluent in Chinese and Spanish. One of the Dominican translators who worked with me on the first project joined me as both a translator and an interviewer on the follow-up. She was the daughter of a Dominican garment worker and was at ease with the workers. The Chinese interviewer I hired was the son of a garment worker. We teamed up at first, and I also had them do mock interviews in English. I taught them to take notes and both interviewers typed their interviews in English for me.

Interviews with the owners usually took place in their garment shops, in their offices or office space. Interviews with workers took place in various locations. The majority of the Chinese workers were interviewed during lunch hours in the various eateries in Chinatown. Some were also interviewed right before or after their ESL classes. I would frequently follow up on our conversations with a telephone interview.

Latino workers were interviewed in the same way. The major difference was that only about a quarter of them received a follow-up telephone interview. This proved difficult because these individuals were hard to keep track of by phone. Frequently, phones would be disconnected, or the individual would not be home. Since I had become spoiled by the ease with which I could obtain information from the Chinese workers, I felt frustrated that I could not ask follow-up questions that would come to mind after the interview.

In my initial study, I had received money from the National Science Foundation to pay the workers a small fee of $10. I did not compensate the employers at all. For my Social Science Research Council (SSRC) postdoctoral research, I paid the employers and workers $25 each for being interviewed. Signed consent forms were difficult to collect from the workers because they wanted the interviews to remain confidential and anonymous. Since it was agreed that the workers did not have to use full or real names, they signed the consent forms with whatever names they wanted. I believe that more than 50 percent of the names were correct. Immigration lawyers also assured the Human Subjects Review Board that I had no obligation to report workers who entered the United States without documentation since I could not determine whether they were covered under any other legal proceedings or were awaiting a change in status.

I increased the amount of money given to the participants between the first and the follow-up study because I felt that the information I was trying to gather the second time around was more sensitive. The hiring process, the check and wage splitting, the wages, and even how undocumented workers got hired were generally known throughout the Chinese, Korean, Mexican, and Ecuadorian immigrant garment sectors. It was not difficult to get that kind of information from the participants. However, for the follow-up interviews, I needed to ask more in-depth and sensitive questions on budgets and spending. I felt the $10 offer really helped the first time because it gave me some breathing room to explain the study to them before they outright refused to be interviewed. Likewise, the $25 offer was a nice amount; it was equivalent payment for four or more hours of garment work. Moreover, I also needed the workers' participation in helping me locate other interviewees. I felt the increased amount would give them an incentive to help me locate other interviewees and it could help them convince others to come forward. Moreover, it was not so much that it would make a huge difference in their family budget but it did give them extra money for purchases like groceries or a nice toy or a treat for their children. I paid the employers for the follow-up as well because I felt that is was necessary and professional. Since I was planning to enlist the employers themselves to help me recruit, I wanted to ensure that they had an easier time as well.

26.6 KNOWING WHEN TO STOP

Throughout the interviewing period, I refined the questions while doing preliminary analysis. I generally interviewed participants until I heard answers being repeated. Sometimes I probed deeper to get clearer answers before I stopped, but the general rule I used was that I was confident when the answers were being repeated by a number of the subjects. As an insider, I can have easier access, but it is just as difficult or sometimes more so to get full answers. Some interviewees were ashamed to share their answers for fear of being looked down upon. Sometimes, they trusted me less, because there were too many people with whom I could share their answers and one of those people could be someone they were trying to hide

558 *Handbook of research methods in migration*

from. Probing questions or comments were ideal for this situation. When I had a sense of clear differences or nuanced similarities between the two groups, I was able to draw conclusions between the groups and the processes they used. I was able to understand how culture or the ethnic social network or the work organization played a role in how each of the groups got their jobs.

26.7 CONCLUSION

In any type of ethnographic work, fieldwork is useful in refining the research questions. In many cases, the situation that is described in the literature no longer reflects the reality. The circumstances in various communities often change by the time of the study, and immigration, new groups, new work, and new laws often affect the communities.

A comparative methodology requires additional work at the data collection stage; however, the analysis is often straightforward. For example, in *Sewing Women* (Chin, 2005b), my analysis indicated that documented Chinese garment workers were not able to get greater pay than undocumented Latino workers, but the Chinese women cherished their flexible work hours so that they could combine household responsibilities with work responsibilities. They wanted this because most of them had their children living with them. The Latino workers, on the other hand, received higher wages, but had very strict work hours. Unlike the Chinese women, most of the Latino workers did not have children living with them in the United States and did not need the flexible hours to accommodate the daily family routine.

The techniques that I developed and refined while in the field were mostly all (except I was not pregnant again after 1998) used again depending on the economic situation in many other subsequent projects that looked at the working poor in various communities (Newman and Chin, 2003) and Chinese garment workers after 9/11 (Chin, 2005a). Analysis is difficult when there is an abundance of data. Getting into the field and refining your subject can also be cumbersome. Gathering the data can only be completed by trying different techniques and those that I have shared here have helped me the most.

NOTES

1. Rob Smith (Baruch College, School of Public Affairs) and DaeYoung Kim (University of Maryland) had worked on this topic.

2. For example, workers were required to punch in the time clock at 8:30 am and punch out at 5 pm. However, workers started work at 8 am and left work at 6 pm. The workers were paid $5.00 per hour from 8:00 to 6:00 (minus 30 minutes for lunch) and were not paid overtime.
3. The Korean owners that he contacted for me quizzed me on what I did in elementary school, middle school, and high school. They wanted to gain some insight or find a formula on how they could get their children to follow my educational path. These Korean owners expressed an interest in sending their children to an Ivy League school. The Chinese were also impressed by my educational background, but seemed much more interested in the US educational process as a whole. They were less concerned than the Koreans were with the process of getting into an Ivy League school.
4. I had sent a thank you card, but then followed up months later with Christmas cards to the owners, letting them know how my family was doing. Since they returned my Christmas card with ones of their own, I kept just about all of them on my Christmas list.
5. I used my laptop to type up interviews as soon as I possibly could. Coffee shops in midtown were great locations to do this in between or right after interviews.
6. 110 workers and ten owners.

REFERENCES

Chin, M.M. (2005a), 'Moving on: Chinese garment workers after 9/11', in N. Foner (ed.), *Wounded City: The Social Impact of 9/11*, New York: Russell Sage Foundation., pp. 184–207.
Chin, M.M. (2005b), *Sewing Women: Immigrants and the New York City Garment Industry*, New York: Columbia University Press.
Newman, K. and Chin, M.M. (2003), 'High stakes: time, poverty, testing, and the children of the working poor', *Qualitative Sociology*, **26**, 3–34.
Reich, J. (2003), 'Pregnant with possibility: reflections on embodiment, access, and inclusion in field research', *Qualitative Sociology*, **26**, 351–67.
Rosaldo, R. (1989), *Culture and Truth: The Remaking of Social Analysis*, Boston, MA: Beacon Press.
Stanfield, J. (1994), 'Ethnic modeling in qualitative research', in N.K. Denzin and Y.S. Lincoln (eds), *Handbook of Qualitative Research*, Thousand Oaks, CA: Sage, pp. 175–88.
Warren, C. and Hackney, J.K. (2000), *Gender Issues in Ethnography*, 2nd edn, Thousand Oaks, CA: Sage.

27 Three mistakes and corrections: on reflective adaptation in qualitative data collection and analysis
Johanna Shih

I recall being told, in a moment early on as a graduate student, that analysing qualitative data was a bit like 'osmosis' because the story 'just suddenly comes to you' (or something to this effect). Since I was, at the time, drowning in data that I could not make sense of, this explanation did not engender the illuminating 'Aha!' that it was meant to (perhaps more of a 'What?!' instead), although I have over time come to truly appreciate the truth in this description. Notwithstanding my belated understanding, this chapter takes a different explanatory tack by offering three examples of mistakes and subsequent corrections that I made during the course of two research projects. Put differently, these examples focus on the process of reflective adaptation at various stages of research, a practice that contributes to producing sound qualitative data analysis.

27.1 TWO EXAMPLES FROM SILICON VALLEY

27.1.1 The Study in Brief

I conducted a case study of hi-tech engineers (focusing on white women and Asian immigrants) in Silicon Valley, based primarily on a set of in-depth, semi-structured interviews. Silicon Valley, a region in Northern California, is home to a hi-tech industry that achieved exponential growth in the past three decades and has been the subject of worldwide attention. Aside from its economic success, the region was also quite interesting from a sociological standpoint for a number of reasons. First, there was a pervasive discourse, both popular and academic, about Silicon Valley that depicted it as meritocratic because the burgeoning hi-tech sector was ready to reward anyone with innovation and talent. Stories abounded of the glass ceiling being 'shattered,' and the administrative assistant who had the 'right idea' and became a multi-millionaire. Second, the region also represented a newer form of economic organization – flexible specialization – that was seen as a move away from the more rigid and hierarchical organization of mass production in the Fordist era. Flexible specialization was characterized by smaller, specialized firms that were geographically concentrated and densely networked. Third, the high-skilled, hi-tech workforce was relatively more diverse than other engineering industries in the USA – it had a larger proportion of women engineers, and a significant proportion of Asian immigrants who had come to the USA to work in the region.

27.1.2 Example 1: Race, Ethnicity, and Gender in the Hi-tech Industry

Given these features, one clear question that emerged was whether the 'old' forms of ethnic and gender mechanisms of inequality survived in this new economy – for example, within the organizations literature, lack of access to key networks and mentorships was consistently cited as a mechanism of inequality. As a flexibly specialized economic region, networks are central to the livelihood of both organizations and individuals – would this feature of Silicon Valley exacerbate inequality? More broadly, did white women and Asian immigrant engineers believe that race, ethnicity, or gender shaped their careers here?

A cursory look at my interviews showed that in response to a specific question about whether their gender, ethnicity, or race impeded their careers, almost no engineers I spoke with believed that these ascribed characteristics affected their mobility in Silicon Valley, and furthermore, those who had worked in other engineering industries previously explicitly stated that they believed that hi-tech was more meritocratic. In other words, to my admitted surprise, the interviewees seemed to confirm the discourse about Silicon Valley. However, when I read the interviews in their entirety (rather than simply the responses to the one specific question), I subsequently found that four fifths of those I spoke with also voluntarily told me, at some point in our conversations, stories of incidents where they perceived that their ethnicity or gender did matter. This included stories of bosses that were clearly gender biased, at least in their attitudes, and experiences from Asian immigrant engineers who felt that they were being concentrated into project groups or tracks that were purely technical (and thus without much room for mobility). This was frankly puzzling, because it rendered most people's accounts internally contradictory – on the one hand, they said that ethnicity and gender did not affect their careers in hi-tech; on the other hand, they readily proffered up stories where, it seemed to me, that these characteristics did matter. What was I missing?

As it turned out, the key to resolving this contradiction was that almost all of these respondents went on to explain how they circumvented the situations they perceived to be discriminatory by job-hopping to firms (and employers) they viewed as more egalitarian. For US born women, this often meant moving within an organization or to a different company that they had 'heard,' through their networks, was more open. For Asian immigrants, this more often meant moving to, or starting a company with co-ethnics, an option that was attractive in this industry where global ties matter. Job-hopping was a particular feature of this flexibly organized industry, and it has been more generally identified as a career mobility strategy of workers and as a necessary characteristic in an industry in which organizations no longer felt any long-term responsibility for their workers. So, in fact, what respondents were saying to me was that they were able to use this feature of the region's economic organization to navigate around discriminatory bosses, colleagues, or workplaces. They also detailed how they were able to do so by forging and leveraging their own ethnic and gender-based networks that had the resources to help their members successfully job-hop. So after struggling with the data and what I perceived to be its initial contradiction, this was the story that I was eventually able to tell.

27.1.3 The Mistake and Correction: Using the Wrong Research Framework

When I think about the circuitous path I took in figuring out what people were telling me, I realized that this path was shaped mostly by an analytic mistake: I had been reading and interpreting the interviews through the lens of the existing body of literature on gender and ethnic inequality, which had been based on the large, hierarchically structured organizations of the Fordist era. In particular, this literature primarily assumes that employees are essentially 'trapped' in organizations, with little means of recourse against discrimination. Thus the emphasis was on whether employers were biased, whether mentorships or key networks within organizations included minorities, or whether structures and policies within organizations were discriminatory. When I first looked at the interviews, I thus assumed that if the engineers were saying ethnicity and gender didn't impede their mobility, this subsequently meant that bosses and organizations were not discriminatory.

However, as I noted above, what respondents really meant was not that issues of race or gender were absent, but rather that they believed they were able to find their way out of the situation. It was only by retracing my steps and reading through the interviews that I was able to see where I went wrong – that I had assumed in my question that the presence of bias also meant that respondents had little recourse to circumvent it, which had been shaped by the prevailing literature on organizational inequality. This was not the case in Silicon Valley during this time period, and my understanding of this situation changed when I looked at how respondents described their experiences using their own frameworks. In fact, even if they said yes (and one can see that if I had rephrased the question, for example, to ask 'have you ever felt that your gender, ethnicity or race mattered in terms of how you were viewed by your bosses, clients, or colleagues?' I might have garnered a lot of 'yeses' in that respondents did give accounts where they believed that race, ethnicity, or gender mattered), I still would have been wrong in my analysis because the presence of discriminatory employers and organizations was not the end or even the heart of the story. The heart of the story in Silicon Valley at the time was the particular confluence of events that allowed for some white women and Asian men and women to forge their own resource-rich networks that allowed them to job-hop into better circumstances, effectively turning the tables on discriminatory employers. (Of course, I did not try to argue that this is always possible; my task from there was to try to root respondents' experiences into the particular characteristics of the region and the particular contexts of their groups that made their job-hopping possible). This was a story I would have missed had I not taken a step back to reconsider whether my own framework as a researcher was submerging what respondents were trying to say. That is, rather than letting respondents tell me about how they viewed the meaning of race, ethnicity, and gender in their careers, I had, with too heavy a hand, imposed frameworks that I had garnered from research literature about other settings. While this was primarily an analytic error, one can also view it as a methodological error too – after all, the strength of qualitative data is the possibility of theory generation from the 'ground up,' whereas I had clearly used far too deductive a lens.

To finish the analytic path, I gained further confidence in my interpretation of the interviews by embedding what respondents had to say in a multi-layered context which included the networks and social relationships in which the individuals were nested in; the characteristics and history of the group with which they identified with respect to Silicon Valley; and the economic organization, ideology, and history of the hi-tech industry. These contexts rooted the experiences of the individuals by providing logical parameters within which the experiences could be understood without claiming that these individuals 'stood' for everyone and provided a certain test for validity.

27.1.4 Example 2: The Pace of Work in the Hi-tech Industry

A second focus of my interest in Silicon Valley was on the widely reported hectic work schedules of hi-tech engineers, and how this might itself be producing gender inequality given women's greater likelihood to be in charge of the 'second shift.' While most of the media attention on the hi-tech industry was on its rapid economic growth, some anecdotal reports emerged that this expansion was paralleled by an acceleration in the pace of work as competition over product and service innovations and the race for time to market dominated life for hi-tech workers. High-skilled, hi-tech workers in particular were roped into this race with the lure of a big 'pay off' from stock options. For me, I was interested in whether this accelerated pace of work interacted with the needs of the private sphere of the home?

Given this interest, one question included in the original interview schedule asked respondents how many hours a week they work. However, a problem quickly became evident – interviewees who had, up until this question, spoke easily and at length about their careers and lives in the region suddenly seemed startled or hesitated in response to this question, saying that they weren't sure or it was 'hard to figure out.' Their reactions were surprising to me; since this was a standard question on surveys, I had not given much thought to the wording of it nor had I expected that it would be problematic. This question might be standard, but it certainly baffled my respondents who were, in other portions of the interview, generally quite articulate and thoughtful. Respondents stopped speaking suddenly, frowned, cocked their heads, stammered, and hesitated in a variety of other ways before saying that they really could not hazard a good guess, because it depended on the project and where they were on the project cycle. It could be 30 hours, or it could be over 100 I was told, it all depended. After pushing them further to explain why they could not give me an answer, I figured out that respondents' work weeks were not organized by any 9-to-5 type of schedule, but rather were determined by the project cycle, which lasted anywhere from a few months to a year or more, and were character-ized by a slow pace in the initial phases that accelerated quickly until the end. Organizing work through project cycles has several implications for people's experiences at work, which I explain further below.

27.1.5 The Mistake and Correction: Asking the Wrong Question

What happened here, which I realized after conducting the first 15–20 interviews, was that the question I was asking was not well suited to the realities of the respondents' lives. I had to recognize this mistake in order to correct the way that I framed the question (which became 'Can you tell me about the pace of work here?'). Part of this shift was moving from a quantitative view of time (that is, how many hours) to a qualitative/non-linear view that was more in keeping with respondents' experiences.

There were a few different issues that interviewees brought up that led to this shift. For one, regardless of the amount (quantitative) of time someone is putting in, it is clear that the leisurely feel that accompanies the beginning of a project is quite different from the harried pace at the end when one is under significant pressure to meet deadlines, and it is indeed these last few weeks that lead to frequent burnout among hi-tech engineers. Second, respondents also explained how, especially in this type of knowledge-based economy, the line between working and not working is increasingly blurred, because there are many times in the day that are not easily categorized. Checking e-mail or answering work-related phone messages at home, or trying to solve a problem when showering, as one respondent put it, represents ambiguous space. Third and finally, a non-linear conception of time is also exemplified in terms of people's perspectives of their life course, where there appeared to be a shift from viewing career and family as simultaneous events to one that is sequenced so that respondents hoped to work very hard right now, put off family until later, and hope to retire early.

Giving respondents the chance to describe their temporal experiences at work in their own words really clued me in to the particular ways in which people's personal time became co-opted in Silicon Valley, and the passion with which this was explained to me (in comparison to the stilted responses to my initial question of how many hours) also indicated that this issue was important to those who worked in the region. It thus became evident that while the hectic pace of work does indeed create gendered results, the more compelling point seemed to be its impact on shaping the experiences of everyone I spoke with. This turned into a story about how high-skill, hi-tech workers' lives in Silicon Valley became synchronized to the escalating rhythms of the global capitalist market and the factors that created and reproduced this synchronization. For example, when I asked people to tell me more about the demands of the project cycles, they explained to me how the pace of innovation and development in the hi-tech industry was accelerating, creating increasingly unreasonable deadlines in the rush to 'get it to market.' The very characteristics of flexible specialization which were seen to give places like Silicon Valley an advantage because it made the region better able to adapt quickly to the changing demands of the global capitalist market were the same characteristics that bound their workers more tightly to the vicissitudes of the global marketplace.

These sets of findings were ultimately guided by two corrections. The first stemmed from my mistake in how I asked the question about time at work, because, as indicated before, my question about a set work schedule did not really make sense from the respondents' viewpoints. So the first correction was to accept that it was best to see the collection of my data

566 *Handbook of research methods in migration*

as an open dialogue in which the initial questions are merely the starting point of the conversation over which I, as the researcher, did not have total control. The second correction was then analytic because what respondents said led me down an unexpected path. As I noted above, the original framework from which I saw respondents' experiences was through the lens of gender inequality, and, more particularly, the literature that argued that both the public sphere of work and the private sphere of home must be taken into account when considering women's labor market trajectories. While I still believed that the demands of the hi-tech industry on workers' time were producing gendered outcomes, I also came to see that this issue was not solely about gender, but was also about labor relations in the new economy. Given this shift in my interpretation, I needed to find the right framework to understand my results. Finding this framework entailed a constant back-and-forth with the actual data, the concepts and themes that I had identified in memos to myself as emerging from the data, and the prevailing research that could be used as a comparison. For example, when I considered what respondents were telling me in terms of how their lives were organized around increasingly untenable project cycles, I began to wonder why they complied. This led me to go back through their interviews to find the answer, from which I realized that another two themes were the individualist ideology in the region that constructed individuals as being entrepreneurs of their own careers, and the managerial effort in blurring the line between private and work time. Both these trends functioned to legitimate and facilitate the hectic pace of work in Silicon Valley. At this point, I went back to reading other research and used as a historical comparison the literature on managerial ideologies of coercion during industrialization (as juxtaposed to coercion in flexibly organized economies), and a comparison between the 'clock time' of industry with the 'project time' of hi-tech. The general point I'm trying to illustrate is that the ongoing dialogue between my data, my preliminary identification of concepts and themes, and other research eventually allowed me to better understand and also contextualize what respondents were telling me and to present a more complete story about the pace of work in Silicon Valley.

27.2 ONE EXAMPLE FROM HEMPSTEAD, NEW YORK

27.2.1 The Study in Brief

I am broadly interested in the relationship between neighborhood characteristics and health outcomes. To explore this question, I conducted interviews with parents in Hempstead, New York in order to understand the challenges which parents face in raising healthy families in this poor and racially segregated neighborhood. Current research clearly documents the association between race, class, and negative health outcomes, and furthermore, quantitative studies have shown how those who live in class or racially concentrated areas have higher morbidity and mortality rates. While these relationships are consistent across a broad range of quantitative studies, what is still unclear are the mechanisms that connect neighborhood with health outcomes. In other words, we don't know why neighborhoods matter.

The incorporated Village of Hempstead (which is part of the larger town of Hempstead) in Nassau County, New York, is a prism through which we can explore this question. Hempstead Village reflects Long Island's history of racial and class segregation, particularly as a product of its post World War II suburban development policies. While technically a suburb located 30 miles outside of New York City, the village is nonetheless as densely populated as most major cities, and also represents one of the emerging 'majority-minority suburbs.' According to the 2000 Census, approximately half of the residents of the village are African American, and almost a third are Hispanic or Latino. In contrast to its relatively affluent neighbors, the residents of Hempstead Village are more likely to be struggling economically as reflected by lower median family incomes, lower per capita incomes, and a higher percent of individuals and families living in poverty. The demographics of the Hempstead Free Union School District magnifies the socioeconomic characteristics of the village. For example, schools in the Hempstead Free Union School District are over 95 percent Black or Hispanic, and more than two thirds of the students in each of these schools are eligible for free lunch (New York State Report Card 2004–05). Thus Hempstead represented a good case study for the research question at hand. Aside from an academic interest, I also hoped that the research findings from this study could help inform health policy recommendations for an advocacy organization I have collaborated with.

27.2.2 The Mistake and Correction: Forgetting My Own Biases

Since one of the goals of this project was to help develop policy recommendations, the questions developed for the interview schedule were informed by the prevailing medical emphasis on lifestyle changes to ensure healthy, long-term living. In particular, this medical framework has shifted from a concern over the prevention and treatment of contagious diseases (that is, epidemics) to a focus on the prevention of chronic illnesses (that is, Type 2 diabetes, hypertension, and so on). Recommendations for the prevention of chronic illness typically entail changes in individuals' 'lifestyle' behaviors such as avoiding risky behavior (such as smoking) and engaging in healthy diet and exercise. My adherence to this framework was also reinforced through earlier interviews I conducted with medical providers in New York that serviced areas of high needs.

As a scholar of inequality, I was aware that the concept of individual choice that formed the basis of medical recommendations about lifestyle changes is misleading because it overlooks the challenges in people's lives, especially for those living in resource-poor neighborhoods. Thus my expectation going into the interviews was that Hempstead parents would detail how their 'built' environment – that is, the availability of affordable and accessible healthy foods near their homes, access to quality medical care, or the absence of safe public spaces and recreational facilities – impeded their ability to lead healthy lives for themselves and their families. In other words, I expected the respondents to be concerned with issues such as the diet and physical activity of their children, but to detail how their personal circumstances and their neighborhood characteristics might make it difficult for them to achieve these 'lifestyle choices.' I made this assumption – that these so-called 'lifestyle issues' would be at the forefront of parents' views on health – both because of the prevailing medical framework, but also from my personal experiences as a middle-class parent living in a middle-class neighborhood. With children in elementary school, I regularly speak to other parents at the neighborhood school, and the issue of healthy diets (that is, limiting junk food at classroom parties) and exercise (that is, how much recess time the children have) frequently comes up. So, in short, I had made assumptions about what parents would be interested in talking about when it comes to the topic of their children and health.

What immediately struck me when conducting a set of preliminary interviews were Hempstead parents' lack of interest in discussing health, at least as narrowly construed by my questions. This silence and (what I perceived to be) disinterest occurred despite the fact that respondents were informed during recruitment and during the introduction of the interview that the research study was about Hempstead parents' experiences with health issues and with healthy living for themselves and their families, and despite the fact that several of the questions in the interview schedule explicitly asked questions about health and health care access. Indeed, these type of specific questions were the most likely to receive either a very brief response, or a one-worded response. Also to my surprise, significant health problems faced by respondents or their families, including hospitalizations for medical issues such as stroke, physical handicaps, diabetes, asthma, and colitis were referred to in passing but not elaborated on. For example, I found out that one respondent was recently diagnosed with diabetes only because he happened to mention as I was walking with him out after the interview that he was going to the doctor's office to get his blood tested. He had also mentioned that his wife had had a stroke only towards the end of our interview and only as a side point to a story, despite the fact that I had asked him a number of specific questions about his family's health and experiences with health care.

When I sat down to reflect upon the first few interviews and as I continued to talk with other interviewees, I saw that the key issue seemed to be that Hempstead parents' definition of health was a far broader one than the narrower definition used by medical practitioners and by myself, or as defined in the academic literature. They said that health to them was 'taking care of everything,' it is 'to be happy,' to 'be self–sufficient,' and 'being in a two parent household. Being able to interact with other children in the same age group. Just being able to enjoy the safety and security – you live on your street, you go to your schools, you know the people that you go to school with, you know the parents. To me that's healthy.'

As I talked more with parents, I saw that this definition of being healthy stemmed from what interviewees viewed as missing from or problematic about their current lives and the lives of their children in this neighborhood. For everyone we talked with, these lives included multiple proximate risks, which included histories of community or domestic violence and family experiences with alcohol and drug abuse. These immediate risks overshadowed those posed by the prevailing discourse about health, which focuses on the long-term effects of individual behavioral choices. The father referred to above, for example, talked quite eloquently about wanting to move (despite his love for Hempstead as the town he grew up in) because he wanted a less stressful life for his wife and daughter. For him, a healthy life first and foremost meant a life free of potential violence, and this was a dominant theme in his talk, rather than any specific concerns about his diabetes or his wife's stroke.

As I came to see it, the mistake I made was not recognizing the bias in my own (middle-class) views about health and parenting, a bias that I think is mirrored and perhaps shaped by the prevailing medical discourse. I used an individualist paradigm in thinking about health, despite the fact, ironically, that I was interested in how neighborhood characteristics might affect people's ability to be healthy. This was in contrast to the experiences of the interviewees, as they detailed it, because for them health could not be understood solely as an individual or family problem but was instead fundamentally intertwined with the neighborhood and the social networks within this neighborhood. In detailing concerns about their ability to give their children healthy lives, parents referred to neighborhood social problems, such as drug dealing in the park and in certain houses or streets near them, and about specific incidences of gun violence that they were witness to. Parents reported reservations as well about the school environment, saying that they could not trust that their child was safe at school and that their children were exposed to fighting, to gun play, and to illicit drug use. In other words, being healthy, or living healthy lives, simply could not happen in an unhealthy neighborhood – it could not be individually defined as I had originally construed it to be. I was not initially able to fully appreciate what parents were saying to me; because I did not recognize the inherently individualist paradigm I had been working from.

27.3 CONCLUSION

The examples detailed here were chosen to illustrate three types of mistakes one can make in the course of qualitative data collection and analysis (and, in particular, the collection and use of semi-structured interviews) and the steps taken to correct these mistakes. In the first case, which focused on mechanisms of ethnic and gender inequality in hi-tech firms in Silicon Valley, the mistake I made was in using an analytic framework that was inappropriate for flexibly organized regions. This initially led me astray, because I assumed that when engineers told me that their race, ethnicity, or gender did not impede their career mobility in Silicon Valley, this meant that there were no mechanisms of discrimination. In contrast, what they were really saying was that from their experiences, bias existed, but that there were specific characteristics in the region that allowed them to circumvent it. Thus correcting my mistake entailed developing a different framework for understanding both the mechanisms of inequality in this flexibly organized hi-tech industry and understanding what accounted for workers' ability to resist it.

In the second example, I described a mistake I made in constructing the data collection instrument, specifically, the mistake I made in wording a question about how many hours hi-tech engineers worked. Here, I used a standard question about hours worked per week that did not reflect in any sense the reality of these hi-tech engineers' pace of work. To correct this error, I had to substantially revise the question and also expand my understanding of 'time' in a number of ways. At the simplest level, the question about hours worked per week was not suitable to the project cycles of engineering work, because the hours worked vary widely between the initial phases of a cycle to the harried end, and the exhaustion experienced by respondents at the ends of these project cycles in a qualitatively different way that went beyond the sheer number of hours worked. On other levels, correcting the question allowed respondents to explain to me how the division of work and home was no longer cleanly divided, which allowed their time to be co-opted more easily by their own ambitions, the pressures of their managers, and the vicissitudes of the global hi-tech market.

In the final example based on my research in Hempstead, New York, I showed how I made a fundamental error by not recognizing the effect of my own class bias (and that of the prevailing medical discourse) in shaping an individualist and overly narrow model of health, which overemphasized changes in individuals' lifestyle behaviors to promote long-term health. Respondents' disinterest in my questions about health (as construed in my narrow sense) and their own broader definitions of health and healthy living clued me in to the fact that because the experiences of people are inextricably linked to the neighborhoods that we live in, it is impossible to fully understand or even define health from an individual lens. Parents' definition of health included the necessity of neighborhood health, a fact that is true in every type of neighborhood, but is obscured for middle-class parents such as myself who take for granted the advantages conferred by healthy neighborhoods.

In the introductory paragraph, I refer to this process of making mistakes and corrections as reflective adaptation, which is defined for me as the ability to be reflexive and open about each stage of the research process, recognizing any discrepancies or dissonances as important, and being willing to concede to and correct for any adjustments that are needed. In a sense, it is misleading for me to use the word 'mistake,' because it strikes me that making, recognizing, and correcting errors is at the heart of sound qualitative data analysis and an integral component of generating new theories. Indeed, one of the strengths of qualitative research and also, to my mind at least, one of the most enjoyable parts of it is to see the research as a collaborative process between you and your respondents in bringing out a part of the social world. By describing the paths I took in making and correcting mistakes in the research process, I hope that I have illuminated to some extent this core component of how qualitative analysis is done.

Index

AAMY (Ashraf, Aycinena, Martinez, and Yang) 262–4
abduction 43
absolute surplus-population 98
abstraction process 94
acculturation 82
accumulation
 by dispossession 97
 distribution 98
action inquiry 288
Adams, R. 188, 190
adaptability 16
additional team members, research projects 468–71
agent-based modelling 389
agentive agency 42, 47
aggregation and coding 238–9
agriculture and social transformation 18
Alcaraz, C. 194
American fast food industry 523–43
American franchises
 access issues 528–31
 and immigrant poverty 523–43
American garment workers 545–58
American Political Science Association 9
American Sociological Association 8–9
Amuedo-Dorantes, Catalina 3
Anaheim asylum office 415, 416–17
Anderson, Bridget 3
Angrist, J.D. 174
anonymity, interview code for 335–6, 457–8
Antecol, H. 167, 168, 169
anthropological research 32, 37, 285
 guidelines 330
anti-immigration policies 109
Antman, F. 258, 260
Apitzsch, U. 38
Appadurai, A. 75
application ranking form 470
Archer, Margaret 27, 28, 36, 40, 41, 42, 44, 45
Ashraf, N. 262–4

Asian garment workers, in US 545–8
Asian immigrant engineers 561
assimilation 82
asylum seekers 46, 62, 104–106, 109, 231, 411–27
 mistrust as survival strategy 459
 one-year rule 419
Atal, Y. 275
atomistic positivism 28
Auriat, Nadia 140, 141, 142
Axinn, W.G. 146
Aycinena, D. 262–4

Bader, V. 37
Baghramian, M. 29
Bakewell, O. 17
Bakhtin, Mikhail 85
Bambirra, Vania 96
Banerjee, Raka 2
Barham, B. 188
Bartram, David 2, 53, 59, 64
Basch, L.G. 72, 277
Beam, E. 265
Bechhofer, F. 52
Becker, H.S. 53
Becoming a Citizen 517–18
Belli, R.F. 145
Bello, W. 95, 101
Belmont Report 453
Benedict, Ruth 83
Bennett, K. 284–5
Bentley, J.H. 69
Berger, P.L. 11
Bernard, Russell 140
Berry, J.M. 329
Bertrand, M. 174
Best, J. 30
Bhabha, H. 75, 86
Bilger, Veronika 3
Bilsborrow, R. 218, 224, 230, 234, 237, 244
biographical research 38–9
birthplace data 234–5

573

574 Handbook of research methods in migration

Black, R. 109
Blanc-Szanton, C. 72
Blau, F. 168, 169
Bloemraad, Irene 3
Bloor, M. 281
Boas, Franz 82
Boccagni, Paolo 2, 22
body language 127–8
Böhning, W.R. 61
booster samples 218
borders
 enforcement 169
 nature of 309
Borgolte, M. 87
Borjas, G.J. 165, 166, 168, 250, 257
Bose, Pablo S. 2
Boswell, C. 33, 34
boundary changes, and internal migration 245
Bourne, Randolph 71, 73, 90
Boyle, Paul 38, 147
Brabha, H.K. 277
Brah, A. 275–6
Braziel, J.E. 275
Brazil
 industrialization 18
 plantation economy 81
Breton, R. 517
Brown, R. 188
Brubaker, Rogers 314
Bryan, G. 265
building trust 288, 289–91
Butcher, K.F. 181–2, 188

Caesar, Mary 3
calendar interviewing 143–7
Callegaro, M. 145
Cameron, A.C. 218
Campos-Guardado, Sofia 412–13
Canada, as bicultural 82
Canales, A. 108
capital
 in general 95
 original accumulation of 97
 and overpopulation 97–8
capitalism 93–5
 globalization of 83
Capoferro, C. 213
Card, D. 171, 174, 175–8
Cardoso, Fernando Henrique 96

Carletto, Calogero 2, 217, 225
Carling, Jorgen 2, 139, 156, 158
Carter, Bob 41, 44, 45
case selection 509
case study definition 327
Castells, M. 18
Castles, Stephen 2, 17, 44, 45, 58, 100, 104, 108, 109, 123, 126, 231
Catlin, G.E.G. 10
causal groups 42
causal impact assessment 250–51
causal mechanisms 42–3
causality
 conceptualisation of 40–41
 mechanisms of 518–19
 positivist notion of 28
 probabilistic causality 510
 social 40
census data 391, 506
census reliability 326
chain-referral sampling *see* snowball sampling
Chamratrithirong, A. 242
Changing Status, Changing Lives? project 397, 399
characteristics of the move 141
Chatham House Rule 335
Chi Square test 134
Chikanda, Abel 3
Chin, A. 263–4
Chin, Margaret M. 3
Chiquiar, D. 194
Chiswick, B.R. 165, 166, 169, 178–83
Choi, H.J. 259
Chouliaraki, L. 42
circular migrants 74, 212
citizenship 237, 505, 506, 517–18
civil organizations 108
Clarke, G. 260
Clemens, M. 253, 254
Clifford, J. 285
climate change 109
cluster sampling 130
co-operative inquiry 288
Cobb-Clark, D.A. 168–9, 169
coding and aggregation 238–9
cognitive turn 314
Cohen, R. 275
cohort parameters 168
Collier, A. 27

colonialism and migration 55, 75, 85
common labour markets 59–60, 66
comparative case studies 22, 327
comparative logic, and small N studies 510–12
comparative qualitative research 421–5
comparative-historical studies 52, 510, 511
comparison as cognitive operation 52
compensation, for research participants 331, 333–5
complex realism 44
complexity theory 44
compliance unknown status 406
conceptualisation 57–62, 65, 85
concurrent embedded designs 321
concurrent triangulation designs 321
conflationist theory 43
confounding factors, in fieldwork 385–6
conjugal stability 160
Constant, A. 257
constructivism *see* social constructivism
container theory of society 300
context-dependent monitoring 391
continuous data-gathering systems 231–4
continuous reporting system *see* Migration Outlook
Contradictory assumptions in the minimum wage workforce 537
Control Function techniques 178
control groups 508
convenience sampling 346
conventional questionnaires 142–3, 152–5
conventionalism 30
core concepts 51
Cornelius, W.A. 53
counterfactual thinking 43
Covarrubias, K. 217
Coven, Phyllis 413
credibility of procedures 16
créolisation 86
Cresswell, T. 121
Creswell, J.W. 281, 320, 321
critical realism 39–46
cross-border practices variability 296
cross-country research 312–13
cross-sectional data 186–90, 202
cross-sectional surveys 15
Cruikshank, J. 27, 30, 39, 44

Crush, Jonathan 16
Cuban migration 82
Cueva, Agustín 96
cultural pluralism 71
cultural stereotypes 34–5
cumulative causation 99

Danermark, B. 28, 39, 40, 41, 42, 43
data
 analysis of 7, 10, 154–5, 336, 404–408, 417–21, 560–71
 categorizing 323
 census 391
 collection 7, 288, 336, 417–21, 560–71
 consistency programming 196
 cross-sectional 186–90
 difficulties in using 505–506
 environmental 391
 fetishism avoidance 289
 global inventory 242–3
 global migrant-origin database 235
 interactive stages in collection/analysis 417–21
 interpretation of 244–6
 limitations of 425–7
 longitudinal 186, 190–204
 mixing 320
 and personal encounters 531
 privacy issues and 345
 qualitative approaches 406–408
 qualitative data collection 560–71
 quality of 14, 229
 quantitative approaches to 404–406
 remittances 432–6
 retrospective data-gathering methods 234–43
 socio-economic 391
 sources 283, 287
 and statistics 9–10, 14
 triangulation of 313, 518
 visual checking 196
datasets 494
Davidson, A. 126
Davis, M. 18
DD (difference-in-differences) estimation 164, 171–5, 181, 201, 202
de Brauw, Alan 2, 224, 225
de Guchteneire, P. 35
de Haas, H. 17
Declaration of Helsinki 453

576 *Handbook of research methods in migration*

deductivism 28
Delaney, D. 122
Delgado Wise, Raúl 2, 95, 97, 100, 102, 103, 104, 108
demography 285
Denscombe, M. 281
departing migrants 233
dependency theories 98
Deren, Eleanora 83
descriptive questions 14
descriptive statistics 133
DeSipio, L. 16
deterministic theory 510
development and migration 99–100
development studies 284
development theory 283
development-induced displacement 283, 284
developmental refugees 278
developmentalist state 63
DeWind, J. 16
Dexter, L.A. 329
DFL (DiNardo, Fortin, Lemieux) reweighting analysis 181–2
diachronic research 312–13
dialectic analysis of society 94–5
dialectical processes 42
diasporas
  Africa–Canada 349–59
  concept of 74, 274–6, 292
  e-recruiting 353–9
  methodological challenges 345
  online 347–9, 359–62
  policy research methods 319–39, 345–63
  questionnaire 324–6, 332
  sampling 346
differently situated participants 414
Dijkstra, W. 146
DiNardo, J. 163, 178, 181–2
discourses 42
discursive practices 30
discursive reductionism 44
discursive relativism 31
displaced persons 76, 104–106
disproportionate sampling 217
dissertations 483–500, 503–504
divergent citizenship 517–18
document analysis 125
documentary research 336–8

documents, fraudulent 407
Dos Santos, Theotonio 96
Drew, D. 233
drill-down phase 338, 339
driver-focused research 381
dual character of society 11
dual labour market theory 54–5, 99
dual life social pattern 307
Dunham, Katherine 83
Durkheim, Emile 10
Dustmann, C. 256, 257
Duval, L. 193
Dwyer, C. 118

e-recruiting 353–9
EA (Emuneration Areas) 216
EACH-FOR 367–92
  case studies 371–3
  census data 391
  control group definition 381–2
  control group measurement 382–3
  environmental data 391
  environmental variables isolation 390
  fieldwork approach 384–7
  further research 388–92
  gaps between enviromental events and site visits 387–8
  intervention measurement 382–3
  locations 374–6
  methodologies 381
  overview studies 371
  project design 373–83
  project findings validity 383
  project research steps 377
  project summary 370–71
  research questions 378–9, 389–90
  research tools 389
  seasonal factors and interviews 388
  socio-economic data 391
  theoretical background 368–70
  two-group post-test design 383
  variables 379–81
  see also environment
Eberhardt, Cassandra 3
ECM (Extensive Case Method) 45–6
econometric techniques 164
Economic Commission for Latin America and the Caribbean (ECLAC) 96
economic geography 283, 284

Index 577

economic migrants 278
economic shock 254–8, 261
EHC (Event History Calendars) 143–7
elite interviews 329–32, 335
Ellis, D.R. 275, 285
embedded units of analysis 327
emergent research process 288, 291
emigrants
 with controls 200–201
 definition 74, 210–11
 without controls 201–203
 see also immigration; migration
emigration state systems 323–4
empirical invariance, principle of 28
employment status 54–5
Engels, F. 92
ENIGH (Mexican Statistical Institute) 432, 435
entrepreneurial capacity 527
entry, categories of 232
enumeration system 216, 242
environmental change
 Environmental Change and Forced Migration Scenarios *see* EACH-FOR
 hotspots 391
 human-induced 369
 and migration 366–92
 variables 379–81
environmental damage 101
environmental degradation 102, 108
environmental factors, isolation of 369–70, 390
environmental problems, categories 373
environmental refugees 109
environmental sciences 89
environmental variables, isolation 369–70, 390
EOC (Everyone Counts Survey) 325–6
epistemological relativism 40
epistemology and methodology 7, 10, 27
Estonia–Finland migration 51
ethics
 post-fieldwork 462–3
 in research 288, 333–4, 451–64
ethnic discrimination 104
ethnic enclaves 524
ethnic migration research 37–8, 45
ethno-cultural associations 87
ethno-religious dummy variables 188

ethnocentric harm 426
ethnographic research 285, 286, 305
ethnographic studies 52
ethnomethodology 417
EU (European Union) Enlargement 397, 398, 399
evaluative ideas 11
exchange rate shocks 254–8, 261
exogenous variables 188
exotic harm 426
expectations, rise of 84
experimental design 508–10
external funding 489
external grants 489–90
extra-local references 300

Facebook 353–9
Fairclough, N. 42
Faist, T. 72–3
Falzon, M.A. 305
family bifurcation 156, 158
Fanning, B. 62
farm subsidies 18
Fast Food Fast Track: Imigrants, Big Business, and the American Dream 523
fast food industry case study 523–43
Faulkner, P. 27
feedback, on published work 488–91
feminist research/studies 414, 461
Fenton, S. 36
Fetterman, D.M. 285
field experiments 261–6
field objectives/tasks 387
fieldwork 384–6, 390
 see also ethics
financialization 101
Finch, T. 233
Fitzgerald, D. 72, 298, 306, 312, 314
fixed effects estimators 193
Fleeing Gendered Harm: Seeking Asylum in America 411
Fleetwood, S. 29, 39
flexibility in research 16
focused interviews 329
Foladori, G. 101, 102
Foner, N. 74
food parameter changes 88
forced migration 104–109
 and unequal development 106–107

578 Handbook of research methods in migration

foreign worker concept 57–61, 65
forgetting function 141
formal interviews 335
formal relations of similarity 42
Foster, A. 213
Foster, J.B. 29, 101
foundationalism 31
Fox, J. 110
Frank, André Gunder 96
fraudulent documents 407
Freedman, Deborah 145
Freeman, Gary 56, 63
French-Canadians 62
Freyre, Gilberto 81
Frisch, M. 58
Fuess, S.M. 53, 61
functionalist sociology 10
funding 472–3, 488–91
funds of knowledge 84
Funkhouser, Edward 2, 194, 199
Furtado, Celso 96
fuzzy set approach 66

Gamio, Manuel 82
Gamlen, Alan 3, 21
Gandini, L. 110
Garfinkle, Harold 417–18
Geertz, Clifford 32
Geiger, S. 290–91
gender bias 80
gender regimes 426
gender-based persecution 411–27
general explanations 51
generalizability 325
generative causal mechanisms 40
geographic patterns 189
geographic regression models 389
geographic relationships 286
George, M.V. 246
George, S. 46
Gibson, J. 188, 252
Gilroy, P. 276, 277
GIS (Geographic Information Systems) 134, 286
Glaser, Barry 416
Glewwe, P. 220
Glick Schiller, Nina 22, 34, 35, 72, 299, 302, 306
global capitalist development 98
global financial crisis, 21st century 102

global migrant-origin database 235
Global North research 19
global origin-destination database 245
global social transformation and human mobility 16–19
Global South research 10, 18–19
globalization 17–18, 19, 21, 83
  neoliberal 101–103
  studies in 524
Goldstein, K. 329
Gordon, J. 110
Gramsci, Antonio 85
Grant, Madison 71
graphical timetables 148
green revolution 18
Grosh, M. 220
grounded theory 416
group interview 123–4
guaranteed anonymity 457–8
Guarnizo, Luis E. 83
guestworker policy 53, 58
Guha, R. 75
Gzesh, S. 104, 108

Hägerstrand, Torsten 147
Halfacree, K.H. 38
Hall, Catherine 75, 85
Hall, Stuart 75, 85, 275, 277
Hallock, K.F. 178
Hämäläinen, T. 64
Hammar, T. 65
Hammersley, M. 30, 31, 32, 36, 37, 38
Handlin, O. 72
Hanson, G. 189, 190, 286
Hartwig, M. 39, 40, 42
Harvey, H. 95, 97, 102, 103
Harzig, C. 71
HCT (Human Capital Theory) 34–5
Heckathorn, D.D. 218
Heckmann, F. 213
Hedberg, C. 45
Held, D. 19
Hempstead, New York case study 566–70
Henze, B.R. 36
Herder, Johann Gottfried von 70
Hesse-Biber, S.N. 291
Hi-tech industry case study 560–71
Hibberd, F.J. 27, 30, 32
hibridación 86

Index 579

high-skilled workers 61
Hildebrandt, N. 189
Hill, Ashley 3
historical narrative approach 45
historical studies 15
historicity of social phenomena, in political economy 94
Hoerder, Dirk 2, 22, 86, 87
Hollifield, J.F. 55
homeland connectivity 307
House, S.R. 41
Household Responsibility System 224
household-level remittance patterns 436–9
Hughes, Everett C. 72, 82
Hughes, Helen MacGill 81, 82
human agency, and migration 22
human capital 34–5, 86
human mobility and global social transformation 16–19
human rights 84, 107, 108
human smuggling 451
human trafficking 105, 451, 459
humanitarian categories of migrant 231
Humanities 88
Humboldt, Alexander von 70
Humboldt, Wilhelm von 70
Hurston, Zora Neale 83

IDB (Inter-American Development Bank) 95
identification strategies on immigration economics 165–71
identity 37
  deconstructing 459–61
  thinking 31
IDP (Internally Displaced People) 278
Iguchi, Y. 53
illegality
  and immigration 59, 65, 233, 396–409, 401–404
  and social integration 408
  tolerance by individuals 407
  types and levels of 407, 408
IMF (International Monetary Fund) 95
immigrant, *see also* emigrant; migrant
immigrant assimilation 163
  study methodology 165–8
immigrant characteristics 169
immigrant earnings 165–8

immigrant selection methodology 168–9
immigrant skills 78–9
immigrant transnationalism key forms 297
immigrants
  arrival age 158
  concept of 57, 65
  definition 210
  effects on labour markets 164, 169–71
  in fast food franchises 523–43
  and illegality 59, 65, 396–409
  inaccurate designations of 73–4
  legal status of 65, 398, 399–401, 459
  political participation 517
  status questions 402–404
  as symbols of globalization 19
  teenagers in fast food work 533–5
  time since arrival 158
  see also interviewing migrants
immobility and migration 65
in-depth interviews 123, 513–17, 525
indirect method of difference 52
individualistic positivism 28
inductivism 28
industrialization 18
inequality 18
inferential statistics 133
informed consent 330, 331, 333–5, 456–7
innovation systems restructuring 101
innovative research 50
institutional frameworks 454
instrumental variables techniques 175–8
instruments performance 190
integrated approach 320
interdisciplinarity problems 9
interdisciplinary approach 88, 273–92
  components 288
  matrix 287
  tools for 280–87
  traditions in 280–87
internal emigrants 210
internal migration 213, 245
internal realism 30
international code of ethics 453
international development studies 283
international emigrants 210
internationalization 101
interpretation of data 244–6
interpretative sociology 11

interpretive-symbolic approach 32
interviewer effects 402
interviewing migrants
　access 401–404
　comparative approach 540–42
　conceptual re-examination 540–42
　data analysis 404–408
　ethical issues 399
　ethnic insiders 538–9
　format 335–6
　grounded theory 416
　in-depth interviews 123, 513–17, 531
　information analysis 132–5
　information transcription 132
　interactive elements of the interview 539–40
　interview guides 416, 526
　interview process 125–32
　interview techniques 122–5
　interviewer bias 567–70
　knowing when to stop 557–8
　lifestyle issues 568–9
　locating interviewees 550
　open-ended questions 525
　participant-observers 337
　participants' environment 337
　participants' perceptions 461
　payments to interviewees 556–7
　personal interviewing 336
　policy knowledge by interviewer 338
　positionality 117–21
　power relations 453
　professional boundaries 537
　question errors 564–70
　questioning types 124
　questionnaires 142–3, 152–5, 220–25, 384–5, 513
　reflective experience 540–42
　relations with franchise managers 535–7
　sampling methods 128–9
　and seasonal factors 388
　semi-structured interviews 526
　spatial considerations 121–2
　status questions 402–404
　trust building 458–9, 531–9
intransitivity 39, 42
inverted foundationalism 31
IOM (International Organization for Migration) 369–70, 384, 386, 472

Iosifides, Theodoros 2, 10, 27, 28, 31, 38, 39, 41
IPCC (Intergovernmental Panel on Climate Change) 381
irrealism 26–7, 28
irregular migration 233, 236, 451, 451–2
IT advances 101
IV (instrumental variables) regression techniques 164, 175–8, 181, 190, 261

James, C.L.R. 82
Jasso, G. 232
Jayaram, N. 275
Jessup, P.C. 71
Johnson, C.A. 63
Jones, B.G. 33, 33–4
Joseph, J. 31
judgemental rationality 40
judgemental relativism 36

Kallen, Horace 71, 90
Karlan, D. 267
Kendall's tau- measure of association 133
Keohane, R.O. 71
Keynesian economics 96
keyword search software 496
Khadria, B. 110
Khosravi, S. 460
Kindleberger, C.P. 53
King, G. 52
King, Russell 148, 157
Kish, L. 217
Kivesto, P. 74
Koenker, R. 178
Komai, H. 53
Kreuger, A.B. 174

labour force surveys 208
labour market primacy 79
labour precariousness 102, 106
labour rights 108
Lacey, H. 46
Lambda measure of association 133
large N studies 511
large scale research project management 467–78
LATE (Local Average Treatment Effect) 177, 260

Index   581

Latin America
  migration 86
  political economy 96–7
Law, Anna O. 3
Leavy, P. 291
Leeves, G. 188
legal residence restrictions 398
legal status of immigrants 65, 398, 399–401
Lester, R. 102
Levitt, Peggy 72, 296, 299, 302
Lewis, P. 122
Lexis diagrams 137, 156, 158, 159
Lieberson, Stanley 510–12
Liempt, Ilse van 3
Life History Calendars (LHC) 143–7, 152–5
life sciences 88
life-cycle considerations 256
lifetime data 235
lifetime migration 239
Limb, M. 118
Limited Information Maximum Likliehood (LIML) 177–8
linguistic relativism 31
liquidity constraints 251
logical empiricism 27
logical positivism 27
Lokshin, M. 189
Lonergan, S. 109, 369, 380
long-term migrants 211
longitudinal data 186, 190–204
longitudinal studies 15
Lopez, M. 168
Lorber, J. 414
lottery process 188
Lozano, Fernando A. 2, 35, 110, 168
LPPR (last place of permanent residence) 236, 237, 238
LSMA 199
LSMS (Living Standards Measurement Surveys) 193, 209, 213, 216, 218, 220, 223, 225, 244
Lu, Y. 193
Lubotsky, D. 167
Lucas, R.E.B. 139, 143, 208–209, 259
Luckmann, T. 11

McAdam, J. 109
McDonaldization 523–43

McKendrick, J.H. 322
McKenzie, David 2, 189, 218, 251, 252
macro trends 17, 20
Magdof, G. 101
mail-out surveys 346
majority-minority suburbs 567
male-headed households 80
Malinowski, Bronislaw 82–3
Manicas, P.T. 36
Mannur, A. 275
Marcus, G. 285
Mariel Boatlift 171–4
Marini, Ray Mauro 96
Márquez Covarribias, Humberto 2, 95, 97, 102, 103, 104
Martin, P.L. 213
Martinez, C.A. 255, 256, 262–4
Marxist political economy 92–3, 94, 95, 97, 98
Massey, Douglas 15, 213, 257, 312, 396
matched sample logic 311
matriculas consulares 263
Mauthner, M.L. 290
Mazzucato, Valentina 313
measurement error 197
measures of association 133
mechanisms of causality 518–19
Meillassoux, C. 97
membership degree changes 66
Mendola, M. 188
mestizaje 86
meta-theory 45
method of agreement 52
methodological framework development 525–8
methodological individualism 33
methodological nationalism 22, 23, 35, 295, 300
methodologies, multiple 498–500
methodology
  approach 455–6
  diversity 312
  and methods 7–23, 493–7
  in migration research practice 13–16
métissage 86
Mexican Migration Project 15, 208, 244, 311–12
migrant identification 213–15
migrant labour markets, illegality in 396–409

migrant savings studies 262–4
migrant stocks 212
migrants
  category membership 66
  characteristics of 210–11
  connectedness and ethnographic
    involvement 305
  definition of 210–11, 222–3, 230
  departing migrants 233
  economic migrants 278
  funds of knowledge 84
  impact of change in economic
    conditions 254–8
  interviewing *see* interviewing migrants
  irregular migrants 233, 236
  legal status of 396
  motivation 211
  and political structures 84
  remittance patterns 77–8, 99, 107
  return migrants 211
  seasonal 211
  self-selection 249
  skills 78–9, 80
  smuggling of 105
  UN migration data 163, 207
  vulnerable 451–64
  women as associational migrants 80
  see also emigrants; immigrants
migration
  and alternative development 107
  causal impact assessment 250–51
  definitions used 137, 210–15, 230
  and demand for labour 110
  as demographic variable 230
  and development 99–100
  effects on labour markets 164, 169–71
  forced migration 104–109
  as interdisciplinary 275
  internal 213, 245
  irregular 233, 236, 451, 451–2
  political economy of 97–9
  as rare event 215–19
  recent research data 163–4
  rotatory migration 89
  transnational *see* transnationalism
  workers' rights 104–105
migration analysis 101–103
  concepts 103–106
migration barriers identification 264–6
migration bias 454

migration data *see* data
migration dynamics 102, 123
migration event duration 224
migration flows 212
  data 84–5
migration histories
  data collection formats 142–54
  informants' memories 139–42
  methodological approaches 137–8
  migration data analysis *see* data
  moves thresholds 138–9
  presentation 155–9
migration history charts (MHC) 147–57
migration lotteries 249, 251–4
migration measurement tools 231–7
migration motivation 198
Migration Outlook reports (OECD,
  SOPEMI) 10, 57, 58, 61, 62, 232
migration patterns 189–90
  difficulty in locating 277–80
migration points systems 267
migration pressures 63
migration projects *see* projects
migration research
  and global hierarchies 75
  proposals 14
  reports 14–15
  and social theory 17–19
  and social transformation 19–22
migration study design 415–17
migration theory 20–21
migration trends 370
migration types 211–13
Milanovic, B. 19
Milkman, R. 110
Mill, John Stuart 52, 56
Miller, M. 17, 123, 231
Mills, C. Wright 8, 9, 23
Miluka, J. 188, 189
Mishra, P. 254, 259
Mistiaen, J. 218
mistrust context in interviews 458–9
Mitchell, K. 121
mixed methods research 281, 320–23
mixed research methods 513–17
Mohammed, R. 119
Moore, R. 32, 46
Mora, J. 189
Morgan, J. 27
multi-layered spaces 76–80

multi-methods 281
multi-sited fieldwork 336–8
multiculturalism, official 517
multinationals 71, 101
multiple comparisons 512
multiple methods research 320
multiple metholologies 498–500
Munck, R. 108, 110
Murdock, S.H. 275, 285
Myers, N. 109
Myrdal, Gunnar 99

Nagar, R. 290–91
narrative analysis 336
nation-state *see* transnationalism
nationhood 44
natural experiments 254–61
naturalization 505
negative labour migration 53–4
négritude 86
NELM (New Economics of Labor Migration) 443
neoclassical approach 33
neoliberal globalization 17, 21, 101–103, 104, 108, 110
networking 488–91
Newbold, K.B. 278, 281
19th century migration control 76
non-immigrant categories 231
nonprobability sampling 128–9, 386–7, 416
Nordic Common Labour Market 59
north-south remittance flow 99
NRI (non-resident Indian) 282
Nuremberg Code 453
Nye, J.S. 71
Nyerges, T. 286

objectivity
  differences in 322
  and social construction 10–11
OECD (Organisation for Economic Co-operation and Development) 10, 57, 58, 61, 232, 243
OLS (Ordinary Least Squares) regression technique 163, 164, 170, 171, 175–8, 179, 180, 181, 190
Ong, A. 276
online diaspora research 347–9, 359–62
ontological flatness, of positivism 28

ontological realism 40
ontology of the self 33
ORG (Outgoing Rotations Groups) 168
original accumulation of capital 97
Ortiz, Fernando 81, 82
Osterhammel, J. 84
overpopulation 97–8
overproduction 102
overqualification 105
oversamples 218
overstayers 233
Oxford, Connie 3

paradigm crisis 95
paradigmatic phenomena 44
parallel cueing 146
Parker Talwar, Jennifer 3
Parsons, C.R. 244
Parsons, T. 10
partial migration registration 233
participative enquiry 288–9
participatory fieldwork methods 390
participatory research 22, 288
The Passing of the Great Race 71
Patel, K.K. 71
Paterson, L. 52
Patomäki, H. 29, 31, 32, 33
Pécoud, A. 35
Pempel, T.J. 55
Pendleton, Wade 3
Percentage Difference measure of association 133
permanent migrants 211
persecution, gender-based 411–27
person-years 154
Petras, J. 95, 101
phenomenons, establishing of 324
Phi Coefficient measure of association 133
Philip, L.J. 322
Pierri, N. 101, 102
Pinto, Anibal 96
Piore, M.J. 54–5, 55, 99, 102
Plano Clark, V.L. 281
policy experiments 251–4
policy variation 56–7
political economy
  foundations of 92–7
  of migration 97–100
political incorporation 505, 515

584 *Handbook of research methods in migration*

political participation 517
political philosophy 283
political transformations 83–4
Portes, Alejandro 21, 72, 307, 308, 310, 324
Portugal–Goa migration 72
Portuguese quasi-experiment 508–10
positionality in interviewing 117–21
positive orthodoxy 33–4
positivism 11–13, 27–9, 46
  positivist thinking central premises 27–8
  and scientism 33, 6
positivist/constructivist dispute 10, 11, 13
post-structuralism 31
Pozo, Susan 3
Pratt, M.L. 75, 86
Pratten, S.B. 28
pre-migration 189
Prebisch, Raúl 96
presumptions and research 502–18
Pries, L. 21, 296
probabilistic causality 510
probability sampling 128–9, 217, 416
probit regression 190
process tracing 513–15
processual geography 78, 86
processual structures 86
professional boundaries 537
project, budgets 475
project cycles 564
project funding 472–3, 488–91
project management, large-scale 467–78
project marketing 471–2
project networking 488–91
project publishing 483–500
project reporting 475–6
project researchers 474–5
projects
  familiarization with local factors 477–8
  initial feedback on 488–91
  interdisciplinary knowledge 484–8
  money management 475
  partners in 473–4
  staff hiring 468–71
  time-lines for 475–6
  working in different countries 476–8
  see also research

Protocol relating to the Status of Refugees (1967) 412
proxy respondents 214, 221
PSU (primary sampling units) 216, 217, 218, 225
publishing research work 483–500
purposive sampling 346
push factors 370

qualitative components 320
qualitative data collection 560–71
qualitative information 132–5
qualitative migration study design 415–17
qualitative research methods 9, 14, 15, 21, 153, 281, 302–306, 322, 326–38, 370, 390, 400, 401, 406–408, 413–27, 495, 513, 518, 525, 555
quantile decomposition 183
quantile regression 178–81
quantitative components 320
quantitative information 132–5
quantitative research methods 9, 13–14, 21, 29, 41, 153, 281, 306–12, 322–6, 390, 400, 401, 404–406, 453, 495, 513, 518
quasi-experiments 508–10
questioning *see* interviewing migrants
questioning migrants *see* interviewing migrants
questionnaires 142–3, 152–5, 220–25, 384–5, 513
quota sampling 129

racial stereotypes 34–5
racism 19
radical scepticism 36
Ragin, Charles 52, 53, 66
random assignments 508–509
random effects estimators 193
random sampling 128–9
random walks 219
randomized treatment-control methodology 263
Rank-Order Correlation 133
Rapoport, H. 251
Ratcliffe, P. 43
Ratha, D. 54
rationality 33

realist methods 41–6
reality, different theories of 31
recall period 224
reciprocal relationships 290
reconstruction in political economy 94
recording devices 555
reductionist theory 28, 43
Reed, Holly 154
reflexive processes 531
refugees 76, 278, 279, 280, 285
regional cooperation 20
regression analysis 12, 133
Reitz, J.G. 517
relativism 29–32, 36–9, 46
remittance 77–8, 99, 107, 137, 197, 198, 207, 208, 249, 255, 258–60, 264, 306, 430–47
research
  conducting 456–61
  as creative venture 518
  dissemination of findings 462–3
  as emergent 288, 291
  external grants 489–90
  initial feedback 488–91
  participative enquiry 288–9
  and vulnerable migrants 451–64
research design 507–12
research ethics 288, 333–4, 451–64
research feasibility 328
research flexibility 16, 288
research framework errors 562–3
research handbooks 502
research limitations 22–3
research methods
  approaches and methodology 11–13, 21, 36–7, 483
  recent developments 178–82
research participants
  compensation for 331
  recruitment 332–3
research planning 454–6
research projects *see* projects
research publishing 483–500
research questions 455–6, 502–18
  definition 524–5
research reflexivity 290
research software 496
research units, appropriateness of 300–301
research variables 495

residency rule 214
respondent attributes 141
respondent, attributes of the 141
restrictive policies 54–5
retroduction 43
retrospective data-gathering methods 234–43
return migrants 211, 212
revelatory case studies 327, 328
revising projects 484–8
Richmond, Anthony 83
Ritzer, G. 541
robotization of the workforce 541
Robson, C. 327
Rogaly, Ben 3
Rosenzweig, M. 213, 260
rotatory migration 89
Rubin, D. 253
Ruhs, Martin 3
Rumbaut, R. 307, 308, 310
rustbelt industries 19

Sack, R. 122
SAE (Small Area Estimation) techniques 218
Said, E. 118
Salzinger, L. 46
Samers, M. 34, 121
sampling 128, 129, 217, 219, 239–42, 243–4, 325, 326, 329, 332–3, 346, 384, 386–7, 398, 416, 427, 527
Sánchez-Ayala, Luis 2
Sapir, Edward 83
Sassen, S. 55
satellite imagery 390
Sawyer, K.R. 28, 41
Sayer, A. 27, 30, 31, 36, 40, 42, 43
scale-dependent monitoring 391
scapes 86
Scheyvens, R. 289, 290
Schienstock, G. 64
Schierup, C.U. 19, 102, 103
scientism 27–9
  and positivism 32–6
  scientific logic 32
seasonal factors and interviews 388
seasonal migrants 211
Sector-Based Scheme visas 401
sedentary bias 17
seed lists 219

selection bias 509
self-reflexivity 118
Sellek, Y. 53
semi-structured interviews 526
sequential explanatory designs 321, 338
sequential exploratory studies 321
service economy poverty 523–43
Sewing Women 547, 555, 556, 558
Shaw, W. 54
Shih, Johanna 3
short-term migrants 211
Shurmer-Smith, P. 284–5
Siegel, Melissa 3
Silicon Valley case study 560–71
simulation/agent-based modelling 389
simultaneity 298, 313, 314
Singer, P. 98
single case studies 327
Siouti, I. 38
Skeldon, Ronald 2, 18, 242
Skocpol, Theda 510–12
slavery 82, 86
small N studies 510–12
Smith, James 140–42
Smith, L.T. 290
Smith, Michael P. 83
SMS (simultaneous matching sample methodology) 313
Snel, E. 308, 310
snowball sampling 129, 219, 325, 326, 332–3, 346, 384, 386, 398, 416, 427, 527
social capital 86
social construction
  and objectivity 10–11
  and reality 38
social constructivism 10–13, 30, 31, 37
social emergence 41
social facts 10
social inequalities 103
social integration and illegality 408
social interconnections 44
social issues, understanding of 8–10
social organization, key relationships 95
social phenomena in political economy 94
social practices 44
social science tasks 8
social theory and migration research 16–19

social transformation 17, 19, 19–22
  agency for 109–10
  generic framework 44–5
  methodology 21–2
  research organization 22
  spatial levels 20–21
  theory 20–21
social whole in political economy 94
socialization 89
The Sociological Imagination 8
Sociological Methodology 8–9
sociology 285
  of knowledge 11
Sokal, A 31
SOPEMI reports *see* Migration Outlook reports (OECD)
Sorensen, T. 168
spaces as scapes 86
spatial dimensions of migration 139
spatial levels of social transformation 20–21
Spearman's Rank-Order Correlation 133
Spivak, G. 75
Sporton, D. 38, 39
Sriskandarajah, D. 233
Stable Unit Treatment Value Assumption 253–4
Stark, O. 256, 259
state concept 70
state policies 63
state-generated refugees 75
states, conceptualization of 85
statistical significance 134
statistics and data *see* data
status questions 402–404
status refugees 279
Steinberger, Michael D. 2, 35
stepwise separation 156, 158
Stiglitz, J.E. 101
Stillman, S. 252
Storey, D. 289
strategic practices and migration 100
stratified random sampling 217
Strauss, Anselm 416
structural adjustment neoliberal policies 95
structural dynamics and migration 100
structured mobilization 515
structured processes 86
structures, conceptualization of 40

Index 587

StudentVoice Canada 361
stylized facts 12
subjective-meaning complex of action 11
subjectivity 37
substantive exchanges 335
Sunkel, Osvaldo 96
survey characteristics 142
Swain, A. 109
Swedish–Finnish migration 45
Switzerland, foreign labour 62
systematic sampling 129

Tarbuck, K. 94
target-earners 256
taxonomic groups 42
Taylor, J.E. 189, 213
Taylorization 78
team members, research projects 468–71
technocratisation 34
technological innovation 83
temporal dimensions of migration 139
temporary migrants 211
territory 122
Thelen, D. 69
thesis presentation 483–500
third space 86
Thomas, Duncan 140–42
transborder relations 298
transculturación 86
transcultural approach 83–90
transcultural perspective 87
Transcultural Societal Studies 69, 87–8, 89–90
transcultural spaces 87
transculturalism 69
transculturation 81–83, 86
transfactuality 42, 47
transit migration 451
transitivity 39
translocal multi-layered spaces 76–80
translocality 299
transmigrant term 73
transnational analysis 306–12, 345
transnational engagement 307
transnational family life 311
transnational migration 276
transnational organized crime 105
transnational social field 301–302
transnational societal units 301

transnationalism 22, 69, 70–76, 96, 138, 276
 actor-focused 299
 boundaries clarity 313
 and concept of society 298
 as conceptual apparatus 296–7
 cross-border practices 296
 economic domain 297
 immigrant key forms 297
 methodology 295, 299–302
 operationalizing 308, 309
 political domain 297
 as research lens 297, 298
 social field 296
 as social phenomenon 296–7
 sociocultural domain 297
 terms of debate 296–9
 units of analysis 301
 units of measurement 301
 units of reference 301
transnationals, changing potentiality of 314
transoceanism 81, 83
transportation geography 285, 286
transregional multi-layered spaces 76–80
treatment groups 508
Treiman, D. 193
Trejo, S.J. 169
triangulation of methods 15, 321
Trivedi, P.K. 218
troubles 8
trust in interviews 458–9
Tsiolis, G. 38
Tufte, E.R. 148
20th century migration control 76–7
two-group post-test design 383
two-phase sampling 217
two-stage sampling 219

UK immigration 55
uncertainty principle 12
undocumented immigrants 459
undocumented international migrants 213
undocumented workers 59
unequal development
 and forced migration 106–107
 in migration analysis 103
 public policy 110

United Nations Convention Relating to the Status of Refugees (1951) 109
United Nations Population Division 232
United Nations Statistics Division 232
University of Melbourne School of Enterprise, project management 467
urban geography theories 282–3
urbanization and migration 213
US BIA (Board of Immigration Appeals) 422–3
US border enforcement 169
US Census (2000) data 166, 167
US Illegal Immigration and Reform Act (1996) 419
US immigration 55, 72, 82
US Refugee Act (1980) 412
US Social Science Research Council 16
US-Canada differences 511

Valentine, G. 119
value freedom 11
value judgements 11
Van Hear, N. 148
Vandergeest, P. 284
variability in remittance income 430–47
variable-oriented comparisons 511
variation in migration 50, 51–7, 62–4
Vartiainen, J. 64
Veltmeyer, H. 95, 101
visa entry 231
visa lotteries 249, 251–4
visas 402, 407, 408
voluntary participation 456
vulnerable persons 452

Walby, S. 37, 37–8, 38, 44
Waldinger, Roger 72, 298, 307, 308, 310
Wallerstein, E. 98
Wallsten, S. 260
Walzer, M. 126
Ware, Caroline 81
Warner, Koko 3
Washington Consensus 100
Watson, James 525
WB (World Bank) 95
weather shock 258–60, 261
Weber, Max 10–11
Wells, P. 36
Where Peoples Meet 81
Wight, C. 29, 31, 32
Williams, Eric 82
Williamson, J.G. 213
Wimmer, A. 22, 34, 35
Withol de Wenden, C. 108
Wolff, F.C. 193
Wolpin, K. 260
women, as associational migrants 80
Wong, L.L. 75
Wood, E.M. 29
Wood, F. 281
Woodruff, C. 189, 190
world-system theory 98–9
WTO (World Trade Organization) 95

Xiang, B. 110

Yang, Dean 2, 189, 194, 255, 256, 257, 259, 260, 262–4
Ybry, Charles 148
Yeung, H.W. 29, 43
Yin, R. 327
Yoshida, K. 31

Zinman, J. 267
Zolberg, A. 58